ISBN=978-0-8122-4639-1

W0008745

American Gandhi

POLITICS AND CULTURE IN MODERN AMERICA

Series Editors:
Margot Canaday, Glenda Gilmore, Michael Kazin, Stephen Pitti, and Thomas J. Sugrue

Volumes in the series narrate and analyze political and social change in the broadest dimensions from 1865 to the present, including ideas about the ways people have sought and wielded power in the public sphere and the language and institutions of politics at all levels—local, national, and transnational. The series is motivated by a desire to reverse the fragmentation of modern U.S. history and to encourage synthetic perspectives on social movements and the state, on gender, race, and labor, and on intellectual history and popular culture.

AMERICAN GANDHI

A. J. Muste and the History of Radicalism
in the Twentieth Century

Leilah Danielson

PENN

UNIVERSITY OF PENNSYLVANIA PRESS

PHILADELPHIA

Published by
University of Pennsylvania Press
Philadelphia, Pennsylvania 19104-4112
www.upenn.edu/pennpress

Printed in the United States of America
on acid-free paper
1 3 5 7 9 10 8 6 4 2

Library of Congress Cataloging-in-Publication Data
Danielson, Leilah.
   American Gandhi : A. J. Muste and the history of radicalism in the
twentieth century / Leilah Danielson.—1st ed.
   p. cm.— (Politics and culture in modern America)
   Includes bibliographical references and index.
   ISBN 978-0-8122-4639-1 (hardcover : alk. paper)
   1. Pacifists—United States—Biography. 2. Quakers—United
States—Biography. 3. Radicalism—United States—History—20th
century. 4. Muste, A. J. (Abraham John), 1885–1967. I. Title. II. Series:
Politics and culture in modern America.
JZ5540.2.M8D36   2014
320.53092—dc23
[B]   2014007120

For Eric and our children, Adin and Mira

CONTENTS

⤶

Contents

ABBREVIATIONS

ACLU	American Civil Liberties Union
ACW	Amalgamated Clothing Workers of America
AFFFHW	American Federation of Full-Fashioned Hosiery Workers
AFL	American Federation of Labor
AFSC	American Friends Service Committee
AFT	American Federation of Teachers
ATWA	Amalgamated Textile Workers of America
AWP	American Workers Party
CALCAV	Clergy and Laymen Concerned About Vietnam
CIO	Congress of Industrial Organizations
CLA	Communist League of America
CNVA	Committee for Nonviolent Action
COFO	Council of Federated Organizations
CORE	Congress of Racial Equality
CP	Communist Party
CPLA	Conference for Progressive Labor Action
CPM	Church Peace Mission
CPS	Civilian Public Service
CRC	Christian Reformed Church
FERA	Federal Emergency Relief Administration
FOR	Fellowship of Reconciliation
IFOR	International Fellowship of Reconciliation
ILGWU	International Ladies' Garment Workers' Union
IWW	Industrial Workers of the World
LID	League for Industrial Democracy
LIPA	League for Independent Political Action
MOBE	Spring Mobilization Committee to End the War in Vietnam
MOWM	March on Washington Movement

NAACP	National Association for the Advancement of Colored People
NLF	National Liberation Front
NSBRO	National Service Board for Religious Objectors
NUL	National Unemployed League
PMA	Progressive Miners of America
RCA	Reformed Church in America
RUMW	Reorganized United Mine Workers of America
SANE	Committee for a Sane Nuclear Policy
SCM	Student Christian Movement
SDS	Students for a Democratic Society
SNCC	Student Nonviolent Coordinating Committee
SP	Socialist Party
SPU	Student Peace Union
TUUL	Trade Union Unity League
UCL	Unemployed Citizens' League
UMWA	United Mine Workers of America
UTW	United Textile Workers
WEB	Workers' Education Bureau
WILPF	Women's International League for Peace and Freedom
WPB	World Peace Brigade
WPC	World Peace Council
WPUS	Workers Party of the United States
WRL	War Resisters League
WTUL	Women's Trade Union League
YMCA	Young Men's Christian Association
YWCA	Young Women's Christian Association

Introduction

ON A RAINY afternoon in May 1957, seventy-two-year-old Abraham Johannes (A. J.) Muste sat down to write his autobiography. Unfortunately, he would never complete the volume, as he was repeatedly interrupted by the pressing work of organizing protests against nuclear testing and aiding the African American civil rights movement. In his "Sketches for an Autobiography" that were published in *Liberation* magazine, the present always intruded, precluding a stable, linear narrative. Writing an autobiography, Muste mused, "relates to the present or immediate past, to the world in which the writer now lives, not the one into which he was born." For Muste, that present was "Hiroshima; Nagasaki; Bikini; Korea; Dienbienphu; Suez; Hungary; Kenya; Algeria; South Africa; Alger Hiss; McCarthy; Oppenheimer; Japanese fishermen caught in a lethal rain; White Citizens Councils; the H-Bomb; the Intercontinental Ballistics Missile." The yawning gap between the horrors of the mid-twentieth century and his childhood as a Dutch provincial seemed insuperable to him. "How far, far away is all this in years, and in more subtle and profound respects, from a little provincial city in Holland in 1885? How long the journey and to what end?"[1]

Muste's comments speak to his long life as a leader of social movements and as an important political, intellectual, and moral presence in American society from World War I to the mid-1960s. In this book, I offer an interpretation of his evolving thought and politics as a window into the history of the American left in the years when the United States became a modern nation and emerged as a global superpower.[2] I argue that Muste was a prophet; he drew upon his Christian faith and the example of the Hebrew prophetic tradition to call the American people to righteousness, to repent of their sins and build a new world where "every man would sit under his own vine and fig tree, and none should make them afraid."[3] His prophetic sensibility underscores the messianic dreams that animated many American radicals, both religious and secular, giving them the courage to challenge the ideological and coercive structures of power, often at considerable personal risk.[4] Yet messianism always threatened to become megalomania; indeed, the history of American radicalism is rich with examples of individuals and movements who succumbed to delusions of grandeur to compensate for political marginality.[5] In Muste's case, a commitment to the pragmatic method—to grounding theory in practice and the individual in community—helped to curb his messianic impulses and allowed him to remain flexible and relevant across and throughout the political and ideological shifts of the mid-twentieth century.[6]

Muste's revolutionary commitment never ceased, but his confidence in the power of structural change to remake human beings and human society declined over time. Like others who came of age in the 1910s, he was a modernist, convinced of the plasticity of the self and the environment.[7] But in the 1930s and 1940s, he shared in the introspective turn of many of his comrades, questioning his assumptions about reason, history, and progress.[8] Rather than retreat from his socialist convictions, however, he remade them for the new era of the "American Century," in which organization, bureaucracy, and conformity appeared to threaten human freedom as much as class inequality and poverty had in earlier decades. The result was a new kind of "prophetic politics" in which action and commitment represented an effort not only to change society, but also to maintain one's humanity against the "anti-human."[9] His existential politics and style resonated deeply with the New Left, making him an ideal figure for exploring change and continuity in radical politics over the course of the twentieth century.[10]

At the same time that Muste represents significant historical formations, he was unique. He occupied an anomalous place in the history of American radicalism: he was a Social Gospel minister yet he was a working-class immigrant; he was an intellectual and idealist yet he was beloved by the practical and down-to-earth workers who rallied to his vision of militant industrial unionism in the 1920s and 1930s; he was an anti-Stalinist yet he refused to condone McCarthyism and opposed the Cold War; he was the foremost theoretician of Gandhian nonviolence in the United States yet he publicly chastised the civil rights leadership for failing to respond to the challenges posed by black power and U.S. empire; he was a devout Christian yet he was held in high esteem by the Marxist, secular left; he was an Old Leftist yet he supported and celebrated the New Left.

This story of Muste's life, thought, and politics thus illuminates familiar stories, while adding new twists and some largely unknown plots. Like other recent scholars, I emphasize the centrality of religion and culture in making the modern left and in forging alternative solidarities to modern nationalism. For Muste, as for others of his generation, exposure to liberal theology and mysticism allowed him to break from the Calvinist theology and worldview in which he had been raised.[11] Rather than leading to a narcissistic preoccupation with the self, as critics have charged, Muste's liberal creed led him outward, toward engagement with modernity and reform.[12] By the time the United States entered World War I, he was a committed pacifist and socialist, views that put him in conflict with the wartime state. Yet these same views also propelled him into an alternative community of radical Christian pacifists and civil libertarians. Together, in groups like the Fellowship of Reconciliation (FOR) and the American Civil Liberties Union (ACLU), they helped to create the modern discourse of conscientious objection and civil liberties.[13]

The evolution of Muste's activist career from Social Gospel minister to pacifist, and from pacifist to labor agitator reveals a history of collaborations between progressive labor, liberals, and the left that continues to be obscured by the ideological legacy of the Cold War. Muste and other pacifists helped to build this "liberal-left tradition" by forging connections to the vibrant labor movement of the World War I era.[14] For example, although scholars often associate the birth of the civil liberties movement with a discourse of individual rights, Muste's example demonstrates the pro-labor orientation of the early ACLU. In 1919, caught up in the "revolutionary ferment of the times," he and other pacifists became involved in a massive strike of textile workers in Lawrence, Massachusetts. Upon winning the dramatic and bloody strike, Muste assumed the leadership of the Amalgamated Textile Workers of America (ATWA), a radical union modeled after Sidney Hillman's Amalgamated Clothing Workers (ACW). The nascent ACLU was a crucial ally in the ATWA's organizational campaigns, particularly with the onset of the postwar Red Scare. Indeed, the modern fight for civil liberties and labor's struggle for the right to organize evolved together quite literally in Muste's ATWA.[15]

This broad alliance of pacifists, progressive unionists, and independent leftists continued into the 1920s. These were not the "tired radicals" of lore, but rather, like Muste, idealists who recognized that the labor movement and the left had entered a period of retrenchment.[16] Many of them had been active in wartime efforts to build the Farmer-Labor Party, founded in 1919, and modeled after the British Labour Party. The postwar Red Scare led to the party's quick demise, but remnants of this "progressive labor network" remained a strong minority presence and real influence in the labor movement. In the 1920s, they channeled their energies into third-party organizing, defense of political prisoners, and workers' education.[17] The workers' education movement in particular offers a window into the rich and dynamic history of labor progressivism in the 1920s, a time usually considered one of quiescence and conservatism in American labor history.[18]

From 1921 through 1933, Muste was probably the most influential figure in the workers' education movement. As head of Brookwood Labor College, the country's only residential college for workers, he oversaw the development of the movement's teaching philosophy, pedagogy, and curriculum, as well as its expansion to include city labor colleges throughout the country and summer schools for women workers. For Muste and other labor intellectuals, workers' education was part of a larger effort to modernize and democratize the labor movement. They constructed a method of inquiry and working-class organization that drew upon the pragmatic method, while rejecting liberal citizenship and parliamentarianism as vehicles for social change. Their efforts disrupt the dominant historiographical narrative in which Randolph Bourne's denunciation of John Dewey for his support for World War I serves as an epitaph, proof "that pragmatism is a philosophy of acquiescence to 'the existing fact,' a philosophy that must validate capitalism, accept imperialism, and repudiate socialism," as James Livingston has summed it up.[19]

Muste and his comrades in workers' education also developed an analysis of education and culture under capitalism that had striking parallels to Antonio Gramsci's ideas about hegemony and culture, viewing their educational programs as counter-hegemonic institutions that would produce working-class meaning and knowledge. Their educational, cultural, and organizational experiments helped to lay the groundwork for the Congress of Industrial Organizations (CIO) and the Popular Front of the 1930s, both of which recognized the crucial role of culture in social movement formation.[20]

The grouping that gave birth to and sustained workers' educational experiments like Brookwood was not without its tensions; there were real philosophical, class, and cultural differences between the various elements that made up the liberal left. Indeed, one reason for making Muste the center of historical inquiry is that he quite consciously embraced the dialectical interaction between the poles of realism and idealism, liberalism and collectivism, that have been a source of creativity and contestation in American liberal-left politics throughout the twentieth century.

For example, pacifists tended to be strongly libertarian in contrast to their more collectivist comrades in the labor movement. Cultural differences also played a role; most pacifists were native-born Protestants from the upper and middle classes who felt uncomfortable in the diverse and contentious world of labor radicalism.[21] In fact, Muste's continued and active engagement in the labor movement was unusual for a pacifist and probably reflected his immigrant and working-class background. Also in contrast to his fellow pacifists, Muste was more of a syndicalist than a parliamentarian; he was deeply skeptical of legalistic and moralistic methods for achieving social change and instead placed his hopes in labor organization, militancy, and solidarity. With the onset of the Great Depression, these differences led to Muste's estrangement from organized pacifism, making it difficult to group him uncritically with other Protestant pacifists of his generation.[22]

This question of divisions on the liberal left inevitably brings up the Communist Party's role in the labor and political struggles of the 1920s and 1930s. For many years, the standard interpretation was that the Communists pursued a policy of "divide and conquer," slavishly following the party line set down in the Soviet Union rather than responding to the American context.[23] More recently, revisionists have shown that race, gender, and region inflected and mediated the Communist Party line.[24] While revisionist accounts have often been persuasive, this analysis suggests a more complex history. In Brookwood's early years, for example, the party had shown a level of toleration for Brookwood, allowing its members to attend the college and inviting Brookwood faculty to lecture at the Party's Workers' School. Yet in 1928, the party entered its "Third Period" in which Stalin ordered a dramatic reversal of the policy of "boring from within" and a shift to dual unionism. In making this shift, the American Communist Party became openly revolutionary, frontally attacking the American Federation of Labor (AFL) and refusing to compromise with elements it dubbed "social fascist," such as Muste and Brookwood Labor College.[25] As a result, Muste, along with other liberals and non-Communist leftists, increasingly found Communists impossible to work with, a sentiment that should be distinguished from "red-baiting," which progressives viewed as a "bogey" that hindered labor's progress.[26]

Despite these differences, Communists, independent leftists, progressive laborites, and religious liberals all shared "a transformative concept of social progress," in the words of historian Doug Rossinow.[27] Muste, for example, placed Christ in the Hebrew prophetic tradition to suggest that he was a revolutionary who stood against the church and state of his time. Like other liberal Protestants of his generation, he adopted a kind of philo-Semitism in which the Jewish view of history as a project of the human and the divine served as the basis for his radical politics. "To be religious," Muste sermonized, "is to get out of Egypt into Canaan," to refuse to be slaves and to seek out the promised land of milk and honey.[28]

Muste's radical ideals remained deeply important to him, despite the fact that he adopted a moderate tone and practical orientation in the 1920s. As economic and political conditions changed, and as the labor movement and the far left began to publicly attack and vilify him, he would revise his ideas about how to strengthen the labor movement and build a socialist America. His efforts gave birth to the Conference for Progressive Labor Action (CPLA) in early 1929, an organization committed to revitalizing the American labor movement through aggressive and militant efforts to organize industrial workers and an unabashed idealism.

Historians typically associate the "Musteite" movement with the American Workers Party (AWP), which was founded in December 1933 only to merge with the Trotskyist Communist League of America (CLA) a year later and become the Workers Party of the United States (WPUS). Yet the movement actually began with the founding of the CPLA as a reaction to the marginalization and persecution of labor progressives within the AFL.[29] As a result of the CPLA's informal character, which was often no more than a progressive caucus within a union, the Musteites' influence on the labor movement has not received adequate scholarly attention. Yet, as we shall see, they played a key role in jump-starting the movement for industrial unionism and were one of the main forces behind the movement of unemployed men and women in the early years of the Great Depression.[30]

The Musteites also made important theoretical and organizational innovations. Drawing upon their efforts in the workers' education movement, they attempted to "Americanize" Marxism by placing praxis at the center of organizing and revolutionary activity. As a result, they would attract intellectuals like Sidney Hook, V. F. Calverton, and Lewis Corey who were eager to reconcile pragmatism and Marxism and to make culture a front in the struggle for a socialist society. Their theoretical framework, in other words, was not imposed from above by late-coming intellectuals, but rather had been developed by the working-class men and women who formed the shock troops of the CPLA.[31] This largely unknown story of the "Musteites" helps fill in gaps in the history of the left and labor from 1929 through 1934 and provides a social history of the independent radicals and industrial unionists who would become the backbone of the CIO and the Popular Front.[32]

Ironically, just as the CIO exploded onto the scene, Muste's own movement was on the verge of collapse. The Musteites had become more openly revolutionary over the course of the 1930s, viewing the widespread labor revolts as a sign of an imminent workers' revolution. But it soon became apparent that the thrust of the revitalized labor movement was toward social democracy rather than communism. Muste sought to resolve this dilemma by adopting the Leninist idea of a vanguard party who would lead the masses in the revolution. In the interest of party building, he welcomed overtures from the Trotskyist CLA to merge their respective parties. But the Trotskyists did not conduct the merger in good faith; over the course of 1935, Muste watched in dismay as his most dedicated supporters left the party in disgust to serve as organizers for the CIO or to join the Communist Party, which had now entered its dynamic united front period. By early 1936, Muste's movement was in shambles.[33]

Muste's options were limited. He could have remained in the Trotskyist movement, yet that would have meant being surrounded by comrades he had come to view as petty, duplicitous, self-interested, and ruthless. He could have joined the CIO, but that would have entailed some reconciliation with his old nemesis John L. Lewis, with whom he had tangled in the civil wars that had wracked the United Mine Workers of America in the late 1920s and early 1930s.[34] It also would have involved some compromise with the Democratic Party. Yet Muste firmly believed, with other Trotskyists, that President Franklin Roosevelt would take the nation into another world war, and that it would not be a war against fascism, but a war for American capitalism and imperialism. It turned out, of course, to be *both* a war against fascism and a war for American global hegemony, yet Muste would prove congenitally unable to make this "Faustian bargain," as Nelson Lichtenstein has called the rapprochement made between socialists, the Democratic Party, and the warfare state over the course of the New Deal era.[35]

It was in this painful and complicated context that Muste had a mystical experience that told him to return to Christianity and pacifism. His "recon-version" was no doubt genuine, as it paralleled a similar moment of tran-scendence that he had during World War I, but it also allowed him to leave the secular left and the labor movement, where he had found himself compromised and marginalized, and to return to the Christian-pacifist community and to mainline Protestantism.

Ever the social activist, Muste derived political meaning from his mysti-cal experience. As he explained in numerous articles, speeches, and a book entitled *Non-violence in an Aggressive World*, the "proletarian movement" had been "corrupted" by "the philosophy of power, the will to power, the desire to humiliate and dominate over or destroy the opponent, the accep-tance of the methods of violence and deceit, the theory that 'the end justifies the means.'" Yet once one assumes that "in some situations, you must forswear the way of love, of truth, must accept the method of domination, deceit, violence . . . there is no stopping place."[36] His return to pacifism thus grew out of a renewed appreciation of pacifists for respecting human dignity and paying attention to means.[37]

Muste's return to the church and to absolute nonviolence involved, on some level, a rejection of his pragmatism and a more unequivocal embrace of moral prophecy. Yet pragmatism would continue to shape his political character; it bequeathed him openness, flexibility, and an experimental attitude that would allow him to transcend bitter intra-left conflicts of the postwar era and to build coalitions that advanced com-mon purposes. Moreover, he continued to view the interaction between his ideals and reality as a sort of scientific project, as a search for truth. At its most creative, this approach would help to make pacifism dynamic and innovative in the post-1941 era. At its most limited, it could lead to pure prophecy, as pacifists judged American society harshly only to with-draw from it.

Muste's renewed appreciation for the prophetic tradition led to a very public and ongoing debate with the theologian Reinhold Niebuhr. In his 1932 book *Moral Man and Immoral Society*, Niebuhr charged that liberals and pacifists were insufficiently "realistic" about the realities of sin and power, and called for compromise with the coercion and violence that char-acterized real relations between social classes and nation-states. He did not, however, condone this reality, but rather hoped that prophets (such as him-self) would act as society's conscience and curb its excesses.[38] Muste sharply disagreed with this interpretation. The problem of the immorality of group behavior was indeed real, but the very "tension" Niebuhr and other "Christian realists" emphasized "exists only if the impossible demand of the Gospel is laid upon them. Otherwise . . . 'the relationship between the Kingdom of Christ and the political sphere' becomes 'a tension of static parallelism' and not 'a tension of dynamic transformation.'" Indeed, in calling for compromise with human limitations, realists had actually renounced the prophetic tradition that they claimed was their inspiration. Without a vision and without a goal, Muste predicted, realism would serve as an apology for nationalism and war.[39]

Muste's preoccupation with making pacifism politically relevant became the basis for his exploration of Gandhian nonviolence as a method for social change. When the FOR hired him as national secretary in 1940, he attempted to transform the organization into a vehicle for building a mass "nonviolent direct action Movement" that reached out to "oppressed and minority groups such as Negroes, share-croppers, industrial workers . . . as Gandhi did in the India National Congress."[40] His efforts helped to lead to a renaissance in American pacifism. As one FOR staffer would recall, the era of World War II was the "golden age of the FOR." The staff and the executive board were "composed of giants" like Bayard Rustin, Glenn Smiley, James Farmer, and George Houser. Muste "towered" over all of them.[41]

With Muste's active encouragement, the main target of these early experiments with nonviolence was American race relations.[42] As a labor progressive, Muste had long been a vocal opponent of racial segregation and discrimination, but he had ultimately subordinated race to class, viewing it as a problem that would be resolved with the inclusion of black workers in the labor movement. Changes in American political economy over the course of the late 1930s and into the 1940s led him to question this analysis. Although he welcomed the social legislation of the New Deal, he feared that it would lead to a rapport between labor and the Democratic Party that would compromise labor's independence and diffuse its radical spirit. American intervention under a Democratic president only increased these concerns, as he predicted that the close relationship between labor and the state would tie the movement to American militarism and imperialism.[43] African Americans and other marginalized groups thus appeared uniquely situated to recognize and mobilize against the contradictions of American society. Gandhi had shown, moreover, how nonviolence could be a powerful tool in confronting the problem of caste.[44]

Although World War II was a time of creativity and dynamism for the pacifist movement, it was also a time of marginalization and defensiveness, as pacifists' opposition to the war brought them the enmity not only of the public, but also of longtime friends and allies. Already on the defensive since the publication of *Moral Man and Immoral Society*, they now faced a full-on assault. As Niebuhr powerfully argued, "Whatever may be the moral ambiguities of the so-called democratic nations . . . it is sheer moral perversity to equate the inconsistencies of a democratic civilization with the brutalities which modern tyrannical States practise. If we cannot make a distinction here, there are no historical distinctions which have any value."[45] As a consequence, pacifism shifted from being at the center of mainline Protestantism to the margins, in the process assuming a more distinct identity of nonconformity.[46]

Muste's analysis of the causes and potentially negative consequences of the war were not unfounded. Yet, as is further explored in Chapter 9 below, it lacked the nuance and complexity for which he was well known. After all, he had long held that it was morally irresponsible for pacifists to refuse to take sides in the class struggle and in the struggle against racism and Jim Crow. And later, during the Cold War, he would qualify his pacifism to accommodate liberation struggles in the global South. But, in the case of World War II, he was unequivocal in his support for neutrality legislation and his opposition to American intervention.

In part, Muste's rigidity can be explained by his career and his biography; he had, just in the late 1930s, found his footing once again within the world of pacifism, something he would have jeopardized had he compromised his pacifism in the name of a war against fascism. But it also speaks to a stubborn optimism about human nature at the core of his pacifist faith, one that made it difficult for him to appreciate the ideological dimensions of the conflict. As Bhikhu Parekh has commented of Gandhi, Muste assumed that all human beings were essentially good and that their hearts would be moved by the power of self-suffering. "*Satyagraha* presupposes a sense of decency on the part of the opponent, an open society in which his brutality can be exposed, and a neutral body of opinion that can be mobilized against him. It also presupposes that the parties involved are interdependent, as otherwise non-cooperation by the victims cannot affect the vital interests of their opponents." Yet the ruthless suppression of public discourse and the sanitized and hidden violence of totalitarian regimes left little room for the power of moral prophecy to have any meaningful effect on centers of power or the course of the war. Moreover, as Parekh comments, "some human beings might be profoundly distorted and beyond hope."[47]

Still, a distinction should be made between opposition to war and resistance to war. Once the United States entered the conflict, Muste urged pacifists not to "sabotage or obstruct the war measures of the government" and instead focus their energies upon building pacifist fellowship, protecting civil liberties and the rights of conscientious objection, and seeking "human betterment and reconciliation" at home, particularly by befriending interned Japanese Americans and fighting for racial equality.[48] Indeed, more so than their contemporaries, pacifists acknowledged the ways in which the Allies, especially the United States, contradicted their own rhetoric. This was particularly evident in their response to the atomic bomb. As Muste asserted in his 1947 book *Not by Might: Christianity, the Way to Human Decency*, the specter of "total, global, atomic war" had rendered the just-war tradition of the Christian church obsolete.[49]

As Paul Boyer argues in his classic history of the atomic bomb and U.S. culture, *By the Bomb's Early Light*, Muste's "eloquent manifesto posed profound dilemmas for the non-pacifist Christian who held with the just-war tradition that some conflicts were morally justifiable, and who believed that World War II fell in this category, but who recognized that it had ended in a orgy of killing almost beyond restraint or limit." Niebuhr, for example, initially agreed with the Federal Council of Churches that the surprise attacks on Hiroshima and Nagaskai were "morally indefensible," but soon thereafter justified their use as having shortened the war. The public dialogue that emerged after the war about the moral, ethical, and political challenges posed by atomic weapons quickly subsided, due in large part to the emergence of the Cold War and the U.S. government's desire to promote a positive image of the atom. The campaign for international control of atomic energy and world government also foundered in the face of worsening relations between the United States and the Soviet Union.[50]

The emergence of the Cold War also brought long-standing tensions between the anti-Communist and Popular Front wings of the American liberal left to the surface. Anti-Stalinists like Sidney Hook and Norman Thomas maintained that the Communist Party represented a totalitarian threat and therefore did not deserve democratic rights of free speech and free association. Similarly, Christian realists accelerated their attack on liberal Protestants who hoped for peace and reconciliation with the Soviet

Union, calling them naive and irresponsible. Realism required a sharp differentiation between the sacred and profane and an acceptance that the ends could justify the means, including the reality and threat of nuclear warfare. By the end of the decade, American liberalism as a whole became more "realistic," moving away from its indictment of corporate capitalism and unabashedly embracing a foreign policy bereft of Wilsonian moral idealism.[51]

Muste occupies a complex place in this history. On the one hand, his pacifist critique of science and technology in the atomic era called elements of the Enlightenment tradition into question. He also shared the anti-Stalinist analysis of the Soviet Union as a totalitarian regime intent on expanding its power. Moreover, many of his closest friends occupied the libertarian wing of the liberal left that was purging organizations like the ACLU of Communists.[52] On the other hand, he recognized early on that a politics of anti-Communism served as a justification for an expansion of American military might and the suppression of civil liberties. As a pacifist and a devout Christian, furthermore, he was deeply troubled by the tendency of his fellow Protestants to identify the fate of Christianity with the nation-state and U.S. foreign policy. It seemed to him that the United States, like the Soviet Union, was guilty of excessive secularism and materialism, manifest most alarmingly in the twin evils of conscription and atomic weaponry.[53]

Muste thus explicitly shunned "realism" and immediate political effectiveness in favor of a long-term campaign designed to appeal to the moral conscience of his fellow Americans. While "common sense and realism" were important, they were not "our first and greatest need," he wrote in an open letter to Niebuhr. For Christian realists to pronounce judgment and doom on Americans for their atomic hubris without also calling on them to "repent, act and so flee from that judgment" allowed socialists and liberals to make their peace with war. The role of a prophet was not only to invoke a realization of God's judgment but also to offer the possibility of escape from that judgment through repentance. Instead of realism, what the world desperately needed was "faith and hope" that it was possible "to build a just and durable peace."[54]

Together with other radical pacifists, Muste formed the Peacemakers, a group dedicated to "holy Disobedience against the war-making and conscripting State."[55] Reflecting their essentially Christian worldview, they believed that by taking suffering upon themselves in individual and collective acts of disobedience, they would cut through the conformist culture of the Cold War and awaken their fellow Americans to their responsibility for the atomic and international crisis. With their themes of sin and suffering, repentance and redemption, Muste and his fellow Peacemakers continued and elaborated traditions of idealism and antimilitarism into the postwar era, both of which were being abandoned by large sections of the Protestant mainline, the labor movement, and the left.[56]

Yet the Peacemakers ultimately proved disappointing to Muste. With the hardening of the Cold War, radical pacifists began to despair that they would ever change American opinion. Most turned inward, toward the building of alternative or "intentional" communities, some of which manifested deeply antimodern and sectarian values. Muste found the movement's cultural politics discomfiting. While he believed in the importance of simple living, he remained a modern, delighting in the diversity, commotion, and cultural life of urban environments; he smoked and danced, and enjoyed Broadway shows, baseball, and the Marx Brothers. Indeed, parallels to Gandhi only go so far, as Muste firmly rejected asceticism and pre-industrial nostalgia. "I believe men are meant to lead the 'abundant life,'" he explained to his more abstemious comrades, "and this means physically, aesthetically, intellectually, spiritually . . . this involves variety, nonconformity, experimentation."[57]

Muste also remained a socialist, and he viewed utopian experiments as, paradoxically, expressions of individualism and anarchism. Civil liberties and decentralism were not ends in themselves, but rather part of a larger effort to democratize and demilitarize the politics of the left. If we "profess to conceive of mankind as a family which should live as a family," he commented, "then our only valid objective is the transformation of society, not the building of a shelter for the saints or a secular elite within a corrupt social order, which in effect is assumed to be beyond redemption."[58]

This difference between radical pacifists and their titular head remained in abeyance until the mid-1950s when world-historical events intervened and persuaded Muste that a political and ideological space had opened up for mass action. He pointed to the Montgomery bus boycott as evidence that nonviolence might appeal to large numbers of people. He also suggested that growing public concern over nuclear fallout might be directed into opposition to the arms race and American foreign policy. In addition to these fissures within domestic political culture, international developments suggested some possibility for easing the tensions between the two superpowers. Soviet premier Nikita Khrushchev's denunciation of Stalin might lead to the humanization of Soviet rule; it might, moreover, be the grounds upon which the "split between Socialists and Communists could be healed" and a new left reborn. The emergence of a nonaligned movement in the decolonizing world was the most promising development of all.[59]

In the late 1950s and early 1960s, Muste sought to build a nonaligned "third way" and antinuclear sentiment through his leadership of and organizational efforts on behalf of the Committee for Nonviolent Action (CNVA) and the World Peace Brigade (WPB), both of which exemplified the prophetic, existential style of political activism he had pioneered in the 1940s. Their dramatic, often transnational campaigns had Muste crisscrossing the globe, engaging in dialogue and building relationships with European and Asian peace activists and clergy that would help lay the foundations for the international antinuclear movement and the revitalization of the international peace movement.[60]

At the same time, he took tentative steps toward rebuilding the United States' shattered and divided left. He helped to found *Liberation* magazine in 1956 as a vehicle for promoting "fresh thinking," and he pursued reconciliation of anti-Communist socialists and Communists through the American Forum for Socialist Education.[61] The latter effort was a failure that illustrated the ways in which the question of Communism continued to divide liberals and socialists. Through *Liberation*, CNVA, and the civil rights movement, however, he would find that the younger generation was far more willing to move beyond the ideological divides of the Old Left and, moreover, that they shared his idealism and his flair for direct action and nonviolence.

The mid-1950s were also a time of personal change in which Muste's assumptions about cultural norms, sexuality, and gender were challenged in a variety of ways. Muste had long had relationships of mutual respect and love with activists who were women, homosexual, and/or people of color. Yet, like others of his generation, he simply did not see the realm of family, gender, and sexuality as having political meanings. This was most apparent in his relationship with his wife, Anne (called "Anna" by her friends and family) whose life had been in service to making his political commitments possible. Yet her death in 1953 did not lead him to question the degree to which his public self had been dependent upon her private labor. Instead, he praised her for her "loyalty," a comment that reveals his patriarchal assumptions about the proper role of women in relationship to men.[62]

At the same time, however, his ideas about morality and sexuality started to shift. One can see this in his evolving views of Bayard Rustin's homosexuality, as well as his reflections upon the cultural changes that had begun to make themselves felt by the end of the 1950s. Muste never politicized sexuality or gender, but his pragmatic sensibility and commitment to nonviolence allowed him to maintain open lines of communication and productive relationships with people whose cultural and sexual identities were far more subversive than his own. Hence the seemingly paradoxical place of honor the Protestant elder occupied in the minds and hearts of bohemian nonconformists like Allen Ginsberg, Paul Goodman, Judith Malina, Julian Beck, and Barbara Deming.[63]

This was how Muste became a cultural and political icon in the 1960s. Bohemian radicals and Freudian psychoanalysts viewed him as a model of the self-actualized personality, delighting in his advocacy of authenticity, spontaneity, and love. Intellectuals dialogued with him about the problems of conformity and organization in contemporary American society, and admired his ability to take the existential leap of faith and action that eluded them. Liberal Protestants increasingly found his critique of realism persuasive, and joined him in signing petitions and marching in demonstrations against nuclear testing and the Vietnam War. Civil rights activists praised him for his pioneering efforts on behalf of nonviolence; as Martin Luther King Jr. told Muste's biographer, the jazz critic Nat Hentoff, "The current emphasis on nonviolent direct action in the race relations field is due more to A. J. than to anyone else in the country."[64]

Pacifists, meanwhile, continued to draw strength and sustenance from what they viewed as his equanimity, expressed through joyfulness and humor, as well as his spiritual constancy and depth of vision. "We are all sons of A. J.," Tom Cornell of the Catholic Worker Movement proclaimed.[65] Muste was "the leader, prophet, confessor and gadfly to us all," recalled Glenn Smiley.[66] Without Muste's leadership, antiwar activists concurred, the coalition against the war in Vietnam would not have been possible. Activists outside of the United States similarly recognized Muste's centrality to struggles for peace and freedom; Indian pacifists referred to him as "the American Gandhi," and when he died, telegrams streamed in from around the world, from places as diverse as Tanzania, India, North Vietnam, England, France, and Chile.[67]

Of course, philosophical, political, and cultural differences continued to inhibit Muste's efforts. Many pacifists remained unwilling or unable to relate to all but true believers in nonviolence, while liberals and social democrats remained reluctant to move beyond anti-Communism and the bipolar worldview of the Cold War.[68] Perhaps Muste shared some responsibility for these difficulties. After all, his political position was a fairly complex and nuanced one that was difficult to enact in practice. He called on peace activists to avoid united fronts, while keeping the lines of communication with Communists open. He called on them to be "prophets," while at the same time instructing them to be "canny" and pragmatic. He called for an absolute commitment to nonviolence, while urging qualified support for third world revolutionaries who embraced violence. For Muste, such were the inevitable contradictions of living as a revolutionary and a pacifist in a sinful world, and he was not personally troubled by them. Yet this made for an unclear and confusing strategy for nonviolent activists to follow.[69]

Starting in 1964, Muste became utterly consumed with ending the war in Vietnam. "I cannot get it out of my head or my guts that Americans are away over there, not only shooting at people but dropping bombs on them, roasting them with napalm and all the rest," he wrote in 1965.[70] In his speeches and publications, he insisted that Vietnam was not a "mistake," but rather an expression of an overall "pattern" in American history and foreign policy. All of us "are trapped in the heritage of the past," he observed, particularly the Western heritage of equating power with the use of force and violence, and of subjugating "others" based on notions of racial, national, and religious superiority. Yet he refused to be trapped by history, insisting that if Americans—"especially white Anglo-Saxon Americans"—genuinely confronted their sins of empire and race, then a "radically new approach" to relations between nations and people would become possible. As he wrote in 1965, "if a power like the United States voluntarily withdraws from the arms race and makes the changes in its own social structure which this entails, this would constitute 'intervention' of historic dimensions."[71]

Muste's efforts to end the war in Vietnam combined his pragmatic and prophetic impulses. On the one hand, he worked relentlessly to overcome the divisions on the liberal left and within the peace and civil rights movements that inhibited taking a strong stance against President Lyndon B. Johnson and the war. In New York, the result was a new coalition, headed by Muste, known as the Fifth Avenue Peace Parade Committee, which managed to bring together groups as diverse as labor unions, women's peace groups, black power revolutionaries, Protestant clergy, young Trotskyists, and liberal peace activists in opposition to the war. In the fall of 1966, the Parade Committee worked with other anti-war groups to form the November 8th Mobilization Committee, which, in early 1967 became known as the Spring Mobilization Committee to End the War in Vietnam (MOBE), with Muste as national chairman.[72]

At the same time, Muste insisted upon his right and the moral imperative of resistance, regardless of its popular appeal. As he wrote to a fellow peace activist, "Are prophets not needed in this age? Should prophets keep silence if they are unpopular and unheeded?" The "real world" was neither the "world of ethics, love, nonviolence" nor "the world of power." Rather, these two worlds were in "perpetual tension," a tension that only became creative "when, in [Martin] Buber's phrase, 'the plowshare of the normative principle' is driven into the hard soil of political [reality], not when the plow is withdrawn from or blunted by the hard soil."[73] Muste thus encouraged and participated in myriad civil disobedience campaigns against the war. His final act of defiance, at age eighty-two, was to bypass the State Department and visit with Ho Chi Minh in order to "convey the spirit of peace to the stricken people of Vietnam." He died in February 1967, soon after his return.[74]

Central to Muste's enduring radical politics was his philosophy of history as a joint project of human beings and God. Drawing parallels to his biblical namesake, he held that history began when Abraham left the city of his ancestors. By going out to find "a city which existed—and yet had to be brought into existence," Abraham demonstrated that divinity was to be found in the history of human work and creation. For Muste, then, "the crucial thing about men, or societies, is not where they came from but where they are going." Indeed, it was precisely when "human communities" decided to "intervene in their own destiny" that history was made rather than lived.[75]

Since the 1960s, the liberal left has faltered and declined, losing faith in transcendent ideas of social progress and in the power of human beings to make change. Muste would have shared these critiques of the Enlightenment tradition and its notions of rationality, universality, and progress, but he also would have insisted on the human and divine imperative to continue dreaming and creating. "Without a vision, the people perish," he wrote in 1955, paraphrasing Proverbs 29:18, at the height of the Cold War.[76] Regardless of whether one shares his pacifism or his religious faith, his

thoughtful and determined efforts to reconcile idealism and realism, collectivism and liberalism, internationalism and Americanism, anti-imperialism
and labor unionism may offer insights on how to reinvigorate the dynamic
and contested liberal left that once so indelibly shaped American political
culture.

CHAPTER 1

⌒

Calvinism, Class, and the Making
of a Modern Radical

Character is built by action rather than by thought.
Contemplation does not beget virtues. But out of the
elements of the daily struggle we mold at last conceptions
of justice, parity and truth and build that temple of
morality which is the chosen seat of true religion. Finally,
it is only through the conflict into which his unrest urges
him that man at last finds God. Revelation is powerless if it
enlightens only the reason. . . . And faith is valid only when
it leads to action, so its ultimate satisfaction is found only
in the active life.

—A. J. Muste, 1905

MUSTE WAS BORN in January 1885 in Zierikzee, a port town in the province of Zeeland in the Netherlands. Zierikzee, Muste learned later in life, was apparently the Dutch "equivalent of our Podunk," small, poor, and remote.[1] Indeed, from the nineteenth century to the present, Zierikzee and Zeeland as a whole have had a reputation for economic backwardness and religious orthodoxy. A series of islands located on the extreme southwestern coastal zone of the Netherlands, much of Zeeland actually lies below sea level and is protected by a system of river and sea dikes. This location gave rise to a paradoxical character. On the one hand, as its reputation as the boondocks of the Netherlands suggests, Zeeland was isolated from the mainland. On the other hand, because it was located in the estuaries of some of Europe's greatest rivers, it was a commercially and strategically important area to control.[2]

This paradox of isolation and interconnectedness provides the backdrop for Muste's experiences in the Netherlands, the reasons for his migration to the United States in 1891, and perhaps even a key to his adult character and politics. A close analysis of his childhood and youth reveals that the Dutch American community was less insulated and conservative than Muste characterized it or than historians of Dutch ethnicity have recognized. Despite their best efforts to isolate themselves, the small world of Dutch American Calvinists intersected with larger processes of global capitalism, industrialization and class formation, international migration patterns, urbanization, and cultural changes related to religion and gender. It is in these intersections that it becomes possible to understand the making of a modern radical.

THROUGHOUT the nineteenth century, Zeeland's economy was like its geography, both remote from and integrated into the world market. As the least urbanized and industrialized province in a country that already lagged far behind its neighbors in its level of modernization, Zeeland had a profoundly rural character. At the same time, however, the development of its rich sea-clay soil was capital and labor intensive, which encouraged concentration and proletarianization. In spite of the expansion in commercial agriculture, Holland's modern industrial sector did not grow fast enough to absorb the increasing rural population. The result was a rising number of day laborers and servants reliant upon a commercial economy vulnerable to world market fluctuations. True to its reputation, Zeeland led the country in child and infant mortality, death and birth rates, and emigration rates.[3]

The Mustes were a quintessential Zeeland family.[4] The patriarch, Martin (also known as Marinus) Muste, was the second oldest child in a poor family of five or six children. When he obtained a job in Zierikzee as a coachman for the local nobility, the sense was that he had risen "a bit in the economic scale."[5] The matriarch, Adriana Jonker, came from a large family of ten or eleven children in the countryside and was, Muste recalled, "very definitely a peasant woman." Unlike Martin, who had completed the fourth grade and who could read and write, Adriana read with difficulty and she could not write. Her and Martin's first child, a son, Abraham Johannes, had died in infancy, and they gave their second child the same name. Soon thereafter, Adriana gave birth to three more children, two daughters, Nelley and Cornelia, and a son, Cornelius.[6]

In spite of his family's poverty, Muste never had a sense of weariness or desperation and recalled having a contented and happy childhood. His mother was "an extremely good housekeeper and a good cook," who kept her family clothed and fed. One St. Nicholas Day—the Dutch equivalent of Christmas—stood out in Muste's memory as being particularly joyful. He must have been about three years old, since only his sister Nelley was present, as they waited by the staircase for Santa Claus. Suddenly, there was a commotion and cinnamon-spiced nuts began rolling down the stairs. "Then Santa Claus himself came stomping down the stairs, distributing gifts. He left by the front door and in a moment or two mother came back laughing happily. It was a most stimulating and yet soothing sensation to have a real Santa Claus and a real mother at the same time and in the same person."[7]

In later years, Muste would attribute the class culture of his Dutch upbringing to Calvinism. The view of his parents and of the broader Dutch culture was that one had to be contented with one's station in life because it had been assigned by God. The "dominant pattern," Muste recalled, was "acquiescence in the will of God rather than rebellion against it."[8] Muste's parents were members of the Dutch Reformed Church (Nederlands Hervormde Kerk), which was established as the state church after the country won its independence from Spain in 1648. John Calvin, of course, was Martin Luther's successor in the Protestant Reformation. Born in France in 1509, Calvin shared Luther's core beliefs but took them even further than the reformer. From Luther's emphasis on God's saving grace alone, Calvin elaborated the doctrine of predestination, which emphasized the utter estrangement of human beings from God and their powerlessness to affect their salvation.[9]

Controversies within the Hervormde Kerk would spill over into the Dutch immigrant communities in the United States. In 1834, there was the first of several major secessionist movements. The separatists opposed the state's recent assertion of supremacy over religious matters, which they viewed as a sign that the church was succumbing to the theological liberalism of the Enlightenment. The Seceder movement grew rapidly in the rural parts of the Netherlands, including Zeeland. State and ecclesiastical authorities viewed the Seceders as a threat and heavily persecuted them. This repression, along with agricultural crises and economic depression, encouraged Seceders to immigrate to the United States, giving them a greater influence in the new country than they had in the old. Although repression waned over the course of the nineteenth century, there was a second secession (known as the Doleantie) in 1886, under the leadership of Abraham Kuyper, and their influence grew tremendously when he was elected prime minister in 1901.[10]

In contrast to Max Weber's thesis that Calvinism constituted the cultural arm of capitalist modernization, Seceders tended to be hostile to liberal ideas, while the most economically prosperous and more liberal tended to be members of the Hervormde Kerk or smaller, more liberal Protestant denominations.[11] Indeed, the Secession was a counterrevolutionary movement in opposition to the trends unleashed by the French Revolution and the Enlightenment. According to Kuyper, the intellectual leader of the Doleantie, the Enlightenment had made three fundamental errors: "'Humanism,' making man the center and measure of reality; 'Pantheism,' identifying man and nature with God; 'Materialism,' denying the reality of the spiritual and non-empirical." Only "a restored spiritual ethos" would provide "ties that could harmonize individuals and groups without enslaving them. Only divine authority could check human power; only the transcendent realm gave hope to the oppressed, sound standards of value for public conduct, and dignity to human life." Kuyper was thus both a conservative and a reformer, calling for a return to an organic, patriarchal order that would have little room for plurality and difference, while at the same time recognizing the oppressive tendencies of the modern state and industrial order.[12]

Calvinism appears severe to modern eyes. Yet it is important to recognize that Calvin did not view predestination as an expression of despair in humanity. Rather, the "sweet and pleasant doctrine of damnation," as Calvin put it, spoke to the utter majesty of God.[13] Certainly Muste did not experience Calvinism or the cultural life of the Reformed Church as stern or dreary. Sunday was for Muste "*the* high day of the week—a day of 'rest and gladness,' of 'joy and light.'"[14] His family, while reserved, was warm and loving, and found amusement in activities that fell within the moral strictures of the church. Indeed, although he would later reject Calvinistic theological doctrines like predestination, his religious heritage shaped his life and politics long after he left the Reformed Church. In particular, he retained "a strong conviction about human frailty and corruption" and the belief that one's life must conform to the "imperious demand" of the gospel. Later, in the 1930s and 1940s, when he developed a critique of

Marxism and the Enlightenment tradition more broadly, he seemed to echo Kuyper in his insistence that belief in God was ultimately the only way to save humankind from destroying itself. His more skeptical relationship to liberalism and more pessimistic view of human nature differentiated him from his fellow Social Gospel clergy. It would also make him the most thoughtful and insightful pacifist critic of neo-orthodoxy, a theological movement that began after World War I as a reaction to nineteenth-century liberal theology and a positive reevaluation of the Reformed tradition.[15]

The overwhelming preponderance of Seceders and lower-class members of the Hervormde Kerk in Dutch migration encouraged an earlier generation of historians to emphasize religious over economic factors in influencing Dutch migration. Yet recent scholarship has established the centrality of structural causes.[16] Certainly economic considerations influenced the Muste family's decision to move to the United States. In the 1880s, Holland experienced an agricultural crisis that accelerated the mechanization and consolidation of commercial agriculture in the sea-clay-soil regions. Zeeland was hit especially hard, and during the years 1880 through 1893, it contributed a larger proportion of emigrants than any other province.[17]

Included among the second wave of Dutch immigration in the 1880s were four of Muste's maternal uncles, poorly paid agricultural laborers eager to improve their livelihood. The Jonker brothers settled in Grand Rapids, Michigan, home to a substantial Dutch community, where they managed to establish small businesses in groceries, drugs, and scrap metal. "Having achieved a measure of security for themselves," Muste recalled, "they considered the plight of their youngest and favorite sister, my mother, and one of them paid us a visit and proposed that our family emigrate."[18]

The journey, which occurred in late January and early February 1891, was long and arduous. Like most immigrants, the family, which included six-year-old Muste and three younger siblings, traveled in steerage, where conditions were cramped and food was scarce. Part of the voyage was stormy; Adriana became sick and had to be taken out of steerage into the ship's hospital. Still, the experience was a thrilling one; Muste recalled the "awe" of viewing the "tremendous expanse" of the ocean and the excitement of disembarking at New York City's Castle Garden (the immigration depot that preceded Ellis Island), bustling with people and boats. The family remained at Castle Garden for a month while Adriana recovered in the hospital. Although concerned about his mother's health, Muste had "only the happiest of recollections" of Castle Garden; the children had the run of the hospital's corridors, the food was better than they were accustomed to, and, most crucially, the "atmosphere was a friendly one."[19]

The Muste family's positive experience at Castle Garden was not unusual. The port was "so commodious, well-run, and protective of the new arrivals that its fame spread throughout Europe."[20] But their warm welcome also reflected the fact that the Dutch were considered especially desirable immigrants, in contrast to southern and eastern European immigrants who would succeed them. As Muste drolly recalled, "there was no barrier of culture as there was to be later with immigrants from Eastern Europe, and no barrier of color as with Negroes or Asians. . . . Almost without exception [the Dutch] were sober and industrious. . . . They were allergic to unions or 'agitators' of any kind."[21]

It was at Castle Garden that Muste had his first initiation into late nineteenth-century American nationalism. When one of the attendants learned that Muste's name was Abraham, he began calling the Dutch boy "Abraham Lincoln," naming him, as it were, as an American. Even though Muste had no idea who Abraham Lincoln was, when he finally arrived in Grand Rapids, one of his first projects "was to find out what this Abraham Lincoln meant." The result was a strong identification with the Great Emancipator, an identification no doubt encouraged by the fact that the midwestern city, so close to Illinois, was Lincoln country. "My education . . . of this country," Muste mused, "was the picture of the trip down the Mississippi and seeing the slave sold on the block in New Orleans and saying, 'If I ever have a chance to hit that thing, I'll hit it hard!' " By the time he was nine years old, he had memorized the entire Gettysburg Address.[22]

In later years, Muste would reflect that his largely positive experience of emigration and immigration might offer a key to understanding his character and adult political commitments. The ocean voyage had "its apprehensions," but it ultimately had a "happy ending." This taught him that "the peril is *not* to move when the new situation develops, the new insight dawns, the new experiment becomes possible." Just as the biblical Abraham went out to find "a city which existed—and yet had to be brought into existence," divinity was to be found in the history of human work and creation. History was, moreover, a "movement toward a goal."[23] As Muste's references to Abraham suggest, this philosophy of history as a joint project of human beings and God toward the city-which-is-to-be is deeply rooted in both Judaism and Christianity and helped to shape the progressive view of history that has characterized Western political thought since the Enlightenment. Certainly it encouraged Muste, along with others of his generation, to view political activism as a religious imperative.

As Muste's rapid assimilation into the drama of the Lincoln republic reveals, many Hollanders quickly identified with the new nation. For them, Muste recalled, the United States was "a land of opportunity and freedom, the land to which God had led the Pilgrim fathers, a land where youth was not conscripted, and a Christian land, though unfortunately not entirely peopled by orthodox Calvinists."[24] Yet Muste's caveat is an important one, and it helps to explain why the Dutch retained a distinct ethnic identity even as they outwardly blended with other northern and western European immigrants. As the rich historiography of religion in nineteenth-century America has shown, the Second Great Awakening in the 1830s spread the idea that individuals had the right of private judgment in spiritual matters and the possibility of salvation through faith and good works. The culture of American Protestantism was, in other words, an evangelical one, imbued with an antinomianism that was anathema to pietistic Dutch Calvinists.[25]

The Dutch Americans' relationship to the new country, and their politics, reflected their differences with mainline Protestantism. On the one hand, they praised the United States, became staunch allies of the conservative wing of the Republican Party and the business community, and, with the exception of temperance, did not participate in the reform movements of the late nineteenth and early twentieth centuries. On the other hand, they often expressed deep ambivalence about American culture; it seemed too individualistic, superficial, materialistic, and Methodist, and appeared to threaten "the very core of the community's existence." The problem, they concluded, was theological: "the substitution of individualistic for covenantal (i.e. corporate) theology." This corporatism encouraged them to sympathize with labor and support pro-labor legislation, even as they opposed unions as anti-Christian institutions.[26]

As the Dutch struggled to define themselves in a new land, their ethnicity and Calvinist heritage became deeply intertwined, giving them a cultural persistence that defies the paradigm of western and northern European assimilation.[27] They did not rapidly assimilate and intermarry with the broader society. Although they integrated into American economic and political life, their cultural life remained largely separate. In church, school, marriage, and recreation, "the Calvinists built an institutional fortress and demonstrated their religious solidarity."[28]

Grand Rapids offers a case study in Dutch cultural persistence. In the 1890s, when the Mustes immigrated to the United States, Grand Rapids was a classic midsized, nineteenth-century midwestern city, with a rapidly growing population of just over sixty thousand residents. A frontier outpost for much of the antebellum period, it had been transformed by the transportation and communications revolution that integrated the nation over the course of the nineteenth century. By the time of the American Civil War, railroad and telegraph lines linked the city with distant urban markets. Soon, Grand Rapids became a manufacturing center, its famous river lined with furniture factories and working-class neighborhoods, peopled by immigrants from the Netherlands, Germany, Poland, and Canada.[29]

The Dutch composed the largest of Grand Rapids' immigrant groups; in 1900, 40 percent of the city's population was of Dutch birth or ancestry.[30] Dutch immigrants first began streaming into Michigan in the late 1840s, when the Reverend Albertus C. Van Raalte led a group of Dutch Seeders to western Michigan, where they established Holland, the first of several Dutch *kolonies*. Gradually, many of these rural pioneers trickled into the village of Grand Rapids, where they were joined by succeeding waves of their compatriots.[31] As the Dutch presence in the city grew, the number of Reformed churches multiplied, along with Christian schools, which maintained instruction in the Dutch language and educated immigrant children in Reformed doctrine.[32]

Within the Reformed Church, doctrinal and cultural questions became inseparable, as quarrels over theology intersected with the thorny issue of Americanization. Despite Van Raalte's reputation as a zealous reformer, he had affiliated and built close ties with the Reformed Church in America (RCA), which had deep roots in North America. Strict on doctrine and religious piety, Van Raalte also stressed the importance of learning the English language and encouraged rapid naturalization. Opposition to Van Raalte's concept of Americanization soon emerged, as dissenters questioned affiliation with the American church, which they charged with insufficient orthodoxy. In 1857, the separatists founded the Christian Reformed Church (CRC), which had "a more gloomy view of the new country," represented by its decision to hold services in the Dutch language into the twentieth century.[33] Nevertheless, whether CRC or RCA, wherever orthodox Reformed pietism was preached, its themes were "human sin and the need for salvation, human dependence and God's mercy, the inevitability of suffering and tribulation and the need for penitence."[34]

The proliferation of Reformed churches and doctrinal disputes between them speak to the vibrancy of the Dutch community that greeted the Muste family when they finally arrived in Grand Rapids.[35] The Mustes settled into a house a block away from the Quimby furniture factory, where the Jonker brothers had obtained a job for Muste's father. Six out of ten families who lived on Quimby Street were Dutch, and approximately 60 percent of the Dutch who lived in the neighborhood were unskilled laborers who hailed from Zeeland. There were also Dutch grocers and butchers and shoe stores and clothing stores. The church the Mustes attended held services in Dutch, and Muste attended a Dutch parochial school.[36]

It would be a mistake, however, to characterize the Dutch American community and particularly the Mustes as thoroughly isolated and remote from the dominant culture. Soon after they arrived, Adriana and Martin decided to join the RCA and not the CRC, despite the fact that several of the Jonker brothers held prominent positions within the latter church. While it is difficult to know the precise reasons for the Mustes' decision, the implications cannot be exaggerated; even though the RCA was theologically orthodox, it was more open to the dominant culture and affiliated with the established and substantial Reformed community on the East Coast, where Muste would later attend seminary and ultimately break with Calvinism. After Muste had attended two years of parochial school, Adriana and Martin also decided to send him and his siblings to public school. Moreover, the neighborhood in which the Mustes lived was more heterogeneous than other Dutch neighborhoods. "We had . . . the impression that these Americans were likely not as orthodox as [us] and that some of their behavior was questionable behavior," Muste recalled, but ultimately the walls between them were "very thin."[37]

Martin Muste's work also brought him in contact with Americans and other nationalities. The furniture industry dominated the city's manufacturing sector and the working-class neighborhood in which the Mustes lived. Down the street and across the railroad tracks were a slew of furniture factories that provided work for an estimated one-third of the city's laborers. Native-born workers provided the skilled labor, while Dutch immigrants, along with a growing number of Poles, provided the semiskilled and unskilled labor. Working conditions were dangerous, hours were long, and child labor was not uncommon.[38] Still, "impersonality" had not yet appeared; Muste recalled of his summers working as a teenager that "the speed up . . . is much greater now than it was then. The factories I worked in were always comparatively small ones. Everybody knew everybody else. They were neighbors and it was pleasant to spend the time with them."[39]

The class culture of the furniture industry was a paternalistic one. Management was vociferously antiunion; it formed an employers' association with detailed records about each worker's wages, productivity, and union sympathies to which banks had access.[40] Much to the dismay of union organizers, Dutch immigrants, including Martin, were largely hostile to unionism, and the mass of the industry's laborers remained unorganized until the 1930s. As Muste recalled, "there was a general attitude in the Dutch churches that labor was associated with socialism and not a thing for Christian people."[41] The strong presence of the conservative Dutch and the dominance of the furniture industry meant that Grand Rapids was known for many years as an "open-shop" town. Still, there was a residual labor culture; the Knights of Labor had been strong in the city until 1886, and skilled workers like the Woodcarvers and the United Brotherhood of Carpenters and Joiners were active in the Trades and Labor Council, which organized a Labor Day parade every year that brought the Mustes and other residents out in droves.[42]

Muste's childhood in Grand Rapids revolved around neighborhood, school, and church. The Mustes, who now had a fifth child, Willemina, lived in a small, drab house that belonged to the owners of the Quimby furniture factory. Next to the house was the lumberyard, where the Muste children played hide-and-seek; to the west was the Quimby lumber mill where Martin worked; and directly across the street was the "big house," where the Quimby family lived. Muste frequently played with Irving Quimby, who was about the same age, despite Adriana's fears that Martin would be fired for the presumption. Irving introduced Muste to the Quimby family library where, "breathlessly," Muste read bound volumes of *Harper's* and *Century*, which had been running series of articles on the Civil War that filled his head with romantic accounts of battles, marches, and sieges. Veterans who lived nearby at the Old Soldiers Home enthralled Muste as they tramped by on their way downtown, where—he later learned—they bought booze. Occasionally he managed to get one of them to talk. "What a day that was!"[43]

School was for Muste an "utter fascination." From the time he started he was the best speller and reader in the class. "School never started too early in the morning for my taste. The school day always seemed to rush by. The start of vacation was in its way an occasion, but the opening day of school after Labor Day was a much more joyful and momentous one." There, his budding identity as an American was imbued with the missionary nationalism that was characteristic of nineteenth-century political culture. As Muste recalled of the ideological milieu in which he was raised, "Americans thought of themselves as the chosen people who were to bring the blessings of Christianity, democracy, prosperity and peace to all mankind." "The Civil War had, of course, been a traumatic experience. . . . By the eighteen-nineties, however, the image that was communicated to us in the schools . . . [was that] God, in his inscrutable Providence, had inflicted upon us the tragedy of the war experience. The nation, North and South, had been crucified on the Cross of War. Did not the Bible teach that 'without shedding of blood there is no remission of sin'?" Now, however, "the union was indissoluble."[44]

Impressed by the Dutch boy's intellectual abilities, Muste's teachers took a special interest in him. In eighth grade, the principal of his school encouraged him to write an essay on child labor for an annual contest sponsored by the Trades and Labor Council that he won. It is tempting to interpret Muste's denunciation of child labor as growing out of his own experience, since, starting at age eleven, he spent his summers laboring with his father at the factory, but the principal furnished him with the research he used to write the essay. But it does tell us something about the twelve-year-old boy's worldview. The essay, which reads like a sermon, begins by suggesting in Social Darwinist fashion that child labor "is the result of the brute nature in man; of the oppression of the weak by the strong." It then provides a subtle yet ultimately conservative class analysis: "the rich oppressed the poor and made the children work," which resulted in the emasculation of the male breadwinner, who becomes a loafer, "blaming the capitalists and the government," while the mother nags incessantly. Fortunately for the American people, child labor was not as widespread in the United States as it was in England. The essay concludes didactically, with an appeal to follow the golden rule.[45]

Muste's prize for winning the contest was $15 worth of books and publication of the essay in the Labor Day souvenir book, "one of the great experiences in my life." Several of the books he chose indelibly shaped his character.

An anthology of poems "helped develop a love for poetry which has been one of life's greatest and most enduring joys"; J. B. Green's *History of England* fostered a lifelong interest in history; and, finally, Ralph Waldo Emerson's *Essays* had a "seminal influence. . . . With Lincoln, Emerson was a creator of that 'American-Dream,' which, along with the great passages of the Hebrew-Christian Scriptures, molded and nourished my mind and spirit."[46]

Muste's reference to Emerson shows how public education exposed him to alternative worldviews. In contrast to the corporatist, determinist, and antiliberal thrust of the Reformed Church, Emerson preached a more modern creed of "self-reliance," of the divinity within each person and of the self's capacity for "an original relation to the universe." His question was not "What can I know?" but "how can I live?"[47] Muste the prepubescent boy was hardly aware of the tensions between transcendentalism and Calvinism, but he was strongly influenced by the Emersonian idea that the divine exists in every person, and that religion is realized in action and experience, not theological verities. These beliefs would eventually draw him—as they did Emerson—away from the formal ministry into Quakerism, nonconformity, and mysticism. They would also draw him to pragmatism, a philosophy developed by Emerson's godson, William James, which held that individual self-realization and democratic practice were inseparable.

Indeed, one of the arguments of this book is that Muste must be placed in the tradition of religious humanism associated with figures like Emerson and William James. Emerson, and transcendentalism more broadly, "insists, first, that the well-being of the individual—of all the individuals—is the basic purpose and ultimate justification for all social organizations and second that autonomous individuals cannot exist apart from others." By making the individual and his or her soul central to the modern project, transcendentalism offers an alternative to "utilitarian liberalism," on the one hand, and to "leader worship" and "collectivism," on the other. "It is the ambition, if it has not yet been the fate," writes one of Emerson's most notable biographers, "of transcendentalism to provide a soul for modern liberalism and thereby to enlarge the possibilities of modern life." This idea constitutes "the central truth of religious—not secular—humanism, the idea that is also the foundation of democratic individualism." Certainly, as we shall see, it was Muste's "central truth," providing form to the many twists and turns of his long public career.[48]

Muste's rhetorical facility was not only fostered by public school, but also by the church, which was at the center of the family's cultural life.[49] When his family entered the church on Sunday mornings, Muste felt as though he had "entered another world, the 'real' world . . . 'to Mount Zion, the city of the living God, the heavenly Jerusalem.'"[50] Years of Sunday school taught him to sermonize and, at age eleven, he gave his first sermon on the meaning of Christmas; the following year he discoursed on "Jesus, as Prophet, Priest and King." There was never a moment of doubt that he was destined for the ministry. In fact, there was no real choice in the matter; as the eldest son, his family and community expected that he would honor them by becoming a minister. But Muste's sense of destiny for the ministry also reflected his religious sensibility. At the age of thirteen, he had a mystical experience in which he was overcome by a sense of wonder and divine presence. "Suddenly," Muste recalled of this moment, "the world took on a new brightness and beauty; the words, 'Christ is risen indeed,' spoke themselves in me; and from that day God was real to me." Soon thereafter, he received confirmation, whereas most were not confirmed until age eighteen. In later years, he would come to see his youthful mysticism as a nascent expression of pacifism.[51]

Having displayed his oratorical talents and religious sophistication, Muste was given a scholarship to attend the preparatory academy attached to Hope College, an RCA denominational college located in Holland, a small, largely Dutch community about twenty-five miles west of Grand Rapids. Hope offered Muste a safe, nurturing environment for the maturation of his intellect and his spirit, while also providing him with experiences and opportunities that drew him outward, away from the known into the unknown.[52]

Hope offered a classical liberal education that was largely isolated from the new intellectual climate of biblical criticism and Darwinian biology. But by the turn of the century, outside currents had begun to creep in. The college created a department of physics and chemistry and a department of biological science, and the library began to accumulate a small collection of science books. Although secondary students were not allowed to read the heretical texts, Muste had access to them because of his job in the library. He also learned a new "point of view" from the new professor of biology Samuel O. Mast, the first and only faculty member "who was a scientist in the modern sense of the term," a vocation that created some tension between him and the college administration. He forced his students, Muste among them, to perform dissections rather than read about them.[53]

Involvement in extracurricular activities such as the YMCA and intercollegiate athletics also exposed Muste to the outside world. When Muste first arrived at Hope, "we didn't have any intercollegiate athletics at that point. That was considered rather unorthodox and rather wild." By the time he entered his freshman year, however, the college had grudgingly admitted that physical exercise, when not taken too far, could promote "Christian character."[54] The idea that new, muscular bodies of Christians would be better equipped to spread the gospel had already made deep inroads into mainline Protestantism, and at the turn of the century had just begun to penetrate conservative churches such as the RCA, due largely to the efforts of the YMCA. Muscular Christianity was the religious counterpart of the redefinition of American manliness associated with Theodore Roosevelt's cult of the strenuous life. While the old model "stressed stoicism, gentility, and self-denial," the new, Progressive model of American manhood stressed action and aggression, attributes intimately connected to Social Darwinist notions of civilization, progress, and race.[55]

Hope students, including Muste, heartily assented to these ideas. He was an active member of the campus chapter of the YMCA, helped lead the campaign for intercollegiate athletics at Hope, and, later, led the college to two state basketball championships as captain of the Flying Dutchmen.[56] He also served on the editorial board of the student newspaper, the *Anchor*, which was suffused with the language of muscular Christianity. As one 1905 editorial, probably written by Muste, put it, "In a college such as ours where so many profess to be Christians one is apt to lose sight of the serious, strenuous side of Christianity, because there is not the incessant conflict with sin that is forced upon one when in the presence of the positive evil in the world of active life."[57] His 1903 oratory on the Polish king John Sobieski, which won the Michigan state championship, similarly reveals a preoccupation with establishing the criteria for Christian manhood: "By what standard shall we determine a man's greatness?" He concludes that what made Sobieski "the Lincoln of Poland" was not just his use of force, but his principled stand for "civilization" and Christianity against the "barbarism" of the Turks.[58]

These treatises provide us with a glimpse of the teenage Muste's worldview. He appears fixated on the question of how to be both manly and Christian. Over and over again, he argues that the man of words can be a

FIGURE 1. A. J. Muste (holding ball) as captain of the Flying Dutchman
basketball team. 1904–5. (*Joint Archives of Holland*)

hero so long as he exhibits character traits like courage, sincerity, and a
willingness to take action and struggle. Like his heroes John Sobieski and
Abraham Lincoln, he pines for an "important mission" that will inspire
him "to conquer and to die on humanity's behalf."[59] These gendered concerns have a weighty quality to them; his writing is heavy with the
nineteenth-century style in which Greek mythology and history, scripture,
Victorian sentimentalism, and notions of Western progress and civilization

FIGURE 2. A portrait of the Muste family a year before Martin Jr.'s death from bronchitis. Front row, left to right: Martin Muste, Martin Jr., and Adriana Muste. Back row, left to right: Cornelia, A. J., Nellie, Cornelius, and Minnie. Circa 1906. (*Marian Johnson*)

blend together in ways that appear self-important to twenty-first-century eyes. Still, a softer side to Muste occasionally makes an appearance, like an Emersonian ode to nature's beauty and another on the importance of honoring poets, not just warriors and statesmen.[60]

Meanwhile, back at home, life continued as usual. The Mustes attended the same church and lived in the same neighborhood, Martin continued to work in the furniture industry, and Adriana continued to keep house and raise children, including a third son, Martin Jr., who was born in 1902 (and who would die of bronchitis in 1907, when he was four years old).[61] Martin and Adriana were proud of their eldest son; after all, "the height of a parent's ambition in that environment [was] that the older son should get an education," especially if he planned to enter the ministry. But they expressed this pride with characteristic modesty and "matter-of-factness."[62]

According to friends, family, and acquaintances, Muste shared his parents' humble and unassuming character, which seems to contradict the confident and masculine image of him that emerges from his college days, suggesting that we must be cautious about drawing neat conclusions based upon the flourishes of a nineteenth-century rhetorical style.[63]

As Muste neared graduation, he began to chafe under the cultural and intellectual limitations of his milieu.[64] As the new editor of the *Anchor*, he called for more intercourse with other schools and for the paper to serve as "the voice of the studentry [*sic*] in earnest criticism and sincere demand for reform."[65] His valedictory speech, entitled "The Problem of Discontent," provides further evidence for his growing restlessness. The speech is a classic statement of Social Darwinism, with its themes of race progress and civilization, struggle and conflict. But, perhaps revealingly, Muste compares the drama of historical progress to the individual, who is filled with doubt, dissatisfaction, and impatience, particularly "in matters of religion." "What is the solution of this problem of unrest? Why this eternal restlessness? Where is surcease from sorrow?" Just as with civilizations, the answer was a "life of action and of usefulness" that builds character and brings the individual closer to God. "The god of philosophy is an abstraction. The God of experience is personality, power, and love."[66]

It is difficult to discern a budding pacifist in martial texts such as these, but one can detect a nascent reformer. Muste had clearly begun to question "his early faith," a drama that would eventually inform his interest in modern theology. He had also imbibed the culture of muscular Christianity, a seedbed both of empire and of reform. Like so many Protestants of his generation, he associated the religious life with engagement, rather than retreat; he was open to the outside world and what it had to offer. His identification with Lincoln and Emerson may have further nurtured a penchant for reform; Lincoln was for him the "great emancipator," while Emerson gave a noble purpose to the realization of self. In the right context, moreover, there were elements within the Calvinist worldview that could encourage a stance critical of the United States and its institutions. Calvinist anti-individualism and ambivalence toward American culture might lead to a sympathy toward labor and collective action and to criticism of the industrial order. Calvinist suspicion of the modern state might lead to support for civil liberties and an expansive, democratic society.

Finally, as much as Muste embraced the conservative ideology of Social Darwinism, he was decidedly working class at a time of great industrial unrest. The turn-of-the-century United States was rife with class conflict, competing political ideologies and worldviews that sometimes even made their way into Grand Rapids. Temperance and suffrage campaigns shook up the city; eastern and southern European immigrants brought traditions of labor radicalism to the furniture industry, leading to efforts at unionization that culminated in the Great Furniture Strike of 1911, which ended in defeat for unskilled and semiskilled factory workers like Martin Muste.[67] With his working-class background, immense thirst for experience, and enormous intellectual talents, it is hard to imagine that A. J. Muste could avoid being shaken by his 1906 move to the New York metropolitan area, alive with cultural and political ferment and change.

But in 1905, on the eve of his graduation from college, Muste was a fairly conventional, conservative young American man. Despite his status as an immigrant and the son of a factory worker, he was a nationalist, imbued with notions of American exceptionalism and mission. In conformity with the expectations of his parents and his community, he was eager to attend the New Brunswick Theological Seminary in New Jersey and become an ordained minister in the Reformed Church in America. His romance with a Dutch Reformed minister's pretty daughter, Anne Huizenga, further promised upward mobility. As we shall see, these ambitions would be amply rewarded, and yet Muste would eventually risk it all for pacifism, civil liberties, and socialism.

CHAPTER 2

Spirituality and Modernity

And now in this new power of the Spirit they began to
consider the grievous state of the world and the multitude
of evils therein.

Many things were natural and possible to them now which
had seemed impossible so long as fear and hate and mistrust
ruled their hearts.

They planned for a world in which righteousness should
reign supreme.

They saw that the way of love was the sure and only way to
bring good to pass on earth, and that ever the Son of Man
if lifted up would draw all to himself.

—A. J. Muste, 1918

WHEN MUSTE GRADUATED from Hope College, he had a choice of attending either Western Theological Seminary in Holland, Michigan, or New Brunswick Theological Seminary in New Jersey. The choice, as Muste understood it at the time, was between the "restricted life" of the Dutch ethnic community and the metropolitan possibilities of the broader United States. He had "come to feel" that his "future was in the English speaking community, part of the United States, and not in the Dutch community of the [Midwest]. In that sense very definitely I wanted to get away."[1] The decision also reflected his craving for intellectual stimulation and rigor. He was to be sorely disappointed by the education offered at New Brunswick, but the institution's mediocrity pushed him to explore the dynamic intellectual and cultural world of New York City. There, he was introduced to modern trends in philosophy and religion that would serve as the fulcrum for his break from Calvinism, the crux of Dutch American identity and ethnicity, and his embrace of the Social Gospel.

The liberal religion that Muste would eventually adopt has received bad press ever since the 1930s, when Reinhold Niebuhr began his sustained attack on it as having a simplistic and naive understanding of human nature and society. Critics have further charged that the liberal emphasis on self-cultivation and self-affirmation led to the therapeutic, privatized, and individualist culture of the twentieth century.[2] Yet the development of American spirituality also led to social commitment; it was, Leigh Eric Schmidt argues, "inextricably tied to the rise and flourishing of liberal progressivism and a religious left." Moreover, far from being naively optimistic, liberals confronted the most perplexing questions raised by modernity, in the process experiencing its "hazards of alienation, lost identity, and nihilism." Their turn inward was "a cosmopolitan quest" to transform the alienation and anomie of modernity for the good of individual and social life.[3]

Muste's career exemplifies the connections between spiritual seeking, cosmopolitanism, and political engagement. After graduating from Hope College in 1906, he gradually became alienated from the institutional church and pietistic notions of salvation, an estrangement that led to despair and ultimately renewal through a mystical experience. From then on, he viewed the life of Jesus and its central themes of love and self-sacrifice as the true essence of Christianity. This view propelled him beyond the institutional church where he found fellowship within mainline Anglo-American Protestantism, with its ethos of spirituality, antimilitarism, and social reform. Muste had scarcely found himself in the American tradition of nonconformity when the United States declared war upon Germany. With war mobilization and conscription in full force, the meaning of American citizenship changed, demanding that the obligation to the nation supersede the religious, civic, and voluntary associations that had organized American public life in the nineteenth century.[4] Muste would ultimately choose God over country, in the process forging an alternative identity and solidarity as a radical Christian pacifist.

BEFORE moving to New Jersey to attend seminary, Muste spent a year teaching English literature and Greek at the Northwestern Classical Academy of the Dutch Reformed Church in Orange City, Iowa. The "city boy" felt out of place in Orange City. But the town's proximity to Anne

Huizenga, who lived with her family twenty miles away near Rock Valley, in northwestern Iowa, made it worthwhile. Muste and Anne had become engaged during his final year at Hope College. For him, it had been love at first sight. "It took a little longer in her case," but by late winter it was clear that they were going to get married. Living and teaching in Iowa gave the couple a chance to spend time together before Muste went to seminary. "In those days," Muste recalled, "you didn't get married when you were in college nor even while you were in theological seminary. In fact, it was regarded as positively an immoral thing to do." For one, it indicated that "you couldn't control yourself," and, second, it was considered irresponsible to marry a woman before attaining the means to support her.[5]

Anne was quite a catch for the working-class Muste. Her family was comfortably middle class; her father was a Dutch Reformed minister and two of her older brothers were physicians. In contrast to Muste's home, where his parents could barely read and write, Anne's had an "intellectual atmosphere" that he eagerly absorbed. Together, he and Anne's family read and discussed Shakespeare, Shelley, Keats, and other texts. It was, he recalled, a year of being "intoxicated" by "intellectual life and experiences."[6]

Ironically, when Muste moved to the New York metropolitan area to attend New Brunswick Theological Seminary, he entered an intellectual community that was less stimulating than his fiancée's home in rural Iowa. It was, he recalled, "a devastating experience" to go there; he would not "have survived it without New York," where he was able to take classes at New York University and Columbia University.[7] One of the oldest seminaries in the United States, New Brunswick had long faced declining enrollment and student complaints about the quality of its education, so much so, in fact, that Reformed congregations in the metropolitan area rarely hired its graduates. New Brunswick's official historian has suggested that one reason for its poor reputation was its conservatism. Yet this explanation overlooks the fact that nearby Princeton Theological Seminary, which was even more orthodox, had a better reputation. One gets the sense that it was the seminary's insipidness, rather than its conservatism, that was the problem; certainly that was what rankled Muste.[8] While other American seminaries were becoming more scholarly, New Brunswick persisted in viewing itself as a school for training ministers and was reluctant to adopt contemporary academic standards. Until 1907, faculty members were hired by the Reformed Church's General Synod, which believed that the best qualification for teaching was holding a successful pastorate.[9]

As much as Muste disdained New Brunswick, it provided him with a supportive environment for mediating between Calvinism and liberalism, and between his ethnic ties and national loyalties. In the first place, despite Muste's low opinion of the faculty, they considered him "the most brilliant student our seminary has had for twenty years," endowed with unique "spiritual power," and awarded him a fellowship that gave him an annual income of $3,500.[10] Second, his classmates, most of whom were Dutch Americans like himself, formed a tight-knit group that provided him with friendship and community. Third, he gained valuable ministerial experience. As the only student who was fluent in spoken and written Dutch, during his first year, the seminary dispatched him for the summer and every other weekend to a Dutch-speaking church in Albany, New York, where he was responsible for preaching a morning service in Dutch and an evening service in English.[11]

This experience made Muste aware of the differences between a Dutch and an American pulpit. In Dutch, he was expected to "expound some passages of scripture rather than preach topical sermons," while in English, the "personal and spiritual needs of people" were paramount, and he found himself moving away from "the typical Calvinist and Reform Church position" in order to appeal to his American parishioners. Through this process he discovered that he preferred the latter; he was "interested in the personal problems of people" and liked relating to them in more intimate terms.[12] In embracing a distinctly American and liberal Protestant homiletics, Muste departed from the tradition in which he had been raised and from what he was learning at New Brunswick.

Muste's evolving views on homiletics relates to the most important advantage of attending New Brunswick Theological Seminary: its location in the New York metropolitan area, which gave him access to the theological and philosophical currents and controversies of the early twentieth century. In fact, it was exposure to American ministers in Manhattan that provided him with a model for the personal style of preaching he practiced in Albany.[13] Most crucially, he was able to take advantage of an agreement between the seminary and New York University and Columbia University that allowed students in high standing to pursue postgraduate degrees for free. Interested in philosophy, Muste traveled two hours by train once or twice weekly to take graduate courses at New York University and, later, Columbia in an effort to fill his "hunger" for knowledge.[14]

Muste began taking classes in the philosophy department at Columbia University at an exciting time. Since being hired in 1902, Nicholas Murray

Butler, the ambitious president of the university, focused on shifting its curriculum away from undergraduate education and the classics to graduate and professional education. As part of this modernizing effort, Butler had recently hired John Dewey.[15] The pragmatist joined a faculty of "friendly critics," philosophers of diverse schools who together offered a well-rounded curriculum. The head of the department was F. J. E. Woodbridge; the other members of the faculty were Felix Adler, William P. Montague, and Wendell T. Bush. In later years, Dewey's pragmatism would exercise a tremendous influence on Muste's thought and politics. At this point, however, it was Woodbridge who made "the deepest impression." Like Dewey, Woodbridge espoused naturalism, a distinctly modern approach to philosophical problems that draws upon the methods of the empirical sciences. However, rather than embrace the democratic creed of pragmatism in which he saw traces of idealism, Woodbridge turned back to Aristotle and classical philosophy. Woodbridge thus provided the young Calvinist Muste an entrée into modern thought without completely challenging his worldview. As Muste commented of Woodbridge's appeal, "I was definitely a Platonist. This tied in with my Calvinism."[16]

Even so, Muste's exposure to naturalism and pragmatism subtly shifted his Calvinist worldview. William James's ideas about religion particularly affected him.[17] In *Varieties of Religious Experience* and his other writings, as well as at several public lectures Muste attended, James defended religious belief against the "intimidation" of positivistic science and, indeed, suggested that religion and science could be reconciled.[18] He pointed out that science, like religion, was a human creation; personal inclination and social context shaped scientific knowledge, making it no more "true" than other truth claims. And he called upon science to evaluate religious belief using the scientific method of inquiry in which experience and results determine the truth of a hypothesis. Based on this criteria, James insisted, religious belief was as real as empirical science because it could "make a genuine difference in our moral life." He made the same demand upon religion, dismissing tradition and doctrine as paths to truth, and emphasizing the "fruits" and consequences of beliefs. James was uninterested in "secondhand religious life" because it was based on tradition, not experience, and he drew his readers' attention to the mystical tradition of spiritual inwardness and direct experience with the divine.[19]

James pointed Muste toward a more modern religiosity and sensibility. Unlike his contemporaries, and certainly unlike his professors and peers at

New Brunswick Theological Seminary, James defined religion broadly and inclusively. Religion was "the feelings, acts, and experiences of individual men in their solitude, so far as they apprehend themselves to stand in relation to whatever they may consider the divine."[20] Indeed, James must be identified "with the Christian 'modernism' of his milieu, according to which religion was a fine thing but specific theological doctrines were felt to be something of a distraction."[21] The impact on Muste was subtle yet dramatic. As he recalled, *Varieties of Religious Experience* "opened up to me a great variety of approaches to life and in that way . . . laid the groundwork for wrestling with . . . the theology [with which] I was brought up."[22] In particular, James's stress on experience over form, and his celebration of spiritual inwardness and mysticism, suggested the possibilities of a religious life stripped of theology and the church.

James further bequeathed to Muste the notion that it was possible to be both an idealist and a realist. Throughout Muste's long career, the ideal of "human brotherhood" and the imperative to bring it about on earth, drove his activism, whether that ideal was rooted in Christianity or socialism (or both). Still, drawing upon pragmatic theory, he insisted that ideals, to be meaningful, had to be grounded in practical analysis and activity. "Ultimate values, ideals which are essential," he reflected in an interview about his early career as a minister and an activist, "have to operate in some political and economic situation and not in a vacuum, not [in the] abstract." Bringing the ideal and the real together and "effecting some kind of an integration . . . is a perpetual and very difficult problem, but it seems to me that this is the problem of human existence and therefore in some way or other I'm trying to work at it all the time."[23]

Muste's move toward a more modern, pragmatic worldview and theology was gradual. For a while he seemed to live in two different worlds. One was in New Brunswick where he continued to see himself as preparing for a life serving the Reformed Church and the Dutch American community. The other was the intellectual and cultural life of the great modern metropolis. There, as we have seen, he took seminars with leading philosophers who stressed the diverse ways of knowing and being. Moreover, as a supply preacher at a Reformed church in Manhattan's Lower East Side in the summer of 1908, he delighted in the "seething" culture of "Italian, Polish, Jewish, recently arrived immigrant[s], children, babies all over the streets and the steps [of tenements]." Reflecting his roots in industrial Grand Rapids, he felt comfortable among the city's immigrant, working-class residents.

He "never had the feeling that some people do[,] that New York is a terrible place to live in. I can put up with almost anything in New York."[24] In this respect Muste differed from the Progressive Era reformers with whom he is often linked. Although he shared their Protestant heritage and commitment to a life of service, his ease in the culture of urban America marks him as part of the modernist generation, which was more ethnically diverse and which celebrated the possibilities of the city.[25]

In 1908–9, of course, Muste had not yet embraced a modern credo, but his inclination was forward rather than backward. His choice of pulpit is illustrative. As valedictorian, he was offered three choice pulpits: one was the newly founded Fort Washington Collegiate Church in the Washington Heights neighborhood of northern Manhattan, and the other two were older, established churches in rural settings outside of the city. The president of the New Brunswick Theological Seminary had also offered him funding for doctoral study in Europe and the promise of an academic position at the seminary when he returned. He made the decision "that New York was the place for me" without "too much difficulty." In the first place, Fort Washington Collegiate Church was only a few blocks away from where the Yankee ballpark was then located. For another, academic life held little appeal: "I was too much interested in action."[26] He would also be able to continue his education, since Washington Heights was located just north of Columbia University and Union Theological Seminary. Finally, the New York church was especially wealthy and well established, with roots in the Dutch colony of New Amsterdam, but it had shed its exclusively Dutch cast, while its Presbyterian structure and Calvinism attracted non-Dutch Protestants. With a single classis (the local governing body, known as a presbytery in the Presbyterian Church) for all four of New York's Reformed churches and substantial investment income, it offered a salary of $2,000 a year, more than twice the average salary for Reformed ministers at the time.[27]

More to the point, Muste chose the Collegiate Church for the "challenge" it represented. It was a world he knew little about: mostly native-born, middle-class professionals who were active in social work and politics, and whose intellectual pursuits extended far beyond his parlance of theology and the classics. The lawyer Raymond Fosdick, then commissioner of accounts for the City of New York, was one of his congregants. Fosdick's older brother was Harry Emerson Fosdick, then a minister in Montclair, New Jersey, who would later become famous as the pastor of Riverside

Church in Morningside Heights and as a staunch defender of modernism against the rising tide of fundamentalism in the 1920s. Another congregant, John A. Fitch, former student of the labor economist John Commons, had just published *The Steel Workers*, an acclaimed sociological study of the steel industry. Fitch also served as industrial editor of Paul Kellogg's *Survey*, the leading journal of social work, and was a professor at the New York School of Social Work. Shelby Harrison, head of the research department at the recently formed Russell Sage Foundation was yet another prominent member of the congregation, as was the Republican congressman William Stiles Bennet. Here, as Muste noted wryly in his oral history, he could not get away with popularizing a Calvin passage as he could have in a "typically Dutch-speaking congregation," and he found the opportunity "decidedly stimulating."[28]

Before Muste could accept his call to the Fort Washington Collegiate Church, however, he had to pass the licensure examinations and be ordained by a classis. He also wanted to marry Anne who remained with her parents in Iowa. The preparation for ordination was lengthy and arduous. Under the care of the Grand Rapids classis, Muste had to return home to take an all-day licensing exam in Greek, Hebrew, church history, theology, and church government, as well as deliver a sermon. His father was present when he received his license, and they celebrated at the Muste home afterward. The occasion was indeed a "very important" and "happy one" for his parents, for whom it had been eleven years since their eldest son had left for Hope Preparatory Academy. On his way back to New York to be ordained by the city's classis, Muste traveled to Iowa to marry and collect Anne. Back in New York, on June 25, 1909, Muste was examined again and then ordained in "a very solemn and impressive service" in which the novitiate knelt while the ministers placed their hands upon his head. The service concluded with a benediction by Muste. It was a "tremendous experience for me," Muste recalled. "I felt a very strong call to the ministry and a very strong urge to preach and a feeling that I had something to give and, of course, [I had] this sense of fulfillment that my parents had."[29]

AT Fort Washington, Muste exhibited the personal traits that would make him a successful minister and, later, a beloved and effective leader. He had an unpretentious and down-to-earth temperament, keen sense of humor, and took pleasure in leisure and commercial amusements, particularly baseball. When providing pastoral care, he was an attentive and nonjudgmental

listener, and when he spoke, he had a direct, personal style that sought to
reconcile different points of view. Moreover, unlike stereotypically charismatic personalities, he had first-rate organizational skills that would make
Fort Washington a dynamic and expanding institution. These two aspects of
his character—warmhearted and catholic, on the one hand, and calculated
and ambitious, on the other—help to explain why, later in his career, he was
often underestimated by political and intellectual foes. At Fort Washington,
it led to personal growth and professional success, endearing him to his congregation and his superiors in the collegiate system and making his break
with the church, when it came, free of mutual recriminations.[30]

As minister, Muste continued to evolve a more modern theology. God
assumed the role of loving father, not judging patriarch; his focus was on
life on this earth, not on the hereafter.[31] Union Theological Seminary,
where he took courses from 1909 until 1913 and obtained another bachelor
of divinity degree, encouraged this move away from Calvinism.[32] The center
of liberal Protestantism, Union had declared its independence from
denominational control in 1892 following the "Briggs controversy." The
controversy began when the Presbyterian Church suspended a faculty
member for advocating the revision of the Westminster Confession, which,
among other things, asserts the doctrines of infallibility and biblical literalism. From then on, Union "moved in an increasingly liberal and non-
denominational direction."[33] It also served as a leader in the move toward
a more academic, historical-critical approach to seminary education.
Reflecting this orientation, its faculty did not necessarily have pastoral experience, and often held advanced degrees from German universities, making
it a striking contrast to the education Muste had received at New Brunswick. At Union, Muste became acquainted with the national and international leaders in mainline Protestantism and made contacts with people
who would later play a significant role in his life, such as Norman Thomas,
later the leader of the American Socialist Party, and Ted Savage, who would
become executive director of the Presbytery of New York.[34]

What Muste learned at Union challenged Calvinist doctrine to its core.
Arthur McGiffert, from whom he took four classes on church history and
with whom he developed a close, personal relationship, used critical historical methods to study the New Testament and early Christian history, an
approach that had earned him some notoriety in the 1890s. McGiffert criticized the Reformed tradition for having a juridical conception of God, and
his research emphasized that Jesus conceived of God as merciful and

fatherly. He explored modern trends in religion, tracing the shift in religious authority from external, legal, and absolute terms to human, vital, changing, and as the product of personal experience. He stressed the key role of William James in rehabilitating faith for the modern world, as well as the German theologian Albrecht Ritschl for his view that religious life is love activated in service to others and in community.[35] Other Union faculty members were similarly modern, stressing the need—and the inevitability—of adapting Christianity to the historical context and turning to the life of Jesus as a model for Christian living in a modern age. Christianity is "the religion of sympathizing love and of self-sacrificing service," asserted George William Knox, Union's professor of the philosophy and history of religion.[36]

Through his courses at Union, Muste's sense of religion's purview expanded, and he soon became deeply interested in politics, though not an activist. McGiffert, Knox, William Adams Brown, and other faculty were part of a larger cultural project of constructing a "radical Jesus" whose ideals of egalitarianism and love stood against the church and state of his time.[37] Like other adherents of the Social Gospel, they understood the King-dom of God to be a redeemed social order. Most important for Muste's politicization was their view of Christianity as a prophetic religion that built upon the historical and ethical foundations of Judaism. As Muste recalled, studying the Hebrew prophetic tradition taught him that religion was not remote, but found "in the here and now" and "in the historical process," thus giving action in this world meaning and ultimate significance. The prophets were "preachers of social justice, fearless agitators, political rebels . . . constantly stirred as was Moses by anger against injustice and dreams of a just nation or society."[38]

Muste's congregants, most of them Roosevelt Republicans, encouraged his exploration of the social and political implications of Christianity in study groups and forums sponsored by the YMCA. He also attended some of the discussion clubs that sprinkled the city where "Socialist and liberal activists and intellectuals" came together to examine such topics as child labor, juvenile justice, peace, and international arbitration. In this context, he read Woodrow Wilson's "New Freedom" and found it persuasive, as well as socialist material that popularized the ideas of Marx.[39]

His politicization moved "very fast"; "by the time the [1912] election came along I voted for [Socialist candidate Eugene V.] Debs."[40] Still, to vote for Debs in the context of progressive New York circles was not a particu-larly radical thing to do. As Muste stressed in his oral history, Debs was "in a way . . . a part of this progressive tradition." He was "a figure associated with Abraham Lincoln," not with un-Americanism or even Marxism; the marginalization of socialism would come later, during and after World War I.[41] Moreover, he remained largely disconnected from the socialist agitation, labor strikes, and political scandal that shook up the city during this period.

Yet politics would not be the fulcrum for Muste's estrangement from the Fort Washington Church. His nascent socialist consciousness was well within the bounds of acceptable political discourse in the context of Progressive Era Manhattan. He still considered himself a minister by vocation and not a reformer; politics rarely made an appearance in his sermons, which remained focused on his congregants' personal problems. And yet even as his church prospered, by 1913 he was in the midst of a profound spiritual crisis that would ultimately compel him to break from the Reformed Church. The theological modernism to which he had been exposed at Union had gradually eroded his faith. He now doubted the doctrines of the Westminster Confession, particularly the virgin birth, original sin, and the literal interpretation of scripture. As he questioned the tenets of the faith in which he had been raised, he fell into a deep depression, fearing that he had "lost religion" and "questioning how you could believe that life was worthwhile at all." He even considered leaving the ministry altogether.[42]

Whether because of his "nervous prostration" or because his wife was sick from a miscarriage (or both; the sources are unclear), in early 1914 he and Anne left the city for the Catskills to reflect and recuperate. There, he had a tremendous mystical experience that reassured him of God's existence and of God's love; "I have now arrived at a perfect religious certainty, a peace of mind after a long period of doubt," Muste proclaimed upon returning to the city.[43] The *New York Times* reported that "he returned to the city restored from the nervous prostration he had experienced, but when he compared his reformed, new-found, faith with the doctrine of his church, he found divergences."[44] Close friends, including Henry Sloan Coffin, a leader in the Presbyterian Church and faculty member at Union Theological Seminary, urged him to find a way to reconcile his new beliefs with the Westminster Confession and then work to reform the church from within. But Muste, setting a pattern that would be repeated throughout his life, would brook no compromise with his conscience, and he honored his contract with the Reformed Church requiring that he report any "doubts or difficulties" to his classis.[45]

On October 20, 1914, the New York Classis met to consider a communication from Muste to the effect that the doctrines of the church were largely "untrue, outworn, or unimportant," and that the real meaning of Christianity was to follow Jesus, "to live by his spirit, to give him free course in one's life." "This past winter has brought me into such communion with God, such peace, such perfect confidence, as I can honestly crave for all men everywhere," Muste explained. While he hoped to continue doing "God's work" within the Reformed Church, he accepted the probable consequences of his apostasy. Though they "loved the pastor," the classis was unwilling to make an exception, and it was clear that Muste had to resign.[46]

Viewed as a preacher of "rare intellectual ability" and "unusual [spiritual] power," his departure from Fort Washington deeply troubled and saddened New York City's Reformed community.[47] "I blame Union Theological Seminary for the whole trouble," the Reverend Dr. David J. Burrell, senior pastor of the Collegiate Reformed Church, told the *New York Herald*.[48] Another minister was more sympathetic, commenting presciently that "we cannot but feel that in an environment in which he feels a little less restraint theologically, he will develop into a very unusual man."[49]

To leave the Reformed Church was also, symbolically at least, to break with the Dutch ethnic community. His parents, who had sacrificed to make his ministerial career possible, found his decision puzzling, even embarrassing, though they would continue to respect and love him. Perhaps they received some consolation from their younger son, Cornelius, who followed Muste into the Dutch Reformed ministry, yet remained within the church. Indeed, "Neal" occupied a sort of parallel universe; he followed Muste to Hope College, New Brunswick Theological Seminary, and a ministerial career in New York City. Yet, as Muste drew deeper into nonconformity and political radicalism, Neal continued his steady rise in the Reformed Church, fulfilling the expectations his parents had for his older brother. In so doing, however, he assumed a class status and identity that separated him from his family of origin. He visited Grand Rapids less frequently than Muste, who made the trip at least twice a year; there, relatives found "Uncle Neal" distant and condescending, preferring the company of "Uncle Bram," who was "quiet," "humble," and "down-to-earth."[50]

In his journey from Calvinism to liberalism, from the Republican Party to voting for Debs, Muste was typical of other Social Gospel progressives. The first generation of progressives, such as Jane Addams, John Dewey, and

George Herbert Mead, shed their Calvinist heritage and turned to secular professions and reform as an outlet for their "quest for religious perfectionism."[51] The Social Gospel similarly shaped the evolving political identities of the next generation of Protestant reformers, such as Norman Thomas and his brother Evan, Kirby Page, Paul Kellogg, Mary Van Kleeck, Reinhold Niebuhr, and others. As Muste and other Calvinists groped toward a new, more authentic Christian faith, they drew upon powerful cultural narratives popularized by figures like William James and the Quaker mystic Rufus Jones, who celebrated spiritual inwardness and ecstatic experience as offering a path out of the dislocating and alienating effects of modernity. The mystical tradition that they helped invent was a cosmopolitan one in which the solitude of mystical experience gave way to a sense of oneness with all peoples, to ideals of "universal brotherhood, and sympathetic appreciation of all religions."[52] It was also a reformist one; James and Jones believed that mysticism unleashed energy for the hard work of social transformation. For James, for example, the measure of religious experience was "its fruits, its production of saintliness and active habits." It was a "way to unleash energy, to find the hot place of human initiative and endeavor, and to encourage the heroic, the strenuous, the vital, and the socially transformative."[53]

Still, there were important differences between these two generations of Protestant reformers. The latter, coming of age during the era of modernist revolt, would prove itself more laborite and more libertarian than the former, which had a deep affinity for top-down, Fabian-style reform. Muste's generation was also more cosmopolitan, decidedly rejecting notions of Anglo-Saxon cultural superiority and embracing cross-ethnic exchange and experiences (Muste was, of course, an immigrant himself). They were, in other words, Protestant modernists; the emphasis is on the adjective, for they largely remained conventional in matters related to morality, sexuality, and gender in contrast to their more secular comrades like Floyd Dell, Margaret Sanger, Edmund Wilson, Max Eastman, and Louise Bryant. In this vein, most Christian modernists supported Prohibition; Unitarian minister John Haynes Holmes bragged that he would "never under any circumstances allow a drop of alcohol to pass my lips."[54] Muste was somewhat unusual in his opposition to Prohibition and his refusal to moralize on the evils of alcohol, as well as in his enjoyment of popular culture. But he shared the moral uprightness of his fellow Protestants, noting later in life that "he had never been drunk."[55]

How Muste related to his wife during this period of spiritual crisis offers another example of the cultural conservatism of Protestant modernists. Though Anne was aware of Muste's estrangement from Reformed doctrine, he did not engage in philosophical or intellectual discussions with her. More to the point, he apparently decided to break with the church without consulting her, setting a pattern that would persist throughout their lives together. Indeed, even as Muste developed close working relationships with powerful women and often worked with them on terms of mutual respect and equality, within his personal life, there was a strict sexual division of labor, with his wife clearly subordinate to him. In this instance, Anne does not appear to have been much disturbed; according to Muste, she was not a particularly "rigid" sort of person, and her own horizons had been broadened by the move to New York. It was several years later, in 1917, when Muste broke with the ministry altogether over his pacifism, that clear differences emerged. Yet there was no question but that Anne would support her husband, even as his choices made her deeply anxious and perhaps even ill.[56]

Gender expectations alone do not explain Anne's support for her husband during this period. Like Muste, she was the product of a deeply religious environment in which her husband's apparent communion with God was culturally acceptable and, indeed, a cause for rejoicing. There is no reason to doubt Muste's recollection that both of them shared "a deep sense of. . . the ultimate rightness of things" when he had another mystical event soon after leaving Fort Washington. While walking along the corridor of a hotel, he suddenly experienced "a great light flooding in upon the world making things stand forth 'in sunny outline brave and clear' and of God being truly present and all-sufficient." It was in this spirit of "having arrived" that the Mustes moved to Newtonville, one of five villages that made up the city of Newton, Massachusetts, to assume the pastorate of the Central Congregational Church.[57]

THE Congregational Church was an ideal theological home for Muste following his break with the Reformed Church. Congregationalism shared the Puritan and Calvinist heritage of the Reformed Church, yet had a more liberal style of church organization in which local churches were autonomous in matters pertaining to faith, worship, and congregational life. It had also decisively broken with Calvinism, with Congregationalists playing a leading role in the development of the "New Theology," a more optimistic, ethical creed that posited Christ as a moral exemplar.[58] Founded in 1868, Central Congregational Church in Newtonville reflected this history of liberalism; as early as 1877, the church did not require that members provide an unqualified assent to the Apostles' Creed. It was also younger and less wealthy than some of the older, more established Congregational churches in New England; it was not one of the "top churches," as Fort Washington Collegiate Church had been. Still, as with Fort Washington, Muste's parishioners were largely progressively oriented professionals, with faculty from local preparatory schools and universities, editors, and people active in philanthropy.[59]

Muste's new pastorate placed him at the center of the Anglo-American tradition of nonconformity. Nearby Concord was the place where Henry David Thoreau went to jail rather than pay taxes to support the U.S.-Mexican War, and Muste's parishioners and larger community felt a deep sense of identification and connection with the tradition of nonresistance and abolitionism that had played such a prominent role in the region. Soon after Muste arrived, he was accepted into a discussion club run by leading Congregational and Unitarian preachers and theologians of the area—and indeed of the United States. George A. Gordon of the Old South Church, who had been a central figure in the Congregational revolt against Calvinism, was a member of this group, as was the Reverend James Brown of King's Chapel Church; the Reverend Ambrose Vernon of the Harvard Church in Brookline; the Reverend J. Edgar Parke, future president of Wheaton College; Willard Sperry, dean of Harvard Theological Seminary; and Bliss Perry, a specialist in the Transcendentalists, who lectured at Harvard and served as editor of the *Atlantic Monthly*. Perry was especially important in bringing Muste "closer to, deeper into Emerson, Thoreau, [and] Channing."[60] As a result of these discussions, "spiritually, as well as physically, I felt myself seeing the places that Thoreau and Emerson had looked upon, breathing the air they had breathed."[61] The link between nonconformity and Americanism was complete: "the mere sight of Boston Common, the State House, Concord and Lexington" came to mean "a great deal" to Muste.[62]

With the spiritualist culture of New England affirming his mystical tendencies, his sense of connection to God and his sureness of God's love deepened. As he wrote a recently widowed parishioner, "I believe with all my being that our lives are in the hands of a God who loves each of us much more than we ever love our dearest ones."[63] In turn, his parishioners adored him, viewing him as "a man of a rarely sweet and sincere nature, a preacher of deep spiritual power," and increasing their benevolent contributions more than four times from 1915 to 1917.[64] It was in this context, early in January 1916, that Muste's first child, Anne Dorothy (called "Nancy"), was born. "She was, naturally, a lovely baby. At heaven's gate the lark sang; the snail was on the thorn, the bird on the wing, God in his heaven, and all was right in the world," Muste recalled.[65]

Muste was indeed "a liberated man" in Newtonville.[66] Feeling "freer in expression" than he had in the Reformed Church, his sermons matured and sounded themes that would be at the center of his political vision throughout his activist career.[67] A 1915 sermon, "Of What Shall We Be Afraid?" began, typically enough, with Jesus Christ and specifically his admonition in Matthew 10:28: "Do not fear those who kill the body, but cannot kill the soul. Fear him rather who is able to destroy both soul and body in hell." Rather than expound upon the passage's implications for the individual moral life, Muste was explicitly political, arguing that Americans' preoccupation with threats from abroad, particularly German aggression, had blinded them to the dangers that "threaten us from within," such as racism and economic exploitation. Referring to "serious labor disturbances in Lawrence, in New York, in Paterson, in Little Falls, in West Virginia, in Northern Michigan, in Colorado," he rejected the notion that revolutionary agitators were to blame: "The only trouble with [them] from Jesus' point of view is that they are not half revolutionary enough, for they are only tinkering away at the outward machinery of life; he would strike at the heart of man and take out of it the very desire for money, for ease, for power, for honor, which creates the outward order of industry and society."[68] This idea—that socialization, to be truly effective, must be accompanied by a change of heart—would be repeated throughout Muste's long career and points to one of the central differences between Christian socialists and their secular comrades.[69]

Muste's evolving politics involved a reworking of his identity. Educated in the imperial culture of "muscular Christianity," his sermons show a preoccupation with squaring his new ideals of peace and justice with an ideology of white manhood that stressed martial prowess and racial struggle. "Many people seem to think that war is hard and makes a rugged, noble race," he observed, and that "peace is easy and makes degenerate men." While he conceded that war might develop certain virtues, it also involved giving into base instinct; a "real man," by contrast, strived for

self-control, the respect of his neighbors, and cared for rather than extermi-
nated the weak. Moreover, if anything, modern warfare spread "degener-
acy" by killing off the "finest men" and leaving the "less fit" to breed.
Social Darwinism thus continued to shape his thought even as he groped
toward a more pacific male identity.[70]

These two sermons, delivered about a year after Europe plunged into
the Great War, also show a growing preoccupation with the threat of militarism and war. The European conflict had seemed distant and unthreatening
at first, as President Woodrow Wilson promised to keep the United States
out of the conflict. But, as American entry grew more likely, Muste, along
with his fellow religious liberals, was forced to confront the question of
whether or not he could reconcile his Christian faith and participation in
war. Muste was on uncertain ground here; even his courses at Union had
never given him the "inkling that there might be such a thing as a pacifist
interpretation of the Gospel."[71] In fact, in the fall of 1914, he had preached
a sermon for the veterans of the Spanish-American War in which he "made
the expected, conventional observations that war is a terrible and wicked
thing . . . but when the strong attack the weak, and democracy and religion
are in danger, then, of course, as good Christians, we must go bravely,
though reluctantly, into battle."[72]

On one level, Muste's conversion to pacifism was simply a question of
"Christian conscience." As he recalled of those difficult days, he ultimately
"could not reconcile the Sermon on the Mount, 1 Corinthians 13, the
whole concept of the cross as the way of redemption, with war."[73] Yet
Muste's pacifism must also be understood within the cultural context of
New England and liberal Protestantism more broadly. His discussion club,
for example, had introduced him to a serious exploration of Christian mysticism and particularly the Quaker Rufus Jones whose work celebrated the
Quakers and their peace testimony as illustrative of mystical religion in
action.[74] Sperry, Parke, and other members of his social group were also
deeply involved in Boston's active peace movement, and they had invited
Muste to attend various antiwar meetings, including one in early 1916 that
featured the founders of the pacifist Fellowship of Reconciliation (FOR).
Soon thereafter, Muste, together with Sperry and Parke, joined the FOR;
their first meeting was held in Bliss Perry's Boston apartment.[75]

Founded in 1914 by the English Quaker Henry Hodgkin, the FOR was
a small yet influential international organization whose members pledged
to build "a world-order based on Love" by following the example of "the

life and death of Jesus Christ."[76] Hodgkin had helped to establish an American branch at a conference in Garden City, Long Island in November of 1915, soon after President Wilson initiated a preparedness campaign. The Fellowship was a "combination of Christian parochialism and expansive sentiment," as one historian has put it aptly.[77] Its members were exclusively Protestant, with strong roots in the Social Gospel movement, highly educated, and often from elite backgrounds. Many of them had been active in the YMCA, and its statement of principles reflected this evangelical heritage. The organization also had a strong Quaker influence, signified by its commitment to individual spiritual autonomy. As one early statement put it, "It is intended that members shall work out personally and in their own way, what is involved in their membership. There is no program or theory of social reconstruction to which all are committed. The chief method is a life lived in loyalty to Christ, expressing itself in every activity and relation of life."[78]

The FOR was, in other words, exactly what its name implied: both a fellowship of Christian pacifists, eager to witness for their beliefs, and a political organization committed to using "the method of Jesus" to resolve vexing industrial, racial, and international problems. There was some tension between these two aims, and what exactly was meant by "the method of Jesus" would soon become a matter of intense debate, but in its founding years the FOR functioned as an important source of support and camaraderie for opponents of war.

In becoming a pacifist in 1916, Muste remained a part of the liberal mainstream, which was largely opposed to American intervention. But all of this changed on April 2, 1917, when President Wilson summoned the Congress and the American people to war, explaining that "the world must be made safe for democracy." Wilson's language of American mission was the language of American progressivism, and the majority of progressives and even most self-described "pacifists" shifted from hostility to interventionism to support for the state. For progressives, the war offered an opportunity for reform. The war, John Dewey declared, was "full of social possibilities"; it would constrain "the individualistic tradition" and teach "the supremacy of public need over private possessions."[79]

The Federal Council of Churches, representing the mainline denominations, similarly viewed the war as an opportunity to modernize and liberalize the country and to extend American values to a decadent and corrupt

Europe. William Adams Brown, one of Muste's former professors at Union, headed up the Federal Council's crusade to uplift the morals of American soldiers and make them "fit to fight." Other Protestant luminaries such as Harry Emerson Fosdick, Shailer Matthews, Sherwood Eddy, and John Mott also joined the effort. Especially devastating was Brown's incisive criticism of pacifism in which he suggested that it was "a kind of fundamentalism." Though he had "the greatest respect" for pacifists, he argued that they were attempting "to apply an absolute ideal" to a progressive, changing society, and thus represented a regression to the orthodoxy and dogmatism against which they had rebelled.[80]

On one level, progressive optimism was not misplaced; the war offered them the opportunity to rationalize American society and to spread their values to the larger world. At home, the wartime state created agencies like the War Industries Board, which assumed greater control over industrial production, and the National War Labor Policies Board, which adjudicated labor disputes, enacted an eight-hour workday, and guaranteed collective bargaining rights for some industries. Abroad, President Wilson expressed his commitment to constructing a postwar international organization that would prevent war through planned reconstruction, liberalized trade, and democratization, and he welcomed the assistance of liberal internationalists in making his dream a reality.[81]

At the same time, the war exposed the dark side of the modern, managerial state and the imperial assumptions behind Wilson's idealism. As critic Randolph Bourne predicted in his famous 1917 essay rebuking his idol John Dewey, a war of rival imperialists could not be molded to "liberal purposes," but would rather empower the least democratic forces in American life.[82] Perhaps because progressives believed so completely in the justness of their cause, they viewed any evidence of dissent as a sign of disloyalty. A repressive atmosphere soon enveloped the country; eager to quash antiwar sentiment, the federal government enacted statutes to restrict freedom of speech with the Espionage Act of 1917 and the Sedition Act of 1918. Approximately one thousand Americans were convicted of violating these statutes, including the Socialist leader Eugene V. Debs. Numerous publications, including FOR's *World Tomorrow*, were denied use of the mails. State governments were even more repressive; thirty-three states outlawed the possession or display of the red flag of Communism or the black flag of anarchism, and twenty-three adopted laws defining the crime of "criminal syndicalism." Private groups, including churches, colluded in stifling dissent. Antiwar clergy faced harassment, were denied civil liberties, and often lost their pulpits. Many of them made their way into the FOR.[83]

For those, like Muste, who placed their religious obligations above national loyalty, the attacks on civil liberties and the acquiescence of the churches came as a profound shock. Many of them had assumed that their "reforming religion was more or less in accord with the enlightened outlook of progressive political leaders such as Woodrow Wilson," and it was distressing to find that their opposition to war and conscription placed them "outside the terms of citizenship."[84] The mistreatment of conscientious objectors (COs) reflected their newly marginal status. The Selective Service Act of 1917 initially only made provisions for COs who were members of the historic peace churches (i.e., Brethren, Mennonites, and Quakers), giving them a choice between noncombatant military service or confinement under military authority. Most of the four thousand COs who were confined to army camps were antimodern scriptural literalists, but a minority of them were pacifists of the FOR type, including Norman Thomas's brother Evan, his friend Harold Gray, and the civil libertarian Roger Baldwin. Without clear guidelines, the military's treatment of COs was inconsistent, ranging from benign neglect to beatings and abuse. At least two COs died during their internment.[85]

Together, these events radicalized pacifists. Though most of them had long supported social reform, their opposition to World War I was based upon religious belief. Yet the use of government power to suppress their Christian conscience, as well as dissent more broadly, gave meaning to traditional American civil liberties to which they considered themselves heirs. During World War I, FOR member John Haynes Holmes recalled, there "suddenly came to the fore in our nation's life the new issue of civil liberties."[86] In October 1917, Holmes, along with Norman Thomas, Hollingsworth Wood, Roger Baldwin, and other pacifists, founded the National Civil Liberties Bureau (later known as the American Civil Liberties Union) to defend the rights of individuals against the state and dissenters against majority opinion. In founding the ACLU, pacifists resisted the obligatory and coercive demands of modern citizenship and "gave voice to a politics that imagined the citizen first and foremost as an individual and as a bearer of rights." In so doing, pacifists invented a "rights-based vision of citizenship" that has competed with and coexisted alongside the growth of the American national government ever since.[87]

In their defense of individual rights, pacifists broke from their progressive roots and drew closer to the modernist, revolutionary milieu known as the "lyrical left." As the above quote by Dewey suggests, the progressive movement had rejected the individualist creed of the nineteenth century, viewing it as the ideological cover for the selfishness, inequality, and class conflict of the industrial capitalist order. Many progressives had almost a blind faith in the federal government as the agent of social progress. But World War I had demonstrated the potentially repressive power of the state, and some progressives (Dewey included) gained an appreciation for civil liberties. Significantly, pacifists and other early members of the ACLU did not believe their support for individual liberty and social democracy was a contradiction in terms. As Doug Rossinow has commented, "the theoretical conflict between legal individualism and social reconstruction that a later generation of political liberals would assert simply did not obtain in the minds of most political activists on the left half of the political spectrum in these years."[88] Indeed, it was an article of faith for these modern "liberal-leftists" that personal liberation and social emancipation were inseparable. Thus, somewhat unexpectedly, pacifists became allied with cultural experimentalists and revolutionary socialists.[89]

THE pro-war hysteria arrived gradually to Central Congregational Church and the Boston area. In part, this was due to the fact that Boston had been the center of a vigorous peace movement. Muste was also on very good terms with his parishioners who had generally expressed respect and sympathy for his antiwar stance.[90] But by Labor Day of 1917, when Muste returned from a two-month summer vacation, the situation had changed dramatically. By this time, the draft was in full effect, as private groups and voluntary associations mobilized to do the coercive work of a national government that lacked a modern administrative apparatus, a situation that fostered a mob psychology. At Central Congregational Church, some seventy parishioners had sons in the service and many others supported the war effort through the YMCA, YWCA, or the Red Cross. The church itself was militarized, actively fund-raising for a War Camp Community Recreation Fund and listing an "honor roll of men in the military and naval service" on the back of Sunday service programs.[91] Some began to question Muste's ability to provide adequate consolation should their sons be killed. As a result, pressure mounted on him to moderate his pacifism. Church officers proposed that he take a leave of absence for the duration of the war. Even his pacifist comrades Willard Sperry and Edgar Parke urged him to modify his pacifism publicly, as they had done, arguing that maintaining the connection between a minister and church superseded the call of prophetic witness.[92]

Muste, however, stood his ground. On December 9, 1917, he affirmed his pacifist faith in a letter of resignation he read to the congregation in lieu of a sermon. Instead of being treasonous, his pacifism showed the utmost concern for "the boys in the service" and, most important, authentically reflected the spirit of Jesus and the early Christian church. Rather than support the war effort, which was the work of fallible men, the church should focus on creating "the spiritual conditions that should stop the war and render all wars unthinkable." He went on to explain that another recent "mystical experience of God" had released him from any doubt; he was "happy and at rest in God. The war no longer has me by the throat." In concluding, he offered his resignation "without the least feeling of bitterness," unless the church was willing to respect their differences. Two weeks later, at a meeting that filled the chapel, church officers affirmed their "honor, respect and love" for Muste, while also passing a resolution supporting the American war effort. They offered him three months leave "to investigate the war situation," presumably with the hope that he would change his mind. Muste accepted the leave, but ultimately tendered his resignation.[93]

Muste stayed long enough to deliver the Christmas Day sermon. A meditation on 1 John 3:2 ("Now are we the children of God, and it is not yet made manifest what we shall be"), it reveals the powerful ways in which his radical Christian pacifism both intersected with and challenged the modernist project. The sermon began with French philosopher Henri Bergson's comments on his 1913 visit to the United States to the effect that there was a gap between technological and industrial achievement, on the one hand, and moral and spiritual development, on the other. Nowhere was this more apparent than in modern warfare, which had multiplied humanity's capacity to kill without a corresponding change in views of war and peace. "Our supreme immediate need," Muste paraphrased Bergson, "is finer, nobler men and women, clearer minds, above all, loftier souls." Modernist social scientists used the term "cultural lag" to describe this idea, and they believed their research would supply the information and knowledge needed to bridge the gap between science and culture. Muste, by contrast, contended that Christianity had already provided "the answer" with its message that "the divine can and does express itself through the human," and he promised that awareness of the divinity within oneself and within others would reveal that social conventions, churches, and nations were just illusions separating people from each other.[94] In Muste's formulation, the path out of the alienation and anxiety of modern times was not the imagined community of the nation, but to live like Christ.

Muste's biographer Jo Ann Robinson has suggested that Central Congregational Church's decision to fire Muste was in part due to his "erratic" behavior over the course of 1916 and 1917, as he alternated between expressions of pacifism and support for the war. She points to an article Muste published in the *Congregationalist* in late 1916 in which he called on readers to "do your bit for Belgium" and a patriotic service he led after the war was declared that included a paean to the "noble American ideals" of freedom, opportunity, and Christianity.[95] Another possible interpretation of this period, however, is that Muste did not initially understand his pacifism as contrary to "Americanism." Government repression, the link made between patriotism and war, was as "unanticipated and shocking" for him as it was for other pacifists and dissenters. As Muste recalled in his memoirs, before the United States entered World War I, the loyalty of its inhabitants, including members of the Socialist Party, was taken for granted; "there were no F.B.I.'s or state loyalty boards to assemble dossiers on thousands of citizens," he commented, adding that these trends have since "endured and gained in strength."[96] Certainly the work of Nick Salvatore and others bears out Muste's perception that citizenship and socialism were not viewed as mutually exclusive until World War I and the subsequent Red Scare.[97] Reflecting these concerns, immediately after leaving Central Congregational Church, Muste became a volunteer for the nascent ACLU, serving as an advocate for COs and other persecuted pacifists in the New England area.

In staying true to his pacifism, Muste consciously chose the life of a prophet and the fellowship of dissenters over that of a minister and the obligations of modern citizenship. His memoirs provide some clues as to why he felt compelled to follow his conscience over the demands of his beloved congregation while others, such as Sperry and Parke, did not. In recalling these years, Muste reflected that, growing up in the Reformed Church, he had "received too solid a dose of Calvinism not to have a strong conviction about human frailty and corruption." Thus, once he had concluded that Christianity and war were irreconcilable, he was congenitally unable to "adapt the Gospel to [external] circumstances" that violated his deepest sense of what was the true meaning of Christianity. Yet he had not become a new sort of fundamentalist, as William Adams Brown's trenchant criticism of pacifism would suggest. The mystical creed he embraced saw religious vitality as growing out of a creative tension between engagement and adaptation to a changing environment, on the one hand, and those "permanent and time-transcending Realities" that emerged from direct communion with God, on the other. Moreover, like his spiritual mentor, Rufus Jones, Muste was fully cognizant of the psychological and cultural factors that might mediate between his experiences of the divine, and he conceded that, for some, mysticism might be a sign of pathological disturbance.[98] However we choose to interpret it, his religious experiences clearly offered him a language for breaking with the ministry, the conventions of middle-class life, and the demands of national belonging in the modern era.

Upon leaving Central Congregational Church, Muste continued his work with the ACLU of providing advocacy and legal help for pacifists throughout New England. In this context, he joined the Religious Society of Friends, a decision that apparently involved no theological crisis. Since his break from the Reformed Church, he had subscribed to the Quaker doctrine of the inner light, which holds that every person has access to God's presence, a sentiment reinforced by his participation in his Boston-area discussion club and membership in the FOR. The Quakers' history of nonresistance and social activism also reflected his own evolving beliefs. Becoming a member of the Society of Friends did not, moreover, exclude other religious affiliations. Indeed, for the rest of his long life (except for his years as Marxist-Leninist), he would remain a member of the Presbyterian Church in the United States of America, an identity and commitment that speaks to his ongoing engagement with the Calvinist tradition.[99]

In January 1918, the Providence Friends' Meeting offered him a small salary and a home in return for teaching and ministerial services and maintenance of a reading room in the meetinghouse, a center for "the various unorthodox, persecuted individuals in the city" to gather and "metaphorically hold hands." Though Providence's Quaker community was affluent and well established, the authorities viewed the meetinghouse as a source of irritation and concern. Reflecting his newly disreputable status, on June 7, 1918, at the annual meeting of the New England Yearly Meeting of

Friends, Muste narrowly escaped arrest when a local Baptist minister charged him with seditious speech.[100]

As this experience suggests, the persecution of dissenters intensified even as the war wound to a close. By the late summer of 1918, so-called "slacker raids" reached a fevered pitch, as patriot volunteers rounded up men suspected of dodging the draft. By the end of the war in November 1918, the country was in the midst of a full-fledged Red Scare, culminating in the "Palmer raids" of 1920 in which Attorney General A. Mitchell Palmer rounded up hundreds of political radicals in the labor movement and deported some five hundred of them.

Yet it would be misleading to emphasize only the repressive atmosphere of the immediate postwar years; for the left, 1918–20 was also a time of expectancy, urgency, and optimism. In Russia, the Red Army defeated counterrevolutionaries and brought their revolution into eastern Europe, while in western Europe trade unions broke free of their exclusivist traditions and became mass movements for democratic control of industry. Meanwhile, in the colonized world, uprisings suggested that the era of imperialism was nearing an end. Even in the United States, where American capital emerged from the war stronger than ever, many believed that capitalism was in its "death throes" and that they were part of an international movement giving birth to a more egalitarian social order. With Soviet Russia as their beacon, they looked to the labor movement to make their dreams of revolution a reality. The eruption of a massive strike wave involving some four million workers throughout the country suggested that labor was indeed realizing its historic role. There were general strikes in Seattle and Winnipeg, strikes among longshoremen, stockyard workers, carpenters, textile and clothing workers, telephone operators, and, most dramatically, the Great Steel Strike of 1919, involving 365,000 steel workers. Proposals for reconstructing the social order came from across the liberal-left political spectrum. Even the conservative American Federation of Labor (AFL) entertained proposals to extend wartime economic controls, establish social insurance, and nationalize the railways.[101]

Muste was deeply affected by the era's revolutionary spirit, as well as by "the visions of the prophets of a new heaven and a new earth, where righteousness would prevail and every man would sit under his own vine and fig tree, and none should be afraid." Convinced that "a new world" was "about to be born," he joined other members of the Boston FOR in founding "the Comradeship," a group committed to examining "the question of how to organize our lives so that they would truly express the teachings and spirit of Jesus."[102] In November, he moved his family from Providence to the Comradeship's headquarters in a rented house in the working-class neighborhood adjacent to Back Bay. They lived on the second floor, while pacifist minister Harold Rotzel, his wife, and three-year-old daughter lived on the third. Other members of the Comradeship included Cedric Long, another minister who had lost his pulpit because of his opposition to the war, and three women of independent means: Anna N. Davis, a Quaker and member of the Hallowell family; Ethel Paine, a prominent Bostonian and descendant of one of the signers of the Declaration of Independence; and Elizabeth Glendower Evans, a socialist and a disciple of William James who believed with the philosopher in the reality and "genius of the trance phenomena." To these women, Muste, Long, and Rotzel were "saintly" characters, and they served as essential sources of support for the Comradeship and for Muste throughout his life.[103]

The headquarters of the Comradeship served as a sort of alternative community for its members and for a hodgepodge of radicals who used it as a meeting space and safe haven. The spiritual atmosphere was intense. Muste and Rotzel arose every morning at five o'clock, bundled themselves in overcoats, and "read the New Testament—especially the Sermon on the Mount—together, analyzed the passages, meditated on each phrase, even each word, prayed, and asked ourselves what obedience to those precepts meant for us." Members subjected themselves to a common "spiritual discipline," while individually setting aside time for Bible study, prayer, and devotional reading.[104] Muste appears to have been in a state of religious fervor. As Elizabeth Glendower Evans described him in the winter of 1918–19, "His face had the inner glow of one fed by spiritual manna."[105]

Evans went on to comment that she "feared that he and his wife and perhaps even their little children went hungry. However, he made no complaint."[106] As this comment suggests, for Muste, the transition from upstanding, respectable minister to impoverished radial agitator was eased by the peace of mind that came from following his conscience and from joining a community of shared believers. The same could not be said for Anne Muste, who did not have "the release of being true to convictions" that he had experienced. "I was imposing a situation on her. What could she do about it?" he commented rhetorically, revealing the gender privilege upon which their marriage was based. Indeed, for Anne, the experience involved a loss of community and identity. As Muste noted in his memoir, she was more of "a social being" than he was, "got more out of the ordinary amenities of life" that came with being the wife of a minister. In Newton, the young mother had enjoyed shaded streets, parks and playgrounds, and the support network provided by the Women's Association of the Central Congregational Church. It was therefore a struggle for her to understand her husband's decisions and to reconcile herself to their consequences. "One night [during this period] as we were in bed and were talking things over," Muste recalled, "she said 'If you'll just keep on talking to me as to why you think these things and why you think you have to do them, it will be all right.'"[107]

By the end of 1918, the Comradeship had drafted a proposal outlining the ideas that had come out of their meetings. As Muste wrote to the FOR, they would form a "preaching order," a lay group of men and women who felt "the call" to "rebuke" the old order and "enter upon the new." Members would live simply, share a common fund, submit to a shared "spiritual discipline," and perhaps even have a "form of dress peculiar to the order." Through their personal example, as well as through proselytizing, pamphleteering, and going to jail for their beliefs, they would explain "the facts as to the present order—extremes of wealth and poverty, unearned income, undemocratic control of industry, lack of the right spirit in international relations" and the need for "a radically new order" based on "the principles of Jesus." They hoped that their message would persuade the "possessing and educated classes" to similarly "renounce the existing order" and support the working class in their struggle for economic justice. Among the workers, they hoped to inculcate the "healthy and divine discontent" that came from envisioning a cooperative commonwealth and recognizing the "futility of violence and the [more promising] way of reason and love." The early Christians clearly served as a model for the Comradeship; just as Paul "had to cut away from old Jewish associations, in order to fulfill [the Christian] mission," so too would they work independently of the organized churches and identify themselves with the impoverished and needy.[108]

Significantly, unlike other utopian movements inspired by the vision of "bringing the Kingdom," the Comradeship did not seek to separate itself from the larger society. There was some discussion of forming an economic cooperative in the country, but only as a base of support and renewal for the preaching order as it brought its message to the masses. Indeed, even as a conservative young college student, Muste had held that character and faith were built through engagement and action, not asceticism and social withdrawal. "I have a deep-seated conviction that the aim and the essence of life is love," Muste explained in 1957. "And love is in its inmost nature an affirmation, not a negation; an embracing and being embraced, not rejection and withdrawal."[109]

In 1918, of course, Muste was still a political novitiate and his thinking on such questions was not fully developed. But, precisely at the moment he and his comrades drafted their proposal, a dramatic textile strike erupted in nearby Lawrence, Massachusetts, giving them an opportunity to translate their ideals of brotherhood and nonviolence into reality. In Lawrence, the diverse and contentious world of labor radicalism returned Muste to his working-class roots and provided him with an outlet for his idealism and his desire for a life of action, struggle, and self-sacrifice. Ironically, however, it also put distance between him and the community of Protestant liberals with whom he had found kindred spirits in Christian mysticism and pacifism.

CHAPTER 3

〜

Pragmatism and "Transcendent Vision"

In every movement or institution that I have ever belonged
to, except the trade union movement, I have felt like a free
lance, an individual who could stand over against it, so to
speak, and whose main concern was to get his ideas uttered
at every cost. In the trade union movement I just feel
different. Of course, I do not agree with many of those who
are in it . . . however . . . I cannot divorce myself from it
any more than I can jump out of my own skin. No matter
how much I differ from many of those prominent in the
trade union movement, I want to differ with them as one
who is just as much a part of that movement as they are.
        —A. J. Muste, 1925

"IT WAS QUITE AN EXPERIENCE," Muste recalled in his memoirs, to be
driven from his pulpit for holding pacifist views, but it was "nothing"
compared to the transition from preaching at a Quaker meeting to the
leadership "of a turbulent strike of 30,000 textile workers in Lawrence,
Massachusetts." In the context of the postwar Red Scare, there was "no
middle course"; by supporting the strike, he had placed himself on the side
of anarchy and violence not only in the eyes of the authorities, but also
among many of the liberals and pacifists whom he had counted as allies
and friends.[1] For Muste, however, the strike was an intoxicating experience.
Like so many of his generation and the next, the labor movement became
his "messiah," destined by history to usher in the Kingdom of God on
earth. Indeed, one can make too much of the religious differences between
Muste and the workers he organized and led. Though his idealism may

have sprung from a different source, all imbibed the ferment of 1919 with a millennial urgency that spoke of the cultural contexts in which they were reared. Anthony Capraro, an anarcho-syndicalist who was one of Muste's closest comrades during this period, wrote in the midst of the strike that the death and destruction of World War I also signaled "the birth-throes" of "a period of creation," of "renaissance and regeneration." "As the gospel of Jesus, so is the revolution," he proclaimed. "It comes from the East."[2] Sidney Hillman, Capraro's superior in the Amalgamated Clothing Workers union (ACW), offered a similar analysis at a mass meeting in 1918: the "Messiah is arriving. He may be with us any minute—one can hear the footsteps of the Deliverer—if only he listens intently. Labor will rule and the World will be free."[3]

Still, the Lawrence struggle and the subsequent challenge of organizing the Amalgamated Textile Workers of America (ATWA) forced Muste, the religious idealist, to deal with practical questions. "What does one do in a strike? How do you organize relief? What about pickets? How do you start negotiations? How do you get national publicity? Where do you get milk for the hungry kids? How do you spot a labor spy? How do you start a union?" To answer these questions, Muste turned to the pragmatic philosophy of William James and John Dewey.[4] Though often misunderstood to mean moderate or sensible, pragmatism seeks to reconcile idealism and realism by holding that "truth" emerges out of the dynamic interaction between the individual and the environment, theory and practice, and thus is always subject to change and revision. A distinctly modern philosophy, pragmatism did not view the decline of the self-sufficient individual of the nineteenth century as a tragedy, instead viewing "the increased interdependence and association determined by a corporate world of large-scale, even global, production" as having cosmopolitan and collectivist possibilities.[5] In these ways, pragmatism dovetailed with the views of Muste's comrades in Hillman's ACW, who sought to combine revolutionary commitment with the creation of stable, efficient unions, a project that entailed rationalizing and modernizing industry. The ACW deeply influenced Muste's ideas about trade unionism and provided the model for the ATWA, which he headed from 1919 through 1921.[6]

The forces of postwar reaction would ultimately destroy Muste's textile union, but his philosophy—which might best be described as "labor pragmatism" or "working-class pragmatism"—continued to shape his thought and served as the theoretical basis for the workers' education movement that he led in the 1920s and, later, the "Musteite" movement of the 1930s. As the chairman of the faculty at Brookwood Labor College, the country's only residential school for workers, Muste and his fellow "labor movement intellectuals" found the pragmatic engagement of modernity, criticism of individualism, and optimisim about social progress as valuable resources in their laborite project. At the same time, they rejected its emphasis on the internal development of the child to the exclusion of collective action and ideals. As Muste put it, teachers must take "their social responsibilities seriously" and articulate ideals of "genuine democracy and an economic collectivism suitable for the machine age."[7] In that spirit, labor educators made their commitment to socialism explicit and viewed their role as fostering the working-class solidarity and militancy needed to make it a reality. With the support of sympathetic academics, liberals, and leftists from across the ideological spectrum, the workers' education movement made up a key constituency of the left-liberal coalition that survived World War I and the Red Scare and that continued to evolve in creative ways through the 1920s.[8]

In many respects, their theory and practice of workers' education "anticipated" Antonio Gramsci's ideas about hegemony and culture. In his prison notebooks, Gramsci would argue that the bourgeoisie maintained its dominance largely through culture and ideology and that cultural institutions such as schools play a role in the hegemonic process by denying the reality of class conflict, producing intellectuals who rationalized the existing order, and giving the impression of facilitating social mobility. Conversely, workers should make education a vital part of a revolutionary "war of position" in which they would "free themselves from their dependence on bourgeois intellectuals [and] develop and disseminate their own conception of the world and of life."[9] Muste and his comrades in the workers' education movement developed a similar analysis of education and culture under capitalism and viewed their schools and colleges as counter-hegemonic institutions that would produce working-class meaning and knowledge. As they put it, effective working-class organization was only possible "when it [was] based upon a labor culture; that is, a mode of feeling, thinking and acting in terms of the problems and aspirations of labor."[10] Their efforts to create a counter-hegemonic labor culture in the 1920s challenge historical narratives of the decade as a period of quiescence and suggest that the seeds of the CIO and the "cultural front" of the 1930s were laid a decade earlier.[11] Not coincidentally, it was a debate over the meaning of working-class education in 1928 that served as a lightning rod around which the movement for industrial unionism began its open revolt against the conservative American Federation of Labor (AFL).

LAWRENCE was the nation's largest textile city, located north of Boston on the banks of the Merrimack River. Its massive textile mills lined the city's skyline and employed over thirty thousand workers, most of them immigrants, who worked and lived under abysmal conditions. Like other mass production industries, textiles were notoriously difficult to organize. The workforce was divided by skill and ethnicity; "older" immigrants dominated lower-level management and skilled positions and "newer immigrants"—predominantly Italians, Russians, Syrians, Walloons, and French Canadians—were largely unskilled and thus easily replaceable. The unwillingness of the AFL's United Textile Workers (UTW) union to organize unskilled workers further undermined and divided Lawrence's working class.[12]

With the UTW indifferent and even hostile, the Industrial Workers of the World (IWW) had managed to gain a foothold in Lawrence in 1912, when they successfully led the "bread and roses" strike, a dramatic and often violent confrontation that made the city "the era's supreme symbol of militant struggle against industrial oppression."[13] The local disintegrated soon afterward, largely because of repression, but also because the IWW proved itself more capable of leading strikes than forming stable unions. "Most of us were wonderful agitators but poor union organizers," Elizabeth Gurley Flynn recalled of their efforts in Lawrence.[14] Still, the legacy of the 1912 strike was important in indoctrinating the revolutionary philosophy of syndicalism among Lawrence's workers. At the same time, its failure bequeathed a sense that organization, when it came, would need to have a more practical orientation by signing contracts and paying close attention to bread-and-butter issues.[15]

The 1912 strike has obtained almost mythic status in the annals of radical history, no doubt in part because of the involvement of IWW luminaries Elizabeth Gurley Flynn, Carlo Tresca, Arturo Giovannitti, and "Big" Bill Haywood. But the 1919 strike was equally dramatic. Like other industries, textiles had experienced wartime prosperity, enjoying record-breaking profits from 1916 to 1918. The greatest beneficiary of all was William Wood's American Woolen Company, the largest company in the entire textile industry, which had extensive operations in Lawrence. For the first time, mill workers enjoyed year-round employment. Recognizing their advantage, they broke traditional patterns of deference on the shop floor and staged a number of small strikes to gain wage increases. Textile workers were eager to hold on to their gains as the war ended. Mill owners, on the other hand, sought to maintain their high level of profitability, and they began to lay off workers and to reduce their hours as soon as wartime orders dropped off.[16]

It was in the context of this tense and volatile situation that the UTW, under its conservative president John Golden, launched a nationwide campaign for the eight-hour day, passing a resolution calling on the textile mills to begin the new schedule on February 3, 1919. When it became clear that Golden was content to leave wage adjustments to the future, a movement emerged throughout New England textile centers to change the demand to 48/54—fifty-four hours' pay for forty-eight hours' work. As workers prepared to strike, the American Woolen Company announced it would honor the forty-eight-hour week but without the wage increase. The tactic succeeded in ending the UTW's involvement and in undercutting the strike movement everywhere except in Lawrence and, to a lesser extent, Passaic and Paterson, New Jersey, which were also major textile centers.[17]

With memories of the violent 1912 strike still fresh, the imminent standoff in Lawrence was front-page news in Boston. Eager to translate their ideals of nonviolence and brotherhood into reality, the Comradeship sent Muste, Harold Rotzel, and Cedric Long to Lawrence to investigate the situation. When the three ministers arrived on a bleak winter day in January, they found a city tense with excitement and fear. In true pacifist fashion, they immediately set about researching the situation from all points of view, interviewing workers, ministers, professionals, and industrialists, including William Wood Jr. They quickly concluded that the strike was justified; the pay was "miserable" even as the mills enjoyed windfall profits, yet the mill owners were utterly opposed to compromise and the native-born public was "paralyzed with fear," viewing the movement as part of a plot to Bolshevize the United States. To show their support, the ministers began passing out leaflets explaining the "facts" to the wider public and raising relief funds for the impending strike.[18]

The strike leaders welcomed the ministers' support. Many of them had been involved in the 1912 strike and knew the importance of outside support and publicity. As Muste recalled, "we were hailed as angels in these circumstances. They had virtually nobody who could talk English straight, nobody who could write English," and they recognized the value of "our connections" in Boston.[19] Strike leaders had already set up a provisional strike committee composed of representatives from the various national and language groups. Under its auspices, for the first week of the strike, the ministers continued to focus their energies on obtaining relief funds and favorable publicity.[20]

Having earned the trust of the strike's leaders, when a general strike committee was formed a week later, the ministers assumed key positions. For his part, Muste was elected executive secretary of the general strike committee, in effect making him the leader of the strike. Though he lacked experience, he had proven a charismatic and inspiring speaker whose ability to reconcile different points of view and construct a cohesive vision out of the strike's "kaleidoscopic" ethnic and ideological diversity quickly endeared him to the workers. At his very first speaking appearance in Lawrence he told the assembled crowd: "You should learn all you can about the textile industry because very soon you are going to take it over for your own."[21]

Muste also "demonstrated an ability to learn on the job" and to adapt his principles to fit the situation.[22] Without a background in labor unions or industrial conflicts, he drew upon the pragmatic method and looked to experience and practice as guides to truth. As he explained of his approach to labor organizing, "there are no absolute roles, formulas. . . . You have, on the one hand, a 'social situation'; [and] on the other hand, an individual. But neither of these terms is set and static; they are fluid and dynamic." Ultimately the "rebel must submit himself to the test of results" and "the test of group discussion . . . in spite of all the risks of compromise involved." Ideals ultimately must not be "petrified dogmas mechanically applied to living situations, but hypotheses fearlessly lived by so long as [no] better are in sight, but constantly made to meet (not evade) situations and thus enriched and corrected." "The moral life" was indeed "an adventure!"[23]

His response to the violence that characterized the strike illustrates his ability to be flexible and adaptable while maintaining his principles. The first day of the strike, on the first Monday in February, provided a harbinger of what was to come; as the strikers gathered at dawn outside the mills, the police attacked the picket lines, clubbing strikers, and even entered their homes, pulling women out of bed and beating them.[24] The repressive, brutal treatment of the striking workers continued throughout the strike and reflected the conviction, held by the city elite, that that the strike represented "Bolshevism, the enemy of democracy, the destroyer of property rights, the breeder of anarchy." They were determined that "Bolshevism" would "get no grip-hold in Lawrence" as it had in Seattle, Winnipeg, and other cities, and they granted the police free rein in handling the strikers.[25]

Police brutality placed the problem of violence squarely before Muste and his fellow pacifist clergy. Though the FOR favored socialism, many of its members opposed strikes, viewing their coercive character as a form of violence. The organization held that "true reconciliation" came from identifying with "both sides of the quarrel" and then drafting a solution "in which the true interest of every party can be satisfied." In the case that one party to a dispute was unwilling to "be converted," they suggested that it was better to let evil triumph than to violate their fundamental principles of nonviolence and love.[26] When Cedric Long defended the right of workers to strike at an FOR conference, he was publicly chastised by John Haynes Holmes who, with the hearty approval of the audience, pointed out that strikes violated the "moral law."[27]

In Lawrence, however, law enforcement was the "creator of violence," and the experience taught Muste, Long, Rotzel, and other left-wing pacifists that the language of peace could function to maintain the status quo. As Muste wrote in the *New Textile Worker*, the organization and agitation of workers may appear to disrupt the "social peace," but in fact brings attention to the class struggle that already exists. Quoting the English economist and historian G. D. H. Cole, he insisted that "the interests of Capital and Labour are diametrically opposed and although it may be necessary for Labour sometimes to acquiesce in 'social peace,' such peace is only the lull before the storm" that must come if a fundamental restructuring of power and privilege is ever to occur.[28] While Muste certainly hoped that the final victory in the class struggle would occur nonviolently, he refused to abandon the Lawrence strike on the grounds that striking workers were not pacifists.

Philosophical questions aside, as the leader of the strike, the problem of violence was also a practical one, for it seemed self-evident that the police were being deliberately provocative in the hopes of undermining the strikers and their cause. Police violence also undermined morale; several weeks into the strike, pessimism set in in the ranks "because of this business that every morning so many people got beat up." "Naturally," the impulse was for strikers "to go back to the mills" and attack strikebreakers. Muste, Rotzel, Long, and other strike leaders urged striking workers to avoid retaliatory violence, but as the conflict between strikers and scabs escalated, it occurred to them that something more dramatic was called for. "Back in the jungle era of 1919," Muste recalled, it was the policy for strike leaders to avoid the picket line because they would be "picked off" by the police. But to boost morale, the strike committee decided that Muste, Long, and several other leaders would lead the picket line.[29]

On the afternoon of February 26, Muste and Long left strike headquarters, leading a throng of thousands on a picket line in front of one of the larger textile mills. No sooner had they begun the picket line when police on horseback swarmed into the crowd. In the confusion, Long and Muste ended up in a side street where police cut them off from the other picketers and began beating them. Long was immediately knocked unconscious, but they were more careful with Muste, systematically beating his legs and body and forcing him to continue walking to avoid being trampled by their horses. When he was finally unable to stand up, they placed him in the patrol wagon where Long was coming back into consciousness.[30]

At the police station, the two ministers were charged with disturbing the peace and loitering (Long received the additional charge of assaulting an "unknown girl"). Placed in separate cells, Muste and Long received another bout of abuse; the police hammered incessantly on the metal bars and even brought in Newton's chief of police, whose son had attended Muste's Sunday school class, to chastise Muste for getting "mixed up" with "all these wops" and "this row." The ministers grew increasingly anxious as night fell because at nine o'clock prisoners were transferred to a facility on the outskirts of town and it was "routine that *en route* prisoners 'tried to escape and had to be beaten into submission.'" Yet their comrades had worked feverishly to raise funds and managed to bail them out before the deadline. The next morning Muste and Long were out on the picket line again.[31]

The tactic proved a tremendous success. The persecution of the ministers turned liberal public opinion toward the strikers, lifted sagging spirits, and firmly established Muste's leadership role. Yet, as the strike wore on, the general strike committee continuously feared that they would lose control of the strike or that the workers would return to the mills. Provocative behavior by the police continued to be a problem. One of their most incendiary acts occurred during the sixth week of the strike when they mounted machine guns at several principle intersections. In response, a member of the strike committee made a speech calling on the workers to turn the machine guns on the police. Much to Muste's relief, the speaker was voted down when others pointed out that "they can't weave wool with machine guns."[32] A week later Muste would find conclusive evidence that the speaker was in the employ of a detective agency and had made the speech at the behest of the police. A similar discovery was made a few weeks later when the strike's financial secretary revealed to Muste that he was a spy involved in a scheme with the mill employers to set him up for murder. Thus Muste learned firsthand about the role of labor spies and agents provocateurs in radical movements, a lesson he would not forget. They always posed "as the most intransigent Marxist and most militant labor fighter of them all," and insisted "upon the most meticulous observance of all the rules," Muste recalled of this perennial problem in labor and radical movements.[33]

But the main problem was dwindling funds. Muste's connections in Boston had raised thousands of dollars and had helped to raise spirits by joining the workers on the picket line.[34] But the strike fund was quickly depleted by the costs of feeding and clothing thousands of striking workers, providing medical care for injured workers, and paying legal expenses for trials such as Long and Muste's (ultimately dismissed for lack of evidence). Early in March, connections were made between the striking workers and Sidney Hillman of the ACW. Hillman had long envisioned a union of all workers in the apparel industry and he was eager to provide assistance. Along with money, the ACW dispatched staff members August Bellanca, Nathan Kleinman, Leo Robbins, Gioacchino Artoni, H. J. Rubenstein, and Anthony Capraro to assist in the strike.[35]

The relationship with the ACW reflected not only a desire for funds, but also the growing conviction that the struggles in Lawrence and other textile centers represented an opportune moment for the unionization of all textile workers, regardless of skill. The ACW appealed to Lawrence's immigrant workforce because of its industrial character and because of its combination of revolutionary élan and practical achievements. Unlike the IWW, the ACW signed contracts through means of an impartial arbitrator and sought to maintain stable, efficient unions that provided tangible benefits to their workers.[36] There were also cultural similarities between clothing and textile workers; both groups were made up of immigrants with anarcho-syndicalist sympathies, giving their movements a spirit of militancy, localism, and democracy. Still, the ACW's impressive victories during the war were the result of Hillman's commitment to collaboration with the state and his willingness to discipline unruly members. As a result, the ACW secured a reliable foothold in the industry, and its membership increased from 48,000 in 1916 to 138,000 in mid-1919. By 1920, the union would be the fourth-largest body of organized industrial workers in the United States, after the miners, machinists, and railroad workers. The question was where this practical orientation would lead: would "industrial democracy" mean workers' control or something more limited like co-management between workers and their employers, which was how Hillman increasingly defined it?[37]

Thus, as the Lawrence strike dragged on into its eighth week, Muste and other strike leaders laid plans for a textile workers convention in New York City under the auspices of the ACW. On April 12–13, seventy-five workers from half a dozen textile centers gathered at Labor Temple at Fourteenth Street and Second Avenue where they voted to give birth to the Amalgamated Textile Workers of America (ATWA) and elected Muste general secretary. The constitution was modeled after the ACW and was explicitly revolutionary: it declared the reality of the class struggle and asserted that the union was the "natural weapon of offense and defense" in the struggle for a socialist society. It rejected the craft orientation of the AFL as outmoded and suggested that democratic, industrial organization would provide the training for workers to assume "control of the system of production."[38] At the same time, reflecting the influence of the ACW, the union also made it clear that it aimed to be "practical." As Muste explained, delegates felt that "former organizations had either been hopelessly conservative and thus played into the hands of the bosses, or, while radical in purpose, had been so extreme and impractical in method as likewise to fail in soundly organizing the industry."[39]

Although the headquarters of the new union were to be in New York City, Muste returned immediately to Lawrence where the situation had grown more desperate. On April 11, the mill owners rejected an offer of mediation that even conservative Massachusetts governor (and later U.S. president) Calvin Coolidge said was "fair." Two weeks later, the city Marshall announced the withdrawal of police protection for the strike leaders, and editorials appeared in local papers calling for vigilante action against "reds and mobs."[40] Meanwhile, strike funds were so depleted that workers went without shoes and milk for their children, leading the organizers to imitate a famous tactic of the 1912 strike of sending children outside of the beleaguered city to stay with families who could afford to clothe and feed them. On May 2, in order to raise morale, the strike leadership snuck Carlo Tresca into town to rally the workers. A lovable, inspiring speaker, Tresca had been banned from Lawrence for slapping the face of the police chief during the 1912 strike. When the authorities learned of his visit, they became so enflamed that they organized a mob that went in search of Muste. Unable to find him, they kidnapped and brutally beat Anthony Capraro and Nathan Kleinman; the former only narrowly escaped a lynching.[41]

Though such acts tended to unify strikers and generate liberal support, the strike leadership began to prepare for defeat. On Monday, May 19, they dispatched Muste to New York City ostensibly to raise more funds; in fact, they wanted the head of the union out of town if and when the workers capitulated and went back to work. As Muste walked despondently to the train station, an incredible turn of events occurred that revealed the personal power wielded by the mill owners, especially William Wood, and also how the solidarity and organization of workers could challenge that power. A man approached Muste and told him that Walter Lamont, the head of Wood's American Woolen Company in Lawrence, wanted to see him. Together, they drove to Lamont's home where the magnate began cursing him as an outside agitator who had created the trouble in Lawrence. After a while, Muste asked, "Is this what you got me here for?" "No," he replied. "How can we settle this goddamn strike?" After Lamont assured him that he spoke for all of Lawrence's mills, Muste returned to the strike headquarters to announce that management was ready to settle with a 15 percent increase in wages and no discrimination against strikers.[42]

After the strikers joyfully ratified the settlement, Muste focused on channeling their enthusiasm into a solid industrial organization. This was a huge educational and cultural undertaking, for workers with traditions of shop-floor militancy and strikes did not necessarily translate into reliable union members.[43] Moreover, as Muste was fond of saying, the ATWA was like a "proletarian League of Nations" and while differences in language, nationality, and custom could be overcome, they presented a constant challenge.[44]

To overcome these ethnic and ideological differences, as well as a culture of resistance centered on the spontaneous strike, Muste and the ATWA leadership drew upon the example of the ACW and the International Ladies' Garment Workers' Union (ILGWU), both of which stressed the importance of building a union culture. Revolutionary idealism alone was not enough, Muste argued; strikes should be supplemented by "a great deal of quiet educational work" to give workers practical skills in union organization and to foster a common workers' culture. By offering members services that met "all their varied needs" as human beings, such as recreation, entertainment, and housing, Muste contended, unions would "hold the worker to his union and so build up labor morale." It was "fundamentally bad to have these services handed to the workers from . . . above." Workers must be prepared for the future, when they would run industry and society by themselves.[45] Thus, in that brief period from 1919 through 1920, the ATWA locals not only led strikes and organized shop committees, they also opened union halls, developed youth programs, sponsored lectures and classes for adult education, formed consumer cooperatives, and hosted festivities like picnics and dances, all in an effort to build up a union culture.[46]

In organizing schools, the ATWA also sought to counter the influence of the Americanization programs set up by employers and the public schools as part of the nativist sentiment that swept the country after the war. According to the ATWA, the language of Americanization "cloaked" a determination to exploit workers and preserve the status quo. In contrast to racist and deferential notions of citizenship, the ATWA and its supporters constructed a pragmatic definition of Americanism, viewing it as an inclusive, collaborative process that was constantly "in the making," as Harold Rotzel put it. "I, for one, am for *a rapidly changing Americanism* which will represent the people of America and make democracy real where the people spend so much of their time—in industry," he wrote.[47] ATWA educational programs thus sought to teach "in a spirit . . . of equals working out a problem together," with the recognition that "what the alien knows" would help make American life "fuller and better."[48] Significantly, its cosmopolitan understanding of Americanism was embedded within a working-class, revolutionary internationalism. Reflecting this spirit, it sought to organize rather than exclude immigrants and to build relationships with textile workers across national borders—such as its mutual union card exchange that it set up with textile workers' unions in Italy and Poland.[49]

The ATWA's concern with Americanization had to do with the very real ways in which hegemonic notions of national identity were used against them. Employers inculcated obsequious ideas about citizenship through their Americanization programs and through welfare capitalist schemes that sought to foster loyalty to the company rather than to expansive ideals of freedom. More coercively, employers used the bugaboo of "Bolshevism" to break their agreements with the ATWA; they discriminated against former strikers, sped up production, spied on their workers, and sometimes moved production to nonunionized regions. Local and state authorities colluded in the hounding of the ATWA. Capitalizing on the hysteria generated by the Palmer raids, they obtained injunctions, arrested organizers, and shut down union halls. In November 1919, repression of striking textile workers in Utica, New York, culminated in an incident in which the police fired 250 rounds of ammunition into an unarmed crowd of men, women, and children, wounding six of them.[50] To put it bluntly, left-wing unionism simply did not enjoy liberties such as free speech and the right of assembly.

The ATWA struggled mightily against the forces of reaction. When ATWA organizer (and ACLU member) Paul Blanshard was arrested in Utica for violating an injunction, he issued his own counter-injunction "against the Capitalist Class of Utica" in which he "restrained" them from "firing on unarmed women," intimidating workers from joining unions, suppressing free speech, and otherwise denying workers "industrial democracy."[51] In Passaic, New Jersey, when the police turned out the lights in their union hall, union members joined representatives of the ACLU in reading the New Jersey Constitution by candlelight.[52] Meanwhile, the ATWA expanded its efforts into the Midwest and Pennsylvania, where some mills had relocated to find cheaper, more docile labor. In an ideological offensive, Muste and other union organizers gave speeches and published articles warning workers not "to be deceived" by welfare capitalism. "Real men have never desired charity, but freedom and justice," Muste wrote in the pages of the *New Textile Worker*.[53]

In the summer and fall of 1919, this hard work generally paid off, and the ATWA could boast of having fifty thousand dues-paying members by the end of the year. The union's most impressive victory, at least in terms of their desire to obtain the sort of foothold in the textile industry that the ACW had achieved in clothing, was in New York City's silk ribbon industry where they hammered out a collective bargaining agreement using an impartial arbitrator.[54] But a postwar economic depression in the spring of 1920 shifted power decisively to the mill owners and forced the union on the defensive. At the first annual convention of the ATWA in April 1920, Muste warned that favorable conditions in industry would not last and urged affiliation with the ACW to provide the union with the institutional strength and stability to withstand the imminent onslaught. He also pursued an alliance with independent textile unions throughout the Northeast and Midwest.[55]

Yet he could not stem the tide; with their arbitrary power legitimated by the retreating wartime state, the mills spied on their workers, fired members of the ATWA, dramatically cut hours, slashed pay, and refused to negotiate with shop committees or the union.[56] When ATWA locals responded with strikes, the mills locked them out. Most dramatically, the American Woolen Company simply shut down production for the summer of 1920, and when it reopened in September, it discriminated against union members. Mills in other textile centers followed suit.[57] Recognizing the ATWA's fragile state and confronting the same forces of postwar reaction, the ACW retreated from its earlier assurances of affiliation. Unlike the former, the latter would manage to survive the Red Scare; a more established institution, it had managed to impress certain sectors of the clothing industry of its usefulness. Hillman had also established some powerful connections in high political places through his cooperation with the wartime state—in sharp contrast to the pacifist Muste.[58]

Anarcho-syndicalist sentiment, as well as ethnic and ideological divisions, compounded the union's woes. It should be noted in this context that syndicalism also shaped Muste's politics: he had a strong commitment to democracy within the union and believed that the path to workers' control lay in the organization and action of labor unions—which is why he did not join the more politically oriented Socialist Party.[59] Yet within the rank and file, syndicalism was often infused with anarchism—a sentiment to which Muste could not abide. Like his mentors Hillman and Joseph Schlossberg of the ACW, he was engaged in a modernist project to bring rationality, efficiency, and stabilization to a highly chaotic and differentiated industry. Anarcho-syndicalism could also intersect with ethnic parochialism and localism. In Lawrence, for example, the local had persistent trouble collecting dues and had to answer to charges that organizers were living high off of the earnings of workers.[60] Likewise, Muste was forced to respond to rumors that he, Long, and Rotzel were secretly in collusion with William Wood to achieve "industrial peace."[61] Ethnic tensions, particularly Polish anti-Semitism, further hindered the union's efforts to unite workers.[62]

One historian has suggested that the "naïve" leadership of the union's "middle-class intellectuals" further contributed to the union's demise. For evidence, he cites the union's reluctance to stage strikes in the spring and summer of 1920, and argues that this reflected a politics of moderation out of step with the militancy of the rank and file.[63] Underlying his argument is the problematic assumption that religious faith leads to moderation. As we have seen, pacifists like Rotzel, Long, Evan Thomas, and Muste risked their careers for their antiwar stance, and showed courage and militancy in organizing and leading the ATWA, which is why they earned the respect and trust of the workers. Muste's ambivalence about striking in the spring of 1920 did not reflect a failure of nerve so much as his pragmatism—with the union facing unilateral reductions in hours and even lockouts, an offensive strike to double the wages of textile workers and obtain union recognition seemed almost certain to end in defeat.[64]

Still, there were cultural differences between Protestant pacifists and the largely immigrant workforce; some of Lawrence's Italian workers, with their strong tradition of anticlericalism, never overcame their suspicion of the ministers.[65] For their part, pacifists often experienced union politics as an "assault" on their affinity for moral consistency.[66] Long would ultimately decide that his ideals found better expression in the cooperative movement, where he remained for the rest of his life. Evan Thomas, who served as the ATWA's organizer in Paterson, observed that his loyalty to individuals rather than to ideas or groups could rouse "real suspicion from some of the workers" in Paterson. "Many of us intellectual radicals are too introspective and ego-centered" to serve the labor movement, he surmised in a letter to his mother. Soon thereafter he turned away from organized politics to focus on his career and family. Likewise, following the demise of the ATWA, pacifists tended to stay on the sidelines of the labor movement, feeling morally compromised in the trenches.[67]

It would, however, be a mistake to exaggerate the divide between pacifism and labor. Left-wing members of the FOR continued to give the labor movement valuable support, and some of them remained actively involved.[68] And John Haynes Holmes may not have liked strikes very much, but he defended the rights of labor to free speech and free assembly as a member of the ACLU. Holmes's approach to the "labor question" was typical of pacifists and mainline Protestants throughout the 1920s: they served as crucial allies of the labor movement, while staking their hopes for industrial and international peace on moral suasion and legalistic formulas like the "outlawry of war" movement and a world court.[69]

Even so, Muste's continued and active engagement in the labor movement was unusual. In contrast to many of his fellow pacifists, he rejected the notion that individual conscientious objection alone would lead to peace. He was also deeply skeptical of legalistic and moralistic methods for achieving social change, instead placing his hopes in labor organization, militancy, and solidarity.[70] The difference probably reflected his immigrant and working-class background. Union organizer James Dick's memories of the ATWA are suggestive: "We had seven or eight ministers in the Amalgamated Textile Workers, and that was six or seven too many. But there was one who did understand the workers and did understand labor organization: that was A. J. Muste. There is no man in the United States that I would rather go on the picket line with where there is real danger of getting heads cracked."[71]

For Muste's part, he felt a "very strong" sense of identification with men like Sidney Hillman, Carlo Tresca, Arturo Giovannitti, Abraham Cahan, and other ethnic leaders and workers with whom he had become closely connected, and his impression was that they felt the same toward him. His early experiences of poverty and factory work gave him empathy for "the conditions under which they had to live, the suffering which they had to undergo, the deprivation," and conditioned him to live simply. Like them, he also enjoyed the camaraderie of East Side coffeehouses and union meetings, often one and the same, though his Protestant heritage made him "congenitally" unable to sit around drinking and playing cards. "I had to get my relaxation going to plays or listening to music, and so when the boys went out to drink I didn't go along." Yet he refused to moralize, reflecting a deeply held conviction that idealists, whether religious or secular, should keep their ideals to themselves in a diverse and multifaceted movement.[72]

Ultimately, Muste found the experience of being part of something larger than the self deeply satisfying, a sentiment that contrasts with the strongly libertarian bent of other pacifists. Like other pragmatists, he believed that the individual could only find himself or herself through and in community rather than over and against it. "There is no such thing as an individual," Muste explained years later in his oral history. "He's a part of a community, a society" and has responsibilities to it.[73]

In 1920–21, as Muste watched the ATWA collapse all around him, he came to believe that the labor movement should combat not only the conservatism of the AFL, but also the increasingly out-of-touch insurrectionary politics of the left. Radicals had fallen "into the formulation of rules, orthodoxies," escaping into "dogmatic radicalism" rather than facing "life and reality."[74] Indeed, one reason the postwar Red Scare was so devastating to the labor movement was that the Palmer raids tended to exacerbate the left's millenarianism; from 1919 to 1921, anarchists entered a conspiracy to avenge their repression, the Socialist Party split into rival right- and left-wing factions, and the subsequently formed Communist Party went underground. These insurrectionary politics deeply affected the ATWA. Union meetings often centered on "doctrinal disputations" rather than "straight-out trade union organization of the workers for the immediate improvement of their conditions." More dramatically, anarchists in textile centers bungled several bombings and the union's Communist Party members became scarce.[75]

Muste's decision to leave the ATWA and turn to workers' education emerged out of this context. It was clear to him that labor's expansive vision for the postwar order had been defeated and that the United States had entered a period of reaction. Yet he found reason to be hopeful. John Golden, the UTW's reactionary president, died in 1921 and was replaced by Thomas McMahon, a more progressive unionist who reached out to Muste and who would fight closely with progressives in the 1922 New England textile strike. Perhaps the ATWA had served its purpose in spurring the UTW into more aggressive action; "for the time being," a more practical approach was to push for a federation of textile unions under the auspices of the UTW. At any rate, the "extraordinary instability" of textiles, the specter of an economic downturn, and the extreme hostility of textile magnates made dual unionism now seem like a suicidal policy.[76] Meanwhile, workers' education became a means whereby he could build a culture of industrial unionism within the American working class, which his experience within the ATWA had taught him would be no easy task. As he reflected, building class consciousness and organizing workers required more than an "evangelistic" method of intensive organization campaigns, big strikes, and generating popular enthusiasm; it was a long-term educational and cultural project. It might also serve as a means whereby he could press his vision for a more realistic left, on the one hand, and a more idealistic labor movement, on the other.[77]

Progressive unionists and independent radicals throughout the United States shared Muste's deep interest in workers' education. The needle and clothing trades were especially supportive, having initiated cultural and educational programs for their members, but so too were the machinists, mine workers and railroad brotherhoods, and central labor councils. James H. Maurer, a machinist who had risen to the presidency of the Pennsylvania Federation of Labor, was one of its most passionate advocates. Mortified by the pro-war, pro-corporate, nationalistic stance of the schools during World War I, Maurer became convinced that labor needed "schools of its own . . . for free and open discussion, from the workers' point of view, of the social and economic questions that are of vital interest to workingmen." Other prominent backers of the movement included John Brophy, the president of the United Mine Workers of America (UMWA) District 2, who served as a center of insurgency against the autocratic leadership of John L. Lewis, and the venerable John Fitzpatrick, head of the Chicago Federation of Labor and partisan of third-party organizing efforts.[78] Their organ was the left-labor monthly *Labor Age*; its statement of purpose encapsulates the ideology of these labor pragmatists: "Presenting all facts about American labor—Believing that the goal of the American labor movement lies in industry for service, with workers' control." Its aim was to serve the labor movement by dealing "with the acts and thoughts of labor, without regard to dogma."[79]

Intellectuals, educators, and pacifists joined these progressive laborites in support of workers' education. Boston's Trade Union College could boast that its teachers included Felix Frankfurter and Harold Laski of Harvard University. The journalist Arthur Gleason was a particularly zealous backer, as were the historian Charles A. Beard and Bryn Mawr's president M. Carey Thomas, both of whom had traveled to England where they had observed an active and flourishing movement. When they returned to the United States, Beard taught classes for the Rand School of Social Science and the ILGWU, while Thomas founded Bryn Mawr's famous summer school for women workers. By the spring of 1921, there was enough sentiment to host a conference of two hundred supporters at the New York School for Social Research. Noting that at least twenty-six workers' education "enterprises" serving some ten thousand students had been established in just two years, the conference voted to found the Workers' Education Bureau (WEB) as a national clearinghouse for research, teaching, publication, and extension work in workers' education.[80]

The movement's nascent philosophy embraced the experimental, non-dogmatic approach of progressive education, while rejecting its individualism. As one proponent put it, academics and liberals implicitly viewed education from a "middle-class point of view" with their tendency to "substitute 'higher spiritual or cultural objectives'" for the "'materialistic' outlook" of workers and trade unions. Workers' education, by contrast, aimed to educate workers to serve their unions and their class, not to educate them out of their class with bourgeois ideals of individualism and upward mobility.[81] Reflecting this perspective, the curriculum of early workers' education programs was largely limited to subjects considered directly useful to workers, such as the English language, trade union instrumentals, and the social sciences, which included sociology, economics, history, and some literature. At this early stage, literature and the arts were seen as something the workers already had access to as human beings, not as an additional "front" in the struggle for "a new social order."[82]

Still, enthusiasts of workers' education remained on the political left. Unlike the conservative trade unionists they had battled for supremacy during the war, their ultimate goal was a socialist society, and they believed that workers' education could help them achieve it. As Fannia Cohn of the ILGWU explained, workers' education must be "flexible, experimental, and reflective of the interests of the groups involved," while also having a "central ideology" of unifying the working class to achieve power.[83] Labor educators were also tired of the factional squabbles of left and right and sought to make workers' education independent of any political party or dogmatic creed, in contrast to the educational programs of the Socialist and Communist parties. As one early theorist explained, the movement was "positively partisan" in its commitment to strengthen the labor movement, but it would not "stereotype men's thoughts, ideals and beliefs . . . substitute one dogma for another." Clint Golden, a machinist who would serve as Brookwood Labor College's field secretary in the 1920s, reiterated this distinction in a 1925 survey of the movement. "Where classes have been organized or conducted primarily for propaganda purposes [such as those offered by the Communist and Socialist parties] they have had but a brief existence. . . . Those efforts seem most directly and permanently felt which are pragmatically conducted—dealing with the individual problems with which the workers are confronted," and allowing for "free investigation, examination and inquiry."[84]

As Golden's comments suggest, pedagogically, this independence was expressed through a commitment to the "factual approach," in which worker-students would be presented with a real, living problem and the data and tools necessary for solving it themselves. Historians have typically interpreted the social science language of "facts" and "neutrality" as a retreat from the values of advocacy and service that had animated the previous generation of intellectuals.[85] But for enthusiasts of workers' education, faith in the tools of the social sciences coexisted with a rejection of academic notions of objectivity and detachment. "There is a great deal of bunk current which suggests that . . . both or more sides must be presented for the students' judgment. Mental gymnastics, however, is not education. . . . Teach students to think by all means, *but thought must have a content and education a purpose.*"[86] Students were given leave to participate in strikes and other labor activities, which were viewed as "laboratories" for testing the hypotheses and methods that they had explored in their classes. As Louis Budenz explained in the pages of *Labor Age*, "It is in the pragmatic field of the workers' trench warfare that workers' education will be worked out."[87]

The alliance between progressive unionists and intellectuals represented by the workers' education movement shows that not all intellectuals retreated from their faith in the masses and social service after World War I, nor did all workers ascribe to the anti-intellectualism preached by Samuel Gompers.[88] Indeed, the movement served as a residual expression of a once robust bond between workers and intellectuals, though laborites made it clear that intellectuals were there to serve the movement and "not as prophets."[89]

The origins of Brookwood Labor College reflect the developments outlined above. Its founders were Christian pacifists who had been converted to labor's cause during World War I. The most important of these was William Fincke, a minister who had resigned his pulpit in opposition to the war. In the fall of 1919, he and his wife, Helen, decided to turn their country estate—complete with a mansion, "white and wooden-grand with high pillars and wide portico"—outside of Katonah, New York, into a secondary school to promote their ideals.[90] For a variety of reasons, the school never really got off the ground, and the Finckes, inspired by the example of Ruskin College in England, decided to reopen the school as a labor college.[91]

In the spring of 1921, they invited a small group of intellectuals, academics, and trade unionists to discuss the founding of a residential school for adult workers.[92] As a pacifist, a socialist, and a trade unionist with working-class credentials, Muste provided the bridge between the various groups and quickly emerged as the most likely candidate to direct the school. At first, he only agreed to teach history, but the demise of the ATWA, his own growing interest in workers' education, and the decision of the Finckes to leave Brookwood at the end of the summer of 1921 all pushed him to assume the chairmanship. It was like "screwing in the spark plug of an engine," the Finckes' son recalled of the recruitment of Muste.[93]

Personal factors also played a role in Muste's decision. The years since he left Newtonville's Central Congregational Church had been chaotic and insecure ones for his family. While he led the Lawrence strike, Anne remained in Boston, pregnant with their second child, Constance, who was born in August 1919. That same summer, Muste moved his family to New York City where the ATWA had set up its headquarters. In some ways, this was a more stable existence. As head of the union, he earned a regular salary, albeit much reduced from what he had received as an upstanding minister. Yet, despite these improvements, Muste was rarely at home and his involvement with the ATWA meant that he constantly faced arrest and even death. As Muste recalled of those years, "I do not recall a single week when there was not a strike on somewhere. . . . There was no strike without labor spies; no strike in which we did not encounter arbitrary, and usually violent, conduct on the part of the police; no strike, hardly a union meeting in those days, where raids by Attorney General Palmer's men were not carried out or at least threatened." Though he found these experiences decidedly stimulating, he began to feel as though he was "running out of ammunition," with never a moment to pause for reflection. Brookwood thus offered some respite from the constant ferment of leading a persecuted union in decline.[94]

Two miles outside of Katonah in Westchester County, "up a winding road through overhanging woods," Brookwood also offered an idyllic, though primitive, environment for raising children. Nancy, Constance, and John Martin (born in 1927) recalled these years as happy ones for the family. Though conditions were initially quite rustic, eventually the campus included a stone cottage for the Mustes, volleyball and tennis courts, and a swimming pool, "nestled in surrounding greenery" and overlooking "the wooded hills and valleys" of nearby estates. Other faculty and staff, along with their children, also lived on the campus, which had a communal atmosphere in which residents took their meals together and often worked cooperatively to improve the campus. The Muste children thrived in the idealistic, community-centered culture of the school. One of their fondest memories was of being asked to act in plays written by students and faculty. As Nancy recalled of one Saturday night, the Muste family "was up on the stage, huddled around some mechanical parts, while we sang a song about [how] 'the Anarchist family threw the bomb-bomb-bomb.'"[95]

Anne also apparently enjoyed "the settled life at the school."[96] She was, however, often sick; sometime in the late 1930s, a doctor would diagnose her with a serious heart condition that resulted from having rheumatic fever when she was a child.[97] Perhaps the combination of having poor health and the sole responsibility for household chores and raising the children explains why contemporaries described her as shy and retiring. Yet her reserve may also have reflected disinterest in the political and ideological concerns that consumed her husband. While other movement wives occasionally make an appearance in the historical record from this period, Anne appears only once—in a letter from her resigning as head of Brookwood's kitchen committee because of the constant squabbling between "the girls."[98]

Under Muste's leadership, Brookwood Labor College quickly outgrew its pacifist roots and became a central institution of the progressive wing of the labor movement. At this point, Muste remained a committed pacifist, viewing "modern" educational methods as reflective of the ideals of nonviolence.[99] Yet he also recognized that workers came from a variety of ideological and political perspectives and would not abide preaching. Thus, he supported the decision to discard the Christian pacifist ethos of Brookwood School and to place it under the control of unionists, a move that pushed pacifists to the margins.[100]

Muste and the other unionists who founded Brookwood worked hard to make it "labor's own school," thus differentiating it from workers' educational initiatives sponsored by private colleges and state universities.[101] The college's board of directors was dominated by trade unionists, all with long, distinguished careers, including Maurer, Fitzpatrick, Brophy, Rose Schneiderman of the Women's Trade Union League (WTUL), Abraham Lefkowitz of the American Federation of Teachers (AFT), Jay G. Brown of the Farmer-Labor Party, Phil E. Ziegler of the Brotherhood of Railway Clerks, and Fannia Cohn of the ILGWU.[102] It only hired faculty members who had a record of service to the labor movement and ran a closed shop in which faculty had to be members of the AFT; in fact, Muste served as one of the international's vice presidents through much of the 1920s. The college only admitted students who had recommendations from their unions and reached out to unionists who could not stay for long-term study by establishing an extension program and by offering short courses where unionists could gather to explore problems in their union or in the labor movement as a whole. In 1925, Brookwood expanded its extension program by offering correspondence courses through the pages of *Labor Age*.

Brookwood also sought to be wholly financed by unions. These efforts paid off: within Brookwood's first year alone, Muste boasted of having thirty endorsements from unions. The college never became financially independent, however; although a number of unions established scholarships, he was forced to turn to old sources of support, like Elizabeth Glendower Evans and Anna N. Davis, as well as to the newly formed American Fund for Public Service (also known as the Garland Fund), from which he managed to obtain a long-term grant. Muste made it clear, however, that these donations came with "no strings attached."[103]

Muste's desire to obtain labor's support partly explains his more moderate tone and cultivation of the AFL leadership during Brookwood's early years, though he was also genuinely eager to find common ground between "lefts and rights" in the movement. In his correspondence and interactions with the AFL leadership, "Brother Muste" explicated Brookwood's pragmatic approach to education and its hostility to sectarianism, and reassured them that the college's goal was simply to make more "effective" trade unionists. He also made it the college's policy not to take official positions on questions facing the labor movement or to publicly align with any given party. In 1924, he even offered the AFL official representation on Brookwood's board of directors, though he was relieved when the federation declined the offer.[104] His efforts paid off. By 1924, the AFL had endorsed the movement and became formally affiliated with the WEB, and articles on workers' education, including some by Brookwood faculty and staff, began to appear regularly in its organ, the *American Federationist.*[105]

Muste's publications during this period espoused loyalty to the AFL, while drawing attention to trends that presaged a more progressive federation. Thus he responded with cautious optimism when, in 1924, the AFL departed from its tradition of nonpartisanship and supported third-party candidate Robert La Follette's bid for the presidency and replaced Gompers with William Green, who many hoped would be a progressive because of his background in an industrial union.[106] In essence, Muste tried to chart a middle course. He continued to call for a more militant and internationally minded American labor movement, while criticizing "lefts" for "crabbing about trade union leadership" and for pursuing a "destructive" policy of dual unionism.[107] To some, recalling his recent stint as head of a renegade union, his reformist posture appeared disingenuous, but Muste saw it as a realistic assessment of the state of American labor in the early 1920s. In this way, he reflected the spirit of reconciliation that animated the progressive wing of the labor movement more broadly during the postwar years. *Labor Age*, for example, rarely explicitly criticized the AFL, instead posing questions for discussion and printing articles that represented a variety of perspectives.[108]

It took Muste two years before he found a stable faculty who shared his teaching philosophy. In early 1922, he hired Josephine "Polly" Colby, who had served as a vice president and full-time national organizer for the AFT, to teach English and public speaking.[109] The other two core members of the faculty were David Saposs and Arthur Calhoun. Saposs was from a working-class, immigrant background and had worked his way through graduate school under the tutelage of John Commons at the University of Wisconsin. By the time he was hired at Brookwood to teach courses on trade union organization and administration, he had extensive experience as a labor researcher and economist and had published widely. Arthur Calhoun, a sociologist by training, taught courses in economics, social problems, and social psychology. Clint Golden took Brookwood's message into the field, finding students, obtaining scholarships, initiating extension classes, and helping Brookwood alumni secure funding for educational initiatives within their unions and their communities. A burly and charismatic man, Golden was tremendously important in expanding Brookwood's connections far beyond the progressive wing of the labor movement.[110]

Muste's commitment to a pragmatic approach to labor education shaped the curriculum. Courses focused on the "actual living problems" that confronted workers and the labor movement; education should begin with the "experiences" of trade unionists and "the problems that arise in connection with them," Muste explained.[111] Faculty preferred free and open discussions rather than lecture, which was seen as passive and authoritative, or debate, which was seen as narrowly confining discussion between two simplified poles. Faculty also presented their subject material as objectively as possible, and then allowed the students to come to their own conclusions, using the research and rhetorical skills they had learned.[112]

Muste's personality encouraged this thoughtful engagement with different sides of an issue. Len De Caux, who attended the college in the mid-1920s (and who would later serve as the Communist editor of the *CIO News*), recalled that Muste "always looked for the center with his 'On the one hand . . . But on the other hand . . . .'" "To us young Brookwooders, A. J. was essentially moderate. We respected his counsels of caution, practicality, a relative labor conformism." He continued, "I would have expected

FIGURE 3. Brookwood Faculty and Staff, 1928. Left to right: Arthur Calhoun,
A. J. Muste, Cara Cook, Helen Norton, Josephine Colby, Tom Tippett, and David
Saposs. (*Walter P. Reuther Library, Archives of Labor and Urban Affairs,
Wayne State University*)

him to progress ever rightward, a typical social-democrat. Youthful impa-
tients, we didn't suspect that fires like our own might burn beneath the
diplomatic calm of this lean and eager man." De Caux's comments must
be understood as the impressions of a student; Cara Cook, who served as a
staff member of the college, suggested that Muste's tendency to present
many sides of an issue was "consciously cultivated . . . more as a teaching
method than as a front for tolerance." It may have reflected "his own
method of thinking through something . . . employed until the crunch
came, when he could be unequivocal—'the time comes when, for the good
of all concerned, you have to make up your mind.' "[113]

Short courses and visiting lecturers from all elements of the labor movement and the liberal left, as well as from abroad, further enriched Brookwood's curriculum and reinforced the inclusive spirit of inquiry that Muste
sought to inculcate in his students and in the labor movement. Trade union

officials representing both left and right perspectives spoke at Brookwood, academics like Rex Tugwell and Selig Perlman participated in summer institutes and workshops, and a wide range of intellectuals lectured on a variety of topics; William Z. Foster, Roger Baldwin, V. F. Calverton, Sinclair Lewis, Elizabeth Gurley Flynn, A. Philip Randolph, Scott Nearing, Reinhold Niebuhr, Norman Thomas, Charney Vladeck, Harry Wood, Bertram Wolfe, and Kate Richards O'Hare were just some of the left-liberal luminaries who spoke at Brookwood in the 1920s.[114]

Brookwood's student body offers further evidence of Muste's ecumenical approach to labor education and his desire to bridge the gap between conservatives and radicals in the movement. The faculty deliberately selected students who would disagree with each other. "What we wish to do is to make our idealists practical, and our practical minded people, idealists," one early member of the faculty explained. They also sought to balance region, trade, and ethnicity, making a special effort to recruit women and African Americans. Foreign students also enrolled at Brookwood. Len De Caux, for example, was from New Zealand; others hailed from Japan, Mexico, Norway, Guatemala, and England. As a result of these policies, Brookwood's student body was quite diverse and became more so over time. As Muste once bragged, Brookwood students "are 'old line trade unionists' and 'wobblies': lefts, rights, ambidextrous ones; reds, yellows, pinks, greens!"[115]

In the first half of the decade, most of Brookwood's students were immigrants who had participated in the great strikes of the war years. Few of them had formal education, having left school as soon as they were legally permitted to work, and were eager to learn. As dedicated trade unionists, they sought practical skills that would help them to strengthen their unions and the labor movement. As one student explained, "the problems uppermost in my mind since I came to Brookwood relate to the failure of the Metal Trades campaign waged last summer [in Pittsburgh]. . . . Why did the campaign fail . . . [and] to find a method whereby it is possible to stir the spirit of the rank and file in the interest of the labor movement." Students further appreciated the opportunity to meet unionists from other cultures and trades, though these interactions could also be fraught with ethnic and cultural tensions.[116]

Len De Caux provides an account of Brookwood that is suggestive of its deeper meaning for the students who arrived there. "Brookwood was beautiful. . . . To the miner, Brookwood was green, clean, all above ground—no coal dust, no cricks in the back. To the machinist, Brookwood was greaseless days far from the grinding roar of metal against metal. To makers of suits, dresses, hats, Brookwood was a fairytale country to which they were wand-wafted from the square, treeless hills, the trash-strewn cement valleys of Manhattan or Chicago. To those who had known poverty, Brookwood offered ease, security, the fresh-air pleasures of the well-to-do." The seasons were sharply defined, with "clear and crisp" air in the fall, sledding and frozen-over ponds for skating in the winter, and "fat, bursting buds, sun-dimpled rivulets, baby-green grass" in the spring that set the stage for romantic dalliances. Indeed, "Brookwood was coeducation at close quarters"; with the average Brookwood student unmarried and in his or her late twenties, romances flowered in the context of intellectual and political stimulation and debate. The overall effect was the spiritual expression of "a labor movement in microcosm—without bureaucrats or racketeers—with emphasis on youth, aspiration, ideals."[117]

By 1925–26, the college was flourishing. Under Muste's able leadership, Brookwood had secured stable financing, improved living and working conditions on campus, and initiated a Building and Endowment Fund to further improve and expand the campus. Its graduates had assumed key roles within their unions as organizers, labor journalists, and educators, while its new students emanated a confidence borne from their status as second-generation immigrants.[118] As we have seen, by 1924, the AFL had "warmly" embraced workers' education.

Relations with the Communist Party were also relatively harmonious at mid-decade. At one point, in 1924, party leader Earl Browder accused the school of Fabian elitism, but generally it was believed that "good Communists can go to Brookwood and come out better Communists." Party members attended the college through their unions, Brookwood faculty were invited to teach at the Communist Party's Workers' School in New York, and leaders of the party occasionally lectured at the college. It almost seemed possible that the college might serve as a fulcrum for the reconciliation between left and right, intellectuals and workers, within the movement.[119]

As Brookwood matured, so did its theoretical understanding of the role of education and culture under capitalism. In the college's early years, it tended to view itself as a medium for communicating expert knowledge to workers. By mid-decade, however, it increasingly saw itself as a site where working-class knowledge was produced. As Muste explained in 1927, knowledge about industry and labor was already "in the heads of the men and women who have been doing the practical work of the [labor] movement." The problem was that it had not "been written down anywhere." Brookwood thus offered workers the opportunity to "to think carefully, comprehensively, critically" about their experiences and problems through collaboration with other workers and "experts." Meanwhile, Brookwood graduates and faculty disseminated that knowledge for the benefit of the labor movement through educational initiatives within their unions, articles in the labor press, pamphlets, and books. In these forums, labor educators presented their views and subject matter in a problem-centered format, as starting points for discussion, rather than as truths handed down from above.[120]

In part, Brookwood's evolving teaching philosophy grew out of its half decade of experience teaching adult workers. But it was also a response to the growing sophistication of capital in the 1920s. The full-scale employer assault on organized labor in the early 1920s had given way "to the gentler methods of paternalistic welfare capitalism." Although its emergence was uneven, welfare capitalism sought to develop a "harmony of interests" between the worker and the company through employee representation plans ("company unionism"), fringe benefits and higher wages, as well as through educational and cultural programs. This was part of a larger project to modernize business methods; just as Frederick Winslow Taylor brought efficiency and rationality to production, corporations sought to do the same with personnel.[121] Muste was deeply concerned about these developments, and his evolving views of workers' education must be placed in this context. "The boss is not afraid of education," Muste often pointed out. Newly formed schools of business management "used expert service of all kinds" to train managers in the skills of industrial efficiency, de-skilling, and company unionism. Unless the labor movement shed its residual anti-intellectualism, he warned, the social sciences would continue to be used in antilabor ways.[122]

The advent of mass culture and its reshaping of working-class culture and institutions further concerned Muste. He read Robert and Helen Lynd's book *Middletown* with great interest, observing that the automobile meant that many workers no longer lived near their places of employment, which "makes it harder to bring them together for organization purposes." This development, "together with the radio, movies and other modern ways of recreation and spending leisure time, is cutting down attendance at union meetings."[123]

Rather than adopt a defensive posture, however, Muste called for engagement and appropriation of the new mass culture within the values of the labor movement. Modern methods of propaganda—such as "modern psychology, advertising, and religious revivalism"—and the new media of mass communication might be utilized to win "individuals and the masses" to the labor movement. Indeed, culture might be an important front in the struggle for a socialist society.[124] The union had to be the primary working-class institution because "the basic fact about a worker is that he is a worker" and all of his "human relations depend upon that fact." But it was also important for labor to create its own history, literature, art, and drama. "When Labor undertakes to write and produce its own movies, to do its own radio broadcasting," Muste opined, "then it gives notice that it expects to do its own dreaming henceforth. . . . And this is of great importance, for the dreams that men dream, the visions that they see, probably have far more to do than their abstract thinking in determining how they shall vote and act."[125]

Other labor progressives shared Muste's interest in culture, taking an approach that differentiated them from their modernist contemporaries and that anticipated the left's engagement with the popular and vernacular arts in the 1930s. Throughout the 1920s, organized workers explored the possibilities of counter-institution building and culture as ways to inculcate the ethics of the labor movement in workers and their families. The AFL's schemes like labor banking and life insurance have often been interpreted as evidence of its "class collaborationist" character during this decade, but it might be more fruitful to interpret them as a conservative manifestation of a much larger and diverse cultural project that included education, cooperative experiments, drama, radio programs, summer camps, and youth groups. One such program, Pioneer Youth, with which Muste was closely connected, was conceived as labor's alternative to the militaristic and patriotic culture of the Boy Scouts. It aimed to instill social idealism, a cooperative spirit, and knowledge of the labor movement in working-class children, but in a nondogmatic and playful atmosphere so that workers children would "become critical, independent, [and] creative."[126]

Brookwood's pedagogy and curriculum changed to reflect this more expansive vision. Starting in 1925–26, the college began to organize "labor sports," volleyball, baseball, hiking, tennis, and horseshoe pitching, to foster physical health and working-class solidarity.[127] It also broadened its curriculum to include elective courses in subjects like social psychology, current events, labor journalism, literature, and dramatics. The *Brookwood Review* announced these changes in December 1925 with a modernized format and a lively lead article: "Can that most dramatic movement in the world, the Labor Movement, be dramatized? And dramatized . . . by the workers themselves? Can the workers, in dramatizing the movement for the world, bring home to their own consciousness the scope and possibilities of the movement? Can they, in effect, create a form of drama characteristic of the new proletarian spirit in production?"[128]

As this quote suggests, labor theater proved the most popular with students and faculty. The new drama teacher, Jasper Deeter of the Provinceton Playhouse, oversaw student writing and production. Like the proletarian cultural production of the 1930s, these plays mixed proletarian realism and modernism, while also drawing upon the formulas of mass culture. While often rather simplistic, they reflected students' actual experiences; one of the authors of the play *Shades of Passaic* had been beaten by the police for participating in an ACW-led strike.[129]

Brookwood faculty also wrote and produced plays. Tom Tippett, a former miner who was hired to teach economics in 1927 and later became the school's extension director, published *Mill Shadows*, a dramatization of how one company town was transformed into a union community.[130] Helen Norton, the school's journalism instructor, wrote a number of plays, one of which was a satire of a faculty meeting that reveals much about the culture and politics of Brookwood during this dynamic period. In the play, Muste introduces the meeting agenda, stating that they need to plan Brookwood's economy. Cara Cook, the school's librarian and tutor, responds, "I thought what we wanted was a revolution, not a planned economy." Yet, to meet costs, they must figure out how to reduce the number of students. One faculty member suggests eliminating students who "get second helpings in the dining room." After realizing that this would eliminate nearly every student, another suggests cutting "out *one* student from *each* political wing represented at the school." But that solution is also seen as impractical since it would mean that "practically everybody would leave, and the few left would have far too much harmony in the class room." At one point, David Saposs offers to economize by not teaching his classes. Eventually, they decide to host a "bazaar," but then immediately start debating how to raise money, the gradual approach or the big campaign, metaphorically discussing the best means of organizing workers. Throughout, the meeting is interrupted by phone calls from various creditors and labor contacts, as well as by Connie Muste, who asks her father for a pencil for her history test the next morning.

The play speaks to "the spirit of fellowship" and "dear love of comrade" that Brookwood sought to inculcate, while its humor serves to release tensions over the perennial challenge of fund-raising, quality of the food, heating problems, and gender; in one scene, when Muste is told that the furnace in the women's dormitory might blow up and destroy the labor posters the students had made, he responds, "Well, it would get rid of the women students, and I'd give a poster a day to get that problem off my hands."[131]

Brookwood faculty and students performed these plays, along with labor songs, poems, and lectures on a variety of topics in traveling "labor chautauquas" that raised money for the school and for various strike funds, while also educating workers in the history and culture of unionism.[132] Yet this cultural turn brought criticism from some quarters that suggested that it would divert working-class militants from the urgent task of industrial organization.[133] As a result, culture remained secondary to the college's main purpose of training trade unionists to more effectively serve the labor movement. The college's refusal to hire V. F. Calverton, the editor of the modernist literary magazine *Modern Quarterly*, as a full-time instructor of literature reveals the dominant place practical courses on trade unionism and the social sciences held in Brookwood's curriculum. As Muste explained of the college's decision to only employ him on a part-time basis, "we are specializing in getting men and women whose interests are not primarily cultural or scholarly but who are practical people who . . . are going to do the practical work of the trade union movement." Perhaps when Brookwood became a full-scale "labor university," it would be able to hire Calverton on a full-time basis.[134]

Muste's dreams for Brookwood and the labor movement thus remained expansive, despite his moderate posture and practical orientation during this period. Between the poles of revolutionary socialist and loyal trade unionist was a pragmatist who recognized the importance of being flexible and adaptable to changing conditions. In the early 1920s, those conditions were corporate intransigence, a hostile state, a conservative labor movement, and a decimated left, all of which made education and conciliation with the AFL seem imperative. Pragmatism also gave Muste a language for reconciling his individualism with his allegiance to the working class; with its emphasis on cooperation and action as the path to freedom, pragmatism helped to temper his sense of historical destiny as a prophet of nonviolence and human brotherhood. Yet those ideals remained deeply important to him. As economic and political conditions changed, and as the labor movement and the far left remained resistant to his efforts at reconciliation, even going so far as to publicly attack and vilify him, he would revise his ideas about how to strengthen the labor movement and build a socialist America.

CHAPTER 4

Muste, Workers' Education, and Labor's Culture War in the 1920s

The most ominous fact confronting us is that the labor movement in this country does not have a policy, a voice, an ideal of its own.

—A. J. Muste, 1930

As Brookwood grew, so did Muste's stature in the labor movement. By mid-decade, he was firmly established as a central figure within labor's progressive wing. Among a myriad of other honors and activities, he was called in to advise and mediate strikes, particularly those involving textile workers; invited to speak on workers' education and other topics to unions and central labor bodies throughout the country; elected a vice president of the AFT and as vice president of the National Association for Child Development; served as a member of the Central Trades and Labor Council of Greater New York and as a member of the executive board of the Workers' Education Bureau; and served on the editorial board of *Labor Age*.[1] He also published widely, with articles appearing in *Labor Age*, the *Survey*, the *Nation*, the *World Tomorrow*, the *New Leader*, the *International Trade Union Review*, the *American Federationist*, and the *Modern Quarterly*, among other publications.

During this period, Muste's primary allegiance was to the labor movement, and his pragmatic approach makes it difficult to discern the dedicated Christian pacifist of the war years. Still, he remained committed to nonviolence and civil liberties; he served on the executive committee of the national FOR, chairing that committee from 1926 through 1929, and continued to serve on the national committee of the ACLU.[2] His political agenda in the 1920s can also be interpreted as an expression of his pacifism, as he focused on promoting mutual understanding between radicals and conservatives in the labor movement and engendering a pragmatic spirit; labor must approach its problems "calmly, objectively, ready to cast aside old ideas and methods and to adopt new ones if necessary, willing to experiment," Muste frequently asserted.[3] His refusal to engage in *ad hominem* attacks offers further evidence of his pacifism, and it served to attract those who were eager to transcend the increasingly divided political culture of the labor movement and the left in the 1920s.

Descriptions of Muste from this period describe him as "happy" and even-tempered, a "square shooter" whose modest, unassuming manner endeared him to the hardscrabble workers who attended Brookwood. At the same time, he was clearly a force to be reckoned with; as a militant in the labor movement, and as an independent on the left, sometimes he was "shot at from both sides. From the hierarchy of the American Federation of Labor. From the Hell-for-leather Communists. And just when the air is thick with critical bullets, you will find A. J. grinning a most winning grin and shooting right back, straight and hard."[4] This characterization of Muste as someone who exuded "moral authority" and equanimity, while also being shrewd and strategic, echoes descriptions of him as a minister and as a leader of the ATWA. As we shall see, they would be repeated again and again in his long career; as David McReynolds would recall of his mentor, he was both a saint and as "sly as a fox."[5]

Though Muste worked hard throughout the 1920s to reconcile right and left elements within the labor movement, by the end of the decade he found himself attacked as a "labor fakir" by the Communists and red-baited by the AFL.[6] On one level, the conflict between Muste and the AFL was about competing visions of unionism—a struggle between those advocating industrial unionism, militancy, and political engagement and those advocating labor-management cooperation, voluntarism, and nonpartisanship, or between what we might call progressive and conservative unionism. But on a deeper level the conflict was cultural and generational. Muste and other labor progressives had adopted a modern worldview that frowned upon dogmatism and orthodoxy of any kind and viewed adaptation and flexibility as virtues in a rapidly changing world. Their supporters were a new generation of working-class youth who were more self-confident, modern in their outlook, and more invested in the United States than their immigrant parents. Union leaders, on the other hand "were ideological prisoners of the past."[7]

By mid-decade, Muste had become more confident and assertive. He continued to espouse loyalty to the AFL, but he lost the deferential tone of the early 1920s and spoke as an authority. His publications generally sounded two interrelated themes. First, he believed that the ideological splits in the labor movement had to be healed, and he offered insights into the causes and consequences of these divisions, and suggestions for their remedy.[8] Second, he called for the modernization of the labor movement; it had to "adapt" to the realities of the new capitalism or die. This latter project was intimately related to the former for it entailed incorporating the younger and more militant members of the labor movement and recognizing that modern developments had rendered older methods of trade union organization archaic.

In an influential series of articles on "dissenters" in the labor movement, for example, Muste assumed the role of an impartial observer, noting that unions often responded in a "primitive" manner to outbreaks of dissent and radicalism rather than "scientifically" and "impersonally" inquiring into their origins. Drawing upon the fields of sociology and social psychology, he pointed out that all organizations had some level of internal strife, and that such strife sometimes indicated that a movement was a "living" one. Unions were particularly prone to internal strife because of their dual role as both "army and town meeting." On one level, the union assumes the character of an army, with the right to conscript and the right to tax, and during strikes, its struggle was replete with "generals," battles, spies, and enemies. At the same time, however, the union was a democratic institution, with the membership enjoying the democratic right to elect its leaders. This tension between the union's "two and incompatible functions" was further complicated by the union's contradictory position of, on the one hand, having a vested interest in society through its role as a collective bargaining agent and, on the other, its opposition to the present order.[9]

While some internal dissension was inevitable, Muste maintained that certain conditions gave rise to the "serious problem" of factionalism—such as an economic depression, an industry undergoing transition, or lack of union control over an industry. Thus, when a union faced discord, the correct response was to inquire into industrial conditions rather than try to quash oppositionists; an economic depression, for example, was often a sign "that the time has come when the union must work out a new program of action, that the conventional tactics will no longer do."[10] The real question was not, then, what was wrong with the "lefts" or "rights" but rather "what measures the union must take to adapt itself to those changes." "Oppositions do not make crises," Muste concluded, "they are created by them."[11]

In these articles and others, Muste suggested that one reason why unions were unable to intelligently and calmly deal with problems such as internal strife was that organizers often had little training or experience for their roles, and he suggested that unions adopt fairly uniform criteria in selecting their organizers, much like modern businesses did. Organizers should, first of all, possess certain personal qualities such as energy, public speaking ability, a fighting spirit, good judgment, a thick skin, and charisma—"He must have the quality variously described as magnetism, personality, 'sex appeal,' which enables him to approach people and to hold them." And yet, Muste cautioned, unions did not want "salesmen," but rather committed and experienced trade unionists; it was essential that organizers have an intimate knowledge of their craft, their union, and their industry; an ability to keep records; and some knowledge of psychology, since "an organizer needs to know himself and to know others." These qualities could be cultivated through organizational experience, consultation with others in the movement, and, more to the point, courses in workers' education.[12]

Another reason for the sorry state of the labor movement was that it had failed to utilize young people. It was natural that older people feared the young; "young people are inexperienced, often hasty, unorthodox, critical, rebellious, great nuisances. The good God or Nature . . . has fixed that. It's no good whining about. We have simply to accept the situation and deal with it." Moreover, "any organization is in constant need of new blood, if it is not to stagnate and die"; young people often had that "spark" of "idealism" that kept movements alive. At the same time, he offered advice to young unionists about how to deal with a labor movement dominated by conservatives, advice that reflected his own journey from revolutionary idealist to labor pragmatist. His maxims are worth quoting at length; not only do they reveal his approach to the problems of labor conservatism and worker dormancy, they illustrate the good humor and evenhandedness for which he was well known:

Don't be somebody who is going to do something TO the labor movement. Be somebody who is going to be and do something IN the labor movement. . . . Don't get the Messiah or the Moses-lead-the-movement-out-of-the-wilderness complex. . . . Don't be in a hurry. . . . Some things have to grow; they can't be made. . . . Don't be a cry baby. . . . A cry baby is anyone who always finds someone else to blame except himself. . . . Don't be a nut. A nut is someone who is so obsessed with his own idea that he doesn't see it in relation to other ideas nor in its effect on the people he is dealing with. . . . Don't play for the limelight all the time. There are still somethings [*sic*] that can't be done effectively in the limelight, such as making love or bringing up babies. . . . Don't be afraid of being called names [such as "Bolshevik"]. . . . Don't become a cynic. Don't grow up; don't get old; don't settle down; don't lose your nerve, your gayety, your willingness to take a risk.[13]

Yet underneath Muste's moderate tone was a growing sense of urgency and frustration with the official labor movement. By mid-decade, it was clear to him and other progressives that their hopes in Green had been misplaced, as the AFL "shifted from militancy to respectability." At its 1926 convention, rather than endorse industrial organization as the answer to Fordism, the federation proposed union-management cooperation through schemes like tying wage increases to high productivity. It also withdrew from its move into electoral politics, retreating into its traditional stance of nonpartisanship and voluntarism. Meanwhile, the labor movement was weak and in disarray. The United States was the only industrialized country without a political party that provided adequate representation for organized workers, as well as the only one in which company unions, injunctions, the industrial spy system, and the yellow-dog contract were used without impunity against workers.[14]

These developments distressed labor progressives like Muste, as well as the liberal left more broadly, and they grew more vocal in their criticism of the AFL leadership.[15] A case in point is Muste's comments on the infamous "Mitten-Mahon agreement" in which the Street Railway Employees' Union agreed not to intrude upon certain company unions. Though Muste stated at the outset that he sought to approach the question in "a spirit of inquiry," he pointedly compared the agreement to the process by which

Benito Mussolini had gained control of unions and workers in fascist Italy. He also began touching upon wider themes, linking labor's fate with struggles against imperialism and racism at home. His response to the execution of Sacco and Vanzetti, in which he compared the two Italian anarchists to Christ, further revealed a latent ardor and millennial urgency.[16]

Starting in mid-1928, Muste began to take his first tentative steps toward reviving the spirit of "militant progressivism" that had characterized the labor movement during the war years. In an article for V. F. Calverton's *Modern Quarterly*, he groped toward the formulation of a "progressive-realist" position (also known as the "practical idealist" position) that would stand somewhere between a complacent labor movement and an ultra-revolutionary left wing. In contrast to the Communists, who had "irritated" laborites and progressives "beyond words" by their use of "verbal mud-slinging" and by seeking to capture movements, progressive realists would exhibit "realism and flexibility" in the struggle for a socialist society; they would recognize that the revolution was not around the corner, at least not in the United States, and would be willing to cooperate with both liberals and the official labor movement. In essence, Muste's vision was a mix of social democracy and revolutionary socialism; he placed primary emphasis on industrial organization over parliamentary politics, embraced coalitions and the possibility of gradualism, while at the same time conceding that conditions might arise in which a more Leninist approach might become necessary—in a counterrevolutionary context, for example, "a compact, centralized, and vigorous party is absolutely indispensable for leadership of the workers."[17]

As this reference suggests, Lenin's ideas had begun to influence Muste's thought. Lenin, he reminded readers of *Labor Age*, was a labor strategist and tactician, who offered insights of the "greatest value to all active labor people quite regardless of their political or economic views." Moreover, despite his criticism of Lenin's disciples in the American Communist Party (discussed in more detail below), he was deeply impressed by their revolutionary dedication, which he saw as a model for other socialists to emulate. He reconciled this move to the left with his pragmatism by insisting that Leninist theory was not infallible and by drawing attention to Lenin's own admonition that revolutionaries must be flexible and adapt their methods to changing conditions.[18]

As Muste compared the activities of the revolutionary left to the politics of mainline Protestantism, the latter increasingly came up short. Where the churches were "identified with the status quo," "the Left had the vision, the dream, of a classless and warless world" that motivated the Hebrew prophets and Jesus Christ. As he later recalled of this period in his life, "This was a strong factor in making me feel that [the revolutionary left], in a sense, was the true church. Here was the fellowship drawn together and drawn forward by the Judeo-Christian prophetic vision of 'a new earth in which righteousness dwelleth.'" Leftists were, moreover, "truly religious" insofar as they "were virtually completely committed, they were betting their lives on the cause they embraced."[19]

Muste was also growing disenchanted with organized pacifism. In 1928, he published an article in the *World Tomorrow* taking pacifists to task for their efforts to dissuade workers from using violence in their struggles against capitalism. Rather than criticize workers, pacifists should denounce capitalism and call on the ruling class to renounce its power and privilege. They should, moreover, disassociate as much as possible from the economic system and identify with workers and their cause. Only then would they be in a moral position to counsel nonviolence. Muste was not prepared to dismiss pacifism entirely, but he insisted that "in a world built on violence, one must be a revolutionary before one can be a pacifist; in such a world a non-revolutionary pacifist is a contradiction in terms, a monstrosity." In 1929, he made a similar argument when he addressed the annual meeting of the FOR.[20] The organization's refusal to unequivocally support labor's right to strike at the meeting further alienated him from pacifism and religious liberalism, though he continued to think of himself as a Christian and retained alliances with more radical members of the FOR and left-leaning Protestants for several more years, occasionally attending FOR meetings and continuing to serve as a contributing editor to the *World Tomorrow*.[21]

As Muste assumed a more forceful presence on the labor left, so too did Brookwood. The college's extension program expanded, and its faculty, staff, and alumni were intimately involved in other workers' education initiatives like the Bryn Mawr Summer School for Women Workers, the Southern Summer School for Women Workers, Highlander Folk School, Commonwealth College, Seattle Labor College, Baltimore Labor College, Denver Labor College, Philadelphia Labor College, and Pittsburgh Labor College; indeed, the syllabi, curriculum, and pedagogy of these educational initiatives were largely based on Brookwood's example.[22] The college's influence also grew as alumni assumed central roles in their unions as organizers, editors, and officials.

Among others, the machinist Charles L. Reed became vice president of the
Massachusetts Federation of Labor; Bonchi Friedman continued to organize
for the ACW; Alfred Hoffman served as an organizer for the American Federation of Full-Fashioned Hosiery Workers (AFFFHW) and the UTW; and Rose
Pesotta began her rise within the ranks of the ILGWU.

Meanwhile, the college continued to hold its popular labor institutes in
which representatives from various industries met to discuss problems facing their unions. Starting in 1926, it also began to host conferences on
more expansive and controversial subjects. In 1927, it held a symposium
on "Negroes in Industry" that included presentations by black workers and
intellectuals—such as Charles S. Johnson, E. Franklin Frazier, Abram L.
Harris, A. Philip Randolph, and Frank Crosswaith—that explored such topics as the history of race and trade unionism, conflicts between black workers and the black bourgeoisie, and the rise of black nationalism. "Negroes
are organizable," the *Brookwood Review* editorialized in its review of the
symposium.[23] Two months later, Brookwood began a series of institutes on
the topic of women and the labor movement; the first one focused on the
plight of unorganized female workers.[24] Soon thereafter, Brookwood hosted
a two-day youth conference that involved representatives from twenty-two
unions, rank-and-file members, and AFL officials on the question of how
to organize young workers.[25]

The gist of these 1927 conferences was that these workers were not
"problems" or obstacles to trade unionism, but rather had their own, distinct experiences that needed to be understood and adapted to if unionism
was to flourish.[26] These relatively progressive views on the black working
class and women workers existed in tension with deeply held racial and
gender ideologies. At the same time that Brookwood decried the existence
of racial prejudice, the Brookwood Players performed a play that had coal
miners dressed up like "horrifying African cannibals." Moreover, as sympathetic as they could be toward the challenges facing black workers, Brookwood faculty, students, and alumni were often reluctant to confront racism
because they feared it would weaken the labor movement as a whole.[27]
Similarly, despite challenging the myth that women just worked for "pin
money," the structure of Brookwood depended upon the unpaid labor of
faculty wives, such as Anne Muste, even as they had little formal say in the
school's governance. More broadly, progressive unionists shared with their
conservative brethren a construction of the worker as a white male and
conflated organization with the attainment of full manhood.[28]

As the college became an intellectual center for labor progressives, it also became directly involved in a series of strikes that occurred over the course of 1926 to 1928. Brookwood's policy had always been to release students for participation in strikes by their unions, but now the college organized as an institution to assist striking workers. This change reflected the growing conviction of Muste that education must "be applied in action," not only in the classroom.[29] Thus Brookwood provided crucial financing and publicity for strikes by New York's garment and fur workers, miners in Pennsylvania and Colorado, midwestern hosiery workers, and especially textile workers. The Passaic strike of 1926 was like a miniature revival of the Lawrence strike of 1919, as liberals supported the rights of the strikers to free assembly and free speech. Muste and other Brookwooders helped organize the "Conference on Relief for the Passaic Strikers" to raise money and relief, while the Brookwood Players performed *Shades of Passaic* to a packed audience of strikers.[30]

At Brookwood's second annual summer textile institute, held in 1928, Muste urged the UTW executive board to step up their efforts to organize the South. Alfred Hoffman spearheaded the organizing drive in the Piedmont region, along with the help of other Brookwood students.[31] Meanwhile, closer to home, in Paterson, New Jersey, the Associated Silk Workers, an independent union, called a strike on October 10, 1928, for the forty-four-hour work week, a uniform piecework scale, and union recognition. As the strike dragged on for several months, Brookwood organized relief for the striking workers, while Muste organized merger negotiations between the independent union and the UTW. The decision to have Muste serve as impartial arbitrator "was the unanimous choice of both sides," President McMahon of the UTW commented.[32]

Brookwood formalized its move "into the field" in 1928 with the formation of an extension department. Under the direction of Tom Tippett, a former miner, the college provided not only classes and lectures to workers throughout the United States, but also participated in organization campaigns and strikes. Brookwood considered these activities "not as interruptions of school work but as genuine education, and students and teachers alike bring wiser judgment and a keener sense of reality to their classes in consequence."[33]

As Brookwood assumed a more substantial presence in the labor movement, the AFL moved to quash any evidence of independence or dissent within the movement. Even though the college worked hard to avoid public criticism of the federation, the very nature of workers' education—as conceived of by labor progressives—conflicted with an official labor movement seeking loyalty and control. On the one hand, Muste and other advocates of workers' education stated their allegiance to the labor movement and their conviction that education would make the movement stronger. At the same time, they were adamant that they would teach their students *how* to think, not what to think.[34] What this meant was that a variety of ideological and political perspectives found expression in workers' education initiatives, including those that were in opposition to the official policies of the AFL. A memorial service Brookwood held for Gompers offers a case in point, as it included speeches by students who favored the nonpartisan policy of the AFL as well as by devoted Leninists. The affair prompted William Green's secretary, Florence Thorne, to write to Muste: while she appreciated "your difficulties in meeting the various tendencies of your Brookwood group," she wondered if the college might refrain from publicizing such events. "This would . . . help to keep the ideals and policies of Brookwood more in line with our American labor movement." In his response, Muste admitted to the "unfortunate" juxtaposition of Gompers and Lenin, but reminded Thorne that the college's policy was "to allow of a certain freedom of discussion [in the college newspaper] which it might be difficult to maintain in the publication of the trade union."[35]

The divergences between a labor movement seeking ideological conformity and an educational movement committed to free discussion came to a head over the course of 1926 to 1928 and ultimately became the seedbed for the emergence of the "Musteite" movement at the end of the decade. In 1926, several of Brookwood's students and instructors joined John Brophy's "Save-the-Union Movement" to wrest control of the UMWA from the autocratic leadership of John L. Lewis. When the insurgent miners organized an anti-Lewis gathering in April 1928, Muste refused to exercise ideological control over students and alumni who attended the conference.[36] The incident tied Brookwood to oppositionists and empowered conservatives in their efforts to seize control over workers' education. As Irving Bernstein has commented, to openly defy John L. Lewis made a break "inevitable."[37]

Another incident occurred in 1926, this one involving workers' education, that foreshadowed a split between Brookwood and the AFL. Unfortunately for progressives who had placed so much hope in workers' education, Matthew Woll, one of the AFL's most conservative vice presidents, had joined the executive council of the WEB as one of the AFL's three representatives. In 1926, the adult education movement, which had emerged concomitantly with the workers' education movement, made overtures to the WEB, offering it a grant of $25,000 from the Carnegie Corporation. Conservatives like Woll favored acceptance of the grant, while progressives viewed it as an effort to co-opt their movement. At a meeting of the WEB in April of 1926, progressives sought to clearly differentiate adult education and workers' education. As James Maurer stated, the former was "designed, for the most part, either to give a bit of culture to the student, or else to lift him out of his present job into a higher one." Workers' education, by contrast, had a class perspective and agenda of educating the worker into the labor movement and of service to the working class. With twenty-one other progressives, Muste voted against accepting the funds, while a majority of forty-six voted in favor of acceptance, so long as the funds were given unconditionally.[38]

Yet the AFL of the mid-1920s simply would not tolerate dissent; Spencer Miller Jr., secretary of the WEB, was so offended by the sentiment against adult education that he questioned the right of Brookwood to remain affiliated with the WEB.[39] Meanwhile, the AFL moved to tighten their control over the bureau. In 1927, at the AFL's annual convention in Los Angeles, the federation recommended that the WEB limit the membership of the executive committee to national AFL representatives, a move that would have essentially stripped the executive board of any representation from those most directly involved in workers' education. Muste went on public record in opposition to this "wrong step in workers' education," pointing out the need to have labor educators involved in executive decision making, and questioning the ability of teachers to maintain academic freedom when their institutions were solely under the control of personnel with no connection to workers' education.[40]

Early in 1928, Brookwood began to anticipate an attack by the AFL. "Subordination, coordination, or independence—these are the terms which describe our choices," labor educators concluded at their annual conference at Brookwood in February of that year.[41] A few months later, Muste published an article in *Labor Age* responding to rumors that the AFL officialdom viewed labor education as "unpatriotic and un-American, atheistic and radical (Bolshevik)." In it, he questioned the worth of a labor movement that was unwilling to allow its rank and file to "examine their own opinions" in order "to develop critical, fearless, open, independent minds!" "Have we now a labor dogma, a labor creed, a labor orthodoxy, to which all must conform? Which must be taught . . . as a given system of doctrine is imparted in a sectarian theological seminary?" Such thinking was based on the assumption "that there is danger in a critical discussion of labor policies," but, in fact, the real danger was in preventing free discussion in the first place.[42]

As the debate over workers' education played out, several disgruntled Brookwood students sought to exploit the controversy over the UMWA in order to undermine the school. Passionate debate had been a central feature of Brookwood student life from the school's inception, but these disagreements were generally expressed and resolved within the culture of ecumenism and academic freedom that Brookwood sought to foster. In 1927–28, however, the school had admitted several students from conservative backgrounds who deeply resented the radicalism of some of their peers, a resentment that was heavily tinged with anti-Semitism and misogyny. One of them was a miner who opposed Brophy's "Save-the-Union Movement." In 1928, he published an account of the fractious UMWA conference that exposed the Brookwood students who attended the conference and accused them of being Communists. The other conservative students rose to his defense and persuaded their internationals, the Brotherhood of Railway Carmen, the International Association of Machinists, and the International Brotherhood of Painters and Allied Trades to withdraw their funding for Brookwood.[43]

For the first time in Brookwood's history, Muste was unable to reconcile the student body; the second-year class voted to bar the offending student from their final seminar on the grounds that he could not be trusted, while the handful of conservative students left the school and refused to attend graduation ceremonies. It was "painful and distressing" to graduate students "out of accord with [what] Brookwood is trying to do," Muste stated at the graduation ceremony, yet he stood firm "on the fundamental things that Brookwood stands for and is trying to do" and accepted "the challenge of those who do not believe in those things." Those "things" were a militant labor movement committed to energetically and courageously organizing the unorganized, raising the political and economic consciousness of American workers, freedom in workers' education, and anti-imperialism. If the American labor movement considered this treasonous, "then let them make the most of it." To be seen as "unpatriotic, irreligious, and red" was to be "in good company"; Jesus and the Founding Fathers had been viewed similarly by their contemporaries. It would be "a pleasant death to die" in the service of militant unionism, he opined in what can only be viewed as a sermon.[44]

In spite of his firm tone, one senses Muste's foreboding as he clarified his position. "One might hope that if we are to fight each other, it might be with a little more mercy and decency and fair play than ordinarily characterizes conflicts in the labor movement."[45] Yet the fight was not to be merciful. On August 7, 1928, the executive council of the AFL, unexpectedly and without warning, announced that it was advising all of its affiliated unions to withdraw their support from Brookwood Labor College. Though this did not emerge until later, its decision was based upon a secret report by Matthew Woll, which had been instigated by the complaints of the same conservative students who had red-baited Brookwood a few months earlier. The report was not released to the public nor was the source of the evidence against the college revealed, but it persuaded Green and the executive council that it was a "propagandistic and communistic" institution that promulgated dual unionism, sexual immorality, and antireligious views. The charge of dual unionism was particularly ironic: when Muste learned of the announcement, he was in the middle of leading negotiation efforts to bring Paterson's Associated Silk Workers into the UTW.[46]

Muste returned immediately to Brookwood and rallied its supporters. The next day, the college's board of directors issued a statement calling the charges "without foundation" and voicing particular concern over the process through which the college had been censured, which violated the "fundamental labor principles of fair play, collective bargaining, and conference about grievances." The board requested a copy of the charges against the college, the evidence upon which they were based, and a hearing to respond to them.[47]

The case quickly became a cause célèbre among progressive unionists, liberals, and educators. Letters of support poured in to Muste, while telegrams of protest flooded the AFL executive office. John Brophy wrote to Muste that "what has been meted out to Brookwood . . . is exactly what the Executive Committee of the UMWA meted out to me. All opposition, no matter of what character, they labeled communistic and expulsions followed." Fannia Cohn protested to Green that Brookwood deserved a hearing because of its affiliation with the WEB, the "the educational arm" of the AFL, because its faculty were members of the AFT, and because its board of directors were all loyal members of the AFL with long records of service and strong anti-Communist credentials. She called it "unintelligible" that only four disgruntled students had been consulted, while the 125 other Brookwood students and graduates who had "a favorable opinion . . . are not questioned or given an opportunity to discuss frankly the charges made."[48] Alumni like Charles Reed, Mary Goff, and William Ross similarly wrote to defend Brookwood's educational methods, explaining how the college taught them "how to read, how to write, and how to talk . . . to examine each situation and all situations in the light of Facts; and to face those facts regardless of the consequences."[49]

Finally, on October 30, the AFL executive council met to consider the question of whether or not Brookwood should be granted a hearing. Woll won the day with the dubious argument that Brookwood should not enjoy a hearing because Communists had "freely" condemned the AFL without giving its internationals a chance for a hearing. The way the AFL handled the entire case was disingenuous; Green even reported to the *New York Times* that Brookwood had not asked to present its side of the case to the executive council.[50]

The controversy reveals the precarious position of progressives within the labor movement in the 1920s and 1930s, as well as the tensions inherent to the workers' education project. Left-leaning unionists like Muste had retreated from their revolutionary stance of the war years and pursued rapprochement with the conservative wing of the labor movement. They rarely criticized the federation's policies openly and instead sought to gradually impress upon the labor movement the need to modernize its methods and framework to meet the challenges of a new era of industrial capitalism. Within the workers' education movement, they allowed for the expression of a range of opinions and emphasized the importance of taking a more experimental and scientific approach to labor's problems, while also holding that the working class must be unified and American society collectivized. Their philosophical approach was a complex one; it drew, on the one hand, from liberal theories of individual freedom and, on the other, from notions of solidarity and collective purpose that animated the labor movement and other cooperative projects. Muste's notion of the labor movement as a combination of army and town meeting was to the point; the poles of authoritarianism and democracy were inevitable by-products of unionism, but they could also be the source of creativity and growth if handled in a spirit of flexibility and adaptability, recognizing that the labor movement was a "living movement." Hence he and other progressive unionists believed that they should have "the right of criticism" while also being considered loyal members of the AFL.[51]

It is revealing that progressives viewed the question of workers' education as one of academic freedom, while the AFL insisted that it had to do "with the fundamentals of trade unionism," as Matthew Woll put it.[52] Underlying this misunderstanding were two very different visions of the role of the labor movement in American society. AFL conservatives had disavowed the "oft-expounded theory that differences between capital and labor" were irreconcilable, while progressives sought to fundamentally restructure American society. Their contrasting views of the role of education in the labor movement reflected this basic disagreement; the AFL viewed education as a "safeguard against revolutionary doctrines," as William Green put it bluntly, and thus ascribed to a narrow curriculum and authoritarian methods.[53] Progressives, by contrast, sought "new educational forms and methods" in order "to change behavior fundamentally to revamp cultural values, and to bring about a new society."[54]

Further complicating this disagreement were the culture wars of the 1920s. Green, Woll, and others in the AFL hierarchy were cultural conservatives who were deeply offended by the cultural politics of modernism. Hence their criticism of Brookwood was not just that it allowed for the expression of views contrary to the official line of the AFL, but also that it freely discussed evolution, questioned religious dogmas, and subjected sex and gender norms to scrutiny. Reflecting this perspective, the *American Federationist* published an editorial in October 1928 stating that workers needed two kinds of education, cultural education and trade union education. The former could be handled by the adult education movement through university extension programs, while the latter should be strictly controlled by unions, with the implication that this focus on trade union issues meant that academic freedom was inapplicable.[55] Such a formula was, of course, anathema to the socialist moderns who had spearheaded the workers' education movement. As they commented in *Labor Age*, dogmatism and orthodoxy "cannot be the marks of a living movement." Moreover, there was a vital need for workers to create their own institutions and build a "labor culture" to compete with the antilabor culture of the dominant society.[56]

These cultural and philosophical issues played themselves out as efforts now focused on appealing the AFL's decision at the federation's annual convention scheduled to take place a month later in New Orleans. Internationals and labor leaders close to Brookwood continued to rally to the college's defense, while also experiencing some trepidation about directly confronting the powerful and increasingly intolerant executive council. The AFT, Muste's own union, offers a case in point; its leadership offered some of the most strident condemnation of the AFL's action, but refused to introduce a resolution at the New Orleans convention calling on the AFL to reconsider its decision.[57]

Leading the charge was Muste's former professor at Columbia University John Dewey, who had been an enthusiastic backer of Brookwood and labor education more broadly. On the eve of the New Orleans convention, Muste organized a public meeting at the New York Society for Ethical Culture that featured Dewey as well as other venerable supporters of Brookwood, including Harry F. Ward of Union Theological Seminary, John A. Fitch of the New York School of Social Work, and Henry Linville of the AFT. The pragmatic worldview was fully in evidence. Fitch called on the AFL to learn to accept "new truths," and to reconsider its action with a more "scientific attitude." Dewey spoke on the difference between training and education, the latter of which was "the awakening and movement of the mind."[58]

Despite widespread liberal sentiment for an appeal, at the convention, the executive council made sure that the issue was kept off of the floor. Finally, on the last day of the weeklong convention, the president of the Street Railway Employees' Union—signatory of the notorious Mitten-Mahon agreement that Muste had dared to publicly criticize—called out, "Let us hear what is the matter with Brookwood." Conservatives dominated the floor; whenever a supporter of Brookwood rose to speak, he or she was ruled out of order. Woll gave a long speech denouncing Muste as a Communist, while Green produced a letter from Brookwood faculty member Arthur Calhoun to the *Daily Worker* endorsing William Z. Foster for president. "Do you want to send members of the A.F. of L. to a school that employs an avowed Communist to teach these trade unionists economics?" he challenged the delegates.[59]

In short, conservatives outmaneuvered and intimidated progressives, with even the UTW, the ILGWU, and the AFT ultimately backing down in fear of a public confrontation with the powerful leaders of the federation.[60] As John Dewey commented, the executive council took steps "which made contrary action possible only if the delegates were ready to declare war on the official management of the Federation. Under the circumstances, it is almost surprising that as many as one-fourth of the delegates were not in favor of confirmation." It was, he concluded, a "scholastic lynching."[61]

Dewey's support certainly raised Brookwood's prestige among liberals, but it also helped to unleash the latent anti-intellectualism of the AFL. At the convention, Woll called Dewey a "propagandist" for Communism," and demanded that the AFL's Education Committee expunge the reference to Dewey in its annual report. Afterward, he gloried in the pages of the *International Labor News Service* that Brookwood had been "socked in the jaw, in the solar plexus, in the small of the back, in both jaws."[62] Others apparently shared his view of the controversy as a reflection of the differences between intellectuals and the "laboring man." After the convention, Muste received a letter from a minor labor official who suggested that perhaps Brookwood faculty could not understand the perspectives of AFL officialdom, who had been compelled to work "at the age of 10 or 11 eleven years . . . suffering all the tortures of hell . . . until relief came through organization." Muste, who rarely made reference to his working-class background, wrote back angrily, "It happens that it was exactly at the age of eleven when I went to work for the first time myself in a furniture factory." He further pointed out that his father, "at the age of 72, still works in a furniture factory every day of his life."[63]

Once again in AFL history, anti-intellectualism functioned as a convenient way to silence and marginalize left criticism and opposition. Yet the break between the AFL and a vibrant workers' education movement was not inevitable. Although the AFL had long distrusted Brookwood, the two institutions had enjoyed a working relationship through the WEB and through international unions that had chosen to affiliate with the college. Brookwood faculty had long expressed their loyalty to the federation and carefully avoided public criticism; even as Muste grew more assertive over the course of the 1920s, his publications evinced a conciliatory spirit. It was only starting in 1926, at precisely the moment when the AFL turned decisively conservative, that conflict became unavoidable. Not coincidentally, 1926 was also the moment when Brookwood was on the verge of moving beyond the "experimental stage" to achieving a level of permanency, as evidenced by Muste's plans to turn the college into a university. The AFL, in other words, attacked "while the school was still vulnerable" and before it could serve as the center of an alternative vision of unionism.[64]

AT precisely the same time Brookwood was attacked by the right, it was attacked by the left. The Brookwood faculty and board of directors were not Communists, but their commitment to the free exchange of ideas meant that they refused to discriminate against Communists, which, as we have seen, much chagrined the AFL. Communist theories were freely discussed at Brookwood, and the college worked with Communists in educational programs and strikes. Early in the school's history, moreover, the Communist Party had shown a level of toleration and even respect for Brookwood, allowing its members to attend the college and inviting Brookwood faculty to lecture at the Workers' School. Such interactions were not without their tensions; like other progressives, Brookwood faculty were often "embarrassed and irritated" by their collaborations with Communists who, as Muste put it, "talked a language" foreign to progressives, as well as "the great masses of American workers," and insisted upon "'capturing' movements and organizations, which thereupon turned out to be mere shells in their hands."[65]

Yet in 1928, the situation "definitely and radically changed." Reflecting its shift to the "Third Period," the Communist Party departed from its history of toleration for Brookwood and began to publicly attack and vilify the college in the left-wing press, at party gatherings, at educational meetings, and instructed its members not to attend the college. How the Communist Party responded to the AFL's attack on Brookwood offers a case in point; rather than defend the college, the *Daily Worker* stated that Brookwood had "consistently functioned as a cloak for the destructive policy of the reactionary labor fakers . . . everybody who has eyes can see that its whole content is the preaching of class collaboration in a 'refined' form."[66]

Even more galling, from Muste's perspective, was how the Communists' policy reversal affected efforts to strengthen and radicalize the UTW. For years, in pursuance of their policy of boring from within, the Communists had worked with other progressive elements to obtain unification between the Associated Silk Workers and the UTW. The process, for which Muste had served as arbiter, was a difficult one in which progressives had to coax and plead with conservatives in the UTW. Finally, when an agreement was hammered out and placed before the membership for a vote, Muste wrote incredulously, "those who had started this movement, nursed it along, toiled for it, turned square around and let it be known that . . . they would not support it" because the Communist Party had decided to change its tactics from "boring from within" to dual unionism. While he was willing to concede that consistency was "the vice of little minds," it was also "childish" to make "frivolous changes of front," particularly when there was such a desperate urge to organize industrial workers. Repeating a frequent theme, he bemoaned that in the United States, the official labor movement was so conservative, while the left wing, which had "courage, amazing vitality," exhibited such "childishness, lack of realism, cheap bickering, mere fury that creates endless turmoil." In between these two extremes were "many afflicted with the malady of defeatism" yet who still dreamed of "a world freed from exploitation and in the control of the workers." Who would be "willing to act" to reignite this dormant idealism, Muste wondered?[67]

Muste was thus in a bind when the AFL attacked Brookwood as a "communistic" institution. On the one hand, he had consistently opposed sectarianism and had tried to maintain comradely relations with Communists. On the other hand, he viewed Communist tactics as destructive of trade unionism and unrealistic in the context of the late 1920s. Moreover, reflecting his laborist agenda, he was far more interested in having good relations with the labor movement than with a small radical sect.[68]

Over the course of December 1928 and January 1929, Brookwood clarified its policy of nonexclusion, while at the same time stating its refusal to become a Communist-controlled institution. Ironically, the college would find itself unable to maintain this policy. Even though the Communist Party prohibited members from attending Brookwood, a handful of them were accepted as students over the course of the next several years. Muste and other Brookwood faculty soon discovered that these students were not attending the college in good faith, but were rather bent upon "disrupting and destroying the school." As they explained, these students "openly expressed hostility" toward Brookwood, left in the middle of the term under party orders, flaunted school discipline, and worked with the party to deprive Brookwood of financial contributions. Moreover, Communists who had graduated from the college "openly repudiated Brookwood and attempted to work against it." Asserting that "no school is under any obligation" to accept students committed to its destruction, Brookwood banned Communists from attendance so long as the party's policy was one of attacking elements it considered reformist, though it continued to invite Communist speakers to lecture at the college.[69]

THUS, as 1928 drew to a close, Brookwood was in the midst of a severe crisis; it had strained relations with the left wing, while its relations with the right had reached a breaking point. More ominously, the entire workers' education project seemed doomed, as the AFL maneuvered for control of the movement. In January 1929, Muste and David Saposs were unseated from the WEB's executive committee and Brookwood was disaffiliated from the WEB. A few months later, at the bureau's annual conference, the executive committee voted to adopt the AFL's recommendation to eliminate all those most intimately involved in workers' education from the governing board of the WEB. When progressives called for trade union control of workers' education, Muste opined, they meant that unions "should control them democratically, as it insists industry should be controlled," with teachers and students in labor classes, local unions, city central bodies, and state federations having some representation. Without democracy, he warned, the WEB would "cease to be a rank and file movement" and would lose its progressive impulse to remake the social order. In protest, James Maurer resigned as president of the WEB and walked out of the annual conference, followed by Muste, Israel Mufson, Charles Reed, and seven others.[70]

As Muste predicted, AFL control over the WEB led to the body's decline; from then on, it met infrequently and articulated a narrow vision of workers' education, viewing it as a means for teaching the fundamentals of trade unionism and leaving other subjects to the extension programs of the universities. In spite of this defeat, labor educators both within and outside the official movement would keep the progressive vision of workers' education alive through the mid-1930s, when most of them were hired by CIO unions and the Federal Emergency Relief Administration (FERA), which initiated a workers' education program in 1934.

Muste found the accumulated controversies and strain emotionally exhausting. As he wrote to Fannia Cohn in January 1929, he had "never in my life been in such poor shape and, I do not know, frankly what the outcome will be." Along with defending Brookwood against the AFL and the Communists, he was teaching an overload of classes and serving as sole director, fund-raiser, and dean of students of the college. "Tragic events in Anne's family" back in Iowa further contributed to his stress. "All this would be enough to carry," he commented, but in addition he faced "on every hand rumors about being dishonest, weak, a conspirator, another irresponsible intellectual, about withdrawing financial support from Brookwood, etc. etc. . . . I am exhausted completely and unless there is a definite change, I shall have to withdraw from activity—or perhaps I ought to say, Anne will drag me out."[71]

Rather than emotionally collapse, however, Muste continued his frenzy of activity, seeking to clarify Brookwood's role in the new context and the place of progressives within the larger movement. In a series of discussions held over the winter of 1928–29, the college decided that its best line of defense would be to reaffirm its loyalty to the AFL, while at the same time reiterating its commitment to "free, critical labor education" and sharply asserting its "profound disagreement with some of the fundamental polices of the AF of L administration."[72] Meanwhile, Muste worked to broaden and diversify the college's base of support, while shoring up its traditional base in unions such as the ILGWU, UTW, ACW, AFFFHW, the AFT, the Pulp and Sulphite Workers, the Railway Clerks, and more progressive city labor councils. Through his efforts, Brookwood retained many of its scholarships and unions continued to send students even as many central labor councils and internationals from around the country accepted the AFL censure and distanced themselves from the college. In 1930, the college had its largest class ever, with forty students, including four African Americans, a mix of Italians, Norwegians, Slavs, Jews, and white southerners, and foreign students from Costa Rica, Guatemala, England, and Germany.[73] Thus, while the AFL's attack, combined with the onset of the Great Depression, cut short Muste's hopes of turning Brookwood into a university, workers' education would remain dynamic into the next decade.

Convinced that workers' education could only "flourish" in the context of a strong labor movement, Muste next set about to rebuild the spirit of "militant progressivism" that had given birth to the workers' education movement in the first place. The controversy with the AFL had made it clear to him that the federation would no longer tolerate dissenters, while recent history had shown that it was unwilling to organize the unorganized. It was therefore necessary for progressives to do the job themselves, he argued in a series of conferences with other labor progressives and Socialists held over the course of the winter of 1928–29.[74]

As a result of these discussions, in February 1929, Muste issued a sixteen-point "Challenge to Progressives" in which he called upon those opposed to both "Communist tactics" and the "reactionary" policies of the AFL to fearlessly pursue a "progressive trade union program." His sixteen points defined labor progressivism as aggressive organization of industrial workers, with special attention paid to women workers, black workers, and immigrant groups; determined resistance to antilabor laws; active campaigns for social insurance and other reforms; formation of a labor party;

recognition of the Soviet Union; opposition to American imperialism and militarism; and working-class internationalism, "since capitalism is internationally organized and conditions of work in one country directly affect workers in other lands." Finally, the sixteen points asserted that only a labor movement "marked by idealism, leading American workers on to freedom and independence," could inspire workers.[75]

As these points suggest, Muste criticized the AFL not only because it had failed to adopt industrial unionism; he contended that the labor movement had lost its distinctive, laborite vision and become beholden to "capitalist culture."[76] He had been deeply influenced by the scholarship of his colleague, David Saposs, who maintained that "an effective labor movement is only possible when it is based upon a *labor culture*; that is, a mode of feeling, thinking and acting in terms of the problems and aspirations of labor." According to Saposs, the labor movement in the United States had been

> well on the way to developing a labor culture . . . including unions, cooperatives, political parties, mutual benefit societies, a press, workers' education, and so on. Then came the American Federation of Labor with its business unionism, which deliberately discouraged all working class organizational activity except unions, and which led the workers to immerse themselves in the capitalistic culture. This attitude automatically destroyed the incipient labor movement and labor culture, with its traditions and customs, finally even resulting in the weakening of the trade union movement, so that in general it is weaker now than it has ever been in its history . . . we must begin by developing a labor culture as the foundation for a completely rounded out labor movement encompassing the organization of the workers on all important fields of human endeavor.[77]

Saposs was cautiously optimistic about the possibilities for reforming the AFL and revitalizing the labor movement. Drawing on his research on the history of left-wing oppositions, he wrote in the essay "The Future of Radicalism in the Labor Movement" that the future "belonged to the radicals" since they appealed to workers' "emancipatory longings." Yet he had serious reservations about the Communists, whose tactics of dual unionism were based upon the faulty assessment that American capitalism was weak. The "moderate radicals," by contrast, recognized that American capitalism was "on firm foundation" and thus focused their efforts on boring from within, adapting their methods to the demands of organization, while also maintaining their idealism. He predicted that this policy had far more potential; for a variety of reasons, progressives may manage to "win over enough unions" to transform the AFL and, in so doing, attract independent unions such as the ACW. On the other hand, he noted presciently, the AFL could so resist progressive efforts that a center for progressive unionism would grow up outside of the federation's orbit, eventually "taking with them a considerable number of A.F. of L. unions also progressively inclined." Whichever alternative ultimately triumphed, moderate radicals had their work cut out for them, and he warned that in trying to balance the evangelical and the practical, the path would be "a devious one and pitfalls abound. There is always the danger of leaning too much toward one or the other of the methods or miserably falling between them." He called on them to remain centered, to plod along, judiciously recognizing those moments for compromise and those for staying firm.[78]

Despite its harsh criticism of the AFL, the new movement Muste envisioned would not actively support dual unionism. For reasons explained above, he viewed Communist dual unionism as divisive and disruptive; the progressive approach, by contrast, would be to take constructive "action," providing "healthy criticism" rather than "heresy hunting." At the same time, it would drop the left's deferential attitude toward the AFL and spearhead the organization of workers on a variety of fronts. Progressive laborites, Muste explained in the *Nation*, "would like nothing more than to see the AF of L reinvigorated." But he reminded readers that the AFL was "a human institution. It had its beginning and will doubtless have its end. It will survive, like any other social institution, if it is flexible, if it can adapt itself to the tremendous social changes taking place." Laborites, therefore, need not turn the AFL into the "devil incarnate" but neither should they "fall into the error of regarding it as something sacred, inviolable, immortal on which no one . . . must lay unholy hands." Indeed, it was precisely this attitude—this fear of alienating the AFL—that had prevented progressives from taking it on and helping it to adapt to modern conditions.[79]

Muste's "Challenge" appeared in the February 1929 issue of *Labor Age*, which reprinted and distributed it to unions and progressive organizations throughout the country.[80] The attack on Brookwood was the final straw, *Labor Age's* editor Louis Budenz proclaimed. It "caused us to take the bull by the horns," and he urged fellow progressives to rise to Muste's challenge and "make the 16 points in the Progressive program live realities in the United States."[81]

Budenz had become an important ally of Muste's. A midwesterner who hailed from a devoutly Catholic, lower-middle-class family, Budenz had moved from Catholic reformer to secular radical over the course of the years 1910 to 1919, and had jettisoned the law to become a labor journalist. Budenz was also active in the field, serving as a sort of roving organizer for the AFFFHW and lecturing occasionally at Brookwood. Like Muste, Budenz's ideological home was somewhere between the Socialist Party and the Communist Party; his syndicalist leanings inclined him toward industrial action rather than the parliamentarianism of the Socialists, while his pragmatism made him view the Communists as erratic and opportunistic in their approach to trade unionism. Also like Muste, he criticized the Communists for their "lack of roots in American soil," and he was well known for suggesting that the labor movement frame the struggles of the working class against the "New Capitalism" as the "third revolution" in American history (the first being the struggle against the British and the second the struggle against slavery).[82]

Still, there were important differences between Muste and Budenz that foreshadow their later parting of ways. Temperamentally, Muste was confident and even-keeled, while Budenz was high-strung and insecure. Both men thrived on action over talk, yet Muste was more of an intellectual and political analyst than Budenz, evincing a nuance and erudition lacking in Budenz's more forceful and bombastic prose. Perhaps the difference was a result of divergences in their religious education: Muste had been educated out of his inherited orthodoxy by fellow Protestants; as a Catholic, Budenz was never exposed to modern biblical criticism, and he continued to view the world in moral absolutes even though he had renounced the church. These differences are exemplified in their "American approach" to working-class mobilization. Patriotism repelled Muste, but he believed that it was imperative for radicals to adapt themselves to the specific structural and ideological conditions they faced, no matter what country they lived in. Budenz's Americanism, by contrast, often devolved into a kind of sentimental nationalism, in which he posited the American tradition of nonconformity as healthy and vigorous in contrast to the "exotic" and "neurasthenic" European left.[83] It is thus not surprising that Budenz would leave the Musteite movement for the Communist Party in 1935, precisely when the former began to de-emphasize the American approach and the latter had adopted the Popular Front, stressing the need to adapt to American conditions and utilize American revolutionary traditions and slogans. When the Communists abandoned the Popular Front in 1945, Budenz left the party, returned to the church, and became an ardent anti-Communist who eagerly supplied information for the House Un-American Activities Committee.[84]

The "Challenge" generated considerable discussion in liberal, left, and labor circles. The *New York Times* and the *World*, among other mainstream newspapers, took notice. Positive responses in the labor and radical press could be found in the Socialist *New Leader*, the *Reading Labor Advocate*, *Montana Labor News*, *Philadelphia Trade Union News*, the *Nebraska Craftsman*, the *Lithographers' Journal*, the Catholic *Industrial Solidarity*, and the Jewish anarchist *Freie Arbeiter Stimme*, among other publications. J. B. S. Hardman, Carlo Tresca, and other radicals associated with the ACW who had known Muste during the Lawrence strike also rallied to the "Challenge."[85]

But the most enthusiastic supporters were students, alumni, and faculty of labor colleges and extension programs, having been exposed to the views of the pragmatic idealists and been frustrated in their attempts to modernize their unions. J. C. Kennedy, the director of Seattle Labor College (who replaced Calhoun as instructor of economics at Brookwood in 1929), commented that the "'Challenge to Progressives' . . . expresses the sentiments of thousands of active workers in and out of the Labor Movement all over the country. It has become increasingly apparent . . . that we could not rally our forces around the banner of the Communist Party, because of its dogmatic spirit, autocratic form of organization and inability to comprehend the psychology of the American worker." At the same time, it had become "equally clear" that the AFL leadership had become "so thoroughly capitalistic in its outlook" that it was unable to build a movement "sufficiently strong to cope with American capitalism."[86]

The left wing of the Socialist Party formed another strong source of support for the nascent movement, at least initially. In the *New Leader*, Norman Thomas commented that the "Challenge" was significant not for its program, which was not new, but that it had appeared in *Labor Age*, an organ that had "standing with organized workers." He called on fellow Socialists to study the statement and to support it through action. James

Oneal, Frank Manning, Frank Crosswaith, and other leading Socialists joined Thomas in waxing enthusiastic about the sixteen points and participated in the discussions leading to the founding of the Conference for Progressive Labor Action (CPLA). Moreover, although rarely acknowledged in historical accounts of the Socialist Party, the sixteen points and the subsequently formed CPLA became the fulcrum for the emergence of the "Militants," the group of younger Socialists who shook up the party in the 1930s with their demands for greater militancy and criticism of the party's parliamentarianism.[87]

The AFL leadership and the Communist Party, predictably, denounced the "Challenge." Matthew Woll accused the nascent movement of dual unionism and Communism, and warned affiliates against "the progressives." "Not since the 1890s," he observed worriedly, had there been so significant an onslaught on the leadership of the labor movement. For their part, the Communists disparaged the "Challenge" as an expression of "social fascism."[88]

But there were also more substantial criticisms of the venture, particularly by those close to the workers' education project. Longtime Brookwood supporter Fannia Cohn was desperately upset about Muste's initiative. Cohn's concerns reflected both her commitment to workers' education and her tenuous position as the only female vice president in the male-dominated ILGWU. In letters to Muste and others, she repeated the prevailing wisdom among progressive unionists that it was fatal to openly confront the labor movement—that to do so would risk being written "out of the movement." She also pointed out that, despite Muste's assurances that Brookwood would remain independent of the CPLA, the AFL would not differentiate between them, and that the college and the workers' education movement would be further enfeebled as a consequence.[89]

FOR Muste, however, the decision to organize a loyal opposition clearly had a liberating effect, even as he found it emotionally wrenching. He had never been entirely comfortable as a labor educator; as faculty and director of Brookwood, his activities always extended beyond the classroom. Moreover, as we have seen, he had been moving toward a politics of progressive action even before the AFL attack. Now, with Brookwood no longer circumscribed by a policy of obsequiousness to the AFL, he felt released to assert his vision for the labor movement, and he would assume the mantle of leader of an insurgent movement with self-assuredness and confidence.

Meanwhile, a labor revolt began in the spring of 1929 that appeared to vindicate Muste's argument that the time was right for a revival of unionism and that the AFL would be incapable of leading it. "There are many indications that events are playing into our hands," Muste commented in an April 1929 article for *Labor Age*. "From South, East, West, and North . . . comes word that workers are revolting."[90]

Textiles, the industry with which Muste was most intimately acquainted, were at the center of the revolt. A "sick," unrationalized industry, textiles had been in a downturn since 1924. Mills responded to their woes by introducing the "speed-up" (known as the "stretch out" in the South) in which workers were forced to operate more machines without an increase in wages. The center of gravity for the textile industry also shifted south, where there was a seemingly limitless supply of cheap labor as poor, dispossessed mountain folk with no experience of industry or unions, migrated to mill towns throughout the Piedmont. Mill owners controlled their workforce with company towns, which they governed, as one mill manager admitted, "like the Czar of Russia."[91] Wages were the lowest in the entire manufacturing sector, the ten- or eleven-hour day was typical, and child labor was common.

In the South, unionization was nonexistent, but Brookwood alumnus Alfred Hoffman's activities as an organizer for the UTW had drawn the attention of the labor movement when, in the fall of 1927, he succeeded in signing up some six hundred mill workers in Henderson, North Carolina, as members of the union. Hoffman's achievement, along with pressure from progressives, had led to the formation of the Piedmont Organizing Council by the North Carolina Federation of Labor and had pushed the AFL to adopt a resolution at the 1928 New Orleans convention committing the federation to map a campaign for the South. Yet the revolt, when it began in Elizabethton, Tennessee, in March 1929, was not the consequence of union organizing, but rather a spontaneous walk out of some five thousand rayon workers in response to increasingly desperate working conditions. Within a few weeks, one strike after another followed, "until the whole Piedmont section . . . was dotted with local walkouts." In the spring of 1929 alone, there were some seventeen thousand textile workers on strike.[92]

Muste and his comrades were deeply involved in these labor struggles. Hoffman had arrived in Elizabethton soon after the strike began; despite being kidnapped at gunpoint and run out of town, he quickly returned, organized a local, and served as a leader of the strike through its denouement in late May. Brookwood's extension director, Tom Tippett, was also in the South in the spring of 1929, investigating mill conditions. The experience would propel him and other Brookwooders, including Muste, to become directly involved in the southern labor struggles that accelerated that summer and over the next several years. Up north, laborites associated with the Labor Publication Society and Brookwood were also active in a wave of strikes involving workers in such industries as textiles, clothing, and cigar making. Budenz, for example, had spent the better part of 1928 leading hosiery workers in a yearlong strike in Kenosha, Wisconsin. Like many of these strikes, Kenosha ended in defeat; but progressives imagined that they would have better success if they could get the AFL machinery to support their agenda.[93]

With events seeming to confirm Muste's analysis, pressure mounted to formalize the "Challenge." On May 25–26, 1929, 151 people from thirty-one cities and eighteen states gathered at Labor Temple in New York City for a conference to discuss how to make the sixteen points a reality. Among them were unofficial representatives from thirty-three unions, labor educators and students, and members of the League for Industrial Democracy and the Young People's Socialist League. Presided over by Muste, the deliberations led to the formation of the CPLA as a provisional organization that would "carry on research, educational work and action among the workers . . . to stimulate in the existing and potential labor organizations a progressive, realistic, militant labor spirit and activity in all its phases—trade union, political, cooperative and educational." The only way to convince American workers "to think and to act as workers . . . to build a labor culture and spirit," its statement of policy declared, was through "working class education for action." *Labor Age*, with a circulation of approximately twenty thousand, was made the CPLA's official organ.[94]

At its first meeting in June, the CPLA's National Executive Committee elected Muste as chairman; James Maurer and Carl Holderman of the AFFFHW as vice chairmen; A. J. Kennedy of the Amalgamated Lithographers of America as treasurer; Budenz as executive secretary; and Leonard Bright, a young Socialist, as secretary. Prominent unionists and Socialists such as Frank Crosswaith, Justus Ebert, Abraham Lefkowitz, Norman Thomas, J. B. S. Hardman, Harry Laidler, Ludwig Lore, Frank Manning, James Oneal, Clint Golden, and Israel Mufson served on the organization's standing committees.

With its headquarters at 104 Fifth Avenue, the CPLA immediately set about distributing literature and organizing branches.[95]

Proponents of workers' education were prominent in the CPLA. Indeed, Brookwood would become one of its most active branches, with all of its faculty and staff, most of its students, and some of its board of directors joining the organization. In the field, alumni formed the nucleus of the CPLA, which spread in concentric circles as they returned to their unions to push for the militant progressivism advocated by Muste. Still, Brookwood would continue to admit students regardless of political affiliation, and Muste always maintained that they were separate entities, but if education was for action and action was education, it was difficult to discern where Brookwood ended and the CPLA began. As Muste would discover, the synergy between the two organizations was dependent upon a certain vagueness and inclusiveness that would become increasingly difficult to maintain as the country sank into the Great Depression and the task of organizing workers and building a socialist society assumed even greater urgency. For Muste, Saposs's advice to stay centered, plodding along somewhere in between the reformers and the revolutionaries, grew increasingly difficult to follow, and he ultimately chose the latter. Yet his decision to more sharply define the CPLA's politics and mission forced his comrades to choose between his movement and other commitments—including workers' education.

⌣

CHAPTER 5

Labor Action

We . . . must resolve to create a new movement, to infuse
the rank and file of the AF of L with courage and
determination to cope with the new problems of industry
and conquer all obstacles which the subtle new capitalism
makes. There is no question of our loyalty to the American
Federation of Labor. We are more loyal to the AF of L than
many of those who attack us. We will show our loyalty to
the AF of L by fighting for the principles of progressive
trade unionism.

—A. J. Muste, 1929

MUSTE AND HIS comrades in the CPLA "stood for what was then hailed as 'practical labor idealism.'" As Len De Caux observed in his memoir, "Between the hidebound right and wild left," they "tried to steer a left-of-center course."[1] Hence they criticized the AFL on a deeper and more profound level than its failure to adopt industrial unionism. Musteites argued that the fundamental problem with the labor movement was its "lack of an intangible virile unifying force in the form of a labor culture and a labor idealism." This analysis unified CPLA activism; whether focused on inter-union politics, organizing drives, mobilizing unemployed workers, or workers' education, the CPLA hoped that their courage and idealism would lead to "the rejuvenation of the Labor Movement as a whole that will eventually discard the antiquated, anarchic philosophy of the Greens and the Wolls, and reestablish Labor as the vanguard of progressivism in America. Mark this period in American labor history as the rebirth of militant unionism," the CPLA predicted in 1930.[2]

At the same time, the CPLA differentiated itself from other left-wing groups in its emphasis on grounding Marxist theory in practice and experience, a project that built upon the labor pragmatist philosophy of the workers' education movement. As Muste put it at the organization's 1932 convention, "the tactics of the CPLA are realistic—not taken from the moon-lit air, but evolved from experience." He contrasted this approach with that of the Communists, who "whether consciously or unconsciously," tried to organize workers on the basis of "subscribing to some social, economic, or political creed." "On this basis you can organize propaganda societies but not unions. Unions must include workers with varied viewpoints." More to the point, no organization could survive if dictated to by an outside group; unions must be run democratically or else morale would suffer. Thus, it was crucial to organize around workers' immediate concerns; class consciousness and solidarity would develop out of the experience of taking collective action. It was, indeed, ultimately "action" and not "propaganda" that was the "great mass educator."[3]

THE CPLA initially envisioned itself as a research and educational organization that would coordinate and centralize progressive activities in the labor movement. Members were directed to educate fellow unionists, unorganized workers, and the public at large on the need for militant industrial action, social insurance, and an independent labor party. Organizers were placed in unorganized industries such as steel and textiles, "with the idea of first carrying on quiet educational work . . . and putting themselves in a position eventually to lead."[4] The CPLA provided support and inspiration for these activities through speaking tours by Muste and executive secretary Israel Mufson, and through the distribution of literature. Within the first year and a half, the CPLA had published seven pamphlets on topics like "Labor's Share in the Late Lamented Prosperity," "Why a Labor Party," "Negro Labor," and "The Need for a Labor Culture."

Muste's hope that the CPLA become "a nerve center of agitation and education for Action" quickly bore fruit. Over the course of the first year, branches were formed in such places as New York, Buffalo, New Bedford, New Haven, Philadelphia, Pittsburgh, Cleveland, Denver, Los Angeles, and Chicago. The organization probably had around four thousand members by 1930, but their influence extended far beyond their size, given the wide distribution of *Labor Age*, the fact that members tended to occupy leadership roles within their unions, and its central role in the curriculum and

pedagogy of workers' education. The goal of CPLA activists was not, moreover, so much to enroll new members, but to politicize and inspire their
fellow unionists into action.[5]

From the beginning, the CPLA emphasized the importance of organizing "neglected groups" like women, African Americans, and young people.
Like other left-wing groups in the 1930s, the CPLA must be described as
labor feminist; it presumed natural differences between men and women,
while seeking to cultivate female leadership and the organization of women
workers because it was believed that such policies would strengthen the
labor movement as a whole. Reflecting this perspective, Muste recruited
women into the CPLA, many of whom were former Brookwood students,
and worked closely with groups like the WTUL, the Affiliated Schools for
Women Workers, and YWCA-sponsored summer camps for female industrial workers, giving speeches, conducting classes, and inculcating a "progressive spirit" in the students.[6]

As a result of these activities, women educators and trade unionists,
particularly in the needle trades, played a prominent role in the CPLA. At
the organization's eastern regional conference in 1931, for example, a session titled "As Women Look at Industry" was "conducted by women themselves." In their analysis, the discussants suggested that female workers
faced their own "peculiar problems" that had to be addressed if they were
to be successfully organized. Specifically, patterns of "insecurity and fear"
and a narrower range of experiences meant that women had to be
approached "on the plane of their interest" and preferably by female organizers. But although working-class women had unique experiences of class
because of their gender, their cause was best served through allying with
men of their own class. "The alignment is, then, not a sexual one of women
against men but a class one of proletarian men and women against bourgeois men and women," a female member wrote in *Labor Age*.[7]

Still, the CPLA reflected the gender politics of the larger labor left. It
fully engaged the masculinist language of class, imagining the worker as a
brawny male and defining itself as the labor movement's "virile" wing. The
structure of the CPLA mirrored its gender ideology. With the exception of
Lucille Kohn, the members of the organization's National Executive Committee were exclusively male, and paid organizers were typically men. As at
Brookwood, if male organizers were married, it was expected that their
wives would serve in an unpaid capacity. In a revealing passage, Muste
wrote to Louise Leonard of the Southern Summer School for Women

Workers that William Ross's problems as an organizer in the southern textile region (discussed below) were not only due to attacks by the AFL; his wife, Tess, "was not able to make any positive contribution in the way of organizing recreation for the women and children, and on the other hand, she insisted on being around all the time, had Bill doing house work when he should have been attending to strike business or resting, etc."[8] Unmarried women workers could also face objectification and condescension by their male comrades. At the 1930 eastern regional conference of the CPLA, when Josephine Kaczor spoke of her activities as a striker and organizer for the AFFFHW, including jail sentences and a hunger strike, it was described in *Labor Age* as a "picturesque interlude. . . . One look at her and the explanation for sheriffs forgetting their duty in her presence was disclosed."[9]

The Musteites' position on black workers was similar: On the one hand, they viewed their precarious status in the labor movement as part of the "larger problem of organizing the unskilled and semi-skilled in the basic industries," while, at the same time, they recognized that organizing black workers required more than "the radical's stock in trade generalization about the solidarity of economic interest between white and black workers." As the prominent black economist and CPLA member Abram L. Harris wrote in *Labor Age*, it was imperative that labor organizers work on two fronts; they should actively combat the "psychology of race prejudice" *and* aggressively cultivate black working-class leadership, helping to wean them away from dependence on middle-class African Americans and the idea that a "conciliatory attitude" toward white elites was the best way to promote their interests.[10] E. R. McKinney, a black CPLA organizer who eventually served on the National Executive Committee, similarly rejected black capitalism and black nationalism as panaceas, while also arguing that organizing black workers was a different project than organizing whites because of the "actualities of race prejudice and misunderstanding."[11]

The CPLA's position on race was thus somewhere in between that of the Socialist Party and the Communist Party. The former tended to reduce race to class, maintaining that racism would fade away as workers obtained more power. The latter, by contrast, viewed the situation of African Americans as an oppressed national group and favored self-determination in the black belt. Harris and McKinney, along with Muste and others in the CPLA, dismissed this idea as bourgeois, while also singling out the situation of black workers and the problem of racism as areas of "vital concern" for all workers.[12]

In addition to recruiting black workers and female workers, Muste was eager to bring young people and intellectuals into the CPLA. As he wrote in August 1930, "there is [currently] a 'theory of the Labor Movement' which is based on the supposed contrast between the role of 'the intellectual' and that of the wage worker. The theory, in my opinion, is contrary to fact, and now more than ever dangerous and harmful." "This is not to suggest that the intellectual is a Messiah or Moses coming from the outside to lead labor into the promised land," he demurred. "They are brothers."[13]

Indeed, long before the "cultural front" of the mid-1930s, Muste recognized that the status of professionals under the "new" capitalism was that of "wage-earners," and that they were "helpless so long as they act as individuals and fail to combine." "These poor worms of 'intellectuals' are also human beings and wage-earners, often not as well-paid as bricklayers or plumbers." In fact, one of the reasons he advocated developing alternative, labor-based cultural activities and institutions was to attract this new class to the ideals and aspirations of the labor movement rather than to the values of individualism and upward mobility engendered by the dominant culture.[14]

Reflecting these perspectives, Muste actively recruited from the League for Industrial Democracy (LID), the youth wing of the Socialist Party that was particularly active on college campuses, and the YWCA's industrial department, with which he had extensive contacts because he and other Brookwood faculty provided instruction, syllabi, and curriculum for their summer camps for women workers. As a result of these efforts, Socialist Militants had a heavy presence in the CPLA, as did working- and middle-class women involved in the YWCA. Muste's comrades in the AFT and the workers' education movement offered another source of intellectual support; faculty and staff at Brookwood, Seattle Labor College, and Commonwealth College in Mena, Arkansas, for example, functioned as active CPLA groups.[15]

Labor intellectuals also played a prominent role in the CPLA. Ludwig Lore, editor of the German-language socialist *New Yorker Volkszeitung*; Justus Ebert of the Amalgamated Lithographers of America; M. H. Hedges, director of research and education for the International Brotherhood of Electrical Workers; and J. B. S. Hardman (a.k.a. Jacob Benjamin Salutsky), editor of the ACW's monthly, the *Advance*, all assumed leadership roles in the new organization. Hardman was especially close to Muste, serving on the CPLA's National Executive Committee and heading the organization's research and education committee. Born in Grodno province in Russia on August 25, 1882, Hardman joined the Bund as a teenager and became active in revolutionary activities until his exile in 1909. Settling in New York, he attended graduate school at Columbia University, where he studied constitutional law under Charles Beard and Frank Good. But, as with other radical intellectuals of his generation, the revolutionary labor movement beckoned, and in 1920 he assumed a prominent role in the ACW, directing the union's educational and cultural activities and editing the *Advance*. The position brought him into close contact with Muste, the ATWA, and, later, Brookwood Labor College.[16]

Like his fellow Musteites, Hardman was unalterably opposed to sectarianism and dogmatism. At the same time, however, he remained convinced of the importance of theory, and he frequently urged the CPLA to sharpen its theoretical and political views to give the movement more definition and clarity. Indeed, he insisted that Marxism, properly understood, would reinforce the CPLA's pragmatic approach to revolutionary activity. "What has 'made' Marx," he instructed the CPLA rank and file, "is above all the fact that he carried his ideas into the 'street,' into the actual struggles of his days. He used theory as an enforcement [*sic*] to his engagement in the practical revolutionary struggle, and the latter as an intellectual feeder for his theoretical work."[17]

But by far the most distinctive element within the CPLA was working-class militants. Among the most active were Israel Mufson of the Railway Clerks; the machinists Clint Golden, William Ross, and Jack Lever; miners Mike Demchak, William "Bill" Truax, William Daech, Gerry Allard, William Stoeffels, Cal Bellaver, and Charles Gardner; textile workers Lawrence "Larry" Hogan, Irene Hogan, and Beulah Carter; Carl Holderman, Eddie Ryan Sr. and Eddie Ryan Jr., and Josephine Kaczor of the AFFFHW; ILGWU militants Rose Pesotta and Anna Kula; Justus Ebert and A. J. Kennedy of the Lithographers (the latter assumed the union's presidency in 1930); Anthony Ramuglia of the ACW; Isador Laderman of the International Pocketbook Workers' Union (who became president of that union in 1931); and Jean Ogden of the Amalgamated Food Workers. The CPLA was proud of its working-class character, describing the delegates to one conference as "definitely working-class, not 'intellectual' or dilettante. The delegates represented the finest type of American worker—serious, wanting to see action, revolutionary, but not taking it out in a long-winded, theoretical discussion."[18]

FIGURE 4. Anne and A. J. Muste (holding son John Martin) with Jack Lever, Brookwood alumnus and "Musteite," 1930. (*Walter P. Reuther Library, Archives of Labor and Urban Affairs, Wayne State University*)

The working-class character of the movement tended to reinforce its pragmatism. CPLA members referred to themselves as "Labor Actionists" to differentiate themselves from a right wing that they viewed as too complacent and a left wing that was too ideological. Thomas Dabney, a black journalist who had attended Brookwood, joined the CPLA because "the watch words of labor now should be *Organize! Agitate! Educate!*" He continued, "We need action as well as philosophy."[19]

The emphasis on "action" over talk also reflected the CPLA's aversion to sectarianism, and it studiously avoided the derisive tone that characterized much intra-radical discourse. "The Musteite type," the writer Edmund Wilson observed, differed from the Communists in their "conventional dress, literate language, and polite approach . . . the influence of Muste himself has perhaps had the effect of making them a little like the students of a divinity school."[20] As Wilson's comments suggest, Muste insisted on the importance of observing "working-class ethics" in the CPLA's relations with other groups. The adjective "working-class" is important, for Muste recognized that ethics were historical and cultural, not "sacred" and "eternal" as most people believed. "All morals," he explained in a 1932 article, "have been class morals," even as they were mouthed as "universal"; only when there was a classless society would there be "true universal morality." Yet this did not mean, as many in the labor movement and on the left seemed to have concluded, that in the conflict with capitalism there were "no rules." In fact, the method employed was "inevitably transferred to every other situation. The same was true for relations between different groups within the labor movement; if "anything goes," then the movement will continue to become endlessly divided and weakened.[21]

In concrete terms, a strong and united labor movement depended upon "a certain willingness to give the other fellow a chance and to remain within certain limits of decency in dealing with him." This did not mean, however, that he wanted a movement "free from all controversy. The only place where there is no controversy is the grave." Nor was it "a plea for softness, a suggestion that people ought to be 'nice' to each other. . . . But if we are to have morale in the labor movement . . . we must have a degree of unity, and, if we are to have that, it follows, for one thing, that we cannot spend all our time in controversy and in fighting each other—maybe 99 per cent of the time, but not quite 100 per cent."[22]

ALTHOUGH the CPLA initially envisioned itself as the research and educational arm of progressive labor, it quickly found itself directly involved in action. In particular, the Piedmont revolt that began in the spring of 1929 beckoned, as it accelerated and spread beyond Elizabethton. As Muste wrote in one of the CPLA's first pamphlets, "No such opportunity has confronted [the AFL] in years. If the textile industry of the South is organized, other industries in this section will follow. With the growing industries of the South won for unionism, the labor movement could sweep the nation."[23]

Less than three weeks after the Elizabethton walkout, textile workers in nearby Gastonia, North Carolina, struck. Led by the Communist Party, the strike led to a vicious season of repression that culminated in the murder of Ella May Wiggins, a twenty-nine-year-old widow and mother of five. The Musteites were not directly involved in Gastonia, though they did help raise money and publicity for the persecuted strikers and their leaders. Early in the summer, Tom Tippett and Brookwood graduate Jesse Slaughter attempted to visit the Gastonia tent colony as part of their investigation of the strike wave, but they were immediately arrested and driven out of town. The pair moved on to Marion where they became caught up in a unionizing drive that had been initiated by workers at R. W. Baldwin's Marion Manufacturing Company.[24]

The drive began in April when two textile workers, Larry Hogan (described by Sinclair Lewis as "a huge square-shouldered Irishman with a quiet voice and a vast efficiency") and Dan Elliott (in Sinclair Lewis's words, "sensationally good-looking . . . like Henry Ward Beecher with his lion's mane") had begun organizing workers with Alfred Hoffman's assistance. In late June, textile workers held a public meeting where they were addressed by Hoffman and Tippett. Baldwin responded by firing twenty-two union members and rebuffed appeals for their reinstatement and for a reduction of working hours from twelve to ten hours per shift. Ridiculing the workers' grievances, Baldwin dared them to strike, offering their leaders $50 each if they could "pull a strike."[25]

Workers responded to his dare by walking out of the Marion mill on July 11. As the strike spread to Marion's other mills, Tippett busied himself organizing strike committees, Hoffman raised money, and Slaughter educated workers in the culture of unionism by teaching labor history and union songs. Hogan and Elliott remained in leadership roles; along with several other strikers, both would shortly thereafter enroll in Brookwood and join the CPLA. William Ross also arrived in Marion to assist them, while Muste visited on several occasions to offer advice and inspiration.

With little support forthcoming from the AFL or the UTW, labor progressives sustained the strike through the Emergency Committee for Strikers' Relief.[26]

Muste, who still identified as a Christian, found the religious atmosphere of the strike deeply moving. As he recalled, the mass meetings resembled revivals: "The union songs were sung to the tunes of spirituals and evangelistic Gospel hymns. I think it was in Marion that summer that the old spiritual *Jacob's Ladder* was first adapted to include these lines: 'We are building a strong union, Workers in the mill.'"[27]

The religious atmosphere of the strike helped maintain morale even in the face of evictions, injunctions, and state troopers, forcing the mill to shut down. In late August, a crowd of strikers carried furniture belonging to a strikebreaker out of a company house from which a striker had been evicted. Hoffman and 148 others were indicted for insurrection following this incident. Finally, after nine weeks on the picket line, an official of the AFL arrived in Marion and negotiated a settlement with Baldwin; workers were to return to work in exchange for a reduction in their hours (along with a reduction in their wages), no discrimination against union members, and a grievance committee of workers recognized by the union. Muste personally viewed the settlement as a weak one and predicted that it would be violated as soon as the strikers returned to work.[28]

Sure enough, immediately after the mills resumed production, Baldwin began to discriminate against union members and continued evictions. Then, early on the morning of October 2, a mill operative working the night shift got into an argument with his foreman that led to a walkout of mill workers. As they gathered outside the mill gates to alert day-shift workers of the strike, the sheriff and his deputies arrived on the scene, fully armed, and ordered the pickets to leave. To make his point, the sheriff shot tear gas into the picket line. In the confusion that followed, three strikers were killed and dozens injured; three more strikers would die of their wounds within the next day. All were shot in the back. Baldwin was unrepentant, commenting that "the sheriff and his men were good marksmen. If ever I organize an army, they can have jobs with me." The sheriff and his deputies were later acquitted of all charges.[29]

Muste's writings and speeches from this period rarely invoked the Christian ideals that undergirded his radicalism, but in the evangelical culture of the Piedmont, they flowed forth at the funeral for the six men. "These men are good soldiers who have fallen in a war that is as old as humanity. They are martyrs in the noblest cause in all the world. The cause for which they died is the cause of labor, the cause of justice and freedom for the plain people who do the work of the world and who bear its burdens." He went on to suggest that, like these martyrs, Jesus Christ had chosen "to side with the common people," which was why the elite of his time called him a "revolutionist" and crucified him. Later on, at the gravesite, with no clergy to deliver a eulogy, Muste stepped forward and said, " 'We consecrate this worker's body to the earth from which it came. He has fought a good fight in a noble cause. He will rest in peace.' "[30]

Muste, along with Tippett and Francis Gorman of the UTW, both of whom also spoke at the funeral, urged the mourners to continue their struggle for unionism and not to allow the martyred workers to have died in vain. Meanwhile, the CPLA sought to exploit the furor over the massacre to push the AFL to aggressively organize the South.[31] In an effort to push the UTW in this direction, Muste offered the union half of Ross's salary to stay in Marion and help keep the union alive. He also stayed in close communication with progressives in the UTW, encouraging them to map out a strong plan to unionize southern textile workers.[32]

Muste also attended the 1929 annual convention of the AFL, held in Toronto a few days after the funeral, where he was pleased to discover an enthusiastic and militant spirit inspired by the Marion massacre. In addition to breaking from tradition and endorsing old age pensions, the AFL unanimously adopted a resolution calling for a great campaign to organize the South. President Green even invited Muste to serve on the planning committee that met on November 11 in Washington, D.C. At the November meeting, delegates agreed that each international union would supply at least one organizer to the campaign and contribute funds to the UTW treasury. They also established a committee to direct the campaign consisting of an AFL organizer, Francis Gorman of the UTW, and a representative from the Tennessee Federation of Labor.[33]

The AFL ultimately conducted the campaign conservatively, and the result was an inconsistent and fainthearted campaign. In Marion, for example, the UTW assigned one organizer who was only rarely in town because of his involvement in the larger campaign. Bill Ross tried to keep the movement alive by conducting educational activities and making provisions for the care of arrested, sick, and evicted strikers, along with the 345 strikers who lost their jobs because of the strike. Meanwhile, Hoffman remained in jail and Hogan and sixty-two other strikers were still under indictment for the furniture incident. "In short," as Tom Tippett wrote in his highly acclaimed account of the Piedmont revolt, *When Southern Labor Stirs*, "the whole situation was permitted to slip downhill without union resistance" even as President McMahon of the UTW gave speeches on the need to remember Marion.[34]

Labor progressives refused to give up on Marion and the South more broadly even as it became apparent that the AFL campaign was to be an ineffectual and halfhearted one. In the winter, Muste sent a Brookwood student, Elmer Cope, to assist Ross. He also raised money among liberal groups like the American Friends Service Committee (AFSC) to provide aid for the persecuted workers. When Ross decided to leave Marion in February, Muste sent Hogan in his place who "immediately assumed the reins as best he could without any official sanction." He put women to work making hooked rugs, set up educational activity, and conducted classes. But soon his "free-lance activities . . . began to bother the national office of the UTW." The union finally sent an investigator, whose report that unionism was now at a standstill prompted UTW president McMahon to make a commitment to renewing the effort. But by this point Hogan was serving his sentence on the chain gang and the AFSC had withdrawn its support.[35]

By the summer of 1930, the strike movement was completely defeated. Where once there had been "a magnificent organization" in Marion, Tippett wrote, now workers "were overcome in a horrible wreck. The United Textile Workers stood on the shore unable to decide whether to throw a life-line, and while it was making up its mind the membership went down under the waves and was drowned." Yet the CPLA remained committed to the hungry and persecuted textile workers. Agnes Sailer arrived in Marion from the Pioneer Youth of America to organize workers' children into clubs that carried on, singing songs, playing games, making toys, and going on hikes. A striker took responsibility for these cultural activities when Sailer returned home. Tippett, along with Helen Norton of Brookwood, also visited Marion that summer where they held a retreat on a lake on the outskirts of town. "Never once did we hear a word of regret or bitterness because of their struggle," Tippett remarked. Soon thereafter, Tippett would write *Mill Shadows*, a play based on the Marion strike that would become one of the classics of the labor theater of the 1930s.[36]

Despite the tragic conclusion of the Marion strike and the southern campaign, the experience served to strengthen the morale and resolve of the CPLA. Members took comfort that their efforts in the South had helped to bring national attention to the plight of southern textile workers. "We need not regret our enterprise," Ross explained to his CPLA comrades. The CPLA had succeeded in its effort "to develop a situation" and had spurred the AFL to greater, albeit woefully inadequate, action.[37] Tippett's poignant account of the strike wave concluded by restating the philosophy at the heart of the CPLA: it was possible to organize industrial workers if leadership was courageous and committed, staying in the field after the battles are over to bind wounds, "so that they will recover with affection for and loyalty to the spiritual ideal of labor-unionism." While recognizing that the AFL had placed a serious handicap on southern organizing with its weak campaign, Muste would continue to put some of the CPLA's resources in the region by appointing Ross and Hogan as field secretaries in the South, focusing Tippett's extension work in the South, and supporting efforts such as the Southern Summer School for Women Workers.[38]

EVENTS within the United Mine Workers of America (UMWA) further spurred the CPLA into direct organizational activity. The onset of the Great Depression in late 1929 had devastated the miners union, already decimated by falling wages and hours and demoralized by John L. Lewis's autocratic control. In early 1930, anti-Lewis forces coalesced in Illinois District 12, "the last bastion of union strength for coal miners and the one district over which the UMW president lacked complete control."[39] The revolt was led by men like John Brophy, Powers Hapgood, Adolph Germer, Alexander Howat, and John Walker, the former president of the Illinois Federation of Labor. All tended to be idealists, with backgrounds in the heyday of American Socialism, and all had been victims of Lewis's autocratic leadership. Taking advantage of a constitutional oversight made by Lewis when he failed to call a convention in 1929, the insurgent group called a convention in Springfield, Illinois, in March 1930 to elect new international officers to what soon became known as the Reorganized United Mine Workers of America (RUMW). The movement posed a real threat to Lewis. With a much larger membership in Illinois than Lewis's, they held "considerable strength . . . they aimed to solidify power in Illinois and then use District 12 as a club with which to smash the Lewis organization."[40]

Tippett, a former Illinois miner with personal connections with the rebels, traveled to Illinois in January 1930 to investigate the insurgency. His detailed report persuaded Muste and other members of the CPLA to attend the March 1930 convention, where they joined forces with the more radical delegates to ensure that the more left-wing Alexander Howat won the presidency and that reliable progressives (including Brophy and Hapgood) were elected officers. Still, the Musteites' optimism was not unbounded; Muste noted with concern the involvement of Frank Farrington, former president of the Illinois miners, who had been ousted from the union in 1926 under charges of corruption. Yet he hoped that, with the CPLA's help, there was a chance that a "progressive, fighting, democratic, clean, intelligent industrial union" would emerge in this basic industry.[41]

Muste knew that the CPLA's decision to back the insurgency was to be in for a fight with one of the most powerful men in the AFL. Before the RUMW gathered in Springfield, Lewis issued his own convention call in nearby Indianapolis to be held on the same date. Both conventions were replete with name-calling and denunciations. "When the shouting and the tumult of the twin conventions subsided, the hand-to-hand and head-to-head warfare began."[42]

With commitments to the RUMW and to the textile workers, among other struggles, CPLA members had a lot to discuss when three hundred of them met for the organization's first annual eastern regional conference in March of 1930. In addition to the typical problems of labor spies and yellow-dog contracts, delegates reported encountering resistance by the AFL, like that experienced in Marion and in the miners' union.[43] Delegates also commented on the prevalence of rank-and-file apathy and a dearth of organized young workers; union meetings had become "conclaves of old men thoroughly cowed who attend the union halls through habit." At the same time, they expressed enthusiasm about the possibilities for a revitalized labor movement. In just a short while, they had gained a strong presence in international unions such as the UTW, the AFFFHW, the Millinery Workers, the Amalgamated Lithographers, the ACW, the International Pocketbook Workers, and the Railway Clerks, as well as in a number of smaller, independent unions. Workers were interested in unionism, delegate Elmer Cope insisted; the problem was "lack of leadership and education."[44]

As a result of this conference, the CPLA institutionalized its move into organizational work by creating an "organization department." Members would continue to stimulate militancy and progressivism within their unions, focusing in particular on young workers, yet now the CPLA would have a mechanism for supporting workers organized in independent unions and workers seeking unionization who were unable to obtain assistance from the AFL. The new department was to be under the direction of Louis Budenz, who had replaced Israel Mufson as executive secretary; by the fall of 1930, he had received requests for assistance from the dyers of Paterson, the neckwear workers of Philadelphia, and the oil workers of Bayonne, New Jersey, altogether numbering about thirty thousand workers.[45]

As the CPLA continued its educational and agitational activities on behalf of militant unionism, it persistently found itself in the dilemma that David Saposs had predicted in his essay "The Future of Radicalism in the Labor Movement," discussed in Chapter 4: On the one hand, when it worked within existing trade unions to support progressivism, it became associated with opposition and disloyalty. On the other hand, when it organized unorganized workers in the basic industries, the AFL refused to lend support, which then placed the CPLA in the unenviable position of supporting dual unionism, despite its opposition to such tactics.[46] Compounding the CPLA's troubles was persistent difficulty raising adequate funds to support organizing drives and strike activities.

This dilemma can be seen in the CPLA's relationship to the miners' reorganization movement. The organization had obtained a strong position in RUMW's left wing with members such as William Daech and Bill Truax secured as officers in the union and close relationships with Howat, Brophy, and Hapgood. It was Muste, in fact, who advised the union to overcome its internal divisions by securing an organizing victory in West Virginia's Kanawha Valley's District 17 where miners were still angry at Lewis for deposing their popular former president Frank Keeney. Yet despite making progress in West Virginia and Illinois, the RUMW remained in a fragile state. The national leadership was preoccupied by a yearlong court case to decide which union was the legitimate miners' union. Meanwhile, Lewis took advantage of the RUMW's decision to include Farrington by associating the insurgents with class collaboration and corruption. At the same time, he exploited Howat's close relationship with Muste, Tippett, and other left-wingers, "accusing them of seeking to 'bolshevize' the mine workers and of subjecting workers to the influence of effete New York left-wing bohemians." Howat's alcoholism exacerbated the problem, as he seemed to spend more time drinking in bars than organizing workers. Lewis further undermined the RUMW by employing "force and violence against the insurgents," including murder and kidnapping. The Communists compounded the RUMW's troubles by refusing to support them;

despite their hatred of Lewis, they continued to pursue the Third Period policy in which Communists were to engage in class war against social democrats and trade unionists as well as capitalists.[47]

The cumulative effect was an extremely fractious and divided movement. Reflecting the AFL's culture of antiradicalism and anti-intellectualism, Germer and Walker were particularly upset by Howat's reliance on Muste and Tippett for advice and direction. As historians Melvyn Dubofsky and Warren Van Tine have observed, "More anti-Communist than anti-capitalist," Germer and Walker "decided that compromise with Lewis was necessary. And as their base of support among coal miners withered, they had to choose among a slow death, coalition with Muste . . . or a compromise with Lewis. In the event, much as they despised Lewis, Walker and Germer considered Muste, whom they falsely linked to communism, a greater evil." When the courts handed Lewis a compromise victory on March 6, 1931, in which District 12 would remain autonomous while the RUMW disbanded, Walker and Germer abruptly surrendered without consulting the other officers, much less the union membership.[48]

The Musteites joined the rank and file of the RUMW in condemning Walker and Germer's hasty decision. Together with Howat, Muste and Tippett drafted a call for a public convention in St. Louis to be held in mid-April of 1931, subsidized entirely by the CPLA. Over the week of March 17–22, Muste and Howat met secretly in St. Louis to draw up plans for a new, dual miners' union to continue the struggle. At the convention itself, the CPLA assumed a central role; Muste, Tippett, Truax, and other CPLA members spoke to great acclaim. Although the convention did not vote to organize a separate union, it did appoint a policy committee to coordinate the activities of those committed to building democratic unionism in the mining industry.[49]

Why did Muste pursue this alliance with Howat, who had proven himself an increasingly inept drunk, and when the prospects for success in Illinois had become dim? In part, the answer has to do with the Musteites' close involvement in Keeney's West Virginia campaign, which they viewed as "an outstanding exception" to the corruption and fratricide of the UMWA. Muste had attended the March 1931 founding conference of the independent West Virginia Mine Workers' Union, where forty-seven delegates representing between 5,000 and 10,000 miners eagerly committed to enrolling thousands more members and reestablishing their former collective bargaining agreement. "These men know what unionism is," Muste reported to Brookwood students. Tippett, Lucille Kohn, Cara Cook, Helen Norton, Katherine Pollak, and other CPLAers who traveled south to aid the campaign were just as enthusiastic.[50] Keeney's endorsement of independent political action, an important progressive plank, only increased the Musteites' enthusiasm for the hardscrabble miners.[51]

As a result, Brookwood and the CPLA poured personnel and resources into the West Virginia miners' movement (upwards of $100,000), particularly during the summer of 1931, when Keeney led some twenty thousand miners in a strike that lasted approximately six weeks. Despite the solidarity of the workers, the CPLA could not provide enough money to support the strikers once the company began evicting thousands of them from company housing. Even though the strike was defeated, the CPLA continued to support Keeney, as he struggled to keep his movement alive as efforts now focused on organizing the Independent Labor Party of West Virginia.[52] But the movement continued its decline. Later in the decade, when John L. Lewis embraced the militant industrial unionism long advocated by progressives, Keeney and the West Virginia miners would rejoin the UMWA. The same was true of other unionists close to Muste; Brophy, Hapgood, and Clint Golden, for example, accepted Lewis's fig leaf and assumed high office in the UMWA and, later, the CIO.[53]

Meanwhile, Walker, now back in charge of Illinois's District 12, red-baited the Howat-Muste organization, which in turn opposed his leadership. When Walker, aided by Lewis, signed a contract that the rank and file opposed, he had a full-grown insurgency on his hands that soon reorganized itself into the Progressive Miners of America (PMA, later renamed the Progressive Mine Workers of America). Once again, Muste, Brookwood, and the CPLA were deeply involved in aiding the new group, only to watch in dismay as it was quickly taken over by reactionaries; a diverse group of "Ku Klux Klanners, pure opportunists, pie-card artists, and the corrupt associates of Frank Farrington" obtained control of the union and ultimately led it into the AFL.[54]

As one historian has observed, Muste "was right to expect a revival of unionism, and to be skeptical that either the AFL or the [Communist Party's Trade Union Unity League (TUUL)] would lead it."[55] Yet his theory that progressive action would force the AFL to reform itself foundered again and again on the reactionary culture of craft unionism and the ideology of labor-management cooperation. Recognizing early on that "dogmatic opposition to dual unionism . . . would mean failure to organize basic industries," Muste encouraged CPLA members to organize industrial workers without the help of the AFL.[56] But as the Musteites built up rank-and-file support for unionism, they often found that they had to support strikes and union activities themselves. Muste's network of liberal clergy and radical intellectuals could provide considerable funds, but, in the context of the Great Depression, they simply could not raise enough to cover the massive needs of impoverished workers such as those in West Virginia.

Even in unions where the Musteites managed to gain a strong foothold, the AFL's conservatism put them in a perplexing dilemma. In the AFFFHW, for example, the Musteites obtained considerable influence and power in the late 1920s and early 1930s, pushing the union to pursue aggressive organization campaigns that garnered thousands of new members. Yet without the AFL's support, along with an industry that continually responded to collective bargaining agreements by opening new shops in nonunion territories, the AFFFHW was in a bind. The worsening economic situation only narrowed their options, and in 1931 the union felt compelled to sign an unpopular agreement cutting the wages of their members by 20 percent and accepting a modified form of the stretch-out, an agreement that opened the door to conservatives to take over the union.[57]

A similar situation occurred within the UTW. Muste had a long and deep relationship with the union's president and other top officials and had played a central role in persuading them to take a strong stand for organizing the South. The UTW often requested help from the CPLA such as in its continuing effort to merge forces with the Associated Silk Workers in Paterson, which finally came to fruition in 1931.[58] At the same time, however, the UTW worked within the context of a conservative labor movement that failed to make good on promises of support, which in turn undermined its efforts in the field. As CPLA forces both inside and outside of the union pushed it to maintain a militant posture, the leadership increasingly viewed them as irritants rather than as advisers, and Muste was often forced to play a mediating role between CPLA members and UTW organizers.[59]

Yet Muste saw no real alternative to continuing the CPLA's industrial policy of building up progressivism within existing unions and spearheading the organization of unskilled workers. The approximately one hundred "active workers" who gathered in New York City in March 1932 to review the CPLA's policies concurred with their chairman, convinced that they were effectively building a counter-hegemonic bloc that would eventually force the AFL to become more militant.[60] After all, their role was not to have a "blueprint" for every situation and union, but rather to advise, educate, inspire, and guide their fellow unionists. More to the point, they saw themselves as having real, concrete achievements. They pointed to their involvement in rank-and-file movements "against reactionary or corrupt tendencies" in various unions such as the UMWA and Local 3 of the Electrical Workers; their leadership of strikes and organizing campaigns among miners, silk workers, textile workers, food workers, electrical workers, steel workers, among others; and the positions of influence they had obtained within their unions.[61]

CPLA members also pointed to their rather unexpected but very real achievements in organizing the unemployed. Indeed, by 1932, the CPLA could boast of having several hundred thousand members in its Unemployed Citizens' League (UCL). As was often the case on the left, the Communists had taken the initiative. Starting in February 1930, the Communist Party began organizing the jobless into Unemployed Councils, hoping that they would become "a cadre of revolution." The party declared March 6 International Unemployment Day and commemorated it by leading dozens of demonstrations that often led to violent and dramatic confrontations with public authorities. Although "they failed to produce the revolution in America," these demonstrations succeeded in converting "unemployment from a little-noticed to a page-one problem in every important city in the United States."[62]

Impressed by the Communists' success, the CPLA also began to focus on the problem of unemployment, though its approach differed markedly from that of the Communists. In the first place, they were not initially focused on organizing the unemployed so much as raising awareness about the extent and causes of unemployment and the need for state and federal unemployment insurance. Second, as with their union organizing, they mimicked the Communists' in their militancy and willingness to take action, while taking a pragmatic approach and rooting the struggle in American language and culture. As Roy Rosenzweig has argued, this made them "more tolerant and flexible," particularly in regard to self-help, than other left-wing groups. "This flexibility and Americanism paid off; the Musteites were able to attract more American and less-politicized members, and to build a following in areas that the Communists and Socialists were unable to penetrate," particularly the small industrial and mining towns of

Ohio, the steel mills of Pittsburgh, the coal fields of eastern Pennsylvania and West Virginia, and textile centers in North Carolina.[63]

Rosenzweig further suggests that the CPLA faced a "dilemma" between their immediate and flexible methods and their socialist goals. Yet, in fact, the CPLA never viewed the leagues as revolutionary organizations; as with their approach to unions, they were driven by their theory that experience in class consciousness and solidarity would help to break down myths of individualism and upward mobility. They did not, in other words, expect that all league members would become socialists, though they did hope that they would win the confidence of the unemployed who would then accept their leadership in a revolutionary struggle. The purpose of the leagues, the CPLA leadership explained, was to serve as a "unifying force in a working-class which is now in a desperately divided state." It was therefore crucial that CPLA organizers avoid making the leagues "a battleground for contending groups . . . [the unemployed] must be 'driven' by their own experience, not by mechanical pressure by propagandists. To interpret their experience and so to educate them is the job of radicals."[64] Hence Ted Selander, a CPLA member and leader in the Ohio Unemployed League, would later comment of Rosenzweig's thesis, "That dilemma [between immediate and long-term goals] is in [his] head because as far as I know there was no contradiction or dilemma in our heads over the separation of these two tasks during the '30s."[65]

Over the summer of 1930, the CPLA began its campaign in earnest. In the process, they found that not just workers, but the unemployed, who gathered by the thousands around factory gates, were "intensely interested in the proposal for compulsory state relief and flock to our open air meetings. . . . Our literature is snatched out of the hands of the distributors with an eagerness that is pathetic." For example, the New York branch of the CPLA held daily open-air meetings throughout the city in which their speakers—typically Muste, Budenz, or Bright—were "mobbed by unemployed who stand for hours on the chilly street corners waiting for a word of hope." The corner of Lafayette and Leonard Streets, just under the shadow of the Tombs prison, found an especially eager crowd. With upwards of two thousand gathered daily, the Communists addressed the crowd on one corner, while the CPLA addressed the crowd across the street. Over the course of the week, the listeners became "more enthusiastic and more militant" and the police more restive and hostile. As "spontaneous cheers and applause interrupt[ed] the speakers," the crowd mobbed the

CPLA to sign its petition, which was being circulated by the thousands across the country to be delivered to Congress when it met in special session on the problem of unemployment in December.[66]

Soon, the CPLA went beyond gathering signatures and drafting model insurance bills to organizing the unemployed themselves.[67] In December 1930, the CPLA's New York branch opened a center at the Church of All Nations where the unemployed could meet with labor progressives to learn how to fight with their allies "for a better future; for greater security and for a world without hunger in the midst of plenty." In one of their first actions, they held a series of open air meetings where the unemployed came up with a list of demands and appointed a committee consisting of CPLA leaders to present them to Mayor Jimmy Walker.[68]

These open-air demonstrations were often quite contentious and dramatic. On the eve of May Day in 1931, for example, the New York CPLA organized a group of unemployed workers to protest outside of the offices of J. P. Morgan on Wall Street only to have the firm's clerks rush the meeting, breaking the CPLA platform beyond repair and knocking over Muste and several others. The police then forced them to disperse.[69] That same month, during the city's annual Easter Day parade along Fifth Avenue, Muste and Budenz led a march of 150 pickets to publicize the plight of the West Virginia miners and the unemployed, confronting the wealthy who lined the streets with signs that read "You Are Warm—West Virginia Coal Miners Freeze" and "You Wear Fine Clothes—Dressmakers Go Half-Clad."[70]

The first Unemployed Citizens League (UCL) was organized in Seattle. Like their New York comrades, CPLA members Hulet M. Wells, Carl Brannin, and others associated with Seattle Labor College initially focused on publicizing the need for more adequate relief and unemployment insurance, helping to draft a model state insurance bill that was introduced in the Washington State Legislature, and circulating petitions. Soon, however, their work extended to organizing the unemployed, initially focusing on self-help and public works. Following a union model, they organized the UCL into twenty-two locals, each of which established a commissary for the distribution and storage of food and fuel and "elected five representatives to sit on the central body, which met weekly."[71] By June 1932, the league was handling 1,200 tons of wood, 100 tons of coal, 400 tons of foodstuffs, and 300 tons of fruit per week, and had approximately 50,000 members. As

Brannin explained, the unemployed "are not interested in radical philosophies, but will not balk at action, which is revolutionary in its implication. . . . Their daily experience in working together and fighting for their bread and butter, develops solidarity and group consciousness."[72]

The league's evolution bore out Brannin's theory. Although it had begun on a nonpolitical basis, by the spring of 1932, it had begun to endorse candidates in municipal elections and had drafted a political program. The city council, "fearful of the organization's growing political power, voted an emergency relief appropriation of $462,000. The commissaries of the Unemployed Citizens' League became Seattle's relief machinery," conducting the operation efficiently and with low overheard.[73] Elated by the league's success, Brannin instructed his CPLA comrades to follow the Seattle example: begin with a series of meetings with the unemployed to discuss the "social factors" that cause unemployment; form an organization to organize self-help activities; and "avoid political entanglements . . . political policy can be worked out later." Most of all, it was critical that organizers "avoid red flag waving. This cannot be a revolutionary organization. It must consist of *all* the unemployed and conform to the level of mass intelligence *and raise that level by the example of deeds, not words.*"[74]

Leagues quickly sprung up all over the country. They typically followed Seattle's organizational plan and structure, beginning with a series of public meetings and then establishing an organization, which was divided into locals, each with its own committees on matters such as housing, grievance, education, child welfare, and entertainment. The most important of these was the grievance committee, which functioned as a union for relief recipients, hearing complaints and conducting investigations. When it had sufficient data, it would confront local officials in public hearings and, if necessary, with direct action. Recognizing that its project was a cultural one as well as an organizational one, the CPLA took the same approach as it did with unions, organizing picnics, dances, and educational activities, including the establishment of several workers' schools. A songbook from the Ohio Unemployed League included a song written by the unemployed themselves as well as left-labor classics such as "Casey Jones," "Solidarity Forever," "We Shall Not Be Moved," and the "Internationale."[75]

The leagues had their greatest success in Ohio and Pennsylvania, ultimately boasting some 100,000 and 50,000 members, respectively, where they combined Brannin's self-help approach with class-conscious militancy

and direct action. Lem Strong and Elmer Cope, for example, began organizing unemployed steelworkers in western Pennsylvania and eastern Ohio into
the Smith Township Council of the Unemployed as a supplement to their
efforts to unionize steel. As in Seattle, they found that organization made the
unemployed "feel good"; obtaining "tangible results" helped them to overcome their feelings of being "down and out" and gave them a sense of their
own power. As Strong explained of their success in obtaining and extending
county relief work, "They won for themselves, in short, all that the township
and county politicians had assured them couldn't be had." The experience persuaded them to organize a UCL, beginning with cooperative work and food
and fuel distribution and moving from there into politics and direct action.[76]

As with the Communist Party's Unemployed Councils, the UCL's use
of direct action was designed to dramatize both the plight of the unemployed and the inadequacy of relief machinery. Evictions proved ideal sites
for staging protests; as soon as a league learned of an eviction, it sent a
team to investigate and then obtained a permit for a street meeting in front
of the home to be vacated. When the sheriff arrived, he found himself
confronted by a large group and a speaker shouting. "Are we going to stand
by while the tools of capitalism throw us out of our homes?" These actions
were largely successful in forcing the police to leave.[77]

It was through incidents such as these that the league gained the
"respect and confidence" of unemployed workers.[78] In Allentown and other
locales, they not only stopped evictions, but they procured and extended
relief services, including appropriations for prenatal and other medical care,
prevented gas and electricity shut offs, and other measures that improved
the material well-being of the poor. E. R. McKinney, who headed the UCL
in Pittsburgh, recalled, "We knew . . . that when one is dealing with masses
of people . . . something has to be done concretely that benefits the members. . . . Therefore we had a very practical program in the unemployed
league. We got them placed on relief, we actually kept them on relief."[79]

Starting in January 1933, the Musteites began to focus on uniting the
various leagues into a national organization. Ohio had taken the initiative in October 1932 when it held a statewide convention to plan for a
statewide organization. These efforts bore fruit in February 1933, when the
Ohio Unemployed League was established with CPLA members in virtually
all of the leadership positions. Other leagues were less successful in consolidating their forces; in Pennsylvania, factional fighting with the Socialist

Party seriously impeded efforts. Latecomers to organizing the unemployed and with weak support from the national leadership, Socialists were often forced to play second fiddle to the CPLA in local initiatives. But as divisions between the party and the CPLA grew (for reasons discussed below), the former increasingly resented its second-class status and began to resist CPLA domination. When the CPLA began pushing for a united front of all unemployed groups, including Communists, in the National Unemployed League (NUL), the Socialist Party became openly hostile. At the Harrisburg convention to form a Pennsylvania Unemployed League, Socialists complained that Muste was controlling the convention from the floor, "transmitting his instructions by nods and shakes of the head and by notes to the chairman, who was one of his followers." The accuracy of this rendition is unclear, but it does speak to the mutual distrust that increasingly characterized relations between the Socialist Party and the CPLA.[80]

Despite these difficulties, the Musteites proceeded with their plans for a national organization, choosing July 4 as the date of their founding convention. On July 3, approximately eight hundred delegates arrived at the Ohio State Fair Grounds in Columbus, Ohio, representing "a broad range of political persuasions, including Musteites, Communists, Socialists, some who were alleged to be Ku Klux Klanners, and many who combined a radical approach to the problems of the unemployed with extreme patriotism and anti-communism." As Muste wrote of the latter group, "They believe that this country is essentially alright, the only trouble is that bankers and bosses are in control and misusing them."[81]

The Fourth of July convention demonstrates how the "Americanist approach" of the Musteites could unintentionally backfire, and how tensions sometimes emerged between their pragmatic approach and their revolutionary goals. The more conservative delegates became resentful of the convention leadership when it refused to open with a prayer and the singing of "The Star-Spangled Banner." The presence of Communists and plans for closer cooperation with the Unemployed Councils only increased their resentment. Soon after the convention opened, a fight broke out on the floor between patriotic and radical delegates. The so-called "Stars and Stripes" group then seized the podium and gave one speech after another in which they "denounced communism, praised the American way, and yet, at the same time, urged a militant fight for the rights of the jobless." The session closed with the singing of "The Star-Spangled Banner" and a warning to all "reds" to stay away from the convention the following day. Rosenzweig concludes, "in one brief day, the CPLA dream of an American revolutionary movement had turned into a nativist nightmare."[82]

Yet the CPLA had anticipated the dangers posed by nationalistic elements in the leagues.[83] Their use of American language was not an attempt to cater to such groups but rather an attempt to redefine American culture as working class and its history as revolutionary. Thus, on the following day of the convention, they quickly regained control of the floor by issuing a strong counterattack on the right-wing delegates and discrediting the leader as a professional strikebreaker. They remained in control for the rest of the convention, drafting a preamble to the NUL constitution entitled "Declaration of Workers' and Farmers' Rights" that embedded radical demands within the language of the Declaration of Independence. The final day of the convention, delegates elected CPLA members to six of the seven top positions in the NUL: Anthony Ramuglia, president; Arnold Johnson, secretary; Bill Truax, first vice president; Elmer Cope, second vice president; Beulah Carter, third vice president; and Karl Lore, treasurer.[84]

How the CPLA managed the convention reflected their pragmatic operating style. When several Trotskyist delegates charged that they had capitulated to conservatives by deleting a reference to workers' control in the NUL constitution, E. R. McKinney "told them that maybe that was the reason we had the unemployed organization and that they didn't have any. We made a compromise. You wouldn't make it."[85] Ironically, however, over the next several years, Muste would increasingly resist the pragmatic logic of the times, which was that the working class, even a newly militant and class-conscious one, was not interested in radical leadership but rather in an alliance with the Democratic Party. Many radicals made the same mistake, but they eventually came to terms with it. Muste, by contrast, refused to compromise, revealing a revolutionary purism that increasingly took precedence over his pragmatic creed.

In addition to organizing the unemployed and industrial workers, the Musteites agitated for the creation of a mass labor party, an idea that had remained popular among progressives and Socialists even after La Follette's defeat in the 1924 election. The CPLA had initially been reluctant to prioritize building a third party; the American masses were too individualistic, too wedded to capitalist culture, to break from the mainstream parties, Muste observed.[86] As a result, when John Dewey organized the League for

Independent Political Action (LIPA) in 1929, the CPLA had responded ambivalently. More liberal and Socialist CPLAers—such as Paul Blanshard, Paul Douglas, and Maurer—tended to be enthusiastic about the new venture, while those closest to industrial workers tended to be skeptical. Muste, for example, agreed that the Democratic Party was a dead end, pointing to its powerful and reactionary southern wing, but he felt that the LIPA was insufficiently rooted in the labor movement and the working class. Any new third party "must be a Labor Party," committed to developing working-class leadership and candidates, and to "a radical program of social ownership and control of basic resources and industries." The LIPA, however, was oriented toward the middle class, and tended to rely upon "a few prominent individuals and including groups with diverse economic interests." Of Paul Douglas's book *The Coming of a New Party*, Muste commented that Douglas failed "to give any consideration to the question of whether the economic problems of the twentieth century can be solved with the methods of eighteenth-century political democracy."[87]

Despite these criticisms, Muste served as a member of the LIPA's executive committee and participated in LIPA-sponsored conferences, where he urged those interested in a third party to adopt a more laborist orientation. But by 1931, he had become disillusioned with the LIPA leadership's emphasis on courting prominent political figures rather than from the ground up. In resigning from the LIPA, he called upon the CPLA to concentrate on building a mass labor party, based on the industrial organizations of workers, and in a united front with other like-minded groups. In calling on CPLA members to enter the political field, he warned them not to fall prey to the "illusions" of parliamentary politics, and to continue to place primary emphasis on industrial action. But, from a pragmatic point of view, mass political organization would serve as a means "of getting American workers out of the habit of voting the Republican and Democratic tickets." "We cannot ignore government. We have to take control of it and use it for labor ends."[88]

Muste had some reason to hope for a third-party movement at the outset of 1932. Progressives continued to view the Democratic Party with suspicion, doubting that its candidate Franklin D. Roosevelt, with his wealth and background as assistant secretary of the navy, would realign the party along pro-labor lines.[89] Labor organizations close to the CPLA were all on record as favoring a mass labor party. From the field, CPLA organizers reported success in promoting third-party sentiment. In Philadelphia, for example, Branch 1 of the AFFFHW, which was affiliated with the CPLA, had formed the Independent Labor Party, which ran a slate of candidates for local office in the 1932 election, in the process attracting considerable Socialist support; CPLA groups in Buffalo, Niagara Falls, and New Bedford, Massachusetts, similarly spurred unionists and Socialists into third-party activism.[90] Unemployed leagues also showed growing interest in third-party politics, putting candidates up for election and endorsing politicians who were pro-labor. A new Farmer-Labor Party in Illinois, along with the Farmer-Labor Party of Minnesota and the Socialist Party, appeared likely to cooperate in such an effort. More broadly, workers appeared more discontented, even as the "tradition of individualism still lingered."[91]

The time, moreover, seemed increasingly ripe for a new political alignment. As the CPLA observed, the capitalist system had been shaken to "its foundations." As the Great Depression entered its third year, unemployment and misery were widespread, while the rich were allowed to escape taxation. Whenever workers protested, they were "brutally terrorized" with outright violence, in addition to coercive tactics such as injunctions and yellow-dog contracts. Meanwhile, financial and industrial leaders were quietly building a "Fascist dictatorship." "In the face of poverty, unemployment, the bosses' offensive against the living standards and self-respect of the workers, and the onrushing tide of Fascism, the American labor movement stands utterly bankrupt, confused and helpless."[92]

This idea—that the United States was on a "stampede" to fascism, as Muste put it—was widespread on the left in the 1930s. The prevailing wisdom was that the world would inevitably become "collectivist," but that it was an open question whether victory would belong to the fascists or to the laborites. "Either the bankers, industrialists, and politicians will set up a Fascist dictatorship in the U.S. or Labor must fight them, assume control and establish a sane and just economic order and a genuine workers' democracy," the CPLA's National Executive Committee asserted. Pointing to the spread of fascism in Europe, Muste called on laborites and the left to unite in a mass labor party to withstand similar threats at home. "Is it purity or death?" he asked rhetorically.[93]

Neither the CPLA nor other groups managed to build enough sentiment for either a mass labor party or a third party in time for the 1932 election, though they were able to unite in defense of Tom Mooney and the Scottsboro boys.[94] Moreover, the emergence of Roosevelt as a progressive candidate posed a distinct challenge; as Muste wrote in October 1932, his candidacy was "unfortunate and confusing and may mean a set-back for many years for the movement for independent political action," especially if liberals and social workers obtain positions within a Roosevelt administration. "What a lovely dream a lot of nice people are going to have, and what a dangerous one!" He continued, commenting that "the Democratic Party cannot be made over, the only chance of building a party that would really offer an alternative to the Republican, rests in smashing [it]."[95]

Muste was indeed intractable in his opposition to working within the Democratic Party, even for labor reforms, a position that alludes to a growing split within the CPLA between its social democratic and revolutionary wings. As if to foreshadow this parting of ways, when the CPLA joined the Socialist Party and the Minnesota Farmer-Labor Party in calling the "Continental Congress of Workers and Farmers," they discovered—to their shock and disappointment—that their longtime comrades David Dubinsky and Sidney Hillman were there to push not for political independence but for an alliance with the Democratic Party.[96]

CHAPTER 6

Americanizing Marx and Lenin

With capitalism organized all over the world, the labor
movement must also be international, but the American
section will have to be built by the courage, solidarity and
brains of American workers. Nobody else can do the job
here, any more than we can do the job somewhere else.

—A. J. Muste, 1931

IN ITS FIRST two years of existence, the Musteite movement represented a range of progressive opinion, including sympathetic labor union officials, militant rank and filers, Socialists, pacifists, and radical Christians. Indeed, it was initially more progressive than revolutionary, with the CPLA's provisional character giving the movement a flexible and democratic quality. But, over the course of the early 1930s, the Musteites increasingly assumed a more revolutionary posture, a position that was reinforced by the influx of Marxist intellectuals into the movement. In 1932, the CPLA institutionalized its move to the left by redefining itself as a permanent, revolutionary vanguard organization. As a result, membership requirements became more stringent and Muste's control over the movement increased.

The CPLA's evolution from 1929 through the mid-1930s paralleled Muste's personal and political development. As director of Brookwood during the worst years of the Great Depression, he faced a major financial crisis as funds dried up, unions reduced their scholarships, the Garland Fund delayed payments, and major private donors such as Elizabeth Glendower Evans and Anna Davis cut their contributions.[1] Back home in Grand Rapids, where he visited whenever traveling through the Midwest, his parents and sisters (now with families of their own) struggled as employers reduced their hours, cut their pay, and laid them off. Now in his eighties, Martin Muste finally retired from his job at the factory, and he and Adriana moved in with their youngest daughter, Minnie, whose husband also worked in Grand Rapids' lumber mills. Times were so hard for the Mustes that they were unable to raise $3.21 to pay a debt Cornelia's son had incurred with the Book-of-the-Month Club. When the club threatened her son with a summons to court, Cornelia appealed to "Bram," who paid the debt.[2]

The worsening economic depression, the growing restiveness of American workers, the AFL's stubborn resistance to change, and the rise of fascism (both at home and abroad) also combined to give Muste a heightened sense of urgency and revolutionary possibility. In this, he was not alone; "the whole structure of American society seemed to be going to pieces," Muste's occasional ally and critic Edmund Wilson recalled of those "tumultuous" and "lean" years.[3]

By the mid-1930s, most radicals—including, ultimately, most Musteites—would reach a sort of détente with American capitalism, hoping that a social democracy could be built out of the New Deal state and the political muscle of the CIO. Sidney Hillman and Walter Reuther, for example, labor leaders who shared Muste's commitment to modernizing the labor movement and regulating industrial relations through an empowered state, would form an alliance with the Democratic Party.[4] Yet, despite his long-held commitment to such a project, Muste rejected the social democratic path, with consequences for himself, his family, workers education, and the social movement he had worked so hard to build.

In his move to the left, Muste increasingly ignored the advice of long-time comrades and friends. Some even accused him of having a "messianic" sense of self-importance, a charge that must be taken seriously in the context of Muste's history of mystical experiences and identification with the prophetic tradition. During this period, Muste no longer considered himself a Christian or a pacifist. However, a few years later, he would publish an article drawing parallels between Lenin's concept of the vanguard party and the Christian notion of the "True Church" that help us to understand the Russian revolutionary's appeal. One passage in particular is worth quoting at length:

> It is astonishing how many of the marks of the True Church are included in [Lenin's] doctrine of The Party. The Party must be revolutionary. The existing order is corrupt . . . it is doomed. The Party

must therefore aim to overthrow it, not to come to an understanding with it. The Party stands over against "the world" therefore. It is despised, it is weak, it is in a hopeless minority, it is outrageously persecuted—until the day of revolution dawns. . . . The Party is the instrument of God—of destiny at any rate, of those "historical forces which make the triumph of socialism inevitable." A force which makes for the reign of righteousness and brotherhood, to which the individual must surrender himself utterly, and which cannot fail—that comes close to being the definition of . . . a Calvinist God. . . . There can on these terms be only one true party. The individual member, if he be a true member . . . will find ineffable joy in its service. Without The Party, the proletariat is lost. Of itself, through its own experience without being led and for its good manipulated by The Party, it will not rise to revolutionary heights and be able to save itself. . . .

The Party, Lenin contended, must be international, universal, in scope and essence. . . . When finally The Party triumphs, history as we know it comes to an end, or rather history begins for the first time. Man will pass, in Engels' great phrase, "from the kingdom of necessity into the kingdom of freedom."[5]

Muste's argument is an intriguing one; not only does it point to similarities between Judeo-Christian eschatology and Marxist-Leninist theory, it suggests that he had displaced his notion of the "True Church" onto the revolutionary party, and that, as a Marxist-Leninist, he viewed himself as one of the elect.

THE CPLA's efforts on the political and industrial fields increasingly made it a force to be reckoned with in the labor-left world. One testament to its growing presence was the entry of "traditional" intellectuals—those who made their living independently of the labor movement from their work as artists, writers, philosophers, and critics—into the movement. Not surprisingly, the intellectuals who became close to Muste and the CPLA tended to consider themselves communists with a lowercase *c*; they were uncomfortable with what they viewed as the Communist Party's rigid interpretation of Marx, while at the same time being critical of the Socialist Party as too respectable, too concerned with vote getting, and not cognizant enough of the class struggle. As a result, they shared the Musteites' interest in Americanizing Marxism "by fusing it with pragmatism."[6]

V. F. Calverton, editor of *Modern Quarterly* magazine, offers an outstanding example of this group. Muste had known Calverton since the mid-1920s, having attended the literary critic's famous Baltimore salon and hiring him to teach several short courses at Brookwood over the course of 1926 to 1928. In contrast to most American intellectuals, who moved to the left with the onset of the Depression, Calverton had long identified as a socialist; his magazine was a sort of holdover of the lyrical left, combining sexual, cultural, and political radicalism, and exhibiting an optimistic, engaged spirit even after the devastation of the Great War.[7]

Like Muste, Calverton was critically engaged with the pragmatic tradition. The heroes of his youth were the cultural critics Van Wyck Brooks, Randolph Bourne, and Max Eastman, who had drawn upon James and Dewey in an effort to create a new kind of democratic community in which free expression and critical discourse would serve as a means of enriching and reconstructing communal life.[8] Also like Muste, Calverton was a pragmatist who viewed the promise of science in its "method and spirit" rather than a particular body of knowledge. As one of his biographers has put it, he was a modern committed to "the notion that critical intelligence can change and shape environment, that thought can be deployed to enable effective action." At the same time he shared with Muste the conviction that Dewey paid insufficient attention to the role of ideology and economic structure in shaping and limiting human action.[9]

Founded in 1922, *Modern Quarterly* appears in retrospect as a kind of literary counterpoint to Brookwood. Just as Muste sought to bring together laborites and radicals across ideological and ethnic divisions, Calverton attempted to build a "beloved community" of the left, moving beyond the WASP culture of the prewar lyrical left to include ethnics and African Americans, and publishing a range of radical opinion, including Earl Browder, Mike Gold, Sidney Hook, Edmund Wilson, W. E. B. Du Bois, and Harry Elmer Barnes. The central premise of his magazine throughout the 1920s "was that various radical factions were merely part of a greater unity of purpose, part of the complete socialism." [10] Similarly to Brookwood, *Modern Quarterly* was particularly concerned with the class character of American culture and explored the possibilities of developing proletarian art, though its efforts revolved around cultural criticism and theory rather than cultural production.

By the mid-1920s, Calverton and *Modern Quarterly* had attained the respect of leftists and liberals across the ideological spectrum. But, as with Muste and Brookwood, political catholicity became increasingly difficult to maintain over the course of 1926 through 1928. Not coincidentally, the first conflict Calverton had with the Communist Party was over his favorable review of David Saposs's *Left Wing Unionism* in which he praised Saposs's thesis that circumstances determine whether dual unionism or "boring from within" was an appropriate strategy for those seeking to build a more progressive labor movement. Calverton's comment that dogmatism on either point was "absurd" especially rankled the Communist Party, which at this point opposed dual unionism, and Communist Party leader William Z. Foster and *Daily Worker* editor William Dunne castigated him for the "detached manner in which you spoke of the party and its program." Ironically, at the same time that he attracted the ire of Communists, Calverton was attacked from the right by James Oneal, editor of the Socialist *New Leader*, for contributing articles to the *Daily Worker* and for suggesting that the Socialist Party had become undynamic and old. Oneal fired him from the *New Leader*: "the *Daily Worker* is the filthiest thing that ever appeared in the United States," he pointedly informed Calverton.[11]

Calverton would manage to repair his strained relationship with the Communist Party, but conflicts would continue to erupt over the next few years and finally break down completely in 1932–33. Scholars have interpreted the tensions between Calverton and the Communist Party as a reflection of his independent streak and the party's move into the third period.[12] Yet it also reflected the Communist Party's recognition that Calverton had become close to Muste, even though he did not officially join the movement until December 1933. Indeed, by 1928, *Modern Quarterly* had established its distinct identity as a magazine committed to bringing pragmatism and Marxism together as part of a larger effort to "transform radical action from something foreign into terms of the American experience." This commitment stemmed directly "from his contact with Brookwood Labor College . . . during the mid and late twenties, and with A. J. Muste." In language that might have come out of *Labor Age*, of which he was a regular reader, Calverton now argued that the way to overcome the individualistic ethos of American workers was by appealing to them in American terms and utilizing the American past. "Here the influence of the Musteites . . . is apparent," a biographer has commented. "America's revolutionary tradition was to be revitalized and reconstituted: Jeffersonian individualism was not to be salvaged but rather the 'progressive spirit of revolt' in the Jeffersonian philosophy should be upheld. Revolutionary figures of the American past were to be resurrected as 'symbols of challenge and advance.' "[13]

As part of this larger project of Americanizing Marxism, in 1928 *Modern Quarterly* initiated the famous, ongoing debate between Max Eastman and Sidney Hook on the relationship between pragmatism and Marxism. Both men were revolutionary socialists who had been students of John Dewey's at Columbia University, yet they were a generation apart and came from different cultural backgrounds; Eastman was the son of Protestant ministers who had become a leading figure in the prewar lyrical left, while Hook was the son of Jewish immigrants from Central Europe who had recently been appointed instructor in philosophy at New York University. In the debate, Eastman maintained that Marx's dialectic was a holdover from Hegel that needed to be purged in order to make Marxism truly scientific and instrumental. Hook countered that Eastman had misunderstood the dialectic, arguing that Marx believed that human action mattered in the historical process, while being constrained by objective conditions. His argument would later be given its fullest expression in his 1933 book *Towards the Understanding of Karl Marx*, which attempted to demonstrate that Marxism was "not an armchair philosophy of retrospection, but a philosophy of social action; more specifically, *a theory of social revolution*."[14]

Significantly, the CPLA recognized the affinity between Hook's analysis and its own. In August 1931, Muste wrote to Hook, "Your view of Marx is the one on which I have for a good while agreed, although I have never felt that I was a sufficiently erudite scholar in Marx or in the literature of Marxism to be sure that this interpretation was the only possible one." A month later, Muste anonymously reviewed Hook's *Towards the Understanding of Karl Marx* in *Labor Age*, praising Hook's recognition of the vital importance of critical analysis and action in the revolutionary struggle as well as his recognition that Marx was as much a revolutionist as a theoretician. "It is obviously possible on this interpretation to accept the validity and permanent importance of Marx's method without feeling bound to use him as a Talmud and Bible," Muste commented approvingly. "If his interpretation of Marx is not the correct one, then it should be."[15] Soon thereafter, Hardman invited Hook to write for *Labor Age*. Over the course of 1932–33, Hook grew closer to the Musteites, ultimately playing a leading role in transforming the CPLA into the American Workers Party (AWP); Muste had him draft the founding statement of principles for the new party.[16]

In the winter of 1930–31, Calverton initiated another controversial symposium, this one on the role of intellectuals in society, that featured a debate between Lewis Mumford and himself, the former holding that intellectuals should preserve "essential" values in opposition to the materialistic and consumerist ethos of modern society and the latter maintaining that intellectuals should analyze the class nature of society and culture and align with the revolutionary struggles of the working class.[17] It was in this context that Calverton began publishing Lewis Corey (a.k.a. Louis Fraina) who was developing his ideas about the emergence of a "new" middle class and its role in the revolutionary struggle. Corey's thesis would profoundly influence Calverton, who in 1933 formally committed *Modern Quarterly* (now *Modern Monthly*) to the radicalization of professionals.[18]

Michael Denning has established Corey's significance to the American Marxist tradition and to left political culture in the 1930s. According to Denning, Corey was unique in combining radical industrial unionism "with an attention to the new middle classes and the cultural front. As a result he is the great theorist of the Popular Front social movement, the American Antonio Gramsci." Just as his contemporary Gramsci insisted upon the importance of culture, of "ethico-political history," in maintaining and challenging hegemony, Corey wrote in his 1934 book *The Decline of American Capitalism* that "every revolutionary class must wage war on the cultural front." While Gramsci focused on the role of intellectuals, Corey looked to the "new" middle class; as he argued in his 1935 book *The Crisis of the Middle Class*, as salaried employees, the new middle class no longer had anything in common with the old middle class of independent property owners. Here Corey went beyond earlier formulations in which intellectuals were envisioned as allies of the working class to conceptualizing them as fellow proletarians.[19]

Corey's ideas grew out of his collaboration with other Musteites. In 1928, Corey worked with Muste, Hardman, James Rorty, Louis Stanley, John Brophy, James Maurer, Arthur Calhoun, and other progressive laborites and intellectuals to produce *American Labor Dynamics*, an edited volume exploring the economic and cultural transformations of the previous decade and their implications for the labor movement. As early as Labor Day 1929, he participated in CPLA conferences and was probably a member of the organization.[20] Over the winter of 1931–32, he, along with Hardman, Saposs, Rorty, William L. Nunn, and Felix Cohen, all members of the CPLA, founded the ostensibly unaffiliated American Labor Associates, an organization committed to serving as a "collateral intellectual body to the labor movement as a whole." In January 1932, the group began to make preparations to publish a new monthly that would be "devoted to fundamental yet undogmatic and experimental research and criticism along the lines of social transformation." Muste and the CPLA supported the effort, recognizing that the widespread unemployment of white-collar workers and the growing radicalization of intellectuals offered a ripe opportunity for organization. In January 1933, their hard work paid off, as the American Labor Associates published the first issue of *Our America*, a newspaper committed to building "an integrated and militant movement of manual and intellectuals workers rallied around a clear-cut and realistic program of action," with contributions from Muste, Corey, Rorty, Hardman, Saposs, Lore, and the Marxist lawyer Louis Boudin.[21]

Corey is more famous for his role as author of the pamphlet *Culture and the Crisis: An Open Letter to the Writers, Artists, Teachers, Physicians, Engineers, Scientists, and Other Professional Workers of America*, which was published in the fall of 1932 by the recently formed League of Professional Groups for Foster and Ford. Signed by fifty-three prominent intellectuals, the pamphlet called on professional workers to use their creativity and skills to serve the working class and to support the Communist presidential and vice presidential candidates, William Z. Foster and James W. Ford. Although the league collapsed with a year, it is seen as the first major theoretical expression of the Popular Front. As Denning has written, "the group of radicals around Corey and Calverton pioneered the major themes of the Popular Front social movement before the Communist Party itself adopted them: the stress on American exceptionalism and on 'Americanizing' Marxism; the appeal to radicalized white-collar workers; and the turn from a rhetoric of 'proletarian culture' to a notion of a 'cultural front.'"[22]

Historians have interpreted the participation of "independent" radicals like Corey, Hook, and Rorty in the League of Professional Groups for Foster and Ford as a sign of their romance with the Communist Party; thus the breakdown of the league a few months later has been seen as part of a larger drama of betrayed innocence.[23] In fact, however, Muste and the CPLA urged members and supporters to vote for either the Communist Party or the Socialist Party tickets in the 1932 election, while simultaneously exploring the possibilities of building a mass labor party. In other words, the endorsement of Foster by Corey, Hook, Rorty, and others was not necessarily to the exclusion of other political affiliations. Indeed, at the same time they that participated in the league, they were busy with publishing *Our America* and with plans to transform the CPLA into the AWP. Calverton, long reluctant to publicly align with any one faction on the left, made his commitment public in February 1934 when he wrote an editorial in *Modern Monthly* calling readers' attention to the formation of the AWP and referring to it as "the most hopeful sign that has appeared on the American horizon for years." A month later, he signed—along with Muste, Hook, Rorty, and Hardman—an open letter calling on intellectuals to repudiate the Communist Party and join the AWP.[24]

Drawing connections between these ostensibly "independent" intellectuals and the CPLA/AWP is not to split hairs but rather to demonstrate the social foundations upon which their ideas were built. Through Muste, these intellectuals had a base in a radicalized section of the working class that had long been exploring similar questions within the workers' education movement and the CPLA. Yet the relationship between the more laborite Musteites and their intellectual comrades was not always harmonious. There were, first, distinct cultural differences that could become a source of tension. Calverton and others associated with *Modern Quarterly* tended to be cultural radicals who espoused the heterodox feminism of the prewar years. Muste and the rank and file of the CPLA, by contrast, were far more typically Old Left in viewing cultural and sexual radicalism as signs of bourgeois decadence. Hardman, who was a sort of bridge figure between the two groups, wrote sardonically to Calverton that he could not publish an essay on women's emancipation that the latter had submitted to the ACW organ, the *Advance*, because "Labor, you know, is sexless—but safe."[25]

Laborites, moreover, were frustrated by the reluctance of intellectuals close to the CPLA to publicly align with the organization. Particularly in the years 1930 through 1932, they expressed skepticism about the apparent leftward turn in American intellectual life. Hardman wrote to Calverton in the summer of 1929 that the critic's interest in the CPLA was "queer: You won't go further than mention it in a note. Why did you not stay at the [CPLA's founding] Conference?"[26]

The writer Edmund Wilson was another intellectual close to the Musteites who shied away from full commitment to the movement. Louis Budenz's review of Wilson's *American Jitters* (1932) was warmly appreciative of the author's poignant descriptions of Depression-era American society, while suggesting that the book reflected the fundamental problem with American intellectuals: they were moved "more by their hearts than by their heads. The worker, however, has to contend with grim realities, many of which are prosaic and even drab from an emotional viewpoint. . . . Mr. Wilson cannot help there as yet, for he has not gotten down to the battle of the workers." Though Wilson "instinctively" recognized the need for "an Americanized version of the Communist movement" like the CPLA, "beyond that he cannot go."[27]

If intellectuals showed "timidity" and "fear" about expressing their political sympathies in action and commitment, they also displayed rashness and arrogance once they set themselves to the task. Intellectuals had often given the labor movement valuable leadership and a broader understanding of society, a CPLA member wrote anonymously in *Labor Age* (probably Hardman), but there were also cases when intellectuals, with "incorrect outlook and training have been most injurious in their influence." Citing Lenin's "Left-Wing Unionism," the author suggested that newly won converts to socialism often exhibited revolutionary "impatience. . . . There seems to be a belief that the overthrow of capitalism can be brought about over night in some miraculous way. . . . But unfortunately for these magicians, history does not work that way. The masses of the workers do not learn through propaganda and agitation alone. . . . *The broad masses learn through their own political experience.*" Without recognizing this crucial fact, intellectuals tended to "treat with contempt . . . everyday struggles over wages, hours, and better conditions, even though these are of intense concern to workers themselves." Indeed, it was precisely these struggles through which "workers are organized and trained for the final struggle against their oppressors."[28]

For their part, intellectuals tended to admire the courage and tenacity of Muste and his adherents, while simultaneously viewing them as rather naively earnest and abstemious, as captured in Edmund Wilson's contemporaneous description of them as having the appearance of divinity students. "On the other hand," Wilson mused, "they also differ from the truly academic radicals in possessing the conviction and courage which carry them into industrial battles and make them do thankless work and venture into situations which few middle-class people care to face."[29]

Wilson's depiction of Muste himself epitomizes the mix of envy and contempt that some intellectuals harbored toward labor activists. Describing an AWP meeting at Calverton's Greenwich Village apartment on January 3, 1934, he contrasted Calverton's "florid and soft" appearance to Muste's, which he described as taut and sexually repressed. He appeared:

worn, tense, and hardworked, one lock of hair down over his fore-
head, his eyes getting round under his pained and dismayed eyebrows . . . like those of an amazed old hick, his cheeks fevered at the
cheekbones and showing hollows below, his mouth dingy darkened
by the traces of his beard (it occurred to me after I came away to
wonder whether he was a virgin) . . . his shoulders hunched up and
sitting on his hands or afterwards during the discussion with one
leg twisted around the other and his hands clasped in front of him—
when somebody asked him a question . . . he would knock the cigarette ashes off his clothes with little pats of rather fine thin fingers
or take a nervous pull on the cigarette.[30]

A few days later, Wilson wrote (in an entry included in Wilson's chronicle of the 1920s and 1930s, *The Shores of Light*) that Muste was one of
the radical movement's "saints" and suggested that he had "something in
common" with the character George Brush in Thornton Wilder's *Heaven's
My Destination*, an evangelist for whom "goodness" was both a vocation
and a source of irritation to others and the powers that be.[31]

A keen observer, Wilson's account captures the moral intensity of
Muste's character as well as the cultural tensions that sometimes arose
between the AWP rank and file and their modernist comrades. But it must
also be read as filtered through Wilson's deep ambivalence about political
commitment; unlike others close to the *Modern Quarterly*, he never joined
the AWP. Moreover, despite the seriousness with which they pursued the
revolution, the Musteites were hardly dour puritans; their movement culture included parties, dances, carnivals, drama, music and singing, and,
when held at Brookwood, "labor sports" and hiking.[32] As for Muste, he
insisted that his moral inhibitions had not made him a "cold fish." "The
best Puritans carry the glow inside," he remarked to a friend, "which is
better than the ice which abides at the heart of some warm exteriors." He
was also nobody's fool; he had a keen sense of humor and razor-sharp
political acumen. In the same account of the meeting in Calverton's apartment, Wilson wrote that Muste opened the meeting by drolly noting that
he was late because he had forgotten "that New York time is not God's
time and that when you spoke to a garment workers' meeting you would
have to answer questions afterwards about how they were to get rid of their
officers."[33]

As the Musteites assumed a more substantial presence on the labor left, the movement began to attract critical attention. Liberals took notice, publishing favorable articles in such magazines as the *New Republic*, the *Nation*, and the *Christian Century*. Socialists increasingly felt challenged by their example; the militants in the party, led by CPLA members Leonard Bright and Louis Stanley, tried to push it along the lines of the CPLA into direct organizational work among the unemployed and industrial workers. For their part, the Communists acknowledged their growing influence by dedicating pages of ink to decrying them as "labor fakirs," even as they began imitating their methods, particularly in their work with the unemployed, finding that flexibility rather than dogmatism was a more effective organizational tool.[34]

In May 1931, New York's John Reed Clubs invited Muste to debate Communist Party leader William Z. Foster at the New Star Casino. The debate, which attracted some three thousand people (another two thousand had to be turned away at the door), focused on their differing approaches to unionization. Not surprisingly, each side declared itself the victor. For our purposes, the debate illustrates why and how Muste gained so much influence on the left during these years. Often underestimated because of his reputation as a pacifist and for his unwillingness to engage in *ad hominem* attacks, Muste showed himself Foster's equal in the verbal style of the Old Left as he skillfully deployed such phrases as "childish petulance" and "Communist sewing-circles." The debate also illustrates Muste's growing ambitions for his movement. From 1931 through 1934, he sharpened the distinctions between the CPLA and other left-wing groups, and oversaw the CPLA's transition into the AWP. In the process, the Musteites shed their progressive and social democratic elements, and redefined their movement in Leninist terms as the revolutionary vanguard. For Muste, the personal and political consequences of this shift would be profound.[35]

The relationship between the CPLA and the Communist Party would remain contentious. In general, the Musteites heeded their commitment to "working-class ethics," diligently focusing on action over criticism and frequently reminding each other to be "over-patient with the Moscow inspired." But conflicts in the field—in textile centers, in the Illinois coalfields, and among the unemployed—occasionally spilled into public, as in September 1932, when an article in *Labor Age* decried Communists as "strikebreakers" and "union wreckers."[36] The Communists, meanwhile, accelerated their attack. In 1931–32, two of the Garland Fund's Communist board members, Robert W. Dunn and Clarina Michaelson, proposed that Brookwood's funds be withdrawn on the grounds that the CPLA had recently declared its intention to "enter the political field." Their evidence included the overlap between the CPLA leadership and Brookwood faculty as well as statements by a secret caucus of Communist students at Brookwood. David Saposs managed to fend off the Communist assault and sustain the funding, but the experience made Brookwood's faculty and board of directors acutely sensitive to the question of the relationship between the college and the CPLA, and in the spring of 1932, the board restated Brookwood's policy of nonpartisanship.[37]

In some respects, the relationship between the CPLA and the Socialist Party was more problematic. Initially, the two groups were quite close, and there is some evidence that Socialists hoped that the CPLA would "serve as a transmission belt for progressive unionists into the party." But there were also critical differences between those close to Muste, on the one hand, and the left-wing Socialists who supported the CPLA, on the other. First, the Socialist Party had a history of maintaining a laissez-faire attitude toward the AFL; eager to maintain relations with labor, it generally avoided taking strong stands on intra-union politics and focused instead on electoral politics. Compounding this history of détente were Old Guard Socialists, who had positions of influence in unions that were deeply reluctant to confront the AFL leadership. These elements issued public attacks on the CPLA even as leading Socialists were members of the organization. They also clashed with the CPLA when it allied with progressive forces in the ILGWU, the silk workers' unions, and other Socialist-dominated unions. Second, young militants and left-wing Socialists believed that it was possible to reform the Socialist Party from within, while Muste and others close to him tended to view it as hopelessly anachronistic and timid, both in its unwillingness to unseat its right wing and in its tradition of parliamentarianism.[38]

The first hint of the impending break occurred in mid-1930 when James Oneal, editor of the Socialist *New Leader*, resigned from the CPLA because of the organization's decision to support Alexander Howat in the RUMW (see Chapter 5). Despite this public rift, the "militants" remained active members of the CPLA and defended Muste to Oneal and other Socialist leaders.[39] But a split became inevitable in August of 1931 when the CPLA moved closer to defining itself as a political party. The initiative largely came from Muste, who had penned several articles raising the question for discussion.[40] Then, at the organization's annual conference over Labor

Day weekend, the CPLA established more stringent requirements for membership.[41]

Leonard Bright was particularly distressed over the decision, warning Muste that the militants would bolt the CPLA, and trying to convince him that it was possible to reform the Socialist Party from within. Muste, however, was committed to building a revolutionary vanguard even if it meant having a smaller membership; as he explained to Bright, it had become clear to him that the CPLA rank and file were "essentially revolutionists . . . more closely in sympathy with the fundamental policies of the Communists than of the Socialists." He remained, moreover, unconvinced that the Socialist Party was moving to the left: "It seems to us that the Hillquit-Milwaukee-*Forward* influence [by which he meant the Party's right wing] is bound to control in the long run. It seems to us, furthermore, that the Thomas leadership is essentially a left-liberal or progressive, and not a revolutionary one, in spite of our personal affection for Norman."[42]

Bright was deeply pained by Muste's determination to transform the CPLA into a political organization, viewing it as a rejection of the militants even as Muste—rather disingenuously—assured him that party members were still welcome, so long as their primary loyalty was to the CPLA. It seemed to him that Muste was "gambling on a long shot" and in the process "alienating honest, militant elements."[43]

Other left-wing Socialists, less sanguine than Bright about the party's future as a radical force, feared that Muste was abandoning his pragmatism, and that the CPLA's new political line would inevitably draw it into the left's culture of sectarianism. Abraham Lefkowitz, Muste's longtime comrade in the AFT and a member of Brookwood's board of directors, wrote in his letter of resignation that although he had "great admiration for [Muste] personally . . . as a realist . . . I cannot delude myself into believing American labor is ripe for another political party. . . . Surely the awakening of this mass of labor is a task herculean enough for the CPLA without launching into another labor party founded on the communist concept of 'discipline.'" A far more realistic policy would be for the CPLA to confine itself to serving as an educational and progressive force within organized labor, helping to build a broad front of leftists and trade unionists.[44]

Other longtime comrades agreed with Lefkowitz. One predicted—rightly, as it turned out—that the CPLA would find itself the victim of other left groups, who would seek to capture it: "You will be bored from without, you may be sure of this," he warned. Like Lefkowitz, he suspected that Muste was losing touch with reality, "following the steps of many a radical of the American vintage who wanted to go his own path. . . . You are simply psychologizing [*sic*] yourself . . . first, into visualizing the SP as the hopelessly reactionary crowd . . . and, second, into looking upon yourself as the *it*, acquiring a sort of Messianic attitude." He further warned, again presciently, that the rift with the Socialist Party would have repercussions for Brookwood. "Throughout all these troubled years, you have skillfully piloted Brookwood off the dangerous reefs and established its fine reputation as a broad radical institution," yet by alienating the Socialists, Muste was making some formidable opponents. Perhaps the radical movement would be better served if Muste assumed the leadership of the militants within the party itself.[45]

Still, Muste's determination to transform the CPLA into a permanent left-wing organization was not entirely wishful thinking. He could reasonably claim that the CPLA had considerable influence over tens of thousands of workers, with its massive success with organizing the unemployed, its role as a leader of progressive and militant elements in the labor movement, and the recent influx of prominent intellectuals.[46] At the same time, as the defection of many longtime comrades and Socialists indicated, it would be no easy task to balance self-definition and comradely relations with other left-wing groups. Thus, over the course of the winter of 1931–32, Muste backed off from the increasingly caustic tone of the debate and instructed his comrades to do the same.[47]

Finally, after more than a year of discussion, the CPLA established itself on a permanent basis at its annual convention on Labor Day in 1932. In contrast to later claims made by Brookwood's faculty and board of directors, the CPLA's aims and strategy did not change that much. It continued to maintain that the path to socialism was through building up the organized power of the working class on various fronts. It also continued to stress the importance of "realism" and of rooting its struggle in American conditions, culture, and history, but without committing what it considered the social democratic "fallacies" of parliamentarianism and thinking in terms of a "national community." The main difference was that it now explicitly defined itself as a "vanguard" organization composed of "militant activists," "not a mass organization." But even as it adopted the Leninist notion of a vanguard, with the disciplinary apparatus implied, the CPLA's pragmatic roots remained apparent, asserting that ultimately morale was built through "experience" and action, not "mechanical discipline and theoretical hairsplitting."[48] The decision to turn the CPLA into a permanent, left-wing organization precipitated a conflict between Muste and the majority of Brookwood faculty that led to his resignation from the college. In short, the faculty charged that Muste's involvement with the CPLA took away from his administrative and financial responsibilities to Brookwood; that, despite claims to the contrary, Muste was intent upon turning Brookwood into a CPLA school; and that to do so would make Brookwood "sectarian" and dilute its original mission of serving the labor movement as a whole. Underlying these charges was anger at Muste for turning the CPLA into a permanent, left-wing organization with a "vanguard" role in the labor movement; as the faculty asserted, the CPLA's decision to become a political organization meant that it had "abandoned its role of united action," and undermined its broad appeal to unionists and radicals alike.[49] Aside from Tom Tippett, Cara Cook, and part-time instructor Lucille Kohn, each faculty member came to this position at varying times and for different reasons: Katherine Pollak and Mark Starr were close to the Socialist Party and resented the CPLA's assessment of it as reformist; Josephine Colby had drawn closer to the Communist Party and now regretted Brookwood's decision to bar party members as students; David Saposs and J. C. Kennedy feared that the CPLA was becoming a sectarian organization, and that its association with Brookwood would undercut the college's influence in the labor movement.[50]

Thus, soon after the CPLA's 1932 Labor Day convention, faculty pointedly challenged Muste to choose between workers' education and the CPLA. When he stressed the latter commitment, discussions of his possible resignation ensued. Yet faculty were fearful of the financial repercussions that would follow Muste's departure from the institution, and they reached a compromise with him in which they would gradually assume many of his duties, while he would take a one-year leave of absence from chairing the CPLA to pursue a major fund-raising campaign for Brookwood. Further complicating matters was the CPLA's resistance to granting Muste a leave of absence for they too wanted him exclusively for their organization. After a month of negotiations, the CPLA finally agreed to free Muste from administrative and fund-raising responsibilities, though he would continue to attend executive meetings and serve as chairman on the organizational letterhead.[51]

The compromise was an ambiguous one, and it quickly led to controversy. In mid-January, the faculty accused him of violating their agreement to keep the two groups separate when they discovered that he continued to preside over executive meetings of the CPLA. In light of this disagreement, a full meeting of the board of directors was set for March 3–5, 1933. With this respite, Muste departed for a planned three-week tour of Ohio to help plan for the upcoming state convention of the Ohio UCL. In the meantime, Louis Stanley, a Socialist militant and former member of the CPLA, published a book review of a series of Brookwood pamphlets in the *New Republic* in which he observed that they should properly be seen as CPLA publications since Brookwood was "indistinguishable" from the CPLA. With the support of board director Fannia Cohn, Pollak, Saposs, and Kennedy released a public statement of protest that included copies of their recent resignations from the CPLA.[52]

The disagreement had now become "irreconcilable," as Muste put it upon returning to Brookwood. Tom Tippett, engaged in extension activities in Illinois, accused his colleagues of violating Brookwood's long-standing policy of working problems out among themselves. Jack Lever, an alumni board member, called on Saposs to disavow the public statement, charging that he had been "carried away by the arguments of a hysterical woman [i.e., Pollak]." Staff and students soon took positions on the dispute, with most siding with Muste and Tippett, and demanded that there be an open meeting to discuss the situation. In the two public meetings that followed, the faculty—with the exception of Tippett and Kohn—repeated their accusation that Muste had violated their agreement to keep Brookwood and the CPLA separate, and they maintained that Brookwood was best served by maintaining its policy of political independence.[53]

For his part, Muste rejected his colleagues' argument that they were concerned with Brookwood's economic stability and institutional integrity. In an atypical display of immodesty, he asserted that it was largely through his actions and status alone that any and all money had been raised for the school and that accounted for its reputation as "the outstanding institution in the American workers' education movement, known not only all over this country but all over the world." He suggested further that Saposs, Pollak, and Kennedy had in fact shown a reckless disregard for the school in widely releasing the January memo, which they must have known "might have an unfortunate effect upon Brookwood contributors and would make the work of money-raising for Brookwood more difficult." He could only conclude that they sent the memo either out of a malicious desire to "wreck both Brookwood and the CPLA" or that "they did not have the sense to realize all this, in which case they [were] plain numbskulls."[54]

Muste further argued that the real issue had to do with Brookwood's move "into the field," and he maintained that to thoroughly disentangle the college from the CPLA would be to retreat from the field of struggle and take "an exceedingly dangerous turn to the right." In making his argument, Muste pointed out that, from its inception, Brookwood "has had a point of view, philosophy . . . of its own," even as it stressed the need for labor unity and sought to foster an educational atmosphere "where free discussion and criticism prevailed." Over the years, "crises have come and decisions have been made," and those decisions had always been to move to the left, rather than to the right. Brookwood had, moreover, never espoused liberal notions of academic freedom and nonpartisanship. The college's decision to hold its ground against the AFL, for example, was not in the service of "academic freedom, impartiality, and objectivity," but rather its right to have its own vision of the labor movement, that "whatever the A.F. of L. might say or do, Brookwood would be a place where, for example, the Red Flag was sung and the anniversary of the Russian Revolution was observed."[55]

Muste concluded by insisting that his own vision for Brookwood was true to the stand the college had taken in 1929, to advance "a particular kind of labor movement" and to select faculty, staff, and students on the basis of "their willingness, enthusiasm and ability to take part in such a task," regardless of political affiliation. To retreat from the field and adopt a philosophy of "non-partisanship" would isolate the college from the working class and would lead it to the right. Brookwood faculty would descend "to the level of the typical school ma'am. They may have opinions of their own, but if so, they will be careful not to express them. . . . It would be 'the seminary of a sect,' a sect of male and female young ladies."[56]

For the next several weeks, Brookwood was divided into hostile camps as the college readied for the board of directors' meeting on March 4. Muste knew that the odds were not in his favor, with four of the five faculty votes, as well as "labor directors" Lefkowitz, Cohn, and Maurer, certain to be against him. Yet he thought he had a good chance of persuading A. J. Kennedy and John Brophy, also on the board, to support him. Much to his dismay, however, only four of the ten labor directors attended the meeting: Lefkowitz, Cohn, Maurer, and Phil Ziegler, with the latter serving as chairman because he was acceptable to both sides. When the board voted the next day, it was fifteen to four against Muste. Muste and Tippett resigned immediately, taking the entire staff and nineteen of the twenty-eight students with them; most alumni sided with them as well.[57]

It is difficult to assess the Brookwood controversy because, as Muste's response to faculty criticism suggests, personality and emotions became involved. Muste clearly had a sense of proprietary rights over Brookwood, and his pride was wounded by the faculty's revolt against his leadership. Feelings of jealousy and resentment on the part of Saposs and Pollak—and to a lesser extent J. C. Kennedy and Polly Colby—also clearly mingled with genuine concern for the college's future. The college's precarious financial status further contributed to the conflict, though whether Muste could legitimately be held responsible for the situation is an open question. Surely his work for the CPLA compromised the amount of time he could spend fund-raising for Brookwood; yet, as the faculty and board of directors well knew, many of the college's most reliable donors gave to the college out of personal loyalty to Muste. The threat from the Garland Fund had less to do with Brookwood's move to the left, as Muste's critics implied, and more to do with its move to the center with its exclusion of Communists; losing Muste would only further compromise this crucial source of funding.[58]

Ultimately, the question came down to whether or not Muste and the CPLA had in fact become "sectarian," for Muste was correct in observing that Brookwood had always been partisan and that its evolution had been to the left. It does appear that Muste's prophetic inclinations, dormant since the Lawrence strike, had returned; close friends commented that he had "a sort of mystical, prophetic sense of his own mission, which made all else secondary," including the well-being of his family.[59] There was also a decided shift in Muste's personality toward intolerance of other opinions. In his rebuttal to faculty criticism, Muste was eloquent as usual, but he also departed from certain ethical standards that had guided his public career, referring to his opponents as "numbskulls" and sarcastically invoking George Bernard Shaw's dictum "Those who can, do; those who can't, teach." When Colby interjected with "I object," Muste retorted, "Go ahead and object, then." Muste later recalled that this was the "only time I can recall having been consciously malicious. . . . I regretted it then and I do now. It was one of those moments in a controversy when you sense that it cannot be 'patched up' anymore."[60] Colby and other faculty were left "rubbing their eyes and wondering if their colleague and comrade A. J. is this

A. J. with whom we are confronted." Abe Lefkowitz was similarly shocked by the "aspersions" Muste cast on his opponents: "I can only regret that honest partisanship and a perplexing economic and political situation seems to have upset the equanimity of one of the finest and most unselfish of persons it has been my great privilege to meet—A. J. Muste."[61] These observations cannot be taken lightly, coming as they did from men and women who had worked with Muste for many years and who loved and admired him.

As for the CPLA, regardless of Muste's claims to the contrary, the decision to define it as *the* left-wing vanguard was a departure from the more catholic spirit that had motivated its founding. Indeed, what appears to have really upset Lefkowitz and other Brookwooders was Muste's conflation of "left" with the CPLA, which was precisely the attitude that they resented in Communist Party members.[62] All "Brookwooders" considered themselves socialists and revolutionaries, but they had different ideas about how socialism should and would be accomplished in the United States; a broadly based and vaguely defined CPLA had allowed all of them to participate, while a more clearly defined theoretical position and rigid membership criteria excluded them. Similarly, the CPLA's status as a political organization made it a competitor with other left-wing groups; as we have seen, both the Communists and the Socialists resented the CPLA's emergence as a political rival and sought various ways to undermine its growing power and influence, including threatening Brookwood's grant from the Garland Fund. The faculty's prediction that Muste and the CPLA would fall prey to sectarianism was also prescient: two years later, Muste would take the organization into a merger with the Trotskyist Communist League of America, despite the opposition of many of his most dedicated supporters, which led it into a morass of factionalism and ultimate collapse.

On the other hand, Muste was not alone in casting aspersions on his opponents. The decision by Saposs, Kennedy, and Pollak to release the January statement without the approval of the full faculty was an underhanded move that undermined Muste, Brookwood, and the CPLA. And throughout the entire controversy, neither they nor their student supporters ever produced any evidence to suggest that Muste had attempted to indoctrinate students into the CPLA, though, of course, his political affiliations were well known. As for the CPLA, relative to the Socialist and Communist parties, the organization was quite restrained in its criticism of other groups, taking seriously Muste's admonition to focus on action over criticism. Certainly David Saposs and J. C. Kennedy were hypocritical in accusing Muste of being critical of the Socialist Party; for years they had helped to construct the CPLA's assessment of its left-wing alternatives. The CPLA's aims and methods also remained essentially the same as they had always been: a commitment to flexibility and Americanism in its approach to organizing workers, and to building a united front with other groups.[63]

Moreover, whether his faculty opponents were conscious of it or not, Muste was correct that his ouster was part of a larger political realignment. In challenging Muste, they were forced into an alliance with Cohn, Maurer, and Lefkowitz, who held that Brookwood should retreat from the field. In their decision in favor of the majority faculty position, the board effectively sidestepped Muste's argument that nonpartisanship was an impossible and essentially reactionary ideal and asserted that Brookwood confine itself to educational activities and avoid controversy. Determined to remain independent of the AFL and various left-wing parties, the board selected Tucker P. Smith, a Socialist and pacifist who had never even led a strike, to replace Muste as director. Without ties to organized labor and with most alumni siding with Muste, the college quickly assumed a Socialist Party identity, including its opposition to the New Deal and its Anglo and middle-class cast. Whereas in the 1920s, almost all of Brookwood's student body far exceeded the requirements of having three years of experience in industry and two years of union membership, by 1934, an increasing number came from middle-class backgrounds, had graduated from high school, and some had even attended college (including two young ministers!).[64]

At the same time that Smith assumed the directorship, the country entered the New Deal. With Brookwood's opposition to "taking stands" and to aligning with the federal government, it could only watch from the sidelines as some of its most experienced faculty and alumni assumed roles in the new federal bureaucracy. Meanwhile, unions began to distance themselves from the college because of its association with critics of the Roosevelt administration. Support from the Socialist Party allowed Brookwood to survive until 1936 when the party split apart over the question of support for Roosevelt and the New Deal, with the "Old Guard" breaking away into the Social Democratic Federation and endorsing Roosevelt and the remaining Socialists descending into factionalism. The Socialist Party declined precipitously thereafter, while the Communist Party assumed greater visibility as it entered its dynamic Popular Front period. Without the support of the Socialists, Brookwood began to collapse.[65]

Smith recognized the potential of allying Brookwood with the newly established Congress of Industrial Organizations (CIO). After all, Brookwooders held a prominent place in the new federation; Brophy, Clint Golden, Pollak, Len De Caux, Julius Hochman, Rose Pesotta, Victor Reuther, among others, all held high office in the new organization, while countless alumni served as officers or loyal members of the revitalized labor movement. Yet John L. Lewis, not surprisingly, was indifferent to Smith's appeals, while individual unions lacked the funds to contribute to Brookwood and were probably more interested in establishing their own educational programs. The school's Socialist identity did not help, as Communists in the CIO regarded Brookwood with suspicion. By March 1937, the school was forced to close.[66]

In the end, a larger hegemonic process was at work. Unions and the federal government initiated workers' educational and cultural programs, often run by faculty and alumni of the workers' education movement, as well as former members of the CPLA, to tie workers to unionism.[67] Historians have illustrated the dynamic character of this cultural front, showing how the CIO and its radical supporters redefined the United States as multiethnic, working class, and antifascist. They have also highlighted its engagement with modern forms of communication and entertainment, both in terms of its cultural production and theory.[68] Yet they have yet to recognize the role of the workers' education movement, which extended far beyond Brookwood, as well as Muste and the CPLA, in pioneering this cultural front.

Sadly, just as the end of World War II led to the narrowing of political discourse and the decimation of the Popular Front, workers' education became similarly constrained in the postwar era. Unions and universities, which established "labor education" extension courses, focused on training workers in the technical skills of union membership and leadership. "Missing from the discourse of labor education was the intense discussion of the problems facing the labor movement, the path of organization of the unorganized, and the possibilities for a 'new social order,' the staples of the workers' education movement," one historian has commented.[69]

In relaying the Brookwood split in his "Sketches for an Autobiography," Muste observed that "there were underlying ideological issues which were not by any means fully discussed or perhaps even realized at the time." He noted that, with two exceptions, all the faculty on both sides of the dispute soon thereafter found positions in the Roosevelt administration or in unions loyal to the Democratic Party "and, after Roosevelt's 'quarantine the aggressors' speech in 1936, supported his foreign policy and, eventually, United States entry into World War II." The same would be true of many of the Musteites who remained in the movement through its alliance with the Trotskyists; one by one, they would make the pragmatic decision to pursue a social democratic path through union activism and the Popular Front. Muste himself would be offered the directorship of the FERA regional program in Atlanta and probably could have obtained the position of educational director of the steelworkers' union. Yet, for Muste, "to have become identified with the New Deal, with the C.I.O. top leadership and, presently, with support of the war—this would have been for me the abandonment of my deepest convictions—even though that was not altogether obvious at the time." "Of necessity," then, "my 'detour' had to be Left."[70]

In early 1933, of course, this was all in the future. At the time, for Muste as for other radicals, it seemed a moment of crisis and conjuncture when a new world was in the making, akin to the American Revolution or the Civil War. Roosevelt had just assumed the presidency, but "the actual conditions were still much the same as in the panic years. Only the atmosphere was different, because there was an impression that the situation was now mobile. But where things were going was still wholly unclear." Muste continued, "the nation was in a state of civil war . . . a war in which every city and section of the country was rent with deep cleavages and in which there was a good deal of fighting, though the guns were almost entirely in the hands of the police and the National Guard."[71] With his resignation from Brookwood, he was now free to dedicate himself full-time to the class war. In his characteristic style, he called on his comrades to refrain from discussing the Brookwood controversy, and instead to throw themselves "unreservedly into action," commenting that "not in years have I felt so much happiness as I do now. . . . Forward then with renewed vigor all along the line! In Unemployed work! In strikes! In organizing the unorganized! . . . Forward to the overthrow of capitalism and the establishment of the workers' republic!" For the next two years, Muste's life would be "marked by intense and almost uninterrupted participation in the mass struggles of that period . . . and equally intense and seemingly continuous involvement in political discussion and maneuvering."[72]

Underneath his claims to "happiness," however, was an uncertainty about the path he had chosen. In later years, he recalled this period as one of exhilaration, but also of suffering and distress, and speculated that he was in the midst of a midlife crisis that was compounded by the trauma and uncertainty of the Great Depression. "The age at which I left Brookwood is said for a good many to be a 'dangerous' one, bringing with it strains, and perhaps catastrophes, in marital and family relationships." While the experience was "painful" for all, "we bore in together. Within the family circle there was no storm, only mutual support against the storm we had run into."[73]

We have, of course, only Muste's perspective and not that of Anne or their three children. Their lives were profoundly upset by his break from Brookwood, as it involved the disintegration of a community in which they had lived for twelve years; in the intimate and communal atmosphere of the college, they had forged deep bonds with people who now occupied hostile camps. That the break occurred in the middle of the school year made the experience even more emotionally wrenching. After quickly packing up their belongings, the Mustes relied on the charity of friends in New York City who allowed them to live rent-free for several months until they found other accommodations. Forced to move yet again soon thereafter, they finally found semipermanent housing in the summer of 1934, when they settled in the Amalgamated Houses in the Bronx, cooperative apartments developed by the ACW in the late 1920s.[74] Their income remained precarious; paid only a "marginal maintenance" salary by the CPLA, Muste wrote urgent letters to Brookwood demanding back pay, but to no avail. His old comrades in the FOR provided some support, and his benefactors Anna Davis and Elizabeth Glendower Evans also provided crucial assistance.[75]

Revealingly, Davis's and Evans's financial support was accompanied by critical commentary on the choices Muste had made, particularly their consequences for his family. Indeed, the Brookwood controversy and its aftermath appears to have adversely affected Anne's already precarious health; in a 1935 letter to Evans asking for help paying the month's rent, Muste commented that she was no longer "in condition to bear shocks of this kind as she used to be." Evans's promises of support for Nancy's college education helped to sustain Anne, as she had long hoped that her oldest child would have the opportunity to attend Swarthmore College.[76]

Anne had also long reconciled herself to a life as "the wife of a crazy radical agitator," and appears to have focused her energies on providing emotional stability and nurturance to Nancy, Constance, and John.[77] Muste was not alone in observing that the family held together well during the "storm." Despite her frustration with Muste for his "unreasonable" behavior at Brookwood and neglect of his family's well-being, Anna Davis commented in a private letter to Evans that the Mustes were "holding true as a family through thick and thin." Perhaps Anne Muste shared with Davis and Evans the view that her husband, notwithstanding his faults, was "a saint . . . like Jesus Christ." Certainly Nancy Muste seems have been inculcated with such a view: in her letter thanking Evans for her help with college expenses, she commented, "Of course I can't expect to be like my father, but I will try to be worthy of him."[78]

CHAPTER 7

୬

To the Left

This whole Social Democratic tendency and philosophy I
am against as I have ever been against anything in my life.
I think I have always, since 1916, been a revolutionist and
not a Social Democrat.

— A. J. Muste, circa 1931

OVER THE COURSE of 1933, Muste and other CPLA leaders made preparations to transform the organization into a revolutionary party. Experience had taught them that the other parties competing for the allegiance of workers and radicals were too consumed by the 1919 split of the Socialist Party and events in the Soviet Union. It was time for a new, fresh approach, free from the entanglements of the past, and rooted in the experiences of American workers. As Calverton remarked to Muste in October 1933, he was "convinced that we are on the right track and that it is you, with the healthy American organization as the CPLA behind you which should take the initiative in the creation of a genuine American radical party. I don't know anyone in the Labor movement . . . who is better situated than you to take the lead in this project."[1] Two months later, the CPLA launched the American Workers Party (AWP). In contrast to third-party formations, like the Farmer-Labor movement, the AWP was not intended to be a mass party, but rather to unify and coordinate the activities of Musteites in mass organizations. In the Leninist perspective they had adopted, they hoped to eventually earn the confidence of American workers, so that, if and when revolutionary conditions emerged, they would have the moral authority to lead them in the overthrow of capitalism.[2]

The formation of the AWP reveals a centralizing tendency within the Musteite movement. The party's membership criteria stiffened, admitting only those who had renounced other political affiliations and who were engaged in "mass activity." While the party would continue to express its commitment to democratic procedures within mass organizations, it now called on members to more aggressively push them toward the adoption of revolutionary platforms. While the party continued to insist that the "demands of mass organizations grow out of local conditions," it also now aimed for a certain level of "uniformity" across the country to prepare workers for eventual leadership by the AWP; thus, "when the AWP raises these issues, the workers will readily accept them because they have already adopted them."[3]

Still, the values that had governed the CPLA from its inception remained central to the AWP's politics and identity. As its name suggests, it remained committed to developing strategies based on the economic, political, and historical context of the United States, as well as the cultural traditions of American workers. Just as Americanism remained important, so did its pragmatic commitment to building revolutionary consciousness through action and experience. The party would refuse to lay down a set of principles and policies "for which we claim perfection and infallibility," Hardman explained in a speech at the founding convention of the AWP. "We mean to evolve our procedure as we go along." Fundamentally, the AWP believed that "fight is the best preparatory training school for acquiring strength" and that power grows "out of the day-in, day-out struggles" of workers, not "devotion to conspirative [sic] methods." It would be a party, "not of dogmatists, not of fanatics, not of conspirators," but of militant workers.[4]

Hardman's emphasis on the AWP's pragmatic creed can be seen as part of a larger struggle for control over the movement that began to emerge in 1934. Early that year, the Trotskyist Communist League of America (CLA) proposed that the two groups join forces, a question that deeply divided the Musteites. In the face of considerable opposition, Muste would use his prestige to obtain the merger, in the process forsaking his movement and many of his closest comrades. Later, he would suggest that he had been duped by the Trotskyists, who reneged on certain promises. This account, while factually accurate, conveniently overlooks the fact that he had been repeatedly warned by Hardman, Budenz, and others that the Trotskyists would be unable to overcome their sectarian heritage and orientation. Why,

FIGURE 5. An International Newsreel Photo of A. J. Muste announcing
the formation of the American Workers Party in March 1934.
(*Friends Historical Library of Swarthmore College*)

then, did Muste support the merger? One explanation, as suggested in the
previous chapter, is that he had come to share the CLA's position that
theoretical purity—in contrast to pragmatism and flexibility—would preclude "fallacies" such as social democracy to which Muste had become
fundamentally opposed.

Another explanation, not mutually exclusive of the first, is that the personal crisis that he entered upon his break from Brookwood had deepened. As comments by his faculty colleagues suggest, his messianic tendencies had reemerged and grown stronger. Intimately related to this change was his estrangement from the Christian pacifist faith that had served as a source of guidance and strength for him as he had navigated the controversies and personalities of the labor left since 1919. As we have seen, Muste had developed a critique of organized pacifism as early as the Lawrence strike, when he rejected the movement's emphasis on individual conscientious objection as the path to social change, as well as its reluctance to support labor unions and strikes. Still, throughout the 1920s, he continued to identify as "a Christian" and remained active in the FOR. It was the onset of the Great Depression that pushed him deeper into the secular left. As he recalled, it was "the people who adopted some form of Marxian philosophy, who were *doing something* about the situation, who were banding people together for action, who were putting up a fight. Unless you were indifferent or despairing, you lined up with them."[5] The left, moreover, "had the vision, the dream, of a classless and warless world, as the hackneyed phrase goes. This was a strong favor in making me feel that here, in a sense, was the true church."[6] Not coincidentally, when Muste returned to pacifism in 1936, he would come to see his experiences with the Trotskyists as a parable for the limitations of the secular left, the labor movement, and, to some degree, the humanist project as a whole. As he would argue, the Enlightenment's emphasis on reason, science, and historical progress marginalized precisely the values of love, empathy, and cooperation that revolutionaries claimed would predominate in a socialist society.

WITH the formation of the AWP, a series of Communist Party splinter groups immediately began to show an interest in merging their forces with the party, including the Trotskyist CLA, headed by Max Shachtman and James Cannon. The CLA had its origins in Joseph Stalin's consolidation of power in the Soviet Union and over the Communist International. In 1928, the party expelled Cannon, Shachtman, and others who sympathized with Leon Trotsky and his criticism of Stalinist leadership and "Russia comes first" policy. The CLA initially hoped that the CP and the Soviet Union could be reformed. By 1933, however, with the triumph of Nazism in Germany, Trotsky called on his followers to prepare for the formation of a Fourth International to compete with the Communist Third International and "to attract and recruit the new layers of workers . . . and to begin building parties that could provide a revolutionary alternative to the Stalinist movement."[7]

Such was the background that led the CLA to seek out the AWP. Intellectuals like Sidney Hook and James Burnham, who were relative newcomers to the party, tended to support the merger in the belief that the CLA would bring a theoretical sophistication lacking in the movement.[8] Longtime Musteites, by contrast, tended to view the CLA suspiciously, particularly outside the environs of New York City. Among other reasons, they argued that the Trotskyists had few connections to industrial workers; that their emphasis on continual revolution and internationalism would compromise the AWP's "American approach"; and that their origins as a faction of the CP had made them destructively negative, dogmatic, and obsessed with the Soviet Union.[9]

Muste appeared to agree with much of this criticism. He was especially concerned by the CLA's criticism of the "American approach" as nationalistic. Over the course of late 1933 through the summer of 1934, he penned a series of articles that almost certainly were directed at the CLA in which he argued that internationalism was imperative, but that there was also the "danger . . . of becoming sentimental and unrealistic in this matter of labor internationalism. . . . An International with nothing but weak and insignificant national sections is only a thing of paper, a discussion group that exercises no real influence over events." Since revolutionaries aimed, presumably, to obtain state power, they had to recognize and adapt their tactics to the "certain conditions . . . certain background, tradition, psychology" of the American people, even while guiding them toward a more international consciousness.[10]

In spite of these misgivings, Muste aligned with Hook and Burnham and supported pursuing negotiations with the CLA, assuring skeptics that the final decision on a merger would be left to the membership to vote up or down. He also obtained the CLA's promise that it would "not persist as a bloc or a faction within the AWP," if and when a merger obtained. With these conditions met, the AWP set up a committee to begin negotiations.[11] But just as the two groups began discussions, the tremendous labor upheavals of 1934 intervened, ripping "the cloak of civilized decorum from society, leaving exposed naked class conflict." In 1934, "a new militancy and solidarity among American working people appeared," as epic labor battles and general strikes inspired radicals to hope that revolution was on the horizon.[12]

Among the most important of these occurred in Toledo, Ohio, a city that had been hit hard by the Depression, with upwards of 80 percent of its population unemployed. In April 1934, for the second time in three months, AFL Federal Labor Union Local 18384 struck the city's Electric Auto-Lite Company, an auto-parts manufacturer, and two smaller related firms. Striking workers charged that the companies had violated an agreement to set up collective bargaining machinery by April 1. With only a minority of workers on strike and the determined opposition of the manufacturers, the strike had scant chance of victory until the Lucas County Unemployed League entered the scene.[13]

As in the rest of Ohio, the Lucas County Unemployed League had a strong presence in the city, belying later accounts that downplay its influence or describe it as dominated by "outside agitators." Headed by Ohioans Ted Selander, Sam Pollock, and Art Preis, who referred to themselves as the "Three *Muste*-teers," the league had been active in Toledo for over a year; Pollock had in fact worked briefly at one of the struck plants until he was fired after joining the union. The Unemployed Leagues had long emphasized working-class solidarity by supporting strikes and dissuading the jobless from scabbing.[14] Reflecting this policy, the Lucas County Unemployed League joined the picket lines outside the factory gates. When the city issued an injunction limiting twenty-five pickets to each factory gate, the league exhibited its flair for direct action by refusing to obey the order, stating that it was "an abrogation of our democratic rights" and that it contravened "the spirit and letter of Section 7-A of the NIRA [National Industrial Recovery Act]" guaranteeing workers the right to bargain collectively. Two days later, on May 7, Selander and Pollock, along with two union members, defied the injunction. The four were arrested, charged with contempt of court, and released the next day. Returning immediately to the picket line, they were now joined by dozens more strikers. A few days later, forty-six pickets were arrested, including Selander and Pollock. At the trial, hundreds of union members and sympathizers showed up and "took possession of the courthouse and cheered and sang while Selander from the witness stand expounded the principles of militant labor." In a confused and indecisive ruling, the judge released the men upon which "the crowd lifted them to their shoulders and bore them off as heroes."[15]

Over the next two weeks, tensions grew on the picket line. Auto-Lite purchased $11,000 worth of munitions and hired armed guards to protect the hundreds of strikebreakers now working in the plant. By then, Muste and Budenz had arrived to help direct the league's activities and to assist in the strike. The strike quickly took on the distinctive features of the Musteite movement, with signs that that said "1776–1865–1934" and "Don't Tread on Me," and with the use of militant, confrontational tactics such as mass picketing, mass meetings, and defiance of injunctions as means of inspiring and mobilizing workers. The strategy worked; by May 23, the crowd in front of factory gates had grown to six thousand people. With the local police clearly sympathetic to the strikers, Lucas County's sheriff decided that it was now time to "take the offensive." He immediately deputized special police, paid for by Auto-Lite, and arrested Budenz and four other pickets. By now, the crowd had grown to ten thousand. When a deputy began beating an older man in the crowd, the "battle of Toledo" was on. As Muste described the scene for the *Nation*, strikebreakers "were rushed out of the plant and [police] turned streams of water on the crowd, which then forced the strikebreakers back into the building with showers of bricks. Deputies who had also retreated to the factory then unloosed the gas attack." The fighting continued from midafternoon through midnight, with scores of injuries.[16]

The fight resumed and intensified the next day. At dawn, with most of the protesters home asleep, 900 Ohio National Guard troops arrived to evacuate the 1,500 strikebreakers from the plant. But within hours, the crowd had returned, taunting and throwing bricks at the troops, who responded with tear gas. The crowd advanced twice, managing to force the troops into the factory, only to be pushed back by a bayonet charge. On the third advance, the troops fired their rifles into the crowd; two men were killed and fifteen others were wounded. But the crowd refused to disperse and rushed the factory once more later that evening, again meeting gunfire. With that, the adjutant general ordered four more National Guard companies to the scene and shut down the factory. In observing the bloody confrontation, labor journalist Heywood Broun commented that it was the closest thing to revolution that had ever occurred in the United States.[17]

Sporadic fighting continued over the next several weeks as the city elite and Charles P. Taft of the Labor Department sought to find a resolution to the conflict. Taft and his fellow mediators conducted their negotiations carefully, making sure to marginalize the Unemployed League and the AWP by dubbing them as "outsiders" and constructing the dispute as strictly a collective bargaining matter between the company and AFL Federal Labor Union Local 18384. An agreement was finally reached on June 4 that signaled a victory for collective bargaining, while also making an allowance for strikebreakers. As Muste and Budenz commented, the settlement represented "an outstanding victory for the workers . . . a union contrast now exists—the first in the automobile industry." It was, indeed, a "tribute" to the militant methods of labor organization that the Musteites had long advocated, though they also recognized certain weaknesses in the agreement.[18]

Historians consider the Toledo Auto-Lite strike a watershed victory in the history of organized labor that helped lead to the birth of the United Auto Workers. The role of the unemployed was pivotal; as Muste observed, it was the violation of the injunction that reenergized the strike and led to the "battle of Toledo."[19] Contemporaries concurred; as publisher Roy Howard explained in a letter to Franklin Roosevelt's secretary, "The point about Toledo was this: that it was nothing new to see organized unemployed appear in the streets, fight police and raise hell in general. But usually they do this for their own ends. . . . At Toledo they appeared on the picket line to help striking employees win a strike, tho' you would expect their interest would lie the other way."[20] Unbeknownst to Roy Howard, of course, was that the leagues had long provided solidarity to striking workers, a fact that may have given them the confidence to strike in the midst of high unemployment.

A few days after the Toledo strike, Muste and two miners who were members of the AWP were arrested in Belleville, Illinois, while talking to pickets on strike at an auto-parts plant. Jailed on the charge of vagrancy and "conspiring to overthrow the United States government," bail was set at $20,000 for Muste and $10,000 each for his comrades. After several days, the AWP finally raised enough money to bail them out; the vagrancy charge was dropped during the preliminary hearing, but the treason charge hung over Muste's head for another year. Muste and his comrades returned to the state a few weeks later to protest "the reign of repression and terrorism" and to present their program to the workers and farmers of the state.[21]

INCIDENTS like his arrest in Belleville and the Toledo strike confirmed Muste in his analysis that the "workers' revolution" was imminent, and his approach to organizing and party building became more controlling. Whereas he had always insisted that the Unemployed Leagues, like unions and other mass organizations, be open to all regardless of political affiliation, he now urged AWP members to deliberately shape their politics and ideology, so as to prevent them from becoming "devoted to mere self-preservation, to become 'pure and simple' unions of the unemployed, bargaining for favors with relief authorities." His language also changed from its tenor of openness and contingency toward firmness and severity. The Unemployed Leagues must have the "correct" approach to mass organizations; mistakes and "dangerous tendencies" (i.e., social democracy) must be faced and "immediately and ruthlessly corrected," he instructed AWP members, while at the same time insisting that "we do not seek domination. We abhor mechanical control and political trickery."[22]

Underlying this change was Muste's growing hostility toward and fears of social democracy—for the Unemployed Leagues had in fact borne out his theory that experience and action served as the foundations for militancy and class consciousness. But they had not become revolutionary; much like the labor revolt that would give birth to the CIO, their politics tended toward social democracy rather than communism. The appeal of President Roosevelt's works programs and the National Industrial Recovery Act, which empowered the president to regulate industry, compounded Muste's frustrations. In article after article, he called the New Deal so much "ballyhoo" that benefitted capital and not labor.[23] As a result, he became disillusioned with the idea of building a mass labor party, and the creation of a revolutionary vanguard assumed primary importance.

The rise of fascism in Europe and the growing specter of another world war added to Muste's sense of urgency. Over the course of 1933 and 1934, the party's organ (now called *Labor Action*) dedicated pages of ink exploring the origins and development of fascism and calling on labor and all left-wing parties to join forces to militantly combat it.[24] In contrast to later in the decade, when he rarely discussed the subject, Muste published a long series of articles excoriating fascism as nationalist, anti-Semitic, misogynistic, and antilabor. His alarm intensified as fascism triumphed in Germany and Austria, suppressing the labor movement and laying waste to once powerful Socialist and Communist parties. He was especially critical of Socialist parliamentarianism, which he contended had compromised their ability to respond with proper militancy to the fascist threat. As he explained, the failures of the European social democracy demonstrated the urgent need to recruit and unify "all advanced workers" into a revolutionary vanguard.[25]

Muste's growing revolutionary fervor and ambitions for the AWP help to explain his support for the merger with the CLA. Over the summer, while he and Budenz had focused their energies on mass action, Burnham and Hook had been busy responding to the CLA's criticisms of the AWP—that it failed to "formulate properly the nature of the state"; failed to offer "principled" criticism of the Socialist Party and the Communist Party; and inadequately articulated its international position.[26] As Hook tangled with the CLA over the question of the state, Burnham drafted the AWP's "position on the international question." Burnham's subsequently released memo caused considerable discontent in the ranks; his highly theoretical language, his use of terms like "correct" and "error," and his focus on the Soviet Union confirmed suspicions that the very process of negotiating with the CLA would infect the AWP with the poison of sectarianism.[27] After reading it, Harry Howe wrote to Hardman of his fears that "we are moving in the direction of that sectarianism which we have so vociferously denied. . . . Are we also to become revolutionary theologians, lunatics who spend their time debating the number of Leninist angels that can dance on the point of a dialectic needle?" It seemed to him that the party was "going 'left' . . . so fast that we will also soon be conducting the revolution from . . . the dining room of the Albert Hotel. . . . I am getting pretty much fed up on this business of competing with all the other little groups for revolutionary purity." Hardman concurred, observing that newcomers to the movement appeared to view themselves as "Leninist angels" and rank-and-file Musteites as "the simple Americans."[28]

More substantial criticism issued from the Los Angeles branch of the AWP. As it correctly observed, the memo represented a "complete 'about face' from what has been the position of the party since its birth." The CPLA and AWP had always stood for "friendship" with the Soviet Union and had criticized the Communist Party on the basis of its tactics, not its principles. They further argued that the memo's call for supporting anti-Stalinists in the Soviet Union was akin to "contributing to civil war in the USSR," a position that would force the AWP to focus its energies on "attacking the USSR" and building a new international "rather than concentrating on the American revolution." It would additionally compromise efforts at a united front with other left groups, thereby making the AWP a faction, precisely what the party had wanted to avoid.[29]

In fact, the AWP leadership remained divided over the question of unifying with the CLA. On August 30, 1934, the Committee on Negotiations with the CLA reported that it was unable to submit a unanimous recommendation; even Hook and Burnham, who continued to support the merger, conceded that there was a "danger" in the CLA's "lack of flexibility, in their attachment to conventional phrases rather than to principles." Budenz and Hardman remained unalterably opposed. Budenz was adamant that the CLA would destroy the AWP's distinct approach of focusing on the American context and interpreting Marxism through the prism of pragmatism, as expressed in Hook's *Towards the Understanding of Karl Marx.* "We must stand four-square on *workers' democracy*—on testing all our views and actions on the working class and not on the Party." Hardman reiterated Budenz's analysis, adding that the CLA's commitment to destroying both the Communist and Socialist parties, as was revealed in their negotiations, was not the sort of attitude that would lead to the rejuvenation and reunification of the left. "For the present, the AWP stands out as a non-factional venture in American radicalism, and therefore it is not intensely distrusted as practically every one of the older factions." Rather than force unity, he and Budenz proposed that the two groups "practice" cooperation through united front actions.[30]

Muste's comments on the negotiations are not extant, but his other correspondence and writings suggest that he shared Hook and Burnham's hope that the CLA would strengthen the AWP's theoretical grounding in Marxism and its consciousness as a "party," as opposed to a group of militant workers. At the AWP's Active Workers' Conference, held in September, he informed delegates that the way to build a vanguard party was for members to have a combination of training in the fundamentals of Marxist theory *and* experience in leading mass struggles. As a result of his influence, the conference issued a resolution calling on the two organizations to begin making "concrete steps" toward merger, though a final decision would not be made until late November, when the AWP met for its annual convention.[31]

Still, like Hook and Burnham, Muste had reservations about the CLA's origins as a faction of the CP and feared that its commitment to building a Fourth International to compete with the Third International would take precedence over party building in the United States. He was particularly concerned about the so-called "French Turn," in which French Trotskyists had recently entered the French Socialist Party in an effort to move it to the left. To Muste, such a policy made no sense in the United States, where the SP was hopelessly reformist. Moreover, it was a violation of "working-class ethics" to enter another left-wing party on false pretenses. Having obtained Cannon's assurance that the CLA opposed the French Turn and had no intention of pursuing it in the United States, Muste actively pursued merger.[32]

Over the fall of 1934, the AWP and CLA continued to work out the details of the merger.[33] Cannon and Shachtman would wield considerable influence as editors of the party organ, the *Militant,* and its theoretical arm, the *New International,* respectively, while Muste would serve as national secretary. Despite concessions made on both sides, the draft "statement of principle and action," when it was released in late October, ultimately bore the imprint of the CLA more than the AWP.[34] The statement itself was directed toward the future rather than the present, toward a new international rather than the American working class; it retained the term "dictatorship" to describe its vision for a socialist society and continued to insist that the best defense of the Soviet Union was to support "revolutionists" in the Soviet Union "who fight for the revival of the Communist Party of Lenin's time." As Hardman complained to Louis Breier, a prominent AWP activist, "Our program has been continually modified to the point where it is full of things we do not hold to be true."[35]

It is thus not surprising that opposition to the merger continued to grow as the AWP made preparations to vote on the question at its annual convention, to be held in late November in New York City. After a tour of midwestern branches in October, Breier wrote to another party stalwart, Munsey Gleason, that outside of New York there was "opposition and plenty of it," and he predicted that the party would lose its "really significant members . . . in its move toward unity [with the CLA]."[36] In *Labor Action,* Allen Stiller from the Los Angeles branch wrote a passionate defense of the AWP's original vision and warned that merging with the Trotskyists would "involve us in endless shadow boxing with the Communist Party" and would "destroy the distinctively non-factional character of the AWP."[37] Similarly invoking the AWP's pragmatic creed, William Montross wrote from New Jersey that the AWP had its *own* theory of revolutionary action that was in decided contrast to the CLA's; theory must be tested through and with workers in real struggles, and from the perspective that the role of revolutionaries was "not only to teach the workers, but to learn from the workers as well."[38]

The social history of the CPLA/AWP makes it impossible to dismiss this criticism as that of a minority and to suggest that the "overwhelming majority" of Musteites approved of the merger, as Muste himself claimed, and at least one historian has repeated.[39] Aside from Muste, Budenz,

Hardman, Howe, and Ludwig Lore (who also opposed the merger) were the most important national leaders of the movement. For their part, Montross, Stiller, Breier, and Gleason were among the leading Musteites in the field, and their sentiments were shared to a greater or lesser degree by McKinney, Bill Truax, Larry Heimbach, Arnold Johnson, Mike Demchak, Anthony Ramuglia, Ted Selander, Art Preis, Sam Pollock, and Bill Reich, among others.[40]

One of the frustrations critics of the merger faced was that Budenz was unable to lead an opposition movement. Apparently a psychosomatic, Budenz had attacks of "sinusitis" at moments of controversy and stress. He had an attack back in the spring, when negotiations began, and it returned in full force in October, just as the merger talks intensified. Confined to bed rest, opponents only had Hardman to make their case, but he had been beaten down by endless rounds of negotiations and had resigned himself to leaving the party when the merger occurred. Louis Breier made a last ditch effort to rally the opposition. "I feel justified in stating categorically that if merger is accomplished this November 28, it will be, not because the AWP favored it, but because an organized minority once again was stronger than an unorganized and leaderless majority," he wrote to Gleason, urging him to rally. Due to his efforts, several branches sent resolutions to the national office requesting a postponement of the convention. Allentown, "the lustiest and largest" AWP branch in the country, charged that the decision to hold the conference in New York City as opposed to the Midwest, where the party was strongest, was a deliberate attempt to exclude the rank and file from attending. On the eve of the convention, Breier, McKinney, and Hardman sent a telegram to the AWP's Provisional Organizing Committee calling on them to discontinue holding joint meetings with the CLA until after the AWP convention.[41]

As the Allentown branch predicted, only fifty delegates managed to attend the late November convention. There, the debate over the merger lasted well into the night, with a unanimous vote secured in the early morning hours. The popularity of the merger proposal among New York comrades, as well as personal loyalty to Muste, was no doubt instrumental in securing the convention's assent. Hardman resigned immediately and, over the next year and a half, Howe, Budenz, Ludwig and Karl Lore, Reich, Ramuglia, Truax, Johnson, Breier, and other key Musteites would leave the party, viewing it as hopelessly factional and an impediment to the organization of workers and the unemployed. Even the intellectuals, who had played such an active role in consummating the merger, drifted away from the party. Aside from Burnham, Hook, Calverton, and Rorty in varying degrees moved to the sidelines. Some former Musteites would become members of the Communist Party, which now embraced many of the tenets espoused by the CPLA and AWP, such as the need to take an "American" approach, working within established unions, and pursuing a united front with groups previously dubbed social fascist. Most, however, followed the lead of unionists who had already defected from the CPLA when it decided to remake itself as the AWP; Hardman, Tippett, Lucille Kohn, and Cara Cook, for example, drifted out of organized left-wing politics and served as the loyal foot soldiers of the revitalized labor movement, recognizing that reform and not revolution was the spirit of the day.[42]

If Muste thought that he would be able to control and reform the Trotskyists, he was soon disabused of that notion. As Roy Rosenzweig observed many years ago, the formation of the Workers Party of the United States (WPUS) through a fusion of the AWP and the CLA "represented more of an absorption of the AWP than a merger of that group with the Trotskyists."[43] The WPUS's organizational structure and lexicon was Bolshevik, with a ruling Central Committee, Secretariat, Politburo (a.k.a. Political Committee), and regularly scheduled Plenums. Its Declaration of Principles included some reference to the need for realism and flexibility but overall expressed an orthodox Marxist-Leninist position that was in stark contrast to the more pragmatic Marxism of the AWP and the CPLA. Also absent was any discussion of culture as a crucial site of struggle.[44] Indeed, a more rigid interpretation of Marxism and a more punitive approach to organizing predominated, as party members claimed access to the objective, scientific truth and accused those who disagreed with them—even those within the party—of committing the "fatal" crime of subjectivity.[45]

Moreover, as many Musteites had predicted, the Trotskyists proved unable or unwilling to transcend their roots as a faction of the CP. Cannon admitted as much in his *History of American Trotskyism* when he explained that the CLA merged with the AWP in order "to prevent the Stalinists from swallowing up [the Musteite] movement, and to remove a centrist obstacle from our path by effecting a unity with the proletarian activists and the serious people, isolating the frauds and fakers, and discarding the unassimilable elements." As this quote suggests, former CLA members tended to view Muste and former AWP members with contempt, used deception to push their agenda, and were consumed by theoretical discussions that fostered factionalism and precluded effective organizing and party growth.[46]

The fate of the Musteite Unemployed Leagues after the merger illustrates the authoritarian and sectarian culture of the WPUS. In March 1935, when Musteite organizers arrived for an Active Workers' Conference, they found themselves subject to what even Cannon later described as "an unrestrained free-for-all factional fight. , . . Forty or fifty innocent field workers . . . who had come there looking for a little guidance in their practical work, were treated to discussions and arguments and factional denunciations, lasting all day and night."[47] The following fall, at the October WPUS plenum, the Musteites active in the unemployed movement again found themselves under attack, this time for focusing work around immediate demands rather than developing the party. Such an authoritarian and factional approach "was not compatible with organizing efforts" and "served only to alienate many of the remaining members and to dissipate the energies of the leaders." Soon thereafter, the Unemployed Leagues "for all practical purposes were never heard from again"; the organizers who had started them "dropped out of organizing the unemployed . . . because of disenchantment with factionalism, involvement in new political activities, and a shift to new tasks," such as helping to organize for the CIO.[48]

A similar analysis can be made for the WPUS's efforts in the industrial field. Comrades in the auto and steel industries, for example, rose to leadership positions in strikes and organizing drives only to be chastised by the party leadership for failing to recruit workers into the party. Cannon's assessment of Muste's role in the Toledo Chevrolet strike in May 1935 sums up how the Political Committee viewed its field-workers: "He was a good administrator, and a good mass worker, gaining the confidence of workers very quickly. But he tended to adapt himself to the masses more than a real political leader can afford to do. . . . In practically every case Muste in his mass work did a good job which some other political tendency, less generous and easy-going than Muste, eventually profited by."[49] In fact, all WPUS organizers confronted Muste's dilemma, yet—unlike Cannon—they tended to conclude that the historical moment was a reformist and not a revolutionary one. Cope, McKinney, Pollock, and Tippett, for example, never abandoned their revolutionary ideals, but reconceptualized their role as one of service to the labor movement.[50]

But the primary cause for the infighting that consumed the movement was the question of the "French Turn." Despite assurances to the contrary, the Cannon-Shachtman caucus appears to have been determined to pursue the French Turn as early as the fall of 1934.[51] Never one to back down from a fight, Muste would work hard to prevent the WPUS from dissolving and entering the SP, only to finally be defeated in early 1936. Broken in body and spirit by the tactics his opponents had used against him, which he believed violated "working-class ethics," Muste would come to view the experience as an allegory for a totalitarian impulse in Leninism—and the Enlightenment tradition more broadly.[52]

In the first few months of the WPUS's existence, Muste and Cannon appeared to work well together. Immediately after the founding of the party, Cannon joined with such luminaries of the liberal left as Roger Baldwin, Stuart Chase, George S. Counts, Margaret DeSilver, Max Eastman, John Haynes Holmes, Sidney Hook, Freda Kirchwey, Ludwig Lore, Reinhold Niebuhr, James Rorty, George Soule, Carlo Tresca, Oswald Garrison Villard, and Stephen Wise in sponsoring a "testimonial dinner" in honor of Muste's fiftieth birthday and his years of "invaluable service in the revolutionary labor movement." Three days later, the two men embarked upon a national tour to publicize the WPUS's program and principles.[53]

When they returned, Muste focused on bringing the divergent organizational and ideological cultures of the AWP and CLA together, and in balancing the international emphasis of the former CLA with the domestic orientation of the former AWP.[54] Yet Cannon undermined his efforts by pursuing a slew of disciplinary actions against former AWP members as well as the party's left wing. In June, when Cannon proposed that the party unite with left-wing Socialists to form a "single independent party," Muste became convinced that he was engaged in a "duplicitous" and "deliberate" campaign to rid the party of opponents of the French Turn and to evade political discussions. Charging them with using "stupid, factional, brutal, individualistic, and unprincipled methods," Muste managed to pass several resolutions making the party more democratic and inclusive.[55]

The main focus of his efforts, however, was the prevention of the French Turn. He managed to win the first round, but Cannon and Shachtman continued to raise the issue and party factionalism intensified.[56] Meanwhile, once-vibrant branches, such as the one in Allentown, Pennsylvania became wracked with internal dissension as participation in "mass activity" declined and members quit in discouragement.[57] No doubt adding to Muste's distress was the recent death of Larry Hogan, one of his most devoted followers, in a car accident while on his way to a strike meeting in Durham. Against huge obstacles, Hogan had continued to organize southern industrial workers and poor farmers, providing a foundation for the massive textile strikes that began in 1933. To Muste, Hogan exemplified the revolutionary potential of the working class, if only the WPUS properly recruited and developed them.[58]

The struggle intensified in the months and weeks before the December 1935 convention. In late October, the party expelled its left wing, which led to further defections. Meanwhile, Muste accused Cannon of violating party discipline by failing to consult him before publishing articles on the French Turn and the Socialist Party. Muste was further angered by revelations that Cannon had sent a secret report to Trotsky asserting that Muste opposed entering the SP because he had yielded "to the pressure of the conservative and even reactionary tendencies of some of the former AWP elements on the question of internationalism."[59] The rift between Muste and Cannon deepened when the latter called for suspending comrades in the Allentown branch because they had attended a meeting at which Budenz had been a featured speaker. Surely a censure was adequate, Muste asserted. In a strongly worded resolution, he charged the Cannonites with fostering factionalism by their "negative and formal conception" of Marxism, which held that the way to build the party was through "verbally slugging" the Communist Party, rather than through "positive organizational work." As if to confirm Muste's argument, Cannon replied that the resolution was a reflection of Muste's "treacherous attitude" and policy of "protecting and shielding outright Stalinist, semi-Stalinists." In the end, Muste's resolution lost, the suspensions were carried out, and more Musteites bolted the party.[60]

By the end of December, the struggle had reached epic proportions. Upon learning that the SP was about to split apart, with its Old Guard leaving the party, Cannon and Shachtman successfully moved to postpone the WPUS's annual convention, scheduled for December, first to January and then to February. Muste correctly viewed this move as a ploy to maneuver for the French Turn. Soon thereafter, Cannon introduced a resolution calling on the WPUS to enter the SP. At around the same time, Muste received a letter from a comrade revealing that Cannon had been secretly negotiating with the SP and was determined to enter the party regardless of how the WPUS voted at the convention.[61] In a desperate last stand, Muste appealed to Trotsky via Maurice Spector, the head of the Canadian Workers Party, who was conferring with the International

Secretariat in Europe. On February 8, a cable arrived from Trotsky stating that he supported entering the SP, but only if the decision was unanimous. As Shachtman explained to a comrade, the Trotsky letter was instrumental in pushing Muste to go along with the French Turn. Now he and his allies "walk around like broken men, with an apparently irrepressible suspicion that somebody has been dealing to them from the bottom."[62]

Recognizing that his defeat was now a *fait accompli*, Muste directed his energies into fieldwork. In February, he traveled to Akron, Ohio, where some ten thousand workers at the Goodyear rubber plant were using the new tactic of the "sit-down" strike in an effort to obtain union recognition.[63] In an ironic twist, he found that organizers for the newly formed Congress of Industrial Organizations (CIO) did not welcome his far left perspective, and in fact used his own organizing principles against him. His former student, Rose Pesotta, now a CIO organizer, rejected his argument that the agreement between the strikers and Goodyear be thrown out because it did not contain provisions for the closed shop. The contract was "the best one yet," with "distinct advantages to the workers" that easily could be exploited later into obtaining the closed shop. "You trained us at Brookwood to organize the mass production workers. You laid stress on both the practical and ethical sides. And you never let us forget that when strikes are settled, they must be settled honorably. I won't fail your teaching now," she perfunctorily informed him.[64] It seems that Fannia Cohn's prediction that he would be written "out of the labor movement" had come true.

Perhaps Muste recognized that another prediction had also come true: his movement had been "bored from without." As Cannon frankly admitted in his account of the merger, the CLA had joined the AWP for sectarian purposes—in order "to prevent the Stalinists from swallowing up this movement, and to remove a centrist obstacle from our path." If the consequence was the loss of "frauds and fakers and the unassimilable elements" like Budenz, Lore, and Hardman, so much the better. And now Muste was party to an effort do the same to the Socialist Party; again, as Cannon explained the objective of the French Turn: "We must frustrate the Stalinists. We must cut in between the Stalinists and this developing movement of Left Socialism and turn it in the direction of genuine Marxism."[65] Thus, when the WPUS convention voted to dissolve the party in March in order to pursue its plan to secretly take over the SP, Muste duly took out a membership in the SP. Then, every Monday, he met with other former WPUS comrades "as a manipulative faction within the Socialist party."[66]

In his *History of American Trotskyism*, Cannon suggests that the reason Muste opposed the French Turn was that he lacked the masculine strength to stomach the harsh political maneuvers necessary in a revolutionary movement. This was due to his "terrible background in the Church, which had marred him in his formative years." As he explained, Muste suffered from "organizational fetishism, perhaps personal pride. Such sentiments are fatal in politics. Pride, anger, spite – any kind of subjectivity which influences a political course leads only to the defeat and destruction of those who give way to it. You know, in the prize-fighting profession – 'the manly art of self-defense' – one of the first lessons the young boxer learns . . . is to keep cool when facing an antagonist." Without this "manly art," Muste was simply unable to reason or act "with the necessary objectivity."[67]

Yet, in fact, Muste did not shy away from taking political risks or engaging in combative debates. From May 1935 until early 1936, he fought Cannon tooth and nail on party principles and methods. His arguments against entering the SP were indeed ultimately subjective, based upon his own experiences and interpretation of Marxist-Leninist theory, but so too were Cannon's. Where Muste held that the most effective way to build the Fourth International was through mass activity and party independence in the United States, Cannon held that it was through combating "Stalinist" influence. Both men could point to the WPUS's Declaration of Principles and to the Fourth International in support of their respective positions. Ironically, despite Cannon's claims to greater objectivity, it was Muste's prediction that was borne out by history: the Cannonites never managed to turn the SP into a movement of the Fourth International but rather found themselves expelled in the summer of 1937 for divisive activities. They went on to found the Socialist Workers Party, which shortly thereafter experienced another factional split over the question of the nature of the Soviet Union, whether it was a "degenerated workers' state" or a new class system altogether, termed "bureaucratic collectivism."[68]

As for Muste's religious background, certain ethical principles that he had adopted as a young Christian minister clearly continued to shape his politics, even as he rejected the church and pacifism. He strongly believed that adversaries within the radical movement should treat each other with a level of "decency," and that community was a vital component of revolutionary action. Indeed, he viewed the revolutionary movement as a "Comradeship," to use the term of his Boston fellowship, a group of fellow believers that "burned away self-centeredness in devotion to the task of making heaven real on earth by building 'the workers' world.'" These convictions influenced his strong reaction to Cannon's more authoritarian organizational style, as well as his opposition to the French Turn, as he thought it was immoral to enter another left-wing party, as much as he disagreed with its policies, on false pretenses.[69] Yet Muste's ethics were not unique to him. Others without his background in the church also ascribed to these principles; the Musteites were, after all, a diverse lot.

The significance of Muste's religious background thus has less to do with his ethics and more with how he ultimately resolved the personal and political crisis that resulted from the French Turn. In early 1936, he found himself surrounded by comrades he viewed as untrustworthy and cruel, and a member of the Socialist Party, which he had long viewed as hopelessly reformist. His once creative and vibrant movement of working-class militants had been destroyed, and largely due to decisions he had made. In breaking with Brookwood, then turning the CPLA into a revolutionary vanguard organization, and finally merging with the Troskyists, he had acted in an increasingly authoritarian manner, disregarding the advice of his friends and comrades in a singular push for revolutionary purity.

No doubt contributing to his sense of displacement and marginalization was the emergence of the CIO as a force in leading the sort of militant industrial unionism that he had long advocated. Yet Muste was on the sidelines, while his former adversary John L. Lewis led the charge, supported by former Musteites and in an alliance with the Democratic Party and the New Deal state. As Muste recalled, "I was brought up hard against the realization that by that very pragmatic test which I had chosen the method [of Marxist Leninism] did not produce the desired results and that furthermore I was undergoing an inner deterioration and was reduced to judging events and making decisions by purely *ad hoc*, opportunistic standards."[70]

Tentatively, Muste began to consider leaving the Trotskyist movement. Yet his options must have appeared quite limited. He could have joined the CIO, but this would have required him, like his old friend John Brophy, to defer to Lewis's leadership. As for the CP, he fully agreed with the Trotskyist analysis of the USSR as a degenerated workers' state and of the Comintern as its corrupted arm. More immediately, the CP was now pursuing an alliance with liberals and Western democracies that Muste believed would lead to war.[71]

Recognizing that Muste was broken in health and spirit, three of Muste's closest female supporters, Cara Cook, Lucille Kohn, and Doris Prenner, began a fund-raising campaign to give him a vacation in Europe. Muste "very much needs a rest and change," they explained.[72] Much to their surprise, so much money poured in that they were able to send Anne as well. Milton Mayer, a prominent journalist who was close to Muste, recalled that the fund "overflowed with contributions from people who hated Musteism and loved Muste," suggesting that he continued to inspire respect and trust across the ideological lines of the liberal left, despite the political and personal rifts of the past few years. Early in June, a crowd of well-wishers gathered at the Hoboken pier to send them off. As the ship left port, Muste raised his "skinny arm in the clenched fist salute of the bloody revolution."[73]

"It was somewhat contradictory but natural enough under the circumstances that our first stop should have been Norway for a week's conference with Leon Trotsky who was there in exile," Muste would recall.[74] Trotsky and his wife were then living in Vexhall, a village just north of Oslo, in the home of Konrad Knudsen, a Norwegian Labor Party editor who had lectured at Brookwood in the 1920s. Muste took an immediate liking to the Russian revolutionary. As he described their first meeting in a letter to Cara Cook,

> We drove out to the farm house, through a broad valley dotted with farms and, on either side, low wooded mountains, something like the foot hills of the Berkshires. As I turned around in the hall, after hanging my coat in the closet within two paces of me was Levidov who in an instant, and before I could get a full look at his face, was by me and grasping my hand, and then with his left, Anne's. Immediately behind him was his wife Natasha, equally cordial and gentle (yes, I think that *is* the word) in her greeting. Thus the (to me) great event had occurred—so simply I had met Leon Trotsky.

The rest of the visit was as warm and friendly as the first meeting. He and Anne were "completely captivated" by the Trotskys, and the foursome soon felt as though they had known each other for years. Intriguingly, Muste's portrait of the Russian revolutionary echoes contemporary descriptions of himself: Trotsky was a "simple, direct, utterly unassuming" man who emanated "calm" and lacked "bitterness in his spirit." Despite his trials and tribulations, he was "not in any sense a defeated man. His faith and courage are undiminished."[75]

The conversation between the two revolutionaries inevitably turned to politics. When Muste explained his growing reservations about the party, Trotsky "tried very hard to persuade me to stay," even going so far as to concede that the French Turn may not have been the right tactic, "but now it had been done and I should not let it drive me out of the party to which I had too much to give." Muste found his position similarly affirmed after he left Norway for a secret meeting of the leaders of the Fourth International in Paris. There, he learned that many of them shared his conviction that the French Turn was not appropriate for their respective countries, though they intended to adhere to the decision out of loyalty to the party line.[76]

After his meeting in Paris, the Mustes began the relaxing part of their vacation, traveling as tourists to Switzerland and then back to Paris. After years of nonstop political activity and emotional strain, Muste gave himself up to rest, leisure, and self-reflection. With his spirit no longer "deafened by the clamor of the demands, the speech-making by ourselves and others, the activities of life," he became aware of how deeply his confidence in the Marxist left had been shaken by the events of the past two years. He began to sense that "the idealism and élan seemed to have largely gone out of [the revolutionary movement]," both in the United States and Europe. It now seemed to him that "factionalism and lack of confidence on the part of the membership in the leadership and in each other" was "eating at [the movement's] vitals." The military buildup and the presence of soldiers "everywhere" in Europe further contributed to his sense of impasse and impotence.[77]

One cannot help but draw a parallel between his European vacation in 1936 and the summer of 1914, when he and Anne retreated to the country to help Muste recover from "nervous prostration," due to his estrangement from Calvinist doctrine. Just as a direct experience of the divine "saved" him then, one saved him now. While walking in Paris one day, he entered St. Sulpice, a medieval church then in disrepair. As he sat alone in the sanctuary, gazing upon the altar and the cross, an inner voice told him, "This is where you belong. . . . I felt as if the hand of God had drawn me up out of those 'titanic glooms of chasmed fears; of which Francis Thompson sings." This epiphany, ironically located in a Catholic church, released him from his doubts about leaving the Trotskyist movement and set him back toward his Protestant roots and to pacifism.[78]

While Muste was undoubtedly genuine in recounting what happened in the church of St. Sulpice, his Christian pacifism also offered a resolution to his dilemma of how to remain an idealist without becoming an ideologue. He had, by his own admission, become increasingly rigid, intolerant, and out of touch with reality in his move to the left. Yet he continued to hold that compromise with social democracy was untenable. Absolute faith in Christ and nonviolence thus provided him with a clear method for drawing the line, as the essential dignity and inviolability of every human being now became the measure for evaluating himself, his comrades, and the larger society. Yet he continued to believe that ideals, to be meaningful, had to be played out in community, action, and experience. His quest to fuse these seemingly irreconcilable positions would serve as the axis for his postwar career.

As we shall see, pacifists would welcome him back to the fold with open arms. Others, however, viewed his reconversion with a mix of puzzlement and cynicism. *Time* magazine commented sardonically that although Muste "has recanted the barricades, he is still vaguely Marxian." Marxists were not so sure. Hook, for one, stated that he "could not have been very well versed in either" Marxism or Christianity to be able to switch back and forth so quickly.[79] Yet Hook was mistaken; Muste would develop a theological basis for his radical pacifism that drew upon larger intellectual currents such as neo-orthodoxy and existentialism. Moreover, his radical pacifism retained elements of Marxist Leninism that he would merge with Christianity and pacifism to create a new theory of revolutionary social change, allowing him to retain political and cultural relevance on the left during the Cold War era.

CHAPTER 8

Muste and the Origins of Nonviolence
in the United States

> [It] seems to me that in the Jewish-Christian revelation the
> Cross is the crucial event in history, our human history;
> that the concept of the Cross, of suffering love as supreme
> redemptive power, was a social concept, which was revealed
> to men who faced overwhelming and bitter historico-
> political and economic dilemmas as a way of meeting
> precisely such dilemmas; that it is impossible to build up a
> scriptural-prophetic theology which does not demand the
> practice of love in all the relationships of life and promise
> the reign of God on earth.
>
> —A. J. Muste, 1940

OVER THE COURSE of the late 1930s Muste would draw upon his experiences in the labor movement and the secular left, his understanding of the prophetic tradition, and his religious faith to craft a new radical politics based on nonviolence. In 1941, when the FOR hired him to lead the organization, he seized the opportunity to translate this vision into action, in the process helping to make Gandhian nonviolence a central feature of American political culture.

The popularity of World War II created a deep chasm between pacifists and the mainstream, but membership in the FOR grew as true believers closed ranks, and Muste inspired them with his vision of pacifism as a transformative force; the American section of the organization grew from

8,600 members in 1937 to over 14,000 several years later.[1] Still, the generation of pacifists who had come of age during World War I remained ambivalent about nonviolence, viewing its tactics as confrontational and
"coercive" rather than reconciliatory. Muste would find more success with
a younger generation of pacifists, men and women who had come of age in
the Student Christian Movement of the 1930s. Like him, they embraced
nonviolence both as a tactic and as a way of life, though tensions between
those respective commitments emerged early on.

The main target of these early experiments with nonviolence was American racial discrimination and segregation. Like others on the liberal left,
pacifists had increasingly identified racism as a major barrier to human
equality and freedom.[2] The first lady, Eleanor Roosevelt, championed racial
justice and the iconography of the New Deal, if not its policies, posited a
more pluralistic and egalitarian vision of America. The struggle against Nazi
Germany and its ideology of Aryan racial supremacy further highlighted
the country's racial wrongs. President Roosevelt had declared that the purpose of the war was "not only to defend America but . . . to establish a
universal freedom under which a new basis of security and prosperity can
be established for all—regardless of station, race, or creed."[3] Such rhetoric
clashed with the harsh reality of racial segregation and discrimination and
pacifists joined African Americans in seizing the opportunity to expand the
struggle against fascism abroad to a struggle for democracy at home. With
the labor movement unequivocally allied with the war effort, Muste joined
his younger comrades in making white supremacy a central political and
moral concern.

MUSTE's return to pacifism did not signify an abandonment of his radical
politics or his commitment to the labor movement. He continued to argue
that economic democracy was the foundation of political democracy, but
he no longer considered the working class the vehicle for the "practical
realization of Christian and prophetic ideals of justice, social righteousness
and brotherhood."[4] It is not surprising that Muste's disillusionment with
labor occurred in 1936, just as Congress passed the Wagner Act, which
protected labor's right to collectively bargain and outlawed many unfair
labor practices. While Muste enthusiastically welcomed New Deal labor
reform, he feared that the labor movement would narrow its agenda in
return for a greater degree of legitimacy in American society. Instead of
focusing on the "so-called standard of living," labor should recognize that

it was "more important for moral and spiritual beings" to have work that was "rational and under conditions which are psychologically and spiritually satisfying."[5] Muste's move away from the "labor metaphysic" thus must be placed within the context of the changing relationship between labor and the state in the mid-twentieth century.[6]

Muste's encounter with Trotskyism played a significant role in his disillusionment with "the proletarian movement." As he reflected on his experience, he concluded that the reason his otherwise courageous and idealistic comrades had been unscrupulous and deceitful was that they held a mechanical and materialist view of human beings that they shared, ironically, with the economic system they sought to replace. Marxism, like capitalism and fascism, "regard[ed] the system rather than the individual as important." Henry Ford, for example, believed that it was "the duty of management to take the load off the worker's back and put it on the machine and to take the load off the worker's mind and put it on the office. Considered from the spiritual and moral point of view just what is left that is human [in] a creature with nothing on its back and nothing on its mind!" Fascism similarly degraded human beings by making them nothing more than pawns of the totalitarian state, as did Communism, which disrespected human life by subjecting the proletariat "to the dictatorship of an absolute Party." In systems that failed to recognize the value and dignity of every human being, "life becomes meaningless at last; human beings cannot respect themselves; they cannot make moral decisions because they do not think there is such a thing as morality apart from expediency."[7]

In numerous speeches, articles, and a book entitled *Non-violence in an Aggressive World*, Muste traced the origins of this materialistic conception of human life to the Renaissance and the Reformation. While the liberation of human beings from the fetters of the church was both necessary and justified, it led to a tendency "to set man at the center of the universe . . . a tendency to conceive of man as really the highest form of moral being and to put any thought of God, of moral Being beyond man, out of the picture." But once human beings believed that there was no law or force higher than themselves, they became incapable of respecting their fellows and of living in community. Lacking faith in others, they soon lost faith in themselves and became vulnerable to totalitarian worldviews. To quote Muste at length:

> Man whose spirit was to have been freed at last from ancient restraint and superstition has not for centuries found himself less

free than he is today: a cog in a machine in our own industrialism;
a pawn in the hands of a totalitarian state under Fascism; or the tool
of a totalitarian party under Communism. . . . This is the result
of inexorable spiritual law. "If there is no God," exclaims one of
Dostoievsky's characters, "then I am God." And when men come to
believe that . . . there is no objective Good for which they can live;
no law of reality to which high and low are truly subject; no One in
all the universe more honest, more dependable, more capable of
living in and building up a free society than they are themselves;
then they cannot respect and trust themselves or one another. The
body of community is broken and life flies apart.[8]

Thus the irony of freedom and individualism was that they led to
totalitarianism.

Muste offered religious faith and nonviolence as answers to the arrogance of humanism.[9] Labor and the left had to recognize the value of the
spiritual, the essential dignity of every human being over and against the
state and the revolution. The "proletarian movement" had been "right in
prophesying that men cannot live the good life under a 'bad system,'" but
they had erred in assuming that a "good system" would automatically create "good men." Questions of ethics and morality, of the relationship
between means and ends, thus had to be faced if they hoped to build a
genuine democracy. Ultimately, the root of the problem was "moral and
spiritual," not primarily political, economic, or organizational, and could
only be resolved through affirmation of the "central truth" apprehended
by pacifism: that "God is love, love is of God. Love is the central thing in
the universe. Mankind is one in an ultimate spiritual reality." At the same
time, the church had to identify with the struggles of workers and support
the labor movement. "Organized religion . . . stands or falls with a free
labor movement," he insisted. "Where there are no genuinely free organizations of workers, there are presently no free churches either."[10]

Muste's argument was not altogether unique. Trotskyists had, of course,
long criticized the Communist movement for being excessively bureaucratic and state centered. Now some anti-Stalinists had begun to draw connections between fascism and Communism, suggesting that both were
"totalitarian" systems that subjugated the individual in service to an absolutist state. Muste was particularly fond of Ignazio Silone, Aldous Huxley,
and Arthur Koestler who called for a revival of moral and spiritual values

to regenerate and democratize socialism. Theological trends—especially personalism and existentialism—further shaped his thinking. Philosophers such as Martin Buber, Nicolai Berdyaev, and Jacques Maritain deeply influenced him with their view of human existence as incomplete and paradoxical, and their argument that action, suffering, and struggle in spite of doubt and uncertainty opened up possibilities for redemption and transformation.[11]

Also influencing his thought was the incisive critique of liberal Protestantism developed by Reinhold Niebuhr. Although Muste would sharply disagree with elements of Niebuhr's analysis, he did share the theologian's conviction that liberals had accommodated themselves too easily to modern, secular culture. In Niebuhr's words, religion was "so busy adjusting itself to the modern mind that it can find no energy to challenge the modern conscience." Instead, religion should exist in dialectical tension with politics, reinforcing morality and restraining the will to power. He called on his fellow Christians to act in the tradition of the Hebrew prophets, who called upon society to recognize its sins and conform to the will of God. For Niebuhr, religion was not compatible with modern culture and society, but rather a challenge to it.[12]

Niebuhr's critique was as much an attack upon pacifism as it was an attack on liberalism. Indeed, he equated pacifism and liberalism, which speaks to the former's widespread appeal among mainline Protestant clergy and laity during the interwar years.[13] In *Moral Man and Immoral Society*, first published in 1932, he argued that although liberals and pacifists often analyzed contemporary society "quite realistically," their solutions to social problems fell short because they failed to recognize the distinction between the morality of individuals and groups. While education, moral persuasion, and conversion to Christianity might change the behavior of an individual, they would not change society, which was a magnification of humanity's lust, greed, ambition, ignorance, and selfishness. Just as coercion held a society of competing interests together, some level of coercion (such as labor strikes and boycotts) would be needed to change it.[14]

Niebuhr's book profoundly challenged the basis of the pacifist faith in the United States because in it he concluded that, once coercion was accepted as ethically justified, "we cannot draw any absolute line of demarcation between violent and non-violent coercion." He offered the example of Gandhi's recent boycott of British textiles to show that even an act that appeared nonviolent could cause suffering and perhaps even death. He concluded that, since the consequences of nonviolence could not be sharply differentiated from violence, then actions could only be judged by whether or not they increased justice. This led him to further conclude that equality was, therefore, "a higher social goal than peace," and that wars for "the emancipation of a nation, a race or a class" were "in a different moral category from the use of power for the perpetuation of imperial rule or class dominance." Since violence was not "intrinsically immoral," the "real question" was "what are the political possibilities of establishing justice through violence?"[15]

Muste shared Niebuhr's prophetic stance, but dissented from his view that there was one law for the individual and one law for society. "Nowhere in the New Testament do we find the slightest hint that while God uses one way to meet evil and redeem the sinner, the Christian . . . is to use another method in dealing with his fellows." In a situation of sin and strife, Jesus, like the prophets, viewed righteousness as more important than power and viewed defeat not as a sign of God's injustice but rather a sign of one's own failure to be righteous and just. Moreover, just as the prophets emphasized the importance of repentance, Christ suffering on the cross was essentially a repentant act; it suggested that taking responsibility for one's own sins would liberate others to do the same. Thus, Muste concluded, by expressing love and accepting that one might be killed, it would be possible to fundamentally transform human society and usher in the day of peace.[16]

Muste did not fail to appreciate the depth of human sin. Indeed, although historians have portrayed Muste as an idealist, who expressed the "pure, unmixed, unadulterated soul of the Social Gospel," in fact, he had always retained elements of his Calvinist past.[17] He had a "strong conviction about human frailty and corruption," and believed that, ultimately, redemption was only possible through Jesus Christ. Yet he insisted that this was "not the Christian last word." "Where *sin abounds, grace much more abounds.*" God was "infinite justice and righteousness," but also "infinite mercy." Forgiveness came, moreover, with the charge "go and sin no more." "The scriptures," he later wrote in an open letter to Niebuhr, "are not simply an extended commentary on the single text, 'Vanity of vanities, all is vanity.' We read in them the commandment, 'Be ye perfect as your heavenly Father is perfect,' and the promise, 'Behold, I make all things new.'"[18]

As Muste and Niebuhr both recognized, these contrasting views had political implications. For Muste, Christian realism (often associated with neo-orthodoxy or "crisis theology") served as an apology for acquiescence and inaction, and was ultimately reactionary. As he explained, a philosophy that sets limits on human aspiration leads to defeatism, not greater pragmatism. "I am convinced," he asserted, that the realists "radically misapprehend basic elements in Biblical prophetic religion." They conceived of history as cyclical, "simply the re-enactment . . . of the drama of conflict between the demonic and the divine. It consists of cycles that return upon themselves. It has no goal. There have been philosophers, of course, who held such a conception. There is not the slightest warrant for it in Jewish-Christian prophetism. In prophetism history has a goal: God's reign of justice, fraternity, and peace."[19]

Muste defended his perfectionism not only in theological terms; he also insisted that it was, in fact, realistic. "Crisis" theologians and Communists alike overestimated the role of coercion and violence in holding societies together and in obtaining social change. As a consequence, the latter had seen the Bolshevik revolution degenerate into a dictatorship and its international beset by sectarianism and dogmatism. Pointing to Gandhi's example, he argued that nonviolence more realistically took account of the psychic and cultural factors in both social control and resistance. He even suggested that it was more scientific in its approach to reality, as it recognized that the "old formulas" and techniques had not worked. Rather than become "tired radicals" and retreat into the ivory tower, the "only hopeful possibility is to adopt a scientific approach, to be willing to look at the situation afresh, to re-evaluate one's aims, strategy, and tactics, and thus find a solution adapted to the new situation." This was, Muste insisted, also the approach of the "Jewish-Christian prophetic religion," as it stressed the importance of repentance, of freeing the mind "from self-righteousness and self-importance," in order to begin anew.[20]

Ultimately, however, Muste conceded that nonviolence could not be proven by logic alone, nor did he rely upon "proof-texts" from the Bible, as was the case with other pacifists.[21] Pacifism was a faith, "a view and a way of life . . . not merely a tool or device which the individual uses in certain circumstances on his environment." Yet this was precisely what made it revolutionary. Unlike other modern creeds, it rejected the notion that "social engineering" or overthrowing the "system" would automatically improve human life. "If we are to have a new world," Muste asserted frequently, "we must have new men; if you want a revolution, you must be revolutionized." Indeed, he sharply criticized his fellow pacifists for failing to recognize this truth; nonviolence was a way of life that required the discipline, commitment, and spirit of self-sacrifice that had been exhibited by Communists.[22]

As this account suggests, Muste was essentially making the case for non-violent resistance, one that shared many of the features of Gandhian non-violence. Just as Gandhi viewed suffering love as revolutionary, Muste believed that by imitating Christ on the cross, it was possible to fundamentally transform human relations. Also like Gandhi, who saw no contradiction between struggling for Indian freedom and regarding the British as friends, Muste believed that siding with workers and oppressed minorities was not an expression of hatred but rather of a love for justice and reconciliation. Just as Gandhi argued that there were limits to moral appeals and reason, Muste insisted that direct action was not incompatible with nonviolence, but rather brought tension out into the open where it could be resolved. Likewise, Muste shared Gandhi's distrust of the modern state; both men believed that it threatened real democracy by assuming responsibility for much that individual citizens could do themselves.[23]

The similarity between Muste's theory of nonviolent resistance and Gandhian nonviolence should not, however, obscure the indigenous roots of Muste's ideas. It was his exposure to liberal theology and the mystical tradition that gave him an abiding faith in the power of love. It was his long held preference for syndicalism over the parliamentary approach of the Socialist Party that led him to emphasize direct action. It was his experience on the left that convinced him that pacifists had to dedicate themselves to fighting oppression with the conviction and spirit of self-sacrifice that motivated Communists. It was his understanding of Christianity as a prophetic religion that encouraged him to interpret Christ suffering on the cross as a social concept. Thus, Muste drew upon the history of American radicalism and the prophetic tradition to make his argument that pacifists had to engage in nonviolent resistance. Moreover, as much as Muste believed that American pacifists could learn from Gandhi, he was willing to discard those elements of Gandhi's program that he believed were arcane, such as, for example, Gandhi's animus toward industrialized society.[24]

The cultural context for Muste's theory of nonviolence accounts for its strengths and its limitations. At the same time that he freely acknowledged its basis in religious faith, he insisted that it offered a universal blueprint for social transformation. In so doing, he inadvertently reinforced pacifist ethnocentrism. After all, most pacifists were neither theologians nor intellectuals. As historian Patricia Appelbaum has commented, in contrast to "the careful theological reasoning of an A. J. Muste," most pacifists failed to recognize that certain assumptions about human nature and the universe informed their commitment to nonviolence. Her analysis of pacifist narratives—such as the oft-repeated story of the intruder who is disarmed by the kindness and openness of his potential victim—is here suggestive. As she argues, "Read without the cultural assumptions that informed them—faith in the direct, this-worldly, applicable power of love and nonviolence—these stories are barely credible, even dangerous. . . . Read without faith, tales of martyrdom seem only to recommend violent death."[25]

Muste's tendency to conflate Judaism and Christianity further speaks to the universalizing impulse within American pacifism. On the one hand, for Muste and other Protestants of his generation, the invention of a Judeo-Christian tradition was part of a recovery of the historical Jesus and Christianity's roots in Judaism. On the other hand, it also involved a process of co-option and ethnocentrism, as can be seen in Muste's statement that "the supreme incarnation of God and the greatest of the prophets of this Jewish-Christian faith was the Carpenter of Nazareth."[26] His notion, moreover, that Christ suffering on the cross offered a universal blueprint for resistance and social transformation is problematic from a Jewish perspective, a point of departure that would become explicit during World War II. When some pacifists called on Jews to practice nonviolent resistance against Hitler, Jews not only saw this as unrealistic, they were hardly inclined to view their suffering as having redemptive meaning.[27]

These tensions within pacifist theory would come to the surface when pacifists attempted to put nonviolence into action. The following chapter discusses the gulf that emerged between pacifists and the American public when they argued that nonviolence offered a realistic means for resisting fascism. To their critics, it seemed that some human beings were deeply damaged and beyond redemption, and that nonviolence was impractical under totalitarian regimes. Most pacifists, however, avoided grappling with these questions, and instead sought to demonstrate that nonviolence was a realistic method of social change. Unable to influence foreign policy, they poured their energies into the country's first nonviolent campaigns against racial segregation. Although they had some success convincing nonpacifists to adopt Gandhian tactics, they failed to impress upon them the "truth" of the pacifist worldview.

MUSTE's return to Christian pacifism was big news in liberal Protestant circles. The *Christian Century*, the central organ of the religious left, along with other, smaller publications, published accounts of his reconversion.[28] Meanwhile, leading clergy sought to channel his considerable talents and energy to bolster the prestige of a community whose credibility in the labor movement and on the left had been undermined by Niebuhr's searing critique. Muste undoubtedly welcomed the attention, as his financial situation had grown increasingly desperate; Anne's fervent desire that their eldest daughter attend Swarthmore College added to his sense of pecuniary strain.[29]

Muste's first offer came from the pacifist community. Immediately after his return from Europe, he renewed his membership in the FOR. "I am again the unequivocal Christian and pacifist I was some years ago," he wrote to the FOR's chairman, John Nevin Sayre. He praised Sayre for maintaining the organization's religious basis in the face of an earlier crisis over its identity and purpose. "The FOR must be and become revolutionary but out of *religious* experience and in a *religious* sense," he declared.[30] The organization eagerly welcomed him back; at its annual conference in October, members elected him to their national council and approved of his appointment as chairman of the committee on industrial relations and as industrial relations secretary, a paid staff position.[31]

Muste appealed to the FOR because of his strong credentials as a labor activist and revolutionist. A source of tension between Muste and the FOR since the Lawrence strike of 1919 had been pacifists' reluctance to unequivocally side with labor against capital. Most pacifists viewed strikes and boycotts as coercive tactics that violated Christian tenets of love and goodwill. True reconciliation and peace could only occur if both sides of a given dispute were free to recognize their guilt and repent for their sins.[32]

Starting in the early 1930s, however, many of them began to seriously reassess these views. This shift can only be understood in the context of a crisis that swept pacifist circles with the onset of the Great Depression and the emergence of the vibrant labor movement of the New Deal era. While some continued to maintain that pacifists should remain neutral in the struggle between labor and capital, most identified with the working class and endorsed strikes and other seemingly "coercive" methods for seeking economic justice. They argued that justice was a higher value than peace and that refusing to use "coercive" methods placed pacifists on the side of the economic status quo. Some of them even went so far as to argue that there was no meaningful difference between violence and nonviolence.[33]

Muste's own estrangement from pacifism around the year 1930 was an early manifestation of this incipient ideological and tactical crisis. As he explained in a 1929 speech at the annual meeting of the FOR, to refuse to support workers in their struggle against class exploitation was to implicitly sanction the violence of the existing order.[34] Soon thereafter, the FOR's southern secretary Howard Kester developed a similar critique. In 1933, his annual report to the FOR's national council stated that "to attempt to emancipate the mass of white and Negro workers in the South . . . only through the methods of goodwill, moral suasion, and education is to invite the continued exploitation, misery and suffering of generations yet unborn." The FOR, he asserted, needed to see itself as a "revolutionary movement" and demonstrate far more "realism and "abandon" than it had in the past. In particular, he called upon pacifists to align themselves with oppressed workers and racial minorities who might engage in behavior contrary to pacifist precepts of love, honesty, and nonviolence.[35]

Kester's views had strong minority support within the FOR. Niebuhr, who had just published *Moral Man and Immoral Society*, was chair of the organization's executive committee. Indeed, he likely still considered himself a pacifist since he opposed wars for power or privilege, which he differentiated from wars for the emancipation of an exploited class, race, or national group. That others agreed with Niebuhr became apparent as the FOR debated the question of its relationship to working-class struggles for economic justice over the course of 1933.

In February 1933, the FOR's two executive secretaries, John Nevin Sayre and J. B. Matthews, proposed two entirely different roles for the organization, and both threatened to resign over the issue. Matthews essentially took Niebuhr's position, while Sayre wanted the FOR to concentrate on "searching for and experimenting with non-coercive practical methods of pure love and persuasion." Adding to the fervor of the debate was Matthews's conviction that the organization should discard its religious basis.[36]

The way in which the debate quickly polarized over the positions offered by Sayre and Matthews suggested that the choice was between two extremes—persuasion or coercion, Christianity or atheism—rather than the real question posed by Matthews, which was whether or not pacifist philosophy should evolve in relation to a changing world.[37] Yet the Fellowship ultimately avoided grappling with these "perplexities," but instead focused its attention on determining precisely how much coercion or violence a secretary of the organization could legitimately endorse. In December of 1933, the FOR resolved that staff members could not take a position on the "class war" that went further than advocating "nonviolent coercion," by which they meant civil disobedience, strikes, and boycotts. It also accepted Matthews's resignation and appointed Sayre national chairman.[38]

In making these changes, the FOR lost some of its most well-known and politically active members—as well as much of its legitimacy and standing on the liberal left. Kester, along with the FOR's industrial secretary Charles Webber, resigned, predicting that the organization would become irrelevant to oppressed workers and racial minorities. Niebuhr also resigned.[39] Soon thereafter, he and Kester founded the Fellowship of Socialist Christians as an alternative to the FOR; its goal was to resurrect Christianity as "a truly prophetic religion" by challenging capitalist inequities with practical achievements in the field. Significantly, it engaged in a frequent "barrage against 'irresponsible' pacifists of the FOR stripe who imagined love to be a viable ethical strategy in the social and international arena."[40]

This move to the left was temporary, however. The threat of fascism in Europe convinced these self-identified "realists" that "maturity" and "responsibility" meant supporting collective security. As Richard Fox has argued, the realists' willingness to use force and even violence quickly changed "from an instrument of class struggle to a tool for resisting fascism and shoring up beleaguered bourgeois democracies." By the end of the decade, realists had abandoned the Socialist Party, which was anti-interventionist, for the Democratic Party, which had finally embraced collective security. The close relationship between Christian realists and the Democratic Party would continue into the postwar era, as American liberalism also became more "realistic," moving away from its trenchant critique of corporate capitalism and unabashedly embracing a foreign policy bereft of Wilsonian moral idealism.[41]

The loss of Niebuhr and the formation of the Fellowship of Socialist Christians was a "demoralizing blow" to the FOR. It placed the organization and its ideology on the defensive and prompted a flurry of introspection among pacifists.[42] Although Sayre may have wanted the organization to focus exclusively on moral persuasion, it was clear to most members that the organization needed to explore other methods for achieving radical social change and a world without war if they hoped to maintain their relevancy in contemporary social movements. In December 1935, the FOR's leaders met to reconsider the organization's "purpose and program" in light of this sentiment and, after a long discussion, stated their commitment to "building up techniques for non-violent resistance." Soon thereafter the FOR began urging members to form discussion groups to study Richard Gregg's recent book *The Power of Non-violence*, which provided a systematic discussion of Gandhian nonviolence and how and why it was an effective and realistic method of social change.[43]

The son of a Congregationalist minister and a trained lawyer, Gregg had spent four years in India, seven months of which he had lived at Gandhi's ashram. In *Gandhiji's Satyagraha or Non-Violent Resistance*, published in 1930, and *The Power of Non-violence*, published in 1934, Gregg explained how nonviolent resistance worked rather than elaborating on it in the sentimental and idealistic terms employed by other pacifists. The essence of his argument was that nonviolence was effective because it functioned as "moral jiu-jitsu." By refusing to use violence and expressing an attitude of love and willingness to endure suffering, nonviolent resisters obtained the moral high ground and threw oppressors off guard and made them unsure of their position. In this sense, nonviolence was not only effective as a technique, it was transformative; it had the power to "convert the opponent, to change his understanding and his sense of values."[44]

The Power of Non-violence was, in many ways, Gregg's response to Niebuhr's critique. In his account, Gandhi was the consummate pragmatist. He stressed Gandhi's understanding of his movement as an "experiment with truth" and explained that an advocate of nonviolence "recognizes that no matter what his beliefs and convictions are, he may possibly be mistaken or at fault." While Western pacifism had become dry and irrelevant with its assertion of moral absolutes, Gandhi had taken the idea of nonviolence and "proved" its validity by applying "it to mass movements in organized corporate fashion." Gregg also attempted to refute Niebuhr's argument that nonviolent resistance and physical coercion amounted to the same thing. Though he admitted that it was not always possible to "draw a sharp line between violent and nonviolent coercion, and between coercion and persuasion," he insisted that nonviolent resistance was different "in-kind" from the coercion of physical force because it relied on psychic as opposed to physical force.[45]

Niebuhr remained unimpressed with Gregg's arguments. "Since his defense of non-violence is consistently pragmatic," Niebuhr observed, "it prompts the question whether it is possible to condemn violence so absolutely within the framework of a pragmatic position." Niebuhr's trenchant critique pointed to the problems pacifists would confront when they attempted to make a purely instrumental argument on behalf of nonviolence. "By eschewing the rhetoric of absolute moral values," pacifists such as Gregg "raised the possibility of political actors who chose nonviolence purely on the grounds of political expediency." In so doing, however, they undermined their own argument on behalf of absolute nonviolence.[46]

Still, *The Power of Non-violence* represented a breakthrough for American pacifists. First, unlike many of his contemporaries who preferred to avoid the issue, Gregg directly confronted the question of whether or not nonviolent resistance was coercive and therefore violent. While his answer failed to satisfy critics like Niebuhr, it was reasonable to suggest that the element of self-suffering made nonviolent resistance different "in-kind" from the coercion of force. Second, Gregg moved away from the progressive ideology that had shaped American pacifism since World War I. While he recognized the value of reason, he argued that sometimes human relationships become so pathological that "sudden and drastic action" was necessary for creating a better social order. Similarly, Gregg was unimpressed with the legislative approach to solving the problem of war. Citing Niebuhr's argument that the "have" nations would never willingly renounce their wealth and power, Gregg argued that peacemakers had to go beyond the externals of world courts, leagues of nations, and peace pacts and address the "deep seated inconsistencies and forces working for war in many parts of the economic, social, educational and organized religious systems." Finally, Gregg's book marked a departure from the ethnocentrism that had characterized Western pacifists' views of Gandhi. The Gandhi of *The Power of Non-violence* was not a mystical Jesus figure, as previous descriptions of him had suggested, but rather an expert strategist and soldier.[47]

Despite this interest in exploring Gandhian nonviolence, the FOR did not put it into practice, largely because pacifists continued to view it as coercive and therefore incompatible with their larger goal of reconciliation. At the same time, however, they remained acutely sensitive about their marginal role in the labor movement and the public perception of them as irrelevant idealists.[48] Muste's return to pacifism thus promised some resolution to these dilemmas. For one, unlike Gregg, who had ascetic tendencies, Muste had the organizational and interpersonal skills to translate ideas into action. But also—and perhaps more importantly for an explicitly Christian organization—where Gregg had evaded the question of whether pacifism relied ultimately on a leap of faith, Muste embraced its religious nature and indeed made it central.[49]

As FOR's industrial relations secretary from October 1936 through early summer 1937, Muste traveled widely, sharing his ideas about nonviolence and social transformation with religious bodies and labor organizations. In this capacity, he observed the sit-down strike movement that swept automobile and steel organizing campaigns in the Midwest. Impressed, in December 1936, he encouraged some of his old comrades at a local of the American Federation of Full-Fashioned Hosiery Workers to attempt a "lie-in" in which they copied the technique of the sit-down strike, yet infused it with the spirit of nonviolence. Muste was pleased to report that soon thereafter the Hosiery Workers appointed a commission to study the question of using nonviolence in labor disputes. This action "opens up a glorious opportunity for all who believe in the way of love and nonviolence to propagate our message in the ranks of the workers," he informed the FOR.[50]

At the same time that he served as industrial relations secretary of the FOR, Muste applied to be minister and director of Labor Temple of the Presbytery of New York. The position offered the family stability after several years of emotional and financial strain. Along with a respectable income of $300 a month, it included an apartment above Labor Temple big enough for the Muste family, including his daughter Nancy's new husband, John Baker. But as soon as the young couple could afford it, Muste asked them to move out. As Nancy recalled, "Dad was a very strong person and didn't mollycoddle people." The same could not be said for Muste's relationship with his younger daughter, Connie, for whom he felt more protective. She lived with her parents until she married at age thirty-three.[51]

Labor Temple also appealed to Muste because he apparently felt a deep longing to return to the church, "to be 'back home,'" as he put it. His "reconversion" experience had encouraged autobiographical reflection and he felt a pull toward his Calvinist heritage. Perhaps his mother's death in 1939 contributed to this sentiment. He viewed the church, moreover, as "the channel through which . . . the grace of God flows" and thus as having a special and divine mission to redeem the world. Muste spoke these words at the 1937 General Synod of the Reformed Church in America where he had recently been reinstated. It was "in a spirit of humility and gratitude" that he accepted the opportunity to address "the church of my fathers and of my own early years," he told the assembled crowd.[52]

At the same time, he remained theologically liberal and committed to the Social Gospel imperative to seek the Kingdom of God on earth. As he informed the Reformed General Synod, "No one would have been more surprised than John Calvin to learn that there might be some sphere of life in which Christians might act by some other standard than that of Christ!"[53] Hence his affinity for the Presbyterian Church, which grew out of the Calvinist tradition, yet had embraced modernism. Labor Temple especially held appeal. Located on the corner of Fourteenth Street and Second Avenue, it had been founded in 1910 as the institutional expression of the Presbyterian Church's commitment to working people. Over the years, it had evolved three distinct roles: as social settlement; as an open forum for the expression of all points of view; and as a place of worship. The Reverend Edmund Chaffee, the longtime director of Labor Temple, had passed away unexpectedly in the fall of 1936. Perhaps "the hand of God" was at work, Muste mused, as Chaffee's death occurred at the same time that Muste planned to meet with him about his St. Sulpice experience.[54]

Meanwhile, the Presbytery of New York, much like the religious liberals of the FOR, felt compelled to strengthen the church's relationship to the labor movement. Although somewhat apprehensive about Muste's recent Bolshevik past, they wanted to hire someone who "could be expected to develop a program more radical and labor-oriented than the 'mind of the Church' would always find easy to accept, a program by which 'we would plunge into the heart of the social crisis.'" Muste's personal relationship with Ted Savage, the executive secretary of the Presbytery of New York, and Henry Sloan Coffin, president of Union Theological Seminary, both of whom sat on Labor Temple's governing board, no doubt helped his case. A number of "searching discussions" with Muste convinced them of his "sincerity, his Christian idealism and his grasp of the problems that confront us," and in the spring of 1937, they issued the call for his appointment.[55]

For Muste, Labor Temple would serve as a sort of institutional and ideological halfway house between the labor movement and the radical pacifist politics he would espouse for the rest of his career. As director, he interacted daily with the ethnic, working-class residents of the Lower East Side, overseeing social services and educational outreach. He also promoted labor's point of view to liberal and religious bodies, assuming a prominent role as an expert on labor relations within liberal Protestant circles; he helped to draft the Federal Council of Churches' 1938 Labor Sunday message, accepted an appointment as lecturer at Union Theological Seminary, frequently addressed young people at seminaries and religious conferences throughout the country, and published numerous articles in the religious press.[56]

Even so, Muste clearly hungered for a return to political activism. His ambitions were rewarded when, in 1940, the FOR offered him the position of national secretary (Sayre remained in charge of the organization's work with the International Fellowship of Reconciliation) and thus a national platform for promoting Gandhian nonviolence. Muste's growing preoccupation with the threat of war provided further incentive for him to accept the FOR's offer. In 1938, he had founded the United Pacifist Committee in New York City to mobilize against naval expansion, industrial mobilization, conscription, and the revision of the country's neutrality laws. The committee held its meetings at Labor Temple, as did the New York FOR. Yet to minister within a church that had not fully endorsed pacifism was a setup for the wrenching struggle between church and conscience that he had experienced during World War I. After "much painful as well as prayerful consideration," Muste decided to accept the position, which became effective on April 1, 1940.[57]

Upon assuming his new post, Muste immediately set about to transform the FOR into a vehicle for the development of Gandhian nonviolence in the United States. He urged the national council to appoint a committee on nonviolent action headed by J. Holmes Smith, a former missionary to India, to explore how the organization might implement Gandhi's ideals in the United States. He also called upon FOR members to form "cells," a term clearly borrowed from his days as a Bolshevik, in which small fellowships of like-minded people would worship together, study nonviolence, develop a common "discipline," and put their ideals into action. Muste himself joined the Mt. Morris cell in which members pledged to strive "to be aware of God's presence in every person, in every event and in everything that I contact." They also dedicated themselves to "personal devotions," such as prayer and meditation and vowed to practice humility, speak truth, live joyously, fearlessly, and simply, and refuse "to earn my livelihood by any form of exploitation."[58] Some of the men and women destined to play a major role in the pacifist movement of the postwar era joined these cells in the early 1940s.

As a way of circumventing the control exercised by the more conservative national council, Muste also hired a dozen or so younger pacifists as organizational secretaries. His staff, as John D'Emilio has commented, had the same "lean and hungry look" as the Musteites in the 1930s.[59] Eager to demonstrate the relevance of their ideals, these young pacifists welcomed— and at times competed for—the elder radical's mentorship and guidance. His energy and enthusiasm were infectious; on days when he was in town, the national office burst with excitement and energy. At noon, after completing his copious correspondence and reading several newspapers, he gathered the staff together for a period of prayer, meditation, and discussion of the issues facing the movement. Just as he had always done, "A. J. would let the discussion go on. And he would be sitting there not saying anything. Then finally he would come out and he would sum up what one group had said. He would say 'there's this and this and this.' And then he'd say 'And on the other hand' and he would give his own position. . . . It just obliterated the opposition."[60]

Indeed, Muste quickly established himself as the head of the pacifist movement. As with the Musteites of the 1930s, his leadership flowed out of his unique combination of charisma and organizational savvy, passion and evenhandedness, flair for action and adroit reasoning. A few would chafe against his authority, but most did not. He was "the figure that just about everybody acknowledged as the leader," remembered Muste's secretary, Marion (Coddington) Bromley.[61]

One of Muste's most promising new staff members was James Farmer, an African American who had been exploring the idea of a mass, interracial, nonviolent movement against racism for several years. He had recently graduated from the divinity school at Howard University, where his mentor had been the black pacifist Howard Thurman. Under Thurman's direction, Farmer produced a master's thesis that distinguished between "priestly" and "prophetic" religion, the former serving to legitimize unequal social relations and the latter posing an egalitarian vision of human equality and brotherhood. Religion thus held out the possibility of providing a prophetic vision around which the "Negro masses" and sympathetic whites could unite to pose an alternative human community that would serve as a radical critique of U.S. society.[62] Thus, when Muste hired him to serve as race relations secretary of the FOR, he focused on conceptualizing how the organization could become a seedbed for such a movement. "Brotherhood Mobilization," the plan that grew out of this thinking, would serve as the foundation for the Congress of Racial Equality (CORE), one of the most important civil rights organizations in the postwar era.[63]

Another important addition to the staff was Bayard Rustin. An African American Quaker, Rustin joined the Young Communist League in the late 1930s only to resign when the Communist Party asked him to dissolve a committee against racial discrimination in the armed forces that he had formed. Communism for Rustin was not the "God that failed," as it had been for Muste, because "he had never worshipped it." However, "it had failed him, and within a few years he was harshly critical of the Communist Party. At the same time, he incorporated a basic economic analysis of society into his religious ethical philosophy."[64] Muste's synthesis of Christian pacifism and Marxist Leninism thus deeply appealed to him, as did his vision of Christianity as a prophetic religion. Indeed, evidence suggests that Rustin, like Muste, fashioned himself a prophet and was seen as such by his pacifist colleagues. The two men were quite close, with Muste serving as Rustin's mentor and father figure throughout the 1940s and early 1950s.[65] When Farmer faltered as an organizer, Muste gave Rustin a larger role in the organization's race relations work. As a result, Farmer and Rustin "didn't get along." As another staffer explained, "in a sense they were in competitive positions, and the greatest competition was for the affection of A.J." In his words, "Bayard won."[66]

Glenn Smiley and George Houser were similarly important additions to the FOR staff. Smiley was a white Methodist minister whose commitment to Gandhian nonviolence grew out of his deep faith in the socially redemptive power of suffering. He would train scores of young people in the philosophy and tactics of nonviolent resistance as an organizer for the FOR in the 1940s and 1950s. Later, he became a close confidant of the Reverend Martin Luther King Jr.[67] Houser, also white, had recently achieved some notoriety as one of the "Union Eight," a group of seminarians at Union Theological Seminary who refused to register for the draft and consequently served terms in federal prison. Houser had gone to Union to study with Niebuhr and Harry Ward, whom he admired for their views of Christianity as a prophetic religion and their emphasis on the need to identify with the "downtrodden." Houser would put most of his energy into CORE; he organized numerous direct action campaigns against segregation and racial discrimination and, along with Rustin, conducted annual summer institutes on race and nonviolence. Unlike Rustin, he never tried to emulate

Muste, but he admired the older man's courage and recalled that "he was always very supportive of whatever I was doing [and] whatever Bayard was doing."[68]

All of the FOR's new staff members, with the exception of Bayard Rustin, had come of age in the Student Christian Movement (SCM) of the interwar years.[69] The SCM was a federation of Protestant student groups committed to putting their Christian ideals into action. It included the FOR's youth group, the student divisions of the YMCA and YWCA, and student youth groups maintained by larger denominations. The SCM frequently sponsored regional and national conferences that brought together Christian college students from around the country. It was at these conferences that many of the pacifists destined to play a central role in the early civil rights movement and the radical pacifist movement forged links that would tie them together for the rest of their lives.[70]

The SCM was responsible for introducing these young Christians to pacifism. Indeed, the most popular leaders of the SCM were either pacifist or sympathetic to pacifism, such as Henry Van Dusen, Kirby Page, Sherwood Eddy, and George Coe.[71] The antiwar sentiment of the SCM also reflected a larger trend among youth to oppose American entry in another European war. Hundreds of thousands of college students took the Oxford Pledge during the 1930s, a statement that signified their refusal to "support the United States government in any war it may conduct." In April 1934, there was a Student Strike Against War that involved almost 25,000 students across the country. The following year over 150,000 students participated and in 1936 more than 500,000.[72]

By participating in antiwar activities, pacifist youth met older pacifists and learned about the peace organizations that had been established during World War I. Through her social service activities with the Young People's Fellowship in Evanston, Marjorie Swann "found out about the Fellowship of Reconciliation [and the] War Resisters League, and I immediately joined them."[73] Dorothy Hassler learned about Labor Temple through her involvement in the YWCA at Hunter College. Finding its commitment to working-class people deeply appealing, she spent a summer serving as an assistant to its director, Lawrence Hosie, who had replaced Muste when the latter became executive secretary of the FOR.[74] Houser's work with the Church of All Nations similarly brought him into contact with Labor Temple. It was there that he met Muste, who later hired him as a secretary of the

FOR.[75] Bill Sutherland also became acquainted with Muste through attending activities sponsored by Labor Temple. Soon he would identify as "a
Muste boy," signifying his commitment to "revolutionary nonviolence."[76]

Joining a "cell" became an important part of these early experiments
with nonviolence. Urged on by Muste, both Farmer and Rustin joined the
Harlem Ashram, which had been founded by Smith for the serious study
and practice of nonviolence. Sutherland became a part-time member of the
Newark Christian Colony (later known as the Newark Ashram), which had
been founded by Dellinger and three other divinity students. Run commu-
nally, the colony "offered hospitality to anyone who came to our door,
sharing whatever food and clothing we had as well as shelter." It also had a
small farm outside the city where members obtained food from two cows,
twenty-four chickens, and a vegetable garden. Surplus vegetables were sent
to Newark, where they were sold at a cooperative store run by fellow members of the colony. The spiritual atmosphere was intense, with daily prayer
and meditation and one day a week set aside for fasting.[77]

The war at once disrupted and fostered these early experiments in nonviolence. Young pacifists, like their elders, opposed American intervention
on the grounds that the war was a clash of rival imperialisms, not a democratic struggle against fascism, and that the United States, with its own
history of imperialism, was hypocritical in condemning German and Japanese expansion. Such an argument was within the mainstream of liberal
Protestant opinion in the mid-1930s, but by the end of the decade, it came
to appear simplistic and irresponsible. As mainline Protestant institutions,
including the SCM, "began to qualify or reverse their earlier antiwar positions," pacifism "became the position of a small and suspect minority
located on the social margins." As a result, it increasingly assumed a
"strong sense of exceptionalism and nonconformity." Pacifist cooperatives
and cell groups grew more important, and more pacifists began to explore
and experiment with nonviolent resistance. Thus World War II was a crucial moment in making "pacifist identity . . . an important point of distinction from other Protestants."[78]

This was particularly the case for the younger generation. While all pacifists faced the dilemma of opposing a "good war," those of draft age appear
to have felt it more intensely, probably because they were frequently
accused of being "yellowbellies." As Houser explained, one of the main
reasons he became an activist was to show that he was not "trying to hide
from injustice" even though he was a conscientious objector (CO). The

FIGURE 6. A. J. Muste with a conscientious objector in the library of the School
of Non-violence at Civilian Public Service Camp #52, circa 1943–44.
(*Swarthmore College Peace Collection*)

reality of Nazism and fascism had forced him to confront the question of
"how do you deal with the problem of injustice?" Nonviolent direct action
"was very satisfying to me . . . as a way proving something of the efficacy
of this approach [for] dealing with a real problem."[79]

In early 1942, soon after his release from prison for conscientious objection, Houser approached Muste with the idea of organizing a cell that

would focus exclusively on applying Gandhian nonviolence to race relations. Muste immediately hired him. Soon thereafter, Houser moved to
Chicago and founded the Chicago Committee of Racial Equality, which
met on Saturday afternoons to study and debate the possibility of using
Gandhian nonviolence as a weapon in the struggle for racial equality.
Farmer, who was also working in Chicago as a secretary for the FOR, often
attended cell meetings. These discussions led to several actions, including a
dramatic effort to desegregate the White City Roller Rink.[80]

While the race relations cell ventured into direct action, Farmer began
drafting a memo to Muste calling on the FOR to "direct and supervise" a
mass, nonviolent movement against racial segregation and discrimination
that he called "Brotherhood Mobilization." The memo outlined an ambitious plan of action. "Brotherhood Mobilization" would begin as a
"nucleus" of pacifists under the wing of the FOR, but would then become
an autonomous movement that would include "masses of people, black
and white, Jewish and Gentile." Its defining feature would be its willingness
to engage in direct action in contrast to the educational and legal approach
taken by organizations like the Urban League and the NAACP.[81]

Much to Farmer's delight, Muste was so impressed that he sent a copy
of the memo to the members of the FOR's national council for discussion
at the upcoming meeting, which was held in Cincinnati, Ohio, in April
1942.[82] Farmer recalled that he, Houser, and several other young pacifists
drove to the conference with "heady talk about *our* giving birth to a revolution in race relations with a technique new to America that would change
the face of this nation." Although Brotherhood Mobilization had Muste's
support, it did not receive the council's immediate endorsement, as some
raised the vexing question of whether or not nonviolent direct action was
essentially persuasive and reconciliatory. In the face of the national council's reluctance to endorse Farmer's proposal, Muste intervened and fashioned a plan that would allow it to go forward. The FOR would create a
"nonviolent direct action committee," with Muste as "active chairman,"
that would serve in an advisory role as Farmer, Rustin, and Houser began
the task of building "Brotherhood Mobilization."[83]

Almost as soon as the nonviolent direct action committee was formed,
A. Philip Randolph announced that his March on Washington Movement
(MOWM) would hold a national conference to explore civil disobedience
as a way of challenging the Jim Crow system. The MOWM had been
formed a year earlier to protest discrimination in wartime industries and

had resulted in President Roosevelt's Executive Order 8802 establishing
the Committee on Fair Employment Practices. Though Randolph called
off the march, the MOWM continued to gain momentum and now, much
to the enthusiasm of pacifists, had begun to consider Gandhian tactics. As
Muste exclaimed, the upcoming conference of the MOWM "may prove as
epoch-making as the launching in 1906 of Gandhi's own campaign in
South Africa." He continued, "That in the midst of a struggle to preserve
democracy the Negroes in this country should continue to be treated as
second-class citizens . . . is nothing short of a national calamity." He
called upon members of the FOR to give the MOWM their enthusiastic
support and released Farmer and Rustin for service to Randolph's
movement.[84]

At the same time, Muste authored several pamphlets for distribution to
the MOWM in which he made the case for nonviolent resistance against
Jim Crow. In the first, "What the Bible Teaches About Freedom," he compared African Americans to the Hebrew slaves and argued that the lesson
of Exodus was that "to be religious . . . is to get out of Egypt into Canaan;
to refuse to be slaves . . . to build brotherhood in freedom—because that is
what men, the children of God, were created to do!" Yet the history of
Israel had shown how the oppressed could, upon obtaining power, become
exploitative and violent themselves. The way to avoid this dilemma was to
follow Jesus's teaching that "the way to overcome your enemy is to love
him." After all, in existential terms, the enemy is really one's "other self."
In refusing to obey Jim Crow laws and practices, there would "be suffering.
. . . There is always the choice of inflicting suffering upon others or taking
it upon ourselves. The Christian way is to refuse to cooperate with evil and
to accept the consequence. The consequence is the Cross. . . . When we are
ready for that, God himself will give us victory." Indeed, it was precisely
the willingness "to suffer unto death on behalf of our fellows" that would
make the nonviolent revolution more enduring and beneficent "than all
the revolutions of the past."[85]

The second pamphlet posed the question of whether civil disobedience
was the "answer to Jim Crow" and featured comments by Niebuhr, Oswald
Garrison Villard, Kirby Page, Roger Baldwin, Richard Gregg, George
Schuyler, and Howard Thurman, among others. The discussion revealed
once again the political implications of the theological debate between Niebuhr and Muste, with the former advocating a policy of gradualism and the
latter suggesting that gradualism degraded the humanity of blacks and

whites. Muste concluded the pamphlet with an exploration of the "tactical problems" involved in fostering the use of Gandhian nonviolence by African Americans. He recommended that pacifists should not impose their commitment to nonviolence as a way of life onto others, but rather recommend nonviolence on the basis of its effectiveness as a method of social change. At the same time, however, they should not be deceitful about their antiwar convictions. To "bore from within," like Communists had often done, was dishonest and indeed "un-pacifistic." There were, moreover, connections between American foreign policy, war, and race that should not be pushed aside or ignored.[86]

The close relationship pacifists developed with the MOWM paid off in July 1943 when delegates at the MOWM convention voted to endorse a national campaign for civil disobedience against racial segregation. The plan, which had been conceived of by Muste, Farmer, and Rustin, designated one day each week in which African Americans would refuse to cooperate with segregation. Much to their disappointment, however, the plan never got off the ground, largely because Randolph withdrew his support.[87] A similar tension emerged after the war when the MOWM threatened civil disobedience as a protest against racial discrimination in the armed forces. When President Harry Truman issued an executive order desegregating the military, Randolph again retreated, much to the dismay of pacifists.[88]

The failure of the MOWM to adopt Gandhian nonviolence reveals a central paradox at the heart of an emergent radical pacifism. On the one hand, Muste and other pacifists hoped to build a mass movement, and Muste in particular was deeply sensitive to the need for compromise when making alliances with other groups. On the other hand, they held such a strict understanding of what nonviolence entailed on a personal and political level that they tended to exclude all but the true believers. This was certainly the case with CORE, which saw itself as a vehicle for a mass movement while at the same time having stringent membership requirements, including the requirement that members manifest Gandhian principles in their personal and group life. Ironically, when a social movement did emerge, later in the 1950s, committed to nonviolent direct action as a tactic for combating Jim Crow, its results were reformist, not revolutionary, and most of the African Americans who joined the organization utilized nonviolence for strategic reasons, not because they were pacifists.[89]

Indeed, although CORE defined itself as an autonomous organization, in fact it was heavily reliant on the FOR. Muste essentially subsidized it by allowing the FOR's paid staff members—such as Farmer, Houser, and Rustin—to serve as officers of CORE and by providing leadership and funding for its interracial workshops under the auspices of the FOR's Industrial-Racial Department. Charter members of CORE were usually members of an FOR cell who had been convinced by an FOR secretary to form a local branch of CORE. As the branches expanded to include non-pacifists, pacifists typically remained the most active members and occupied leadership positions, thereby profoundly influencing "its philosophy and style."[90]

The pacifist origins of CORE help to explain the organization's philosophy and practice of nonviolence. As we have seen, pacifists differentiated themselves from other reformers in their emphasis on the importance of changing individual hearts and minds as well as institutions. Thus, not surprisingly, the founders of CORE regarded the conversion of the opponent to be as important as, if not more important than, changing racist practice. Houser, who served as executive secretary of CORE from 1945 through 1954, stressed the importance of conversion and reconciliation through an ongoing process of negotiations and the use of direct action only as a last resort. "A non-violent campaign cannot be considered a total success unless attitudes are changed in the process of changing policies."[91]

CORE groups were viewed not only as a means for achieving racial equality, they were seen as vehicles for expressing the reality of racial equality. Pacifists like African American Erna Harris frequently warned fellow "direct actionists" not to become so enamored of direct action that they neglected the important work of getting acquainted with other participants in CORE groups. Such fellowship was an important means of overcoming consciousness of racial difference.[92] In fact, CORE had initially viewed Randolph's MOWM movement with suspicion because of its all-black character. Yet excitement at the prospect of a mass movement utilizing Gandhian nonviolence helped them overcome their misgivings. Muste's analysis proved critical: "From the standpoint of the whole religious pacifist movement as well as from the point of view of race relations in the United States," he wrote, "it is of great importance that we maintain this connection and that we render the maximum contribution to the [MOWM]."[93]

CORE's failure to become a mass movement was not for lack of trying. Over the course of the 1940s, it conducted scores of workshops and directed dozens of direct action projects, in the process breaking down segregation in hotels, skating rinks, department stores, YMCAs, and restaurants throughout the North. One of the organization's most ambitious projects was the 1947 Journey of Reconciliation, which it cosponsored with the FOR and coordinated with the help of Muste. Eager to test compliance with a recent Supreme Court decision declaring segregation in interstate travel illegal, the Journey involved sending an all-male interracial team across the upper South. All of the white participants and half the blacks were pacifists. Much to the satisfaction of CORE, the Journey received both local and national publicity as participants were arrested on numerous occasions over the course of the two-week trip. While most of the arrests resulted in fines, three of the participants ended up serving twenty-two days of hard labor on a chain gang in North Carolina.[94]

Direct actionists viewed the Journey as a success for their movement. Rustin and Houser, for example, believed that the "courteous and intelligent manner" in which they challenged segregation discouraged police brutality. They also suggested that the interracial character of the group meant that the struggle was not interpreted in terms of black against white, "but rather that progressives and democrats, white and black, were working by peaceful means to overcome a system which they felt to be wrong."[95] In terms of the history of the struggle for black civil rights, the Journey became the model for the Freedom Rides of 1961, which resulted in CORE's emergence as one of the most important civil rights organizations of the 1960s.

Despite these achievements, the Journey must be viewed as only moderately successful. It did not lead to the desegregation of interstate travel nor did the publicity lead to any discernible rise in membership or financial viability. Until the late 1950s, the organization rarely had more than a dozen active affiliates spread across the North. Most of these groups tended to be small, tightly knit, and deeply committed to Gandhian nonviolence. Though they had important victories in attacking discrimination in public accommodations, they often foundered when their targets were housing and employment discrimination. Historians August Meier and Elliott Rudwick have offered several reasons for CORE's "modest" achievements during this period, including lack of support from the white public and a black community that remained unconvinced that such tactics held much promise. They also cite "the tendency for chapters to focus on the reconciliatory aspects of their strategy. . . . They took seriously Houser's advice that nonviolence should 'incarnate the spirit of understanding, of goodwill, of humility,' and in fact during these first four years only half the chapters attempted to move beyond negotiations."[96]

Early CORE's attachment to conversion and reconciliation speaks to the organization's roots in pacifism. Even though they offered practical reasons for their use of nonviolence, the pacifists who were at the heart of the organization held a particular worldview, one that had a deep faith in the transformative power of love and self-suffering. Yet CORE activists increasingly tended to disavow the Christian origins of their beliefs, in part because those connections had become obscure to them.[97] Indeed, with the marginalization of pacifism within mainline Protestantism, there was a paradigm shift in pacifist religious culture in which they increasingly "organiz[ed] their religious culture around pacifism rather than Jesus."[98] Thus, although CORE's rejection of education and formal politics marks an important shift in the history of American pacifism, there remained a fundamental continuity in how pacifists approached the problem of social injustice, a continuity rooted in the Protestant origins of its theoreticians and founders. Muste, of course, freely admitted the religious basis for his faith in nonviolence, but many others did not and, as a result, found themselves puzzled by accusations that they were illogical and idealistic.

Ironically, despite this emphasis on reconciliation, pacifist direct actionists continued to face criticism from the older generation. After the Journey of Reconciliation, Muste and Rustin were forced to respond to the charge that they were just "stirring up trouble" and being "meddling outsiders."[99] In a similar vein, when the FOR's nonviolent direct action committee picketed the British embassy for Indian freedom, Sayre wrote angrily to Muste that such tactics were obstructionist and tarnished the FOR's image.[100] These differences spoke to a larger struggle with the FOR over its purpose and direction. As we shall see, these differences emerged most forcefully over the question of the relationship between the pacifist movement and the wartime state, a question that would become magnified after the war as some pacifists, led by Muste, called for civil disobedience to protest atomic weaponry and the militarization of American society. While some argued that it was a time for pacifists to beat a "strategic retreat," Muste called for creativity and direct action.[101] He managed to win the debate during the war, in the process making nonviolent direct action an institutionalized component of American pacifism. In the postwar period, however, as he continued to push a more radical agenda for the organization, he faced increasing push back. As a result, he would pursue his prophetic politics outside of the confines of the FOR in a desperate effort to shake Americans out of their complacency about nuclear proliferation and the Cold War.

～

CHAPTER 9

Conscience Against the Wartime
State and the Bomb

To abolish war it is not enough to say that war must be
abolished. War is so much a part of our culture and of our
economic and political and spiritual being that to say war
must go is obviously the equivalent of saying that a
revolution must take place in ourselves and in our world.
Something has to occur in the political and spiritual realm
which is comparable to the fission of the atom and the
release of atomic energy.

—A. J. Muste, 1947

IN THEIR OPPOSITION to American intervention in World War II, Muste
and his fellow pacifists would fail to adequately grapple with the ideological
and moral challenges presented by the rise of fascism. Still, their thought
had a deeply self-reflexive quality that provided them with an acute sensi-
tivity to the ways in which the United States violated its own democratic
ideals. We have already seen how this led them to experiment with Gandhian nonviolence and American race relations, but it was also evident in
their opposition to the militarization of American society during the war.
While their predictions of an incipient dictatorship may have been over-
wrought, they recognized more than most the ways in which total war
mobilization threatened democratic institutions and might morph into an
oppressive welfare/warfare state. As Muste wrote in early 1941, "we are
asked to believe that somehow when the war is over . . . we shall scrap
our armaments." More likely, however, was that the "armament economy"

would appeal to policymakers as a solution to the problem of unemployment and become a "Super-Arsenal" that would serve as an adjunct of American imperialism and power.[1]

The explosion of two atomic bombs confirmed Muste's worst fears about the deleterious effects of modern warfare on democratic institutions and practices. Over the course of 1945–47, he evolved a penetrating critique of modernity that became the basis for the emergence of the radical pacifist movement in the early Cold War era. This critique involved not only direct resistance to the national security state, but also the building of alternative or intentional communities. Muste was never entirely comfortable with the movement's antimodern thrust, but this difference did not become a source of conflict until the mid-1950s when he became persuaded that it might be possible to build a new left.

Muste was thus one of the first radical intellectuals to foresee the emergence of "a bureaucratic, manipulative, and authoritarian nightmare" in which the capitalist West was transformed "into something not all that different from the Stalinist East."[2] Not coincidentally, he—along C. Wright Mills and Herbert Marcuse, who would develop similar critiques of postwar American society—would be considered an elder statesman of the New Left when it emerged in the early 1960s.

MUSTE and his fellow pacifists viewed World War II as essentially a repetition of World War I; in their analysis, the conflict was a straightforward story of conspiracy by war profiteers and rival imperialists for markets and power. Of course he wanted "to blot fascism and Nazism from the face of the earth," Muste stated at a 1940 conference of the FOR, but the "so-called democracies" had been fundamentally compromised by the "terrible peace" they had imposed upon Germany after World War I, and by their own history of race and empire. The only effective and long-standing way to obtain peace was for the United States, France, and Britain to unilaterally disarm, renounce their colonies, and move toward a more cooperative economic system. Such positive action would throw the Axis powers "off guard" and would undermine the appeal of war making and nationalism among their followers. As for the argument that disarmament and neutrality would leave weaker countries vulnerable, Muste recommended nonviolent defense.[3]

Muste also opposed the war on the grounds that American intervention would create a militarized, authoritarian state at home, and serve as the fulcrum for a postwar "American empire."⁴ The passage of the Selective Service Act of 1940, which established the nation's first peacetime draft, only increased these concerns, as did the War Powers Act of 1941, which gave the president the authority to censor all news and information, limit civil liberties, and seize property owned by foreign nationals. Of course, the most blatant violation of civil liberties was the internment of Japanese Americans, which Muste and his fellow pacifists condemned as a "grievous violation of Christian attitudes."⁵

Over the course of the war, Muste viewed the negotiations that took place between the Allied powers as a confirmation of his analysis that the United States, like Britain and the Soviet Union, viewed the war as a means of increasing its global hegemony. As he wrote of the Dumbarton Oaks proposals, which would give birth to the United Nations, the notion of a "Big Three" and the "superpower veto" showed that the United States was pursuing a policy of "isolationism and neo-imperialism. . . . In pursuance of this policy we shall be putting down independence movements in Latin America . . . [and] we shall be joining with Britain, Holland, and France in crushing independence movements in the Orient. More or less directly we are getting practice now in Greece and Belgium." At home, "the nation will be militarized, as the proposal for peace time conscription suggests," and "reactionary and demagogic elements" will make "scapegoats" of radicals and minority groups.⁶

Muste's analysis of the causes and potentially negative consequences of the war were not, of course, unfounded. Historians have long established that the Treaty of Versailles, economic imbalances and depression, and the history of colonialism all colluded to provide a fertile ground for the rise of nationalism and militarism. It was also a real question whether Britain, the United States, and the Soviet Union were indeed fighting for democracy. The tensions that emerged between Winston Churchill and Franklin Roosevelt in the drafting of the Atlantic Charter are just one illustration of the ways in which the West continued to view democracy as a "whites only" affair. There was, moreover, a strong case to be made for the pacifist argument that the nature of modern warfare tended to eradicate the distinctions between the Allies and the fascist powers. While attacks on civilian populations began with the fascist powers, the Allies adopted obliteration bombing early on in an effort to undermine German morale. While total war might not have led to totalitarianism in the United States, many of the wartime measures passed by the federal government foreshadowed the rise of the national security state and growth of executive power that would culminate in the Watergate scandal. Finally, as Muste predicted, the war helped to create the so-called "American century," in which the United States used its military and economic might to open markets and obtain a "sphere of influence" in Western Europe, Latin America, and the "emerging nations" in Asia and Africa.[7]

Yet Muste's critique of the war also had its limitations. He never grappled with the reality that it was highly unlikely, to say the least, that the Allied powers would respond to Nazism by unilaterally disarming and renouncing their claims to spheres of influence. Nor did he come to terms with the fact that it was possible to agree with his analysis and still believe that the Allied powers represented a "lesser evil."[8] He could also be criticized for inconsistency; he had long maintained, with Gandhi, that "where there is only a choice between cowardice and violence," then the latter was preferable.[9] He had applied this maxim to the labor movement and would do so again after World War II in defense of anticolonial struggles in the third world. Yet surely the horrific persecution of European Jewry met Gandhi's criteria, thereby warranting violent self-defense and the intervention of the Allied powers, morally corrupted though they may have been. The point is that the war was far more complex, contested, and dynamic than Muste's analysis allowed. Indeed, in the United States alone, it had different meanings for different participants: Liberals and laborites viewed it as an opportunity to build a "New Deal for the world"; African Americans transformed it into a war against racism and imperialism; and human rights activists turned it into a struggle for international law.[10]

In the last analysis, although pacifists insisted that their opposition to the war was realistic and that nonviolence offered a concrete, political alternative, their ultimate rationale was that war violated their "foundational beliefs." This comes out most clearly in the statements that COs made to their draft boards, including those who identified as "secular"; they mixed political arguments against war and conscription with truth claims about the nature of human beings and the universe.[11]

More so than others, Muste conceded that his antiwar stance was ultimately based upon his faith in the redemptive power of suffering love. As Donald Meyer has commented, "in Muste, processes of thought universal among the semipacifists and pragmatic non-interventionists—but in them blurred, slurred, unspoken, often unsuspected—were brought out and carried through to final grounds; Muste, unlike the others, knew what it was to hold to a fixed principle without secret inner concessions."[12] To put it another way, Muste viewed pacifism as a realistic political choice, but only because he fully believed in the realism of the cross. With the threat of World War II, he wrote, the West had arrived at a moment of *kairos*, a crisis and an opportunity for a saving act to redeem humankind. "I believe with all my soul that the embattled peoples of the earth . . . are waiting for a nation that would have the sublime horse sense, the divine foolishness, to break the evil spell that is on mankind" and lay down its arms. It was a moment like the one faced by the Jews in the early Christian era. "The hour of judgment has again struck for mankind," he asserted. Peoples and nations must become "fools for Christ" by renouncing might and embracing the way of suffering love. Through their martyrdom they would nourish "the seeds of a new and ampler age" based on brotherhood and peace.[13] It was this commitment to practice a radical form of love that helps to explain his infamous 1940 statement, "If I can't love Hitler, I can't love at all."[14]

These comments reveal the evangelistic and ethnocentric heart of American pacifism, which presupposed its values were universally applicable and which relied, in the last analysis, upon the hope that others would be converted to the truth of nonviolence. Muste's prescription for the threat of tyranny and war was for nations and individuals alike to take up the cross. Only Christianity, and not its "erstwhile 'rivals,'" such as Buddhism and Confucianism, was capable of overcoming the crisis of "secularism" represented by the rise of Nazism and the threat of another world war. The only "genuine" alternative to "world domination" by one nation is "Christian universalism," inspired by the ideals of love, goodwill, and self-sacrifice.[15] At the same time, however, he viewed himself as an internationalist and a democrat. This contradiction illustrates how Christianity shaped the political culture of pacifism, even as pacifists viewed their creed as universally applicable. It also, perhaps, helps to explain why absolute nonviolence held little appeal for Jews, since it was unlikely to stop Hitler and his allies from killing them, and whose theology discourages martyrdom, yet who would be most affected by a policy of crucifixion.[16]

It was precisely the pacifist tendency to measure political realities against the love ideal that was the substance of the Christian realists' all-out attack in the late 1930s. As Niebuhr wrote, "When a religious and moral absolute such as 'perfect love' is introduced into politics as an alternative to power which is the very nature of politics, it breeds confusion. One form that this confusion takes is the disinclination of the pacifists to look at the horrible consequences of tyranny lest they be shaken in their conviction that nothing can possibly be worse than war." In the last analysis, Christians had to balance the law of love against the depth and reality of human sin; in so doing, they would realize that war against Germany was "a negative task which cannot be avoided."[17] From 1938 on, Niebuhr threw himself into the work of leading the Protestant mainline away from pacifism and neutrality and toward a more "realistic," interventionist stance. By 1941, when the first issue of his *Christianity and Crisis* magazine appeared, his supporters included such liberal Protestant churchmen as John C. Bennett, William Adams Brown, Henry Sloan Coffin, Sherwood Eddy, and Henry Van Dusen, all of whom had been pacifists or sympathetic to pacifism during the interwar years.[18]

Yet Niebuhr's own position was not free of moral ambiguities. As Muste pointed out, by dismissing the Gospel as a standard of social and political behavior, Niebuhr and other Christian realists did not solve the perennial problem of where to draw the line.

> The question now is: If we may condone the fact that we ourselves and others live by some other standard than that of the love-ethic of the New Testament, what is that other standard? To admit, eagerly and in all humility, that we do not meet the Gospel standard and are therefore sinful men, is one thing. To conclude that we may, therefore, in a given situation, use another standard, is a totally different thing. By what standard is our compromising to be measured and kept from being too "realistic"? Just what is the workable compromise between the prophets and Machiavelli?

This question was particularly relevant when one considered the total nature of modern warfare, which obviated just-war guidelines for proportional means and distinctions between combatants and noncombatants. It was those theologians who thought there was a middle ground between pacifism and total war that were "unrealistic," Muste asserted. "You are either for or against total war."[19]

As Muste's comments suggest, questions of when to draw the line, of the relationship between the prophet, the nation, and war, were not resolved with the invention of realism. During World War II, Niebuhr would struggle rather unsuccessfully to reconcile his understanding of Christian vocation with the reality of obliteration bombing and the atomic bombing of Hiroshima and Nagasaki.[20] Similarly, during the Cold War, he would frequently inveigh against American illusions of omnipotence and power, while at the same time insisting that realism required taking a hard line against the Soviet Union. Indeed, his very notion of international politics as "a battle in which the Children of Light would 'have to play hardball' if they were to survive" made it difficult for him to oppose anything the United States did in order to prevail over the Soviet Union.[21]

Moreover, as civil libertarians, pacifists did not use coercion to force compliance with their point of view. As Muste observed, his creed may have been an absolutist one, but it was also democratic, as it held that relationships between human beings "must be free relations, fellowships, communities."[22] His response to his seventeen-year-old son John's desire to join the navy illustrates his commitment to human freedom. Although he and Anne made their own position clear, they refused to subject him to "undue emotional pressure" and granted the requisite parental permission. Such was Muste's approach to personal and political questions alike; even the most profound differences were not allowed to exclude someone from the family, whether personal or metaphorical. His relationship with John, for example, remained close even though his son disagreed with him about the war. While they discussed politics, the substance of their relationship was that of a father and son. In fact, their correspondence can be described as affectionately mundane; it shows Muste giving John help with his dissertation on the literature of the Spanish Civil War, waxing enthusiastic about baseball, expressing affection for his grandchildren, and wondering if he should delay an operation for cataracts.[23]

FOR pacifists, fears of the coming authoritarian state first played out in debates over the provisions for conscientious objection allowed by the Selective Service Act of 1940. In contrast to World War I, the law provided exemption from service for those who "by reason of religious training and belief" were conscientiously opposed to participation in war. The first and most popular option for COs was to accept noncombatant service. The second was to perform "work of national importance" in Civilian Public Service (CPS) camps under the supervision of the historic peace churches (i.e., Quakers, Brethren, and Mennonites) and established peace organizations such as the FOR. A third option was to refuse to register altogether and serve time in a federal penitentiary. For most pacifists of the World War I generation, the law represented a step forward in the struggle to obtain government recognition of the right of conscientious objection. Younger and more radical pacifists, however, viewed the arrangement as a compromise with conscription and thus with an increasingly authoritarian state. This conflict became representative of the growing rift between pacifists over the relationship between the individual and the state and the use of direct action. During the war, Muste attempted to keep these two wings of the pacifist movement together, yet the explosion of the atomic bomb convinced him that resistance was imperative of all pacifists, Christians, and Americans.[24]

COs' dissatisfaction with the CPS system grew over the course of the war as the government increasingly asserted its authority over the camps.[25] At first, they expressed their unhappiness with the CPS arrangement through conventional methods like writing letters to the historic peace churches, asking them to stop administering conscription. They also called on the FOR to recall its representative on the National Service Board for Religious Objectors (NSBRO), the body that mediated the relationship between pacifists and Selective Service. Soon, however, some began to take more drastic action by engaging in nonviolent resistance. Their tactics included work slowdowns and stoppages, as well as walkouts in which they accepted prison instead of alternative service. The most militant expressions of nonviolent resistance occurred in federal penitentiaries where COs made up about one-sixth of the prison population. Here their target was less the CPS system, but certain rules and regulations, such as segregation, that they viewed as dehumanizing.[26]

As COs became increasingly radicalized, they felt a sense of estrangement from older pacifists and established peace organizations that had cooperated with the administration of the CPS system. Paton Price, former chairman of the New York Youth Council of the FOR, resigned because he could "no longer identify . . . with an organization which deliberately contributes to the war effort and the perpetuation of that vicious system." While he recognized that his stand would help push "the pacifist movement into two groups poles apart," he had come to believe that "he who accepts [conscription] is molded by it in its own image."[27]

Muste defended the FOR's policy of giving "vigorous but critical support" until the spring of 1943, when he began to rethink his position. In addition to moving beyond the terms of the original agreement between pacifists and the Selective Service by forcing COs to work for private employers, the government had not adequately addressed CO concerns about lack of provisions for dependents, work without pay, and their desire to perform work of national importance. It now seemed to Muste that the camps had become "conscript labor pure and simple" instead of experiments in civilian control that would lead to government recognition of the right of conscientious objection.[28]

At a meeting in May 1943, members of the FOR's national council and staff discussed a memo that Muste had circulated calling on the organization to withdraw from administrative connection with NSBRO if CPS was not "made a genuinely 'civilian program'" with provisions for those COs unwilling to accept CPS by October 31, 1943. After a long discussion, a compromise was struck: the executive committee would present the various points of view to the membership, who would in turn express its "will" for FOR action.[29]

How the FOR ultimately acted in response to the "will" of its membership became a source of controversy. Although most indicated that they favored withdrawal, the council voted to remain affiliated with the NSBRO, albeit with the caveat that they were opposed to participating in a similar setup after the war.[30] Muste justified the decision in terms of the need to maintain pacifist unity, but critics were not appeased. In February 1944, sixteen COs—including Dave Dellinger—imprisoned at Lewisburg Penitentiary in Pennsylvania wrote an open letter to the FOR challenging the process through which the decision was made and disputing Muste's suggestion that remaining affiliated with NSBRO was somehow "neutral." The letter went on to suggest that the FOR was in danger of becoming "a sentimental, impotent organization which, like the Boy Scouts and the AFSC, performs many 'good deeds' but offers no serious challenge to the violent, exploitative society of which it is a part."[31]

Muste knew a challenge to his leadership when he saw one. After all, the young militants had, in effect, suggested that his very manhood was at stake in how he responded to their letter. Moving quickly, he took a two-pronged approach. First, he stood by the FOR's record. As he pointed out in his reply, rather than regress, the FOR had grown substantially and had "been by far the most important channel throughout this period for disseminating information about and popularizing the idea of Non Violent Direct Action." He also suggested that the young militants were acting in a sectarian spirit that was inappropriate in the context of the inclusive and democratic culture of the pacifist movement: "I am done forever, and on the basis of long and painful and carefully considered experience, with political sectarianism."[32]

At the same time that he vigorously defended the FOR's record, he worked to establish the organization's radical bona fides. At the next meeting of the FOR national council, he persuaded the organization to withdraw from its voting membership on the NSBRO, the major source of CO dissatisfaction, though this would not be formalized until December 1944. He also obtained the FOR's approval to organize a series of conferences on the "philosophy and strategy of revolutionary pacifism," which would be explicitly directed at younger pacifists.[33]

The ensuing conferences, held in September 1944 and February 1945, illustrate Muste's profound influence on the nascent radical pacifist movement. In summing up the conference proceedings, participants stated that their models for personal and political action would be the Hebrew prophets, "the life and teachings of Jesus and the 'Way of the Cross,'" and Gandhi. They asserted that nonviolence was a worldview and way of life based upon faith in "the unity of all life." Citing the writings of Berdyaev, Huxley, and Koestler, they argued that their affirmation of spiritual and transcendent values challenged the "prevailing materialism of the time" and the "erroneous notion," held by left and right alike, "that rational thought alone could comprehend the nature of reality." Hence they stressed the need for a "spiritual revolution" to accompany a political revolution.[34]

Their political goals followed from their view of contemporary society as regimented and materialistic. While most of them conceded that the means of communication and transportation should remain centralized, albeit under government ownership and control, they argued that wide-ranging decentralization was necessary to "restore the individual to the autonomy he loses where authority is excessively delegated and rigorously [sic] centralized." This interest in decentralization led to an emphasis on the formation of intentional communities in which there would be common ownership of larger units of production and distribution, and, at the same time, individual ownership of small tools and homes. Radical pacifists hoped that their efforts would serve as a model for their fellow Americans on the virtues of decentralism and simple living, and help to restore a sense of personal responsibility, which they differentiated from "rugged individualism," "a perverted development of this value, isolating and exploiting other people."[35]

Pacifists' concern with unity and integration suggests the influence of Christian existentialism. As we have seen, since his "reconversion," Muste had shown some appreciation for "crisis" theology insofar as it criticized

Enlightenment notions of reason and human progress. Now he began to sound existentialist themes; he quoted from Søren Kierkegaard in his sermons and speeches, and circulated excerpts from the philosopher's writings among FOR members. Reflecting this influence, conference participants maintained that the separation between human beings and the divine was the root of sin and evil. "The unity or the organic nature of life is fundamental in our philosophy," they stated. Without equal rights for all, "division is created, that is, community broken." The way to repair these divisions—to create what they called the "beloved community"—was to take action, to commit their whole selves to fighting for peace and equality. By taking "personal responsibility" for sin and evil, they would create and reaffirm the existence of a moral universe and thereby inspire other Americans to do the same.[36]

Despite Muste's efforts, dissension within pacifist ranks over the CPS issue continued. Dellinger, along with six of the original signatories, resigned from the FOR in the summer of 1944, charging that the organization had failed to meet the war crisis with "courage and imagination." The letter concluded with a call for sympathizers to join them in building "a working-class, revolutionary, socialist movement which will be true to the noblest emphases of religious pacifism."[37]

This letter represented a small minority of pacifist opinion; only seven Lewisburg prisoners actually resigned from the organization. But it points to divides within pacifist ranks that would become more important later on. Whereas younger pacifists had become committed to Gandhian nonviolence through their experience in CPS, prison, and CORE, many older pacifists continued to find such tactics contrary to the spirit of pacifism. The response of Caleb Foote, the FOR's West Coast secretary, to the letters written by Dellinger and the other Lewisburg prisoners offers a case in point. Though he found their tone contrary to the spirit of religious pacifism and their characterization of the FOR unwarranted, he wrote to Muste that they spoke to a profound difference of opinion among pacifists over how to create social change. As he put it, the conflict over the FOR's affiliation with NSBRO was ultimately an expression of "a fundamental conflict as to method. We agree that we want to change the minds [of those] that disagree with us rather than destroy them, but some of us want to use satyagraha and some service. Or, to put it [in] other terms, some want to super-cooperate and some to non-cooperate." Given that the two methods were "almost mutually exclusive," Foote doubted that it was possible to maintain unity.[38]

In addition to disagreeing as to the method best suited to ending war and violence, pacifists held different views of the state. While not all of the younger rebels were anarchists, their experience in CPS and jail had made them deeply suspicious of government and bureaucracy in general.[39] Older pacifists, by contrast, with their roots in the progressive tradition, tended to view the state as a potentially ameliorative force in society. In his October 1946 column in *Fellowship*, for example, John Haynes Holmes differentiated between the "perfect" and the "imperfect" pacifist, stating that the former "aims his shaft at WAR!" whereas the latter was against war only because "he is opposed to government. Nay, opposed to authority of any kind!" Indeed, Holmes suggested, the "perfect" pacifist might be in favor of conscription "under conditions of proper pay etc., if it were instituted in the spirit and to the end of William James' 'moral equivalent of war.' It is *military* conscription that outrages the pacifist."[40]

Yet for the younger generation, it was increasingly difficult to isolate war from injustice or military conscription from the growing presence of the state in all aspects of American society. As Foote explained in an article for *Fellowship*, the problem with prison was not so much physical brutality, which was not as much of an issue as it had been in the past, but the "psychological torture" of isolation, separation from family, and the meaninglessness of daily existence. Such "de-personalization" made prisoners and former prisoners "fruit ready for the picking by the native fascist." This was something that Americans—and, implicitly many pacifists—failed to grasp: "An America sophisticated in thus transforming physical into psychological torture, which calls its concentration camps 'relocation centers,' finds this fact hard to understand."[41]

Dellinger's letter was significant, then, not so much for its attack on the FOR's relationship to NSBRO, which had in effect become a dead issue, but because it identified a growing split between older and younger pacifists over the philosophy and methodology of pacifism. Roy Finch put it succinctly in a letter to Muste in May 1944. The "fundamental" question was whether or not pacifists were "really close enough together in broad political and social philosophies to establish an effective unity?" Or, to put it another way, "Is pacifism . . . to be the touchstone for unity and action? Or is perhaps non-violent 'revolutionism' itself a better touchstone?" For growing numbers of COs, he noted, the answer to these questions was that they had "far more in common with certain non-pacifist radicals and progressives [than with other pacifists]." In this way, the issue of the FOR's affiliation with NSBRO was symbolic. The organization's reluctance to disrupt pacifist unity by withdrawing from the administration of conscription suggested a deeper affinity with "more conservative, more quietistic pacifists" from whom the younger generation felt increasingly alienated.[42] Muste would manage to hold liberals and radicals together for the next several years, but the onset of the Cold War persuaded him that radicals would have to form their own social movement that more accurately reflected their commitment to "non-violent 'revolutionism.'"

"It is a day of judgment," Muste wrote in response to the atomic bombing of Hiroshima and Nagasaki. If he suspected that modern warfare had rendered the just war tradition of the Christian church obsolete, now he was certain. If he thought "Western civilization" was in crisis, now he knew for sure. Now really was the moment of *kairos*, the last opportunity for Americans, already burdened by their history of racism and economic exploitation, to repent and renounce of their power. Like his eighteenth and nineteenth-century counterparts, Muste used the prophetic language of the jeremiad to alert his fellow Americans to their historic role: citing Walt Whitman's "Song of the Universal," he argued that the country could either become a "savior nation" by relinquishing its atomic arsenal or usher in the "apocalypse." People throughout the world were asking whether the United States was "the incarnation of Satan, or is he indeed the symbol of Everyman, the Common People, who by the grace of God may at last inherit the Kingdom? Never in all history has a people been faced with such a responsibility and such an opportunity."[43]

Muste viewed the bomb as the culmination of the existential crisis wrought by modernity that he had identified in his 1940 book *Non-violence in an Aggressive World*. It was, as he put it in December 1945, the "end-product of an age of mechanism, of power, of mass action, of totalitarianism, an age which looked down upon the individual and placed its faith in systems." The problem was both ideological and structural. No longer believing in God or the existence of a moral universe, human beings had come to doubt that their lives had any ultimate meaning. They even doubted the reality of their own existence. This alienation encouraged them to think of themselves as objects rather than as "responsible and creative spirits." As a result, they located power in "the irrational forces of nature" and in the machine rather than in themselves. What exacerbated this sense of fragmentation and depersonalization was the bureaucratization and centralization of modern life. The fact that many of the scientists who worked on the Manhattan Project appeared not to know that they were building an atomic bomb exemplified "this process of depersonalization and mechanization."[44]

Whether liberal or radical, Catholic or Protestant, pacifists agreed with Muste that the bomb signaled a crisis of epic proportions. Dorothy Day's denunciation of the bomb on the front page of the *Catholic Worker* was one of the most eloquent. Citing "What you do unto the least of my brethren, you do unto me," she suggested that Americans could not escape accountability for the bomb. While the Japanese may have been vaporized, "we will breathe their dust into our nostrils, feel them in the fog of New York on our faces, feel them in the rain on the hills of Easton [Pennsylvania]."[45] John Haynes Holmes asserted that the fact that the bomb shattered "not merely a city, and an Empire, but the whole system of moral law. . . . Not by such means will humanity, or any nation, be ultimately saved. Not in the realm of sheer brute force lies the remedy we seek. [Recall] the words of the ancient prophet, Zechariah, 'Not by power, nor by might, but by my spirit, saith the Lord.'"[46]

The younger generation was particularly affected by the bomb. CO Bent Andersen went AWOL from a CPS camp in California as a protest against the bomb. Hitchhiking across the country, he distributed some four thousand flyers that stated: "Nearly half a million people were obliterated recently in a mere matter of seconds. . . . Now is the time for the people of America to cry out that the first atomic bombs in history shall be the last! That war be waged no more!" COs at a CPS camp in Oregon also responded to the bomb by calling on men in CPS camps to go AWOL and for all pacifists to unite and engage in strikes, fasts, and protests at factories producing nuclear weapons and at government offices. As they wrote Muste, "Upon hearing of the introduction of atomic bombing, we were shocked to action geared to stopping the present conflict and aiming to eliminate all war . . . this moment may be the crucial time for us to speak."[47]

Pacifists across the ideological spectrum further agreed with Muste that the bomb was a sign that the modern faith in reason, science, and progress had gone too far. Sayre viewed the bomb as the natural consequence of the "coming of modern science and the dazzlement of men by the scientific method and wonders of technological achievement," and he called for a new generation of saints eager to prove that the "spirit" too had power. The young radical pacifist Marion (Coddington) Bromley asserted that the bomb "was the inevitable product of an inhuman, competitive industrial order in which millions are brutalized by monotonous work," and she argued that the task before pacifists was to find new ways of affirming their faith that "man is bigger than masses."[48]

Although pacifists generally agreed on the causes of the atomic and international crises, they disagreed as to the best method for achieving disarmament and international cooperation. Liberal pacifists believed that it was still possible to work within the system. They emphasized the importance of allying with nonpacifists and working for universal disarmament. They also viewed world government—the idea, first enunciated by Immanuel Kant, that nations relinquish a level of sovereignty to a world body—as the first step toward the control of atomic weapons and world peace.[49]

Those who identified as radical pacifists, on the other hand, were skeptical of world government as a panacea for the current crisis. Some, like Muste, were theoretically in favor of world government, but doubted that it could be accomplished in the climate of mutual suspicion between the United States and the Soviet Union. Rather than place their hopes in world government, pacifists should instead focus on revolutionizing institutions and values, thereby laying the foundations for a world government that would be genuinely democratic.[50] Others opposed world government on anarchistic principles. M. Palmer Bryant, for example, related that his experience in a CPS camp during the war had made him distrustful of government and law as democratic mechanisms. Instead of world government, "the world's great need is bigger and better individual consciences, not bigger and better government."[51]

During 1945–47, Muste became the chief proponent of the radical pacifist position. In numerous sermons, speeches, articles, and a book titled *Not by Might: Christianity, the Way to Human Decency*, he insisted, in existential terms, that redemption would only be possible if human beings asserted their freedom against the depersonalization of modernity. The crisis could not be resolved on a political basis or by political methods, but only by "the individual conscience against the bomb," as suggested by the famous *Life* magazine article of the same name. In real terms what this meant was that pacifists and others should refuse to register for the draft, refuse to pay income taxes, and otherwise not go along with the system. When individuals took "personal responsibility" for evils engendered by the bomb in this way, they forced others to recognize that their feelings of depersonalization were not real—that they existed, and thus they shared responsibility for the current crisis. They also gave others the courage to break with the conformity of modern life. "The moment a man thus acts as a responsible moral being and not a cog in a machine," Muste wrote, "all doubts about the reality of his own existence vanish." Moreover, "soul power" was "released into human life, into history" when individuals courageously refused to subordinate their conscience regardless of the consequences.[52]

In making this argument, Muste again drew upon Protestant theologian Paul Tillich's idea that *kairos* was possible when a group of people seized the transcendental idea of love and renounced power. Such an event "would perhaps create 'mankind.'" As Muste explained, as more and more Americans recognized and repented of their own personal responsibility for the atomic crisis, the nation as a whole would do the same by unilaterally abolishing the country's atomic arsenal. Only by laying "down its life that mankind may live" could the United States become a force for peace:

> It is clear that [calling for unilateral disarmament] is asking the nation to act upon the principle that he who would save his life must be willing to lose it, and to undertake a redemptive mission based on the faith that goodwill, or love, is the ultimate force in the universe. I believe that there is a very real possibility that a nation which had power and renounced it in this spirit . . . would by God's grace open a new and blessed era in human history. But I am certain that even if the United States should be attacked and crucified after having undertaken such a mission, it would still be better to disarm unilaterally. . . . To suffer terribly, and perhaps even to perish as a nation, after having undertaken a spiritual mission. No one who professes any belief in the Judeo-Christian tradition can doubt that the ultimate verdict of God and history would be with that nation.[53]

Muste was certain that just such a moment confronted the United States after World War II, and he spent the next several years trying to convert atomic scientists, liberal Protestants, and his fellow pacifists to his point of view.

Muste was especially interested in the atomic scientists as potential converts because he saw them as the core of the problem confronting humankind: the mystification of individual responsibility caused by a reliance on bureaucracy and mechanization. It was, he suggested in reference to the atomic bomb, the scientist "who incarnates power; it is in the brain or

mind that power is to be found. . . . It was the result of a distortion . . .
that modern man should believe in, never question, never think of questioning, the reality of the machine but not conceive of either the builder or
the tender of the machine as equally and indubitably real."[54] He hoped that
if he could convince scientists to cease production of atomic weapons, then
Americans would recognize that the bomb did not exist outside of human
history, but was a creation of human beings whose fate was in their own
hands.

The scientific community's response to the bomb gave Muste good reason to hope that he would be heard. With "one world or none" as their
slogan, they had united in a campaign to secure international control of
atomic energy and world government.[55] For Muste, however, such a campaign was doomed so long as scientists continued to conduct research that
contributed to the production of atomic weapons. In his letters to Albert
Einstein, for example, he argued that educating the public on the dangers
of atomic war was "not the proper first step in such a campaign. It is
indeed, in the absence of a prior personal and moral act on the part of the
scientists, a trivial and in effect . . . a dishonest thing to do." Echoing Don
Paolo, the hero of Silone's *Bread and Wine*, he asserted that there was "a
deep cleavage in our souls and in our society because our moral and social
development has not kept pace with technological advance. That cleavage
must be healed first and basically within the morally responsible human
being. It will be healed in the scientist who becomes a prophet, that is, a
man who assumes responsibility for what he creates and what is done with
it, a man whose words and actions are in true accord."[56]

Although Einstein found Muste's criticism "justified to a high degree,"
he insisted that the "real solution" was "not refusal of military service but
supranational organization of all military power."[57] This was the general
response Muste got from scientists. Although they welcomed his suggestions and invited him to participate in a number of their conferences, only
a few of them ever took the radical step of disassociating themselves from
activities related to the production of atomic weapons.[58] For Muste, however, it was precisely the scientists' unwillingness to take this kind of risk
that exemplified the paradox in liberal thinking about the bomb and international cooperation. Even as they desperately wanted peace, liberals continued to support a large military budget in the name of national security.
As Muste commented, "the very means nations use to provide themselves
with apparent or temporary 'defense' and 'security' constitute the greatest

obstacle to the attainment of genuine or permanent collective security. They want international machinery so that the atomic armaments race may cease; but the atomic armaments race has to stop or the goal of world order recedes beyond human reach."[59]

Muste found this paradoxical support for military security and desire for peace especially prominent among liberal Protestants, among whom Christian realism had become increasingly popular. His debates with them reveal that a wide gulf had opened up between pacifists and mainline Protestants, and that the latter's realism devolved into a kind of American moral complacency and self-satisfaction that exempted the United States from any responsibility in the rising tensions of the Cold War. Henry Van Dusen, the recently appointed president of Union Theological Seminary, wrote to Muste that "so long as the United States possesses exclusively the secret of the atomic bomb, peace is secure since we shall certainly not employ it aggressively and no other nation will dare threaten us. There is even a faint hope that this instrument may actually accomplish what all of our decades of labor for peace have failed to accomplish—the abolition of war, because no nation will be fool enough to risk involvement in conflict." He concluded by asserting that the possibility for peace rested "on Russia, and on Russia alone." Reinhold Niebuhr made a similar argument. While agreeing that the development of the atomic bomb was "terrible," he wrote to Muste that he saw "little chance" of outlawing it. "The fact that the instrument has been created may increase the fear of war sufficiently so that we can build a real world organization. Therein lies our hope. Nations do not deprive themselves of new sources of power and prestige, once it has been placed in their hands. This is a terrible fact but it is so."[60]

Muste responded by accusing Niebuhr and Van Dusen of failing in their role as prophets. As he wrote in an open letter to Niebuhr, Christian realism fostered not tension, but "*anxiety* or a pervading sense of futility, for tension in the biblical sense is surely characteristic of a situation where man stands before his God and makes a *decision*."[61] Instead of realism, what the world desperately needed was "faith and hope" that it was possible "to build a just and durable peace." Such prophecy was, on one level, an expression of "divine foolishness," but on another it was pragmatic, since it rested on a view of "the universe, life, human history" as "dynamic things, not static. There is, therefore, no set of rules . . . which is eternally valid. Circumstances change and the organism must adapt itself to them or perish."[62]

Without an attitude of humility and contrition, moreover, Niebuhr and other Protestant liberals fell into the trap of nationalism. By thinking that "no one could possibly be afraid of the United States," "realists" failed to recognize that the United States had introduced a profound tension into international relations by developing and using the bomb. Observing that German military might made other nations feel "insecure and afraid," he suggested that it was reasonable to assume that much of the Soviet Union's behavior could be attributed to fear of "our tremendous military establishment and on top of that the atomic bomb." The idea that the United States could intimidate the Soviet Union into becoming more tolerant was equally arrogant and nationalistic. "If Russia could not be kept down after 1917 and all that intervened between then and 1939, what can we expect if now she is compelled by force to 'back down' temporarily?" If anything, a massive arms buildup and monopolistic control over the atomic bomb would further contribute to the climate of fear and mutual suspicion. Moreover, once the Soviet Union acquired the secret of the bomb there would be an arms race that might "be the end of our civilization and perhaps even the end of mankind; for the atomic bomb of today is by no means the ultimate in weapons of self-extermination which man might invent."[63]

Muste's conviction that the United States and the West were at least as responsible as Russia for the emerging Cold War led to a confrontation with John Foster Dulles. As head of the Federal Council of Churches and future secretary of state under Eisenhower, Dulles was not so much a realist as a "priestly nationalist," as one biographer puts it, and realist criticism of his excessive moralism and nationalism is well known.[64] But it also crucial to recognize, as Muste did, that these were differences over tactics, not aims; realists believed in the superiority of liberal democracy and were committed to extending its influence vis-à-vis the Soviet Union. As Muste chided Niebuhr in 1948, "in essential matters—support of the Marshall Plan, the need of fighting communism and Russia by both military and 'peaceful means,' your political position today cannot be distinguished from that of John Foster Dulles."[65]

In a spirited exchange of letters, Dulles took issue with Muste's attempt to "explain Soviet methods as being due to fear of us and of our atomic bombs. Resort by Soviet leaders to . . . forceful coercion has been characteristic [of them] for nearly thirty years." The United States, by contrast, lacked any pretensions to dominate or exploit other peoples: "Throughout our 170 years of national life, [we] have rarely resorted to intolerant methods in the sense of forcibly eradicating people who disagreed with our political system."[66] Muste sharply dissented from Dulles's American exceptionalism. The United States was an "expansionist power-state" just like any other nation. It had "pursued a driving expansionist course throughout most of its history and is doing so now. We did not resort to tolerant methods in dealing with the Indians. . . . We were not tolerant in our war against the Filipinos or in seizing the Panama Canal. We would not tolerate any possible rival to the north or south of us."[67]

As this correspondence illustrates, the conflict between radical pacifists and other Protestants went deeper than the question of the United States' role in the world; it was also about national identity, race, and historical memory. To Muste, when policymakers posited the United States as the representative of democratic civilization, they effectively erased its history of racism and the history of Western imperialism. It was this same blindness that prevented Americans from recognizing the belligerency of U.S. foreign policy. Was it not time, he asked rhetorically, for Americans to develop "a modicum of objectivity and humility and stop thinking that we and our preponderant might constitute an exception among all nations and in all history? That, in other words, we are the master race, the *Herrenvolk*, the supremacy all men will, and must, hail with delight?"[68]

Muste never gave up hope that realism would lose its hegemonic position within Protestant liberalism. Throughout the postwar era, he led efforts both nationally and internationally to maintain the legitimacy of pacifism within theological and clerical circles. He participated in the 1947 World Conference of Christian Youth, held in Oslo, and the 1948 Assembly of the World Council of Churches, held in Amsterdam. At the latter meeting, he and other pacifists managed to obtain recognition of pacifism as a valid "third position" within Christendom. He would continue to participate in assembly meetings in subsequent years, as well as other ecumenical and transnational gatherings of Christian leaders that considered questions of peace and war.[69]

He followed up on these efforts at home. In May 1950, he organized a conference in Detroit on the topic of "The Church and War" that attracted some four hundred delegates representing the historic peace churches, the FOR, and a number of denominational pacifist or peace fellowships. The result was the Church Peace Mission (CPM), an ecumenical effort to more effectively bring the Christian pacifist witness to bear on contemporary problems and to the attention of "Christian people." Aside from Muste, who was elected "chief missioner," its active members included Protestant leaders such as Paul Scherer, Henry Hitt Crane, and John Oliver Nelson. Under Muste's leadership, the organization was quite active, focusing in particular on holding seminars for pastors and laity, outreach to Christian youth, and developing pamphlet literature and resources on such topics as global peace and nuclear weapons testing. Among its most significant achievements was the pamphlet *A Christian Approach to Nuclear War*, a critical response to efforts by the World Council of Churches to articulate its position on just war and pacifism in an atomic age.[70]

As a result of efforts such as these, Christian pacifism managed to survive the early years of the Cold War. While attending Crozer Theological Seminary from 1948 through 1951, for example, the young Martin Luther King Jr. was introduced to pacifism by his mentor George W. Davis and by attending a speech given by Muste and reading his book *Not by Might*. According to Taylor Branch, "King never accepted pacifism at Crozer," siding with Niebuhr against Muste's argument that nuclear weapons "had transformed the essential moral questions of war and peace." Later, however, King's views became closer to Muste's, and the two would collaborate in the civil rights movement and the antiwar movement.[71]

The same was true for other Protestants of King's generation; realism would begin to lose appeal as the arms race proceeded apace and as the United States escalated its war in Vietnam. As early as 1954, *Christianity and Crisis* magazine, which had all but condoned the use of atomic weaponry, published an article by Muste that attacked the logic of deterrence with such forcefulness that the editor, John C. Bennett, was forced to rethink his position. "An armaments race is not in any basic sense . . . a deterrent but the opposite," Muste wrote. The "*fear* engendered by the awful nature of modern weapons" was more likely to induce "suspicion, bitterness, recrimination, hysteria," not bring the Soviets to the negotiating table in any meaningful sense. Brandishing nuclear weapons would also serve to alienate Africans and Asians, "who probably believe we would never use atomic bombs except on colored people." Indeed, in the context of American military bases in Japan and military aid to Indochina, third world peoples were likely to view the United States "as a military interloper in Asia, the 'new imperialism.'" Besides, Muste queried, "on what ethical or Christian ground can the *threat* of H-bomb war, in *the absence of any intention to carry it out*, be justified?"[72]

Bennett took Muste's criticism seriously, writing that it was "entirely sound," and represented "real questions in my own mind about my position."[73] In 1958, he and other leading liberal churchmen agreed to sign a petition circulated by Muste calling for a moratorium on nuclear testing.[74] By the early 1960s, Bennett, along with many others in the magazine's inner circle, had moved away from deterrence and began to support the notion of "peaceful coexistence" and an end to nuclear testing, positions that represented a move to the left for Christian realists. In 1966, with the intensification of the war in Vietnam, virtually all of the *Christianity and Crisis* insiders turned against the war, in the process questioning many of the tenets of realism. Muste must have felt some satisfaction as he watched these developments unfold.[75]

IN the immediate postwar period, however, Muste had much better luck persuading his fellow pacifists of the importance of a radical response to the bomb than he did with either the Christian realists or the atomic scientists. In 1947, he worked with the Consultative Peace Council, a federation of pacifist groups, to organize a "retreat-conference on pacifist organization and strategy." The conference, which met in both May and November 1947 at Pendle Hill, a Quaker retreat in Wallingford, Pennsylvania, attracted a wide range of pacifists; the historic peace churches sent a number of their leaders, including M. R. Zigler of the Mennonites and leading Quakers Clarence Pickett, Ray Newton, Harold Chance, Douglas Steere, and Cecil Hinshaw. In addition to Muste, the FOR sent staff members John Nevin Sayre, John Swomley, and Muste's secretary, Marion Coddington. The FOR was also represented by Robert L. Calhoun, professor of systematic theology at Yale Divinity School, and Allan Hunter, a well-known pacifist minister. Frank Olmstead of the War Resisters League (WRL) and Frederick Libby of the National Council for the Prevention of War also attended the conference, as did Isidor Hoffman, rabbi and cofounder of the Jewish Peace Fellowship, Milton Mayer, editor of the *Progressive* and a self-identified Jewish-Christian, and John Oliver Nelson of the Federal Council of Churches. Mildred Olmstead of the Women's International League for Peace and Freedom (WILPF) was unable to attend.[76]

In a series of workshops and seminars, participants wholeheartedly agreed with Muste that "spiritual life and commitment" had to be at the center of any viable pacifist movement in the atomic age. Quaker Harold

Chance commented that "reform at the political level alone . . . does not go deep enough to heal the hurt of our day." But the goal of spiritual life was engagement, not retreat. As Chance put it, the purpose of meditation and prayer was not only to seek perfection but also to "expand the boundaries of the self." When individuals commit themselves to God, Quaker theologian Douglas Steere commented, they begin "to seek fellowship. . . . Niebuhr says there are two worlds: This inside world and the outside world, and there are different laws. That violates our fundamental belief." That was why the fellowship and discipline imposed by cells were so important; they helped to prevent Christians from committing the greatest "heresy" of all: "separating the life of contemplation from the life of action."[77]

Although there was consensus on the importance of spiritual regeneration and cell organization as the foundation for pacifist action, the conference divided on the question of what precisely pacifists should do to overcome the stalemate between the United States and the Soviet Union. There was unanimity that, ideally, the United States should "take up the Cross" and unilaterally disarm. Americans had to recognize that "no nation must wait until another nation acts, and that a special responsibility rests upon the United States to break the present deadlock of fear, distrust and self-righteousness" because it had dropped atomic bombs on Japan. If the universe was orderly, it was also "characterized by spontaneity. It holds the possibility of new departures and of the release of hitherto untapped energies." This meant that, when a people acted "in conformity with the laws of the universe," and took a leap of faith such as unilateral disarmament, "undreamed of spiritual power will be at their disposal." Such a sacrifice "could be redemptive. . . . This could mean the dawn of a new era."[78]

Still, a difference of opinion emerged between those pacifists who, like Muste, believed that the usual political methods were helpless in the face of the atomic crisis and those who favored lobbying and education in an effort to achieve piecemeal changes. The former were less concerned about immediate political success than they were with dedicating their lives to what was right, with the hope that their example would convert others to the imperative of radically transforming their values and institutions. Marion Coddington, for example, asserted that "ordinary politics were not adequate to meet the present situation" and that "men were looking for a spiritual direction and meaning to life which has been lacking almost since the beginning of the scientific method and the industrial revolution."[79]

By the end of the conference, it had become clear to participants that they were fundamentally divided on the question of tactics; radical pacifists advocated resistance, while liberal pacifists remained committed to working within the system and making alliances with nonpacifists.[80] Recognizing that they would have to start a separate movement, the radicals, led by Muste, drafted a manifesto that specified how they believed pacifists should respond to the nuclear arms race and emerging Cold War. Since all Americans were "personally involved in the war system and the other evils of our day which stand in the way of One World," pacifists had to assume "personal responsibility" for these evils through draft resistance, refusal to pay taxes, refusal to attend segregated institutions, and reducing their standard of living. Such action, the manifesto declared, was "revolutionary" in the context of an "absolutist *state*" that relied on conformity and fear for its existence. It was not, they insisted, an assertion of an anarchistic philosophy, but rather a protest against authoritarian trends that were leading to "the break-down of government and orderly society." In addition to taking direct action, pacifists would belong to cells, which would cultivate "spiritual power" and fellowship. By pursuing internal peace as well as revolution, they hoped to overcome what Arthur Koestler had called the "commissar's" dilemma of seeking only change from without and not from within. Most important, cells would become bases for evangelical activity in the larger society. By sharing economic resources, various members would be able to "go out from their cells" and draw others into the fold.[81]

In the spring of 1948, these pacifist radicals called another conference, this one on "more disciplined and revolutionary activity" to be held in Chicago that April. The conference would help solidify an emerging union between older, more militant pacifists and young radicals. Former COs such as Dellinger, Rustin, Houser, Larry Gara, Francis Hall, and Catholic Worker Robert Ludlow affixed their signatures to the call and encouraged their comrades to attend. Many of these younger pacifists had participated in the FOR's 1944 conference on revolutionary pacifism, and, in February 1946, about ninety-five of them had met for a "Conference on Non-Violent Revolutionary Socialism" in which they founded the Committee for Non-Violent Revolution (CNVR). For a variety of reasons, CNVR never really got off the ground, but younger pacifists remained committed to radical nonviolence and therefore responded enthusiastically to Muste's efforts to formalize the nascent movement in Chicago.[82]

The well-known writer and critic Dwight Macdonald's signature also raised the prestige of the Chicago conference. Like Muste, Macdonald had roots in the Trotskyist movement and had long been suspicious of bureaucratic, state-centered politics. But it was the mass violence of World War II that turned him decisively against Marxist teleology and indeed the entire Enlightenment project. As he argued in his small magazine *politics*, the war had "leveled . . . the whole structure of Progressive assumptions on which liberal and socialist theory has been built up for two centuries." The end of scientific progress had proven to be "the end of man himself." In terms of political action, he suggested that radicals dispense with mass parties and mass action, and instead focus on "symbolic individual action, based on one person's insistence on his own values." These values included pacifism, which was imperative because war was no longer a rational means to an end, and decentralism, which was necessary because governments had grown increasingly centralized and undemocratic. Rather than look toward the future, radicals should gather themselves into small groups where they would attempt to act on their values in the here and now. At the same time, they should continue to engage with the larger society, serving as "prophets" who "put forward ideas which the majority of men of their time think nonsense or worse—and yet which these same men also feel are true."[83]

Macdonald and *politics* magazine have received attention from scholars as signaling an important transition in the history of American radicalism from the laborite and statist politics of the Popular Front toward a new left. Yet, as we have seen, Muste had long been developing a similar understanding of the nature and workings of power in a highly militarized state like the United States and had maintained that prophetic action was a revolutionary tool in this context. Moreover, in contrast to intellectuals like Macdonald, Muste worked to create the organizational apparatus to put these ideas into action with his leadership of the FOR, the Church Peace Mission, and, later, the Peacemakers and the Committee on Non-violent Action (CNVA), among other groups. Macdonald himself acknowledged the influence of radical pacifists on his own thinking when he celebrated those "anarchists, conscientious objectors, and renegade Marxists like myself . . . who reject the concept of Progress, who judge things by their present meaning and effect, who think the ability of science to guide us in human affairs has been overrated." Not surprisingly, Muste was a devoted reader of *politics*, and in fact circulated Macdonald's seminal essay "The Root Is Man" long after Macdonald himself retreated from politics.[84]

The 1948 Chicago conference gave birth to the Peacemakers, a group committed to the program of action outlined in the Pendle Hill manifesto; Muste served as executive secretary. Peacemakers restricted membership to those who were willing to take "personal responsibility" for the contemporary crisis by cutting themselves off as much as possible from the "war-making state." Citing Paul Tillich, they asserted that only when individuals took direct action against the old order would there be a real possibility for "revolution, of breaking down the old" so that a "new world" would come into being. Peacemakers also restricted membership to cells as opposed to individuals, though this structure became more flexible over time. Cells could only become affiliated with the group if they attempted to realize a measure of "economic sharing" and accepted a "common discipline" compatible with the Peacemaker discipline. That discipline required that members, at a minimum, accept nonviolence "as a way of life and as the means for resisting totalitarianism and achieving basic social change," recognize the importance of inner transformation "as a means to effectiveness in revolutionizing the social order," refuse to serve in the armed forces, and live simply.[85]

Thus, although Muste was unable to persuade atomic scientists and other liberals to assume personal responsibility for the atomic bomb and the Cold War, he found a small group of pacifists for whom his message resonated deeply. Like him, they believed that relying on "spiritual" rather than material power was a revolutionary act in the context of a society that had become overly dependent on science, rationality, and the state. They also shared his faith in the redemptive power of self-suffering, and embraced an image of themselves as modern-day prophets whose individual and collective acts of civil disobedience would awaken their fellow Americans to their responsibility for the atomic and international crisis. Indeed, their politics had an essentially evangelical character; instead of seeking to reform institutions or to overthrow the system, they looked to convert individuals in the hope that, by touching the hearts of others, change would be deeper and more far-reaching.

THE Peacemakers thus both departed from and reflected larger trends in the history of the American liberal left. On the one hand, they shared the widespread notion that leftists in the 1930s had relied too heavily on mass

parties, mass action, and the historical process as a means of changing society. On the other hand, they refused to moderate their idealism; in contrast
to many of their contemporaries, they believed that the real problem with
the left was that it had not been radical enough. By looking to the state to
solve social problems, by refusing to renounce violence and war, and by
having faith in historical progress, radicals had not departed from the values of the order they were seeking to overthrow. True radicalism, particularly in the context of the nuclear arms race, consisted of insisting on one's
moral values over and against the demands of the state. In this way, radical
pacifists helped to shift the meaning of radicalism away from socialism
toward an identity that signaled one's stance vis-à-vis American society. As
we shall see, Muste would be uncomfortable with the individualist thrust
of postwar radical political culture, but his own shift toward a more exclusively prophetic politics suggested that he too was unsure of precisely how
"the revolution" would occur.

Reflecting this perspective, the Peacemakers made a point of differentiating themselves from other pacifist organizations, which often had large
"paper" memberships and which favored lobbying, education, and other
conventional methods of political action.[86] Muste, who retained his role in
the FOR and continued to feel deeply connected to liberal pacifists, warned
his fellow radical pacifists against a "sectarian" spirit, of an "inner-
haughtiness and contempt" toward those who did not witness in the same
way.[87] Yet, there was some tension between the two groups, due mainly to
the fact that Peacemakers emerged largely out of the failure of the FOR to
adopt a more radical program. Relations between the Peacemakers and the
other leading pacifist organization, the War Resisters League (WRL), were
less strained, since radicals like Muste, Macdonald, Dellinger, Houser, and
Rustin now sat on the latter organization's executive committee. But even
as the WRL became rhetorically committed to "political, economic, and
social revolution by non-violent means," its old guard continued to view it
as an enrollment and educational organization for COs.[88]

Perhaps the closest ideological ally of the Peacemakers was the Catholic
Worker movement. Dorothy Day and her comrades drew upon European
Catholic thought to develop a non-Marxist radical politics that emphasized
the importance of decentralism, pacifism, and direct action. Reflecting this
ideological concurrence, the Catholic Worker movement responded to the
development of nuclear weapons and the Cold War in virtually the same
terms as other radical pacifists. They called for unilateral disarmament,

refused to support either the United States or the Soviet Union, opposed conscription, and called for draft resistance as a means of expressing penance for the atomic bomb and for protesting nuclear proliferation and the growing power of the nation-state.[89]

The passage of a new Selective Service Act in 1948 requiring compulsory military service bolstered radical pacifists' commitment to direct war resistance. Arguing that the act represented "the same turning-point in American development as was the advent of Hitler to power in Germany," they called for "total rejection and all-out resistance." By October, some 1,500 men had gone on record indicating their refusal to register for the draft. This act had been preceded by a 1947 protest in which Muste, Mayer, Dellinger, Houser, Gregg, Rustin, Macdonald, and others had either burned their draft cards or mailed them to President Truman as a way of protesting the specter of peacetime conscription. Peacemakers also advocated refusal to pay income taxes or keeping one's income intentionally below the withholding level, a way of protesting the massive military budget that would become more widespread in future years. Some of them, in fact, viewed tax resistance as potentially more of a threat to the government's authority to wage war than draft resistance.[90]

In refusing to register for the draft or pay taxes, Peacemakers placed themselves in a long tradition of American and religious nonconformity. Muste, for example, enclosed a copy of the gospels and Thoreau's *Essay on Civil Disobedience* as "supporting material" in his letters to the Internal Revenue Service notifying them of his refusal to file a return or pay any taxes.[91] No one did this more dramatically than Ammon Hennacy, whose "one-man revolution" was a source of inspiration—and, at times, irritation—for many Peacemakers and Catholic Workers. His statement to the tax collector asserted that he was "acting in the tradition which Jefferson, Paine and Emerson gave to this country. I am acting in the tradition of the early Quakers who refused to pay taxes for war and openly broke the law by hiding escaped slaves. I am practicing the same ideas as Thoreau who refused to pay taxes for the Mexican War and slavery." While he recognized that the refusal of a few individuals to pay taxes would not prevent another world war, he believed that in an age where politics had been reduced to "pressure groups," it was essential to keep the idealism of prophets like Eugene V. Debs and William Lloyd Garrison alive. Those who truly believed in a Christian "Way of Life" had to "change themselves: to refuse to be a part of the dominant lie; to live the truth no matter what the consequences." Every year, on the anniversary of Hiroshima, Hennacy fasted and picketed local branches of the Atomic Energy Commission as "*penance for* our sin of exploitation and atomic war."[92]

Peacemaker protest was not only individual in character, though that was its prevailing tendency. One collective action jointly sponsored by the Peacemakers, the Catholic Workers, and the New York branch of the FOR was the Fast for Peace, held the week before Easter Sunday in 1950 in Washington, D.C. The idea of a fast grew out of a sense of urgency that beset the pacifist community when President Truman announced plans to develop a hydrogen bomb. A letter from Bayard Rustin to Muste captures their alarm. Pacifists had to be "prepared to *make terrible sacrifices now, to look mad now,* to give up *all now if necessary,*" he wrote. "We must find some way to let people know that *now* we are prepared to go to jail or even to give up all—to get shot down if necessary—but to cry out. . . . In this way we say to the American public and to the world: When do you begin to draw the line?"[93] Thus, when he and Muste, together with Wally Nelson, Francis Hall, and Dellinger, organized the fast, their goal was to communicate "their willingness to give life itself if necessary in the cause of peace." In addition to having a "prophetic impact," they viewed the fast as an opportunity to express their "penitence" for the atomic bombing of Japan as well as achieve "self-purification" to fortify them in their struggle for peace.[94]

Fifty-four pacifists ultimately gathered at the nation's capital for the fast, with similar actions taking place in fifty-one other cities in the United States and in England, Japan, Canada, Puerto Rico, and Hawaii, where they distributed leaflets calling on men and women everywhere to "draw your own personal line against war *now*." A spiritual atmosphere permeated the event. The group rented a house, where they kept a candle burning day and night for the duration of the fast and set aside a room for meditation and prayer. On Good Friday, twenty-six members of the group went to the Pentagon where they held a silent vigil during the three hours when Christ was reputed to have hung on the cross. Rustin commented, "Through the ages it's the very small thing which turns the course of history. Jesus and his disciples fasted when they sought power. Now [we] seek power for peace."[95]

The Peacemakers also had a "constructive" program in which they attempted to build the new society "in the shell of the old." For example, a group of Peacemakers founded the Kingwood Community in Frenchtown, New Jersey, in which they instituted daily meditation and group worship,

Figure 7. Dave Dellinger, Bayard Rustin, Winifred Rawlins, and A. J. Muste discuss the "Fast for Peace," held in Washington, D.C., Easter 1950. (*Swarthmore College Peace Collection*)

contributed all earnings to a common purse, and attempted to achieve self-sufficiency through activities such as writing, making homemade bread, gardening, and developing a mail-order business in books. Glen Gardner, New Jersey, was another such community. Founded in 1947 by four families (including the Dellingers), the seventeen-acre "homestead" had a laboratory for chemical research, a printing press, and a workshop for children's toys.[96]

Muste was deeply ambivalent about the tendency of many Peacemakers to separate from the mainstream, particularly in rural settings. With his urban, working-class background, he could not help but think that many community experiments were really just "outlets for certain types of intellectuals and disoriented middle-class people which are therefore inherently incapable of expansion beyond very narrow limits."[97] These differences did not assume much importance in the immediate postwar period; as a whole, they retained a strong social purpose, viewing their communities as the "growing edge" in the "non-violent revolution" and continuing their protest activities on behalf of world peace and racial equality. But around 1950, with the development of the hydrogen bomb, the deepening of the Cold War, and the emergence of a full-fledged Red Scare, Peacemakers began to despair of ever changing American opinion and increasingly turned inward, focusing on realizing their goals of egalitarianism and fellowship within their own communities. As a result, members faded away, dropping from probably around three thousand persons in 1948 to several hundred in 1952. Indeed, radical pacifism seemed increasingly a marker of identity rather than a reference to an actual revolutionary program; they judged American society harshly and sometimes withdrew from it, or else they used nonviolent direct action to create reform, not revolution.[98]

The growing quietism of his comrades deeply disturbed Muste. He recognized that the intense nationalism and the relative affluence of American society made it now highly unlikely that Americans would recognize their special burden and responsibility for ending the arms race. At the same time, however, he viewed the turn inward as an expression of despair and urged his comrades to remain political. In particular, after meeting with Gandhians at the 1949 World Pacifist Meeting in India, he became increasingly intrigued by the idea of building a "third camp" of unaligned elements and nations. While the context of the intense power struggle between the United States and the Soviet Union made such a movement unlikely, he proposed that the Peacemakers endorse it as a way of remaining dynamic and engaged.[99]

With the appearance of the South African Campaign for the Defiance of Unjust Laws in 1952, he also began to consider the possibility that nonviolence might have a role to play in African liberation movements. No doubt encouraging him in this view was a letter from Gandhi's son, Manilal, who observed that "Father's spirit seems to be watching over and guiding them."[100] Yet the group, already scattered and decimated by the hostile, conservative climate of the early Cold War, divided on the question and refused to give it their unequivocal support. Muste remained magnanimous in his defeat. While warning pacifists to be wary of retreating into havens in a corrupt world, he reflected that sainthood still had its purpose: "even if we are destined in our lifetime to be a tiny and harassed and seemingly irrelevant minority, it will still be true that a truly human society will be possible on earth in the future only if there are those who do not yield to the seductions of violence . . . who march steadfastly 'to the music of another drum.'"[101]

〜

CHAPTER 10

Speaking Truth to Power

Our political task is precisely, in Martin Buber's
magnificent formulation, "to drive the plowshare of the
normative principle into the hard soil of political reality."
— A. J. Muste, 1960

UNABLE TO PERSUADE the Peacemakers to fully endorse the idea of a third
way in opposition to the foreign policies of both the United States and the
Soviet Union, Muste supported his young protégés George Houser and Bill
Sutherland when they gave up on trying to change American race relations
and decided to focus their energies on building support for the anti-
apartheid movement in South Africa and for African independence more
broadly. In 1952, Houser resigned as a secretary of the FOR to found
Americans for South African Resistance to raise money and awareness
about the Defiance Campaign, and in 1953, he founded the American
Committee on Africa, which attempted to familiarize the American public
with African struggles against colonialism. Sutherland worked closely with
Houser in these efforts, and in late 1953 permanently settled in Ghana in
order set up training centers for "positive action."[1]

Muste also pushed the FOR to consider reorienting some of its
resources toward building alliances with and support for African liberation
projects. In 1952, he sent Rustin to London and Africa to meet with African
leaders and to explore how American pacifists might work in solidarity with
their struggles. Upon his return, Rustin made a twofold proposal: the FOR
should build awareness of African independence movements at home,
while simultaneously training Africans in the tactics of nonviolence; he volunteered to spearhead the second part of his proposal by spending a year
in Nigeria setting up the first nonviolent training center.[2]

Both Rustin's proposal and the American Committee on Africa contained some of the contradictions in the pacifist view of Africa and third world revolutions that would play themselves out in the late 1950s and 1960s. On the one hand, radical pacifists were deeply inspired by and sympathetic to African struggles for freedom and self-determination. More so than their contemporaries, they recognized, as Muste put it, the "close tie between the issue of civil rights and the issue of foreign policy and war.[3] They also hoped, as did many Africans themselves, that African liberation might serve as a redemptive force in a world defined by two power states. On the other hand, they were deeply ambivalent about the exclusionary and separatist tendencies within nationalism, which existed in tension with their commitment to break down divisions of self and other. As anti-Communists, moreover, pacifists at times framed their arguments within a Cold War paradigm. Rustin, for example, explained that the FOR must support African independence in order to prevent Africans from turning to Communism and violence, while Houser placed fiercely anti-Communist social democrats on the American Committee's board, such as Norman Thomas, James Farmer, and A. Philip Randolph.[4]

These tensions were more latent than real in the early 1950s, since pacifists—and Americans more broadly—had scant connection to or knowledge about Africa, but they formed the backdrop for intra-pacifist and intra-radical debates about violence and nationalism, anti-Communism and third world revolution in the late 1950s and 1960s. While some pacifists would withdraw active support for revolutionary nationalism, Muste would evolve a more nuanced approach. He insisted on the right of revolution and self-determination, yet held that pacifists could be most helpful in contesting American power and working to build a movement of nonaligned peoples and nations against nuclear proliferation and the Cold War. Contemporaneous events—in particular, Soviet premier Nikita Khrushchev's revelations about Stalin's crimes, growing concerns about nuclear fallout, and the emergence of the African American civil rights movement—seemed to confirm his analysis that a space had opened up for the expression of alternative and oppositional views.

IMPRESSED with Rustin's African proposal, Muste presented it to the FOR's executive committee in January 1953. He and Rustin had to draw upon all of their rhetorical and charismatic skills to obtain the committee's

approval. Indeed, even though Muste remained in the role of national secretary, his position within the FOR had grown precarious. He had just
turned sixty-eight, the organization's age of retirement, and members of
the executive committee had come to view his radical activities as an
embarrassment for the organization. They also increasingly viewed the
struggle for racial inequality as a distraction from the more compelling
need for disarmament and world peace. Sayre opposed the plan vehemently
and was so angry when it passed that he "lost [his] temper with A.J."[5]

Such was the backdrop for Rustin's tour of the West Coast in which he
was jailed for sixty days on a morals charge. There to give a series of speaking engagements before leaving for Nigeria, he was arrested in Pasadena,
California, when police officers found him in a car with two other men.
The news devastated Muste. For over a decade, the two men had formed a
powerful team within the small world of pacifism. "Muste and Rusty," as
they were known, had a deep emotional bond that contemporaries compared to that of father and son. They also had a shared political vision; no
one in the movement was more like Muste in his intellectual and political
views than Rustin. The arrest, however, signaled that their long-standing
alliance within the FOR had come to an end. As Muste explained to Glenn
Smiley by phone, "this has happened so frequently that I have given Bayard
an ultimatum that if it happened again he would have to resign." Despite
Muste's resolve, the experience took a deep toll on him; he viewed it as
nothing less than a personal and political betrayal. When, about six months
later, the WRL proposed hiring Rustin as program director and office secretary, Muste opposed it so vehemently that he resigned from the organization's executive committee when he was outvoted.[6]

Muste's response to Rustin's arrest has been interpreted as an expression of homophobia, as well as a reflection of the straitlaced Protestant
culture of the FOR.[7] Yet this explanation implies that Muste had an irrational aversion or fear of homosexuals and homosexuality that simply was not
the case. In fact, there were several layers to Muste's reaction to Rustin's
arrest. He was indeed heteronormative in his views of sexuality. He believed
that sexual relations between men and women were natural and that their
purest expression occurred in a monogamous marriage. These beliefs grew
out of his historical and cultural context as well as his background on the
left, which tended to view homosexuality as an expression of the decadence
of bourgeois culture and thus as a diversion from the hard work of building

the revolution.[8] Still, he was not a prude; despite his emphasis on the need for self-discipline and "inner revolution," he was determinedly opposed to asceticism, which he believed was based upon "a profoundly wrong separation between body and soul, flesh and spirit, and a classifying of the 'flesh' as evil."[9]

Muste explicated his philosophy of love to Rustin when the latter faced sexual misconduct charges while in prison for conscientious objection during World War II. Since love was "the essence and supreme value in life," it could not be truly realized in promiscuous sexual relations: "How utterly barren and horrible when not spontaneous; how utterly horrible and cheap where there is no discipline, no form in the relationship." Just as "the artist with the freest vision, the most powerful creative urge . . . submits to the severest discipline," so too must the lover tame spontaneity in order to reach "the discipline, the control, the effort to understand the other." Yet promiscuity denied the "depth" and "understanding" of love. "Physical relationship, yes . . . but this is not love. Since it involves an essential indifference toward the person . . . unconscious impulse to use and exploit rather than to understand and nourish, it is the opposite of love."[10]

These comments speak to the breadth and the limits of Muste's vision. For him, all relationships—whether personal or political—had to be characterized by love for each person's spiritual and physical integrity. It was a vision that allowed him to have friendships with many different kinds of people, including homosexuals such as Rustin, Barbara Deming, David McReynolds, and Paul Goodman.[11] But it also failed to recognize that the pressure on homosexuals to refrain from acting on their homosexual desires—or to keep such desires secret—created a barrier between themselves and others that precluded the kind of nonviolent, beloved community he envisioned. It also called upon them to practice a level of asceticism that Muste himself viewed as unhealthy. Thus Muste could argue with all sincerity that Rustin should refrain from homosexual acts because they caused him to deceive and lie to his friends, rather than recognizing that it was social repression of homosexuality in the first place that placed Rustin in an untenable position. Ultimately, as John D'Emilio has commented, Muste was unable "to imagine homosexual love."[12]

Further influencing Muste's response to Rustin's 1953 arrest was the revolutionary culture of radical pacifism. Like the Marxist-Leninists Muste had led briefly in the 1930s, radical pacifists viewed themselves as a revolutionary vanguard; they adopted strict personal and collective disciplines in

order to capture the confidence of the public and lead them to an egalitarian future.[13] Rustin was among the most ambitious of the group, yet his
predilection for daring and often attention-seeking sexual behavior presented a barrier to the leadership he so craved. Indeed, a pattern of "choosing quick physical pleasure" over his "hope of bearing witness against
injustice" emerged early on, as D'Emilio has observed. While in Ashland
penitentiary during the war, for example, he had enlisted Muste's help in
planning a concerted campaign against segregation only to jeopardize it by
overtly pursuing sexual relations with other men. After he was caught, he
lied to Muste even as the elder man defended him to the prison authorities.
Rustin "had deceived everybody, including your own comrades and most
devoted friends," Muste wrote sternly. "You have made the 'mistake' of
thinking you could be the leader in a revolution" while at the same time
engaging "in practices for which there was no justification, which a person
with a tenth of your brains must have known would defeat your objectives."
After an exchange of letters and visits, Rustin finally confessed to his "weakness and stupidity that defeated the immediate campaign and jeopardized
immeasurably the causes for which I would be willing to die. . . . When
success was imminent in our racial campaign my behavior stopped progress. I have misused the confidence the negroes here had in my leadership;
I have caused them to question the moral basis of nonviolence."[14]

Despite promises to refrain from promiscuity (he apparently never con-
sented to Muste's suggestion that he try to live as a heterosexual, though he
did consider it), Rustin continued to engage in sexual behavior that inter-
fered with his own ambitions to lead the Gandhian movement in the
United States. Though he lived with his lover, Davis Platt, he also participated in the underground homosexual culture of cruising. On several occasions after his release from prison, he was arrested for solicitation. At a
time when the stigma of homosexuality was at its height, and an association
between homosexuality and subversion had been made, incidents such as
these endangered both Rustin and the larger movement. Muste confronted
him directly about his behavior on several occasions, making Rustin fully
cognizant that the Pasadena arrest would lead to his resignation.[15]

Within a few years the two men would rekindle their political alliance
and their friendship (and Muste would return to the executive board of the
WRL). Several forces were at work here. For one, both men needed the
other; as Rustin emerged as an adviser to Martin Luther King Jr., he relied
upon Muste's advice as well as his connections to wealthy donors. For his

part, Muste found Rustin a useful ally in his efforts to restrain the more libertarian wing of the radical pacifist movement.[16] Perhaps more important, Muste's views on sexuality continued to evolve. He read "Toward a Quaker View of Sex," a pamphlet published by the London Yearly Meeting of Friends in 1963, which convinced him of the need to adopt a more flexible understanding "as to what constitutes ethical behavior, how love should and can be expressed, and what these things mean for the kind of communities we try to build." These views placed him on the more culturally liberal wing of radical pacifism; he would resist efforts by some to strictly control the sexual behavior of participants in CNVA direct action projects, and he criticized civil rights leaders when they attempted to marginalize Rustin for his homosexuality.[17] Still, the cost of Rustin's reintegration into the movement was the suppression of his ambitions to public leadership, and no doubt Muste's acceptance of him was predicated on this fact. Such was the tragedy of homosexuality within left politics in the years before the gay liberation movement.

The 1953 incident with Rustin was one of many losses and transitions Muste experienced in the early 1950s. Throughout 1952, the Muste family had a series of health crises. Anne's heart condition continued to deteriorate, making her a "semi-invalid," while Muste was hospitalized for several weeks that spring for a prostate operation. Soon thereafter, their son, John, contracted polio in Mexico and returned home to recuperate. Meanwhile, disappointed in the decline of the Peacemakers, Muste resigned as the group's national secretary. He also faced his imminent retirement from the FOR. In October 1953, John Swomley took over as national secretary of the organization and Muste was appointed secretary emeritus. He would continue to serve as a "staff representative" of the New York FOR, a position that included secretarial services, and would draw a small pension. Yet he was "if not shaken, at least a little wounded" by the experience. Although the organization had not evolved as he had hoped, it had remained a source of fellowship and sustenance throughout much of his adult life. "I did not know in my bones that people reach retirement age and younger men take their place," Muste would write in his autobiographical sketches a few years later. "I did not know either that, when this happens, you just keep on. I did not know that a being you love and have loved for years on end can die, and that a home can cease to be."[18]

As these comments suggest, Anne died in September 1954. Muste always represented his relationship with Anne as a deeply loving one, at times appearing to recognize the stress his political commitments placed on her, while at the same time taking comfort in their devotion to each other. Contemporaries concurred in describing her as shy, "always in the background," as one of Muste's nieces put it, kindhearted and patient, even in the face of her children's inevitable foibles and the strains of being married to a nonconformist. Rustin described her as having been "a bundle of giggles. We had some marvelous parties with Anna as hostess. There would be a lot of singing, stories, and some comic monologues from A.J. Anna would goad A.J. to perform, and although she had heard his parody of 'To Be or Not to Be' scores of times, she'd sit back in the corner and giggle again."[19]

Yet, ultimately, Anne remains an enigma. Most likely, she suppressed her own desires in service to her husband's personality and politics, taking comfort perhaps in a religious and cultural context that made a virtue of female self-sacrifice. Muste was stoic in her death, though family and friends sensed he was lonely. He lived with his eldest daughter and her family for several years, until they moved for a time abroad, and then lived alone in New York City. Still, he remained close to his three children and eight grandchildren, maintaining an active correspondence and visiting them frequently.[20]

Intriguingly, the woman with whom Muste took companionship in subsequent years was Anne's opposite. Bold in appearance and personality, Cara Cook had been educated at Mount Holyoke College, served as a member of Brookwood's faculty and a devoted Musteite, and subsequently worked in an administrative capacity for various labor and liberal organizations. Pictures show a tall, broad-shouldered woman, with a "flapper" hairstyle and comportment. Sometime around 1956, her and Muste's friendship took a more romantic turn "by way of theater, opera, baseball, movies, anagrams and Brookwood reminiscences." The couple vacationed several times at Cook's cabin in Maine, and traveled together to Europe and the Soviet Union in 1958. At some point during this period, Muste proposed marriage, but Cook declined. Yet they would remain on close terms through Muste's death in 1967. She organized his well-attended eightieth-birthday celebration in 1965 and spoke at his official memorial service.[21]

FOR Muste, 1956 would be an important year, not only personally as he rekindled his friendship with Cook, but also politically. Though he had been inspired by the South African Defiance Campaign, in fact he had been pessimistic about the possibilities for third camp alternatives and radical social change, particularly from within the United States. Starting in the mid-1950s, however, he began to argue that a political and ideological space had opened up, and he called upon pacifists to shift from their emphasis on the individual conscience toward developing mass action. "Until recently," he had thought it was "unrealistic" to engage in much more than "ad hoc" activism, he wrote to his fellow radical pacifists, but recent developments had changed his "mind to an appreciable extent." "Not to go overboard," but perhaps it was time "to begin talking seriously about the possibility of working toward the formation of a democratic socialist 'party' or 'movement' and about steps which might be taken toward this end." He pointed to the Montgomery bus boycott, which had begun in December 1955, as evidence that nonviolence might appeal to large numbers of people. He also suggested that growing public concern over nuclear fallout might be directed into opposition to the arms race and American foreign policy.[22]

In addition to these fissures within domestic political culture, Muste pointed to international developments that suggested some possibility for easing the tensions between the two superpowers. Soviet premier Nikita Khrushchev's denunciation of Stalin might lead to the humanization of Soviet rule; it might, moreover, be the grounds upon which the "split between Socialists and Communists could be healed" and a new left reborn. The emergence of a nonaligned movement in the decolonizing world was especially promising. The approach that emerged out of the 1955 Bandung conference of Asian, Middle Eastern, and Asian leaders, Muste wrote excitedly, "was that there are two kinds of military power regimes in the world and both are dangerous, and there are two kinds of colonialism and both are bad." He called upon pacifists to align with Asian and African peoples "to resist both [power blocs], not indeed by military might which we do not possess, but by following an essentially independent course and developing an alternative way for dealing with our problems." He differentiated this approach from "a simple neutralism which wants to keep from any involvement and to avoid taking sides."[23]

In making this argument, Muste expressed concern that American pacifists might recoil at the anti-American and pro-Soviet sentiment often expressed by third world revolutionaries. Yet it was imperative that pacifists not fall into a defensive pattern of implicitly condoning "U.S. militarism" and "the American power-state." The "allure" of Soviet Communism to developing nations had to do with its history of swift economic transformation and state formation, whereas the United States was associated with racial segregation and Western imperialism. While it was rather "fantastic" to think of the Soviet Union as a force for peace and freedom, given its history of suppressing civil liberties and its massive military establishment, it offered "a world-view, a philosophy of life and history, a faith or 'myth,'" as well as an ethos of solidarity and internationalism, that naturally appealed to countries with a history of racial oppression and economic underdevelopment. Rather than criticize anticolonial movements for not appearing in their own image, pacifists should instead help to foster expressions of independence in the Cold War by working for disarmament and contesting American foreign policy. "The American government and the American economic and cultural regime will not do this job," he stated unequivocally. Only "what some call a Third Camp, others, perhaps, democratic socialism, others the Gandhian revolution."[24]

Muste sought to exploit these openings by building alliances between his perfectionist comrades and other groups, as well as between liberals, socialists, and Communists. In early 1955, he began to urge his fellow radical pacifists to found a bimonthly magazine that would "reach out and speak" to "wide circles" of people. It would engage in serious and lively discussions of "fundamental, economic, political, cultural and ethical problems." At the same time, it would take a pragmatic approach of joining theory to action. "Action should serve as an expression of and test of theory," he wrote. "It is hoped . . . that groups of students and others would be stimulated to study and action by the magazine and thus a living movement may develop."[25]

As these comments suggest, Muste was in many respects reviving his political vision of the late 1920s and early 1930s, albeit with important modifications. Much in the style of *Labor Age*, he called for the new magazine to be inclusive, "experimental and not dogmatic or doctrinaire," to strive to "avoid old clichés of the radical movement," while at the same time having a clear "ideological foundation, not equivocating about such issues as dictatorship, war, racism and exploitation." These comments echo Muste's criticism of the Communist Party when he led the CPLA and the AWP, only now he placed greater emphasis on antimilitarism and decentralism; in the past, radicals tended to rely upon "inevitable" historical forces, upon capturing the state, and on technology and bureaucracy, yet this new left would emphasize "decentralization, direct participation" of all workers and citizens, and on ensuring that technology would be used for human ends. It would aim to create "a classless society in which the armed, nationalist, highly centralized State has disappeared (not the same as saying there would be no 'government' of any kind). . . . The touchstone would be the extent to which each individual could develop his own talents and personality. This society would be genuinely inter-national in character, not nationalist. It would be built upon responsible freedom, mutuality and peace." The magazine, in short, would attempt "to constitute or reconstitute a non-totalitarian movement of the left."[26]

While some radical pacifists preferred to continue focusing on individual resistance and community, others found Muste's argument for mass action persuasive. The result was *Liberation* magazine, founded in March 1956 and edited by Muste, along with Rustin, Dellinger, Roy Finch, and Charles Walker. The magazine's lead editorial, "A Tract for the Times," essentially restated Muste's original proposal. Liberalism and Marxism alike had shown themselves inadequate to address the crisis engendered by nuclear weaponry and by the rise of totalitarianism. While the liberal tradition was praiseworthy for its emphasis on civil liberties, it had failed "to come to grips with war, poverty, boredom, authoritarianism and other great evils of the modern world." While Marxism rightly demanded "economic justice," it had failed to anticipate "the growth of the state and its emergence as an instrument of war and oppression." Both traditions, they argued, were rooted in nineteenth-century modes of thought that were "now hopelessly out of date." In order for a new radicalism to emerge, it was necessary to return "to root traditions from which we derive our values and standards." Those traditions were the "Judeo-Christian prophet tradition," which offered "a vision of human dignity and a reign of righteousness"; the American democratic tradition of a "nation conceived in liberty, and dedicated to the proposition that all men are created equal"; the heritage of the radical movements of the late nineteenth and early twentieth century; and the tradition of "pacifism or non-violence," best represented by Gandhi, whose experiments with truth "joined non-violence and revolutionary collective action."[27]

The "creative fusion" of these traditions had implications for how the editors conceived of the struggle for social change. First, they were uninterested in conventional methods for achieving political influence or in capturing the state. In the context of an overly bureaucratized and centralized society, the most radical politics consisted of taking direct action, both through individual acts of resistance and "collective effort and struggle." Second, they rejected "the faith in technology, industrialization and centralization per se, characteristic of both the contemporary capitalist and Communist regimes." Instead they were eager to explore the possibilities for decentralization, industrial democracy, and the use of technology "for human ends." Third, they called for a revival of "utopian" thinking as a way of challenging dominant trends in American political culture, such as realism and notions of a vital center. Finally, they argued that the reality of nuclear weapons meant that any new radical movement had to be pacifist. This meant not only using nonviolence as a means of social struggle, but also rejecting the military policies of both the United States and the Soviet Union. They expressed their interest in building a "third camp" across national boundaries that would nonviolently oppose the Cold War.[28]

There was a distinctly existential character to their politics; an obituary for Albert Camus in a 1960 issue of *Liberation* praised the Frenchman for refusing to give up the search for meaning despite the loss of old faiths and the inadequacies of new ones. "Unlike the Neo-orthodox of many creeds . . . who successfully sink back to an old Order, finding there solace and comfort; and unlike the 'beatnicks' [*sic*] who simply (too simply) and stupidly give up the search for meaning, Camus confessed his loss and continued his search."[29]

As this obituary for Camus suggests, *Liberation*'s historical significance lies in its blending of concern for the alienation and conformity of American life with a radical political agenda. Although intellectuals during the late 1940s and 1950s worried about the negative effects of bureaucracy and organization on traditional American virtues of independence and self-reliance, few of them were politically radical; most of them "praised or at least accepted the stability and benevolence of contemporary institutions."[30] *Liberation*'s editors and contributors, by contrast, tended to advocate various ways of challenging American society, from intentional communities and refusal to pay taxes to collective protest. They also actively supported the black civil rights movement, rejecting the calls for moderation and gradualism espoused by their liberal counterparts. Rustin, of course, became a close adviser to Martin Luther King Jr., but Muste also served in an advisory capacity; later, in the 1960s, he would become particularly close to figures such as James Lawson and James Bevel, and would play a key role in persuading the civil rights leadership to take a public stance against the Vietnam War.[31]

In making a virtue of political radicalism and engagement, the magazine served as a residual expression of the "movement intellectual" of the Old Left years. As we have seen, although he had broken with the politics of the Old Left, Muste had never rejected the idea of a symbiotic relationship between the life of the mind and political action. Indeed, he held that it was precisely the divide between mental labor, on the one hand, and the fruits of that labor, on the other, that was at the heart of the existential crisis of modernity—or, as he increasingly called it, "post-civilization."[32] *Liberation* was thus part of a larger effort on his part to foster connections with intellectuals and social theorists who had been in political retreat. At around the same time as the magazine's founding, he helped to establish the Council for Correspondence, an effort to encourage intellectuals to engage with the "critical issues" of the day. The group, which included sociologist David Riesman, historian H. Stuart Hughes, and psychoanalyst Erich Fromm, discussed and publicized their concerns about nuclear weapons and foreign policy, yet they resisted Muste's entreaties to take direct action.

The contrast between their response to New York City's compulsory civil defense drills and Muste's highlights the difference between how academic intellectuals conceived of political action and how radical pacifists defined it. While the Council for Correspondence provided a strongly reasoned case against the policy, Muste joined his fellow pacifists in refusing to take cover and facing arrest and jail time. Muste "was always trying to get me to do things for which I had no time," H. Stuart Hughes recalled. "While this used to embarrass me, he took it in good grace. I found him a curious combination of stubborn and insistent Dutchman and a man sensitive to the different life style of a person like myself."[33]

The Quaker pamphlet *Speak Truth to Power* represents another effort by Muste to foster intellectual discussion and exchange. The American Friends Service Committee (AFSC) had traditionally focused on lobbying and peace education, and offered policy analyses and recommendations that fit within the mainstream of liberal opinion. But as the arms race continued apace, Muste's more radical analysis of international affairs and U.S. foreign policy gained appeal, as did his calls for direct action. In 1955, the AFSC's new secretary, Robert Gilmore, formed a working committee that included Muste, Rustin, Cecil Hinshaw, and Milton Mayer and asked them to draft a new policy analysis and a more dynamic vision of peace activism.

The result of this collaboration, *Speak Truth to Power*, essentially summarized Muste's thinking since the 1940s.[34] It called for an explicitly utopian approach to the East-West stalemate, in which individuals, groups, and then the nation itself would progressively embrace nonviolence. It offered a practical rationale for its advocacy of nonviolence, but it also conceded that its argument was ultimately based on faith. Drawing explicitly on a mix of Quaker theology and the prophetic tradition, it asserted that God was in every person, and that indwelling endowed him or her with "inalienable worth and dignity." "We must turn from our self-righteousness and arrogance and confess that we do that which is evil in the sight of the Lord." While this might lead to suffering and even death, Jesus Christ had shown that "to risk all may be to gain all."[35]

As with the Council for Correspondence and *Liberation* magazine, the aim of *Speak Truth to Power* was to initiate dialogue and action. The AFSC distributed the pamphlet widely among prominent liberal intellectuals, including Robert M. Hutchins, Lewis Mumford, Erich Fromm, and Hans J. Morgenthau, and invited their comments. Meanwhile, Milton Mayer's *Progressive* published a symposium on the pamphlet with responses from Karl Menninger, Reinhold Niebuhr, George Kennan, Norman Thomas, and Dwight Macdonald. Whether commenting on *Speak Truth to Power* or *Liberation*'s "Tract for the Times," liberals tended to praise pacifists for their insightful analysis of foreign affairs and for their faith in the "individual," while at the same criticizing their strategy for being "unrealistic" and "irresponsible."[36] The Marxist and former Catholic Worker Michael Harrington criticized them from another perspective, suggesting that the "Tract" represented a "facile rejection of Marxism," and a tendency to equate Marxism and Stalinism that replicated Cold War ideology. In fact, he asserted, Marxist theory provided a method for understanding exactly "those things *Liberation* aims to make its own . . . the alienation of man in modern society, of his de-spiritualization. I can think of no analysis of this process which goes as deep as that of Marx." Harrington further criticized the editors for failing to identify the agent of social change; Marxism had shown that "revolutions are made by social classes," not vaguely defined groups of people.[37]

Muste's solicitation of feedback from Harrington reflected his larger commitment to rebuilding the American left. It was unconscionable that in the present crisis—the hydrogen bomb and the nuclear arms race, the confrontation between African Americans and white supremacy, and the passivity of the trade union movement—that the left was "emasculated" and "irrelevant." "Where is the Left in this crisis which obviously cries out for leadership?" he queried. Yet, precisely because there was "movement and ferment there was hope." He called upon the existing groups on the left to come together in a spirit of inclusion and flexibility to discuss their problems and attempt to move forward. "Where there is rigidity there is no hope, for rigidity on the part of existing groups on the left can only be the rigidity of stagnation or death."[38] Thus, in May 1956, he obtained funding from the FOR to organize a forum at Carnegie Hall involving socialists from across the ideological spectrum. Participants included Muste, Norman Thomas, W. E. B. Du Bois, and Eugene Dennis, the general secretary of the American Communist Party, who had recently been released from prison after serving time for violations of the Smith Act. Several more open-air meetings followed and, in December, they were formalized in a structure called the American Forum for Socialist Education that lasted until around 1959.[39]

Muste's hopes for a reconciliation of the American left had been influenced by his deepening friendship with the trade unionist Sidney Lens, who encouraged his reengagement with the Marxist tradition and his hopes that the crisis in the world Communist movement would serve as an impetus for rebuilding democratic socialism. Lens was a Marxist, but he did not view it as an infallible theory; it had, for example, failed to predict the superstructural developments that had made Western democracies so powerful and stable in spite of their many contradictions. Rather than "advance the Marxian theory . . . in tune with the times," Lens wrote, socialists had either retreated into a "tepid liberalism or nihilism" or "clung to their leftism as a dogma, not as a scientific guide to continued search for truth." In so doing, they had facilitated both the destruction of their movement and the emergence of a conservative political culture built around anti-Communism. It was time, he asserted, for the left to study and modify its principles and program "to bring them up to date." This would require hard thinking about such questions as the meaning of socialism, the nature of the state, the relationship between radicals and the labor movement, internationalism in an age of nationalist revolution, and the relationship between democracy and social revolution.[40]

Moreover, Lens maintained, any new left would have to consider the role of "love or humanism" in its philosophy. "A generation ago such a question would lead to nothing but mirth on the part of radicals. . . . But life has proven here too that the Left can go astray with its own dogmas. Utopianism, humanism, was precisely the feature lacking in the Soviet experiment. . . . I don't think that any new Left will emerge in America, or elsewhere, without defining an attitude of tolerance towards others, and an immediate goal of love of our fellow man. The Left, in tossing aside religion, has been ashamed to accept some of the good moral features of religion. The results are written large in the internecine wars between Leftists." Lens's analysis, not coincidentally, placed Muste's politics at the cutting edge of a new radicalism, and he often cited the elder radical by name in his calls for a nondogmatic, humanistic, and antimilitaristic socialism.[41]

Yet this effort by Lens and Muste proved so controversial both within and outside the left that it collapsed after only two years. Soon after the American Forum was formed, Muste, along with several others, attended the annual convention of the Communist Party as "impartial observers" in an effort to facilitate dialogue and to determine the degree to which the party was questioning old dogmas in light of Khrushchev's revelations.[42] Immediately afterward, J. Edgar Hoover of the FBI initiated a smear campaign against Muste and the Forum that led to an investigation by the Senate Internal Security Committee. When the chair of the committee, Mississippi Democrat James Eastland, sent Muste a questionnaire about the presence of Communists in the Forum, he publicly refused to answer it, pointing out that Eastland's opposition to racial integration provided far more grist for Communist propaganda but that no Senate committee was investigating him.[43]

More distressing from Muste's point of view (he was, after all, long used to being the target of such inquiries) was the fact that anti-Communist socialists—such as Norman Thomas, Irving Howe, and Max Shachtman—declined his invitation to join the national committee of the American Forum when they discovered that one of the seven officers of the new organization was a "fellow traveler" and that a handful of the forty-one members of the national committee were members of the Communist Party. Even pacifists opposed the Forum on these grounds; Roy Finch, for example, maintained that Communists should not be allowed to join the committee because they were not civil libertarians.[44] More astute was Roy Kepler's critique of the Forum: Noting that the socialists who refused to join were secular in orientation whereas those who joined were "primarily Christians," he argued that "Dellinger, Muste, et al hope that through 'merciless public attack' [they will] bring the Communists to a sense of their 'sins,' so that they may be 'converted' into social democrats with a libertarian tinge." While members of the Forum certainly had the prerogative of being "fools for Christ," he suggested that they be more sensitive to those who did not share their "missionary zeal." He closed by remarking that they ought to rename the American Forum the "Christian Forum for Communist Rehabilitation."[45]

Kepler's analysis was a shrewd one. Despite their commitment to pacifism and libertarianism, Muste, Dellinger, Dorothy Day, and other members of the Forum approached Communists within a Christian paradigm in which they hoped and expected Communists to acknowledge and repent of their sins. Yet this was not the whole story. As Muste pointed out, his aim had not been to rehabilitate Communists per se but to stimulate fresh thinking across the spectrum of the liberal left. Indeed, the reaction of Kepler, Finch, Thomas, and others to the Forum only served to affirm his conviction that anti-Communism had become a cover for a politics of anti-radicalism even among self-identified socialists. It was also deeply out of touch with reality: The Communist Party was so small, so utterly "irrelevant," as was the left as a whole, that he found their arguments to be almost "incomprehensible."[46] Dellinger, whose relationship with Muste had grown closer since the founding of *Liberation* magazine, offered a similar rebuttal to critics of the Forum, observing insightfully that anti-Communism had its own elements of ritualism and religiosity. "Having rejected the 'Utopianism' of trying to practice their ideals today, [anti-Communist socialists] can only convince themselves and others of their ultimate integrity by a fevered attack on Communist excesses and by a scrupulous dissociation from men of ill repute. Stained by the blood of past and future Hiroshimas, they make a fetish of perpetual cleansing in which they publicly wash their hands of Communist bloodshed. Their words and their list of enemies must try to prove what their lives fail to show."[47]

Despite these setbacks, Muste continued to push forward with the American Forum. But without the participation of leaders of the Socialist Party, the Independent Socialist League, *Dissent* magazine, and other left-wing groups, his efforts were seriously hindered. Within the Communist Party, moreover, dissenters failed to wrest control from the dogmatic leadership of William Z. Foster and Gus Hall, which led to the party's further disintegration. Muste's real hope was that "third camp" figures and independent radicals would join the Forum, but this did not happen in any significant sense, much to his disappointment. The left consisted of "people who are holding their heads in bewilderment and outrage and who are fumbling for a clue to guide them out of the dark tunnel in which they find themselves," Muste commented. "I do not for a moment suggest that this does not apply to myself."[48]

MUSTE faced a similar dilemma within the peace movement, both at home and internationally, as he tried to negotiate a space between pro-Western and pro-Soviet positions. In the early 1950s, in his role as a leader of the FOR, he had attempted to chart a delicate course for the international peace movement; he recommended that the International FOR and other peace groups refuse to join the World Peace Council (WPC) on the grounds that it was dominated by the Soviet Union, while at the same time attending council meetings as impartial observers and communicating with other peace workers "as the spirit leads."[49] Although the IFOR affirmed this policy in 1953, its European members increasingly criticized their American counterparts, arguing that the policy was counterproductive to the cause of peace and reconciliation. As Henri Roser of France wrote to his American friends, "there are many of us in Europe who feel, rightly or wrongly, that the position of the East is sustained by a great hope, while that of the West appears to us conservative." He called on the IFOR to "brave the risk" and engage the Soviet-dominated council with "an attitude which is open, generous, charitable, without fear."[50]

As a result of conversations like these, Muste's position gradually became more flexible and, starting in 1955, he and other pacifists began holding informal meetings with the WPC and Eastern European peace groups. In so doing, he came to "a very deep and in a sense painful realization of the extent to which those in the East and the West live in different milieus, different 'universes of discourse' and how important it is that each should understand the other's position and condition in order that genuine discussion of controversial questions may take place."[51]

Even so, he remained suspicious of peace sentiment that cast either of the two superpowers as occupying a purely defensive position, and stayed firm in his refusal to join the WPC. It was "romantic, unrealistic, and un-Marxian to assume that an arsenal of H-bombs" did not affect "the very nature and structure" of the Soviet state and its foreign policy, he asserted. He offered similar criticism of American peace activists; they tended to hold "American-centric" assumptions about the Cold War and the Soviet Union and failed to recognize that "war is the health of the state."[52] More fruitful would be the development of a third camp, and his efforts in Europe focused on building up such sentiment among religious leaders and peace groups. He found Martin Niemöller, the German theologian, especially responsive, and the two collaborated throughout the late 1950s and 1960s in various peace and antiwar projects. Karl Barth also seemed amenable to his ideas about the Cold War, though the theologian questioned Muste's radical pacifist stance as rather unrealistic. "So what shall we do—stand on the street-corner and cry: 'Madness, madness, madness?'" he queried Muste when they met in 1955. "Perhaps that is what the Old Testament prophets did," the pacifist replied.[53]

But Muste spent the bulk of his energy in the late 1950s and early 1960s on building a radical peace movement in the United States. Here he would have more success than in his efforts to "regroup" the American left, though, as we shall see, tensions over Communism continued to persist. As part of his larger effort to reach out beyond the pacifist community, he had been part of a working group of pacifists who gathered in April 1957 to discuss how they might channel recent concern over hydrogen bomb tests into support for disarmament. In addition to Muste, the group included Quakers Robert Gilmore, James Bristol, and Lawrence Scott; Mildred Scott Olmstead and Emily Parker Simon of WILPF; and Marjorie Swann and Ernest Bromley of Peacemakers. Agreeing that opposition to the tests "could become a break-through in the attempt to reverse the arms race," the group identified three possible approaches to building opposition to nuclear testing: an educational campaign, political action through lobbying Congress and the United Nations, and "action of the Gandhian type (satyagraha)." The group ultimately decided to combine the educational and political approach into an ad hoc committee called the Committee to Stop H-Bomb Tests; *satyagraha* would be pursued separately by "those who feel the leading in that direction."[54]

The Committee to Stop H-Bomb Tests ultimately became the National Committee for a Sane Nuclear Policy (SANE), a coalition of nonpacifists and pacifists committed to raising public awareness of the dangers of nuclear testing. Initially intended to serve a temporary educational purpose, SANE's first advertisement in the *New York Times* calling for the immediate suspension of nuclear testing started a movement. By the summer of 1958, SANE had 130 chapters representing some 25,000 Americans and had attained a significant public presence. At the same time, more radical pacifists such as Muste put together another ad hoc committee called Non-Violent Action Against Nuclear Weapons to organize *satyagraha* campaigns against nuclear testing (in the fall of 1958, the committee was reorganized as the Committee for Nonviolent Action (CNVA), with disarmament as its larger goal). With Lawrence Scott—and soon thereafter Muste—as chairman, the new group brought together pacifists from Peacemakers, the FOR, the WRL, the Catholic Worker movement, and the Society of Friends who wanted to focus on direct action above all else. As Lawrence Scott put it, "Speaking words has become so cheap in this age that only the literal act has much meaning."[55]

Muste's ideological imprint was everywhere on the CNVA. He proposed its first action: a vigil outside the gate of an Atomic Energy Commission bomb project in Nevada on the twelfth anniversary of the bombing of Hiroshima. Muste arrived in Las Vegas early to coordinate the action, build community support, and help provide training in nonviolent tactics. On the morning of the vigil, he was there "all through the torrid day and the long night until the next morning when the nightmarish bomb exploded and the vigil ended," pacifist Jim Peck recalled. He also joined ten of the approximately forty participants who committed civil disobedience by walking into the restricted test site area. The project succeeded in "driving home the fact of personal responsibility," the Quaker Robert Pickus reflected. When the protesters asked the guards what they thought of the explosions, the guards replied, "'I am not authorized to have opinions,' and 'I have no feelings about the tests.'" By accepting personal responsibility for opposing the government's action, project members "demonstrated the fact and possibility of moral choice" both to the guards and to millions of other Americans.[56]

Muste played a similarly central role in other CNVA actions. Among the most successful was the 1958 voyage of the *Golden Rule*, commanded by Albert Bigelow, into the area of the Marshall Islands where the United States intended to conduct nuclear tests. Bigelow and the three other Quakers who made up the crew explained their reasons for sailing into the test-bomb area in a letter to President Eisenhower: "For years we have spoken and written of the suicidal military preparations of the Great Powers, but our voices have been lost in the massive effort of those responsible for preparing this country for war. We mean to speak now with the weight of our whole lives."[57] Too old to serve as a member of the crew, Muste raised money and publicity, and served as the sailors' adviser in Honolulu when they were served with an injunction to prevent them from sailing into the test-bomb area. When they sailed anyway, the government arrested them and placed them on probation. Again, they sailed and again they were arrested. This time, however, they were imprisoned for the remainder of the bomb-test period. In contrast to pacifist activities of the previous decade, the voyage of the *Golden Rule* attracted intense media attention and widespread public sympathy. "Picket lines sprang up around federal buildings and [Atomic Energy Commission] offices across the nation with signs proclaiming: 'Stop the Tests, not the *Golden Rule.*' "[58]

With the success of these "actions" in piquing public awareness about the dangers of nuclear testing, CNVA broadened its efforts to include the arms race and weapons production more generally. In the summer of 1959, pacifists committed civil disobedience at Mead Missile Base in Omaha, Nebraska. As with the Nevada protest and the *Golden Rule*, the "action" exemplified the religious and political culture of radical pacifism: It began with the Gandhian practice of being open and aboveboard with the authorities. As Muste explained in a public letter to President Dwight Eisenhower, their goal was to speak "at the point" where the government was carrying on its "nuclear military program, which we believe to be both profoundly evil and practically suicidal." More fundamentally, they rejected the government's right to despoil the land: "Men are now preparing destruction, which . . . may actually wipe out vegetation and poison the soil. This is a desecration of God's own gift to mankind which must not be permitted to happen." Therewith, starting the last week of June 1959, pacifists held a weeklong vigil for a period of fasting and prayer. Then, on the morning of July 1, 1959, Muste delivered a sermon calling on the United States to disarm, quoting Isaiah 6:1–13 and 30:13, and climbed over the fence, along with two others, whereupon he was promptly arrested for trespassing. For days afterward, pacifists continued to climb the fence until most of them were in jail. The judges handed out suspended sentences; several of them would break the terms of their parole and consequently served up to six months in prison.[59]

As antinuclear sentiment spread, Muste urged CNVA to internationalize its movement by connecting with peace activists in Europe, Asia, and Africa. One of the group's first transnational efforts involved a 1959 demonstration to protest French plans to test an atomic bomb in the Saharan

Desert, a project that had been initiated by British Gandhians Michael Scott, Michael Randle, and April Carter. The goal of the demonstration was twofold: to raise African awareness about the impending test and to appeal to the conscience of the French people in the hope that the French government would call it off. In early October, CNVA and WRL sent Rustin to London and then to Ghana to help expatriate Bill Sutherland and others coordinate and plan the protest. Muste joined them in late November. Despite his advanced age, he threw himself into the project, exhibiting once again his skills at reconciling different points of view. "I was fearful for him the first couple of days," Rustin commented, "but he quickly adjusted to the climate and plunged into a rigorous schedule that left him little sleep."[60]

On December 6, 1959, nineteen people (eleven Ghanaians, one Nigerian, the president of the Basutoland Congress Party, one Frenchwoman, three Englishmen, and Rustin and Sutherland) journeyed in Land Rovers from Accra, Ghana to French territory where they attempted to gain entrance to the test-bomb site. The protest was extremely popular among the Ghanaian people. Kwame Nkrumah contributed $1,000 to the project, and large rallies of people shouting "Freedom!" greeted the team as they traveled to the test-bomb site. Altogether there were three attempts to enter French territory, all of which failed to prevent the test on February 13, 1960. Muste was not, however, discouraged, enthusing that this was "the first international, direct action program against nuclear war and certainly the first in which Western European and American pacifists sought to enlist and train people of other continents . . . in 'positive nonviolent action' (a phrase common in West Africa)." He hoped that the example would encourage those struggling for national liberation to make opposition to nuclear weapons a central part of their agenda.[61]

Encouraged by the Sahara protest, starting in the summer of 1960, CNVA began planning the "San Francisco-to-Moscow Walk for Peace" as "an experiment in international action by pacifist groups, which for the most part have so far operated only within their respective national borders." The Walk for Peace, which began in San Francisco on December 1, 1960, ultimately involved peace activists from the United States and eight European countries. Walkers distributed leaflets stating CNVA's "program of peace," which urged each country they entered to disarm "regardless of what other nations do," to explore the possibility of defense by nonviolent resistance, to develop an economy that was not based on the production of armaments, and to provide aid to "underdeveloped nations." While the primary aim of the walk was to spread CNVA's message, it also had symbolic meaning. Barbara Deming, a writer who had recently converted to pacifism and who had become quite close to Muste, reflected that the real meaning of the walk was to demonstrate that "We are not just mouthing words. We care enough to stir ourselves. To walk from morning to night. Through the bitter cold. Through the drenching rain. Through the stifling heat." It was, moreover, "a walk of penance" in which they repented of their involuntary commitment to their government's military policy.[62]

In terms of developing international contacts, the Walk for Peace was a success. England's Committee for Nuclear Disarmament (CND) and the Committee of 100 (an organization explicitly modeled after CNVA) organized a rally of four thousand peace activists in Trafalgar Square to welcome the "team." The Americans then led the group in a mass march through London. Smaller but equally enthusiastic crowds greeted them as they walked through Belgium and West Germany on their way to Moscow. The only country that refused them entry was France, but French supporters fulfilled the walk's itinerary by walking through France. They also found a warm reception in East Germany, Poland, and the Soviet Union, where national peace councils provided hospitality and allowed them to present the case for unilateral disarmament in open meetings with citizens. The Soviet Union even permitted them to hold a two-hour vigil in Red Square against the Soviet Union's resumption of nuclear tests. The most difficult problem they encountered was maintaining their independence from peace councils that sometimes joined the walk carrying their own signs attacking Western, but not Soviet, militarism. In these instances, pacifists would refuse to continue walking until the signs were removed, explaining that they were "an independent team advocating unilateral disarmament and Gandhian nonviolence." When the walk ended on October 8, 1961, the team had covered six thousand miles and had crossed six national borders. The team had also developed a relationship with the Soviet Peace Committee, which ultimately led CNVA to support the latter's efforts to come to the United States. The U.S. State Department, however, refused to grant visas to the group's representatives; it would not be until 1964 that the group managed to gain entry.[63]

Muste found the Walk for Peace both exhausting and exhilarating. The organizational details and interpersonal and international relations involved in coordinating a walk that covered some six thousand miles and took 310 days were enormous, and they took a toll on the seventy-six-year-old, already fatigued by a persistent virus and worsening eyesight. At the conclusion of the walk, he was unable to stay awake for a massive civil disobedience demonstration against nuclear weapons being held at Trafalgar Square. And, yet, despite these challenges, Muste waxed enthusiastic about the walk, seeing it as a great experiment in nonviolence and internationalism. East and West had held the entire world captive for so long that people failed to see that they lived under an illusion, that they were trapped by a fear of the other that was exacerbated by nationalist ideology and military production. And yet neither Communism nor capitalism would survive nuclear war: "Is this not the abyss of nothingness before which, according to the Existentialists, modern man of East and West stands?" he queried. By rejecting nationalist thinking, by crossing borders, by working with others despite profound differences in language, culture, and politics, the walk had shown a way to begin crossing the abyss.[64]

As these comments suggest, CNVA was representative of radical pacifist thought since World War II, with its blend of Christian notions of suffering and repentance, existentialism, and Gandhian nonviolence. Like the Peacemakers, CNVA activists believed that by taking personal responsibility for the nuclear arms race and embodying the values of truth, love, and nonviolence, they would inspire others to do the same. Direct action was also imperative, they asserted, because it was the only way that "moral concern and political conviction" could "cut through the mazes of a compartmentalized society, establish that personal confrontation and provide that personal example" that would give others a sense of their responsibility for the arms race. They hoped that, as more and more people were converted, one of the nuclear powers would recognize that unilateral disarmament was the only way out of the Cold War. "When one country disarms first, it opens the way for others to do the same," one of their leaflets put it. "Some nation must find the courage to act first."[65]

The main difference between CNVA and the Peacemakers was that it emphasized collective efforts over individual action and tended to be more media savvy. Their "acts of conscience" were quite deliberate performances designed to capture the attention of the press.[66] But they were also profound acts of political unrealism. As Muste explained, people needed their "saints" to show them that the "age" in which they lived was ultimately "not permanent, not real. It is a house built on sand." Like Christ, they would be "deemed foolish, weak, defeated, dead," but therein lay their power and, indeed, their wisdom. Their suffering love would provide the leaven for the world to break "loose" from its attachment to power politics, nuclear weapons, and war, and to open itself to "change," to "possibility."[67]

CNVA was not without its tensions, however. As with the Peacemakers, questions of philosophy and organization emerged early on. Some opposed the use of noncooperation on the grounds that it was "obstructionist" and therefore not "really Gandhian."[68] A related issue had to do with the move beyond nuclear testing to include missile production, as some maintained that pacifists would alienate the public with their radical stance of opposition to the arms race. These questions came to a head during the Polaris Project in New London, Connecticut, which included efforts by pacifists to board nuclear submarines. *Golden Rule* skipper Albert Bigelow resigned from the CNVA national committee in protest, arguing that such tactics were "attention getting" and self-righteous, and would preclude the conversion of opponents.[69]

In his letter of resignation, Bigelow further maintained that CNVA was in danger of becoming overly "organized" and centralized. This was a critique that came up frequently and emerged in myriad and often contradictory ways; thus Bigelow could at once call for greater regulation of action projects and for a more decentralized structure. At its heart was the strongly libertarian impulse within pacifism that could conflict with the desire to work collectively and have a political impact.[70] One particular source of tension had to do with the "group disciplines" that were developed to guide action projects. As the movement gained attention, pacifists welcomed the participation of nonpacifists, only to find that they ignored and even resisted communal regulations. The tendency of younger participants to flout social and sexual mores proved especially trying for pacifists, with some maintaining that CNVA adopt stricter selection criteria and others arguing that the movement's growth depended upon the loosening of such controls.[71] The place of community life within the larger movement similarly attracted debate, as proposals for group living often came with strict policies that could conflict with individual self-expression and the "leading of the spirit."[72]

In each case, Muste rejected the dichotomy pacifists drew between the individual and the community and between freedom and organization. For one, based on his long experience of organizing, CNVA barely even qualified as an organization; it was rather a national committee that enacted policy on a largely consensus basis and with considerable autonomy for

FIGURE 8. Left to right: Miriam Levine, A. J. Muste, and Judith Malina sit in front of the Atomic Energy Commission, 1963. In the fall of 1993, the A. J. Muste Memorial Institute's published the first issue of its newsletter, *Muste Notes*. It featured this photo and included a brief recollection of the sit-in by Judith Malina: "A. J. chose the moment to cross the barricade and sit down. Miriam Levine and I followed a moment later. We were very aware of the police behind us, their hands at ready with gun and club, and we were aware of the Atomic Energy Commission behind them." (*War Resisters League*)

local and regional groups. More to the point, he strongly believed that human association was a fundamental part of life, and that antiorganizational sentiment often served to mask individualistic and antisocial feelings; it was not, in his view, coincidental that those most opposed to "organization" were often those most in favor of strictly regulating personal and group relations. "I wonder if you are aware of how highly organized" the Gandhian movement was, Muste wrote rhetorically to Bigelow, who, like many pacifists, invoked Gandhi's example to bolster his arguments. Thus Muste could call for organizational structure while at the same time occupying the more inclusive, flexible wing of CNVA. "I don't take Gandhi to be infallible and certainly not as having provided formulae to be applied at all future times in every country where nonviolence may be practiced," he explained to Bigelow. This perspective shaped his response to the question of "obstructionism"; he refused to "recognize some kind of eternal, principled difference between climbing over a fence at a missile base and sitting in the road in front of the fence." There were many ways of "bearing witness," some that may seem extreme, but a living movement required a "loose," experimental, open-minded approach rather than hairsplitting.[73]

The same was true of questions of group discipline and community life, which Muste criticized for being prescriptive in their views of nonviolence and love and for having a purist, antiurban, and anticosmopolitan bent. "I attach great importance to the fact of variety (among human beings) and the principle of non-conformity. I do not think there can be one mold or mode of life into which individuals can or ought to be fitted. To try to make them fit by one or other kind of pressure seems to me to be a fundamental denial of pacifism. 'Pressuring' the individual, thinking in a mold, limiting experimentation may be the worst sin ('the sin against the Holy Spirit.')." While it might be necessary to adopt some kinds of restraints or discipline on action projects, these should be constructed loosely to allow for spontaneity and diversity and should be understood as "an artificial and temporary situation which does not necessarily require or allow for relations at the deepest level with other human beings."[74]

Muste's ability to find a reconciling space between the personal and political divisions within CNVA and to find a way forward in times of apparent stagnation and uncertainty made him seen indispensable to the movement. Indeed, the comments about Muste by fellow radical pacifists echoed those made by Brookwooders in the 1920s and Musteites in the 1930s. The only reason the Peacemakers survived from 1948 through 1953, commented Lawrence Scott, was that Muste's "ability of reconciliation was so great, and still is, that he was able to pull us through each annual conference without undue violence." Scott, who would grow disillusioned with CNVA as early 1959, predicted that the committee would survive only because of "A.J. again the master reconciler of the irreconcilable."[75] Dellinger offered a similar account of Muste's "remarkable qualities" of dialogue and reconciliation. He consistently brought "his own wisdom to [an] encounter, without being enslaved by it or intimidating others with it. There was seldom a strategy session of the organizations he headed . . . in which most of the others did not speak before he did."[76]

As these comments suggest, Muste was not only the intellectual and political head of the peace movement, but also its spiritual leader. Contemporaries drew strength and sustenance from what they viewed as his equanimity, expressed through joyfulness and humor, as well as his spiritual constancy and depth of vision. David Riesman, who did not share Muste's radical pacifism, "admired his purity; his lack of vindictiveness; his rare combination of single-mindedness with personal decency and courtesy, even courtliness." Erich Fromm likewise stated in a contemporaneous interview that the existence of people like Muste were the only reason he was able to stay "sane" in the modern world. At around the same time, the jazz critic Nat Hentoff published a biography of Muste that offered a similar assessment. "A. J. is the spiritual chairman of every major pacifist demonstration in the country and often is the actual chairman," he quoted Bradford Lyttle as saying. "He is the number one peacemaker in America."[77]

The sense of deep attachment his fellow peace activists had for him intensified as he grew older and frailer. As the decade of the 1960s began, he started making references to his own mortality and attempted to reduce his organizational responsibilities accordingly.[78] His sense of his own frailty increased as his cataracts worsened. In the summer of 1964, just as he opened a health insurance policy to cover his upcoming eye surgery, he was mugged near his apartment on 103rd Street and West End Avenue. Yet he found strength in the fact that his reaction to the experience was only physical, not emotional. "Achy and numb" for a few days because of a hard punch in the mouth, he viewed it as an expression of the "epidemic" of violence in the world, which he believed was "coming to a head" in the nuclear age. Even if "mankind" was ultimately incapable of reversing the trend, at least there was some comfort in being a victim and not an executioner, as suggested by Camus's famous essay.[79] For his friend and comrade Barbara Deming, the incident "exploded" her "shyness" at expressing her love for him. "Perhaps you do know how very much people love you, or perhaps you don't. People do.. . . I do—always more and more and more."[80]

Similarly, Edith May Snyder, his secretary during this period, expressed her love for him in poetical tones. In a letter to Deming, probably written in 1963, she explained how she had initially viewed a recent statement by Muste as "too theological," but then, "in a moment of illumination, I understood what it meant." In the same letter, she wrote that Muste had "gifted me with one beautiful red rose to welcome spring. i [*sic*] can almost feel it slowly unfolding before me. i suppose aj is aj because he can feel so joyful that it is the first day of spring, even if the weather here in nyc [*sic*] doesn't know it yet."[81] A year later, writing to Muste from Albany, Georgia, where she had initiated an innovative antiracist organizing campaign among the city's white community, expressions of love for the beloved community intermingled with feelings of spiritual love for him. A representative letter began with "oh sweet heart dost thou feel the love spilling out of me towards thee?" and followed with statements of her fervent belief in the power of nonviolence.[82]

CHAPTER 11

⤳

Muste and the Search for a "Third Way"

I forbear speculating on "what the decade of the Sixties will
bring."

—A. J. Muste, 1959

STARTING AROUND 1960, Muste's efforts to internationalize the peace
movement increasingly focused on involving nationalist leaders in the
decolonizing world. He had long harbored hopes that anticolonial movements might serve as the fulcrum for building a nonaligned, "third way."
Yet his efforts in this direction had been hindered by the intensity of the
Cold War, both at home and abroad, as well as the reluctance of the FOR
and the Peacemakers to fully endorse these efforts. The Sahara protest,
however, rekindled his hopes. In Accra, much to his surprise, some nationalist leaders had not only welcomed pacifist assistance, but asked them to
share their ideas about nonviolence and revolution. As a result, his ambitions grew, and he began calling for an international nonviolent revolutionary movement that would focus on eliminating the causes of war, building
a third camp, and opposing nuclear proliferation in an attempt to "somehow affect the centers of power in contemporary society."[1]

But even as Muste developed relationships and alliances with activists
in India and Africa he doubted the feasibility of this vision. He feared that
the East-West bloc was so powerful that the emerging nations would be
unable to escape the ideological tug-of-war between the United States and
the Soviet Union. He was also uncertain about the relationship between
nonviolence and nationalism, and whether the place of pacifists was within
a nation-building paradigm. Finally, he believed that it was desperately
important for nonviolence and antinuclearism in the third world to develop

organically without the interference of "outsiders," particularly those from
the West, given the context and legacy of colonialism, white supremacy,
and American responsibility for instigating the nuclear arms race. Thus,
when interest in both declined in the early 1960s, Muste would not be
unduly distressed; rather, it would reinforce his long-standing conviction
that American activists had to primarily focus on challenging U.S. foreign
policy and expressing solidarity with those oppressed by it.[2]

MUSTE found his experience in Ghana during the Sahara protest encouraging for good reason. The interest aroused by the project encouraged President Kwame Nkrumah, along with the governments of other independent
African nations, to call the All-African Conference on Positive Action for
the Peace and Security of Africa, which took place in Accra from April 7
through April 10, 1960.[3] Muste, along with Ralph Abernathy of the Southern Christian Leadership Conference (SCLC), attended the conference, as
did peace activists from across Europe, Japan, and India. Although the delegates refused to unequivocally endorse nonviolence, they drew up a manifesto stating that the Sahara protest and the larger struggle against the
nuclear arms race were "an integral part of the African liberation struggle."
It further invited more "nongovernmental" actions against "nuclear imperialism" in Africa, and called for the renunciation of nuclear weapons by
independent African nations. Finally, it reaffirmed the importance of independence in the power struggle between the United States and the Soviet
Union, and expressed its support for the founding of training centers for
"positive action" in Africa.[4]

Even before he left for Accra, Muste knew that there was scant possibility the delegates would embrace Gandhianism en masse. He shared the
analysis of his friend Sidney Lens, who maintained that the racial history
of colonialism made African struggles unique in world history. As Lens
explained, "Africa pursues its own special course. It pays little homage to
'free enterprise.' It is for socialism, but it rejects the concept that the
working class is the pivot of social advance. And where it practices nonviolence, it practices it as a tactic, not as part of a social philosophy."[5]
Muste thus warned his fellow pacifists not to become overoptimistic. The
purpose of the conference was to explore "specific projects" whereby
nonviolence might be successfully employed, he explained. "There will
be differences of opinion." In particular, the defeat of the South African
Defiance Campaign had posed "the question as to whether there is a

viable nonviolent alternative for those who will no longer passively submit to slavery enforced by machine guns."[6] This realistic assessment probably explains why Muste downplayed the rhetoric on behalf of revolutionary violence that permeated the conference, including a dramatic speech by Franz Fanon on the need for armed resistance in Algeria. He recognized that the conference gave pacifists access to power on a scale hitherto unimagined, and that the onus was on them to prove the relevance of nonviolence to people long oppressed by empire and race. Moreover, he viewed it as highly significant to the international peace movement that the conference had endorsed nonalignment and expressed its opposition to "nuclear imperialism."[7]

As it turns out, plans for setting up centers for positive action never really got off the ground (only one was ever established). There were three main reasons why the project failed. First, the crisis in the Congo diverted the attention of Nkrumah and other interested African leaders. Second, pacifists themselves became ambivalent about the idea when it became clear that the centers would be closely connected to governments, some of which were not as cognizant of civil liberties as they would have liked. Third, and probably most important, colonized peoples did not find the nuclear disarmament issue as urgent as the struggle for national liberation. As Muste commented, his sojourn in Africa had shown him that the issue of nuclear catastrophe did not impress upon colonized peoples much as it did upon East and West.[8]

Nevertheless, he continued to hope that stronger linkages might be made between pacifists and anticolonialists. In December 1961, he joined approximately sixty other pacifists in Beirut, Lebanon, to discuss the question of transnational action against war and oppression. The idea of a "nonviolent army" had first been proposed at a 1949 meeting of pacifists in New Delhi that both Muste and Rustin had attended, but there had been little follow-through.[9] This time a deep sense of urgency pervaded the proceedings, largely because of the influence of Muste, Michael Scott, and M. G. Ramachandran, an Indian politician and well-known movie star. The meeting concluded with the unanimous decision to found the World Peace Brigade (WPB), an international "peace army" that would oppose war preparations and assist anticolonial struggles through nonviolent protest, with Muste, Scott, and the veteran Gandhian and Socialist Jayaprakash Narayan as cochairmen and respective heads of the three regional councils (North American, European, and Asian).[10]

FIGURE 9. A. J. Muste (center) and Bayard Rustin (far right) with other members of the World Peace Brigade in Tanganyika, Africa, 1962.

Muste had some basis for hoping that the formation of the WPB could "prove epoch-making." The decision to launch the brigade had been unanimous and the WPB could boast of having the sponsorship of prominent figures such as Kenneth Kaunda of Northern Rhodesia (Zambia), Julius Nyerere of Tanganyika, Martin Buber of Israel, Bertrand Russell of England, and Martin Niemöller of Germany. Yet it would prove a failure, at least in part because of pacifists' discomfort with the world of high politics and power. Muste himself exemplified the paradox at the heart of the undertaking: He called on pacifists to move beyond their "Anglo-Saxon" heritage of individualism and make collective efforts to affect the centers of power, while at the same time insisting that they remain "unreconstructed and uncompromising unilateralists" who should appeal to others on the basis of morality and not political power.[11]

This paradox can be seen in the WPB's first major project, a demonstration to express solidarity with the Northern Rhodesia Independence Movement led by Kaunda, a proponent of nonviolence with whom pacifists had established friendly relations. With Muste heading up operations, the plan was to have an international team march across the border from Tangan-yika (which became Tanzania in 1964) into Northern Rhodesia (now Zam-bia) in support of Kaunda's call for free elections. Although Muste raised the necessary funds and recruited volunteers, Kaunda ultimately called off the march because the British agreed to hold elections. As the African leader explained to Brigade-member Bill Sutherland, "it's quite clear now that we're going to have an election which will provide for majority rule, and the end of British control. I have been with you all this time. I have been nonviolent in principle and I've appreciated and wanted to thank you for all you have done. But I have decided that I am going to be a politician, and to go into government." Kaunda's decision to forego the protest in the interest of consolidating the Zambian state foreshadowed the fate of other WPB initiatives in Africa, including setting up another "positive action" training center in Dar es Salaam, Tanganyika, which closed after only a year in operation due to lack of funds.[12]

When Muste returned from Tanganyika, he found an invitation from the Gandhi Peace Foundation to attend an antinuclear-arms convention in New Delhi in mid-June 1962. He eagerly accepted, recognizing the unique opportunity to discuss questions of disarmament with leaders of a major nation (the Indian representatives included not only Narayan, Ramachan-dran, and Vinoba Bhave, with whom he was well acquainted, but also Prime Minister Jawaharlal Nehru, President Sarvepalli Radhakrishnan, and other high officials) as well as prominent international peace activists such as Abbé Pierre, Danilo Dolci, and Martin Niemöller.[13] Muste saw it as espe-cially significant that former President Rajendra Prasad appeared to favor unilateral disarmament: "If any one country taking courage in both hands unilaterally disarmed, it would break this vicious circle of mutual fear and distrust and pave the way for universal disarmament," Prasad proclaimed. Yet Muste's own account of how Nehru responded to "Prasad's challenge" at the New Delhi convention suggested how unlikely it was that India would embrace such a policy. While affirming his faith in nonviolence as the "ulti-mate solution," Nehru suggested that the masses would view it as an act of cowardice and fear, an offense to national pride, and a violation of the democratic process.[14]

The patriotic reaction of the Indian people to Chinese excursions in the Himalayas several months later placed these tensions between nonviolence and nationalism in stark relief. As the government moved to defend its borders, Narayan asked Muste to return to New Delhi to participate in discussions about how Gandhians should respond to the national crisis. There, Muste showed that he recognized the complexity of the situation. On the one hand, he viewed the Chinese as the primary aggressors and maintained that the Indian reaction was understandable in the context of their recent struggle for independence. Yet he remained firm in his stance that self-proclaimed Gandhians should refuse to support the war, asserting that it would be impossible for those "who sit in on the game of nationalism and power" to avoid becoming compromised by supporting military defense and national unity.[15]

Together, he and other WPB activists conceived of a project that they hoped would ease the tension between India and China, an "International Friendship March from New Delhi to Peking" that would express "the friendship and unity of peoples, irrespective of the policies pursued by their governments" and call upon the two countries to resolve their dispute without violence. Yet the international team, which began its trek in March 1963, faced criticism from Indian nationalists who saw them as apologists for Chinese aggression and resolute opposition from the Chinese who refused to let them cross into the People's Republic of China through the border area. Internal debates further complicated matters, as Indian Gandhians had "a much greater sense of identification with the nation-state than most Western pacifists do."[16] In fact, Indians themselves were divided over the question of Gandhi's legacy for national defense. Vinoba Bhave, for example, maintained that Gandhians should provide nonviolent assistance for national defense, while Narayan argued that India should resist militarism and strengthen its commitment to nonviolence. These questions played themselves out every time the marchers arrived in a new village, as public meetings became scenes of passionate debate about the role of nonviolence in national defense, the future of the nonaligned movement, the implications of a nuclear-armed China, and so on.[17]

In October, the team was stopped at the Burmese border by officials fearful of alienating China. In desperation, they appealed upon Muste to return, whereupon he spent three weeks in India and another week in London, attempting to negotiate a mutually agreeable solution to the impasse. Yet the Chinese remained unmoved, and he had to concede defeat. At the same time, the WPB faced a dearth of funds, as its financial sponsors prioritized aiding the African American civil rights movement. Regional concerns also drew attention away from transnational projects. The question of Kashmir's status and relations between India and Pakistan absorbed Narayan,

Muste's cloest ally, while the conflict between Cuba and the American government preoccupied Muste. The WPB soon thereafter fell into disuse.[18]

The WPB faced the recurring problem of its relationship to "centers of power." For obvious reasons, the newly independent countries in Asia and Africa were deeply concerned with providing for their national security. Their dilemma was aptly summed up by Kaunda in a conversation with Sutherland. Although he was a "believer in nonviolence," as head of state, he faced the problem of how he was "going to be able to defend the country against the South Africans and the southern Rhodesians and all of these people who are coming in with their spies and attempting to destabilize us from the south."[19] Pacifists were ultimately unable to respond to Kaunda's critique. Some proposed defense by nonviolent resistance, yet this inevitably struck nationalists as naive and impractical. Muste tended to shy away from making this argument, recognizing that it operated within the discourse of nationalism and power that pacifists aimed to transcend. But he had little to offer in its stead; to call on independence leaders to simultaneously seek liberation and transcend nationalism was to ask for the extraordinary, particularly in the context of big-power rivalries and ambitions. Beyond the inadequacies of theory, pacifists were at heart uncomfortable with the project of nation-state formation. As Bill Sutherland put it in a letter to Muste, although he supported national liberation, he did not "feel at home [with nation-building projects]. I just can't find room within modern statehood for basic nonviolence."[20]

The question of how radical pacifists should relate to independence movements in the third world—and, indeed, the aspirations of oppressed racial minorities at home—was revived by the Cuban revolution and the U.S. government's response to it. Most pacifists—radical and liberal alike—agreed with Muste that it represented a genuine popular movement for human dignity and hoped that it "might set the example of a substantially new type of revolution."[21] He also supported, though did not join, the American Fair Play for Cuba Committee, which had a strong contingent of pacifists, and worked closely with intellectuals such as C. Wright Mills, Erich Fromm, and David Riesman to protest growing sentiment for American intervention.[22] Pacifists, of course, were more inclined toward direct action than their more academic comrades; Muste, Dellinger, and Dorothy Day, participated in several public fasts to express their support for Cuban independence, while the FOR focused on delivering humanitarian aid to the island.[23]

With the consolidation of the Cuban revolutionary state, however, debate emerged over the nature of the regime and how pacifists should respond to it. For his part, Muste maintained that the undemocratic aspects of Castro's rule were related to the context of the Cold War rivalry and that pacifists' primary responsibility lay in convincing the United States to change its foreign policy. To intervene in the Cuban revolution was "utterly deplorable" and morally "indefensible," he wrote in response to the Bay of Pigs invasion. It meant no less than "the death of the Republic, the open advent of the American Empire."[24] Some, like Roy Finch, however, argued that the revolution had become totalitarian and explored ways of nonviolently engineering Castro's overthrow. Disagreement over the issue became so sharp that Finch resigned from *Liberation*'s editorial board.[25]

The issue emerged in somewhat different form during the Quebec-to-Guantanamo Walk for Peace, which CNVA organized in 1963 as a way of protesting the superpower dispute over the island, manifested alarmingly in the recent Cuban missile crisis. Walking from Canada along the East Coast, through the South to the Florida Keys where they hoped to sail to Cuba, the walk lasted from May 1963 through October 1964. One reason it lasted so long was that the walkers were imprisoned in an Albany, Georgia, jail from December 23, 1963, through February 24, 1964, for disobeying a city ordinance. Trouble between the marchers and southern officials had begun in Griffin, Georgia, when local police responded brutally to the spectacle of white women and black men walking side by side. Incidents such as these culminated with their arrest in Albany, when they refused to compromise with a ban restricting their free movement on the main streets of the city.[26]

Throughout the Quebec-to-Guantanamo Walk, conflicts emerged between pacifists and black activists that illustrate the dilemmas pacifists faced in relating to marginalized groups and their quest for political power. As the group entered the South, one of the walkers held up a sign that called for "no federal troops in Cuba, Vietnam, and Dixie." Surely the sign would be misunderstood by African Americans, Muste and Deming demurred, ultimately prevailing upon the walkers to remove it.[27]

A few weeks later, the Washington, D.C., chapter of CORE attempted to offer solidarity to the besieged walkers in Griffin, Georgia, by calling upon the Department of Justice to investigate. Yet when FBI officials arrived on the scene, the walk's coordinator, Bradford Lyttle, refused to confirm the story and his secretary "*denied that there was any police brutality in*

Albany!!!!" a CORE member wrote incredulously to Muste. "What is the sense of denying what happened in Griffin? . . . They have been torturing people for years, and unless the public is aroused and made aware of what is going on; unless the Justice Department steps in and does something, they will go on torturing and maiming, and violating every decent human right known to man. . . . Can you let us know what the group wants us to do? What's the point of [the walkers'] seeking publicity only to deny what happened?"[28] Soon thereafter, when the walkers arrived in Albany, they again alienated the local African American community by organizing a protest at the Turner Air Force Base, one of the few racially integrated employers in the state.[29]

Muste was circumspect in his response to criticism of the walkers, but he was clearly disturbed by what he saw as their inability to deal with "paradox" and "complexity." More concretely, he believed that the Justice Department did, in fact, have "certain obligations under the law and in a democratic society" to investigate and prosecute civil rights violations. Muste would spend the next several months in the "wild south," hoping that his presence would help to resolve "some of the problems which have emerged." In so doing, he helped to give meaning and shape to a narrative that increasingly seemed incoherent and contradictory to CNVA's presumptive allies.[30]

Even as Muste repaired relations with Albany's African American community, another conflict arose.[31] Bradford Lyttle, still in his role as organizer of the walk, intended to hold demonstrations at Cuban military installations as a way of protesting Cuba's commitment to armed self-defense. Dave Dellinger, however, strongly opposed this plan, particularly after visiting the island and observing a popular revolution that was "fighting for its life against American blockade and aggression—and against Stalinist influences." "We must recognize," he wrote to CNVA's executive committee,

that the phenomenon of armed defense by a tiny minority . . . is very different than that of U.S. militarism, which is linked not only with capitalism but with the suppression of colonial movements for freedom and for economic justice. Personally I am not interested in the walk's taking false action here—in this besieged revolutionary country—in order to impress the American public, government, or liberals with the "fairness" or "impartiality" of our position. Cuban

militarism is not American militarism and we can be total advocates
of nonviolence . . . and still be realistic about the differences between
Cuban defense and U.S. "defense."

Dellinger called on the walk's organizers to cancel their plans to picket
Cuba, which he argued had a legitimate concern with defending itself from
superpower aggression. It would be far more appropriate, he suggested, for
the walk to offer "to take specific actions of our own, nonviolently, against
invasion or in support of revolutions in other Latin American countries. In
other words, offer them our nonviolent help but don't condemn them out
of hand for their method."[32]

In making this argument, Dellinger drew a parallel to the pacifist movement's relationship to the civil rights movement; just as he would not picket
civil rights demonstrations in the United States "at which violent 'self-
Defense' was advocated," neither would he picket Cuban bases. Referring
specifically to the tensions that had emerged between pacifists and black
activists when the Guantanamo walkers entered the South, he accused
Lyttle of holding an "extremely narrow, rigid and self-righteous attitude
which is appalling." The right to self-determination belonged to Cubans,
just as it did to African Americans fighting for freedom at home.[33]

Muste sided with Dellinger, as did most other members of the executive
committee.[34] As a result, instead of demonstrating at Cuban military installations, the walkers planned to go to the U.S. naval base in Guantanamo
Bay where they would call on the United States to close the base and withdraw its troops as a symbol of goodwill for the Cuban people. Ironically,
after all of their discussions on the proper course of action in Cuba, the
State Department refused to grant them visas. After exploring various legal
avenues and holding protests at the State Department's Miami office, five
walkers attempted to sail to Cuba in a boat they dubbed the *Spirit of Freedom*, which was promptly confiscated by the authorities.[35]

The debate between Dellinger and Lyttle over how CNVA should relate
to the civil rights movement and the Cuban revolution exemplifies the
dilemmas pacifists faced as they became involved in anticolonial projects.
As pacifists, they were conscientiously opposed to the use of violence even
in self-defense and were often uncomfortable with state-centered politics.
As radicals, however, they supported social justice and national liberation.
Over the course of the 1960s, they resolved these apparent contradictions in

a variety of ways. Some, like Roy Finch, viewed expressions of revolutionary violence as signs of incipient totalitarianism and remained deeply suspicious of a politics of solidarity. Others tried to find a way of nonviolently supporting popular revolutions. As George Houser recalled of his work for the American Committee on Africa, "I always figured that . . . we're not in the position to call the tune. I am against colonial regimes. I am really in favor of these guys who are struggling against it. My assistance is not raising arms and munitions for them to win, but to support them politically."[36]

For his part, Muste expressed solidarity with these movements, while foregrounding the imperative of building opposition to the Cold War and the nuclear arms race. As he pointed out, these positions were not mutually exclusive, since the Cold War rivalry placed a stranglehold on third world revolution and struggles for self-determination. Moreover, he strongly believed that the task of the peace movement was not to criticize or blame others but to "concentrate on truly liberating itself and in so doing liberate its adversary."[37] These views would shape his response to the political developments of the 1960s and positioned him to take the lead in the movement against the Vietnam War.

In the end, the regional turn and subsequent breakup of the WPB was not only a result of philosophical tensions. Poor communication networks and a dearth of funds also presented obstacles to international action.[38] Most especially, the Vietnam War would increasingly preoccupy antiwar activists in the United States and elsewhere. Significantly, Asian and European members of the WPB encouraged and supported American pacifists as they turned their attention to U.S. foreign policy in Southeast Asia, as did South Vietnamese and Japanese Buddhists with whom American pacifists had developed networks of solidarity.[39]

IN addition to facing the dilemma of how a pacifist movement with a predilection for decentralism and internationalism could relate to national liberation projects, radical pacifists had to grapple with how to relate to the larger peace movement that had emerged in opposition to nuclear testing. Initially, CNVA had hoped to have a close working relationship with SANE—Muste, Gilmore, and other radical pacifists sat on its national and local committees—yet profound differences over questions of ideology and tactics emerged almost immediately. As early as 1959, *Liberation* magazine criticized SANE for assenting to the Eisenhower administration's insistence that inspection guarantees precede a test ban. Rather than appeal to the "power elite," SANE should appeal to the people; after all, it was widespread popular indignation that had raised the issue of testing in the first place.[40] Differences between radical pacifists and SANE emerged again in the summer of 1960 when Senator Thomas J. Dodd of the Senate Internal Security Committee charged that the organization had been infiltrated by Communists, and Norman Cousins, Norman Thomas, and other board members followed by adopting a resolution that excluded from membership those who adhered "to communist or other totalitarian doctrine."[41]

Muste was among the most perceptive and outspoken critics of SANE's anti-Communist policy, resigning in protest. While opposed to the Communist Party's history of using dissimulative tactics in united front activities, he believed that the party was a far too marginal force in the 1950s to represent a serious threat. Now, in contrast to the 1930s, pacifists were the "controlling element" in the peace movement. "If there are people thinking of bringing people around to a Soviet line, I don't know where in the world that would take them! Any peace movement in the U.S. today with such a line would be dead before it was born." More to the point, by colluding with the politics of anti-Communism, SANE had hindered rather than helped the peace movement. The practices of the Dodd committee were, Muste wrote, "part of the mechanism by which the Cold War is carried on. A peace organization that does not maintain an absolutely clear position of opposition to them is abetting the Cold War and stultifying itself." It was, moreover, imperative for SANE to stop thinking in "nationalist terms," and recognize that the United States was at least as responsible for the Cold War as the Russians or else it would be unable to build a long-lasting, effective movement.[42]

Radical pacifists further departed from the liberal peace activists over the question of whether the movement should focus on nuclear war or warfare in general. Muste maintained that an exclusive focus on nuclear weapons would make the movement vulnerable to being co-opted if the government actually began reducing its nuclear arsenal.[43] This criticism turned out to be quite prescient. The similarity between SANE's position on nuclear testing and the government's appears to have hindered its long-term effectiveness. SANE and other liberal peace activists fully supported the Kennedy administration when it created the Arms Control and Disarmament Agency in 1961 and negotiated a limited test-ban treaty with the Soviet Union in August 1963, viewing these actions as first steps toward disarmament. As a result, "the tide of protest action began to ebb" and grew more respectable, merging "into the liberal wing of the Democratic Party. SANE, the largest, most powerful peace organization, increasingly substituted lobbying and 'responsible criticism' for demonstrations, causing its grassroots vitality to dry up." The truth, however, was that "the peace movement had less cause for rejoicing than it believed. By focusing on the issue of thermonuclear warfare, as it had done since 1957, it was peculiarly vulnerable to a shift in military strategy taking place during the 1960s." That shift involved decreasing the risk of nuclear war while at the same time increasing the country's ability to wage "conventional" warfare. As historian Lawrence Wittner has commented, "H-bombs were out, napalm was in." Thus, by the fall of 1963, the peace movement lost "the momentum that it had briefly gained at the turn of the decade."[44]

Over the course of 1963–64, CNVA vigorously debated various proposals for maintaining their relevance and building up a stable constituency in the new climate of public indifference. Some, like Lawrence Scott, called on pacifists to appeal to liberals by dropping their language of unilateralism and by foregrounding the importance of international law and supranational institutions like the United Nations. This position gained traction when Republican presidential candidate Barry Goldwater stated his support for first use of nuclear weapons.[45] Others called for maintaining CNVA's unique identity as a unilateralist and direct action organization, but suggested that the group shift away from dramatic national and international projects and instead focus on local projects that cultivated grassroots involvement. "The question is," Theodore Olson asked, "are we really interested in people?" Still others, most notably Marjorie Swann and Barbara Deming, proposed that CNVA forge greater connections between the peace movement and the civil rights movement, contending that the two struggles "were fundamentally one." Yet there remained concern that black activism would become more closely identified with the state and lose its radical edge. As one CNVA member put it, "Civil rights victories will tend toward Negro patriotism and support of national ambitions."[46]

For their part, Muste and Dellinger insisted that a spiritual and ideological "rupture" with liberalism was imperative. Once upon a time the liberal-left tradition had been driven by a vision of "a classless and warless world," but ever since the outbreak of World War I, liberals, socialists, and unionists had become increasingly identified with the state and capitalist culture. "As tends to happen, philosophical and theological rationalizations have emerged which appear to justify this attitude," Muste wrote. "Former radicals write about 'the end of ideologies' from chairs in vast educational institutions" with deep ties to nuclear weapons research. Theologians "emphasize 'power'" and "decry utopianism," placing the "realization of the beloved community 'beyond history.'" Having lost their moral compass, they had been seduced by the idea that "the situation" was under control. The optimism that greeted Kennedy's announcement of a test ban exemplified this delusional thinking, for the state continued to spend enormous sums of money "on research into weapons of mass destruction" and to police "the world on behalf of 'freedom,'" most ominously in Vietnam.[47] "We must abandon our fascination with . . . the word, of talk, of negotiations, which do not correspond to the realities," Muste asserted. "We have to see steadfastly that the arms race is real . . . the rest is unreal, [an] illusion."[48]

Pacifists should, therefore, maintain their distinct antiestablishment identity as unilateralists and direct actionists, while building alliances among the "creative" forces in black America and the decolonizing world. After all, "the problems of racial equality, economic and social order, and peace are integrally related and at one level constitute a single problem." To bolster his argument, Muste pointed to the history of the civil rights movement. Just as the Supreme Court decisions outlawing segregation would have been "a dead letter" if it had not been for mass direct action, the same was true for peace activism. While it might seem unthinkable that mass numbers of Americans would accept a radical peace program, "thirty years ago most people would have equally considered a massive revolt of Negroes against segregation unthinkable. What brought the latter about was not a more skillful practice of gradualism, but the *rejection* of that approach."[49] It was, moreover, the vision of the "beloved community" that had inspired black people, not a language of realism. In the same way, pacifists had to fearlessly articulate their moral values and faith. "It is not possible to arrive by way of a calculus of expediency at a moral standard. . . . It is by way of a moral commitment, of setting a limit beyond which one will not perpetrate atrocities and deface the human image, or the image of God in man, that new possibilities emerge in politics."[50]

In the end, Muste conceded that it was impossible to predict whether in fact a "revolutionary society" would come into being or even what such a society would look like. Yet rather than give up hope, he continued to believe in the power and imperative of human beings to make history, and he invoked Abraham to suggest that radicals had to continue to "go out" to build the city, even if they were not entirely sure where they were going. Indeed, as a socialist and a democrat, it was important to him *not* to provide a blueprint because he believed that to do so would lead to the authoritarianism and dogmatism he had come to despise about the left. To "go out" was in any case the only way to preserve one's humanity in a world "debauched by violence." Quoting a recent speech by the philosopher Herbert Marcuse, he insisted that it was time "to become sentimental again, to have the courage to believe in the unmanipulative language of our feelings! . . . Refuse to make yourselves the accessories to the crimes of inhumanity which are daily committed and daily concealed. Rather try to remake this world a little in your own image, in the image of your own uncompromising hopes and dreams."[51]

CNVA's executive committee thrashed out these questions at a thirteen-hour discussion in December 1964. By the end of the meeting, Muste's vision had triumphed; they decided that CNVA should continue to emphasize their total opposition to war and support for unilateral disarmament while also focusing on "opposition to American imperialism in the Congo, Vietnam, and elsewhere; and only a peripheral involvement in civil rights." Rather than pursue long, expensive national and transnational projects, CNVA would develop local group activities, which would be tied to the larger goal of opposing the Vietnam War.[52]

This decision proved prescient. As a result, Muste and other radical pacifists were posed to serve an important leadership function and to shape the tactics and philosophy of the emerging movement against the war in Vietnam. Muste would find that he had much in common with the student leftists who became the backbone of the movement, with their shared hostility toward Cold War liberalism, penchant for direct action, and affinity for nationalist revolutions. Meanwhile, his anti-Communist bona fides allowed him to maintain open lines of communication with social democrats and liberal peace activists as he sought to build a movement to end the war. Hence his subsequent ability to pull together the most remarkable coalition of liberals and leftists since the days of the Popular Front, the Fifth Avenue Peace Parade Committee, and to unite the civil rights and peace movements in the Spring Mobilization to End the War in Vietnam (MOBE).

At the same time, however, Muste recognized that the antiwar movement was not against war in general, but against the war in Vietnam in particular. Thus, even as his stature and influence grew, his relationship to the antiwar movement would parallel his relationship to the civil rights movement, the antinuclear movement, and anticolonial struggles in the third world. While serving a vanguard role and helping to shape the movement's ideology and tactics, he was unable to channel it into a nonviolent revolutionary movement against war in general. Perhaps his inability to do so had to do with the vagueness of his program for social transformation in the first place; though he continued to avow socialism, his program for how to achieve it relied, in the last analysis, upon the hope that his fellow Americans would experience a religious conversion, a "spiritual rebirth" that would provoke the crisis and opportunity for divine intervention in history. But, in the end, he would not be much preoccupied with these limits, as ending the war in Vietnam absorbed every fiber of his being.

⤳

CHAPTER 12

The "American Gandhi" and Vietnam

For each of us the first consideration is to look into himself
or herself and determine scrupulously whether he or she
has made the unrepeatable decision, performed the act
of faith and commitment and humility which is required of
each of us now—and I mean especially for white Americans
and Europeans who have acquired a habit of domineering
and arrogance—if we are to live and not perish in the day
of judgment, which is today.

—A. J. Muste, 1965

MUSTE'S CRITICISM OF Cold War policy in Asia had been long-standing.
He observed as early as 1946 that French resistance to Vietnamese self-
determination did not augur well for the region. With the defeat of France
at Dien Bien Phu in 1954, he warned that the American obsession with
preventing the spread of Communism would lead it into an unwinnable
war. The massive buildup of aid to the South Vietnamese during the Kennedy administration, even in the face of the reactionary policies of the Diem
regime, convinced him that the peace movement, as well as activist forces
more broadly, should focus all of its energies and resources on opposition
to American intervention.[1]

Yet the American liberal left continued to be divided, hindering Muste's
efforts on this front. Civil rights leaders were reluctant to criticize American
foreign policy at the same time that the movement gained access to national
political power. Debates about the politics of nonviolence and interracialism created further tensions within the movement. Meanwhile, the question of Communism remained fraught and unresolved. Old Left socialists

and peace activists criticized New Leftists for their apparent naïveté about working with Communists and proved reluctant to view the war in Vietnam outside of a Cold War paradigm. More broadly, generational and cultural differences made it difficult for the different wings of the "Movement" to find common ground. Yet Muste pushed on, determined to overcome the divides that prevented Americans from taking a united stance against what he viewed as a criminal war. His efforts, organizational, political, and intellectual, laid the basis for one of the most powerful and diverse antiwar coalitions in American history.[2]

OVER the course of 1964, Muste helped to set the terms of the debate that would consume the American liberal left for the next decade. In the summer, he and David McReynolds published a historical evaluation in which they laid out what would become the "radical" analysis of the war. In it, they argued that American intervention in Vietnam stemmed directly from the faulty assumptions of the containment policy. The refusal of the United States "to recognize the reality of China," they declared, became the basis for a series of aggressive acts toward the mainland, such as refusal to admit China into membership in the United Nations and support for Taiwan, as well as efforts to prop up the illegitimate government of South Vietnam. As a result, the United States was on the side of counterrevolution, even as it declared itself in favor of democracy and self-determination, and two historical enemies, China and Vietnam, had drawn closer together, making it less likely that the Vietnamese would, in fact, follow an independent course. Apart from these historical considerations, sea power was of no use in an Asian land war, and air power would only further alienate civilians "because the Vietcong cannot be spotted." "We are trapped in a situation where no traditional military victory can be won in South Vietnam regardless of how many more troops and how much more equipment is poured in."[3]

Still, peace activists and liberals were reluctant to take a strong stance against American foreign policy in Asia. For many of them, Republican presidential candidate Barry Goldwater, with his talk of "nuking Asia" represented a greater evil than Lyndon Johnson, who had, moreover, recently helped to pass the Civil Rights Act of 1964. Muste was not, however, persuaded from departing from his "long-time practice of not voting." As he wrote during the campaign, it was not "Goldwater and Right extremists" who had built up a "vast military establishment" and had set an "unsavory record in relation to Cuba and other regions," but, rather, the current "regime."[4] The rapid escalation of the war soon after Johnson's reelection served to confirm this analysis and persuaded some of the president's supporters to join Muste and other radical pacifists in protesting the war. On December 20, 1964, Norman Thomas and A. Philip Randolph spoke alongside Muste at an antiwar rally in New York City that had been organized by CNVA, WRL, the FOR, and the Student Peace Union.[5]

At this early stage in the war, however, most liberals recoiled from the idea of protesting the war. For example, in an article for the *New York Times* in November 1964, George Kennan sought to chasten this emerging antiwar sentiment by suggesting that the United States had "not done too badly" in Asia and that it was necessary to place "limitations on the standards of our criticism." In making this argument, he suggested that the Chinese were "embittered fanatics, wedded to a dated and specious ideology" from which other Asians needed protection. While he counseled patience and pragmatism, he conceded that the ultimate objective of American foreign policy should be the "destruction of Communism as a political force in China and everywhere—the overthrow, in other words, of the Chinese Communist government."[6]

In an exchange of letters that was later reprinted in *Liberation* magazine, Muste challenged Kennan's analysis, and suggested that it was based upon notions of national and racial superiority. The history of Western imperialism and of white supremacy was crucial for understanding Chinese ideology and foreign policy. Indeed, "Westerners, people 'developed in the Judaic-Christian tradition,' to use a phrase of Mr. Kennan's by which [he implies] a certain moral superiority . . . have certainly given Chinese and other non-Westerners many lessons in violence, brutality, and violation of human dignity." He continued: "people who emphasize political realism ought to expect the new Chinese regime . . . to behave just as it does." He found it "utterly appalling" that "a man of Kennan's stature should exhibit the same blindness to the United States' role that most Americans are afflicted with and that, for all his deprecation of 'moralism,' he should confirm America's image of itself as by and large virtuous, innocent, only seeking to see that Communists are 'contained' and do not make trouble. This smugness and self-righteousness means that the 'others,' the Communists, etc., are always the aggressors, fanatics, and sinners." What Kennan and American policymakers more generally had to recognize was that "the day of domination by any Western power" in Asia was "over!"[7]

The debate between Muste and Kennan inevitably turned to the war in Vietnam. Kennan suggested that Muste's criticism of the United States' China policy and calls for unilateral withdrawal from Vietnam amounted to isolationism. Without a U.S. presence in Asia, Kennan wrote, Asians would be left to the "mercies of . . . fanatical, power-hungry and wholly intolerant minorities." Muste responded by suggesting that it was precisely Kennan's characterization of the Chinese that made U.S. foreign policy imperialist rather than internationalist. "When is the moment to cease basing policy on the concept of opponents as 'embittered fanatics, power-hungry, and wholly intolerant' and to predicate it instead [on] their 'ultimate humanity and sobriety?'" To equate withdrawal and an end to military interventionism with isolationism reflected "our (bad) habit of thinking that the only relevant or 'real' relationship with other peoples is in the realm of 'power' and essentially military in character." In the end, Kennan conceded that perhaps the United States "had done little good anywhere," but he saw no alternative except the admission of "complete failure and helplessness on our part."[8]

Within a year, Kennan would become a vocal opponent of the war in Vietnam, but not for the reasons Muste opposed it. The main difference was that the former viewed Vietnam as a mistake, while Muste viewed it as an expression of an overall "pattern" in U.S. foreign policy.[9] Other self-described realists shared Kennan's views. Hans Morgenthau, for example, argued that the war was a "consequence of a series of human failures and mistakes, and of a lack of greatness in our leaders, who refuse to admit the mistakes and liquidate a losing enterprise." Niebuhr condemned the war as "futile," both because it reflected the "illusion of American omnipotence" and because Asian peoples lacked the cultural "pre-requisites for self-rule" and democratic government. Even so, he maintained that the war was an "insoluble problem" in which there were few alternatives besides staying the course.[10]

Even more troubling from Muste's point of view was the reluctance of socialists to unambiguously support an immediate American withdrawal. In the summer of 1964, *Dissent* magazine published an editorial declaring the war unwinnable, while at the same time urging the United States to provide aid to a genuinely reformist South Vietnamese government. At issue, of course, was Communism; as Muste pointed out, the reason the editors balked at "a simple proposal to withdraw American troops" was that they feared South Vietnam would reunite with the North and align with China. "Underlying this argument is the thesis that there is a momentous struggle going on between a free, democratic world (good) and a Communist totalitarian world (evil)." As a result, the *Dissent* proposal was "distorted and unrealistic," containing logical errors and contradictions that undermined its own antiwar stance. In fact, the Vietcong represented a "bona fide movement of national liberation," and it was the United States, not China, that was "the interloper and aggressor in Asia." Until Americans could recognize these realities, the United States would continue to "keep the world on the brink of annihilation."[11]

As these comments suggest, to confront the bipolar worldview of the Cold War also involved confronting the political culture of anti-Communism at home. Muste had attempted to initiate dialogue on the left in the 1950s and had vehemently opposed Red Scare tactics on the part of liberal peace groups such as SANE. Yet, based on his experiences in the 1930s, he remained unsure about how to conduct united front actions. He also found it problematic that far left groups often viewed the Chinese and other Communist bloc countries as purely defensive, as pacific and "angelic beings," though their leaders "make no such claims."[12] Reflecting this rather delicate balancing act between anti-Stalinism and anti-anti-Communism, CNVA's policy had been to sponsor joint actions only with groups that shared their commitment to pacifism and to nonalignment, while inviting the participation of individuals and groups regardless of their political affiliation, so long as they abided by nonviolent discipline.[13]

Muste's shifting response to plans by the Students for a Democratic Society (SDS) for an antiwar march in April 1965 exemplifies this ambivalence. He had become close to student leftists over the years, addressing the annual conferences of SDS in 1964 and 1965, serving on the National Advisory Council of the Student Peace Union (SPU), and being arrested with them in anti-civil-defense protests.[14] The elder pacifist and the young radicals shared an obvious affinity for each other; like them, he was an outspoken critic of Cold War liberalism and the conformist culture of postwar America, and embraced a "politics of authenticity," in which action served as the path out of the alienation of the modern age.[15] Thus he eagerly supported their plans for what would become the first March on Washington to End the War in Vietnam, helping them to organize and raise funds, and putting his name to a list of supporters that included Kay Boyle, James Farmer, Erich Fromm, Alfred Hassler, H. Stuart Hughes, Dorothy Hutchinson, Staughton Lynd, Norman Thomas, Arthur Waskow, and Dagmar Wilson.[16]

Meanwhile, he and other radical pacifists matched their zeal by organizing the Declaration of Conscience campaign, which called for an immediate American withdrawal and for "the development of nonviolent acts, including civil disobedience, in order to stop the flow of American soldiers and munitions to Vietnam." Their goal was to obtain the signatures of leading American intellectuals and clergy to present to President Johnson on the twentieth anniversary of the bombing of Hiroshima and Nagasaki.[17] They also began planning a speak-out at the Pentagon for June 15–16, in which they planned to barrage Pentagon employees and the public with leaflets, speeches, and open-air meetings.[18]

Then, on the eve of the march, Muste was called into a meeting by Rustin, Norman Thomas, Robert Gilmore, H. Stuart Hughes, and other peace activists who expressed concern about SDS's policy of nonexclusion. At the end of the meeting, the group released a short statement of support for the march, while noting that it was not in agreement with some of its "elements." Critics of SDS immediately seized upon the statement as evidence that the group was dominated by Communists, while SDS accused the signers of sabotage.[19] This experience was the final straw in persuading Muste to thoroughly break with the exclusionary politics of the peace movement. Over the next several months he repaired his relationship with SDS and urged CNVA and other pacifist groups to reconsider their opposition to joint action with nonpacifist groups. Rather than be distracted by controversies over "fronting," pacifists should stay focused on the task of ending war. Working in solidarity with other groups should not mean "ignoring or trying to cover over differences" but rather "bringing them to the surface and facing them," a process that would heal the rifts that divided the peace movement and the left. At any rate, SDS was "in a category of its own. Like [the Student Nonviolent Coordinating Committee] . . . it is a genuinely spontaneous movement of youth [and] is not the product of any movement of grownups out of the American past."[20]

From that point on, Muste's overriding goal was to build an effective and diverse coalition against the war. Over the course of the summer of 1965, pacifists invited SDS and the Student Nonviolent Coordinating Committee (SNCC) to jointly sponsor the Declaration of Conscience campaign and the Assembly of Unrepresented People, which culminated in a march on the Capitol and a sit-in demonstration. Muste played a central role in these protest activities and in transforming the experience into the basis for coalition.[21] The result was the National Coordinating Committee to End the War in Vietnam, a short-lived organization that sponsored the International Days of Protest in October 1965, and that led to the formation of a new coalition in New York City called the Fifth Avenue Peace Parade Committee, with Muste at its helm. The Parade Committee brought together pacifists, liberal peace activists, New Leftists, civil rights workers, Communists and Trotskyists, and others who agreed to seek unity in their opposition to war, while at the same time acknowledging and respecting their differences.[22] The result, Muste commented, was "the widest spread of viewpoints that has collaborated on any such activity in my memory." As such, it would have to be conducted on an "experimental" basis, with recognition of its "risks" as well as "potentialities."[23] This pragmatic approach served him well. As his contemporaries commented, "What made such a broad based coalition possible was the personality of A. J. Muste." "While few of the groups had ever agreed, worked with, or much less trusted one another, they were all united in their respect for A.J."[24]

Muste was particularly eager to attract nonpacifist intellectuals, clergy, and the civil rights community.[25] Drawing upon the relationships and connections he had established over the years in organizations like the Committees of Correspondence, he urged intellectuals and academic professionals such as Erich Fromm, David Riesman, Benjamin Spock, Irving Louis Horowitz, William Davidon, Anatol Rapoport, Sidney Peck, and Eric Bentley to sign the Declaration of Conscience and join the "Speak Out at the Pentagon." For those reluctant to align with such radical activities, he developed the alternative of serving as "moral" supporters.[26] To further cultivate these relationships, he joined or sponsored antiwar initiatives by professional and cultural groups, such as the University Circle Teach-In Committee, the Action Committee of Artists, Writers, and Professionals Against the War, and the Center for the Study of Democratic Institutions, and accepted invitations to participate in "teach-ins" and other antiwar gatherings on university campuses.[27]

In addition to organizing intellectuals and artists, Muste sought to legitimize his radical analysis of the war through collaboration with academics and other policy experts. For example, he served as part of a working committee of social scientists and peace activists sponsored by the AFSC to study the questions of how the United States became involved in a military struggle in Vietnam and how it could "get out." The subsequently published report demonstrated in carefully measured tones and with documentary evidence how American policy rested on "distortions" of historical and political "realities." Muste's imprint could be seen throughout, especially in its analysis of the role of China and its concluding argument that genuine negotiation rested on the willingness of the United States to take unilateral steps to de-escalate the conflict, combined with a genuine commitment to national self-determination for South Vietnam, including members of the National Liberation Front (NLF).[28]

Meanwhile, Muste continued to hammer away at realism, participating in conferences, such as those sponsored by the World Council of Churches and the Church Peace Mission, on questions related to religion, war, and peace. His incessant critique of Christian realism bore fruit, as liberal Protestant clergy, such as John C. Bennett and William Sloane Coffin, moved closer to his views, and organized Clergy and Laymen Concerned About Vietnam (CALCAV).[29] The organization would join Muste's Spring Mobilization Committee to End the War in Vietnam (known as the MOBE), which was founded in November 1966 and came into full public view in April 1967. By 1968, the group would advocate such radical, "Mustean" tactics as draft resistance and tax refusal.[30]

In 1966, in recognition of his efforts, the nominally secular group Promoting Enduring Peace, led by Yale Divinity School's Jerome Davis, awarded him their annual Gandhi Peace Award.[31] That same year, even liberals like Reinhold Niebuhr, George Kennan, and *New York Post* columnist James Wechsler began to incorporate Muste's analysis into their understanding of the war and American foreign policy, though they continued to doubt the "realism" of unilateralism.[32]

Together with Sid Lens, Muste also reached out to organized labor. As the two men suspected would happen, these efforts often foundered on the "Cold War liberalism" of the labor movement, which was closely aligned with the Johnson administration, as well as by labor's dependence upon jobs created by the defense industry. They sought to alleviate these fears by addressing issues of employment, cybernation, and automation, and by helping to popularize the "triple revolution," the notion that "the problems of racial equality, economic and social order, and peace are integrally related and at one level constitute a single problem," as Muste explained.[33]

Notably, they found that the unionists most responsive to their advances knew Muste from the 1930s. According to David McReynolds, Muste was unique among peace activists in having so many close connections to labor. He recalled visiting New York City locals and being waved inside by cigar-smoking, heavyset unionists once they learned that he was one of "Muste's boys."[34] The Amalgamated Clothing Workers, with whom Muste had worked closely since the Lawrence strike of 1919, proved particularly open to such overtures. In 1966, for example, Muste arranged to have U Thant, secretary-general of the United Nations and critic of U.S. foreign policy, speak at the union's annual convention.[35] Arnold Johnson, the old Musteite who had joined the Communist Party, was present during the speech, having reunited with Muste in joint actions to protest the war. Similarly, Sam Pollock, one of the "Three Muste-teers" from the Toledo Unemployed League, sponsored the 1966 International Days of Protest in his capacity as president of Cleveland's Meat Cutters Union.[36] Despite these inroads, antiwar sentiment within the labor movement would remain rather inchoate until after Muste's death, when the rift between Walter Reuther and George Meany and between doves and hawks within the Democratic Party became more pronounced.[37]

The civil rights movement was another target of Muste's efforts to build a coalition against the war, as he had long held that peace and civil rights were inextricably connected. He gently nudged Martin Luther King Jr. on the issue on numerous occasions, commenting, for example, on the civil rights leader's 1959 visit to India that it would not long be "possible to separate the struggle for basic social justice . . . from the struggle to prevent and end war." In 1961, he tried to convince the SCLC to hire James Lawson, with whom he was close, as a full-time staff member, hoping that the young black pacifist would help the organization to broaden its agenda.[38] Yet the SCLC proved an obstacle to these efforts. Fearful of alienating northern liberals at a time when the movement was on the verge of obtaining civil rights legislation, the organization backed down from promises to hire Lawson and chastened King to keep race and peace separate issues.[39]

As these examples suggest, the political culture of anti-Communism and the Cold War complicated Muste's efforts to attract the civil rights community, as it had with the peace movement and the liberal left. African Americans had long been critical of American foreign policy and had made links between their own struggle for freedom and movements for national liberation. Yet the ideological imperatives of the Cold War suppressed this perspective, and the black critique shifted from anticolonialism to the notion that the maltreatment of African Americans at home undermined the struggle against Communism abroad. The argument was politically effective, but also constraining, as it tied them to the domestic anti-Communist consensus and alienated them from allies abroad.[40]

Further complicating Muste's efforts were racial and philosophical differences between white pacifists and African Americans, differences that
paralleled the tensions between Western pacifists and nationalist movements in the decolonizing world. The former opposed racism often at considerable personal risk, while holding strongly individualist and antistatist
views that conflicted with the more immediate and pragmatic concerns of
the latter. As he had in Albany, when tensions emerged between the largely
white pacifist Guantanamo walkers and the local black community, Muste
attempted to find a middle ground, while also continuing to emphasize the
transformative power of nonviolence.

Toward the pacifist community, Muste maintained that African Americans, as with other oppressed peoples, should lead and direct their own
liberation. The pacifist contribution laid "in supporting and commending
nonviolence in popular struggles rather than in developing struggles ourselves." In 1959, he and other *Liberation* editors chastened their readers
that it would be "arrogant" for pacifists to criticize African Americans who
defended themselves with arms. Instead, they should identify with the
oppressed and rise to the challenge of building a viable pacifism. He also
admonished whites that the growing attraction of black power was understandable in the context of the history of white supremacy and imperialism.
"Many people in the U.S. have in recent weeks expressed surprise at the
militancy and bitterness expressed by many Negroes," he commented in
the summer of 1963. "Had we earlier put ourselves in their place and been
in some degree aware of what it is to suffer contempt and incessant humili-
ation, this would not surprise us." Rather than recoil, white Americans
should simultaneously support civil rights legislation *and* confront the history of white supremacy by changing their own attitudes of superiority and
by organizing the white community.[41] Thus he was particularly supportive
of initiatives like the Assembly of Unrepresented People, which linked the
antiwar movement to domestic struggles against poverty and racism.[42]

Such was the background of the famous essay he wrote in early 1964 on
the question of whether or not the movement should adopt more "realistic" methods such as armed self-defense in light of the federal government's
failure to protect civil rights workers in the South. The essay, entitled "Rifle
Squads or the Beloved Community," began by stating unequivocally that
ultimate responsibility for the tense and unsettled situation lay with white
peoples who had exploited and humiliated others for centuries, and who
had failed to take demands for "freedom now" seriously. It further accused

liberal whites of holding a double standard, as if "Negroes had a peculiar obligation to be nonviolent," and for failing to appreciate the enormous restraint African Americans had shown in the face of extreme provocation.[43]

Still, Muste insisted that the movement remain nonviolent for practical and idealistic reasons. For one, a revolutionary situation simply did not exist in the United States. While the desire of African Americans "to control their own civil rights movement and not have it run by whites" was "legitimate," African Americans "as a people want to live in the United States; they don't want to migrate and they don't seriously want to live in a Negro nation-state in some corner of American soil." Thus, it was imperative for blacks and whites to continue the project of working together, of confronting and attempting to overcome the historical "wounds" of white supremacy. As for the role of the federal government, he rejected the idea of relying upon federal troops or self-defense as a *strategy* for the movement, while at the same time suggesting that the federal government—in its legislative, judicial, and executive branches alike—should act to remove discrimination and promote equality. He concluded on an ambiguous note, observing that it would be difficult for a movement that stood for the "breakdown of society" to also depend upon "federal agencies that are supposed to hold society together."[44]

This was delicate territory, as his equivocation suggested. Muste had been one of the original sponsors of the Council of Federated Organizations (COFO), which had recently formed the Mississippi Freedom Democratic Party to challenge the legitimacy of the segregationist state party organization.[45] To help with its efforts, COFO recruited one thousand northern volunteers for what became known as Freedom Summer. At their training session in nonviolence, volunteers received copies of Muste's essay, which COFO had reprinted by the hundreds in pamphlet form, and heard testimony from James Lawson about the spiritual imperative of nonviolence, a speech that—portentously, at least from the point of view of pacifists—provoked derisive comments from Stokely Carmichael.[46] Andrew Goodman, James Chaney, and Michael Schwerner were among these volunteers, and their disappearance soon after their arrival in the Magnolia State prompted more calls for federal troops and criticism of nonviolence. Later that summer, when the Democratic Party refused to seat delegates from the Mississippi Freedom Democratic Party at its national convention, the radicalization of the movement accelerated. In the process, nonviolence became associated with moderation rather than militancy, sentimentalism rather than pragmatism.[47]

Muste found these developments deeply unsettling, as did other pacifists.[48] On the one hand, his sympathies were with those calling for the escalation of protest rather than working within the system, for those questioning the American power structure rather than those seeking a seat at the table. On the other hand, he was a pacifist who believed deeply in the importance of interracial dialogue and solidarity as an instrument of redemption and revolution. In this context, Bayard Rustin's idea of focusing greater attention on the problems of black poverty and unemployment held some appeal. In a proposal he circulated for the formation of the A. Philip Randolph Institute, Rustin called for fostering connections between the civil rights movement and the labor movement and for developing genuine black political power through institution building.[49]

To Muste, however, it was one thing to develop mechanisms for the political and economic empowerment of African Americans and the poor, but quite another to align with the Johnson administration, which was an "instrument of oppression" of nonwhite peoples throughout the globe. But coalition politics turned out to be exactly what Rustin had in mind. In a controversial essay published at the same time he launched the Randolph Institute, he argued that it was time for the movement to shift "from protest to politics," building upon its nascent political power to turn the Democratic Party to the left. In terms reminiscent of Reinhold Niebuhr's attack upon the "children of lightness," Rustin chastised black radicals and white pacifists alike for relying upon a language of morality. "They seek to change white hearts," he wrote, "by traumatizing them." But "neither racial affinities nor racial hostilities are rooted there. It is institutions—social, political, and economic institutions—which are the ultimate molders of collective sentiments."[50] In making this argument, Rustin's essay amounted to a rejection of nonviolent philosophy and to a political culture of radicalism that had grown increasingly individualist and identity-driven.

Muste recognized a rebuke when he saw one.[51] While he shared some of Rustin's concerns, much of his political career, particularly after his return to Christian pacifism, had been based precisely upon the need for morality in politics and for placing the person over and against institutions. More immediately, the escalation of the war after Johnson's election placed him squarely on the side of radicals, black and white, who increasingly called for a complete break with American liberalism. He made his views clear in February 1965 with an article entitled "The Civil Rights Movement and the American Establishment" that focused on the problematic "tie-in" between civil rights leaders and the Johnson administration. The article began by deconstructing James Farmer's recent announcement that he planned to tour Africa under the auspices of the recently formed American Negro Leadership Conference on Africa. According to Muste, Farmer revealed the trip's "political character" when he stated that he would serve as a "free agent," "interpreting" the United States to Africans, emphasizing the "massive strides" the country had made on civil rights, as well as the progress yet to be made, and that he would present a "report" on his findings to President Johnson and the State Department when he returned.[52]

Using Farmer as a foil, Muste challenged the notion that it was possible to build upon civil rights gains and make progress toward the "triple revolution" through an alliance with the Johnson "regime." Comparing the decision faced by the civil rights movement with that of the labor movement in the 1930s, he maintained, as he had then, that an alliance with the Democratic Party would make it complicit with American militarism and empire. Indeed, he suggested that civil rights leaders would do well to take the criticisms of black nationalists seriously: "What people like Le Roi Jones are underlining," he asserted, "is that Mississippi represents on a small scale what has obtained on a vast scale for several centuries in other parts of the world. In Asia and Africa white men have proclaimed and lived the doctrine of white supremacy and have humiliated the non-white peoples." While he could not abide by black-nationalist sentiments that advocated guerrilla-style warfare or that seemed "not to regard white people as human beings," he was firmly in their camp when it came to an assessment of "the role of the United States today," which was "largely that of obstruction." The civil rights movement "for Freedom Now has to be for *liberation* of subjugated and humiliated people everywhere, or carry a cancer in its own body," Muste proclaimed.[53]

Farmer viewed the article as a personal attack and responded angrily that he had been misrepresented. His position was, indeed, more complex than Muste's analysis allowed. Since the founding of CORE, he had insisted that civil rights remain separate from other issues because he feared—not without reason—that white radicals would subordinate race to other issues, making civil rights the "tail" rather than the "kite." Hence he had opposed a 1964 proposal by Rustin that would have explicitly aligned CORE with the labor movement and the Democratic Party on the grounds that it would subsume the fight for racial equality under the class struggle. At the same time, Farmer's position was closer to Rustin's than he admitted. He feared alienating the Johnson administration at precisely the moment when the movement was on the verge of obtaining a place within the halls of power, having achieved important civil rights legislation and access to the president. His response to the war reflected this attempt to find a balance; he opposed it as an individual, while vehemently resisting efforts by militants within CORE who attempted to pass an antiwar resolution.[54]

Yet the middle ground that Farmer attempted to hold was no longer tenable. As Farmer quickly discovered, Johnson insisted upon loyalty on the war issue, while radicals like Muste had drawn a line in the sand.[55] Indeed, soon after the publication of Muste's essay, *Liberation* carried an article by Dave Dellinger criticizing the "the equivocations and divided loyalties of some peace leaders tragically compromised by their devotion to a liberal-labor-Negro coalition within the Democratic Party," by which he meant, unmistakably for those in the know, Rustin. The next month, Staughton Lynd issued an even more stinging rebuke, calling Rustin "a labor lieutenant" of American capitalism and militarism.[56]

While Muste refrained from publicly commenting on Lynd's article, which caused an uproar in pacifist-socialist circles, his own position had become unequivocal: "Where is the integrity of Negroes in the United States insisting on equality with whites—economic and human—if they are indifferent to the abject inequality of the non-whites part of the world?" he stated pointedly in a 1965 speech. "If the war in Vietnam escalates further are they going to acquiesce in that course and join in killing Vietnamese and perhaps Chinese? Is this the equality with white Americans they seek or can stomach?"[57]

Muste thus "rejoiced" as black criticism of the war intensified. Within CORE, militants circulated his essay as part of a larger effort to pass an antiwar resolution that directly linked the war in Vietnam to racism at home. Farmer managed to stave off the challenge until July 1966, when Floyd McKissick replaced him as national director. A similar evolution had occurred about six months earlier within SNCC. Although individual activists had already signed the Declaration of Conscience and participated in the Assembly of Unrepresented People, now it appeared that SNCC would play a more formal role in the nascent antiwar coalition. Meanwhile, Martin Luther King Jr. became more openly critical of the war, against the counsel of Bayard Rustin and other advisers.[58]

Muste actively encouraged these developments. Already close to black figures in CORE and to Bob Moses, he wrote personal letters to John Lewis, Julian Bond, James Bevel, and other young militants, inviting them to join the coalition.[59] He also stepped up the pressure on King, inviting the civil rights leader to join a CNVA-sponsored trip to South Vietnam, scheduled for mid-April 1966. When Muste returned from Saigon, he wrote to King that there was "lynching going on in Vietnam" and that it was of "critical" importance that he direct his energies toward protesting American intervention. Soon thereafter, he arranged a public meeting between King and the Vietnamese Buddhist monk Thich Nhat Hanh and helped CALCAV to secure King as co-chair of the organization.[60] Mostly, though, he "brought his influence to bear person to person, prodding, in conversation, by phone," James Lawson recalled of Muste's approach.[61] At the same time, he pressured the peace movement to make a special effort to reach out to civil rights groups and to broaden its agenda to include "freedom" as well as peace.[62]

Within CORE and SNCC, especially, antiwar sentiment was often accompanied by calls for black separatism and armed self-defense. This association of nonviolence with obsequiousness and servility saddened Muste, but he otherwise shared their "basic view about America's role in the world today" and the need for revolution, not reform. Hence he would remain on CORE's National Advisory Committee, even as the organization retracted its nonviolence clause and adopted "Black Power" as its guiding platform.[63]

More immediately, ending the war had become his overriding concern, and his approach to African Americans reflected his larger conviction that the only way to build an antiwar coalition on the divided American liberal left was to secure cooperation between existing groups, not to merge them. Participating organizations should have the freedom to "determine the extent and manner of their activity," he declared. The aim was not to replace existing organizations but to "stimulate increased activity everywhere." His strategy, as Beverly Sterner, his secretary during this period, recalled, was "simply to bring people in."[64] As a result of efforts such as these, the Fifth Avenue Peace Parade Committee and the MOBE, both of which Muste presided over, secured large black participation. Muste would also manage to obtain SCLC leader James Bevel as MOBE's national director.[65]

IN spite of this progress, Muste would continue to face criticism of the antiwar movement's nonexclusionary approach. The peace federation Turn Toward Peace, under the leadership of the Quaker Robert Pickus, refused the invitation to join the Fifth Avenue Peace Parade Committee on the grounds that it included nonpacifists and Communists. The issue continued to divide pacifists within the FOR and AFSC, and Muste often found himself defending the coalition. For example, in August 1966, after the Parade Committee's most recent Hiroshima Day demonstration at the Capitol, the FOR's fieldwork director expressed his concerns about the presence of NLF flags and the absence of expressions of "nonviolence and love." Muste's response—that the committee neither sanctioned flag waving nor approved of it, yet also determined that it should not serve a "police function"—satisfied his critic.[66]

But other peace activists remained unsure, in part because far left groups persisted in the sort of maneuvering and factionalism that had alienated them from their liberal and pacifist allies in the past.[67] Muste labored to convince them otherwise. While conceding that building "a radical antiwar coalition" was "a difficult and delicate task," he insisted that a policy of nonexclusion was essential both because Communists deserved the same political rights as all Americans and because anti-Communism inevitably fed into the Cold War. Only through the process of engagement and working together would it be possible for the various groups to overcome a history of mutual suspicion.[68]

Muste was least successful in persuading liberals and socialists with deep roots in the anti-Stalinist left to join the antiwar coalition. In an article for the *New York Review of Books* on November 25, 1965, his friends Bayard Rustin and Lewis Coser, along with Irving Howe, Michael Harrington, and Penn Kemble, suggested that the presence of far left groups and draft resisters at antiwar demonstrations, as well as calls for immediate withdrawal, alienated the American public and gave "explicit or covert support to the Vietcong." At the same time, Berkeley faculty issued an "Open Letter" accusing antiwar protesters of "obscuring the genuine achievements and promise of this country." "When I read such a sentence," Muste responded with a sharpness of wit reminiscent of his labor movement years, "I think automatically of Arthur Schlesinger's famous phrase about 'the bland leading the bland.'" More pointedly, to suggest that the war was the result of "errors of political judgment" and not part of a larger "pattern" was utterly myopic. "If the signers of the Open Letter have in mind that Johnson has 'shown restraint' by not actually following the advice of the hawks in the Pentagon or the psychopathic anti-Communists in the country at large to drop atomic bombs on China now," he wrote caustically, "then my amazement and depression are further intensified."[69]

As these comments suggest, Muste grew increasingly frustrated with those elements on the liberal left who seemed to spend more time criticizing the antiwar movement than they did the Johnson administration. It was the tone that they assumed—that of wise counsel to wild youth, of reasonableness to irrationality—that especially rankled. Trapped in a political culture of consensus, in which conflict had been flattened out and political "ideology" had become irrelevant, they failed to recognize the degree to which they had become ideologues themselves, upholding the power of the "corporate state" with their calls for maturity and restraint. "Young Tom Hayden" had expressed it well, Muste exclaimed. The United States appeared to be advancing toward a "post-revolutionary stage . . . in which all major organizations are openly or tacitly coordinated in support, extension and defense of the largest institutions. . . . Above all, the real clue to the corporate state lies in its ability to undercut or isolate all positions of potential revolt."[70]

Critics of the antiwar movement followed this logic when they called upon protesters to moderate their criticism in order to appeal to a wider public. This idea struck Muste as "completely wrong." For one, it showed no understanding of social movement formation; as he explained, it was precisely when polarization occurred that a movement had achieved some degree of success, because contradictions and differences had been brought to the surface where they could now be "faced up to, with all the angst and hostility which this entails."[71] It also implied that the Americans and the North Vietnamese and NLF were equally complicit in the war and equally responsible for renouncing violence and beginning negotiations. "There is something about the way [such a position] comes out which makes it seem as if we are all on an equal footing. Before God? Yes. Before each other? Not so clear." To his thinking, the United States was primarily responsible for starting the war and thus had primary responsibility for ending it. Instead of preaching to the Vietnamese to lay down their arms, Americans should focus on the task of opposing their own country's foreign policy. "I think you have to be for the defeat of the United States in this war," he suggested in early 1966. "I just don't see how anybody can be for anything except withdrawal and defeat."[72]

From a more immediate, practical perspective, it was plain to see that "conventional methods" had not worked. Even senators who condemned the war had been ignored. The "speechlessness of slaughter" just went on and went on, Muste observed, invoking Martin Buber's turn of phrase. The choice, therefore, was either to accept this "tragic predicament" or to take action. Ultimately, he insisted, as he had many times before, the only human choice was to do the latter. In a widely read essay, published by *Liberation* in November 1965, he quoted heavily from the philosopher Hannah Arendt to make his point: "'Thus action, seen from the viewpoint of the automatic processes which seem to determine the course of the world, looks like a miracle. In the language of natural science, it is the "infinite improbability" which occurs regularly.'" In the language of Christianity, the possibility of "new birth and new beginning" found its most "succinct expression in the few words with which the Gospels announced their 'glad tidings': a child has been born unto us."[73]

MUSTE's references to nativity in late 1965, and the need for faith even in the darkness, may have reflected his own personal tragedy, the painful illness and death of his middle daughter, Connie. Despite his constant activity, he was close to his children and grandchildren, corresponding with them and visiting often.[74] Connie was his only child to become a pacifist, and she had worked with him for many years within the FOR. When she was diagnosed with liver cancer and given only a short time to live, he did "whatever he could" for her, John Muste recalled. "She was in considerable pain much of the time, and I remember being there one day when he took her aside and assured her that none of the family would think any the less of her if she decided to end her own life. He was the only one who could have done this since she was especially close to him and would have found it very difficult to do anything she thought would make him think the less of her." Connie chose a natural death, and Muste was with her for the final weeks of her life. "Mercifully, she was free from pain during the last couple of weeks of her life," he wrote to friends. John Swomley, his longtime colleague in the FOR, said that the occasion of Connie's death was the only time he had known Muste to cry.[75]

Muste kept his personal life separate from his public one, making it difficult to assess the impact of Connie's death on his worldview and politics. But during her illness and after her death, he became increasingly "obsessed" with Vietnam and with impressing upon his fellow Americans the need "for radical action now."[76] In November, he presided over a draft-card burning in Union Square and made statements of conditional support for two Americans who set themselves afire as a protest against the war. Increasingly, it seemed to him that the United States, with its ideology of "self-satisfaction," was the biggest "obstacle" to peace in the world today. The president's announcement, as 1965 drew to a close, that there would be another pause in the bombing campaign to allow for negotiations, confirmed these fears, as it seemed so obviously a ruse to justify further expansion of the war.[77]

Other antiwar activists shared Muste's sense of dismay and disillusionment. The National Coordinating Committee to End the War seemed to "deteriorate" after the protest activities of October and November, with young people coming to a "nagging realization that no matter what we seem to do, the administration accelerates the war."[78] Muste urged them to rally in the face of despair and helped to lay plans for antiwar demonstrations and civil disobedience as soon as the United States resumed bombing North Vietnam. Thus, when President Johnson announced that bombing would begin again on January 31, 1966, Muste and the Fifth Avenue Peace Parade Committee were ready, with plans for a protest march and a "sit-down" demonstration at Times Square on February 2. Once again, the diversity, inclusiveness, and militancy of the coalition were apparent, as participants were given the freedom to carry and distribute any form of literature they liked, while agreeing—whether for practical or for idealistic reasons—that nonviolent tactics were most effective.[79]

Muste clearly felt a deep sense of urgency and desperation about the war in early 1966. When the bombing of North Vietnam resumed, he wrote to his friend Sid Lens that "every form of dissent is valid now and ought be pushed to the limit."[80] He also felt a growing sense of identification with the Vietnamese people and their struggle against the corrupt South Vietnamese government and the American military presence. In February, inspired perhaps by his friend Staughton Lynd, who had recently returned from Vietnam with Herbert Aptheker and Tom Hayden, Muste began to explore the idea of holding an antiwar demonstration in Saigon. Together with other members of CNVA, he developed a plan that would bring a small yet diverse group of Americans (Muste advocated at least one woman, a member of SNCC, and someone from the "student movement") "to witness for peace and to call men to justice," while expressing their "particular" opposition to the Vietnam War. As he explained, as pacifists, they rejected

war and violence, yet they also had the obligation to make "political judg-
ments. . . . We do not, for example, equate the violence employed by peoples who have been subjugated . . . with the violence used against them by
their oppressors or by foreign powers."[81]

While Muste hoped that their demonstration would have an impact
on international public opinion, his main goal was to make connections
with the Vietnamese people, and especially the peace movement and the
NLF. "We want to communicate at firsthand with Vietnamese and other
people," Muste explained. "We covet a better understanding of what they
think and feel." Lest this goal seem sentimental, he recognized the very
real dangers and obstacles in the way of such communication, particularly
to the Vietnamese, who had "already suffered so much." If they failed to
establish their antiwar bona fides to "the NLF in South Vietnam, to North
Vietnam, and to Communist China," perhaps they would "open the way
for others."[82]

In this way, the group appears to have been successful. On April 11,
1966, Muste, along with fellow pacifists Bradford Lyttle and Barbara Deming, Karl Meyer of the Catholic Worker movement, the prominent physicist
William Davidon, and student activist Sherry Thurber, departed from Kennedy airport for Saigon. They stopped in Tokyo on the way, meeting with
members of the Japanese FOR and the Japan Peace for Vietnam Committee, who introduced them to peace activists who had recently visited Saigon
and gave them the names of potential contacts in South Vietnam. On the
morning of their departure, they received news that the Saigon airport had
been attacked by the Vietcong, killing nine Americans and injuring about
150 more. The airport reopened a day later, and the American pacifists
arrived in the early afternoon.[83]

The group immediately went to central Saigon. Half of them focused
on finding accommodations, while Muste, Lyttle, and Thurber departed for
the headquarters of the Vietnamese Christian Service. There, they learned
there had recently been a large Buddhist demonstration against the war and
that Americans had been urged to stay indoors. They also experienced the
violence of the war-torn city firsthand; soon after they arrived, "two tremendous explosions," followed by small-arms fire, shook the building and
forced them to the floor. Apparently, a nearby police station had just been
blown up by the Vietcong. The next day, after settling in to their accommodations, they resumed their search for contacts and explored their options

for holding a demonstration in the city. Among their discoveries was the nearby American embassy, which seemed an appropriate site for a protest.[84]

Perhaps the most important contact they made was with the Buddhist monk Thich Nhat Hanh, whose open letter to Martin Luther King Jr. had recently been published in *Liberation* magazine. Initially cautious about the group, Thich quickly warmed up to them, explaining the complexity of the political situation and expressing his hope that American religious leaders would help to end the war. Thich, among other informants, maintained that the withdrawal of American military support for Prime Minister Nguyen Cao Ky would allow for the formation of a coalition government that would include the NLF. As for the argument that this would lead to a purge of non-Communist elements, Thich expressed his doubts. Anyway, he explained, such was for the Vietnamese to decide. "You Americans must not think that we regard the Vietcong as foreigners and you as Vietnamese. The Vietcong are our countrymen. They are patriots according to their own lights. They have fought against foreigners."[85]

After a couple of days of discussions with Buddhist and Catholic monks, intellectuals and students, and journalists, the group made plans to hold a press conference at their hotel on Wednesday, April 20, and to picket the U.S. Embassy the following day. Thich, along with a Catholic priest, approved of their leaflet and offered to translate and copy it for them. Meanwhile, other Vietnamese volunteered "to translate all of our press material too and paint signs in English and Vietnamese." On Wednesday morning, as the group prepared for the press conference, they learned it had been canceled by the police because they lacked a permit. Taken to city hall, they consulted with the head of the local security forces, who offered the use of the Saigon council chamber, on the second floor. The group demurred and headed back to the hotel to discuss the matter, whereupon local security forces arrived to inform them that their visas had expired and that, if they hoped to hold a press conference, it would have to be later that afternoon. The group relented and carried their leaflets and signs to city hall, where they introduced themselves, made statements, and then asked for questions. After two questions from reporters, self-described students barraged them with hostile questions, asking them to take a stand for or against Communism. Soon "pandemonium" ensued, as the crowd shouted and threw objects at them, and then rushed the platform to pin their own signs on the wall, reading "The War in South Vietnam Is a War of Self-Defense" and "We Cannot Live with Assassins. American Troops Are Welcome." "One said to A.J. 'I'll kill you with my own hands!' "[86]

After the press conference, the group returned by police escort to their hotel, where they met with reporters and readied for plans to demonstrate at the embassy the following day. Hotel officials woke them early the next morning to inform them that there was a car waiting outside to take them wherever they wanted. Recognizing that this was a ploy to bypass the embassy and whisk them to the airport, the group began to walk toward the embassy. Ultimately, the police brought a paddy wagon, lifted them into it, and took them to the airport. On the way, several Vietnamese— including one of the "students" at the press conference from the day before—surreptitiously apologized for their behavior. More apologies arrived after they returned to the United States, with explanations that the time and place of the press conference had been concealed from the public and that the authorities had arranged for the "group of fanatical government supported youngsters" to be there, as well as expressions of "deep appreciation and gratefulness" for their act of "solidarity."[87]

Predictably, most newspaper reports seized upon the details of the press conference to suggest that few South Vietnamese supported the peace mission.[88] For Muste, however, the trip confirmed his opposition to the war and motivated him to continue his work building a radical antiwar coalition. As he explained, the "only heckling we encountered was from young Vietnamese put up to it by the Chief of Police in Saigon and some of them apologized to us the next day." Moreover, virtually all of the people with whom he spoke—"Buddhists, Roman Catholics, intellectuals, peasants— who are non-Communist and not under Vietcong control" expressed their opposition to the Ky regime and to American military intervention. While withdrawal presented a "terrible predicament" for the Johnson administration, he insisted that it was "in the true interest of the American people and of mankind," and he reiterated his call for Americans, especially opinion-makers and intellectuals, to "clog" the system "with their whole weight," as Thoreau had said many years before.[89]

Over the course of the summer and fall of 1966, Muste threw himself into the task of reinvigorating the fledgling coalition against the war. He helped to organize another round of protests in New York City scheduled for the twenty-first anniversary of the bombing of Hiroshima and that culminated in a rally at Times Square, where he spoke to the crowd of the importance of unity in their diversity.[90] He also participated in meetings called by the University Circle Teach-In Committee of Cleveland over the course of the summer and fall of 1966 to discuss a proposal to "mobilize the antiwar sentiments of the American people on a truly massive scale." The subsequently formed November 8 Mobilization Committee, with Muste as chairman, coordinated four days of protests that preceded the national elections. Soon thereafter, another conference was called to reconstitute the group as the Spring Mobilization Committee to End the War in Vietnam, which planned to broaden the peace movement's base and to organize "a mass action in the spring—on April 15—on a scale that would render it 'qualitatively different' from previous anti-war demonstrations." Once again, Muste was elected chairman.[91]

The conferences that gave birth to the MOBE had not been easy. Participants were extremely diverse, with representatives from trade unions, the CP, WILPF, FOR, AFSC, CALCAV, SANE, SDS, SNCC, W.E.B. Du Bois clubs, the Catholic Peace Fellowship, the University Circle Teach-in Committee, and the Young Socialist Alliance, among others. Once again, there were debates on the policy of nonexclusion and strategies for broadening the movement's base, through moderate or radical appeals, through a top-down or bottom-up approach. Once again Muste helped to bring divergent forces together and to develop an inclusive, yet radical approach to peace organizing. Rather than focusing on "converting" the "man on the street," he called for concentrating attention on already existing groups, such as student leftists, unionists in revolt against the Meany machine, and "radical sections of the civil rights movement. . . . These people do not need to be 'converted' to an antiwar position." He doubted that churches would realize their "prophetic function" and take a strong stand against the war, but liberal religious leaders might be persuaded to translate their antiwar sentiments into action.[92]

Despite the challenges of building the coalition, he viewed it as the most significant development in the struggle to build a movement against the war. Beverly Sterner, his secretary, observed that in the four years she had worked with him, she had never seen him "as optimistic, as enthusiastic, and as inspired," as he was by "by the potential of a nonviolent movement spearheaded by the combined forces of civil rights, the academic community, and the traditional peace groups." He was, Nat Hentoff recalled, "positively ebullient" about the emergence of the coalition.[93]

Muste also encouraged and participated in more dramatic action, such as civil disobedience and draft resistance, a stance that endeared him to

young people and students who sought counsel and support as they confronted the machinery of Selective Service.[94] A case that particularly caught
his attention was the "Fort Hood Three," which involved GIs who faced
court martial for refusing to fight in Vietnam. Despite the fact that the
three men were not pacifists, Muste argued that they should enjoy the rights
of conscientious objection on the basis of the Nuremberg principles. "The
fundamental question involved in this case is the right of soldiers, as citizens of the United States," to refuse to serve in the Vietnam War, "which
they consider to be 'immoral, illegal and unjust.'" As co-chair, with
Staughton Lynd, of the Fort Hood Three Defense Committee, Muste helped
to raise publicity and obtained legal advice for the young men. He attended
their military trial and continued to work on their behalf after they were
convicted and sent to the Fort Leavenworth penitentiary.[95]

In addition to organizing resistance and opposition to the war, Muste
made plans to visit Vietnam again. His hopes that the Saigon trip would
open up lines of communication with the NLF and the North Vietnamese
had been realized. Soon after his return, he had received "urgent calls"
from the North Vietnamese Peace Committee to come to Hanoi and determined, along with Dellinger and Lynd, to make the trip right away.[96] U.S.
bombing raids over Hanoi and Haiphong in July interrupted these embry-
onic plans, but, finally, after months of consultation with fellow peace activists in Great Britain and France, as well as figures close to the North
Vietnamese, a plan was finalized: Muste and three other elder statesmen of
the international peace movement—Martin Niemöller of Germany, Bishop
Ambrose Reeves of England, and Rabbi Abraham Feinberg of Toronto—
would spend ten days in Hanoi in January 1967.[97] With his eighty-second
birthday on January 10, Muste was to be the oldest of his companions.

The trip was planned as a protest against the war, but Muste also felt
an underlying personal compulsion to connect with the North Vietnamese
people, to express his shame and outrage at the conduct of the United
States toward their country. At a press conference in Paris on the eve of his
departure, he explained that his overriding hope was to "convey the spirit
of peace to the stricken people of Vietnam. If it is the last thing in my life
that I am able to do, I shall be content." As this reference to his mortality
suggests, the trip was dangerous not only because it involved entering a
war-torn area, but also because it would place extreme strains on his
increasingly frail body.[98] Indeed, traveling to Hanoi proved excruciating,

with delayed and missed flights and unplanned detours. Muste, Feinberg, and Reeves arrived four days late, just missing Niemöller, who had traveled separately.[99]

From January 9 through 19, the three clergymen investigated conditions in and around Hanoi. What they discovered was a "very beautiful city," with few soldiers and policemen, and a sense of solidarity among its residents. It offered a stark contrast with Saigon, Muste observed, a city that lived "under terrible tension," with police, soldiers, violence, corruption, and crime "omnipresent."[100] The clergymen also discovered that parts of the city had been reduced to rubble by American bombs, contrary to statements by the Johnson administration. On four separate occasions, they were forced to hide in shelters while bombs hit the surrounding area. Tours of the countryside showed utter devastation, with many women and children forced to live underground. Deeply shaken by the scenes of destruction and death, Muste cabled the following message to Washington: "For God's sake stop lying! Let us stop this bombing practice or else say honestly to our government, to the world, and to ourselves, 'We are trying to bomb [the] hell out of the Vietnamese people!' "[101]

Throughout the trip, the three clergymen met with various civilian groups, as well as Nguyen Van Tien, the NLF's representative in North Vietnam, who insisted that unification was not a precondition for peace. The highlight of the trip was a meeting with the North Vietnamese premier Pham Van Dong and president Ho Chi Minh. Together, they shared their impressions of China and Saigon, as well as New York City, where Ho Chi Minh had once lived for several years. He "seemed to know that we had demonstrations" in Times Square, Muste observed. "He also asked about Harlem; he said he's spent a lot of time there." Then, after gifting them hand-carved walking sticks, President Ho stated that he would welcome peace talks with President Johnson. "Let President Johnson come here and I will talk with him just as I am talking with you people now," Muste quoted him as saying. "Only let him not come with his gun, or with his generals and admirals."[102]

Muste was deeply impressed by Ho Chi Minh. He seemed "a very great human being" about whom "there are no trappings of government and show." Taking the leader at his word, Muste conveyed his message at press conferences on his way back to the States and in a letter to President Johnson on January 31, 1967. While he could not guarantee that a cessation of bombing would compel the North Vietnamese to give in to all of the U.S. demands, he was certain that it would "enhance" the possibility of a ceasefire and peace talks. Still, he had obviously been moved by the righteousness of the Vietnamese cause and their determination to continue their struggle: "Neither the Democratic Republic of Vietnam nor the National Liberation Front could be forced by military means . . . into surrender and submission," he declared.[103]

When Muste returned to the United States in late January, he immediately settled into his usual routine of antiwar organizing. He gave talks about his experiences in numerous forums, including a gathering held in his honor at the Church Center for the United Nations and hosted by Dr. Benjamin Spock, and prepared official reports for publication in *Liberation* and *WIN*. With James Bevel, he stayed up all night drafting the official announcement of the April demonstration and made plans for a press conference to take place later that month. There was no indication that he was anything but his usual self, except that he used a heating pad in the evenings, as his friends and neighbors, Joyce and Robert Gilmore recalled.[104]

Then, on February 10, he went to his doctor complaining of sharp back pain. He returned home after receiving a prescription for painkillers, yet was unable to sleep. The next morning, he telephoned the Gilmores, who lived upstairs from him. When they came down, they found him sitting down with a sharp pain in his lower back and so nauseous that he could not swallow his pain medicine. They called his doctor, who injected him with a sedative, which allowed him to sleep for a short time. Meanwhile, they made plans to take him to the hospital for tests. An ambulance took him to St. Luke's that afternoon. The pain and discomfort worsened, yet nurses would not give him another sedative until a doctor had examined him. After about twenty minutes, he gasped that he was "going to pass out," put his head back and fought for breath. "He probably lost consciousness immediately, and within a few seconds his heart had stopped," Joyce Gilmore commented.[105]

The hospital's emergency team managed to resuscitate him, though he never regained consciousness, and made plans for surgery to correct what they now believed was an aneurysm. His daughter Nancy arrived shortly after six o'clock and Muste died about half an hour later, before they had attempted surgery. It seemed to his friends that this last trip to Vietnam had finally killed him. As Cara Cook recalled, despite his decision, made about a year ago, "not to go tramping about Europe" anymore because it would "knock me out," he had gone "tramping off to Europe again and to Asia—twice, and he was finally knocked out: he didn't quit."[106]

Two days later, Muste was cremated at Ferncliff Cemetery in Westchester and laid to rest next to his wife, Anne. There was a brief private service, attended by Nancy and her family, the Gilmores, Bayard Rustin, David Dellinger, Beverly Sterner, and David Schwartz.[107] That night, a tribute was held at the Community Church of New York in which some 1,500 people turned out to hear minister Donald Harrington, James Bevel, and Dave Dellinger speak of Muste's legacy for the peace movement. A more formal memorial service was held a week later, at the Friends Meeting House in New York City. "It was a most heterogeneous audience—many from the young, 'new left,' element," Cara Cook wrote in a letter to Brookwood's former comrades and students. "The poet Allen Ginsberg was one presence which caused a stir . . . a telegram from Bobbie Kennedy . . . young men who had 'walked' and 'sailed' and 'sat in' with A. J."[108] Similarly, James Wechsler, columnist and editor of the *New York Post*, observed that "hundreds of all ages crowded the main meeting room and spilled out to the balcony. What was most notable about the assemblage was the generational gap it spanned. . . . It was Muste's ecumenical quality that enabled him to serve as peacemaker among warring factions and inspire even the most dogmatic to rise momentarily above ideological vindictiveness."[109]

More tributes followed, in New York City and elsewhere. For example, a few weeks later, some seven hundred people, composed mostly of "gray-haired peace lovers and a minority of bearded youth," gathered in Greenwich Village to memorialize him with poetry. About a month thereafter, Paul Knopf's jazz trio and singers presented "The Faith of a Radical" at the Judson Memorial Church in the Village. With biblical verses from Isaiah set to minor blues and the free swing style of mezzosoprano Sheila Jordan, the piece sought to capture Muste's unique combination of firm moral vision and spontaneity.[110]

In these tributes, peace activists, revolutionaries, and liberals alike memorialized him as a figure of great significance in the history of American radicalism. He was "an Authentic Great Man," as Paul Goodman put it; as "the Thoreau of his time—or perhaps even a prophet," Hugh Black of London's *Peace News* declared; as a genuine "Christian Revolutionary" in the tradition of William Lloyd Garrison, according to his antagonist and friend Reinhold Niebuhr; and as a "truly liberated man," in the words of Bayard Rustin. It was, they insisted, his integrity as a man, not as a saint, that held so much appeal. After all, there was a "sensuality" to him; he smoked "innumerable cigarettes," ate meat, lived in and loved New York City, and enjoyed opera and poetry, as well as popular culture. "Historians of the future who want to know what it meant to live with integrity in the twentieth-century era of wars and revolutions," Staughton Lynd declared, "will very likely begin with the life of A. J. Muste."[111]

But they also feared what his death would mean for the future of the American left and the antiwar movement. AFSC organizer Ellen Wertheim wrote to Beverly Sterner of the confusion and despair that beset the peace movement after Muste's death. "A. J.'s power" was rooted in "his consistency, his way of holding on and following through to make dreams reality." No one else "could be a bridge between just about all sections of the radical non-community," lamented Nat Hentoff. Without Muste, Max Lerner observed, antiwar forces lacked "any great leadership." He was the "spiritual backbone of resistance" to the war in Vietnam, Irving Louis Horowitz commented. "The cliché-ridden phrase—who will replace him?—is temporarily unanswerable."[112]

Comments like these make it tempting to interpret the last years of Muste's life as a tragedy. As newspapers reported in the United States and around the world, the "American Gandhi" had died, but without having realized his dream of ending the war in Vietnam—or, for that matter, of abolishing organized violence on any level. Indeed, it seemed that Gandhian nonviolence lent itself more toward reformism than revolution. Moreover, by the time of his death, Muste had come to see the United States as nearly unredeemable, incapable of recognizing and taking responsibility for its sins of empire and race, manifested most atrociously in Vietnam. He had even seriously considered remaining in Hanoi with the Vietnamese people, rather than returning home with his companions.[113] As if to confirm his disillusionment with American democracy, the United States did not withdraw from Vietnam for another six years, despite the fact that protests against the war grew ever larger and more dramatic. Partly as a result, the American left grew increasingly cynical, factionalized, and isolated; some retreated into "pure prophecy" or academia, while others embraced piecemeal reform as the best that could be hoped for.[114]

Meanwhile, with King's death about a year after Muste's, the appeal of nonviolence declined precipitously.[115] Some effective liberal-left coalitions have emerged since the 1960s, particularly around single issues, but they have quickly dissipated, evidence of fragmentation and self-doubt. At the same time, global capitalism and American empire have grown even more powerful and destabilizing, and myths of American exceptionalism continue to hold a grip on the national consciousness.[116]

Yet Muste's friends did not remember him as a tragic idealist. Barbara Deming, writing soon after he died, recalled waiting with him in a detention room at the Saigon airport. The day had been "broiling hot" and "we had spent some time just sitting in the paddy wagon out under the full sun, and that hadn't been easy for him." Worried for his health, she looked across the room at him, "and he looked back with a sparkling smile, and with that sudden lighting up of his eyes which many of his friends will remember and he said, 'It's a good life!' That is realism, too, isn't it?" Deming asked rhetorically. "He had done what he thought had to be done (that trip was above all his idea), and he had done it as well as he knew how; and then—he was able to be happy. What more could he do—until the next time." Thus, though his life was a "hard one," it was also a "particularly happy" one "because he never tried . . . to fool himself about himself with words. What he told himself that he believed, he turned into acts, into acts of belief."[117]

More concretely, Muste's legacy was the Spring Mobilization, which famously brought together a diverse group of liberals and leftists, pacifists and black power militants, religious leaders and counterculturalists, veterans and women peace activists, in a massive, nationwide coordinated protest against the war. The march, which took place on the morning of April 15, 1967, had been preceded by Martin Luther King Jr.'s famous speech at the Riverside Church in which he formally broke with the Johnson administration over the war. Sounding very much like Muste, King accused the American government of being the "greatest purveyor of violence in the world today" and stated that the initiative for peace must come from the United States and must include a cessation of bombing. The war, he observed pointedly, was but a "symptom" of "a far deeper malady within the American spirit. If we are to get on the right side of the world revolution, we as a nation must undergo a radical revolution of values. We must rapidly begin the shift from a 'thing-oriented' society to a 'person-oriented' society." A week later, he gathered with hundreds of thousands of protesters in New York's Central Park. After about one hundred men burned their draft cards, he linked arms with Dave Dellinger, Harry Belafonte, Benjamin Spock, James Bevel, Stokely Carmichael, student mobilization leader Linda

Figure 10. Float in honor of A. J. Muste in the Spring Mobilization to End the War in Vietnam March, New York City, April 15, 1967. (*John C. Goodwin*)

Dannenberg, among others, and led the crowd in a twenty-block march to the United Nations plaza. It seemed that a coalition between the peace and freedom movements was finally bearing fruit, yet, as Muste would have reminded his comrades, this would not have been possible without both a vision and a conviction of the capacity of human beings to work together and make history.[118]

Epilogue

FEW AMERICANS RECOGNIZE A. J. Muste's name today, though his influence can be found in both the dominant culture and its radical and pacifist margins. A mural of Muste by the radical cartoonist and muralist Christopher Cardinale now graces the outer wall of 339 Lafayette Street in New York City, a building known to the local activist community as "the peace pentagon" and which houses the A. J. Muste Memorial Institute, the national offices of the WRL and WILPF, and other activist groups. In 2010, the *New York Times* published an article on the "grannies," a group of elderly men and women who gather weekly in front of New York's Rockefeller Center to protest the wars in Afghanistan and Iraq. When a protester was asked if she really thought their demonstrations had an effect on national policy, she invoked Muste, who was asked a similar question while maintaining a candlelight vigil outside the White House to protest the Vietnam War: "I don't do this to change the country," he said. "I do this so the country won't change me."[1] In Thich Nhat Hanh's book *Peace Is Every Step*, he writes, "A. J. Muste, the mid-twentieth century leader of the peace movement in America who inspired millions of people, said, 'There is no way to peace, peace is the way.'"[2] The same quote appears in bold letters outside Flagstaff's local Quaker meetinghouse that I drive by every day on my way to work.

Within the academy, although Muste has yet to receive the in-depth scholarly attention other figures of his stature have received, he makes an appearance in almost every book on the history of the peace movement, the civil rights movement, and American Protestantism, engaging in such actions such as directing a demonstration, advising Martin Luther King Jr., mentoring draft resisters, chairing an antiwar committee, and penning theological rebukes of Christian realism.

Significantly, both academic and popular recollections of Muste portray him as a peace activist and as an advocate of nonviolence. There is virtually no historical memory of him as a labor leader, despite his leadership of the famous Lawrence textile strike of 1919, the Amalgamated Textile Workers of America, the workers' education movement of the interwar years, the movement for progressive, militant industrial unionism in the late 1920s and early 1930s, and the small but influential revolutionary group known as the "Musteites."

What accounts for our culture's failure to remember Muste as a labor leader? In part, it reflects the relegation of the labor movement to the margins of Americans' collective historical memory. Contrast the prominent place of the civil rights movement in contemporary American culture with the labor movement—everyone has heard of Martin Luther King and Malcolm X, while few have heard of Walter Reuther, Sidney Hillman, or other giants of labor history. But it also has to do with Muste's decision to leave the labor movement in 1936 just before it rose to the peak of its prominence and influence within the corridors of power. Though he welcomed the new protections for workers and collective organizing under the New Deal, he feared that the labor movement's emerging alliance with the Democratic Party and the federal government would have a deradicalizing effect. He predicted that labor would lose its oppositional role in society, become beholden to business and governmental elites, and collude with American militarism and foreign policy.

Muste was thus one of the earliest American radical intellectuals to come to see unions as "little more than self-aggrandizing interest groups, no longer a lever for progressive social change." As Nelson Lichtenstein has shown, this perspective would become dominant among post–World War II radicals, as critics such as C. Wright Mills argued that labor had become "big labor," another bureaucratic institution in the vast military-industrial complex that ruled American society. The New Left, when it emerged as a social movement in the 1960s, would share this view. In the Port Huron Statement, the young New Leftist Tom Hayden complained that labor unions had become bureaucratic institutions, "cynical" and "afraid of rank-and-file involvement in the work of the union." This attitude would change in the 1970s, when the New Left turned to organizing the working class, but residues of suspicion remained strong.[3]

Radical intellectuals like Muste had legitimate reasons for holding this view of labor. The success of organized labor in the 1930s and 1940s—its achievement of some real bargaining power—undermined its social movement character, as did the Taft-Hartley Act of 1947 in which union leaders were forced to sign statements swearing they were not Communists. As a result of these factors, more conservative unionists became dominant in the AFL-CIO; labor only halfheartedly supported the black civil rights movement and largely condoned U.S. foreign policy during the Cold War, including the Vietnam War.[4]

The labor movement did indeed grow more conservative, but, as Lichtenstein has argued, Muste and other radical intellectuals were mistaken in assuming that labor's gains under the New Deal were irreversible and that the "labor question" was no longer of central importance. Labor did become a big player in the Democratic Party, but its role was a subordinate one, evident by its failure to win any major concessions from either President Kennedy or President Johnson. Moreover, as early as 1947, it faced a concerted counterattack by the business community and a resurgent right wing. Combined with the shift of well-paying manufacturing jobs to low-wage regions of the United States and overseas, labor has assumed an increasingly defensive position. At the same time, the shift of American politics to the right has made policies that once seemed moderate or centrist—such as the defense of Social Security, public education, and collective bargaining—appear liberal and even radical.[5]

In response to its increasingly precarious position, and with the Democratic Party an increasingly unreliable ally, the labor movement has begun to seek out new friends. In 1996, when John Sweeney became the head of the AFL-CIO, he sought to expand labor's base of support to include intellectuals, academics, and even old-time radicals. As Robert Welsh, Sweeney's top assistant, explained, "The labor movement needs to win the war of ideas in addition to other wars that are going on. The whole conversation with progressive scholars, writers and artists is critically important to having a vibrant, outward-looking labor movement as opposed to an inward-looking, moribund one."[6]

Many left-leaning intellectuals have been responsive to Sweeney's call, recognizing that the welfare state and protections for labor have turned out to be neither inevitable nor irreversible. What can Muste's career tell us about the possibilities and potential pitfalls of this fledgling alliance? Throughout his long career, whether in the labor movement or the peace movement, Muste was more effective and influential when he combined his idealism with pragmatism—when he focused on coalition building and worked for immediate as well as long-term goals. Thus, the height of his influence in the labor movement was in the 1920s and the early 1930s, before he became a Trotskyist, and when he pursued a broad, united front with liberals, social democrats, and unionists. Similarly, as a pacifist, his advocacy of nonviolence had its biggest impact and was most relevant when he moved beyond his community of true believers to include nonpacifists, such as in CORE, the antinuclear movement, and the MOBE, all of which were organizations or coalitions that welcomed nonpacifists, so long as they were willing to abide by nonviolence.

At the same time, the difficulties Muste faced as a labor radical—such as being viciously red-baited by the AFL in 1928—shows the need for inclusiveness and toleration within the labor movement and the liberal left more broadly. Early on, moreover, he recognized that social democracy could become an "iron cage," diluting labor's oppositional role and sapping its idealism, particularly in the context of American militarism and global hegemony. These insights can serve as reminders of the importance of retaining a vision of social transformation and moral prophecy, even as we work for limited goals. Indeed, it was precisely in the 1920s and the early 1930s, when progressive labor, liberals, and leftists shared this vision that they were at their most dynamic and creative, even in the context of a weak labor movement, conservative dominance of American politics, and vast economic inequalities—much like the conditions we face today.

NOTES

ᔐ

The following abbreviations appear in the notes.

ACP Anthony Capraro Papers, 1891–1975, Immigration History Research Center, College of Arts and Letters, University of Minnesota

ACTW Amalgamated Clothing and Textile Workers Union Papers, 1914–1990, Kheel Center for Labor-Management Documentation and Archives, ILR School, Cornell University

AJMP Abraham Johannes (A. J.) Muste Papers, 1920–1967 (microfilm edition), Swarthmore College Peace Collection, Swarthmore College

AJMP-LA Abraham Johannes (A. J.) Muste Papers, Later Accessions, Swarthmore College Peace Collection, Swarthmore College

BCP Bert Cochran Papers, 1913–1984, Tamiment Library and Robert F. Wagner Labor Archives, New York University

BDP Barbara Deming Papers, 1908–1985, Schlesinger Library, Radcliffe Institute for the Advanced Study of Women, Harvard University

BLCC Brookwood Labor College Collection, 1921–1937, Archives of Labor and Urban Affairs, Walter P. Reuther Library, Wayne State University

BRP Bayard Rustin Papers, 1942–1987 (microfilm edition), Manuscript Division, Library of Congress

CL Congregational Library and Archives, Congregational Christian Historical Society, Boston, Mass.

CNVA Committee for Nonviolent Action Records, 1958–1968, Swarthmore College Peace Collection, Swarthmore College

DDCW Dorothy Day–Catholic Worker Collection, Special Collections and University Archives, Raynor Memorial Libraries, Marquette University

DSP David J. Saposs Papers, 1907–1968, Library Archives Division, Wisconsin Historical Society

ECP Elmer Fern Cope Papers, 1903–1965 (microfilm edition), Ohio Historical Society

EGEP Elizabeth Glendower Evans Papers, 1856–1937 (microfilm edition), Schlesinger Library, Radcliffe Institute for the Advanced Study of Women, Harvard University

EMBP	Ernest and Marion Bromley Papers, 1920–1997, private collection, Voluntown, Connecticut (now at Swarthmore College Peace Collection)
FOR	Fellowship of Reconciliation Records, 1915–current, Swarthmore College Peace Collection, Swarthmore College
GRH	Grand Rapids History and Special Collections Center, Grand Rapids Public Library
HCP	Horace Champney Papers, 1906–1990, Swarthmore College Peace Collection, Swarthmore College
JAH	Joint Archives of Holland, Theil Research Center, Hope College, Holland, Michigan
JBSHP	J. B. S. (Jacob Benjamin Salutsky) Hardman Papers, 1882–1968, Tamiment Library and Robert F. Wagner Labor Archives, New York University
JCP	Josephine Colby Papers, 1912–1933, Tamiment Library and Robert F. Wagner Labor Archives, New York University
JLFP	James Farmer and Lula Peterson Farmer Papers, 1908, 1920–1999, Briscoe Center for American History, University of Texas at Austin
JNSP	John Nevin Sayre Papers, 1885–1992, Swarthmore College Peace Collection, Swarthmore College
LC	Labadie Collection, Harlan Hatcher Graduate Library, University of Michigan
LSP	Lawrence Scott Papers, 1955–1965, Swarthmore College Peace Collection, Swarthmore College
MOBE	National Mobilization Committee to End the War in Vietnam Records, 1966–1969, Swarthmore College Peace Collection, Swarthmore College
MSP	Max Shachtman Papers, 1917–1969 (microfilm edition), Tamiment Library and Robert F. Wagner Labor Archives, New York University
Muste, COHC	Oral Memoir, Reminiscences of Abraham John Muste (1954), Oral History Collection of Columbia University
NHM	Newton History Museum, Newton, Massachusetts
OHAL	Oral History of the American Left, 1920–1990, Tamiment Library and Robert F. Wagner Labor Archives, New York University
PBP	Paul Blanshard Papers, 1912–1979, Bentley Historical Library, University of Michigan
PMR	Peacemakers Movement Collected Records, 1948–1980, Swarthmore College Peace Collection, Swarthmore College
RCA	Archives of the Reformed Church in America, Gardner A. Sage Library, New Brunswick Theological Seminary, New Brunswick, New Jersey
VFCP	V. F. (Victor Francis) Calverton Papers, 1923–1941, Research Collections, New York Public Library

Introduction

1. "Sketches for an Autobiography" (1957–60), reprinted in Nat Hentoff, ed., *The Essays of A. J. Muste* (New York: Simon and Schuster, 1967): 3, 12–13 (hereafter "Sketches").

2. I approach Muste as a historian, interested in what his life and thought can tell us about American politics and culture in the twentieth century, and particularly the rise and decline of the liberal left. It is an attempt to write a "historian's biography," to use the term suggested by Alice Kessler-Harris to differentiate between popular and historical approaches to biography. See Kessler-Harris, "Why Biography," in "AHR Roundtable: Historians and Biography," *American Historical Review* 114, no. 3 (June 2009): 625–30. The two existing biographies of Muste, Jo Ann Ooiman Robinson's *Abraham Went Out: A Biography of A. J. Muste* (Philadelphia: Temple University Press, 1981) and Nat Hentoff, *Peace Agitator: The Story of A. J. Muste* (New York: Macmillan, 1963), stand on their own and have been invaluable resources for my own research. Indeed, there remains much more work to be done on Muste, particularly his relations with the Protestant community and the broader peace movement, both in the United States and internationally.

3. Muste, "Sketches," 85.

4. See, for example, Michael Kazin, *American Dreamers: How the Left Changed a Nation* (New York: Knopf, 2011); Doug Rossinow, *Visions of Progress: The Left-Liberal Tradition in America* (Philadelphia: University of Pennsylvania Press, 2007); Edward J. Blum, *W. E. B. Du Bois: American Prophet* (Philadelphia: University of Pennsylvania Press, 2007); David S. Gutterman, *Prophetic Politics: Christian Social Movements and American Democracy* (Ithaca, N.Y.: Cornell University Press, 2005); Steve Fraser, *Labor Will Rule: Sidney Hillman and the Rise of American Labor* (Ithaca, N.Y.: Cornell University Press, 1992); Robert Hyfler, *Prophets of the Left: American Socialist Thought in the Twentieth Century* (Westport, Conn.: Greenwood Press, 1984); and Nick Salvatore, *Eugene V. Debs: Citizen and Socialist* (Urbana: University of Illinois Press, 1982).

5. See sources cited in note 4 above. See also James R. Barrett, *William Z. Foster and the Tragedy of American Radicalism* (Urbana: University of Illinois Press, 1999); and John H. M. Laslett and Seymour Martin Lipset, eds., *Failure of a Dream? Essays in the History of American Socialism*, rev. ed. (Berkeley: University of California Press, 1984).

6. Muste's ideas have parallels to philosopher Cornel West's more recent formulation of a "prophetic pragmatism" as the basis for a democratic left politics. See West, *The American Evasion of Philosophy: A Genealogy of Pragmatism* (Madison: University of Wisconsin Press, 1989). Discussions of pragmatism that emphasize its radical possibilities can be found in Louis Menand, *The Metaphysical Club* (New York: Farrar, Straus and Giroux, 2001); Robert Westbrook, *John Dewey and American Democracy* (Ithaca, N.Y.: Cornell University Press, 1991); David Hollinger, *In the American Province: Studies in the History and Historiography of Ideas* (Bloomington: Indiana University Press, 1985); Christopher Phelps, *Young Sidney Hook: Marxist and Pragmatist* (Ithaca, N.Y.: Cornell University Press, 2005); and James Livingston, *Pragmatism and the Political Economy of Cultural Revolution, 1850–1940* (Chapel Hill: University of North Carolina Press, 1994). Others have emphasized its risks, pointing out that it could devolve into a crude instrumentalism or "realism" that stripped politics of questions of morality and ethics. The most well-known critique of pragmatism is Randolph Bourne's "Twilight of Idols" (1917), reprinted in David Hollinger and Charles Capper, eds., *The American Intellectual Tradition*, 5th ed. (New

York: Oxford University Press, 2006), 2:181–88. For similar critiques, see also Max Horkheimer, *Eclipse of Reason* (New York: Oxford University Press, 1947); and Christopher Lasch, *The New Radicalism in America* (New York: Norton, 1965). Ironically, as Christopher Phelps points out, many of the same liberals who drew upon pragmatism to make the case for professional and scientific elites "to govern in the benevolent interest of a befuddled, gullible public" would later identify as "realists" and took pleasure in rejecting John Dewey's philosophy as excessively optimistic about human nature and society. See Phelps, *Young Sidney Hook*, 252. Muste occupies a complex place in this history. On the one hand, he shared Bourne's criticism of Dewey during World War I. On the other hand, he defended idealism against realist attacks in the 1930s. See especially Muste, *Non-violence in an Aggressive World* (New York: Harper and Brothers, 1940); Muste, *Not by Might: Christianity, the Way to Human Decency* (New York: Harper and Brothers, 1947)); Muste, "Theology of Despair" (1948), and "Pacifism and Perfectionism" (1948), both reprinted in Hentoff, *Essays of A. J. Muste*, 302–7 and 308–21.

7. Doug Rossinow has made an important distinction between the progressive generation and the new generation of liberals and "lyrical" leftists who came of age in the 1910s. Muste belonged to the latter group. Although less bohemian than the Greenwich Village crowd, he shared their pro-labor orientation, cultural pluralism, and anarchist and civil libertarian impulses. See Rossinow, *Visions of Progress*, 55–59. For the links these moderns made between the personal and the political, see Christine Stansell, *American Moderns: Bohemian New York and the Creation of a New Century* (New York: Henry Holt, 2000); and Michael McGerr, *A Fierce Discontent: The Rise and Fall of the Progressive Movement in America, 1870–1920* (New York: Oxford University Press, 2003), chapter 7.

8. The rise of the anti-Stalinist left has received much attention from historians. See, for example, Ann Douglas, "The Failure of the New York Intellectuals," *Raritan* 17 (1998): 1–23; Harvey Teres, *Renewing the Left: Politics, Imagination, and the New York Intellectuals* (New York: Oxford University Press, 1996); Michael Denning, "New York Intellectuals," *Socialist Review* 88, no. 1 (January–March 1988): 136–47; Alan Wald, *The New York Intellectuals: The Rise and Decline of the Anti-Stalinist Left from the 1930s to the 1980s* (Chapel Hill: University of North Carolina Press, 1987); Richard H. Pells, *The Liberal Mind in a Conservative Age: American Intellectuals in the 1940s and 1950s* (New York: Harper and Row, 1985); and Christopher Lasch, *The Agony of the American Left* (New York: Knopf, 1969).

9. Muste, quoting Martin Buber in a letter to the editor of the *New York Times Book Review*, January 7, 1964, AJMP, reel 36.

10. For the intellectual, social, and cultural origins of the New Left, see Daniel Geary, *Radical Ambition: C. Wright Mills, the Left, and American Social Thought* (Berkeley: University of California Press, 2009); Nelson Lichtenstein, ed., *American Capitalism: Social Thought and Political Economy in the Twentieth Century* (Philadelphia: University of Pennsylvania Press, 2007); Doug Rossinow, *The Politics of Authenticity: Liberalism, Christianity, and the New Left in America* (New York: Columbia University Press, 1998); James J. Farrell, *The Spirit of the Sixties: The Making of Postwar Radicalism* (New York: Routledge, 1997); and Maurice Isserman, *If I Had a Hammer: The Death of the Old Left and the Birth of the New Left* (Urbana: University of Illinois Press, 1993).

11. See, for example, Leigh Eric Schmidt, *Restless Souls: The Making of American Spirituality* (San Francisco: HarperCollins, 2005); Kip Kosek, *Acts of Conscience: Christian Nonviolence and Modern American Democracy* (New York: Columbia University Press, 2007); and Rossinow, *The Politics of Authenticity*.

12. Critics include Christopher Lasch, *The Culture of Narcissism: American Culture in an Age of Diminishing Expectations* (New York: Norton, 1978); and Robert Bellah, *Habits of the Heart: Individualism and Commitment in American Life* (Berkeley: University of California Press, 1985).

13. See Kosek, *Acts of Conscience*; and Christopher Capozzola, *Uncle Sam Wants You: World War I and the Making of the Modern American Citizen* (New York: Oxford University Press, 2008).

14. I borrow this term from Doug Rossinow, *Visions of Progress*, 2–3. See also the contributions by Eric Foner et al. to the seminar "Liberalism and the Left" in *Radical History Review* 71 (Spring 1988); Michael Kazin, "What Liberals Owe to Radicals," in Neil Jumonville and Kevin Mattson, eds., *Liberalism for a New Century* (Berkeley: University of California Press, 2007): 119–30. Works that emphasize the overlapping and linked histories of the pre?Cold War left include Michael Denning, *The Cultural Front: The Laboring of American Culture* (New York: Verso, 1997); Penny Von Eschen, *Race Against Empire: Black Americans and Anti-Colonialism* (Ithaca, N.Y.: Cornell University Press, 1997); and Patricia Sullivan, *Days of Hope: Race and Democracy in the New Deal Era* (Chapel Hill: University of North Carolina Press, 1996).

15. Muste, "Sketches," 85. For the founding and early years of the ACLU, including some discussion of its links to the ATWA and other labor insurgencies of the era, see Samuel Walker, *In Defense of American Liberties: A History of the ACLU*, 2nd ed. (Carbondale: Southern Illinois University Press, 1999). Only later, with the rise of anti-Stalinism and the Cold War, did the ACLU's understanding of civil liberties become more libertarian and absolutist. Steve Fraser's biography of Hillman provides a discussion of efforts to unify the two unions, as well as the ACW's expansive and modernist vision for the labor movement. See Fraser, *Labor Will Rule*, chapter 6.

16. See Walter Weyl, *Tired Radicals and Other Papers* (New York: Huebsch, 1921).

17. The term "progressive labor network" comes from Jonathan Bloom, "Brookwood Labor College and the Progressive Labor Network of the Interwar United States, 1921–1937" (Ph.D. diss., New York University, 1992). Muste provided a brief historical retrospective on progressive unionism in "'Where to from Here?' Muste Asks Regarding Brookwood's Future Goal," *Brookwood Review* 7, no. 1 (October–November 1928): 1–2. For a recent discussion of the third-party efforts of the 1920s, see Rossinow, *Visions of Progress*, chapter 3.

18. By the end of the decade, however, conservatives clearly dominated the organized labor movement. For labor during World War I and the 1920s, see Joseph A. McCartin, *Labor's Great War: The Struggle for Industrial Democracy and the Origins of Modern Labor Relations, 1912–1921* (Chapel Hill: University of North Carolina Press, 1997); Dana Frank, *Purchasing Power: Consumer Organizing, Gender, and the Seattle Labor Movement, 1919–1929* (London: Cambridge University Press, 1994); David Montgomery, *The Fall of the House of Labor: The Workplace, the State, and American Labor Activism, 1865–1925* (Cambridge: Cambridge University Press, 1989); and Irving Bernstein, *The Lean Years: A History of the American Worker* (New York: Houghton Mifflin, 1960).

19. James Livingston, "War and the Intellectuals: Bourne, Dewey, and the Fate of Pragmatism," *Journal of the Gilded Age and Progressive Era* 2, no. 4 (October 2003), 438–39. My argument about the pragmatic thrust of workers' education and Muste's central role in the movement is demonstrated below. For the history of workers' education in the 1920s, see Annelise Orleck, *Common Sense and a Little Fire: Women and Working-Class Politics in the United States, 1900–*

1965 (Chapel Hill: University of North Carolina Press, 1995); Karyn Hollis, *Liberating Voices: Writing at the Bryn Mawr Summer School for Women Workers* (Carbondale: Southern Illinois University Press, 2004); Richard Altenbaugh, *Education for Struggle: The American Labor Colleges of the 1920s and 1930s* (Philadelphia: Temple University Press, 1990); and Kenneth Teitelbaum, *Schooling for Good Rebels: Socialism, American Education, and the Search for a Radical Curriculum* (New York: Teachers' College Press, 1995). These labor intellectuals were working against the tide of the AFL leadership, which espoused strongly anti-intellectual views, as became evident in 1928, when the federation began a full-scale assault upon Brookwood and independent labor education more broadly. For the AFL's views on intellectuals, see Richard Hofstadter's classic account, *Anti-Intellectualism in American Life* (New York: Vintage, 1966), esp. 284–88.

20. Denning and other scholars, particularly Nelson Lichtenstein, have suggested that Brookwood served as a sort of "cadre school" for the CIO, but, until now, there has been no systematic analysis of the relationship between the workers' education movement (which included not only Brookwood but educational programs in local and state labor federations, city labor colleges, summer camps, and extension courses throughout the United States) and the CIO. See Lichtenstein, "Falling in Love Again? Intellectuals and the Labor Movement in Postwar America," *New Labor Forum* (Spring–Summer 1999): 21; and Denning, *The Cultural Front*, 68–72. See also Altenbaugh, *Education for Struggle*; and Lizabeth Cohen, *Making a New Deal: Industrial Workers in Chicago, 1919–1939* (New York: Cambridge University Press, 1990). Gramsci's ideas about education and hegemony can be found in Antonio Gramsci, *Selections from the Prison Notebooks*, ed. and trans. Quintin Hoare and Geoffrey Nowell Smith (New York: International Publishers, 1971). For a useful discussion, see Carmel Borg, Joseph Buttigieg, and Peter Mayo, eds., *Gramsci and Education* (Lanham, Md.: Rowman and Littlefield, 2002).

21. See Kosek, *Acts of Conscience*, 47.

22. For a discussion of the pacifist movement in during the interwar years, see Kosek, *Acts of Conscience*; Charles Chatfield, *For Peace and Justice: Pacifism in America, 1914–41* (Knoxville: University of Tennessee Press, 1971); and Charles DeBenedetti, *Origins of the Modern American Peace Movement, 1915–1929* (Millwood, N.Y.: KTO Press, 1978). Muste's laborite politics and the reasons for his estrangement from organized pacifism are discussed below. See also Robinson, *Abraham Went Out*; Hentoff, *Peace Agitator*; and Leilah Danielson, "'In My Extremity I Turned to Gandhi': American Pacifists, Christianity, and Gandhian Nonviolence, 1915–1941," *Church History: Studies in Christianity and Culture* 72, no. 2 (June 2003): 361–88.

23. Classic works in this vein include Theodore Draper, *American Communism and Soviet Russia* (New York: Viking, 1960), and Harvey Klehr, *The Heyday of American Communism: The Depression Decade* (New York: Basic Books, 1984).

24. See, for example, Dorothy Healey and Maurice Isserman, *California Red: A Life in the American Communist Party* (Urbana: University of Illinois Press, 1993); Robin D. G. Kelley, *Hammer and Hoe: Alabama Communists During the Great Depression* (Chapel Hill: University of North Carolina Press, 1990); Maurice Isserman, *Which Side Were You On? The American Communist Party During the Second World War* (Middletown, Conn.: Wesleyan University Press, 1982); and Mark Naison, *Communists in Harlem During the Depression* (Urbana: University of Illinois Press, 1983).

25. For the CP's shifting trade union policy, see James R. Barrett, "Boring from Within and Without: William Z. Foster, the Trade Union Educational Leagues, and American Communism in the 1920s," in Eric Arnesen, Julie Greene, and Bruce Laurie, eds., *Labor Histories: Class, Politics,*

and the Working-Class Experience (Urbana: University of Illinois Press, 1998); Bernstein, *The Lean Years*, 140–41; Barrett, *William Z. Foster*, 156–58; and Draper, *American Communism and Soviet Russia*, 278–94.

26. Muste, "Education and the Unorganized," *Labor Age* 17, no. 4 (April 1928): 8–10. See also Muste, "Mother Throws Out the Baby," *Labor Age* 17, no. 10 (October 1928): 20–22; and Muste, "Militant Progressivism?" *Modern Quarterly* 4, no. 4 (May–August 1928): 333–34. Doug Rossinow makes the same argument in his book *Visions of Progress*, 121–22. See also Eric Arnesen's important discussion in his "A. Philip Randolph, Black Anticommunism, and the Race Question," in Donna T. Haverty-Stacke and Daniel J. Walkowitz, eds., *Rethinking U.S. Labor History: Essays on the Working-Class Experience* (New York: Continuum, 2010): 137–67.

27. Rossinow, *Visions of Progress*, 5.

28. Muste, "What the Bible Teaches About Freedom" (1943), in Hentoff, *Essays of A. J. Muste*, 279–95. Indeed, Muste held that "that there isn't such a thing as a Jewish religion and a Christian religion, that there is one Jewish-Christian or Hebrew-Christian prophetic religion." See Muste, lecture notes for "The Church and Social Action," which he taught at New Brunswick Theological Seminary in 1938 and 1944, AJMP, reel 3. See also Muste, COHC, 217, 243–46. Some scholars have argued that the invention of a Judeo-Christian tradition was a form of appropriation that failed to recognize the differences between the two religious traditions. See, for example, Arthur A. Cohen, *The Myth of the Judeo-Christian Tradition* (New York: Harper and Row, 1970). Still, in the interwar period, it reflected an effort by liberal Protestants to combat anti-Semitism by recognizing the Jewish roots of Christianity and by seriously engaging Jewish theology. See, for example, Martin E. Marty, "A Judeo-Christian Looks at the Judeo-Christian Tradition," *Christian Century*, October 5, 1986, 858–60; and Mark Silk, "Notes on the Judeo-Christian Tradition in America," *American Quarterly* 36, no. 1 (Spring 1984), 65–85.

29. For discussions of the Musteites that tend to associate the movement with the AWP rather than the CPLA, see Denning, *The Cultural Front*; Phelps, *Young Sidney Hook*; and Judy Kutulas, *The Long War: The Intellectual People's Front and Anti-Stalinism, 1930–1940* (Durham, N.C.: Duke University Press, 1995). Conversely, some historians use "Brookwood" synonymously with Muste's movement. See, for example, Lichtenstein, "Falling in Love Again?" 21–22; Melvyn Dubofsky and Warren Van Tine, *John L. Lewis: A Biography* (New York: Quadrangle, 1977), 157–67; and Bernstein, *The Lean Years*, 34–36, 358–90.

30. Roy Rosenzweig's articles on the Musteites and the unemployed are an important exception to this tendency of historical neglect, though he does not discuss the movement's roots in workers' education and labor progressivism. See Rosenzweig, "Radicals and the Jobless: The Musteites and the Unemployed Leagues, 1932–36," *Labor History* 16, no. 1 (Winter 1975): 52–77, and "Organizing the Unemployed: The Early Years of the Great Depression, 1929–1933," *Radical America* 10 (July–August 1976): 37–60. Rosenzweig also mistakenly claims that "Many [CPLA members] were college graduates who had completed postgraduate training at Brookwood," and cites as evidence the prominent CPLAer Elmer Cope who had studied at Brookwood after attending Swarthmore College. In fact, as is demonstrated below, the vast majority of Brookwood graduates came from working-class backgrounds and had no experience with higher education aside from courses in workers' education programs offered by their unions; Cope was, in other words, the exception and not the rule. The same was true of most CPLA members; almost all were members or officers of AFL or independent unions. I prefer to think of them as "labor movement intellectuals," a term I have borrowed from Denning, *The Cultural Front*, 73.

31. Discussions of efforts by left-wing intellectuals to "'Americanize' Marxism by fusing it with pragmatism" can be found in Denning, *The Cultural Front*, 425–34 (quote is on p. 425); Leonard Wilcox, *V. F. Calverton: Radical in the American Grain* (Philadelphia: Temple University Press, 1992); and Phelps, *Young Sidney Hook*. The difference between these accounts and my own is that I emphasize the social historical roots of these ideas in the 1920s and among organized workers.

32. For an account of the 1930s that similarly emphasizes the role of CIO militants and non-Communist leftists, see Denning, *The Cultural Front*. The period 1929–34 continues to be a sort of enigma in labor-left history, since the AFL was wracked by internal conflicts and the Communist Party was tiny and fractious, having entered its ultra-revolutionary third period. See Chapters 6 and 7, below, for details on Brookwood alumni and former CPLA members who assumed prominent roles as organizers and educators in the CIO and the federal bureaucracy created by the New Deal.

33. As we shall see, there had been an earlier exodus from the Musteite ranks in 1932–33. Many of these former Musteites similarly found work as organizers and labor educators in the CIO, as well as in the New Deal bureaucracy. Accounts of this period in American Trotskyism, some of which contrast with my own interpretation, can be found in Rosenzweig, "Radicals and the Jobless"; George Breitman, Paul Le Blanc, and Alan Wald, eds., *Trotskyism in the United States: Historical Essays and Reconsiderations* (Atlantic Highlands, N.J.: Humanities Press, 1996); Constance Myers, *The Prophet's Army: Trotskyists in America, 1928–1941* (Westport, Conn.: Greenwood Press, 1977); James P. Cannon, *The History of American Trotskyism: Report of a Participant*, 3rd ed. (New York: Pathfinder Press, 1995); Tim Wohlforth, "Trotskyism," in Mari Jo Buhle, Paul Buhle, and Dan Georgakas, eds., *Encyclopedia of the American Left* (New York: Garland, 1990), 782–85; and Phelps, *Young Sidney Hook*, 52–140.

34. Muste had been closely associated with John Brophy and the reorganized miners' movement, which earned Lewis's wrath. See Dubofsky and Van Tine, *John L. Lewis*, 163–201.

35. See Nelson Lichtenstein, *Walter Reuther: The Most Dangerous Man in Detroit* (New York: Basic Books, 1995), 132–93; and Fraser, *Labor Will Rule*, 259–323.

36. Muste, "Return to Pacifism" (1936), reprinted in Hentoff, *Essays of A. J. Muste*, 199–201. For a thoughtful discussion of Muste's critique and its implications for the Marxist tradition, see Paul Le Blanc, *Marx, Lenin, and the Revolutionary Experience* (London: Routledge, 2006), esp. 24–25.

37. Kip Kosek astutely observes that Muste's reconversion was "a kind of performance, retold in numerous speeches, letters, and essays." Kosek, *Acts of Conscience*, 147–49.

38. See also Reinhold Niebuhr, *Moral Man and Immoral Society* (1948; reprint, New York: Charles Scribner's Sons); and Niebuhr, *The Children of Light and the Children of Darkness* (1944; reprint, Chicago: University of Chicago Press, 2011); Richard Wightman Fox, *Reinhold Niebuhr: A Biography* (1985; reprint, Ithaca, N.Y.: Cornell University Press, 1996); June Bingham, *Courage to Change: An Introduction to the Life and Thought of Reinhold Niebuhr* (1972; reprint, New York: Scribner); and Donald Meyer, *The Protestant Search for Political Realism, 1919–1941* (Berkeley: University of California Press, 1960). For the history of pacifism during this period, see Kosek, *Acts of Conscience*; Patricia Appelbaum, *Kingdom to Commune: Protestant Pacifist Culture from World War I to the Vietnam War* (Chapel Hill: University of North Carolina Press, 2009); Chatfield, *For Peace and Justice*; and Danielson, "'In My Extremity I Turned to Gandhi.'"

39. Muste, *Non-violence in an Aggressive World*, 33–34; Muste, "Theology of Despair," 302–7. As Muste predicted, many mainline Protestants would find realism ultimately inadequate

for dealing with the ethical and moral problems presented by nuclear proliferation and third world interventions by the U.S. military. See Paul Boyer, *By the Bomb's Early Light: American Thought and Culture at the Dawn of the Atomic Age* (New York: Pantheon, 1985); and Mark Hulsether, *Building a Protestant Left:* Christianity and Crisis *Magazine, 1943–1991* (Knoxville: University of Tennessee Press, 1999).

40. Muste, "The World Task of Pacifism" (1941), reprinted in Hentoff, *Essays of A. J. Muste*, 223–25. A helpful introduction to Gandhi's thought is Bhikhu Parekh, *Gandhi: A Very Short Introduction* (Oxford: Oxford University Press, 2001).

41. Glenn Smiley, quoted in John D'Emilio, *Lost Prophet: The Life and Times of Bayard Rustin* (Chicago: University of Chicago Press, 2004), 40. For pacifist experimentation with Gandhian nonviolence, see Kosek, *Acts of Conscience*; Scott Bennett, *Radical Pacifism: The War Resisters League and Gandhian Nonviolence in America, 1915–1963* (Syracuse, N.Y.: Syracuse University Press, 2003); Lawrence Wittner, *Rebels Against War: The American Peace Movement, 1933–1983*, rev. ed. (Philadelphia: Temple University Press, 1984); and Danielson, "'In My Extremity I Turned to Gandhi.'"

42. The efforts by pacifists to combat racial discrimination and segregation led, most notably, to the formation of the Congress of Racial Equality in 1942. For details on CORE's organizational history, see August Meier and Elliott Rudwick, *CORE: A Study in the Civil Rights Movement* (Urbana: University of Illinois Press, 1975).

43. See, for example, A. J. Muste, "Address for CBS's *Church of the Air*," typescript, September 3, 1939, AJMP, reel 3; Muste, "Winning Industrial Workers to Christ and His Program" (ca. 1937–38) and "Foundations of Democracy: The Role of Economic Groups" (ca. 1945), typescripts, both in AJMP, reel 4. Muste proved prophetic in his analysis of the consequences of labor's alliance with the Democratic Party and the wartime state, and during the postwar period many radical intellectuals would come to share his critique. The causes and consequences of this estrangement between radical intellectuals and the labor movement, as well as its legacy for the labor movement today, have been explored in Nelson Lichtenstein, "Pluralism, Postwar Intellectuals, and the Demise of the Union Idea," in Sidney Milkis and Jerome Mileur, eds., *The Great Society and the High Tide of Liberalism* (Amherst: University of Massachusetts Press, 2005); Lichtenstein, "Falling in Love Again?"; Lichtenstein, *State of the Union: A Century of American Labor* (Princeton, N.J.: Princeton University Press, 2003); and Ellen Schrecker, *Many Are the Crimes: McCarthyism in America* (Princeton, N.J.: Princeton University Press, 1999).

44. See, for example, Muste, "The Fellowship of Reconciliation," typescript (1945), AJMP, reel 4; Muste, "The World Task of Pacifism"; and Muste, "What the Bible Teaches About Freedom." For an insightful discussion of Americans' tendency to equate race and caste, see Nico Slate, *Colored Cosmopolitanism: The Shared Struggle for Freedom in the United States and India* (Cambridge, Mass.: Harvard University Press, 2012).

45. Reinhold Niebuhr, "Why the Christian Church Is Not Pacifist," in *Christianity and Power Politics* (New York: Charles Scribner's Sons, 1940), 16, 9, 29.

46. See Appelbaum, *Kingdom to Commune*, 3, 34–38; and Gerald Sittser, *A Cautious Patriotism: American Churches and the Second World War* (Chapel Hill: University of North Carolina Press, 1997), 30–98. Appelbaum provides a brilliant analysis of pacifism as a "folk culture," and maintains, persuasively, it "survived [the war] in ideas and practices formed within Protestant pacifist culture, some of which later lost or severed their ties with the Protestant context."

47. Parekh, *Gandhi*, 74–75.

48. "The Course Before Us," Statement of the FOR Executive Committee, December 10, 1941, reprinted in *Fellowship* 8, no. 1 (January 1942): 2; and Muste, "Some Fellowship Objectives," *Fellowship* 7, no. 10 (October 1941): 165–67.

49. Muste, *Not by Might*, 159. For an insightful discussion of pacifists and World War II, see Kosek, *Acts of Conscience*, 146–90.

50. Boyer, *By the Bomb's Early Light*, 220, 43, 291–351. Niebuhr quote is on page 43. See also Leilah Danielson, "Christianity, Dissent, and the Cold War: A. J. Muste's Challenge to Realism and U.S. Empire," *Diplomatic History* 30, no. 4 (September 2006): 645–69. For a transnational history of the postwar peace and antinuclear movements, see Lawrence Wittner's multivolume series *The Struggle Against the Bomb* (Stanford, Calif.: Stanford University Press, 1993, 1997, 2003).

51. For the history of liberalism during this period, see Alan Brinkley, *The End of Reform: New Deal Liberalism in Recession and War* (New York: Vintage, 1996); Rossinow, *Visions of Progress*; Meyer, *Protestant Search for Political Realism*; Pells, *Liberal Mind in a Conservative Age*; Steven Gillon, *Politics and Vision: The ADA and American Liberalism, 1947–1985* (New York: Oxford University Press, 1987); and Arthur M. Schlesinger Jr., *The Vital Center: The Politics of Freedom* (reprint; 1962, Boston: Houghton Mifflin Co.). For a discussion of Niebuhrian realism and U.S. foreign policy during the Cold War, see Jason W. Stevens, *God-Fearing and Free: A Spiritual History of America's Cold War* (Cambridge, Mass.: Harvard University Press, 2010); Campbell Craig, *Glimmer of a New Leviathan: Total War in the Realism of Niebuhr, Morgenthau, and Waltz* (New York: Columbia University Press, 2003); Joel H. Rosenthal, *Righteous Realists: Political Realism, Responsible Power, and American Culture in the Nuclear Age* (Baton Rouge: Louisiana State University Press, 1991).

52. See Rossinow, *Visions of Progress*, 162–65; Walker, *In Defense of American Liberties*, chapters 6 and 7.

53. See, for example, Muste, *Not by Might*; Muste, "On Understanding Russia," *Fellowship* 12, no. 11 (December 1946); Muste, "The Spiritual Menace of Russian Communism," *Fellowship* 10, no. 6 (June 1944): 104–5; and Muste, "Communism and Civil Liberties" (1948), reprinted in Hentoff, *Essays of A. J. Muste*, 322–30. Muste led efforts to oppose the Smith Act and McCarthyism more broadly. See essays above and, for example, FOR, "Statement Against Attorney General's List of Subversives," December 4, 1953, FOR, box 3, folder 12; FOR National and Executive Council, Minutes of Meetings, May 13–14, 1954, FOR, box 4, folder 8; and his lead signature on "A Petition to the President of the United States on Amnesty for Smith Act Victims and Postponement of Trials" (ca. 1955), AJMP-LA, box 2.

54. Muste, "Theology of Despair," 303, 305; Muste, "Is Our Only Hope Dumbarton Oaks or Chaos?" *Fellowship* 11, no. 4 (April 1945): 70.

55. Muste, "Of Holy Disobedience" (1952), reprinted in Hentoff, *Essays of A. J. Muste*, 355.

56. It was "an ominous sign . . . that those regarded as liberals and Progressives" advocated and defended American military might, Muste commented. "This would not have happened 'in the old days.'" See Muste, *Not by Might*, 10. For radical pacifists in the postwar era, see Marian Mollin, *Radical Pacifism in Modern America: Egalitarianism and Protest* (Philadelphia: University of Pennsylvania Press, 2008); Kosek, *Acts of Conscience*; Bennett, *Radical Pacifism*; and Leilah Danielson, "'It Is a Day of Judgment': The Peacemakers, Religion, and Radicalism in Cold War America," *Religion and American Culture: A Journal of Interpretation* 18, no. 2 (Summer 2008): 215–48.

57. Muste to CNVA, March 26, 1963, BDP, box 9, folder 151. See also Muste, "Sketches," 90; Muste, COHC, 176–84, 353, 412–13; Muste, "The World Task of Pacifism"; Cara Cook's comments on Muste for radio station WBAI, New York, on February 23, 1967; Hentoff, *Peace Agitator*, 141–48; and Robinson, *Abraham Went Out*, 98–99. For the pacifist critique of modernity, see Applebaum, *Kingdom to Commune*; Kosek, *Acts of Conscience*; and Mel Piehl, *Breaking Bread: The Catholic Worker and the Origin of Catholic Radicalism in America* (Philadelphia: Temple University Press, 1982).

58. Muste, "Sketches," 87–90. See also Muste, COHC, 412–13.

59. Muste, typescript of position paper, 1956, PMR; Muste, "Neutralism or Third Force," typescript, April 1955, AJMP, reel 4; and Muste, "Whither Communist Russia?" *Liberation* 1, no. 3 (May 1956): 3–7.

60. See Wittner, *The Struggle Against the Bomb*; Wittner, *Rebels Against War*; Mollin, *Radical Pacifism in Modern America*; and Bennett, *Radical Pacifism*.

61. Editors, "Tract for the Times," *Liberation* 1, no. 1 (March 1956): 3–6. For the American Forum, see my discussion below, as well as Robbie Lieberman, *The Strangest Dream: Communism, Anticommunism, and the U.S. Peace Movement, 1945–1963* (Syracuse, N.Y.: Syracuse University Press, 2000), 141–42; and Robinson, *Abraham Went Out*, 101–5.

62. For her loyalty, see Muste, COHC, 225–27, 311. For descriptions of Muste as egalitarian and "non-judgmental" in his attitudes, see Cara Cook to Jo Ann Robinson, March 22, 1979, and Barbara Deming to Jo Ann Robinson, March 25, 1979, both in AJMP-LA, box 2; and Bayard Rustin's comments in *WIN Special Supplement on A. J. Muste, 1885–1967*, p. 16, copy in AJMP-LA, box 2. Muste's son, John, suggested that his father was theoretically in favor of women's rights but was less egalitarian in practice. He observed that "no woman ever had an important management position in the organizations he led." At home, Muste encouraged his daughters to pursue careers, but gave his son far "more latitude in behavior." John's sister Nancy, however, disagreed with his account of family life, insisting that Muste treated her equally, as he did all women. See John Muste to Jo Ann Robinson, February 6, 1979, and Nancy [Muste] Baker to Jo Ann Robinson, February 8, 1979, both in AJMP-LA, box 2. For gender and the left, see Mollin, *Radical Pacifism in Modern America*; Van Gosse, *Where the Boys Are: Cuba, Cold War America, and the Making of a New Left* (London: Verso, 1993); Mari Jo Buhle, *Women and American Socialism* (Urbana: University of Illinois Press, 1983); Kate Weigand, *Red Feminism: American Communism and the Making of Women's Liberation* (Baltimore: Johns Hopkins University Press, 2002); and Sara Evans, *The Roots of Women's Liberation in Civil Rights and the New Left* (New York: Random House, 1979).

63. See Chapter 10, below, for my interpretation of Muste's evolving views on sexuality, as well as his relationship with Rustin, which differs somewhat from John D'Emilio's. See D'Emilio, "Homophobia and the Trajectory of Postwar American Radicalism: The Career of Bayard Rustin," *Radical History Review* 62 (Spring 1995): 81–103. The intellectual and cultural innovations of the 1950s are discussed in Daniel Belgrad, *The Culture of Spontaneity: Improvisation and the Arts in Postwar America* (Chicago: University of Chicago Press, 1998); and Wilfred M. McClay, *The Masterless: Self and Society in Modern America* (Chapel Hill: University of North Carolina Press, 1994).

64. Martin Luther King, Jr., quoted in Hentoff, *Peace Agitator*, 18.

65. Tom Cornell, quoted by David McReynolds in *WIN Special Supplement*, 2. McReynolds concurred and added: "We were also his lieutenants. But we were not . . . his disciples. We were

co-workers and comrades as well as being his children." See also Tom Cornell, interview with author, June 16, 2006, New York City; and David McReynolds, interview with author, June 6, 2006, New York City.

66. Smiley, quoted in Robinson, *Abraham Went Out*, 186.

67. Copies of contemporary appreciations, telegrams, and obituaries can be found in the AJMP, reels 1, 36, and 37. See also articles in *WIN Special Supplement* and *Liberation* 12, nos. 6 and 7 (September and October 1967), a special issue on A. J. Muste.

68. For the postwar peace movement and the politics of anti-Communism, see Lieberman, *The Strangest Dream*; and Wittner, *Rebels Against War*.

69. See Robinson, *Abraham Went Out*, 185. See also Lieberman, *The Strangest Dream*, 84–86.

70. Muste, "Who Has the Spiritual Atom Bomb?" (1965), reprinted in Hentoff, *Essays of A. J. Muste*, 500.

71. Ibid., 480. See also Muste and George F. Kennan, "An Exchange: A Policy for the Far East," *Liberation* 10, no. 2 (April 1965): 6–11, 24; and Muste, "Crisis in the World and in the Peace Movement" (1965), reprinted in Hentoff, *Essays of A. J. Muste*, 465–78.

72. For Muste's central role in building the coalition, see my discussion below; Robinson, *When Abraham Went Out*, 212–15; and Simon Hall, *Peace and Freedom: The Civil Rights and Antiwar Movements in the 1960s* (Philadelphia: University of Pennsylvania Press, 2005).

73. Muste to Lawrence Scott (ca. 1962), BDP, box 29, folder 581. Muste often cited Buber to this effect. See, for example, "Pacifism Enters a New Phase," *Fellowship* 25, no. 7 (July 1960): 25; and Muste to the editor of the *New York Times Book Review*, January 7, 1964, copy in AJMP, reel 36.

74. Muste, quoted in the *New York Herald Tribune*, December 29, 1966, copy in AJMP, reel 36. See also Robinson, *Abraham Went Out*, 216.

75. Muste, "Sketches," 15, 27; Muste, "Who Has the Spiritual Atom Bomb?" 501. See also Muste, "What the Bible Teaches About Freedom," 279–95; and Muste, "Saints for This Age" (1962), reprinted in Hentoff, *Essays of A. J. Muste*, 414–15.

76. Muste, "Proposal for a Bi-Weekly Magazine," February 21, 1955, PMR.

Chapter 1. Calvinism, Class, and the Making of a Modern Radical

Epigraph: Muste, "The Problem of Discontent," Hope College *Anchor* 18, no. 17 (July 1905), no page numbers.

1. Muste, "Sketches," 15.

2. Michael J. Wintle, *Zeeland and the Churches* (Middelburg: Commissie Regionale Geschiedbeoefening Zeeland, 1988), 3–4, 212–13.

3. Ibid., 41. See also Robert Swierenga, *Faith and Family: Dutch Immigration and Settlement in the United States* (New York: Holmes and Meier, 2000).

4. Muste, COHC, 1–6; Swierenga, *Faith and Family*, 53.

5. Muste, COHC, 5–6.

6. Ibid., 8–9, 17–18; Robinson, *Abraham Went Out*, 3.

7. Muste, "Sketches," 17.

8. Muste, COHC, 15–16.

9. Peter W. Williams, *America's Religions: From Their Origins to the Twenty-first Century* (Urbana: University of Illinois Press, 2008), 95–97. The nature of predestination had been fully developed in 1618–19 by the Synod of Dort, which had been called in response to the teachings of Jacobus Arminius, who held that the faithful had some hand in their salvation. The decrees of Dort held that, first, human beings are totally depraved; second, that salvation occurs irrespective of personal merit or faithfulness; third, that Jesus Christ's sacrificial death was for the benefit of a select few and not the whole of humanity; fourth, that the elect had no choice but to accept God's saving grace; and, fifth, that the "saints," or the elect, would obtain salvation regardless of lapses in their earthly lives. See also Wintle, *Zeeland and the Churches*, 148.

10. Robert Swierenga, ed., *The Dutch in America: Immigration, Settlement and Cultural Change* (New Brunswick, N.J.: Rutgers University Press), 3–4.

11. Swierenga, *Faith and Family*, 18.

12. James D. Bratt, *Dutch Calvinism in Modern America: A History of a Conservative Subculture* (Grand Rapids, Mich.: Wm. B. Eerdmans, 1984), 21–25. See also Bratt, *Abraham Kuyper: Modern Calvinist, Christian Democrat* (Grand Rapids, Mich.: Wm. B. Eerdmans, 2013).

13. Williams, *America's Religions*, 95.

14. Muste, "Sketches," 5.

15. Ibid., 46.

16. Swierenga, *Faith and Family*, 14 and 61. The only exception to this was the first great wave of immigration, in the 1840s, in which the Seceders had a heavy presence. Still, even then, they only composed 24 percent of the migrating population; moreover, as a predominantly lower-class group, they were also driven by economic distress caused by the depression of the 1840s.

17. Ibid., 66.

18. Muste, "Sketches," 19–20; Muste, COHC, 10.

19. Muste, "Sketches," 28.

20. Swierenga, *Faith and Family*, 134.

21. Muste, "Sketches," 27. Historians have shown that the division between the "old" and "new" immigrants has been somewhat exaggerated; rural and urban differences, for example, also played a role in how immigrants were treated. See Roger Daniels, *Coming to America: A History of Immigration and Ethnicity in America*, 2nd ed. (New York: Harper Perennial, 2002), esp. chap. 6.

22. Muste, COHC, 26–31. For an excellent discussion of how Americans have viewed Abraham Lincoln and his legacy, see Merrill D. Peterson, *Lincoln in American Memory* (New York: Oxford University Press, 1994).

23. Muste, "Sketches," 23–27.

24. Ibid., 28.

25. See, for example, Jon Butler, *Awash in a Sea of Faith: Christianizing the American People* (Cambridge, Mass.: Harvard University Press, 1992); Nathan O. Hatch, *The Democratization of American Christianity* (New Haven, Conn.: Yale University Press, 1989); and Paul Johnson, *A Shopkeeper's Millennium: Society and Revivals in Rochester, New York, 1815–1837* (New York: Hill and Wang, 1983). As James Bratt comments, the Dutch Reformed theology was *not* "the energetic, optimistic, progressive thing so familiar to American Protestantism. . . . The Dutch pastoral ethic was not one of perfectionism but of penitence, of tribulation . . . of pilgrimage . . . daily life was to be regarded under eternal truth, which meant that believers would never conquer the sin in themselves or in the world." See Bratt, *Dutch Calvinism in Modern America*, 43.

26. Bratt, *Dutch Calvinism in Modern America*, 57, 59.

27. The centrality of Protestantism in the maintenance of Dutch ethnicity can be seen when comparisons are made with Dutch Catholic immigrants, who were quickly absorbed into multiethnic parishes. See Swierenga, *The Dutch in America*, 5.

28. Swierenga, *Faith and Family*, 213.

29. James Bratt, *Gathered at the River: Grand Rapids, Michigan, and Its People of Faith* (Grand Rapids, Mich.: Grand Rapids Area Council for the Humanities/Eerdmans, 1993), 58. See also Gordon Olson, *A Grand Rapids Sampler* (Grand Rapids, Mich.: Grand Rapids Historical Commission, 1992), 95–96.

30. Swierenga, *Faith and Family*, 82.

31. David G. Vanderstal, "Neighborhood Development in Grand Rapids," in Swierenga, *The Dutch in America*, 131.

32. Ibid., 149.

33. Elton Bruins, "Americanization in Reformed Religious Life," in Swierenga, *The Dutch in America*, 184, 186–87.

34. Bratt, *Dutch Calvinism in Modern America*, 42.

35. Muste, "Sketches," 22.

36. Muste, COHC, 37–38. See also Vanderstal, "Neighborhood Development in Grand Rapids." The Mustes moved at least seven times between 1891 and 1912, but all within the same neighborhood. See city directories, GRH.

37. Muste, COHC, 40–41; Vanderstal, "Neighborhood Development in Grand Rapids."

38. Olson, *A Grand Rapids Sampler*, 87; Michael Johnston, "Non-Union Grand Rapids: 150 Years of the Great Lie" (master's thesis, Central Michigan University, July 2005). Thank you to Gordon Olson for bringing Grand Rapids' labor history to my attention.

39. Muste, COHC, 124.

40. Local historian Michael Johnston writes that "the local men who owned the factories ran them as paternalistic fiefdoms while they acted as benevolent barons." See Johnston, "Non-Union Grand Rapids," 22. Workers were also moved from job to job and company to company to discourage unionization. Martin Muste, for example, was hired as a common laborer, teamster, machinist, yardman, and sawyer by at least five different firms during some three decades working in Grand Rapids' furniture industry. See city directories, GRH.

41. Muste, COHC, 122. See also Johnston, "Non-Union Grand Rapids," 14–18. In contrast, the labor and socialist movements in the Netherlands were fairly large in the late nineteenth century. Perhaps the antiunion character of the Dutch American community reflected the rural background of the Dutch who came to the United States.

42. Johnston, "Non-Union Grand Rapids," 64. Muste recalled that the Labor Day parade was "one of the important days of the year. We always went downtown to see the parade" (COHC, 74).

43. Muste, "Sketches," 31–32.

44. Ibid., 30, 40–41.

45. Muste, "Child Labor," in Trades and Labor Council of Grand Rapids, *Labor Day Souvenir Program*, September 6, 1897; copy in GRH, Collection 38, box 1.

46. Muste, "Sketches," 38. See also Muste, COHC, 74–75; and Muste, "Child Labor." Reflecting the paternalistic culture of Grand Rapids, the Quimby widow and Muste's school principal took him downtown to pick out the books.

47. Robert Richardson, *Emerson: The Mind on Fire* (Berkeley: University of California Press, 1995), 226; for Emerson's question, see p. 16. See also Robert Richardson, ed., *Ralph Waldo Emerson: Selected Essays, Lectures, and Poems* (New York: Bantam, 1990).

48. Richardson, *Emerson: The Mind on Fire*, 250–51. See also Robert Richardson, *William James: In the Maelstrom of American Modernism*, reprint ed. (Boston: Mariner Books, 2007); Philip F. Gura, *American Transcendentalism: A History* (New York: Hill and Wang, 2008); Menand, *The Metaphysical Club*; and West, *The American Evasion of Philosophy*.

49. Information about the pastors, members, and activities of the church during this time can be found in the Eric O'Brock scrapbook, Fourth Reformed Church of Grand Rapids, Grand Rapids, Michigan.

50. Muste, "Sketches," 6.

51. Muste, COHC, 91. See also Muste, "Fragment of Autobiography," *Christendom* 4, no. 3 (Summer 1939): 334; and Muste, "Sketches," 17–18, 35–37.

52. Information about Hope's faculty, students, and curriculum can be found in Catalogue of the Officers and Students of Hope College (Holland, Mich., 1898–99), 23; and "Minutes of the Proceedings of the Faculty of the Preparatory Department of Hope College," 1889–1919, 24, Hope Preparatory School Department Collection, box 1. Both in JAH. See also Muste, COHC, 55, 97–114.

53. Muste, COHC, 115. See also John W. Beardslee III to Jo Ann Robinson, November 8, 1971, A. J. Muste vertical file, RCA. A summer job assisting the town coroner further exposed Muste to the scientific method and to liberal thinking more broadly. See Muste, COHC, 129.

54. Muste, COHC, 95.

55. Clifford Putney, *Muscular Christianity: Manhood and Sports in Protestant America, 1880–1920* (Cambridge, Mass.: Harvard University Press, 2003), 5 and 66. See also T. J. Jackson Lears, *Rebirth of a Nation: The Making of Modern America, 1877–1920* (New York: Harper Perennial, 2010); Kristin Hoganson, *Fighting for American Manhood: How Gender Politics Provoked the Spanish and Philippine-American Wars* (New Haven, Conn.: Yale University Press, 2000); and Gail Bederman, *Manliness and Civilization: A Cultural History of Gender and Race in the United States, 1880–1917* (Chicago: University of Chicago Press, 1995).

56. In 1931, when being interviewed for a book about "adventurous Americans," Muste stated that he wants "to be sure any biographer of him puts this down." See Devere Allen, "Labor Must Learn: A. J. Muste," in *Adventurous Americans* (New York: Farrar and Rinehart, 1932).

57. Editorial, *Anchor* 18, no. 12 (February 1905): 11–12. For Muste's membership in the YMCA, see *Hope College Annual*, 1905, JAH, 62.

58. Muste, "John Sobieski," *Anchor* 16, no. 7 (April 1903): 118–21. See also Muste, "The Orator," *Hope College Annual*, 1905, 127–29.

59. Muste, "John Sobieski," 118.

60. See for example, Muste, "Alfred Lord Tennyson, Some of His Claims to Greatness," *Anchor* 18, no. 8 (October 1904): 1–5; and Muste, "Ramblings," *Anchor* 18, no. 14 (April 1905): 1–4. See also *Anchor* 16, no. 6 (March 1903): 107–8; "Mr. Muste," *Anchor* 16, no. 7 (April 1903): 138; and "Antigone," *Hope College Annual*, 1905, 155.

61. Fairplains Cemetery, Grand Rapids, Michigan, where Martin Jr. is buried, has a record indicating that he was born on August 14, 1902, and died from bronchitis on January 12, 1907. The only reference I have found by Muste regarding the death of his youngest brother was in a sermon he preached entitled "The Hope of Immortality" (Union Theological Seminary pamphlet, 1912) at the Fort Washington Reformed Church in New York City in 1912: "I had a little

brother who fell on sleep before he was five years old; but he had some unnatural intelligence and spiritual penetration that seems sometimes to be given to those who leave while they are yet young, and in his last hours he seemed to be reaching out dimly, yet almost consciously for a better land." Quote is on page 9.

62. Muste, COHC, 119. Muste's younger brothers and sisters also took pride in his accomplishments, reflecting the gender hierarchy that allowed him to attend college in the first place. The Grand Rapids city directory indicates that, while Muste was at Hope, his sisters lived at home and worked as clerks to help support the family. His younger brother Cornelius also lived at home, working variously as an apprentice, helper, and bench hand in a furniture factory. See city directories from 1900, 1903, 1905, 1906, 1908, 1910, 1911, 1912, 1917, and 1919, GRH. See also Muste, COHC, 198.

63. This characterization of Muste as modest is ubiquitous in both manuscript records and oral histories. For his relationship with his family, see Marian Johnson (Muste's niece by marriage), interview with author, October 17, 2005, Grand Rapids, Michigan; Doris Emelander and Henry Emelander (Muste's niece and her husband), interview with author, October 17, 2005, Grand Rapids, Michigan; Edwin E. Henry Jr. (Muste's nephew by marriage), interview with author, October 18, 2005, by phone; and Chuck Johnson Muste, interview by author, October 14, 2005, by phone.

64. A conviction as to Hope's limitations had been fostered by a summer friendship with Frank Bryant, the son of one of his family's neighbors in Grand Rapids who was an associate professor of English literature at the University of Kansas. Impressed by the younger man's victory in the state oratorical contest, Bryant persuaded Muste that Kansas would offer him far more opportunities than a denominational college. It was only the intervention of Hope's president, who appealed to his "duty as a Dutchman," that kept Muste from transferring. See Muste, COHC, 117–18.

65. *Anchor* 17, no. 4 (April 1904): 330.

66. Muste, "The Problem of Discontent."

67. See Olson, *A Grand Rapids Sampler*, 117–33. It is unclear if Martin Muste participated in the strike, though it's doubtful; Dutch immigrants tended to be wary of labor organization and he does not appear to have been blacklisted, which happened to many of the strike's participants.

Chapter 2. Spirituality and Modernity

Epigraph: Muste, "Shall This Dream Come True?" *World Tomorrow* 1, no. 8 (August 1918): 197–99.

1. Muste, COHC, 155–56.

2. See, for example, Niebuhr, *Moral Man and Immoral Society*; and Niebuhr, *The Children of Light and the Children of Darkness*. For examples of historians who have tended to agree with Niebuhr's characterization of Protestant liberals, albeit with important modifications, see Christopher Lasch, *The True and Only Heaven: Progress and Its Critics* (New York: W. W. Norton, 1991); Meyer, *Protestant Search for Political Realism*; and Fox, *Reinhold Niebuhr*. For links between liberal religion and the "culture of narcissism," see, for example, Lasch, *The Culture of Narcissism*; and Bellah, *Habits of the Heart*.

3. Schmidt, *Restless Souls*, xii and 7, 58.

4. See Capozzola, *Uncle Sam Wants You.*

5. Muste, COHC, 197, 137.

6. Ibid., 143. See also John Muste to Jo Ann Robinson, March 12 [1979], AJMP-LA, box 2. The heady climate did not indicate a crisis in his Calvinist faith. After all, as he explained in his oral history, "good Calvinism" and intellectual curiosity went hand in hand. See Muste, COHC, 141–42.

7. Muste, COHC, 153.

8. As Muste put it, New Brunswick was "lukewarm, not a strong orthodox or fundamentalist institution but not something different and inspiring either . . . that was at the bottom of my disappointment with it, my boredom part of the time." See ibid., 166.

9. Howard G. Hageman, *Two Centuries Plus: The Story of New Brunswick Seminary* (Grand Rapids, Mich.: Eerdmans, 1984), 104–10, 126–30; and Elton Bruins, "The New Brunswick Theological Seminary, 1884–1959" (Ph.D. diss., New York University, 1962). See also the course catalog *Theological Seminary of the Reformed Church in America, 1906–1907* (New Brunswick, N.J.: Theological Seminary, 1906), 4, copy in RCA. For Muste's recollections of New Brunswick, see Muste, COHC, 150–52. Muste would reestablish a relationship with the seminary in the 1940s, when he was hired on a part-time basis to teach courses on Christianity and society. His lectures can be found in AJMP, reel 3.

10. *Theological Seminary of the Reformed Church in America, 1906–1907*, 34; Henry S. Cobb to Central Congregational Church, reprinted in "Report of the Standing Committee to the Church on a New Pastor," November 20, 1914, Newton, Massachusetts, Central Congregational Church Records, CL, box 19.

11. Muste, COHC, 155–62.

12. Ibid., 155–56, 160–62.

13. Ibid., 163.

14. *Theological Seminary of the Reformed Church in America, 1906–1907*, 33. See also Muste, COHC, 158.

15. Board of Trustees, Columbia University, quoted in Westbrook, *John Dewey and American Democracy*, 118. See also Kenneth Jackson, *The Encyclopedia of New York City* (New Haven, Conn.: Yale University Press, 1995), 259.

16. Muste, COHC, 169. See also Westbrook, *John Dewey*, 116–20.

17. Muste, COHC, 170; Muste, "Sketches", 43.

18. Hollinger, *In the American Province*, 12.

19. William James, *The Varieties of Religious Experience: A Study in Human Nature* (New York: Longmans, Green, 1911), 55, 6.

20. James, *Varieties of Religious Experience*, 31.

21. Hollinger, *In the American Province*, 8. See also Richardson, *William James*.

22. Muste, COHC, 171.

23. Ibid., 413.

24. Ibid., 176–78.

25. For a discussion of Progressive Era reformers and their views of the city, see Paul Boyer, *Urban Masses and Moral Order in America, 1820–1920* (Cambridge, Mass.: Harvard University Press, 1978); and Robert H. Wiebe, *The Search for Order, 1877–1920* (New York: Hill and Wang, 1966). See also Hollinger, *In the American Province*, 56–73; Rossinow, *Visions of Progress*, 52–56; and Stansell, *American Moderns*, 11–72

26. Muste, COHC, 190

27. See ibid., 191; *Minutes of the Classis of New York*, vol. 14, p. 134, RCA; and Russell Gasero, *Historical Directory of the Reformed Church in America, 1628–1992*, Historical Series of the Reformed Church in America 23 (Grand Rapids, Mich.: Wm. B. Eerdmans, 1992).

28. Muste, COHC, 200. In 1919–20, Raymond Fosdick would serve as undersecretary-general for the League of Nations. For the culture of Protestantism in New York City during this period, see Matthew Bowman, "The Urban Pulpit: Evangelicals and the City in New York, 1880–1930" (Ph.D. diss., Georgetown University, 2011).

29. Ibid., 199, 192–97. Muste recalled the date as June 27, but the records of the classis indicate that it was on June 25. See *Minutes of the Classis of New York*, vol. 13, pp. 406–8, RCA.

30. The minutes of the New York Classis contain frequent references to the "steady activity and growth" and "forward movement" at Fort Washington, and, at least as early as the winter of 1914, Muste had been given an assistant minister to help him with his growing and active congregation. See *Minutes of the Classis of New York*, vol. 14, pp. 56–134; "Fort Washington Reformed Church," *Collegiate Yearbook* (1910), 113–15; and Muste, COHC, 202–10. For Muste's pastoral style, see Muste, COHC, 145–47; John Browaler Voorhey to Wallace C. Boyden, October 22, 1914, and Rev. J. Nichols to Wallace C. Boyden, October 22, 1914, both in Newton, Mass., Central Congregational Church Records, CL, box 19; and Central Congregational Church of Newton, Newtonville, Mass., *A Centennial History, 1868–1968*, 17. My characterization of Muste's leadership style comes from numerous sources and is further explored throughout this book. See, for example, Allen, "Labor Must Learn: A. J. Muste," in *Adventurous Americans*, 99–117; Len De Caux, *Labor Radical: From the Wobblies to the CIO* (Boston: Beacon Press, 1970), 94–100; James Farmer, *Lay Bare the Heart: An Autobiography of the Civil Rights Movement* (New York: Arbor House, 1985), 85–86; Robinson, *Abraham Went Out*, esp. 186, 200–201; and my interviews with Marian Johnson (Muste's niece-in-law), October 17, 2005; Doris Emelander (Muste's niece), October 17, 2005; Beverly Sterner, by phone, August 16, 2006, and in Flagstaff, Arizona, December 2006; and David McReynolds June 6, 2006.

31. See Muste, COHC, 145–47, 207–8; and Muste sermon, "The Hope of Immortality."

32. Registrar's Log Book, 1906–10, vol. C, Union Theological Seminary Records, Burke Archives. Muste's course grades were consistently among the highest. See also Muste, COHC, 226–40.

33. Robert Handy, *A History of Union Theological Seminary in New York* (New York: Columbia University Press, 1987), 112.

34. Muste, COHC, 235.

35. See, for example, McGiffert, *The Apostles' Creed: Its Origin, Its Purpose, and Its Historical Interpretation* (New York: Charles Scribner's Sons, 1902); McGiffert, *The Rise of Modern Religious Ideas* (New York: Macmillan, 1915); and McGiffert, *The God of the Early Christians* (New York: Charles Scribner's Sons, 1924).

36. George William Knox, *The Gospel of Jesus, the Son of Man: An Introduction for the Modern Man* (Boston: Pilgrim Press, 1909), 16. There is a vast literature on the Social Gospel. Important classics in this field are Henry May, *Protestant Churches and Industrial America* (New York: Harper, 1949); and William Hutchison, *The Modernist Impulse in American Protestantism* (New York: Oxford University Press, 1976).

37. Dave Burns's dissertation reminds us of the centrality of Jesus Christ in progressive thought and shows us that the "radical Christ" was constructed by workers, socialists, as well as Social Gospel ministers. See Burns, "The Radical Rites of Christ: Jesus and the Social Revolutions of the Progressive Era" (Ph.D. diss, Northern Illinois University, 2009).

38. Muste, lecture notes for "The Church and Social Action," AJMP, reel 3. See also Muste, COHC, 217, 243–46.

39. Muste, COHC, 210–12. For an illuminating discussion of these clubs, see Rossinow, *Visions of Progress*, 46–47.

40. Muste, COHC, 212.

41. Ibid., 246.

42. Ibid., 218. See also "Unable to Hold Church Doctrine, Pastor Muste Resigns His Pulpit," clipping from the *New York Times* [ca. fall 1914], RCA, A. J. Muste vertical file. See also Muste, "Fragment of Autobiography," 334–35.

43. "Pastor Yields to 'Heavenly Vision'; Goes to New Field," clipping from the *New York Herald* [ca. fall 1914], in Newton, Mass., Central Congregational Church Records, CL, box 19. See also Robinson, *Abraham Went Out*, 18. Nancy Baker, Muste's eldest daughter, recalled that, before she was born, her mother had "at least two miscarriages and perhaps one was at the time they were leaving Ft. Washington." See Nancy Baker to Jo Ann Robinson, February 8, 1979, AJMP-LA, box 2.

44. "Unable to Hold Church Doctrine, Pastor Muste Resigns His Pulpit"; Muste, "Fragment of Autobiography"; and Muste, COHC, 219.

45. Muste, COHC, 255.

46. *Minutes of the Classis of New York*, vol. 14, pp. 159–61, RCA.

47. John Browaler Voorhey to Wallace C. Boyden, October 22, 1914.

48. "Pastor Yields to 'Heavenly Vision.'"

49. Rev. J. Nichols to Wallace C. Boyden, October 22, 1914. See also "Fort Washington Reformed Church," *Collegiate Yearbook* (1915), 130–32.

50. My interviews with Marian Johnson, October 17, 2005; Doris Emelander, October 17, 2005; and Edwin E. Henry Jr. (Cornelius's son-in-law), October 18, 2005. See also letters from Muste's nephew Arthur C. Johnson to Jo Ann Robinson, February 3, 1970, and July 27, 1970, AJMP-LA, box 2. Information on Cornelius Muste's career obtained from Gasero, *Historical Directory of the Reformed Church in America*; and from my interview with Donald Bruggink, October 20, 2005, Holland, Michigan.

51. Leon Fink, *Progressive Intellectuals and the Dilemmas of Democratic Commitment* (Cambridge, Mass.: Harvard University Press, 1997), 16–17. See also Robert M. Crunden, *Ministers of Reform: The Progressives' Achievement in American Civilization, 1889–1920* (Urbana and Chicago: University of Illinois Press).

52. Schmidt, *Restless Souls*, 9.

53. William James, quoted in ibid., 56.

54. John Haynes Holmes, quoted in Kosek, *Acts of Conscience*, 65. Kosek also provides this revealing quote by Protestant reformer Edmund Chaffee, with whom Muste was quite close: "No social system . . . can dispense with the ordinary virtues of honesty, fair-dealing, persistent work and good will. They are not as frequently said, 'bourgeois virtues.'"

55. Muste, quoted in Hentoff, *Peace Agitator*, 31. See also Muste to Rev. J. E. Everett, December 29, 1931, in which he explained that, while he personally abstained, he had opposed Prohibition "and thought it a great mistake to put it over. . . . The passage of the prohibition amendment certainly was part of a general tendency on the part of government to invade the rights of individuals." It also disregarded the fact that "drink" was an expression of local and ethnic "sentiment." The best way to reduce alcohol consumption was through "good jobs." See

BLCC, box 28, folder 14. For Muste and baseball, see Muste, "Sketches," 43. In a March 12 [1979] letter to Jo Ann Robinson, John Muste stressed that "in the area of sexual morality, my family was thoroughly conventional and rigidly respectable." See AJMP-LA, box 2.

56. Muste, COHC, 225; A. C. Johnson to Jo Ann Robinson, July 27, 1970, AJMP-LA, box 2.

57. Muste, quoted in Robinson, *Abraham Went Out*, 18.

58. One of the most famous was Henry Ward Beecher, who declared that the central doctrines of the Westminster Confession were "extraordinary specimens of *spiritual barbarism*." Other leaders in the movement included ministers in the Boston area whom Muste would count soon among his inner circle. Beecher, quoted in John Von Rohr, *The Shaping of American Congregationalism, 1620–1957* (Cleveland: Pilgrim Press, 1992), 349.

59. Muste, COHC, 261. For information on Newtonville's Central Congregational Church, as well as the town itself, see *The Newton Directory*, no. 25 (Worcester, Mass.: Drew Allis, 1917), Newton History Museum; Henry K. Rowe, *Tercentenary History of Newton, 1630–1830* ([Newton, Mass.]: City of Newton, 1930), 391; Thelma Fleishman, *Newton* (Charleston, S.C.: Arcadia,1999); and Annual Report of the Standing Committee of Central Church, January 14, 1916, Newton, Mass., Central Congregational Church Records, CL, box 4.

60. Muste, COHC, 262. For information on Sperry and his circle's conviction that, as Sperry put it around 1914, "we might be on the edge of some general revival of religion," see William L. Fox, *Willard L. Sperry: The Quandaries of a Liberal Protestant Mind, 1914–1939* (New York: Peter Lang, 1991), xi.

61. Muste, "Sketches," 45.

62. Muste, COHC, 262.

63. Muste to Mrs. Van Drezer on September 22, 1917, JAH, Muste Collection, box 1.

64. Central Congregational Church of Newton, Newtonville, Mass., *A Centennial History*, 17.

65. Muste, "Sketches," 45.

66. Robinson, *Abraham Went Out*, 18.

67. Muste, COHC, 264.

68. Muste, "Of What Shall We Be Afraid," in Muste, *Tracts for the Times* (Boston: George H. Ellis, 1915), 10. In another sermon delivered that same year, "Peace—At What Price?" he argued that war with Germany would not lead to peace, but would draw the United States further into the "struggle for commercial supremacy, for trade, markets, colonies, profits," which had given rise to the war in the first place. The only real, lasting solution, he argued, was again to imitate Jesus through a great act of renunciation and repentance such as unilateral disarmament, an argument he would repeat, with more sophistication, during the Cold War. See Muste, "Peace—At What Price?" in Muste, *Tracts for the Times*, 19.

69. See also Muste, "Christianity: The Only Hope of the World" (1918), copy in ACP, box 2.

70. Muste, "Peace—At What Price?" 27.

71. Muste, "Sketches," 45.

72. Ibid.

73. Muste, COHC, 284.

74. See, for example, Rufus M. Jones, *Studies in Mystical Religion* (1909; reprint, London: Macmillan, 1923).

75. Muste, COHC, 272 and 317. He was also attending meetings of the Socialist Party, which, of course, was antiwar. See Allen, "Labor Must Learn: A. J. Muste," *Adventurous Americans*, 105.

76. "Minutes of the Garden City Conference on the Fellowship of Reconciliation," Garden City, Long Island, November 11–12, 1915, FOR, box 1, folder 3.

77. Kosek, *Acts of Conscience*, 27.

78. Quote is from Kosek, *Acts of Conscience*, 27.

79. John Dewey, quoted in McGerr, *A Fierce Discontent*, 282. See also Westbrook, *John Dewey and American Democracy*, 195–227.

80. William Adams Brown quoted in Kosek, *Acts of Conscience*, 32. For "fit to fight" quote, see Charles DeBenedetti, *The Peace Reform in American History* (Bloomington: Indiana University Press, 1984), 100. For the Protestant churches and World War I, see John F. Peper Jr., *The American Churches in World War I* (Athens: Ohio University Press, 1985).

81. See McGerr, *A Fierce Discontent*; DeBenedetti, *Peace Reform in American History*; Thomas J. Knock, *To End All Wars: Woodrow Wilson and the Quest for a New World Order* (New York: Oxford University Press, 1992); and McCartin, *Labor's Great War*.

82. Bourne, "Twilight of Idols" (1917), in Hollinger and Capper, *American Intellectual Tradition*, 2:183.

83. For example, John Nevin Sayre, an Episcopal priest in Suffern, New York, found that his pacifist convictions prevented him from becoming a military chaplain despite his personal connections to the president (his brother, Francis Sayre, was married to President Wilson's daughter). He, along with other dissenting clergy, made his way into the FOR. See Kosek, *Acts of Conscience*, 35. On the repressive laws passed by state governments, see Eric Foner, *The Story of American Freedom* (New York: W. W. Norton, 1998), 177–78. See also Capozzola, *Uncle Same Wants You*; and the classic account by H. C. Peterson and Gilbert Fite, *Opponents of War, 1917–1918* (Madison: University of Wisconsin Press, 1957).

84. Kosek, *Acts of Conscience*, 17; Capozzola, *Uncle Sam Wants You*, 81.

85. DeBenedetti, *Peace Reform in American History*, 103. See also Capozzola, *Uncle Sam Wants You*; Peterson and Fite, *Opponents of War*; Chatfield, *For Peace and Justice*; and C. Roland Marchand, *The American Peace Movement and Social Reform* (Princeton, N.J.: Princeton University Press, 1972).

86. Holmes, quoted in Foner, *The Story of American Freedom*, 183. For the role of religion in Muste's opposition to the war, see his "Sketches," 46.

87. Capozzola, *Uncle Sam Wants You*, 144–45, 14. See also Foner, *The Story of American Freedom*; Walker, *In Defense of American Liberties*; Robert C. Conttrell, *Roger Nash Baldwin and the American Civil Liberties Union* (New York: Columbia University Press, 2000); and David M. Rabban, *Free Speech in the Forgotten Years* (New York: Cambridge University Press, 1997).

88. Rossinow, *Visions of Progress*, 62–63.

89. Not coincidentally, *The Liberator*, the successor magazine to Max Eastman's *The Masses*, was edited upstairs from the New York headquarters of the ACLU. For a discussion of the modernist politics of personal liberation, see McGerr, *A Fierce Discontent*, 221–78; and Stansell, *American Moderns*.

90. There was some evidence of growing estrangement in early 1917. A few members had withdrawn from the congregation after he joined the FOR and, in late spring, a nearby minister refused to hold a joint service with Muste after learning that he had attended an anti-conscription demonstration in Washington, D.C. See Muste, "Fragment of Autobiography," 335; and Muste, COHC, 317.

91. Central Congregational Church of Newton, Newtonville, Mass., *A Centennial History*, 17; Central Congregational Church calendar for the week of November 11, 1917, Newton History Museum.

92. Muste, COHC, 306–8, 316–17; Muste, "Sketches," 50–52. See also Robinson, *Abraham Went Out*, 21–23.

93. Robinson, *Abraham Went Out*, 22.

94. Muste sermon, Christmas Day, 1917, and Muste, "The Present Crisis: The Position of the Conscientious Objector to War," February 18, 1917, both in Newton, Mass., Central Congregational Church Records, CL, box 19.

95. Muste, "Do Your Bit for Belgium," *Congregationalist*, December 14, 1916, 825–26. See also Robinson, *Abraham Went Out*, 21–22.

96. Muste, "Sketches," 48. See also Muste, COHC, 246–47.

97. See Salvatore, *Citizen and Socialist*; and James Weinstein, *The Decline of Socialism in America, 1912–1925*, 2nd ed. (New Brunswick, N.J.: Rutgers University Press, 1986).

98. See Muste, COHC, 269–70, 289; and Jones, *Studies in Mystical Religion*, xviii.

99. On the history and theology of the Society of Friends, see Margery Post Abbott, Mary Ellen Chijioke, Pink Dandelion, and John William Oliver Jr., eds., *Historical Dictionary of the Friends (Quakers)*, 2nd ed. (Lanham, Md.: Scarecrow Press, 2011); Geoffrey Durham, *The Spirit of the Quakers* (New Haven, Conn.: Yale University Press, 2010); and Susan Sachs Goldman, *Friends in Deed: The Story of Quaker Social Reform in America* (Washington, D.C.: Highmark Press, 2012).

100. Muste, "Sketches," 54; Muste, COHC, 321.

101. Fraser, *Labor Will Rule*, 148–49. On the labor insurgencies of 1919, see McCartin, *Labor's Great War*; David Brody, *Steelworkers in America: The Nonunion Era* (New York: Harper Torchbooks, 1969); and Frank, *Purchasing Power*. For an illuminating discussion of the emergence of anticolonial nationalism during World War I, see Erez Manela, *The Wilsonian Moment: Self-Determination and the International Origins of Anticolonial Nationalism* (New York: Oxford University Press, 2007).

102. Muste, "Sketches," 85, 57. See also Muste, "Christianity: The Only Hope of the World."

103. Elizabeth Glendower Evans, unpublished memoir (1936), EGEP, reel 1.

104. Muste, "Sketches," 85.

105. Evans, "Interesting People I Have Known: Three Young Crusaders," magazine title obscured, August 1929, copy in EGEP, reel 11. See also Muste, "Shall This Dream Come True?" 197–98, which described a religious vision he had in which "the multitudes" recognized the "evils" of the world and committed to a world "in which righteousness should reign supreme. They saw that the way of love was the sure and only way to bring good to pass on earth, and that ever the Son of Man if lifted up would draw all to himself."

106. Evans, "Interesting People I Have Known."

107. Muste, COHC, 310–12. For Newton's shaded streets and many playgrounds, see Rowe, *Tercentenary History of Newton*, 349. For Anne Muste's involvement in the Women's Association, see CLA, box 23.

108. Muste, "Suggestions for a Proposed New Preaching Order to Disseminate Fellowship of Reconciliation Principles," December 31, 1918, FOR, box 1, folder 8.

109. Muste, "Sketches," 91. See also Muste, "Surfeit and Famine," *World Tomorrow* (1919), in which he argued that a Christian must lead a "disciplined and self-denying life" to identify with the poor and oppressed. At the same time that he recognized the need for an equal distribution of wealth, however, he warned against the "grave danger in cultivating in men an obsession with the economic problem, a concentration of attention on material things.' "

Chapter 3. Pragmatism and "Transcendent Vision"

This chapter title borrows from Lichtenstein's article in *New Labor Forum*, "Falling in Love Again?" in which he argues that there is a need for both pragmatism and transcendent ideals to revivify the labor movement.

Epigraph: Muste to Scott Nearing, quoted in Bloom, "Brookwood Labor College," 64.

1. Muste, "Sketches," 55; Muste, COHC, 363–67.

2. Anthony Capraro, "Thus Spake Labor," *New Textile Worker*, April 12, 1919, 1.

3. Sidney Hillman, quoted in Fraser, *Labor Will Rule*, 144.

4. Allen, "Labor Must Learn: A. J. Muste," in *Adventurous Americans*, 109.

5. As historian James Livingston explains, pragmatists hoped to create a new, "post-artisanal moral universe," augmenting "the sources and meanings of subjectivity by multiplying the kinds of identifications available to individuals, and by putting the capacities of collective entities, corporate bodies, at the disposal of individuals." See Livingston, "War and the Intellectuals," 438. See also Livingston, *Pragmatism and the Political Economy of Cultural Revolution*; Menand, *The Metaphysical Club*; Westbrook, *John Dewey and American Democracy*; and James T. Kloppenberg, *Uncertain Victory: Social Democracy in European and American Thought* (New York: Oxford University Press, 1986).

6. For the ideology of the ACW, see Fraser, *Labor Will Rule*. For the influence of the ACW on Muste's thinking about trade unionism, see Muste, COHC, 420–23.

7. Muste book review, " 'Progressive' Education," *Labor Age* 21, no. 7 (July 1932): 27–28.

8. For the continued vibrancy of this "left-liberal tradition," see Rossinow, *Visions of Progress*, 102–3 and Eugene Tobin, *Organize or Perish: America's Independent Progressives* (Westport, Conn.: Praeger, 1986).

9. Borg, Buttigieg, and Mayo, *Gramsci and Education*, 4–5; Gramsci, *Selections from the Prison Notebooks*. See also Altenbaugh, *Education for Struggle*, especially his introduction and 271 n. 1; and Muste, "Some Notes on Workers' Education," *New International* 2, no. 7 (December 1935): 225–26.

10. David Saposs, "The Need for a Labor Culture," *Labor Age* 18, no. 11 (November 1929): 23.

11. For the centrality of the CIO in the culture and politics of the Depression decade, see Denning, *The Cultural Front*; and Cohen, *Making a New Deal*.

12. Bruce Watson, *Bread and Roses: Mills, Migrants, and the Struggle for the American Dream* (New York: Viking, 2005); David Goldberg, *A Tale of Three Cities: Labor Organization and Protest in Passaic, Paterson, and Lawrence, 1916–1921* (New Brunswick, N.J.: Rutgers University Press, 1989).

13. Theodore Draper, quoted in Goldberg, *A Tale of Three Cities*, 91. On the history of the IWW, see Melvyn Dubofsky, *We Shall Be All: A History of the Industrial Workers of the World* (New York: Quadrangle, 1969).

14. Flynn, quoted in Watson, *Bread and Roses*, 244. Note that there were 16,000 members of the union at the end of the strike in January 1913, but only 700 by summer 1913.

15. See Muste, COHC, 420–21; David Saposs, *Left Wing Unionism: A Study of Radical Policies and Tactics* (New York: International Publishers, 1926), chap. 1; and David Montgomery, *Workers' Control in America: Studies in the History of Work, Technology, and Labor Struggles* (1981, reprint, New York: Cambridge University Press), 105–6.

16. Even with these gains, the wages of textile workers remained among the lowest of all industrial workers. See Goldberg, *A Tale of Three Cities*, 6–8, 95–99.

17. Ibid., 99–100. See also Muste, "The Truth About Lawrence," *Forward Supplement* 3 (February 1919). Copy in ACP, box 8.

18. Muste, "The Truth About Lawrence"; Muste, "Sketches," 57–59; and Muste, COHC, 363.

19. Muste, COHC, 365. See also Goldberg, *A Tale of Three Cities*, 101–3.

20. Muste, "The Truth About Lawrence"; Muste, COHC, 363–66.

21. Muste, quoted in Goldberg, *A Tale of Three Cities*, 105. See also Rudolph J. Vecoli, "Anthony Capraro and the Lawrence Strike of 1919," in George E. Pozzetta, ed., *Pane e Laboro: The Italian American Working Class* (Toronto: Multicultural History Society of Ontario, 1980), 3–28; Muste, COHC, 360–66; and Muste, "The Truth About Lawrence." Harold Rotzel became chairman of the general relief committee and Cedric Long served as a member of the general strike committee where he was in charge of youth activities and the strikers' guard, which kept order on the picket lines and watched for cases of police misconduct.

22. Goldberg, *A Tale of Three Cities*, 210.

23. Muste, quoted in George Soule, *The Intellectual and the Labor Movement* (New York: League for Industrial Democracy, 1923); 21; Muste, "Contradictions the Rebel Faces," *World Tomorrow* 7, no. 5 (May 1924): 141–44. See also Allen, "Labor Must Learn: A. J. Muste," in *Adventurous Americans*, 109.

24. Muste, "Sketches," 61.

25. Muste, "The Truth About Lawrence."

26. "FOR: A Constructive Policy" (ca. 1915), FOR, box 1, folder 3.

27. Eugenie A. Rettinger to Friends, September 15, 1920, FOR, box 5, folder 1. See also Henry Cadbury, "The Strike: An Unethical Means of Coercion," *World Tomorrow* 3, no. 5 (May 1920): 131–32. Even pacifists who supported strikes were fond of lecturing workers on the futility of violence. See, for example, Scott Nearing's pamphlet *Violence or Solidarity; or, Will Guns Settle It?* (New York: People's Print, 1919).

28. Muste, "Labor's Condition and Aims," *New Textile Worker*, August 16, 1919, 4. See also Muste editorial, *New Textile Worker* September 15, 1919, 5; Muste, COHC, 368; and Norman Thomas, "The Strike: A Justifiable Form of Passive Resistance," *World Tomorrow* 3, no. 5 (May 1920): 133–34, in which he argues that the status quo of capitalism was based on violence and coercion.

29. Muste, COHC, 367–70; Muste, "Sketches," 62.

30. Muste, COHC, 370–75; Muste, "Sketches," 62–63; "Muste and Long on Trial in District Court," *Lawrence Daily Eagle*, March 13, 1919, copy in ACP, box 8.

31. Muste, "Muste, COHC," 475, 370–75; Muste, "Sketches," 62–63; and "Muste and Long on Trial in District Court."

32. Muste, "Sketches," 71.

33. Muste, COHC, 376–88; quote is on p. 387.

34. Goldberg, *A Tale of Three Cities*, 105; Muste, COHC, 364. For Elizabeth Glendower Evans's recollections of the strike, see Evans, "People I Have Known," EGEP, reel 11.

35. See Muste to George Rower Jr., March 19, 1919, appealing for the ACW to make good on its promise of more funds ("promise of money etc. won't do anymore, we must have at least $8000 in cold cash here on Friday or ——!") and pointing out that there "is a great opening for

the Amalgamated in Lawrence." See also "Dear Brothers" from Muste, Rubenstein, Artoni, et al. (ca. April 1919). Both in ACTW, box 218, folder 4. See also Muste, COHC, 401; and Fraser, *Labor Will Rule*, 158.

36. See, for example, Minutes of the First Convention of the Amalgamated Textile Workers of America, April 12–13, 1919, ACP, box 8. See also Muste, COHC, 420–21; Fraser, *Labor Will Rule*; and Montgomery, *Workers' Control in America*, 105–6.

37. Fraser, *Labor Will Rule*, 115, and 170–79.

38. The convention also affirmed May Day as International Labor Day, extended greetings to the newly created Soviet Union, and protested the imprisonment of Socialist Party leader Eugene V. Debs and IWW leader William D. Haywood. See Minutes of the First Convention of the Amalgamated Textile Workers of America, April 12–13, 1919.

39. Muste editorial, *New Textile Worker*, June 7, 1919, 2. See also Muste, "A New Day for Textile Workers," *New Textile Worker*, April 23, 1919, 1; and Muste "Factors of Success," *New Textile Worker*, April 12, 1919, 4.

40. See Muste, "The Truth About Lawrence."

41. Ibid. See also Anthony Capraro, "Lawrence Teaches Me American Democracy," *New Textile Worker*, May 24, 1919, 3–4. For Carlo Tresca and his charismatic personality, see Nunzio Pernicone, *Carlo Tresca: Portrait of a Rebel* (Oakland, Calif.: AK Press, 2010).

42. Muste, "Lawrence Strike Ended After Mills Grant 15 Percent Wage Increase," *New Textile Worker*, May 24, 1919, 1. See also Muste, COHC, 402–5; and Muste, "Sketches," 75–77.

43. As Steven Fraser has observed of the cultural perspective of Hillman's clothing workers, "Anarcho-syndicalist in intent, it was localist in perspective, decentralized, averse to long-term contractual obligations, accustomed to semi-spontaneous action in a firm-specific context, rarely conscious of the industry as a whole, and sometimes infected with the craft-conscious parochialism it criticized in the AFL. It was demonstrably militant, but its militancy was in large measure conservative. . . . In the nineteenth century, unionism often grew up on the basis of such defensive insularity. The 'new unionism,' however, was predicated on the process of its disintegration and reabsorption into a new and characterological structure of behavior." See Fraser, *Labor Will Rule*, 135.

44. Muste editorial, "The Present Task," *New Textile Worker*, May 24, 1919, 2.

45. Muste, *The Kind of Unionism That Will Not Organize the Basic Industries; The Kind of Unionism That Will Organize the Basic Industries; The Organization of the Textile Industry* (Katonah, N.Y., 1927), 31, 14. This pamphlet reprinted a series of articles Muste had published earlier on the nature of the textile industry and the challenges it presented to unionism—e.g., "The Kind of Unionism That Will Not Organize the Basic Industries," *Labor Age* (April 1927); "The Kind of Unionism That Will Organize the Basic Industries," *Labor Age* (May 1927); and "The Organization of the Textile Industry," *Textile Worker* (August 1926).

46. In Paterson, for example, the local hosted dances and public lectures, including one on the history and art of textiles, and held classes on the English language, citizenship, economics, duties of shop committees, debating, and public speaking, and organized a dramatic club to perform plays and organize entertainment. See "Start Work of Education," *New Textile Worker*, October 25, 1919, 1–2. See also Cedric Long, "Local Lawrence Building Up Its Strength," *New Textile Worker*, September 27, 1919, 2; and "Lawrence Local of ATW Celebrate World Labor July 4," *New Textile Worker*, July 12, 1919, 2.

47. Harold Rotzel, "What Lawrence Needs," *New Textile Worker* 1, no. 1 (April 12, 1919): 3 (my emphasis).

48. "Perverted Conceptions of Americanization," *New Textile Worker*, February 28, 1920, 8; Bert Emsley, "What the Alien Knows," *New Textile Worker*, August 30, 1919, 4. See also Stephen S. Wise speech ("Americanization is a matter of standards, not standardization," he asserted), reprinted in *New Textile Worker*, November 18, 1919, 7. The union also appropriated certain historical figures, like Abraham Lincoln, suggesting that they represented the ideals of the radical labor movement. See "Abraham Lincoln—Radical," *New Textile Worker* 2, no. 3 (January 31, 1920): 5–7.

49. "Textile Workers of Italy Soon to Convene," *New Textile Worker*, March 27, 1920, 6.

50. "Strikers Answer Bosses' Cunning," *New Textile Worker*, November 22, 1919, 2; "Quotes from Utica Press" by Paul Blanshard, PBP, box 8, folder 4. See also "Paterson Office of ATW Union Raided by Police," *New Textile Worker*, July 12, 1919, 1; "Local Lawrence Protests Arrests," *New Textile Worker*, January 17, 1920, 1; "Federal Investigator Spied Upon by Agents of Passaic Wool Bosses," *New Textile Worker*, February 28, 1920, 1; "Arrest of ATW Organizer to Break Allentown Strike Movement," *New Textile Worker*, March 13, 1920, 1; "Passaic Kills Free Speech," *New Textile Worker*, April 10, 1920, 1. See also *Nation* 109, no. 2821 (July 26, 1919): 1–2; and no. 2822 (August 2, 1919): 1, which discusses the attacks on the civil liberties of union organizers in Paterson, quoting the city's chief of police: "That's the way we do things in Paterson. We don't need no warrant. We think you fellows are undesirable citizens and, boy, we can close up your place and take your things away from you to examine any time we want." At one point, Muste was arrested for speaking at a strike meeting in Passaic. See Muste, COHC, 417–20. On Americanization programs and the new immigrants, see Gary Gerstle, *Working-Class Americanism: The Politics of Labor in a Textile City, 1914–1960*, 2nd ed. (Princeton, N.J.: Princeton University Press, 2001); and John Higham, *Strangers in the Land: Patterns of American Nativism, 1860–1925*, 3rd ed. (New Brunswick, N.J.: Rutgers University Press, 2002).

51. "An Injunction Against the Capitalist Class of Utica," issued by Paul Blanshard from the Oneida County Jail at Utica, PBP, box 8, folder no. 4.

52. "Fight for Free Speech in Passaic," *New Textile Worker*, April 10, 1920, 2.

53. Muste, "Charity?" *New Textile Worker*, June 21, 1919, 2; Cedric Long, "Propaganda in Lawrence," *New Textile Worker*, November 22, 1919, 2.

54. The "agreement" between silk companies in New York City and Long Island and their respective unions, which were affiliated with the ATWA, was dated April 19, 1920, and can be found in the ATWA vertical file at the Tamiment Library, New York University. Muste called this the ATWA's biggest achievement. See Muste, COHC, 424.

55. Muste, "One Year Old," *New Textile Worker*, April 10, 1920, 1, 4. He also pursued affiliation with the American Federation of Full-Fashioned Hosiery Workers (AFFFHW), which did, ultimately, affiliate with the ATWA. See "Hosiery Union Taking a Vote on Affiliation," *New Textile Worker*, June 19, 1920, 1. On his efforts to secure an alliance with independent textile unions, see "Minutes of an Informal and Confidential Conference of Independent Textile Unions," New York City, May 21–22, 1921, vertical subject file, Labor-US-Unions-Textile, LC.

56. Muste, "They Cannot Stop Us!" *New Textile Worker*, May 8, 1920, 3. See also "No Silk Slump in Allentown," *New Textile Worker*, May 8, 1920, 1; Russell Palmer, editorial, "Palmer's Poor Method," *New Textile Worker*, May 8, 1920, 4.

57. See "ATWA Asks Probe of Wool Mill Shutdown," *New Textile Worker*, July 31, 1920, 1; Russell Palmer, editorial, "Lawlessness in Industry," *New Textile Worker*, July 17, 1920, 4; and Muste, *The Kind of Unionism*. In West Hoboken, New Jersey, for example, ATWA silk workers

were locked out for refusing a reduction of wages. See *New Textile Worker*, September 25, 1920, 2. See also "Labor Finds Out for Itself," *Nation* 112, no. 2901 (February 9, 1921): 208–9, an article on Philadelphia's textile mills, which shut down for several months and then refused to hire union members when they reopened with 20–30 percent wage cuts.

58. Fraser, *Labor Will Rule*, 158–61.

59. The only period when Muste joined the Socialist Party was briefly in 1936 when he was compelled to do so by the WPUS. As discussed below, he had been outvoted in a discussion of whether or not the party should follow the French turn of infiltrating and taking over the SP. Following party discipline, he joined the party but within a few months left it to return to the pacifist movement. Soon thereafter, he allowed his SP membership to lapse. See "Interview with Mr. A. J. Muste," Socialist Movement Project, May 31, 1965, Oral History Research Office, Columbia University. This is a separate interview from the Reminiscences of Abraham John Muste (Muste, COHC), which were conducted in 1954.

60. Anthony Capraro eventually resigned from the union in disgust when Lawrence workers accused him of spying for the ACW. See Anthony Capraro to Muste, March 1, 1920, ACP, box 2. For the "leaderlessness," disorganization, and ultraradicalism of the Lawrence local, see Capraro to Muste, October 18, 1919, ACP, box 2; and Minutes of the First Convention of the Amalgamated Textile Workers of America, April 12–13, 1919, ACP, box 8, which shows that some locals opposed the idea of contributing dues to fund a central office and national organization.

61. See Capraro to Muste October 18, 1919, ACP, box 2; Muste editorial, *New Textile Worker*, October 25, 1919, 3. As Capraro's letter to Muste suggests, these rumors were often instigated by officials of the American Woolen Company; the fact that Lawrence's workers would be susceptible to such rumors reminds us that militancy and a commitment to unionism were not one and the same. Similar problems beset the union in Passaic, though here the challenge came from the right rather than the left, when an independent textile union and the UTW local charged the national leadership of the ATWA with misappropriation of funds and favoring a "Soviet form of government." See "Who and What Are the Amalgamated Textile Workers of America?" by the United Textile Workers of America, ACP, box 8.

62. Goldberg, *A Tale of Three Cities*, 170–71.

63. Ibid., 166–68.

64. Goldberg admits as much when he says that the union's spring 1920 campaign for a 50 percent increase in wages and union recognition was one it "could not win" (ibid., 212). For Muste's thinking on this issue, see Muste to Hillman, April 26, 1920, ACTW, box 4, folder 13. See also Muste, "They Cannot Stop Us!" *New Textile Worker*, May 8, 1920, 4; and "The Present Situation," *New Textile Worker*, June 19, 1920, 4.

65. See Capraro to Muste, October 18, 1919, ACP, box 2. In his letter to Muste, Capraro admitted that he once took offense when Cedric Long suggested that the general strike committee disassociate from strikers who attacked scabs. The decision by ATWA delegates to the union's founding convention to only allow textile workers to serve as officers of the union may also have been a reflection of class tensions (though they made an exception for Muste). See Minutes of the First Convention of the Amalgamated Textile Workers of America, April 12–13, 1919, ACP, box 8.

66. Kosek, *Acts of Conscience*, 47.

67. Evan Thomas to his mother, February 28, 1921, Louisa Thomas private collection. For the story of the role of conscience in the personal and political histories of Evan and Norman

Thomas, see Louisa Thomas, *Conscience: Two Soldiers, Two Pacifists, One Family—A Test of Will and Faith in World War I* (New York: Penguin Press, 2011). See also Cedric Long's comments in Soule, *The Intellectual and the Labor Movement*, 29; and Kosek, *Acts of Conscience*, 46–47.

68. Paul Blanshard, for example, served as educational director for the ACW in Rochester from 1920 through 1924, and then as field secretary for the League for Industrial Democracy; while Robert Dunn, another former organizer for the ATWA, served for decades as executive secretary of the Labor Research Association.

69. For a discussion of the peace movement in the 1920s, and especially their emphasis on moral, legal, and parliamentary methods to achieve peace, see Kosek, *Acts of Conscience*; Chatfield, *For Peace and Justice*; DeBenedetti, *Origins of the Modern American Peace Movement*; Linda Schott, *Reconstructing Women's Thoughts: The Women's International League for Peace and Freedom Before 1941* (Stanford, Calif.: Stanford University Press, 1997); and Carrie Foster, *The Women and the Warriors: The U.S. Section of the Women's International League for Peace and Freedom, 1915–1946* (Syracuse, N.Y.: Syracuse University Press, 1995).

70. See, for example, Muste, "Contradictions the Rebel Faces," 143.

71. "James M. Dick on Problems of the Organizer," January 16, 1931, BLCC, box 1, folder 2.

72. Muste, COHC, 450–57. See also Muste, "Contradictions the Rebel Faces," 141–44; and his comments in George Soule's *The Intellectual and the Labor Movement*, 21: "I believe that the labor movement is fundamentally the idealistic movement of our time. . . . Undoubtedly, intellectuals with high ethical ideals can make a contribution [to the labor movement] . . . provided that they *never preach* ethical ideals to labor unionists and *almost never* speak of them" (emphasis in original).

73. Muste, COHC, 412–13.

74. Muste, "Contradictions the Rebel Faces," 142.

75. In late February 1919, anarchists blew themselves up while planting a bomb at the American Woolen Company in Lawrence and in June 1919, anarchists bombed the home of a silk company executive in Paterson. Paul Avrich documents this in *Sacco and Vanzetti: The Anarchist Background* (Princeton, N.J.: Princeton University Press, 1991), 139–40, 151–52, while also discussing the dialectical relationship between anarchist violence and state repression. Muste briefly discussed the impact of the Red Scare on the ATWA and particularly its Communist members in Muste, COHC, 434–36.

76. For the "extraordinary instability" of the textile industry, see Bernstein, *The Lean Years*, 3. For relations between Thomas McMahon and Muste, see Bloom, "Brookwood Labor College," 103–4. Muste brilliantly summed up the problems faced by textile workers in his *The Kind of Unionism*, 21–32.

77. See Muste, *The Kind of Unionism*, 31. This idea that education would not only teach the principles of trade unionism and organization, but also "keep [workers] organized" in the long term was a central driving principle in the workers' education movement. See, for example, editorial, *Labor Age* 16, no. 12 (December 1927): 23.

78. James Maurer, quoted in Bloom, "Brookwood Labor College," 40. See also Daniel Jesse Goroff, "James Maurer: Socialist Labor Leader" (master's thesis, University of North Carolina, 1969). Or, as *Labor Age* explained, while nations used education to "strengthen extreme nationalism" and employers used it to "spread anti-labor ideas," workers have learned to use it for themselves. See "Our Own Education vs. the Other Fellows," *Labor Age* 14, no. 3 (March 1925): 5. For a discussion of workers' education and its appeal to female trade unionists, particularly in

the needle trades, see Orleck, *Common Sense and a Little Fire*. For a discussion of the Bryn Mawr School for Women Workers, see Hollis, *Liberating Voices*. None of these authors has identified the pragmatic foundations of labor education.

79. The statement of purpose appeared on the first page of every issue and the "aims" appeared on the last page.

80. Bloom, "Brookwood Labor College," 40–42; Leon Fink, *Progressive Intellectuals and the Dilemmas of Democratic Commitment* (Cambridge, Mass.: Harvard University Press, 1999), 43–50.

81. David Saposs, "An Instrumental View of Labor Education," June 1921, DSP, box 6, folder 8. See also Muste, "Progressive Education," *Labor Age* 21, no. 7 (July 1932): 27–28; and his editorial, *Brookwood Review* 6, no. 3 (December 1927–January 1928): 2, in which he explained that "the foremost task of workers' education is to break down [the] fears, illusions, and obsessions," such as the ideology of individualism, that prevented workers from identifying with their class.

82. As one supporter put it, "appreciation of beauty knows no class distinction. There is no capitalistic sunset to be tabooed by the proletariat." See Alexander Fichlandler, "Workers' Education—Why and What?" *Socialist Review*, April–May 1921, 49–50.

83. Fannia Cohn, "Workers' Education Aims at Power," *Labor Age* 16, no. 11 (November 1927): 9–10.

84. Clint Golden, "Across America: A Workers' Education Pilgrimage," *Labor Age* 14, no. 7 (September 1925): 4–5. Or, as Muste put it, "It is not so important to teach young laborites precisely what to think as how to think." See Allen, "Labor Must Learn: A. J. Muste," in *Adventurous Americans*, 115.

85. See, for example, Dorothy Ross, *The Origins of American Social Science* (New York: Cambridge University Press, 1991); and Peter Novick, *That Noble Dream: The "Objectivity Question" and the American Historical Profession* (New York: Cambridge University Press, 1988). But, as Leon Fink points out, while most academics retreated from their political commitments, there was an alternative realm outside the university, particularly around workers' education, where intellectuals sought to bring their social scientific expertise to bear on social problems. See Fink, *Progressive Intellectuals*, 43–50. Fink does not, however, include working-class intellectuals in his study.

86. Mark Starr, "Workers' Education in Britain: Can It Teach Us Any Lessons?" *Labor Age* 18, no. 3 (March 1929): 12–13 (my emphasis). See also, for example, Alexander Fichandler, "Our Minds and Behavior," *Labor Age* 15, no. 10 (October 1926): 18–19, in which he uses the terms "facts" and "experience" interchangeably.

87. Preface, *Labor Age* 15, no. 2 (February 1926): 1–2. In workers' education, workers and their struggles for economic justice became "vast laboratories of the first really vital sociology," stated Herbert Ellsworth Cory, quoted in Fink, *Progressive Intellectuals*, 45. See also letter from Louis Budenz to Muste, January 3, 1928, BLCC, box 42, folder 6; and Louis Budenz, "Success! Through Workers' Education," *Labor Age* 14, no. 5 (May 1925): 1–3.

88. The first generation of the "new economists" in the 1880s had openly identified with the labor movement. Over the course of 1890 through the 1920s, under pressure to appear scientifically reputable, academics increasingly channeled their energies into more acceptable roles as policy experts. See Leon Fink, " 'Intellectuals' Versus 'Workers': Academic Requirements and the Creation of Labor History" *American Historical Review* 96, no. 2 (April 1991): 405,

395–421, as well as his *Progressive Intellectuals*. In this article, Fink suggests that labor economist Selig Perlman's rejection of idealism borrowed from Deweyan pragmatism. Clearly, pragmatism was interpreted and applied in many different ways. But it is important to remember that pragmatism emerged out of Dewey and William James's preoccupation with making idealism relevant in a modern world. For an enlightening discussion of pragmatism and its critics, see Phelps's appendix in *Young Sidney Hook*, 44–57.

89. Budenz, "Success! Through Workers' Education." See also Abe Lefkowitz's book review of Selig Perlman's *A Theory of the Labor Movement* in which he rejected Perlman's argument that intellectual radicals were out of touch with the job consciousness of the American worker. It was not their faith in workers' control that was problematic, but rather their tendency to have a "Messiah complex instead of the service complex." See *Labor Age* 17, no. 8 (August 1928): 14.

90. De Caux, *Labor Radical*, 95.

91. "Death of Brookwood Founder a Great Loss," *Brookwood Review* 5, no. 5 (June–July 1927): 1; Muste, "William Mann Fincke," *Brookwood Review* 5, no. 5 (June–July 1927): 2.

92. Unionists who attended the founding meeting included Brophy of the mine workers; Rose Schneiderman of the Women's Trade Union League (WTUL); Jay G. Brown, a leader in the 1919 steel strike and national secretary of the Farmer-Labor Party; Abraham Lefkowitz of the American Federation of Teachers (AFT); Joseph Schlossberg, the general secretary of the ACW; and Muste in his capacity as head of the ATWA. See also "Memorandum on Brookwood History and Policy," May 29, 1930, BLCC, box 1, folder 1; and also John Dewey, "Labor Politics and Labor Education," *New Republic*, January 29, 1929, 211–14.

93. William M. Fincke, Jr., quoted in Bloom, "Brookwood Labor College," 62. See also Charles F. Howlett, *Brookwood Labor College and the Struggle for Peace and Social Justice in America* (Lewiston, N.Y.: Edwin Mellen Press, 1993).

94. Muste, "Sketches," 79. See also Muste, COHC, 443.

95. Nancy Muste, quoted in Robinson, *Abraham Went Out*, 34.

96. Bloom, "Brookwood Labor College," 320. This assessment was based upon an interview Bloom conducted with John Martin Muste.

97. Robinson, *Abraham Went Out*, 70.

98. Anne Muste, memorandum to the faculty (ca. 1923), BLCC, box 7, folder 10. By contrast, Julia Blanshard, wife of the ATWA organizer Paul Blanshard, spoke passionately at a November 1919 rally of textile workers. Mildred Calhoun, wife of Brookwood's economics professor, Arthur Calhoun, also assumed a more public role as a part-time instructor during her first two years at Brookwood, though she would eventually find the combination of teaching and managing a household impossible to maintain. See newspaper clipping (ca. November 1919), PBP, box 8, folder 4; and "Mildred Calhoun Resigns," *Brookwood Review* 4, no. 3 (January 1926): 3.

99. Muste, draft of article for *Religious Education* 19 (October 1924), AJMP, reel 4.

100. For example, the poet Sarah Cleghorn, who had been hired to teach English, resigned after only a year because she felt that her pacifist ideals were out of step with the tenor of the school. See Bloom, "Brookwood Labor College," 87. See also Cara Cook to Jo Ann Robinson, May 31, 1977, in which she recalled that Muste's religious nature was "not overt" at Brookwood. AJMP-LA, box 2.

101. There was considerable exchange between Muste, Brookwood, and university-sponsored workers' education, with Brookwood faculty often teaching classes and providing curriculum for these endeavors. Yet Brookwooders also criticized university extension and workers'

summer schools for not being under the control of workers themselves. In this, they were in agreement with unionists engaged in workers' education through their unions, local and state federations, and central labor bodies. See, for example, Charles Moore, "Workers' Education in the United States," *Brookwood Review* 1, no. 3 (March 20, 1923): 1; Muste editorial, *Brookwood Review* 3, no. 4 (May 1925): 4; and Arthur Calhoun, "Civic or Social?" *Brookwood Review* 4, no. 4 (February 1926): 2.

102. In order to appeal to the AFL, the board did not include Joseph Schlossberg of the ACW, an outlaw union. There were nineteen members of Brookwood's board of directors. Ten of these were designated for trade unionists, five for faculty members, and two each for Brookwood alumni and students. Given that students and faculty were also trade unionists, the board was exclusively made up of union members. See "Outline of Plan for Incorporation of Brookwood," November 14–December 30, 1924, BLCC, box 7, folder 8; and "By-laws of Brookwood, Inc.," BLCC, box 1, folder 14.

103. Muste speech (ca. 1929), BLCC, box 7, folder 6. See also Muste, "Workers' Education in the United States," *Nation*, October 1, 1924, 333–36. Among the unions who established scholarships were the International Association of Machinists, John Brophy's District 2 of the United Mine Workers, the ACW, the UTW, the AFFFHW, and the United Cloth, Hat, and Cap Makers. For the role of the American Fund for Public Service in the labor and radical movements of the 1920s and 1930s, see Gloria Garrett Samson, *The American Fund for Public Service: Charles Garland and Radical Philanthropy, 1922–1941* (Westport, Conn.: Greenwood Press, 1996).

104. See Muste, "Introducing Ourselves," *Brookwood Review* 3, no. 1 (December 15, 1924): 6. The AFL preferred to have its connection with workers' education through the WEB, and feared that official representation on the Brookwood board might be interpreted as favoritism by other labor colleges and endeavors. See "Memorandum on Past Relations Between Brookwood and the Workers' Education Bureau," undated, BLCC, box 42, folder 22.

105. For the AFL's hearty endorsement of workers' education, see editorial, "Workers' Education Bureau," *American Federationist*, 32, no. 11 (November 1925): 1079–80; and Spencer Miller Jr., "Workers' Education—Its Achievements and Its Future," *American Federationist*, 29, no. 12 (December 1922): 881–87. Articles in the *American Federationist* by Brookwood faculty and staff include Muste, "Brookwood Labor Institute," *American Federationist* 32, no. 10 (October 1925): 939–43; E. J. Lever, "Possibilities of Workers' Education," *American Federationist* 33, no. 2 (February 1926): 172–76; Cara Cook, "Women Who Work for Wages," *American Federationist* 33, no. 4 (April 1926): 454–59; and Tom Tippett, "Workers' Education Among Illinois Miners," *American Federationist* 33, no. 9 (September 1926): 1055–59. The April 1934 issue of the *American Federationist* was devoted entirely to workers' education.

106. Muste, "Preface to the AFL Convention," *Nation*, October 16, 1935, 440–41. See Muste, editorial, *Brookwood Review* 3, no. 4 (May 1925): 2; and editorial page, *Brookwood Review* 3, no. 3 (April 1925): 2. See also William Green circular, May 12, 1926, BLCC, box 16, folder 10. It was quickly evident that these hopes had been misplaced. See Bernstein, *The Lean Years*, 94–97; and Craig Phelan, *William Green: A Biography of a Labor Leader* (Syracuse, N.Y.: Syracuse University Press, 1989), 24–30.

107. Muste, "What's to Be Done in the Labor Movement?" *Brookwood Review* 4, no. 7 (May–June 1926): 2.

108. For example, in September 1926, *Labor Age* hosted a forum on the question of whether industrial unionism was "the answer to merger and mass production." Only one article (by

Arthur Calhoun) openly criticized the AFL, and *Labor Age's* editors asked for "come backs" to Calhoun's contention that the AFL was "a bulwark of conservatism." See "Industrial Unionism?" *Labor Age* 15, no. 9 (September 1926): 1–5.

109. Colby to Muste, December 20, 1921; *American Federation of Teachers Semi-Monthly Bulletin* 1, no. 5 (November 20, 1921): 1–8; Constitution of the American Federation of Teachers, adopted in 1925; "Teachers and Independence," reprint from 13th annual convention, all in JCP, box 1, folder 1. The AFT shared Dewey's commitment to democracy in education while insisting that it was dependent upon the empowerment of teachers through their unions and alliances with other workers in their communities. See Marjorie Murphy, *Blackboard Unions: The AFT and the NEA, 1900–1980* (Ithaca, N.Y.: Cornell University Press, 1990). In Colby's classroom, modern epistemology quite literally fused with the practical needs and agenda of the labor movement. In her first-year English class, for example, she structured her lesson on "definitions" around terms like "trade" and "boycott." Similarly, in a lesson on how to write history, she asked students to determine the structure and argument of William James's famous essay on pragmatism in which he defines theories as instruments, "not answers to enigmas, in which we can rest." See Colby's English course plans, 1923–24, JCP, box 1, folder 29.

110. See Thomas R. Brooks, *Clint: A Biography of a Labor Intellectual* (New York: Atheneum Books, 1978).

111. Muste, "Report of Brookwood Executive Committee," April 18, 1931, BLCC, box 1, folder 1. See also Muste, "Workers' Education in the United States," 333–35; Muste, "Brookwood's Sixth Year," *Brookwood Review* 5, no. 1 (August 1926): 2.

112. See the works cited in the preceding note. See also, for example, Axel Bjorg, "Discussion vs. Debate, Lecture or Discussion," *Brookwood Review* 3, no. 3 (April 1925): 5; Golden, "Across America"; and Muste, editorial, *Brookwood Review* 5, no. 1 (August 1926): 2.

113. De Caux, *Labor Radical*, 94; Cara Cook to Jo Ann Robinson, February 20, 1978, AJMP-LA, box 2.

114. See, for example, "Economic Freedom in Russia Says Baldwin," *Brookwood Review* 7, no. 1 (October–November 1928): 3; "Literature Depends on Economic Trends," *Brookwood Review* 5, no. 3 (December 1926–January 1927): 4 (re V. F. Calverton); "Women Labor Leader Active for 20 Years," *Brookwood Review* 4, no. 5 (March 1926): 1 (re Elizabeth Gurley Flynn); "Sinclair Lewis Sees Unionism Urgent Need," *Brookwood Review* 8, no. 1 (October–November 1929): 1; "Fight for Economic Supremacy Coming?" *Brookwood Review* 7, no. 1 (October–November 1928): 2 (re Scott Nearing); "Can Religion Help in Reconstruction?" *Brookwood Review* 7, no. 3 (February–April 1929): 4 (re Reinhold Niebuhr); "Europe Restless, [Jay] Lovestone Finds," *Brookwood Review* 9, no. 3 (May 1931): 3; "Unions Must Face Industries' Problems," *Brookwood Review* 6, no. 1 (September 1927): 4 (re Norman Thomas); "Which Way the American Labor Movement?" *Brookwood Review* 6, no. 6 (June–August 1928): 1 (re Harry Ward); "Economic Conditions in Russia Described," *Brookwood Review* 4, no. 3 (January 1926): 3 (re Bertram Wolfe); and Muste editorial, "Looking Back at the Summer School," *Brookwood Review* 4, no. 1 (October 1925): 4 (re Rex Tugwell and Selig Perlman).

115. Toscan Bennett, quoted in Bloom, "Brookwood Labor College," 80; Muste, quoted in Bloom, "Brookwood Labor College," 74. For the diversity of the student body, as well their roots in trade unionism, see "A Census of Brookwood Students: Study Made by a Class in Statistics," March 1927, BLCC, box 1, folder 1; "Workers Flock to School's 10th Year," *Brookwood Review* 8, no. 3 (September 1930): 3.

116. Andrew Schmolder, "Fumbling in the Workshop of the World," *Brookwood Review* 3, no. 4 (May 1925) : 8. See also, for example, "Why They Come to Brookwood," *Brookwood Review* 11, no. 1 (December 1932): 2; Bessie Friedman, "Back to Duty," *Brookwood Review* 1, no. 4 (April 15, 1923): 1; and Letters, *Brookwood Review* 3, no. 1 (December 15, 1924): 5.

117. De Caux, *Labor Radical*, 94–107. See also Nancy Baker (Muste's daughter) to Jo Ann Robinson, February 8, 1979, who recalled that "there were all kinds of things that Brookwood students got into, from getting drunk to sexual entanglements. When [Muste] spoke to the family about them, it was always with a tolerant attitude, although he had to spend many hours listening and talking to various individuals with problems." AJMP-LA, box 2.

118. "A Census of Brookwood Students: Study Made by a Class in Statistics." The study concluded from their statistical analysis that the students came from diverse industrial, racial, and home backgrounds; came "almost wholly from industrial families, are nearly equally divided between native and foreign-born students, and native, mixed and foreign-born parents, with a slight indication of increasing native stock among the newer students." They were also "typical of the great majority of workers in entering work life at young ages. All have been trade union activists."

119. Browder's critique of Brookwood can be found in Bloom, "Brookwood Labor College," 112–13. Quote is from De Caux to Muste in 1924. See Bloom, "Brookwood Labor College," 113. Bernstein discusses the Communist Party and Brookwood in *The Lean Years*, 105.

120. Muste, *The Kind of Unionism*, 12. See also "Studies in Curriculum," *Brookwood Review* 1, no. 4 (April 15, 1923): 2; "The American Bureau for Industrial Freedom," *Labor Age* 16, no. 1 (January 1927): 9; E. J. Lever, "Training Labor's Army," *Labor Age* 14, no. 9 (November 1925): 18–20; and Esther Lowell, "Research for What?" *Labor Age* 17, no. 3 (March 1928): 8–10. The Labor Age Service Bureau, founded by progressive unionists in 1927 to collect and disseminate data on the unorganized industries for use by organizers, funded many of these efforts.

121. Bernstein, *The Lean Years*, 146, 164–74; Cohen, *Making a New Deal*, 162–83.

122. Muste, *The Kind of Unionism*, 9.

123. Muste, "So This Is Middletown," *Labor Age* 18, no. 4 (April 1929): 27.

124. Muste editorial, "Dramatizing the Labor Movement," *Brookwood Review* 4, no. 2 (December 1925): 2. As he put it, "To be a truly cultured person [does] not mean acquiring an Oxford accent or learning to read high-brow books." Rather, "true culture" occurred when one figured out one's place and role in the modern world, and built institutions that reflected this knowledge. Muste, address to Ethical Culture Society, November 9, 1928, BLCC, box 7, folder 6.

125. Muste editorial, "Are Trade Unionists Human Beings?" *Brookwood Review* 4, no. 5 (March 1926): 2. See also his editorial "Dramatizing the Labor Movement."

126. Fannia Cohn, "Workers' Education for Workers' Children," *Labor Age* 15, no. 1 (January 1926): 15–17. See also "Some Summerings: Vacations Secured by Labor for Its Own Folks," *Labor Age* 14, no. 6 (August 1925): 9–11, which describes the opening of summer resorts for organized workers, Unity House and Anita Gairbaldi House on Staten Island. For a discussion of how unions might utilize mass culture for their own benefit, see, for example, Louis F. Budenz, "Labor History in the Making," *Labor Age* 15, no. 2 (February 1926): 26; and Theodore N. Brainard, "Conferences—What For?" *Labor Age* 18, no. 3 (March 1929): 14–15. An early cultural theorist was M. H. Hedges, research director of the International Brotherhood of Electrical Workers, contributor to *Labor Age*, and later a member of the CPLA. See M. H. Hedges, "Organizing the Hidden Men," *Labor Age* 15, no. 12 (December 1926): 2–3; and M. H. Hedges, "Under the

Telescope," *Labor Age* 16, no. 2 (February 1927): 18–19. That same year, Hedges published a novel, *Dan Minturn* (1927), about a working-class socialist who is elected to Minnesota's state legislature only to have his ideals corrupted by the climate of political opportunism. Hedges had been a professor of English and rhetoric at Beloit College from 1913 until he was fired in 1920 for publishing *Iron City* (New York: Boni and Liveright, 1919; reprint, Beloit, Wis.: Beloit College Press, 1994), a novel that criticized the college's educational philosophy and methods. Recently republished with an introduction by Alan Wald, the novel, along with Hedges's decision to leave academia to serve the labor movement, should be placed within the context of the workers' education movement.

127. See Muste, "Brookwood's Sixth Year," 6; Eva Shafran, "A Good Beginning—What Next?" *Labor Age* 17, no. 1 (January 1928): 4; and editorial, "Labor Sports Get Attention," *Brookwood Review* 9, no. 1 (December 1930): 2.

128. "To Dramatize Workers' Lives," *Brookwood Review* 4, no. 2 (December 1925): 1.

129. This analysis draws upon Denning's analysis of the proletarian cultural production of the 1930s. See Denning, *The Cultural Front*, esp. chapters 4 and 5. See, for example, *What Price Coal?* JCP, box 1, folder 34; Tippett, "Workers' Education Among Illinois Miners"; *Shades of Passaic*, JCP, box 1, folder 33; "Passaic Strikes Like 'Shades of Passaic,'" *Brookwood Review* 4, no. 7 (May–June 1926): 3.

130. Tom Tippett, *Mill Shadows: A Drama of Social Forces in Four Acts* (1929), reprinted in Lee Papa, ed., *Staged Action: Six Plays from the American Workers' Theatre* (Ithaca, N.Y.: Cornell University Press, 2009).

131. Helen Norton, *Faculty Meeting*. In another satirical play written by Norton, the Muste family drives to a picnic in a car that "was old and the seats were very Muste: There was Abraham John Muste and Anne Muste and Nancy Muste and Connie Muste and John Martin Muste—oh, the interior of that car was very Muste indeed!" Both are in JCP, box 1, folder 34.

132. A wonderful description of a chautauqua held in District 2 of the UMWA, including a reference to its pragmatic method, can be found in Louis F. Budenz, "The Gospel Comes to Hastings," *Labor Age* 14, no. 4 (April 1925): 1–3. See also "A Workers' Chautauqua," *Labor Age* 14, no. 1 (January 1925): 5–6.

133. Margaret Daniels tried to find "a common meeting ground for 'class strugglers' and 'protecults'" in an article for *Labor Age*. Pointing out that modern scientific research had shown that human beings were not made of "neat compartments," she argued that the labor movement needed "well rounded" union members with "an understanding of the deepness and richness of life" as well as the "grim reality of it." See "Shall We Wage the Class War 'Strictly'?" *Labor Age* 14, no. 9 (November 1925): 22–23.

134. Muste to Calverton, April 24, 1926, VFCP, box 11.

Chapter 4. Muste, Workers' Education, and Labor's Culture War in the 1920s

Epigraph: Muste, "Critic or Lackey of Big Business?" *Labor Age* 19, no. 1 (January 1930): 12–14.

1. "Muste Called in Utica Labor Trouble," *Brookwood Review* 4, no. 3 (January 1926): 4; "Faculty Notes," *Brookwood Review* 3, no. 4 (May 1925): 7; and "No Swivel Chair for Muste," *Brookwood Review* 4, no. 3 (January 1926): 3.

2. As Rossinow points out, the makeup of the ACLU's national committee demonstrates the "broad front of laborite liberalism" during this period, with members as diverse as Oswald Garrison Villard, Crystal Eastman, Rose Schneiderman, Elizabeth Gurley Flynn, and William Z. Foster. See Rossinow, *Visions of Progress*, 85.

3. Muste, "What Price Labor Education?" *Labor Age* 17, no. 9 (September 1928): 15–16.

4. Allen, "Labor Must Learn: A. J. Muste," in *Adventurous Americans*, 100. For Muste's "happy manner," see "The American Bureau for Industrial Freedom," *Labor Age* 16, no. 1 (January 1927): 9.

5. The "fox" quote comes from McReynolds, interview by author. See my discussion of Muste's tenure at Fort Washington Church and as leader of the Lawrence strike, above, for similar characterizations of his leadership style.

6. In 1928, the Communist Party declared that capitalism had entered a "Third Period" of crisis and collapse. According to this analysis, social democrats and other non-Communist leftists stood in the way of an imminent working-class revolution and therefore had to be opposed as vehemently as genuine fascists. See Bernstein, *The Lean Years*, 140; Barrett, *William Z. Foster*, 156–58; Barrett, "Boring from Within and Without"; and Draper, *American Communism and Soviet Russia*, 278–94

7. Bernstein, *The Lean Years*, 91. On this younger generation of workers, see Cohen, *Making a New Deal*; and Gertle, *Working-Class Americanism*.

8. See especially Muste, "Whither American Labor?" *Labor Age*, 15, no. 7 (July 1926): 5–6. The issue of factionalism within unions was indeed a pressing one in the 1920s; the ILGWU, with which Muste was closely connected, was in a civil war with its Communist and Socialist members throughout the decade, and the collapse of the coal industry had turned the once powerful UMWA into a fractious, deeply divided union.

9. Muste, "How Shall Labor Deal with Dissenters?" *Labor Age* 15, no. 12 (December 1926): 15–18; Muste, "Factionalism in Trade Unions," in J. B. S. Hardman, ed. *American Labor Dynamics in Light of Postwar Developments: An Inquiry by Thirty-Two Labor Men, Teachers, Editors, and Technicians* (New York: Hartcourt, Brace, 1928); Muste, "The Opposition's Why," *Labor Age* 16, no. 1 (January 1927): 15–17. The latter article was reprinted in pamphlet form.

10. Muste, "How Shall Labor Deal with Dissenters?" 15–18. See also Muste, "The Opposition's Why," 15–17.

11. Muste, "Factionalism in Trade Unions." See also Muste, "Radicals and Conservatives: Can They Work Together?" *Labor Age* 17, no. 6 (June 1928): 4–6.

12. Muste, "Who's Your Organizer?" *Labor Age* 16, no. 10 (October 1927): 9–10. See also Muste, *The Kind of Unionism*.

13. Muste, "Appeal to Youth," *Labor Age* 16, no. 7 (July 1927): 2–4. As he argued, for unions to "meet the challenge of company unionism," they had to organize along industrial lines and offer recreational and cultural activities that would appeal to young workers. See also Muste, "Radicals and Conservatives: Can They Work Together?"; and Muste, "Organization Begins at Birth," *Labor Age* 16, no. 9 (September 1927): 2–3.

14. Bernstein, *The Lean Years*, 97. Moreover, only 12 percent of American workers were organized in contrast to over 50 percent of workers in Australia, over 40 percent in Austria, and around 35 percent in Great Britain and Germany. See Muste, "What Price Labor Education?" 15–16.

15. This can be seen in a review of the articles in *Labor Age* over the course of the 1920s, which grew increasingly assertive, while still expressing loyalty to the AFL.

16. Muste, "Mitten Management and Union," *Labor Age* 17, no. 5 (May 1928): 4–7. Muste published a similarly penetrating critique of the agreement in "Collective Bargaining—New Style," *Nation* 126, no. 3279 (May 9, 1928), 537–38. See also Muste, "Whose Job?" *Labor Age* 17, no. 2 (February 1928): 6–8; Muste, "Them Foreign Relations," *Labor Age* 16, no. 8 (August 1927): 7–9; and Muste, editorial, "Sacco and Vanzetti," *Brookwood Review* 6, no. 1 (September 1927): 2. Brookwood sent two carloads to Boston the night of the execution, "arriving there in time to stand in silent protest outside the Charlestown prison at midnight." See Cook to Robinson, February 20, 1978, AJMP-LA, box 2.

17. Muste, "Militant Progressivism?" *Modern Quarterly* 4, no. 4 (May–August 1928): 332–41.

18. Muste, "Lenin, the Strategist," book review of Valeriu Marcu's *Lenin* (New York: Macmillan Company, 1928), in *Labor Age* 17, no. 10 (October 1928): 29. For his admiration for Communists' "courage and vitality," though not their "childishness," see, for example, Muste, "Mother Throws Out the Baby," 20–22. See also Muste, "Sketches," 134–35.

19. Muste, "Sketches," 134–35.

20. Muste, "Pacifism and Class War" (1928), in Hentoff, *The Essays of A. J. Muste*, 179–82; Muste, "Fellowship and Class Struggle," FOR, box 5, folder 1. Another sign of Muste's growing estrangement with the FOR was his letter to the editor of the *World Tomorrow* calling that magazine's coverage of U.S. intervention in Mexico "sentimental." Copy in BLCC, box 42, folder 6.

21. Left-leaning members of the FOR would join the CPLA, and Protestant radicals like Harry Ward and Niebuhr often lectured at Brookwood. Also, the Church League for Industrial Democracy donated money to the CPLA. Muste to the Church LID (headed by W. B. Spofford), February 21, 1930, BLCC, box 28, folder 7; "Can Religion Help in Reconstruction?" *Brookwood Review* 7, no. 3 (February–April 1929): 4. Left-leaning Protestant pacifists stood up for Muste and Brookwood when both were condemned by the AFL. See "Ministers Appeal for Support for Brookwood," *Brookwood Review* 7, no. 2 (December 1928–January 1929): 2, which notes that ministers including John H. Holmes, Sherwood Eddy, Jerome Davis of Yale Divinity School, Paul Hutchinson and Charles Morrison of *Christian Century*, Harry F. Ward, and Kirby Page issued a statement opposing the "summary treatment accorded Mr. Muste and his associates" and expressing their confidence in him and Brookwood.

22. Examples of alumni who later assumed prominent roles in the workers' education movement include William Ross, who served as president of Baltimore Labor College; Margaret Wall, who founded the Southern Summer School for Women Workers; Jack Lever and Israel Mufson, both of whom were active in Philadelphia Labor College; and Leonard Craig, who set up labor colleges in Pittsburgh and Shenandoah. For reasons discussed above, workers' education enthusiasts were suspicious of experiments such as Bryn Mawr and YWCA schools, though they also lent a helping hand.

23. "Negroes Can Organize Is Conference Feature," *Brookwood Review* 5, no. 5 (June–July 1927): 1–2. Muste had initiated the conference based on a discussion about black workers at the 1926 annual convention of the AFL. See letter from Muste to R. W. Jelliffe, March 15, 1927, and Muste to C. A. Barnett, December 15, 1925, BLCC, box 44, folder 22. The conference program and text of some of the papers presented can be found in BLCC, box 44, folder 4. As discussed below, Brookwood would hold a similar conference in 1931, under the auspices of the CPLA.

24. Grace Butler Klueg, chair of Educational Committee of the Ladies' Auxiliary, International Association of Machinists, discussed plans for the institutes in the *American Federationist*.

See Klueg, "Educating Workers' Wives," *American Federationist* 34, no. 4 (April 1927): 431–35. Fannia Cohn was especially committed to organizing women workers and to including workers' wives in union activities. See, for example, Cohn, "Can We Organize the Flappers?" *Labor Age* 16, no. 12 (December 1927): 18–19.

25. See Helen Norton, "Youth Speaks Its Mind," *Brookwood Review* 6, no. 4 (February–March 1928): 7; Muste, "Appeal to Youth," 2–4.

26. For example, at the conference "Negroes in Industry," the black trade unionist A. Philip Randolph provided a sympathetic account of black nationalism, arguing that it was an understandable response to the "very peculiar" situation of black workers in the United States. "Every cultural effort on the part of a submerged group . . . will help that group in working out his economic problems on industrial fields also," Randolph asserted. In the meantime, it was imperative for unionists to organize black workers, regardless of whether the AFL provided support; unionization would build their collective power and give black workers a "background" and experience in labor organization that they lacked. See A. Philip Randolph, untitled paper, BLCC, box 44, folder 11. See also Thomas L. Dabney, "Negro Workers at the Crossroads," *Labor Age* 16, no. 2 (February 1927): 8–10; Harvey O'Connor, "Facing the Unorganized: Pawlowski and Goscka," *Labor Age* 16, no. 2 (February 1927): 6–7; Muste, "Appeal to Youth"; and Muste, "Whose Job?"

27. See *Brookwood Review* 5, no. 5 (June–July 1927): 2. For example, Brookwood alumnus Israel Mufson of the Railway Clerks was personally opposed to barring blacks from his union, but deferred to his white membership's "social" views and maintained the Railway Clerks' exclusionary policy.

28. Arthur Calhoun explained Brookwood's policy of the family wage in Calhoun to V.F. Calverton, October 10, 1925, VFCP, box 3. . See also See Brooks, *Clint*, 89, which shows that Dora Golden performed stenographer duties for her husband, Clint, without being paid for her labor.. On their masculine construction of the working class, see, for example, Louis Budenz editorial, *Labor Age* 17, no. 2 (February 1928): 1–2.

29. Editorial, "What's This—Education?" *Labor Age* 16, no. 9 (September 1927): 1. See also Muste, "The Real Thing in Workers' Education," *Brookwood Review* 6, no. 6 (June–August 1928): 2, in which he argued that education occurred in the "heat of the struggle." Or, as Louis Budenz put in *Labor Age*, workers' education remained committed to a "pragmatic and liberal view of education" and hostile to "Dogma," while also moving "away from the academic, and into those things about which workers are vitally concerned." See "Success! Through Workers' Education," *Labor Age* 14, no. 5 (May 1925): 1–3. As is discussed below, Budenz became close to Muste during this period and occasionally taught courses at Brookwood.

30. For information on the Passaic strike, see Louis Budenz, "Labor History in the Making," *Labor Age* 15, no. 5 (May 1926): 24–27. For Muste's involvement in the New Bedford textile strike in the early summer 1928, see Muste, "The Real Thing in Workers' Education," 2.

31. Alfred Hoffman, "Hell in Henderson," *Labor Age* 16, no. 11 (November 1927): 2–5; "Organization of the Textile Industry: Extracts from Talk by A. J. Muste to the Executive Council, UTW, at Brookwood, July 12, 1928," *Brookwood Review* 6, no. 6 (June–August 1928): 1 and 6. See also Muste, "The Call of the South," *Labor Age* 17, no. 8 (August 1928): 5–6; and *Brookwood Fellowship Bazaar: Twelfth Anniversary Review; Brookwood Labor College, December 2, 3 and 4, Irving Plaza, New York City* (Katonah, N.Y.: Brookwood Labor College, 1932), 3–5.

32. See Harold Z. Brown, "Silk Strikers Fight Small Bosses," *Labor Age* 17, no. 12 (December 1928): 8–10; and Muste's address to New York Society for Ethical Culture, November 9, 1928.

33. *Brookwood Fellowship Bazaar*, 4–5.

34. See Muste to Florence Thorne, August 30, 1924, BLCC, box 16, folder 2.

35. Florence Thorne to Muste, May 18, 1925, and Muste to Thorne, June 1, 1925, BLCC, box 16, folder 17. Brookwood's annual celebration of May Day, which included tributes to Gompers, Marx, Rosa Luxemburg, Debs, and Lenin, also raised the AFL's eyebrows. See "International Import of Labor Symbolized," *Brookwood Review* 4, no. 7 (May–June 1926): 3. It was perhaps inevitable that the AFL would become an object of criticism given Brookwood's commitment to explore labor's challenges in a spirit of openness and free inquiry. See, for example, "'Welfare Capitalism' Conference Subject," *Brookwood Review* 6, no. 6 (June–August 1928): 1.

36. Muste did, however, ask them to attend the conference as members of the UMWA and not as representatives of Brookwood. See Bloom, "Brookwood Labor College," 173–75.

37. Bernstein, *The Lean Years*, 106. For Lewis's corrupt and autocratic leadership of the UMWA, see Dubofsky and Van Tine, *John L. Lewis*; and Joseph E. Finley, *The Corrupt Kingdom: The Rise and Fall of the United Mine Workers* (New York: Simon and Schuster, 1972).

38. See Bloom, "Brookwood Labor College," 159–62. Over the next couple of years, labor progressives continued to refine the distinction they drew between adult education and workers' education, essentially contrasting the "civic ideal" of the former with the class agenda of the latter. See, for example, Calhoun, "Civic or Social?" 2; Muste, "What Is Adult Education?" *Brookwood Review* 4 (April 1926): 2; and Spencer Miller Jr., Clint Golden, and E. J. Lever, "Who Should Pay for Workers' Education?" *Labor Age* 15, no. 6 (June 1926): 1–6. Notably, the workers' education movement in England had a similar split dating from 1908. On the right was the Workers' Education Association, which took an impartial approach and allowed students to choose whatever courses they wished, formed a relationship with university extension, and used faculty with academic pedigrees. On the left was the National Council of Labour Colleges, which believed that impartiality was impossible and that the bias toward the working class must be at the center of labor education. It focused in particular on courses in the social sciences because of its aim to strengthen labor unions and was far more selective in choosing its faculty, viewing university extension with suspicion. See Mark Starr, "Workers' Education in Britain: Can It Teach Us Any Lessons?" *Labor Age* 18, no. 3 (March 1929): 12–13. See also Lawrence Goldman, "Intellectuals and the English Working Class," *History of Education* 29, no. 4 (July 2000): 281–300.

39. See Muste to Maurer, September 20, 1926, BLCC, box 16, folder 20. In the summer of 1926, when Muste sent the WEB the college's annual affiliation dues, Miller wrote back to say that Brookwood would have to appear before the executive committee before its affiliation would be renewed.

40. Muste, "A Wrong Step in Workers' Education," *Brookwood Review* 6, no. 2 (October–November 1927): 2–3. See also "Teachers Take Stock of Labor Education," *Brookwood Review* 6, no. 4 (February–March 1928): 1, 3, which reported that a conference of labor educators was held in late February in which they criticized the notion that teachers should be stripped from representation on the executive board. As we shall see below, the WEB would follow the AFL's recommendation in April 1929; previously, five of the eleven seats were held by teachers and local and state federations, while six were reserved for the AFL executive council and international unions; the decision eliminated the former from the committee. See Muste, "Rubber Stamp Education," *Labor Age* 18, no. 5 (May 1929): 5–6.

41. "Teachers Take Stock of Labor Education," 1 and 3; E. C. Lindeman, "Relation of Workers' Education to the Labor Movement," *Brookwood Review* 6, no. 4 (February–March 1928): 2–3.

42. Muste, "Back Up Labor Education!" *Labor Age* 17, no. 7 (July 1928): 5–6.

43. Details about this can be found in *Still More About Brookwood College* (February 1929) which provides the text of the infamous letter, BLCC, box 19, folder 1. See also Muste to Green, December 10, 1928, and Muste to Green, December 19, 1928, BLCC, box 16, folder 18. For information on the anti-Semitic and anti-Catholic views of one of the disgruntled students, see "Green's 'Irrefutable Charges' Answered," *Brookwood Review* 7, no. 2 (December 1928–January 1929): 1 and 4. In 1925, a bitter dispute arose between Communist students and more conservative students over the election of two student representatives to the Brookwood board of directors. Faculty were forced to become involved in the conflict, yet it was resolved with an appeal to importance of taking a nonsectarian, nondogmatic, and "factual" approach to intralabor squabbles. See Memorandum, March 24, 1925, BLCC, box 7, folder 7; and Memorandum, April 2, 1925, BLCC, box 7, folder 8.

44. "A. J. Muste's Address to 1928 Graduates," *Brookwood Review* 6, no. 6 (June–August 1928): 1–4. See also "Brookwood Victim of Convention Lynching Bee," *Brookwood Review* 7, no. 1 (October–November 1928): 1–2.

45. "A. J. Muste's Address to 1928 Graduates," 3–4.

46. See *Still More About Brookwood College*. This pamphlet followed another, *Brickbats and Bouquets on Brookwood Labor College* (1928), which had compiled crucial documents related to the controversy. Both can be found in BLCC, box 19, folder 1. It noted as well that the AFL's charges were also ironic in light of Brookwood's loan of $100,000 to the ILGWU for its 1926 strike. See also Bernstein, *The Lean* Years, 106

47. Brookwood Board of Directors, letter to delegates at the AFL Convention, 1928, BLCC, box 16, folder 20; Muste to William Green, August 9, 1928, BLCC, box 16, folder 13. See also Abraham Lefkowitz to Woll, October 16, 1928, BLCC, box 16, folder 22; James H. Maurer et al. to Woll, October 15, 1928, BLCC, box 16, folder 15; and Muste to John Brophy, October 18, 1928, BLCC, box 16, folder 23.

48. See John Brophy to Muste, August 13, 1928, BLCC, box 16, folder 20; and Fannia Cohn to William Green, October 10, 1928, BLCC, box 16, folder 21. See also Muste to Green, August 30, 1928; Green to Muste, September 6, 1928; Muste to Green, September 11, 1928; all in BLCC, box 16, folder 14.

49. See *Brickbats and Bouquets on Brookwood Labor College*, 13–18. Current Brookwood students also circulated an open letter of protest, calling the action "entirely unjust," and pointing out that they represented workers from a range of crafts and regions. They further noted that the college raised funds for local unions in times of crisis and released students to serve their unions when needed. See William Seligman, Annie King, et al. to the AFL and Affiliated Organizations, November 9, 1928, BLCC, box 16, folder 17. In another appeal, a trade unionist wrote that the labor movement was succumbing to dogmatism and orthodoxy, thereby inhibiting "growth" and leading to "decay." See Aloysius Senefelder Jr., "Against Labor Orthodoxy," *Labor Age* 17, no. 9 (September 1928): 21.

50. See telegram from Muste to Green, October 31, 1928, and Green to Muste, November 1, 1928, BLCC, box 16, folder 15. The members of the AFL executive council who supported Brookwood were Frank Morrison, AFL secretary, and J. P. Noonan, president of the International Brotherhood of Electrical Workers. See Muste's address to New York Society for Ethical Culture, November 9, 1928.

51. Muste, quoted in Bloom, "Brookwood Labor College," 186. See also Muste, "The Devil and the Deep Sea," *Labor Age* 17, no. 11 (November 1928): 17–19.

52. Matthew Woll to Henry R. Linville, August 24, 1928, BLCC, box 16, folder 14.

53. William Green, quoted in Charles Madison, *American Labor Leaders: Personalities and Forces in the Labor Movement*, 2nd ed. (New York: Ungar, 1962), 112; William Green editorial, *American Federationist* 34, no. 4 (April 1927): 401–2.

54. Lindeman, "Relation of Workers' Education to the Labor Movement," 2–3.

55. William Green editorial, "Workers' Education," *American Federationist* 35, no. 10 (October 1928): 1170–71. Green was a Baptist, and the disgruntled Brookwood students were evangelical Protestants. See also Phelan, *William Green*, 21–23; Hofstader, *Anti-Intellectualism in American Life*, 284–88; and Bernstein, *The Lean Years*, 94–97; 104–6.

56. Editorial, *Labor Age* 17, no. 10 (October 1928): 4; Muste, address to New York Society for Ethical Culture, November 9, 1928. See also Senefelder, "Against Labor Orthodoxy," 21; and Muste, "Shall Workers Education Perish?" 18, no. 1 *Labor Age* (January 1929): 5–6.

57. See, for example, comments by Mary Barker, president of the AFT, in *Brickbats and Bouquets*, 11–12. See also Bloom, "Brookwood Labor College," 195–99.

58. See "New York Teachers Protest AFL Action," *Brookwood Review* 7, no. 1 (October–November 1928): 4; John A. Fitch, "Workers' Education and the Spirit of Progress," *Brookwood Review* 7, no. 1 (October–November 1928): 3. Correspondence between Muste and Dewey regarding the controversy can be found in BLCC, box 17, folders 12 and 17. See also *Brickbats and Bouquets*, 5–9.

59. The only other evidence presented were letters from the three or four disgruntled former students; no reference was made to the dozens of letters from loyal Brookwood students and graduates that had flooded the AFL national office. See Carl Haessler, "A.F. of L. Convention High Lights," *Labor Age* 18, no. 1 (January 1929): 3–4. See also "Brookwood Victim of Convention Lynching Bee," 1–2.

60. Haessler, "A.F. of L. Convention High Lights," 3–4. In addition to Reed, the delegates who pleaded for a hearing from the floor included Tobias Hall, member of the executive council of the UTW; J. Bannister of the Brotherhood of Railway Clerks; John Burke, the president of the Pulp and Sulphite Workers; Thomas McMahon, president of the UTW; and Florence Hanson, secretary-treasurer of the AFT. See "Brookwood Victim of Convention Lynching Bee," 1–2. See also the *New York Herald Tribune*, December 3, 1928, clipping in BLCC, box 16, folder 17.

61. Dewey, "Labor Politics and Labor Education."

62. Haessler, "A.F. of L. Convention High Lights." Ironically, the AFL's Committee on Education originally stated that "sound" education "must be experimental" and independent. Citing John Dewey, "the most outstanding figure in the educational field in the world today," it suggested that public education might be "capable" of meeting the needs of adult education, but that, for the time being, there was an urgent need for workers' education. See AFL Committee on Education Report, original draft, sect. 1, AFL Convention, New Orleans, 1928, BLCC, box 16, folder 3. Matthew Woll quote can be found in "Brookwood Victim of Convention Lynching Bee," 1–2. On the anti-intellectualism of the labor movement, see Hofstader, *Anti-Intellectualism in American Life*, 284–90.

63. Muste, quoted in Bloom, "Brookwood Labor College," 211.

64. Ibid., 212–13.

65. Muste, "Militant Progressivism?" 333–34; and "Where 'Workers' Control' Is Law," *Labor Age* 14, no. 6 (August 1925): 18–19. See also Louis Budenz, "Labor History in the Making," *Labor Age* 14, no. 7 (September 1925): 28; and A. Rosebury, "Disruption in the Name of 'Revolution,'" *Labor Age* 14, no. 3 (March 1925): 20–22. Aside from their tactics being unrealistic in the

context of a conservative working class, Rosebury commented that Communists "even deny and discard certain ethical rules of social conduct" through "killing of reputation, to moral 'knifing,' to slander and libel with intent to kill morally and politically. All which the Communists scoff at as 'Bourgeois morality.'" See also Prince Hopkins's review of Emma Goldman's *My Further Disillusionment with Russia*, in which he wrote: "To me, a very noteworthy thing is that Emma, like Kropotkin, has got from the Russian experiment a very powerful sense of the importance of Ethics." *Labor Age* 14, no. 3 (March 1925): 29.

66. Bloom, "Brookwood Labor College," 201. More humorously, the Jewish-Communist *Frieheit*, commented that "Only Matthew Woll could charge [Brookwood faculty] with Communism. The Communists themselves know very well that Muste is as far from Communism as a pious Jew from pork." Quoted in *Brickbats and Bouquets*, 3.

67. Muste, "Mother Throws Out the Baby," 20–22.

68. Muste "Comment on the Use of the Communist Odium" to Helen, Dave, Polly, Arthur, November 13, 1928, BLCC, box 42, folder 6; Special Minute, Annual Report, Brookwood 1931–32, BLCC, box 28, folder 27. The issue came to a head in the month preceding the AFL's New Orleans convention, when faculty member Arthur Calhoun charged that the method by which Brookwood had defended itself against the AFL camouflaged its own "revolutionary" attitude. The dispute intensified and became ugly, with Calhoun calling his colleagues "puppets," Muste a "crook," and the board of directors "betrayers of labor." With a feeling of "extreme agony," the board fired Calhoun. See Muste, "For Your Information," June 11, 1929, BLCC, box 1, folder 11; Muste handwritten note, BLCC, box 1, folder 11; and Clint Golden to Muste, June 20, 1929, BLCC, box 42, folder 6. It is difficult to assess the significance of Calhoun's resignation because personal factors clearly also played a role in his disillusionment with Brookwood. See Calhoun to Calverton, April 1, 1926, and Calhoun to Calverton, March 30, 1926, VFCP, box 4.

69. Special Minute, Annual Report, Brookwood, 1931–32. See also Muste, Memorandum on Brookwood History and Policy, May 30, 1929, BLCC, box 1, folder 1.

70. Muste, "Rubber Stamp Education," 5–6; Muste to Brookwood Friends, February 7, 1929, BLCC, box 16, folder 19. See also Muste, "Workers' Education Bureau Surrenders to Reaction," *Labor Age* 18, no. 3 (March 1929): 5–8; and Muste, "What the W.E.B. Convention Did to Workers' Education" *Brookwood Review* 7, no. 3 (February–April 1929): 1–2. See also David Saposs, "Which Way Workers' Education?" *Survey* 62 (May 15, 1929): 250–51, explaining the way the AFL seized control: "Prior to this . . . the bureau was an autonomous body, giving wide latitude to the colleges . . . affiliated with it. Moreover . . . labor colleges and local unions from which students were recruited were permitted . . . to nominate their own representatives to the executive board of the bureau. . . . But the convention changed the constitution to put control of the bureau under the national unions, safely purged of opposition elements and farthest removed from workers' education activities. This was done by giving them the majority share in representation at conventions. The representation for the rank and file of students was materially reduced and rigidly circumscribed. . . . Local unions, where students are recruited and classes formed, are no longer entitled to representation. Not only have labor colleges have the representation reduced, but, to make control trebly certain, it is provided that labor colleges can only become affiliated with the bureau when they are approved by the central labor union of the locality and by the state federation. Further, they must be acceptable to the executive board of the bureau as not being hostile to the A.F. of L." Copy in BLCC, box 19, folder 15.

71. Muste to Fannia Cohn, January 19, 1929, BLCC, box 26, folder 10.

72. In a letter from Muste to Jacob Billicopf, December 31, 1928, he noted that they lost about $3,000 in scholarships that year, "not directly as a result of the action of the AF of L Executive Council, but as part of the general situation which had been brewing for some time. On the other hand, we gained $1000 in new scholarships from the Brotherhood of Railway Clerks." In the expectation that the college would lose more union scholarships, he stated that Brookwood's policy would be "to broaden the base of their support." See BLCC, box 16, folder 18. See also Memorandum on Brookwood History and Policy, May 30, 1929; "Where Brookwood Stands Now," BLCC, box 19, folder 1; and William Green, "Labor's Answer to Its Critics, Brookwood Defenders," January 26, 1929; BLCC, box 19, folder 1.

73. "Workers Flock to School's 10th Year," *Brookwood Review* 8, no. 3 (September 1930): 3. See also Bloom, "Brookwood Labor College," 216–17. Black activists Thyra J. Edwards and Oscar Hunter were two of the African Americans who attended Brookwood during this period. The former praised Muste for his strong opposition to racism within the labor movement. See Gregg Andrews, *Thyra J. Edwards, Black Activist in the Global Freedom Struggle* (Columbia, Miss.: University of Missouri Press, 2011), 38. For Oscar Hunter and Brookwood, see Robin D. G. Kelley, *Race Rebels: Culture, Politics, and the Black Working Class* (1996, reprint, New York: The Free Press), 127.

74. See, for example, Muste, "Shall Workers' Education Perish?" 5–7. The first conference called by Muste was held on December 30, 1928, at Brookwood; about forty people attended, including Louis Budenz, Leonard Bright, Paul Blanshard, Fannia Cohn, Jerome Davis, Abe Epstein, Abe Lefkowitz, E. J. Lever, Cedric Long, A. J. Kennedy, James Maurer, Israel Mufson, Rose Schneiderman, Norman Thomas, Harry Ward, and Phil Ziegler. They drafted a statement of aims and formed a committee for the discussion of labor problems that continued the discussion over the next several months until agreement was reached to form the CPLA. Documents relating to these conferences can be found in BLCC, box 12, folder 1.

75. "The Challenge to Progressives," *Labor Age* 18, no. 2 (February 1929): 1–4; Muste, "Progressives Can Win," *Labor Age* 18, no. 2 (February 1929): 8–9.

76. Muste, "Progressive Movement Moves," *Labor Age* 18, no. 4 (April 1929): 15–16. See also "Challenge to Progressives"; and Muste, "Critic or Lackey of Big Business?" 12–14.

77. Saposs, "The Need for a Labor Culture," 19. See also David J. Saposs, "The Future of Radicalism in the Labor Movement," DSP, box 7, folder 12.

78. Saposs, "The Future of Radicalism in the Labor Movement," 11–20.

79. Muste, letter to the editor, *Nation* 128, no. 3334 (May 29, 1929): 647. See also Budenz editorial, *Labor Age* 18, no. 1 (January 1929): 2.

80. The name was an obvious echo of the Conference for Progressive Political Action, founded in 1922 by six major railway unions to push for independent political action. The difference in name speaks to Muste's emphasis on industrial rather than political action. For the wide distribution of the "Challenge," see Justus Ebert, "Progressives Accept Challenge," *Labor Age* 18, no. 3 (March 1929): 18–20.

81. Budenz, "We Reach the Age of Reason," *Labor Age* 18, no. 3 (March 1929): 1–2. See also J. M. Budish, "The Strategy of Disintegration," *Labor Age* 18, no. 2 (January 1929), in which he interpreted the AFL's action toward Brookwood as a moment of kairos or conjuncture. "History is a continuous process" of slow change and then "some outstanding event [occurs] which conveniently enables us to fix historical dates," and he asserted that the AFL's 1928 convention was one such date, indicating the need for "forceful and aggressive militancy," not conciliation.

Budish was on the board of the Labor Publication Society and editor of the *Headgear Worker*, organ of the Cloth, Hat, Cap and Millinery Workers' Union. He would become prominent in the CPLA. See also Israel Mufson's article for the *Railway Clerk* on December 1, 1928, in which he argued that the crisis with Brookwood brought to the fore the real issue confronting the labor movement. Copy in BLCC, box 19, folder 5.

82. For Budenz's background, personality, and politics, see Jimmy Grant, "Louis Francis Budenz: The Origins of a Professional Ex-Communist" (Ph.D. diss., University of South Carolina, 2006); and Budenz, *This Is My Story* (New York: McGraw-Hill, 1947). See also Muste to Cope, July 27, 1931, and August 2, 1931, ECP, reel 5, which indicates something of Budenz's erratic personality; after being made executive secretary of the Joint Action Committee of the Associated Silk Workers, the UTW, and the CPLA in Paterson, he "decided suddenly and without any real warning, that he was forever through with the UTW, that he thought the only thing to do was to tell the workers rally to the National Textile Workers' Union . . . and resign as secretary of the CPLA!" A few days later, Budenz changed his mind, but his erratic behavior was a source of concern for Muste, who thought it might be necessary to find someone else to be executive secretary of the CPLA, "leaving Louis free for the strike work administrations, etc. at which is his genius." See also Muste, "Not So Long Ago: Encounters with Trotzky [*sic*] and Budenz," Autobiography Part 22, *Liberation* (March 1960): 15–17. For Budenz's teaching at Brookwood, see Louis Budenz, "Outline of Organization Lectures," see JCP, box 2, folder 11.

83. See, for example, Louis Budenz, "Labor History in the Making," *Labor Age* 15, no. 8 (August 1926): 24–26; Budenz, "For an American Revolutionary Approach," *Modern Monthly* 9, no. 3 (March 1935): 14–18. See also, Budenz, "Winning America," *Modern Monthly* 9, no. 5 (May 1935): 142–46. Muste's contrasting understanding of Americanism can be found in his "The American Approach," a brilliant series of articles that appeared over the summer of 1935 in the *New Militant*, and was later published as a WPUS pamphlet. Copy of it can be found in AJMP, reel 6. As is discussed below, these differences between Budenz and Muste were more implicit than explicit until the Musteite movement merged with the WP, when they served as a source of controversy and ultimately the pretext for Budenz to leave the WP for the CP.

84. See Grant, "Louis Francis Budenz"; and Budenz, *This Is My Story*.

85. Ebert, "Progressives Accept Challenge," 18–20.

86. J. C. Kennedy letter, reprinted in ibid., 18–22. See also William Mahoney to Muste, January 1, 1929; Colston E. Warne to Muste, January 30, 1929; Joseph Kucher of the International Labor Alliance to Louis Budenz, February 6, 1929; Alfred Bernheim of the Labor Bureau to Muste, May 28, 1929; William Chalmers to Muste, June 10, 1929; and Charles Gardner to Muste, June 27, 1929; all in JBSHP, box 38, folder 3.

87. This is clear in the Socialists who were elected as officers of the CPLA and who actively participated in the organization. For details, see my discussion below. See also, especially, Ebert, "Progressives Accept Challenge," 21; Norman Thomas comments, *New Leader*, January 26, 1929, 3; Muste, "Socialism and Progressive Trade Unionism," *New Leader*, April 6, 1929, 4; Muste and Louis Stanley, "CPLA Before Two Labor Bodies," *New Leader*, July 20, 1929, 3; Leonard Bright, "CPLA Organizes: Deliberations and Accomplishments of Two Day Conference," *Labor Age* 18, no. 6 (June 1929): 4; and "CPLA on the Job," *Labor Age* 18, no. 7 (July 1929): 19–20. See also correspondence between Muste and Leonard Bright, among other Socialist militants, in BLCC box 28, folders 13 and 14; Minutes of the CPLA National Committee, September 9, 1929, BLCC, box 28, folder 22.

88. See Ebert, "Progressives Accept Challenge," 18–22; Muste, "Progressive Movement Moves," 15–16; "CPLA on the Job," 19–20. See also Minutes of the Administrative Committee, CPLA July 17, 1929, JBSHP, box 38, folder 4.

89. See Fannia Cohn to Phil Ziegler, April 2, 1929, and Ziegler to Cohn, April 1, 1929, both in BLCC, box 15, folder 25; and Muste to Cohn, June 27, 1929, BLCC, box 16, folder 25. For the challenges faced by Cohn and other female unionists, see Orleck, *Common Sense and a Little Fire*.

90. Muste, "Progressive Movement Moves," 15–16.

91. Bernstein, *The Lean Years*, 7.

92. Tom Tippett, *When Southern Labor Stirs* (New York: J. Cape & H. Smith, 1931), 1.

93. Ibid; Muste, "Progressive Movement Moves," 15–16; "Brookwooders Active in Marion, NC Strike," *Brookwood Review* 8, no. 1 (October–November 1929): 1; and Bright, "CPLA Organizes," 3–6.

94. Muste, "Progressive Movement Moves," 15–16; Bright, "CPLA Organizes," 3–6; "Statement of Policy of the CPLA," *Labor Age* 18, no. 6 (June 1929): 6–7. The Rand School of Science Labor Research Department's *American Labor Press Directory* (New York: Rand School of Social Science, 1925), 55, lists a circulation of 10,031 for *Labor Age* in 1925. Its circulation rose likely thereafter, probably reaching a peak of 20,000 in 1929, only to decline with the onset of the Great Depression. I thank Tim Davenport for helping me to find this information.

95. "CPLA on the Job," 19–20.

Chapter 5. Labor Action

Epigraph: Muste, speech at the CPLA founding convention, May 1929. Quoted in Bright, "CPLA Organizes," 3–6.

1. De Caux, *Labor Radical*, 101.

2. Saposs, "The Future of Radicalism in the Labor Movement," 7; "All Hands on Deck," *Labor Age* 19, no. 11 (November 1930): 19–21. See also Muste, "Critic or Lackey of Big Business?" 12–14; and Muste, "Who Shall Organize—and How?" *Labor Age* 19, no. 9 (September 1930): 9–11.

3. Tess Huff, "Notes on the Convention," *Labor Age* 21, no. 9 (September 1932): 19–20; Muste, "Who Shall Organize—and How?" 9–11; and "The Job Ahead" *Labor Age* 22, no. 1 (December–January 1933): 3. See also Report of the National Executive Committee to the CPLA Convention, September 3–5, 1932, JBSHP, box 38, folder 4.

4. Muste to Cecil Headrick, May 22, 1930, BLCC, box 42, folder 11. See also Muste, "Progressives on the March," *Labor Age* 18, no. 6 (June 1929): 7–8; "What CPLA Members Can Do," *Labor Age* 18, no. 12 (December 1929): 13; Memorandum "Methods of Work for the Guidance of CPLA Officers and Workers," Minutes of the National Executive Committee, July 21, 1929, BLCC, box 28, folder 22; and Muste, "Outline of CPLA Program of Action—Nationally and in New York City in Particular" (ca. 1930), BLCC, box 28, folder 11. Most CPLA members were members or officers of the AFL or independent unions, most prominently, ILGWU, UMWA, AFT, ACW, UTW, Bookkeepers, Stenographers and Accountants Union, International Brotherhood of Electrical Workers, International Association of Machinists, Amalgamated Lithographers, Federation of Post Office Clerks, Brotherhood of Railway Clerks, Brotherhood of Locomotive Engineers, Pocketbook Workers' Union, and the Amalgamated Food Workers. Delegates from thirty-three unions attended the founding convention of the CPLA. See sources above and Bright, "CPLA Organizes," 3–6.

5. See Muste, "Outline of CPLA Program of Action." See also "CPLA at Work," *Labor Age* 18, no. 8 (August 1929): 20–22; "Progressives Are Organizing," *Labor Age* 18, no. 11 (November 1929): 22–23; "CPLA Wins Warm Approval," *Labor Age* 18, no. 12 (December 1929): 10–12; "CPLA Activities Extended," *Labor Age* 19, no. 1 (January 1930): 19–21; "Progressive Cause Advances," *Labor Age* 19, no. 2 (January 1930): 21–22; "CPLA Covers Wide Area," *Labor Age* 19, no. 3 (March 1930): 22–24. This estimate is based the number of CPLA branches organized by 1930 (approximately twenty), the fact that its organ, *Labor Age*, had a circulation of around 20,000 in 1930; the CPLA had members in at least thirty-four unions by 1930; the number of CPLA representatives who managed to attend their eastern regional conferences (approximately three hundred) in 1931, even at the height of the Great Depression; and the heavy involvement of Socialists in the organization in its early years.

6. Muste to Mary W. Hillyer, September 21, 1929, PBP, box 30, folder 5. For the close relationship between CPLA, Brookwood, and the YWCA's educational programs for women workers, see Muste to Louise Leonard, head of the Southern School for Women Workers, March 13, 1929, and October 21, 1929, BLCC, box 42, folder 10; "CPLA Organizes," 3–5, which indicates that representatives from Barnard, Bryn Mawr, and WTUL attended the founding convention of the CPLA; "Summer Brings New Opportunities to CPLA" *Labor Age* 19, no. 8 (August 1930): 22–25; "Faculty Members Have Busy Summer Schedules," *Brookwood Review* 8, no. 3 (September 1930): 10; and editorial, *Labor Age* 19, no. 6 (June 1930): 2–3. In the summer of 1930 alone Muste lectured at YWCA industrial conferences at Camp Merrie Woode, North Carolina, Camp Gray, Michigan, Lake Okoboji, Iowa, and Lake George, New York; as well as the Bryn Mawr, Barnard, Wisconsin, and Southern summer schools. Davis Saposs, Josephine Colby, William Ross, Tom Tippett, and others were similarly involved in teaching and developing curriculum for the YWCA and the summer schools. Muste was the featured speaker at the WTUL's annual convention in 1930. See "Progressive Cause Advances," 21–22. For labor feminism, see Orleck, *Common Sense and A Little Fire*; and Dorothy Sue Cobble, *The Other Women's Movement: Workplace Justice and Social Rights in Modern America* (Princeton, N.J.: Princeton University Press, 2004).

7. Miriam Bonner, "Proletarian Women," *Labor Age* 20, no. 12 (December 1931): 28. See also Lucy Carner, "Doing and Growing," *Labor Age* 20, no. 1 (January 1931): 18–22.

8. Muste to Louise Leonard, March 13, 1929.

9. See "CPLA Potent Force in Labor World," *Labor Age* 19, no. 4 (April 1930): 21–25.

10. Abram L. Harris, "The Negro Worker," *Labor Age* 19, no. 2 (February 1930): 5–9. W. E. B. Du Bois was so impressed with this article that he wrote Muste requesting his permission to reprint it in the *Crisis*. See Muste to Du Bois, January 2, 1930, BLCC, box 28, folder 3. A year later, Harris co-authored with Sterling Spero the famous study of African American labor history entitled *The Black Worker: The Negro and the Labor Movement* (New York: Columbia University Press, 1931).

11. E. R. McKinney, "The Negro's Road to Freedom," *Labor Age* 21, no. 9 (September 1932): 12–13, 29. See also McKinney, "Negro Workers Need CPLA," *Labor Age* 21, no. 5 (May 1932): 12.

12. See, especially, Report of NEC to CPLA Convention, September 3–5, 1932. In 1931, the CPLA sponsored a "Black Workers' Conference" at Brookwood that reflected these views. Chaired by W. E. B. Du Bois, the participants included Muste and the rest of the Brookwood faculty; the college's four black students; Abram Harris; Bertram C. Taylor, organizer of the

Mechanics' Association of Harlem; Floria Pinkney of the ILGWU; Frank Crosswaith, a black Socialist, member of the CPLA, and a founder of the Sleeping Car Porters; and the poet Langston Hughes. The conference concluded that the CPLA should take a two-pronged strategy of educating whites out of their racism and educating blacks on the need for labor organization. The conference further directed the CPLA to appoint an organizer to deal with situations of racial conflict between workers and issued a statement protesting the AFL's policy of segregated locals and blaming the lack of black unionism on white workers' racism. "Negro Workers' Problems Conference Subject," *Brookwood Review* 9, no. 2 (February 1931): 2; "Negro Labor Conference," *Labor Age* 20, no. 1 (January 1931): 17. The CPLA also invited Walter White of the NAACP to speak at one of their conferences on the horrors of racism; there, he praised the work of the CPLA. See "Doings and Growing," *Labor Age* 20, no. 1 (January 1931): 18–22. For the Socialist Party and race, see, for example, Sally M. Miller, "For White Men Only: The Socialist Party and Issues of Gender, Ethnicity and Race," *Journal of the Gilded Age and the Progressive Era* 2, no. 3 (July 2003): 283–302. For the Communist Party, see especially Kelley, *Hammer and Hoe*; and Naison, *Communists in Harlem During the Depression*.

13. See Muste, "Wild Intellectuals and Sober Workmen," *Labor Age* 19, no. 8 (August 1930): 4–6, in which he argued that the need for intellectuals and utopians in the labor movement shifted according to shifts in productive relations. See also Abraham Epstein, "The Intellectual and the Labor Movement," *Labor Age* 19, no. 8 (August 1930): 6–8. Muste viewed anti-intellectualism as a ploy for undermining an opponent without having to engage in "sound argument." He also saw it as a manifestation of mainstream labor's hostility to new ideas and resistance to change.

14. See Muste, "Going Over to the Other Side," *Labor Age* 16, no. 12 (December 1927): 9–10. See also Muste, "Progressive Movement Moves," 15–16, in which he explained that his service to the AFT reflected his commitment to organizing white-collar workers.

15. For Commonwealth College as a CPLA group, see correspondence between Muste and Bill Reich, BLCC, box 42, folder 19. Muste served on the LID's National Council, while Harry W. Laidler, the executive director of the LID, was a member of the CPLA and published in *Labor Age*, as was Frank Manning, the head of the Young People's Socialist League (a.k.a. "Yipsels").

16. See Hardman, OHAL.

17. J. B. S. Hardman, "Marx and Marxism After Fifty Years," *Labor Age* 22, no. 1 (February–March 1933): 4–5; Hardman, OHAL.

18. "The Active Workers Conference," *Labor Age* 21, no. 4 (April 1932): 4–6.

19. Thomas Dabney to Leonard Bright, July 11, 1929, JBSHP, box 38, folder 3; "Progressives must be in the field of action," Louis Budenz frequently asserted. See, for example, "CPLA Potent Force in Labor World," 21–25.

20. Edmund Wilson, quoted in Rosenzweig, "Radicals and the Jobless," 55.

21. Muste, "Working-class Ethics," *Labor Age* 21, no. 11 (November 1932): 16–18.

22. Ibid., 18.

23. Muste, funeral address, in *The Marion Murder: The Story of the Tragic Day of October 2, 1929*, Progressive Labor Library pamphlet no. 2 (New York: National Executive Council of the Conference for Progressive Labor Action, 1929), 16.

24. Tom Tippett, "War in Gastonia," *Labor Age* 8, no. 7 (July 1929): 15–16; Tippett, *When Southern Labor Stirs*, 50–100.

25. Tippett, *When Southern Labor Stirs*, 117–20; Bloom, "Brookwood Labor College," 238. Lewis's descriptions of Hogan and Elliott can be found in Bernstein, *The Lean Years*, 29.

26. Tippett, *When Southern Labor Stirs*, 117–50; Francis Gorman Jr., Tom Tippett, and A. J. Muste, funeral addresses, in *The Marion Murder*, 14–17; "Brookwooders Active in Marion, N.C. Strike," *Brookwood Review* 8, no. 1 (October–November, 1929): 1.

27. Muste, "Sketches for an Autobiography," 144.

28. Muste, "A.F. of L.'s Biggest Task," *Labor Age* 18, no. 10 (October 1929): 3–6.

29. Baldwin, quoted in "Flashes from the Labor World," *Labor Age* 18, no. 11 (November 1929): 20–21. See also Muste, "A.F. of L.'s Biggest Task"; and Tippett, *When Southern Labor Stirs*, 120–28.

30. Muste's funeral address, *The Marion Murder*, 14–17; and Muste, quoted in Tippett, *When Southern Labor Stirs*, 145.

31. Muste, "A.F. of L.'s Biggest Task." See also Muste, "After Toronto—What?" *Labor Age* 18, no. 11 (November 1929): 8–10; and Muste, "Militancy and Money," *Labor Age* 18, no. 12 (December 1929): 15–17.

32. Bloom, "Brookwood Labor College," 240. Although Muste praised these moves by the AFL, he feared that the campaign would not be conducted in the proper spirit. Particularly in light of the recent stock market crash, it was essential that the campaign be "large-scale, militant, coordinated," he warned. "Anything else spells failure." See Muste, "Militancy and Money," 15. See also Bernstein, *The Lean Years*, 34.

33. See "After Toronto—What?" 8–10 and Muste, "Militancy and Money," 15–17.

34. Tippett, *When Southern Labor Stirs*, 157–62. See also Muste, "No Strike: The Policy in the South," *Labor Age* 19, no. 5 (May 1930): 14–15; Bernstein, *The Lean Years*, 35.

35. Tippett, *When Southern Labor Stirs*, 164–65.

36. Ibid.; Tippett, *Mill Shadows*; Helen G. Norton, "The Marion Massacre in Retrospect," *Brookwood Review* 8, no. 3 (September 1930): 5–6; and *Brookwood Fellowship Bazaar*, 5–10.

37. "Address of William Ross at Eastern Regional Conference," March 16, 1930, BLCC, box 28, folder 8.

38. Tippett, *When Southern Labor Stirs*, 172. See also "Report of Extension Department," 1931–32, BLCC, box 28, folder 27; Lawrence Hogan, "Rumblings in Southern Textiles," *Labor Age* 21, no. 3 (March 1932): 8, 17; and Muste, "Southern Labor Stirs," *Nation* 135, no. 3501 (August 10, 1932): 121–22.

39. Dubofsky and Van Tine, *John L. Lewis*, 157. See also Bernstein, *The Lean Years*, 358–90; and Finley, *The Corrupt Kingdom*, 42–119.

40. Dubofsky and Van Tine, *John L. Lewis*, 163.

41. Muste, "The Crisis in the Miners' Union," *Labor Age* 19, no. 3 (March 1930): 4–8. See also Bloom, "Brookwood Labor College," 250–53.

42. Finley, *The Corrupt Kingdom*, 68. For Muste's assessment, see Muste, "Miners Grapple with Lewisism," *Labor Age* 19, no. 4 (April 1930): 17–20.

43. In Pittsburgh, for example, the AFL refused to support a strike by taxicab drivers, compelling the CPLA to assume leadership. Similarly, when the CPLA helped to organize black postal workers in Cleveland, they had trouble obtaining a charter from the AFL. See "CPLA Potent Force in Labor World," 21–24.

44. Ibid. See also "Healthy Response to Latest CPLA Campaign," *Labor Age* 19, no. 7 (July 1930): 22–24.

45. See "CPLA Potent Force in Labor World"; "Healthy Response to Latest CPLA Campaign"; *The Call to Action: 2nd Year of CPLA* (pamphlet; New York: CPLA, 1930); and Louis Budenz, "The Lesson of the Hour," *Labor Age* 20, no. 2 (February 1931): 10–11.

46. For example, starting in the fall of 1930, Muste and the New York branch of the CPLA came to the aid of a group of unorganized electrical workers in Brooklyn that the local had ignored. By the spring of 1931, they had formed the Brotherhood of Brooklyn Edison Employees, but the Brotherhood of Electrical Workers refused to give them support. See Horace B. Davis, "Unionism in Receivership," *Labor Age* 20, no. 1 (January 1931): 4–5; S. W. Levich, "Organization Comes to Brooklyn Edison," *Labor Age* 20, no. 6 (June 1931): 14–16; "Sloan Declares War," *Labor Age* 20, no. 10 (October 1931): 1–2; Louis Budenz, " 'Little Caesar' Broach and Local 3," *Labor Age* 21, no. 4 (April 1932): 15–16; and Jerome Count, "Blazing Trails in Brooklyn," *Labor Age* 22, no. 1 (February–March 1933): 13–14. Jonathan Bloom provides a more extended discussion of this campaign in his dissertation, "Brookwood Labor College," 258–62.

47. For details, including Howat's alcoholism, see Dubofsky and Van Tine, *John L. Lewis,* 163–67.

48. Ibid., 167; "The Miners' Crisis . . . and Progress," *Labor Age* 20, no. 4 (April 1931): 3.

49. "The Miner's Crisis . . . and Progress," 3; Tom Tippett, "The Miners Try for a Clean Union," *Labor Age* 20, no. 4 (April 1931): 5–7; Israel Mufson, "The Rank and File Convention at St. Louis," *Labor Age* 20, no. 5 (May 1931): 11–12; and "The Future in the Miners' Union," *Labor Age* 20, no. 5 (May 1931): 3, 26.

50. Cara Cook, "The Union Returns to Kanawha," *Labor Age* 20, no. 5 (May 1931): 5–7, 29 and "Report of Extension Department," 1931–32, BLCC, box 28, folder 27. See also Muste, "Slavery in West Virginia," *Labor Age* 20, no. 5 (May 1931): 8–11; letter from the West Virginia Mine Workers to Brookwood, May 13, 1931, reprinted in *Brookwood Review* 9, no. 3 (May 1931): 1–2; and Lucille Kohn, "There Are Classes in the W. Va. Hills," *Labor Age* 21, no. 9 (September 1932): 11. For a historian's account of Keeney and the miners' movement, see David A. Corbin, " 'Frank Keeney Is Our Leader, and We Shall Not Be Moved': Rank-and-File Leadership in the West Virginia Coal Fields," in Gary M. Fink and Merl E. Reed, eds., *Essays in Southern Labor History: Selected Papers, Southern Labor History Conference* (Westport, Conn.: Greenwood Press, 1977), 144–56. For Howat's alcoholism, see Dubofsky and Van Tine, *John L. Lewis,* 163–67.

51. Muste and Tippett quotes come from Bloom, "Brookwood Labor College," 254–55. See also Bernstein, *The Lean Years,* 385; and "The Independent Labor Party of West Virginia," *Labor Age* 21, no. 2 (February 1932): 5–7.

52. Muste, Tippett, Norman Thomas, among others, spoke at the party's founding convention, which went on record favoring compulsory unemployment insurance, the nationalization of the mines, and other progressive demands. See "CPLA Widens Its Activities" *Labor Age* 20, no. 5 (May 1931): 2–6; "The Independent Labor Party of West Virginia."

53. Tom Tippett, "A New Miners' Union in Illinois," *Labor Age* 21, no. 10 (October 1932): 4–5; Dubofsky and Van Tine, *John L. Lewis,* 200–201; Finley, *The Corrupt Kingdom,* 85–86; and Brooks, *Clint,* 138–97.

54. Dubofsky and Van Tine, *John L. Lewis,* 170. Gerry Allard served as editor of the PMA's organ, and Tippett would briefly serve as educational director of the union after leaving Brookwood in March of 1933. For the CPLA/AWP's response to these developments, see, for example, "Mine Union Slips as Officials Oust Honest Militants," *Labor Action* 1, no. 12 (November 8, 1933): 1. See also Stephanie Elise Booth, *Gerry Allard: Miner's Advocate* (Chicago: Illinois Labor History Society, 1981).

55. Bloom, "Brookwood Labor College," 262.

56. Muste, "Memorandum on the Middletown, Ohio Situation," JBSHP, box 38, folder 3.

57. "The Dilemma of a Militant Union," *Labor Age* 19, no. 9 (September 1930): 4; Edmund Ryan, "The Hosiery Workers Convention," *Labor Age* 21, no. 8 (August 1932): 12–13.

58. "The Firing Line Extends," *Labor Age* 20, no. 7 (July 1931): 19.

59. For example, in December 1931, Sam Bakely, a CPLA member who organized for the UTW, published an article in *Labor Age* criticizing the union's leadership of a recent strike in Lawrence. When UTW organizers protested to Muste that Bakely's analysis was "inaccurate and unfair," Muste tried to strike a middle ground between support for the union and sympathy for Bakely's critique. See Muste, "Strike and Organizing Strategy," *Labor Age* 21, no. 2 (February 1931): 8–11. The CPLA also found that organizers sometimes attempted to cover up deficiencies "by criticism of militants who demand action." This was the case in Allentown and Paterson, where Muste was forced to hold conferences with McMahon and other UTW officials because of such charges. See Report of the National Executive Committee to the CPLA Convention, September 3–5, 1932.

60. Delegates included representatives from "steel, cotton, silk, wool, hosiery, public utilities, anthracite, bituminous, carpenters, electrical workers, garment workers, milliners, clothing workers, food workers, and printers." "Our position [is] that wherever an A.F. of L. union is in existence we regard it a part of our function to stimulate and force that union into progressive and militant activity. At the same time it was definitely recognized that the unorganized must be organized, and that where the A.F. of L. unions simply refuse to act, the work must nevertheless be carried on independently." See "The Active Workers Conference," Labor Age 21, no. 4 (April 1932): 4. See also "CPLA Program for Industrial Activity in the Present Period," *Labor Age* 21, no. 4 (April 1932): 21–22.

61. Report of the National Executive Committee to the CPLA Convention, September 3–5, 1932; see also "Labor Realism," *Labor Age* 21, no. 10 (October 1932): 24–25.

62. Bernstein, *The Lean Years*, 427. See also Daniel J. Leab, "'United We Eat': The Creation and Organization of the Unemployed Councils in 1930," *Labor History* 8, no. 3 (1967): 300–315.

63. Rosenzweig, "Organizing the Unemployed," 50. See also editorial, *Labor Age* 19, no. 4 (April 1930): 1; "Unemployment Insurance: The Next Step," *Labor Age* 19, no. 6 (June 1930): 21–22; "Healthy Response to Latest CPLA Campaign," 22–25; Budenz, "The Lesson of the Hour," 10–11, 29.

64. Editorial comment, *Labor Age* 22, no. 1 (February–March 1933): 2–3.

65. Ted Selander, quoted in Roger H. Hall, "Sam Pollock, Labor Activist: From Radical to Reformer, 1932–1972" (Ph.D. diss., Bowling Green State University, 1993), 24.

66. "'All Hands on Deck,'" *Labor Age* 19, no. 11 (November 1930): 19–21; Louis Budenz, "Working with the Jobless," *Labor Age* 19, no. 12 (December 1930): 9–11, 29; *The Call to Action: 2nd Year of CPLA*.

67. Budenz, "Working with the Jobless"; "Our Unemployment Insurance Bills," *Labor Age* 19, no. 10 (October 1930): 22–23.

68. Demands were for emergency action—such as city administration going on record for unemployment insurance; public works; public welfare through short-term bonds; and so on. "CPLA Focuses Attention on Extent of Unemployment," *Labor Age* 20, no. 1 (January 1931): 20–21.

69. "The Fight Grows Hotter," *Labor Age* 20, no. 6 (June 1931): 20–21.

70. "CPLA Widens Its Action," *Labor Age* 20, no. 5 (May 1931): 20–22.

71. Bernstein, *The Lean Years*, 417.

72. Carl Brannin, "Northwest Unemployed Organize," *Labor Age* 21, no. 6 (June 1932): 5–7.

73. Bernstein, *The Lean Years*, 417. The Seattle UCL's political program called for county, state, and federal relief for every unemployed person, unemployment insurance, no evictions because of inability to pay rent, no light, water or gas shut off because of inability to pay bills; lowering of interest rates, a decent minimum wage for public works, and the expansion of such public works; free medical, dental, burial services for the poor; the five-day work week and six-hour day in public employment.

74. Brannin, "Northwest Unemployed Organize," 5–7 (my emphasis). Model bills based on the CPLA draft were also introduced in the state legislatures of Michigan, Pennsylvania, New York, and Massachusetts.

75. Ohio Unemployed League Songs, Columbus, Ohio, Vertical Subject File:—Unemployed—Ohio Unemployed League—Songs, LC. See also Bystander, "Unemployed Citizens' League of Tacoma," *Labor Age* 21, no. 6 (June 1932): 7–8; Harry A. Howe, "Unemployed Begin to Act," *Labor Age* 21, no. 8 (August 1932): 8–9, 29, in which he contended that most leagues were less likely to emphasize self-help than Seattle.

76. Lem Strong, "Smith Township Gets Going," *Labor Age* 21, no. 8 (August 1932): 10.

77. John Godber, "Philadelphia Unemployed Act," *Labor Age* 21, no. 9 (September 1932): 9. See also Louis Breier, "Allentown Stops Evictions," *Labor Age* 21, no. 10 (September 1932): 6–7, 25; NEC minutes, August 9, 1932, JBSHP, box 38, folder 4.

78. Breier, "Allentown Stops Evictions."

79. McKinney, quoted in Rosenzweig, "Radicals and the Jobless," 57. In making public spectacles of their organizing efforts, the leagues managed to gain political influence and even power. See, for example, Breier, "Allentown Stops Evictions." On the other hand, attaining political influence could also lead to repression. In Seattle, where the league managed to obtain control over the administration of relief, it soon faced a vicious counterattack in which the city elite deposed them from their posts and even threatened to use machine guns against them in demonstrations. See Carl Brannin, "Seattle UCL Fights Back," *Labor Age* 21, no. 11 (November 1932): 10. See also Bernstein, *The Lean Years*, 417.

80. For details about the formation of the Ohio Unemployed League, see Truax to Muste, December 7, 1932, and Truax to Muste, November 13, 1932, in BLCC, box 28, folder 17; and Louis Budenz, "Ohio Jobless Take State Action," *Labor Age* 21, no. 11 (November 1932): 4–5, 22. For Pennsylvania, see Sarah Limbach, "The Tactics of the CPLA," *World Tomorrow*, February 15, 1934, 90–91; "Memo on Policy in Connection with Harrisburg Convention of Unemployed," JBSHP, box 38, folder 4; and Edmund Ryan Jr., "Philadelphia UCL Carries On," *Labor Age* 21, no. 12 (December–January 1933): 11, 28.

81. Muste, "The Columbus Convention of the Unemployed," *Labor Action* 1, no. 8 (July 15, 1933): 3–4. See also Rosenzweig, "Radicals and the Jobless," 60.

82. Rosenzweig, "Radicals and the Jobless," 61.

83. For the CPLA's extensive discussions of how to deal with these elements, see "The Job Ahead," 3; NEC minutes, March 13, 1933, JBSHP, box 38, folder 4; editorial comment, *Labor Age* 22, no. 1 (February–March 1933): 2–3; Louis Budenz, "Organizing the Jobless" *Labor Age* 21, no. 12 (December–January 1933): 9–10; Budenz, "We Can Organize the Jobless," *Labor Age* 22, no. 1 (February–March 1933): 11. The consensus that emerged was that the experience of struggle would help to build their consciousness as workers. As Budenz put it in "Organizing the

Jobless," it was of "utmost importance" that *the growing demands of the unemployed must develop out of their experience and not be foisted upon them*" (emphasis in original). Quote is on page 10.

84. Rosenzweig, "Radicals and the Jobless," 62.

85. McKinney, OHAL, 8.

86. Muste, *Why a Labor Party*, Progressive Labor Library pamphlet no. 2 (New York: Conference for Progressive Labor Action, 1929).

87. Muste, "Independent Political Action—Yes, But What Kind?" *Labor Age* 19, no. 6 (June 1930): 6–8; Muste, book review, *Labor Age* 21, no. 10 (October 1932): 29. See also editorial, *Labor Age* 19, no. 12 (December 1930): 2. The LIPA was essentially a precursor to the realignment of the Democratic Party later in the decade. See Rossinow, *Visions of Progress*, 118–20; and Tobin, *Organize or Perish*.

88. See "Muste Drops Out of Dewey League: Resigns from Executive of Third Party Group," *Revolutionary Age* 2, no. 5 (January 3, 1931): 2; and Muste, "The CPLA: A Positive Statement of Program and Action," *Labor Age* 20, no. 12 (December 1931): 18–21. See also J. C. Kennedy, "Summary of the Political Program of the CPLA," BLCC, box 28, folder 25; editorial comment, "Socialist Party and Labor Party," *Labor Age* 21, no. 2 (February 1932); and editorial comment, *Labor Age* 21, no. 8 (August 1932): 2–3; "Report of the Active Workers Conference," *Labor Age* 21, no. 4 (April 1932): 4–6, 20–22; and "Our Job," *Labor Age* 21, no. 9 (September 1932): 26. Norman Thomas and the SP were similarly disillusioned by Dewey's cultivation of elected political figures. See Frank A. Warren, *An Alternative Vision: The Socialist Party in the 1930s* (Bloomington: Indiana University Press, 1974), 70–71.

89. See, for example, Benjamin Mandel, "Franklin Roosevelt: Jingo-Liberal," *Labor Age* 21, no. 6 (June 1932): 13–14.

90. See David J. Pivar, "The Hosiery Workers and the Third-Party Impulse, 1929–35," *Labor History* 5, no. 1 (Winter 1964), 18–28. In addition to the AFFFHW, the Railway Clerks, the Machinists, the ACW, the Lithographers, and the West Virginia Mine Workers' Union were all on record as favoring a third party. Not coincidentally, these unions were close to the CPLA.

91. See Kennedy, "Summary of the Political Program of the CPLA"; Muste, "For a United Labor Party," *Labor Age* 21, no. 5 (May 1932): 5–7, 29; and Muste, "Memorandum on Political Activities," September 20, 1933, JBSHP, box 38, folder 4.

92. Report of the National Executive Committee to the CPLA Convention, September 3–5, 1932; "Our Job," 26.

93. Report of the National Executive Committee to the CPLA Convention, September 3–5, 1932; Muste, "The Need for a United Labor Party," *Labor Age* 22, no. 1 (February–March 1933): 8–10. For Americans' evolving views of dictatorship and the invention of the concept of totalitarianism, see Benjamin Alpers, *Dictators, Democracy, and American Public Culture: Envisioning the Totalitarian Enemy, 1920s–1950s* (Chapel Hill: University of North Carolina Press, 2003).

94. Muste, "Conventions, Platforms, and Political Power," *Labor Age* 21, no. 8 (August 1932): 15–16.

95. Muste, "The Race for Votes," *Labor Age* 21, no. 10 (October 1932): 14–16.

96. Editorial comment, *Labor Age* 22, no. 1 (February–March 1933): 4–5; "United Political Party of Labor Chief Need in America Today: CPLA Message to Continental Congress," *Labor Action* 1, no. 3 (May 1, 1933): 3; "Congress of 2,000 at State Capital," *Labor Action* 1, no. 4 (May 15, 1933): 1–2. For Hillman and Dubinsky's views, see Fraser, *Labor Will Rule*, 278.

Chapter 6. Americanizing Marx and Lenin

Epigraph: Muste, "The CPLA: A Positive Statement of Program and Action," 18–20.

1. Particularly devastating was a loan Brookwood had made to the ILGWU, which the union was unable to pay back. See Muste to David Dubinsky, April 30, 1932, ATWA, box 1, folder 25. By the fall of 1932, Brookwood's financial situation had become extremely precarious. See Muste to Jack Lever, October 31, 1932, BLCC, box 28, folder 16.

2. Muste to the National Association of Schools and Publishers, April 13, 1932, BLCC, box 42, folder 16; interview with Doris Emelander; interview with Marian Johnson; and phone directories, Grand Rapids, Michigan, GRH.

3. Edmund Wilson, quoted in Leon Edel's introduction to Wilson's *The Thirties: From Notebooks and Diaries of the Period* (New York: Farrar, Straus and Giroux, 1980), xv. See also Bernstein, *The Lean Years*; and Irving Bernstein, *The Turbulent Years: A History of the American Worker, 1933–1940*, reissue ed. (Chicago: Haymarket Books, 2010).

4. Fraser, *Labor Will Rule*; Lichtenstein, *The Most Dangerous Man in Detroit*; Tobin, *Organize or Perish*; and Cohen, *Making a New Deal*.

5. Muste, "The True International," *Christian Century*, May 24, 1939, 668.

6. Denning, *The Cultural Front*, 425.

7. In this sense, he was also similar to Muste, both of whom challenge the narrative of the Lost Generation, espoused by Malcolm Cowley and repeated by historians. See Wilcox, *V. F. Calverton*, 22. Christine Stansell persuasively places gender and sexuality at the center of the lyrical left's revolutionary project in her book, *American Moderns*.

8. In Bourne's famous phrasing of the project: "the good life of personality lived in the environment of the Beloved Community." Randolph Bourne, quoted in Wilcox, *V. F. Calverton*, 22. See also Stansell, *American Moderns*; and Casey Blake, *Beloved Community: The Cultural Criticism of Randolph Bourne, Van Wyck Brooks, Waldo Frank, and Lewis Mumford* (Chapel Hill: University of North Carolina Press, 1990).

9. See Wilcox, *V. F. Calverton*, 33–34.

10. Ibid., 46.

11. Ibid., 51–52.

12. See, for example, ibid., esp. 139–56; and Philip Abbott, *Leftward Ho! V. F. Calverton and American Radicalism* (Westport, Conn.: Greenwood Press, 1993): 94–128.

13. Wilcox, *V. F. Calverton*, 157–59. See also Budenz to Calverton, May 29, 1927, VFCP, box 2; Budenz, Outline of Organization Lectures, 1930, BLCC, box 2, folder 11. Indeed, Calverton published CPLA members, including Muste, Budenz, and Hardman, in *Modern Quarterly/Monthly*.

14. Quoted in Phelps, *Young Sidney Hook*, 78. See also Wald, *The New York Intellectuals*, 115–30.

15. Muste letter to Hook, quoted in Phelps, *Young Sidney Hook*, 109. My certainty that Muste was the author of the book review is based on (1) my familiarity with his writing style, and (2) the use of the exact same phrasing in his letter to Hook as in the review. See "Something Intelligent About Marx," *Labor Age* 20, no. 9 (September 1931): 27–28. Calverton, it should be noted, also shared Hook's interpretation, writing angrily to the *New Masses* that "the great danger which Marxism faces today is exemplified in [by the CP's] approach. Marxism is dynamic and not static; it is significant as a scientific method but dangerous as sterile dogma." Quoted in Wilcox, *V. F. Calverton*, 151.

16. Phelps, *Young Sidney Hook*, 109.

17. "A Challenge to American Intellectuals: A Controversy; Lewis Mumford vs. V. F. Calverton," *Modern Quarterly* 5, no. 4 (Winter 1930–31): 407–21 (Mumford, "The Evolutionary Approach"; Calverton, "The Revolutionary Approach").

18. Editorial, "The Pulse of Modernity" *Modern Quarterly* 6, no. 3 (Autumn 1932): 5–12; and Lewis Corey, "The American Revolution," *Modern Quarterly* 6, no. 3 (Autumn 1932): 13–29. See also Wilcox, *V. F. Calverton*, 161–63; and Denning, *The Cultural Front*, 100–102.

19. Denning, *The Cultural Front*, 99–102. Further quoting Corey, "The university, science, technology, and learning were in general manifestations of bourgeois development . . . waging the bourgeois cultural struggle against the feudal order. But now all these forces . . . are opposed to the proletariat; its revolutionary culture, while it includes many concrete achievements, is necessarily and mainly potential, a culture of revolutionary criticism and ideological struggle, interpreting, clarifying, projecting, capable of becoming dominant only after the revolution." For more on Corey, see Paul Buhle, *A Dreamer's Paradise Lost: Louis C. Fraina/Lewis Corey (1892–1953) and the Decline of Radicalism in the United States* (Atlantic Highlands, N.J.: Humanities Press, 1995).

20. See, for example, "Progressive Labor's Institute," *Labor Age* 18, no. 9 (September 1929): 17–19, which indicates Corey's involvement in the CPLA and his attendance at their annual meeting where he presented a paper. Corey's article, "The American Revolution" in the autumn 1932 issue of *Modern Quarterly* echoed the ideas long promoted by Muste, Budenz, and the CPLA. Notably, Hardman's book received a favorable review in *Modern Quarterly*. See Nathan Fine's book review in *Modern Quarterly* 5, no. 1 (November 1928–February 1929): 123–25. Another intellectual close to the CPLA and AWP was Louis Adamic. In January 1932, he published an article titled "The Collapse of Organized Labor" in *Harper's* that sounded like a CPLA publication, though he never mentioned the group by name.

21. See Lewis Corey, Felix Cohen, J. B. S. Hardman, William L. Nunn, James Rorty, and D. J. Saposs, "The XYZ Monthly," January 22, 1932, JBSHP, box 6, folder 3; Minutes of CPLA National Executive Committee Meeting, May 10, 1932, JBSHP, box 38, folder 4; Report of the National Executive Committee to the CPLA Convention, September 3–5, 1932; *Our America* 1, no. 1 (January 1933). Muste, Hardman, and Calverton had been discussing the idea since 1928. See Hardman to Calverton dated January 30, 1928, VFCP, box 7.

22. Denning, *The Cultural Front*, 102.

23. See, for example, Phelps, *Young Sidney Hook*, 72–78; and Kutulas, *The Long War,* 64–70. Historians have also suggested that they were closer to the Trotskyists and other dissident Communists than to the Musteites. In fact, as will be seen in the next chapter, Calverton, Corey, and others often found them to be as dogmatic and sectarian as the Communists.

24. See Wilcox, *V. F. Calverton*, 181.

25. Hardman to Calverton, June 14, 1929, VFCP, box 7. See also Hardman to Calverton, March 2, 1928: "Your story is published in the current ADVANCE. When you write the next story please think of the tailors having to consult a dictionary too often." VFCP, box 7. In a revealing passage, Muste wrote to Louise Leonard that a person interested in the CPLA was not only mentally unstable, but also "one of the kind interested in sex and Greenwich Village radicalism, rather than economic radicalism. (Newbury flexions on 'personal morality' intended)." Muste to Louise Leonard, October 21, 1929, BLCC, box 42, folder 10.

26. Hardman to Calverton, June 14, 1929. Writing in 1930, Muste commented that it was ironic that the AFL feared "wild" intellectuals since, in his experience, they were overwhelmingly

timid and fearful about speaking up and taking action. See Muste, "Wild Intellectuals and Sober Workmen," *Labor Age* 19, no. 8 (August 1930): 4–6. See also the CPLA's criticism of Louis Adamic in M. Howe, "Groping in the Jungle," *Labor Age* 21, no. 7 (July 1932): 25–26.

27. Louis Budenz, "Bourgeois Bolsheviki," *Labor Age* 21, no. 8 (August 1932): 26–27.

28. Commentator, "Short Cuts to the Revolution," *Labor Age* 20, no. 10 (October 1931): 17–18 (my emphasis).

29. Edmund Wilson, quoted in Rosenzweig, "Radicals and the Jobless," 55.

30. Wilson, *The Thirties*, 415.

31. Edmund Wilson, *The Shores of Light: A Literary Chronicle of the Twenties and Thirties* (1952; reprint, New York: Farrar, Straus and Giroux, 1967), 591–92. See also Kosek, *Acts of Conscience*, 114.

32. See, for example, Tess Huff, "Notes on the Convention," *Labor Age* 21, no. 9 (September 1932): 19–20; advertisement for the Brookwood Bazaar, *Labor Age* 21, no. 11 (November 1932): 29; "Labor Sports Get Attention," *Brookwood Review* 9, no. 1 (December 1930): 2. It's unclear what the Musteites meant by "labor sports," since their athletic activities included such mainstream sports as baseball, volleyball, swimming, and hiking. The difference, I suppose, was that they were conducted by organized workers and that they were intended to build up movement morale and camaraderie.

33. Muste, quoted by Cara Cook to Robinson, August 22, 1978, AJMP-LA, box 2; Wilson, *The Thirties*, 415.

34. See Rosenzweig, "Organizing the Unemployed," 37–60.

35. A week earlier, Budenz debated the CP's second-in-command, Albert Weisbrod, at the Fourteenth Street Labor Temple. See "The Fight Grows Hotter," *Labor Age* 20, no. 7 (June 1931): 22. For the arguments made by Foster and Muste during the debate, see William Z. Foster, *Little Brothers of the Big Labor Fakers* (New York: Trade Union Unity League, 1931); Muste, "The Communists and the Unions," *Labor Age* 20, no. 6 (June 1931): 5–8; and "Flashes from the Labor World," *Labor Age* 20, no. 6 (June 1931): 22.

36. Louis Budenz, "Following the Fight," *Labor Age* 19, no. 1 (January 1930): 15; "Communist Strike-Breaking and Union-Wrecking," *Labor Age* 20, no. 9 (September 1931): 2–3: "The CPLA does not often engage in criticism of other progressive or radical elements in the labor movement," but it was time "to speak out about the strike-breaking and union-wrecking tactics which have recently been pursued by the Communist party." "Whenever Communists have gone into unorganized situations, progressives and radicals have refrained from interfering with them, under many instances have given help; but whenever some other group makes a strike or an organizing effort, Communists break violently into the situation, confuse the minds of the workers, set them to fighting against each other and so help the bosses and the state to crush the efforts being made."

37. Bloom, "Brookwood Labor College," 281–82.

38. Ibid., 265. See also Warren, *An Alternative Vision*, 21–25; and Muste, "Socialists and the Conference for Progressive Labor Action," typescript (ca. 1931), and Muste to "Militant Socialists," January 11, 1932, both in BLCC, box 29, folder 2; Confidential Memorandum on Relations Between the CPLA and the SP (ca. 1931), box 28, folder 24; Muste, "Note on Memorandum Re: CPLA in Relation to Other Organizations and Groups" (ca. 1931), and other related documents in BLCC, box 28, folder 26.

39. The rift between Muste and Oneal became quite public and contentious. See James Oneal, "Liberalism in the SP," *Labor Age* 20, no. 8 (August 1931): 14–16; and Bloom, "Brookwood Labor College," 268–70. Militant Leonard Bright called Oneal's attack on Muste "bitter,

unreasonable." See letter from Bright to Adolph Warshow, December 4, 1931, BLCC, box 28, folder 14.

40. See, for example, Muste, "Do We Need a New Political Party in the United States?" *Labor Age* 20, no. 4 (April 1931): 11–14. See also "Report on Political Organization," *Labor Age* 20, no. 7 (August 1931), 4–8; and editorial, "Do We Need a New Party," *Labor Age* 20, no. 10 (October 1931): 21–22. The CPLA also began to publicly criticize Norman Thomas. J. C. Kennedy wrote in *Labor Age* that "it is scarcely an exaggeration to say that Thomas has no socialist philosophy at all." See J. C. Kennedy, "Whither Socialism?" *Labor Age* 20, no. 7 (June 1931): 25–26.

41. The CPLA called for an active, disciplined membership, free from "ties that might compel them to subordinate CPLA activities or principles to those of another political group." See "Statement of Purpose," *Labor Age* 20, no. 11 (November 1931): 26. Norman Thomas and other SP members were quite critical of the decision to turn the CPLA into a political organization because they believed it would compete with the Socialist Party for the allegiance of the American working class, which was, indeed, Muste's ambition. Thomas resigned over the issue in 1931. See "Norman Thomas, the Communists and Our Political Discussion," *Labor Age* 20, no. 8 (September 1931): 3–4.

42. Muste to Bright, October 21, 1931, and October 14, 1931, both in BLCC, box 28, folder 13, BLCC. See also Muste to Bright, November 6, 1931, BLCC, box 28, folder 14; Muste to Militant Socialists, January 11, 1932; and "Socialist Militants and the CPLA," *Labor Age* 21, no. 2 (February 1932): 3–4, in which the CPLA criticized the January 1932 convention of the SP, which rejected militant proposals. Note that the CPLA was particularly critical of the Socialist Party's hostility to any method aside from parliamentarianism. Developments in the Socialist International, which he criticized for being "gradualist" and "class collaborationist," further alienated Muste from the party. See Charles Kramarsky, "Socialist Congress in Vienna," *Labor Age* 20, no. 10 (October 1931): 19–20; A. Cupelli, Ludwig Lore, David Saposs, and Mark Starr, "Left Trends in the International Labor Movement," *Labor Age* 20, no. 11 (November 1931): 20–22; and "Common Action by 'Left' Socialists," *Labor Age* 21, no. 6 (June 1932): 22.

43. Bright to Muste, October 26, 1931, and August 12, 1931, both in BLCC, box 28, folder 14. In his letter of resignation, Bright promised to continue working "wholeheartedly for the CPLA principles as they were before the N.P.P.—NEW POLITICAL POLICY" (emphasis in original).

44. Lefkowitz to Muste, November 16, 1931, BLCC, box 28, folder 14.

45. [Name unclear] to Muste, November 26, 1931, BLCC, box 28, folder 14. For more criticism of Muste's plans, see Charles Gardner to Muste, January 12, 1932, BLCC, box 28, folder 14; and Israel Mufson to Muste, February 8, 1932, BLCC, box 28, folder 15. For Muste's response to these critics, see Muste to Bright, October 20, 1931, BLCC, box 28, folder 14 and Muste to Chas. Gardner, February 17, 1932, BLCC, box 28, folder 15.

46. Muste, "The Meaning of the Convention," *Labor Age* 21, no. 9 (September 1932): 3–5.

47. See Muste, "The CPLA: A Positive Statement of Program and Action," 18–21. Not coincidentally, Muste published "Working-class Ethics" soon after this article appeared. See also the editorial "A Challenge to Militants," *Labor Age* 20, no. 11 (November 1931): 4–5.

48. Report of the National Executive Committee to the CPLA Convention, September 3–5, 1932. See also "Labor Realism" from report of the NEC to the Labor Day Convention, *Labor Age* 21, no. 10 (October 1932): 22–23.

49. Josephine Colby, David Saposs, J. C. Kennedy, Helen Norton, and Mark Starr, "Supplement to Statement with Regard to the Brookwood Situation"; see also Josephine Colby et al., "Statement with Regard to the Brookwood Situation," February 9, 1933; both in BLCC, box 29, folder 5.

50. See Josephine Colby to Sid [last name?] and Ruth [last name?], March 6, 1933, JCP, box 1, folder 2; Katherine Pollak letter to the editor, *Labor Age* 21, no. 2 (February 1932): 24; David Saposs to Louis Budenz, January 17, 1933, BLCC, box 1, folder 20; J.C. Kennedy to Louis Budenz, January 4, 1933, BLCC, box 1, folder 20. The problem all of them confronted was that Brookwood had indeed become associated in the public mind with the "Musteite" movement, but whether that was Muste's fault was another question. After all, they had all been party to the 1928 decision to extend the college's activities into the field; all had worked with Muste to craft a statement of purpose for the college that was almost identical to that of the CPLA's; all had been founding members of the CPLA, with Saposs and Kennedy serving on the NEC until their resignations in January 1933; and all had enthusiastically and eagerly participated in CPLA activities, which they combined with the fieldwork emphasis in Brookwood's curriculum.

51. See Colby to Sid and Ruth, March 6, 1933; Pollak letter to the editor, February 1932; Saposs to Budenz, January 17, 1933; Kennedy to Budenz, January 4, 1933. See also "Statement of A. J. Muste to Brookwood Students and Faculty" on behalf of himself, Tom Tippett, Lucille Kohn, Cara Cook, and Cal Bellaver, February 11, 1933, and "Rebuttal to Statement with Regard to the Brookwood Situation by Josephine Colby et al.," both in BLCC, box 29, folder 5; and "Recommendation of the Brookwood Faculty and Executive Staff to A. J. Based on Meetings of October 27–28, 1932," JBSHP, box 6, folder 7.

52. David Saposs to Friend, January 18, 1933, BLCC, box 1, folder 20; Louis Stanley book review, *New Republic*, January 14, 1933.

53. "Additional Remarks of Tom Tippett," in "Statement of A. J. Muste to Brookwood Students and Faculty," February 11, 1933; "Statement Issued by the Majority of the Students," March 3, 1933, and "Statement of the Minority of the Students to the Board of Directors," BLCC, box 1, folder 3; statements by Doris Prenner and Cara Cook in "Rebuttal to Statement with Regard to the Brookwood Situation by Colby et al.," in BLCC, box 29, folder 5. Muste and Lever quotes come from Bloom, "Brookwood Labor College," 304. See also Cara Cook, memoir, AJMP, reel 6.

54. "Statement of A. J. Muste to Brookwood Students and Faculty," February 11, 1933.

55. In presenting his educational philosophy, Muste quoted the radical educator George Counts, who was, incidentally, a member of the CPLA and the AWP: "'all education contains a large element of imposition, that in the very nature of the case this is inevitable . . . and that the frank acceptance of this fact by the educator is a major professional obligation. I even contend that the failure to do this involves the clothing of one's own deepest prejudices in the garb of universal truth and the introduction into the theory and practice of education of an element of obscurantism.'" See ibid.

56. Ibid. See also "Statement Requested by Brookwood Policy Committee," undated (ca. March 1933), by Muste, Tippett, Kohn, Cook, and Bellaver, BLCC, box 29, folder 5.

57. "Statement of the Majority of the Student Body of Brookwood Labor College with Regard to Action Taken at the Meeting of the Corporation on March 5, 1933," JBSHP, box 6, folder 7. As they explained, "Brookwood turned right, and we left." In supporting Muste, Thrya Edwards maintained that he was far more progressive on racial questions than his opponents on

the faculty. See Andrews, Thyra J. Edwards, 38. On the staff, see J.C. Kennedy, "Report to the Labor Members of the Board of Directors," March 10, 1933, BLCC, box 29, folder 3; Cara Cook to Acting Director, March 6, 1933; Cal Bellaver to Acting Director, March 6, 1933; and Tom Tippett to J. C. Kennedy, March 6, 1933, all in BLCC, box 28, folder 19. For the tendency of the alumni to favor Muste, see "Vote on Bd. of Directors Report," BLCC, box 1, folder 19. Some alumni formed the Brookwood Honor Roll Club as a pro-Muste alternative to the official alumni association known as the Brookwood Fellowship. See Cara Cook to Fellow Worker, March 21, 1933, BLCC, box 42, folder 22. See also Muste, "Whither Brookwood?" *Labor Age* 22, no. 1 (February–March 1933): 14–16.

58. For the left-wing bias of the Garland Fund, see Jack Lever to Labor Board of Directors, March 5, 1933, BLCC, box 1, folder 3; and Colby to Sid and Ruth, March 6, 1933. That some donors contributed out of personal loyalty to Muste can be gleaned by Elizabeth Glendower Evans's letter to the Temporary Finance Committee, April 14, 1933, in which she stated that "it is impossible for me to decide between you and Mr. Muste, and that if I had to decide I should stay with Mr. Muste—for old time's sake and because it was his valiant struggle for labor that first interested me in him and through him in Brookwood." See BLCC, box 28, folder 20. See also Lefkowitz memo (ca. March 1933), BLCC, box 28, folder 20, in which he states that the labor directors "knew Mr. Muste had the sympathy of the contributors, they knew his ability, persuasiveness and force of his personality."

59. Anna Davis to Evans, August 2, 1933, EGEP, reel 7.

60. Muste, "Sketches," 151.

61. See Colby to Sid and Ruth, March 6, 1933; Lefkowitz memo, undated (ca. March 1933), BLCC, box 28, folder 20.

62. Like others of Muste's opponents, Lefkowitz angrily defended his history of "militancy," as well as that of James Maurer, John Brophy, and Fannia Cohn. See Lefkowitz memo, undated (ca. March 1933). Within a year, the AWP was condemning such figures as A. J. Kennedy of the Lithographers, who had been a founding member of the CPLA, because he went to a dinner hosted by the WTUL in which Eleanor Roosevelt was the featured speaker. See "Red," "WTUL Gives Dinner to 'Friends of Labor,'" *Labor Action* 2, no. 6 (April 2, 1934): 8.

63. See Report of the National Executive Committee to the CPLA Convention, September 3–5, 1932. Indeed, for years, many suspected that Kennedy was a Communist and that Saposs was close to the Communists. Muste interpreted their changing position as a reflection of their "sudden" friendliness to the SP. See Muste, "Whither Brookwood?" 14–16. The NEC of the CPLA issued a statement ("What Is Sectarianism?") during the Brookwood controversy in which it rejected the notion that having a "clearly defined position and theory" constituted sectarianism. To be sectarian was to spend excessive energy in criticizing others, which the CPLA did not do, and "to impose dogmas and theories on mass organizations," again which the CPLA did not do. See editorial, *Labor Age* 22, no. 1 (February–March 1933): 25–26, 29.

64. See "Statement Adopted by the Board of Directors of Brookwood," May 5, 1933, BLCC, box 1, folder 3. See also Maurer to Kennedy, March 11, 1933, BLCC, box 29, folder 3; and Bloom's discussion in "Brookwood Labor College," 335–38. On the SP's evolving views and controversies over its relationship to Roosevelt and the Democratic Party, see Warren, *An Alternative Vision*, 124–33, 158–75. On the political realignment taking place in the 1930s, see Tobin, *Organize or Perish*; Rossinow, *Visions of Progress*; Lichtenstein, *The Most Dangerous Man in Detroit*; and Fraser, *Labor Will Rule*.

65. Bloom, "Brookwood Labor College," chapter 7.

66. Ibid., chapter 8. Other examples of Brookwooders who held positions in the CIO include Larry Heimbach, who led the ACW in Allentown, Pennsylvania; Griselda Kuhlman, who served as an organizer for the ACW; Elmer Cope, who served as a staff member for the CIO's Steelworkers Organizing Committee; and Merlin Bishop and Frank Winn of the United Auto Workers.

67. For example, Tom Tippett taught for FERA and then became education director of the Machinists; Amber Arthun (Brookwood staff member in the early 1920s) was on the staff of FERA's workers' education program; Robert Fechner, a member of Brookwood's board in the late 1920s, was appointed head of the Civilian Conservation Corps (CCC); John Jacobsen, instructor of economics at Brookwood from 1936 to 1937, became an instructor for FERA and the Work Projects Administration (WPA); Hilda Smith, a leader in the summer school movement who was close to Muste and Brookwood, became prominent in FERA's workers' education program; David Saposs became a labor official in the New Deal; Rose Schneiderman assumed prominence in the New Deal state; Mark Starr was educational director of the ILGWU; and M. H. Hedges served as a labor information officer for the United States in Europe after the war. In Philadelphia, the hosiery, textile, and clothing workers who were members of the CPLA and who had some success organizing the third-party movement decided in 1935 to support FDR. See Pivar, "Hosiery Workers and the Third-Party Impulse," 18–28.

68. See Denning, *The Cultural Front*; and Cohen, *Making a New Deal*.

69. Bloom, "Brookwood Labor College," 394.

70. Muste, "Sketches," 152–53. According to B. J. Widick, "The day that A. J. returned from Europe [in 1936] I was at his house—having come from Akron to inform him that the SWOC—through Clint Golden—was considering him for the job of educational director of the steel workers." See Widick's letter to the editor, *Labor History*, June 5, 1975, 563–64.

71. Muste, "Sketches," 155–56.

72. Muste, "Message to CPLA Organizers, Branches and Active Workers," March 10, 1933, JBSHP, box 38, folder 4; and Muste, "Sketches," 155–56.

73. Muste, "Sketches," 148–49.

74. Muste to Evans, September 18, 1934, EGEP, reel 7.

75. Sherwood Eddy and Reinhold Niebuhr authored an appeal for "Mr. Muste personally without any question about the use to which he makes of his time." See Eddy, Niebuhr, and Rev. W. B. Spofford appeal, May 6, 1933, EGEP, reel 7. For support from Evans, Davis, as well as Ethel Moors, see Davis to Evans, August 2, 1933; Evans to Muste, June 6, 1934; Muste to Evans, July 10, 1933; and Muste to Evans, July 24, 1933, all in EGEP, reel 7. For the quote, "marginal maintenance" in describing Muste's pay, see letter from Cara Cook et al. to friends, April 1936, EGEP, reel 7.

76. See Muste to Evans, July 10, 1933, and July 24, 1933, both in EGEP, reel 7. In a letter to Jo Ann Robinson dated August 22, 1978, Cara Cook quoted from a letter she received from Muste on February 1, 1935, in which he expresses concerns about his daughter Connie's health: "she has grown like a beanpole, and had insufficient physical reserves." See AJMP-LA, box 2.

77. Muste to Evans, September 18, 1933, EGEP, reel 7. See also Nancy Baker to Jo Ann Robinson, February 8, 1979, AJMP-LA, box 2; and Peter Muste, interview by author, New York City, June 2006.

78. See Evans to Muste, June 6, 1934, EGEP, reel 7; Nancy Muste to Evans, September 14, 1933, EGEP, reel 7.

Chapter 7. To the Left

Epigraph: Muste, "Note on Memorandum Re: CPLA in Relation to Other Organizations and Groups."

1. V. F. Calverton to Muste, October 28, 1933, VFCP, box 11. Sidney Hook wrote to Calverton in early 1934: "The future belongs to the W.P.—don't you think?" See VFCP, box 8.

2. See "Historic Road to the New Party," *Labor Action* 2, no. 21 (December 1, 1934): 3.

3. See *Build the American Workers Party* (New York: Provisional Organizing Committee of the American Workers Party, 1934); Muste and Budenz, "Letter to CPLA Branches and Members" and "Instructions to Organizers and Branches of the American Workers Party," both in JBSHP, box 38, folder 4; "Why the New Party," *Labor Action* 1, no. 13 (December 20, 1933): 1–3.

4. Hardman, "What Kind of Party?" *Labor Action*, ca. December 1933, 3–4; Hardman, "More About the Kind of Party We Are Building," *Labor Action*, ca. February 1934, 3. Both clippings found in JBSH, box 38, folder 6. See also *Build the American Workers Party*; and "Why the New Party."

5. Muste, "Sketches," 134–35.

6. In its "Declaration of Principles," the WPUS, formed through the fusion of the CLA and the AWP in December 1934, held that "the policy of folded arms, passive resistance, 'conscientious objection' etc. is completely futile as a means of struggle against imperialist war, regardless of the sincerity and courage of those who resort to it." See "Declaration of Principles" and "Constitution of the Workers Party," both in *Labor Action* 2, no. 22 (December 15, 1934): 5–7.

7. Breitman, Le Blanc, and Wald, *Trotskyism in the United States*, 17. See also Myers, *The Prophet's Army*, 112–15. Myers estimates that the AWP had about two thousand members at the time of the merger. In addition to the Trotskyists, in December 1933, a delegation from Benjamin Gitlow's Workers Communist League approached Muste with a merger proposal. Like the CLA, the Gitlow group grew out of power struggles within the American Communist Party and the Communist International. In 1928, the Comintern intervened in a factional fight between Benjamin Gitlow, Bertram Wolfe, and Jay Lovestone, on the one hand, and William Z. Foster, on the other, siding with the former only to expel them in 1929 for allegedly supporting Nikolai Bukharin in the power struggle that consumed the Soviet party. For the Gitlow group's proposal for a merger, see Minutes of CPLA (AWP) National Executive Committee Meeting, December 10, 1933, JBSHP, box 38, folder 4; for the CLA, see "Many Groups Discuss AWP Program," *Labor Action* 2, no. 5 (March 15, 1934): 4.

8. Hook and Burnham, "Analysis and Recommendations," appendix to the "Summary of Negotiations," submitted by the AWP's Negotiating Committee to the membership, August 30, 1934, JBSHP, box 38, folder 5. Max Shachtman later recalled of Hook and Burnham, "they were much more interested in the sort of thing that preoccupied us—theoretical questions, programmatic precision, internationalism, an active struggle against Stalinism, a clear differentiation from reformism—in a word, things that were not quite uppermost in the minds of the traditional followers of Muste." Shachtman, quoted in Phelps, *Young Sidney Hook*, 121.

9. See, for example, Howe to Hardman, June 21, 1934; Hardman to Howe, June 28, 1934; Budenz and Hardman memos, appendix to the "Summary of Negotiations," submitted by the AWP's Negotiating Committee to the membership, August 30, 1934. All in JBSHP, box 38, folder 5. See also "Many Groups Discuss AWP Program"; and Grant, "Louis Francis Budenz: The

Origins of a Professional Ex-Communist." James Cannon maintained that Hardman, Lore, and Budenz opposed the merger because they were "fake" revolutionists. See his *History of American Trotskyism*, 210–13.

10. Muste, "Labor Internationalism," *Labor Action* 1, no. 13 (December 20, 1933): 3; Muste, "Building Labor Internationalism," *Labor Action* 2, no. 13 (July 15, 1934): 5. See also his "The American Approach."

11. "Many Groups Discuss AWP Program." See also Phelps, *Young Sidney Hook*; and Grant, "Louis Francis Budenz," 214.

12. Bernstein, *The Turbulent Years*, 217; Denning, *The Cultural Front*, xiv.

13. Bernstein, *The Turbulent Years*, 217–25; and introduction to Philip A. Korth and Margaret R. Beegle, *I Remember Like Today: The Auto-Lite Strike of 1934* (East Lansing: Michigan State University Press, 1988). See also Muste, "The Battle of Toledo," *Nation* 138, no. 3596 (June 6, 1934): 639–40; and Muste, "Terror in Toledo," *Labor Action* 2, no. 10 (June 1, 1934): 1–3.

14. *Labor Action* is full of references to these actions. See, for example, "Bosses Hit by Militant Food Strike," *Labor Action* 1, no. 7 (July 1, 1933): 2; and "Lehigh City Jobless League Helps Strikers," *Labor Action* 1, no. 11 (October 11, 1933): 2. An example of how contemporaries later disassociated themselves from the strike's radicals can be seen in the collection of oral histories taken by Korth and Beegle, *I Remember Like Today*. This issue of radicalism and historical memory is thoughtfully explored by Jacquelyn Dowd Hall in "Open Secrets: Memory, Imagination, and the Refashioning of Southern Identity," *American Quarterly* 50, no. 1 (March 1998), 109–24.

15. Roger H. Hall, "Sam Pollock, Labor Activist," 1–3. See also Muste, "The Battle of Toledo"; and Muste, "Terror in Toledo."

16. Muste, "The Battle of Toledo." See also "Workers Demand General Strike," *Labor Action* 2, no. 10 (June 1, 1934): 3; Louis Budenz, "Toledo," *Labor Action* 2, no. 11 (June 15, 1934): 1–2; and Bernstein, *The Turbulent Years*, 224–30.

17. See Grant, "Louis Francis Budenz," 216.

18. "The Auto-Lite Agreement," *Labor Action* 2, no. 11 (June 15, 1934): 2. See also Bernstein, *The Turbulent Years*, 224–29.

19. See Muste, "The Battle of Toledo"; and Muste, "Terror in Toledo."

20. Roy Howard, quoted in Rosenzweig, "Radicals and the Jobless," 68.

21. "Muste Arrested," *Labor Action* 2, no. 11 (June 15, 1934): 1; "AWP Leaders Face Trial," *Labor Action* 2, no. 12 (July 1, 1934): 1–2; "AWP Leaders Defy Illinois Repression; Muste Back in State," *Labor Action* 2, no. 13 (July 15, 1934): 1–3; and Muste, "Sketches," 161.

22. Muste, "The Party and the Leagues," *Labor Action* 2, no. 14 (August 1, 1934): 5. See also editorial, "Political Strikes," *Labor Action* 2, no. 10 (June 1, 1934): 4.

23. See, for example, Muste, "Roosevelt's 'Revolution,'" *Labor Action* 1, no. 12 (November 8, 1933): 3. See also Rosenzweig, "Radicals and the Jobless."

24. See, for example,"Germany, Hitler, and US," second zero issue of *Labor Action*, February 25, 1933, 4; and "What Does Fascism Do?" *Labor Action* 1, no. 1 (April 1, 1933): 4.

25. Muste, "Building the Party," *Labor Action* 2, no. 15 (September 1, 1934): 2–3.

26. "Summary of Negotiations" between the AWP and the CLA, August 30, 1934, JBSHP, box 38, folder 5; "Letter from CLA to the AWP," *Labor Action* 2, no. 17 (October 1, 1934): 3.

27. Hook and Burnham, "Analysis and Recommendations," appendix to the "Summary of Negotiations." See also Hook, "Marxism and Democracy," *Labor Action*, May Day Supplement

1934. As Hook explained, the notion of a dictatorship suggested that the party would rule a workers' state, as in the Soviet Union, rather than workers' councils, with the party serving as one group among many, seeking leadership by "by virtue of the correctness of its line and not by choking off all other working-class elements that may be opposed to it." For James Burnham's controversial memo, see JBSHP, box 38, folder 5.

28. See Howe to Hardman, June 21, 1934, and Hardman to Howe, June 28, 1934, JBSHP, box 38, folder 5. See also Grant, "Louis Francis Budenz."

29. Memo from Los Angeles branch of the AWP to the AWP's Provisional Organizing Committee, August 1, 1934, VFCP, box 1. They were further angered when Muste failed to make good upon a promise to share their criticism with the larger membership, thus essentially depriving them "of any opportunity whatsoever to present our objections or our views."

30. Budenz and Hardman memos, appendix to the "Summary of Negotiations." Emphasis in original.

31. See "Party Building Is Discussed" and "Letter from AWP to CLA," *Labor Action* 2, no. 17 (October 1, 1934): 1–6, and 3. Further evidence for his position can be found in Muste, "The Workers Party Is Founded," *New International*, December 1934, 129, in which he explained that "elaboration of theory" would help to ensure that revolutionary action would not become "merely opportunistic. . . . [Theory] leads, therefore, to practical work in the labor scene. On the other hand, a group which seeks to act in a responsible and not an adventurist spirit in the revolutionary movement . . . may indeed scorn Talmudic theologizing and debates which lead simply to more debates, but it cannot be indifferent to theory."

32. In late September 1934, the AWP's Provisional Organizing Committee sent a letter to Cannon demanding that the CLA oppose "a similar policy in the United States." The CLA promised that it would not follow the policy of the French Turn. See Provisional Organizing Committee minutes, September 25, 1934, JBSHP, box 38, folder 5; "Significance of French Trotskyists Action," *Labor Action* 2, no. 18 (October 15, 1934): 4–7; Muste, "The Road to the New Party," *Labor Action* 2, no. 18 (October 15, 1934): 5–6.

33. "Letter from AWP to CLA," *Labor Action* 2, no. 17 (October 1, 1934): 3; "Letter from AWP to CLA," *Labor Action* 2, no. 18 (October 15, 1934): 8. See also Muste, confidential memo, October 10, 1934, and Harry Howe's suggestions for merger conditions, both in JBSHP, box 38, folder 5. In addition to demanding the CLA's assurance that it did not intend to follow the French Turn, the AWP wanted to retain its name, Muste's leadership, and an allocation of leadership positions that corresponded to their greater influence in mass organizations. Eager for consummation, the CLA acceded to making Muste national secretary and demurred that the two groups agreed on the "fundamentals."

34. In his *History of American Trotskyism*, Cannon explains why the CLA was willing to let the AWP have the post of national secretary: "We knew what it meant to them, with their overemphasis on purely organizational matters, to have the secretaryship because the secretary, theoretically at least, controls the party machine. We were more interested in the editorship because that shapes more directly the ideology of the movement" (p. 217).

35. "For the New Party," *Labor Action* 2, no. 19 (November 1, 1934): 5 and 8; AWP and CLA, "Proposed Program for New Party," and Hardman to Breier, October 29, 1934, both in JBSHP, box 38, folder 5. Breier agreed, writing to Munsey Gleason that "we have intellectually been sold down the river to the Trotskites [*sic*]" who had been "evasive" about the French Turn. See letter from Breier to Munsey Gleason, October 30, 1934, JBSHP, box 38, folder 5. Hardman

was so incensed by the proposed program that he wrote a sarcastic memo detailing its flaws, such as "the significance of the new party will not come as a result of using capital [letters]" in referring to it. See Hardman, "Suggested Changes to Proposed Joint Statement," JBSHP, box 38, folder 5.

36. Letter from Breier to Gleason, October 30, 1934, JBSHP, box 38, folder 5.

37. Allen Stiller, "Trotsky Merger Fatal," *Labor Action* 2, no. 19 (November 1, 1934): 6. In making this case, Stiller cited Muste's argument that revolution in the United States must be birthed out of the "experience" of American workers. In a private letter to Calverton, he complained that it appeared that the merger was "merely a matter of time," rather than a real debate to be resolved at the convention in late November. "I sincerely believe your statement that the Trotskyists 'will be allowed to come only on AWP terms,' is a bit naïve. . . . I am absolutely convinced that no American party will be built unless it makes a complete break with past factionalism and sectarianism. . . . I consider it inevitable, absolutely that the CLA guys will get control of the organization."

38. William Montross, "Pre-Convention Discussion," *Labor Action* 2, no. 20 (November 15, 1934): 6–7.

39. Phelps, *Young Sidney Hook*, 122.

40. Letter from Breier to Gleason, October 30, 1934; Breier to Hardman, October 21, 1934; Breier to Hardman, November 2, 1934; all in JBSHP, box 38, folder 5.

41. Breier to Gleason, October 30, 1934. See also telegram to the Provisional Organizing Committee from Breier, McKinney, and Hardman on the eve of the convention; Allentown Resolution re: Party Convention, November 2, 1934; Hardman to Muste, November 1, 1934, all in JBSHP, box 38, folder 5. Similar resolutions apparently arrived from Toledo and Pittsburgh. For Budenz's sinusitis and its possible psychosomatic origins, see Grant's discussion in "Louis Francis Budenz," 215–16.

42. "AWP Convention Votes Unanimously for Merger," *Labor Action* 2, no. 22 (December 15, 1934): 3; Hardman to Muste, November 1, 1934, JBSHP, box 38, folder 5. Never in favor of the merger, Budenz joined the Communist Party and later became a famous ex-Communist. See Grant, "Louis Francis Budenz"; and Budenz, *This Is My Story*. Others who joined the Communist Party included Arnold Johnson, Bill Reich, Winslow Hallett, and Anthony Ramuglia. Hardman continued to serve as editor of the ACW's organ, the *Advance*, and later served as chair of the Inter-Union Institute for Labor and Democracy; Cara Cook went on to work for the New York WTUL; and Tippett became education director of the Machinists union.

43. Rosenzweig, "Radicals and the Jobless," 69.

44. "Declaration of Principles" and "Constitution of the Workers Party," 5–7; "WP Program of Action," *New Militant* 1, no. 10 (February 9, 1935): 3. The WPUS did set up an international workers' school, but its focus was on building the party rather than building a working-class culture. See Muste to Branches, December 24, 1934; and "Report of the IWS Administrator on First Semester," probably for the June 1935 plenum; both in MSP, reel 12.

45. For example, Cannon wrote to a comrade who opposed the French Turn that he had approached the "problem with some elements of subjectivity. This is the most fatal thing in politics." See Cannon to Comrade Heisler, January 1, 1936, MSP, reel 12. This language was used by all members of the WPUS, including Muste.

46. Cannon, *History of American Trotskyism*, 213. See also "Resolution for the New York Membership [CLA] Meeting to Elect Delegates" (ca. fall 1934), MSP, reel 12, which states that

the goal of merger discussions was to isolate "the right wing of the AWP and in bringing the AWP steadily closer and eventually securing an agreement for fusion without a single concession in principle." Paul Le Blanc disputes the notion that there was a "sectarian impulse within the tradition of American Trotskyism" (Breitman, Le Blanc, and Wald, *Trotskyism in the United States*, xi), but my research has suggested otherwise.

47. Cannon, *History of American Trotskyism*, 240.

48. "The once militant, growing, and effective National Unemployed League lies handicapped," Arnold Johnson told a congressional committee in the mid-1930s. "There is not one section of the mass movement that has not been injured by these recriminations." Johnson, quoted in Rosenzweig, "Radicals and the Jobless," 71, 74–75. By 1936, membership in the Unemployed Leagues was about a third of what it had been in 1933. The crisis in the leagues reached its apogee in the winter of 1935–36 and the spring of 1936. See Minutes of WPUS Political Committee Meeting, December 27, 1935, December 30–31, 1935, January 8, 1936, April 13, 1936; and Muste to National Committee members, June 9, 1936. All in MSP, reel 12.

49. Cannon, *History of American Trotskyism*, 247. Organizers like Selander and Pollock in Toledo and Bert Cochran similarly attained leadership roles and gained the trust of the workers only to be criticized by the party leadership for not translating that trust into gains for the party. See, for example, Arne Swabeck to Cochran, July 19,1935, Muste to Cochran, August 29, 1935, and Muste to Cochran, October 31, 1935, all in BCP, box 1, folder 1.

50. See, for example, Hall, "Sam Pollock, Labor Activist"; biographical sketch of Elmer Fern Cope, in *Guide to the Microfilm Edition of the Elmer Fern Cope Papers* (Wilmington, Del.: Scholarly Resources, 1995); and Rosenzweig, "Radicals and the Jobless," 74.

51. Even then, the question was divisive among members of the CLA, with the "Oehlerites," led by the Bolshevik purists Hugo Oehler and Tom Stamm, and the "Weberites," led by Jack Weber, deeply opposed to entering the SP. See "Resolution for the New York Membership [CLA] Meeting to Elect Delegates" (ca. fall 1934) and Hugo Oehler, "Proposed Amendment to the Draft Thesis of the NEC on the New Party" (ca. fall 1934), both documents in MSP, reel 12. In the summer of 1935, Jack Weber revealed that the CLA had entrusted Cannon with "the responsibility of winning the Musteites to the favor of the French Turn," and that the decision to postpone all political discussions for six months after the merger was a strategy for securing Muste's assent. In his *History of American Trotskyism*, Cannon denied that his support for the French Turn in the United States was premeditated, while also admitting that the issue had divided the CLA as early as September 1934 (see pp. 222–24 and 254). As far as Muste and other former members of the AWP were concerned, the policy of the WPUS toward both the Socialist and Communist parties was to recruit their members through the cultivation of "fractions" who would at opportune moments leave their respective parties and join the WPUS. See "Report by Sub-Committee on Fraction Work," in Minutes of WPUS Political Meeting, January 7, 1935; "Recommendation on Communist Party Fraction Work" (ca. January 1935). All documents in MSP, reel 12.

52. For Muste's conviction that the Trotskyists' methods violated working-class ethics, see "Interview with Mr. A. J. Muste," Socialist Movement Project, May 31, 1965, Oral History Research Office, Columbia University, 11; Muste, "My Experiences in Labor and Radical Struggles of the Thirties," in Rita Simon, ed., *As We Saw the Thirties: Essays on Social and Political Movements of a Decade* (Urbana: University of Illinois Press, 1967), 147; Muste, "The True International," 668–69.

53. "Muste and Cannon Start National Tour, Jan. 13," *New Militant* 1, no. 1 (December 15, 1934): 1; "Big Meeting Hears Muste and Cannon on WPUS Program" and "Muste Dinner," *New Militant* 1, no. 3 (December 29, 1934): 1.

54. Muste's commitment to unifying the party can be seen in a series of articles he wrote for the *New Militant* and the *New International* that were clearly intended to complement the editors' overriding concern with the international question, such as "Labor in 1935: Panorama and Prognoses," *New International* 2, no. 3 (May 1935): 102–3; "Some Lessons of the Toledo Strike," *New International* 2, no. 4 (July 1935): 127–29; "Strikes on the 1935 Horizon," *New International* 2, no. 5 (August 1935): 153–56; and "Trade Unions and the Revolution," *New International* 2, no. 5 (August 1935); and, most significantly, "The American Approach," which, as noted above, appeared in series form over the course of the summer of 1935 in the *New Militant* and later as a WPUS pamphlet. His commitment to unifying the party can further be seen in his initial support for disciplinary action against former AWP comrades whom the Cannon-Shachtman faction charged with failing to accurately present the party line. He quickly regretted this decision and thereafter focused on trying to prevent factionalism.

55. For the efforts of the Musteites to create a more democratic movement, see, for example, Muste, McKinney, Johnson, Selander, Karl Lore, and F. King, "Statement on the Internal Party Situation," June 1935 Plenum; Muste, "Motions on Internal Party Situation"; Minutes of WPUS Political Committee Meeting, July 1 and August 27, 1935; Muste, "How C-S Builds the Party" (ca. October 1935). All in MSP, reel 12. For the disciplinary actions of the Cannon-Shachtman faction and Muste's growing opposition to it, see Minutes of WPUS Political Committee Meeting, February 4 and 21, 1935, March 25, 1935, April 9 and 28, 1935, May 27, 1935, December 30–31, 1935, January 7 and 16, 1936; and Muste letter to branches, March 27, 1935. All in MSP, reel 12.

56. The MSP contain voluminous materials regarding this ongoing battle. See especially Muste, "Resolution on SP Work," June 1935 Plenum; Jack Weber, "Resolution on the SP and CP" for the June 1935 Plenum; "Resolution on Attitude of WPUS Toward SP and CP by Cannon and Shachtman," June 1935 Plenum; Minutes of WPUS Political Committee Meeting, July 1, 1935, August 27, 1935, October 28, 1935; Muste and McKinney memorandum, August 12, 1935; internal bulletins of August 13, 1935, August 29, 1935, and September 6, 1935; Muste, "How C-S Builds the Party"; Political Committee to Branches, October 29, 1935. All in MSP, reel 12. See also "Plenum Report," *New Militant* 1, no. 28 (July 6, 1935): 2; Cannon, *History of American Trotskyism*, 213.

57. Budenz resigned from the party in May 1935, charging that it was "moving via Trotsky-ism into the SP." Less than a year later, he would join the CP, along with Arnold Johnson, Bill Reich, Munsey Gleason, and several other Musteites. Howe and Breier resigned soon after Budenz, while Lore was finally expelled because he refused to meet with the Political Committee to discuss disciplinary charges against him. Truax would resign in October, disgusted by the way comrades "undermined" each other, as well as the party's "foolish factional sectarianism." Meanwhile, the intellectuals who had played such a central role in pushing for the fusion dropped away from active involvement. Both Calverton and Rorty decided that they would serve as sympathizers, not members, while Hook remained distinctly on the sidelines. All of this is documented in Minutes of WPUS Political Committee Meeting, April 28, 1935, May 27, 1935, June 10, 1935, August 27, 1935, and October 14, 1935. All in MSP, reel 12. See also McKinney, OHAL, 13. For Calverton's decision to be a sympathizer and not a member, see "Meeting of Secretariat," April 14, 1935, and Jack Weber, "Statement on Internal Situation," June Plenum, MSP, reel 12. Hook's reasons for not playing an active role in the WPUS are unclear, but it was probably due to its greater interest in philosophical and academic pursuits. Whatever the reason, it was a source of irritation to the Political Committee. See Minutes of WPUS Political Committee Meeting, March 9, 1935, MSP, reel 12. See also Phelps, *Young Sidney Hook*, 127–28.

58. Muste, "A Forerunner of the Revolution," *New Militant* 1, no. 36 (August 31, 1935): 3. Muste traveled to North Carolina for the funeral where he gave an address to a crowd of

hundreds of mourners. See Minutes of WPUS Political Committee Meeting, August 27, 1935, MSP, reel 12.

59. See Minutes of WPUS Political Committee Meeting, October 28, 1935; Muste, "Political Aspects" (ca. December 1935); Minutes of WPUS Political Committee Meeting, December 9 and 30–31; Jack Weber to "Ray," December 7, 1935. All in MSP, reel 12. See also McKinney, OHAL.

60. Minutes of WPUS Political Committee Meeting, December 23 and 27, 1935, MSP, reel 12.

61. Muste and Jack Weber, "Comments on C-S Efforts to Postpone Convention," Workers Party Internal Bulletin, January 10, 1936; Minutes of WPUS Political Committee Meeting, January 22, 1936; and Albert Glotzer to Muste, in the Minutes of WPUS Political Committee Meeting, January 22, 1936, MSP, reel 12.

62. Maurice Spector to Martin Abern, February 8, 1936; Leon Trotsky to Muste, February 8, 1936; Shachtman to V. R. Dunne, February 17, 1936. All in MSP, reel 12. See also Cannon to Bert Cochran, February 10, 1935, BCP, box 1, folder 2.

63. As Muste explained, he wanted to focus on "field work and writing," and allowed Arne Swabeck to handle administrative work. See Minutes of WPUS Political Committee Meeting, March 3, 1936, MSP, reel 12; Muste, "Fragment of Autobiography," 329.

64. Pesotta was right: the union soon thereafter obtained the closed shop. See Rose Pesotta, *Bread Upon the Waters* (Ithaca, N.Y.: ILR Press, 1987), 223–25.

65. Cannon, *History of American Trotskyism*, 213, 233.

66. Muste, "My Experiences in Labor and Radical Struggles of the 30s," 141.

67. Cannon, *History of American Trotskyism*, 235, 207.

68. See Breitman, Le Blanc, and Wald, *Trotskyism in the United States*, 22–25. See also Myers, *The Prophet's Army*, 113–14; and Warren, *An Alternative Vision*, 77–85.

69. See, especially, "Interview with Mr. A. J. Muste," Socialist Movement Project, May 31, 1965, Oral History Research Office, Columbia University.

70. Muste, "The True International," 667.

71. For the Communist Party and World War II, see Isserman, *Which Side Were You On?*

72. Cara Cook, Lucille Kohn, and Doris Prenner, appeal letter, April 1935, copy in EGEP, reel 7.

73. Quotes are from Robinson, *Abraham Went Out*, 61.

74. Muste, "My Experience in Labor and Radical Struggles," 146.

75. Robinson, *Abraham Went Out*, 62–63; Muste, "My Experience in Labor and Radical Struggles," 146.

76. Muste, "My Experience in Labor and Radical Struggles,"145–46.

77. Muste, "Fragment of Autobiography," 338.

78. Muste, "The True International," 668.

79. Kosek, *Acts of Conscience*, 149.

Chapter 8. Muste and the Origins of Nonviolence in the United States

Epigraph: Muste, *Non-violence in an Aggressive World*, 21.

1. Kosek, *Acts of Conscience*, 146. Similar statistics can be found in Muste memorandum for Percy Bartlett, secretary of International Fellowship of Reconciliation (IFOR), [1947], FOR, box 1, folder 5.

2. See, for example, Paul Jones, "The Philosophy of a Madman," FOR pamphlet, 1923, JNSP, box 9, folder 2; Bruno Lasker, "A More Perfect Union," FOR pamphlet, 1925, FOR, box 5, folder 1; Anna Louise White, "Reconciliation at Work," *Fellowship* 2, no. 4 (April 1936); and Sherwood Eddy, "The Delta Cooperative Farm," *Fellowship* 2, no. 5 (May 1936).

3. Roosevelt quoted in James L. Roark et al., *The American Promise: A History of the United States*, 4th ed., vol. 2, *From 1865* (Boston: Bedford/St. Martins, 2009), 926. For the New Deal's ethnic pluralism, as well as the growing importance of antiracist politics on the liberal left, see, for example, Gary Gerstle, *American Crucible: Race and Nation in the Twentieth Century* (Princeton, N.J.: Princeton University Press, 2001); Von Eschen, *Race Against Empire*; and Sullivan, *Days of Hope*.

4. Muste, "Address for CBS's *Church of the Air*," typescript, September 3, 1939. Copy in AJMP, reel 3.

5. Muste, "Foundations of Democracy: The Role of Economic Groups" typescript (ca. 1945), AJMP, reel 4.

6. The term "labor metaphysic" was coined by C. Wright Mills to refer to the notion that the working class was the agent of social change, a notion that he argued was made obsolete by the development of a welfare state. See his famous "Letter to the New Left," *New Left Review* 1, no. 5 (September–October 1960): 18–23.

7. Muste, "Winning Industrial Workers to Christ and His Program," typescript (ca. 1937–38), AJMP, reel 4.

8. Muste, typescript (ca. 1941), copy in AJMP, reel 3. See also his *Non-violence in an Aggressive World*. Muste's closest ideological ally was the radical Catholic Dorothy Day, though the two appear to have only met each other a few times before the Cold War. In fact, Day's spiritual, intellectual, and political journey mirrored his in remarkable ways, and the two would collaborate frequently in the postwar era. See Dorothy Day, *The Long Loneliness: The Autobiography of Dorothy Day* (New York: Harper, 1952); Dorothy Day, *From Union Square to Rome* (Silver Spring, Md.: Preservation of the Faith Press, 1938); Dorothy Day, "The Catholic Worker Stand on Strikes," *Catholic Worker* 4, no. 3 (July 1936); William D. Miller, *Dorothy Day: A Biography* (San Francisco: Harper and Row, 1982); and Piehl, *Breaking Bread*. Muste himself recognized the affinity between his ideas and those of the Catholic Workers when he was invited to speak at a round-table discussion at their New York house of hospitality in 1937. "Nowhere has the Fellowship message as I have been trying to state it to all kinds of audiences this winter met with a more sympathetic hearing." See Muste, "Catholic Workers Unite," *Fellowship* 3, no. 6 (June 1937).

9. I borrow this turn of phrase from David Ehrenfeld, *The Arrogance of Humanism* (New York: Oxford University Press, 1982).

10. These quotes are from Muste, "Return to Pacifism," 199–201, and Muste, *Non-violence in an Aggressive World*, 3–5, but virtually the same language can be found in all of his speeches and articles from this period. See, for example, Muste, "Peace Is Indivisible," *Fellowship* 2, no. 8 (October 1936); Muste, "Winning Industrial Workers to Christ and His Program"; and Muste, address to the Women's Association, April 1938, AJMP, reel 3.

11. As Muste put it, citing many of these authors, "The conviction is being expressed by a growing number of writers of the Left that in large measure the crisis in the movement is due to the neglect of ethical factors." See *Non-violence in an Aggressive World*, 90–91. When Muste assumed the post of minister of Labor Temple in 1937, discussed below, he focused in particular

on organizing forums that featured ex-Communists who were asking the same sorts of questions that preoccupied him. See Muste, "Labor Temple's Mission," *Brick Church Record*, May 1938, clipping in AJMP, reel 3, in which he asserted that his goal was to preach the "relevance of the Christian faith today to people who have been under the influence of modern currents of thought." See also Muste to V. F. Calverton, October 24, 1938, VFCP, box 11; Muste, Christmas Greetings, December 26, 1937, AJMP, reel 6; and Muste, "Beyond Marxism," *Fellowship* 3, no. 8 (October 1937): 9. Jo Ann Ooiman Robinson makes this point as well in "The Pharos of the East Side, 1937–1940: Labor Temple Under the Direction of A. J. Muste," *Journal of Presbyterian History* 48, no. 1 (Spring 1970): 18–37. For an important anthology of anti-Stalinist thought, see Arthur Koestler et al., *The God That Failed* (New York: Columbia University Press, 2001). On American anti-Stalinism and the idea of totalitarianism, see Pells, *The Liberal Mind in a Conservative Age*; Wald, *The New York Intellectuals*; Alpers, *Dictators, Democracy and American Public Culture*; and Hannah Arendt's classic, *The Origins of Totalitarianism* (New York: Meridian, 1958). On existential theology, see Will Herberg, *Four Existentialist Theologians: A Reader from the Work of Jacques Maritain, Nicolas Berdyaev, Martin Buber, and Paul Tillich* (Westport, Conn.: Greenwood Press, 1975).

12. Reinhold Niebuhr, "Would Jesus Be a Modernist Today," *World Tomorrow*, 7, no. 3 (March 1929): 123.

13. For the widespread appeal of pacifism to mainline Protestants during the interwar years, see Sittser, *A Cautious Patriotism*; and Heather Warren, *Theologians of a New World Order: Reinhold Niebuhr and the Christian Realists, 1920–1948* (New York: Oxford University Press, 1997).

14. Niebuhr, *Moral Man and Immoral Society*, esp. xx and xvii–xix.

15. Ibid., 172, 180, 234–35. See also Warren, *Theologians of a New World Order*; and Fox, *Reinhold Niebuhr*.

16. Muste, *Non-violence in an Aggressive World*, esp. chap. 4.

17. Quote comes from Meyer, *Protestant Search for Political Realism*, 369.

18. Muste, "Pacifism and Perfectionism," 312, 319; and Muste, "Theology of Despair," 307.

19. Muste, *Non-violence in an Aggressive World*, 33–34. See also Muste, "Pacifism and Perfectionism," 308–21 and Muste, "Theology of Despair," 302–7.

20. Muste, *Non-violence in an Aggressive World*, 7–8, 12–13, 107–9.

21. For Muste's refusal to rely on "proof-texts," see ibid., chap. 2. For the tendency of his fellow pacifists to selectively use such proof texts, see Appelbaum, *Kingdom to Commune*, 62–65. Ironically, as Appelbaum points out, pacifists often accused their opponents of literalism.

22. Muste, *Non-violence in an Aggressive World*, 174–75. See also Muste, "The World Task of Pacifism," 222–25.

23. For Gandhi's political thought, see Parekh, *Gandhi*; Bhikhu Parekh, *Gandhi's Political Philosophy: A Critical Examination* (London: Macmillan, 1989); B. R. Nanda, *Gandhi and His Critics*, reprint ed. (Delhi: Oxford University Press, 1994); and Joseph S. Alter, *Gandhi's Body: Sex, Diet, and the Politics of Nationalism* (Philadelphia: University of Pennsylvania Press, 2000).

24. See Muste, "The World Task of Pacifism." As is discussed further in the next chapter, Muste never shared many of his pacifist comrades' aversion to urban, industrial life or their interest in alternative communities.

25. Applebaum, *Kingdom to Commune*, 182–83.

26. Muste, *Non-violence in an Aggressive World*, 2–3. On the invention of the "Judeo-Christian tradition," see Marty, "A Judeo-Christian Looks at the Judeo-Christian Tradition," 858–60; and Silk, "Notes on the Judeo-Christian Tradition in America," 65–85.

27. As one Jewish leader remarked, a "Jewish Gandhi in Germany" would last "about five minutes." Quoted in Kosek, *Acts of Conscience*, 160.

28. See, for example, Muste, "Return to Pacifism," 195–202; and Muste, "Peace Is Indivisible," *Fellowship* 2, no. 8 (October 1936).

29. For the desperate shape of the Muste family's finances, see Muste to Tucker Smith, April 30, 1936, BLCC, box 12, folder 2. For Anne's aspirations for their daughter Nancy, see Muste to Evans, July 10, 1933; Muste to Evans, July 24, 1933, EGCP, reel 7.

30. Muste to Sayre, excerpt in Robinson, *Abraham Went Out*, 66.

31. Muste, "Peace Is Indivisible," *Fellowship* 2, no. 8 (October 1936). This article was based upon the speech Muste gave at the FOR annual conference in October.

32. As Sayre explained at a 1933 meeting of the FOR, they placed "pressure and punishment on innocent and guilty alike with no regard for individual personality." See FOR National Council and Executive Council, of Meetings, 1933–1941, October 13, 1933, FOR, reel 102.02. See also John Haynes Holmes's criticism of labor strikes in the *World Tomorrow* 10, no. 3 (March 1927). Despite claims to the contrary, they were also deeply uncomfortable with the confrontational nature of nonviolence. For example, Emily Greene Balch of WILPF criticized the *satyagraha* campaigns Gandhi led in 1930 because they lacked "the spirit of goodwill" that made repentance possible. "An *ultimatum* is in essence a war method and issues from a war mentality. One never presents an ultimatum to a friend and if Gandhi does not consider the British as friends— however wrong and however wicked—then he has surrendered something more precious than the non-violence principle—the good will principle." Balch to Mrs. Cousins, quoted in Schott, *Reconstructing Women's Thoughts*, 102 (emphasis in original). See also Foster, *The Women and the Warriors*, 6–7; and Danielson, "'In My Extremity I Turned to Gandhi.'"

33. For intra-pacifist debates during the Great Depression, see my discussion below, as well as Danielson, "'In My Extremity I Turned to Gandhi'"; Kosek, *Acts of Conscience*; Bennett, *Radical Pacifism*; Chatfield, *For Peace and Justice*; and Meyer, *Protestant Search for Political Realism*.

34. Muste, "Fellowship and Class Struggle," FOR, box 5, folder 1. See also Muste, "Pacifism and Class War," 179–82.

35. Annual Report of Howard Kester, Southern Secretary, Annual Conference of the FOR, October 1933, JNSP, box 9, folder 6. See also FOR National Council and Executive Council, Minutes of Meetings, 1933–1941, October 13, 1933, FOR, reel 102.02.

36. See FOR National Council and Executive Council, Minutes of Meetings, 1933–1941, January 6, 1933, March 3 and 13, 1933, FOR, reel 102.02 (note that several of these pages are unreadable on the microfilm version, but legible print versions can be found in FOR, box 2). See also *Newsletter of the Fellowship of Reconciliation*, no. 3 (July 1929), FOR, box 2, folder 5; and J. B. Matthews, *Odyssey of a Fellow Traveler* (New York: Mount Vernon Publishers, 1938).

37. At a meeting of the national council Tucker P. Smith warned the FOR not to retreat from these difficult questions. As he put it, the council was in danger of rigidly "congeal[ing] the organization into its original set-up." Pacifists had adopted "tactics and attitudes of nonparticipation" in the context of their opposition to World War I that were "wholly inapplicable to the class struggle where positive action is necessary." The FOR should not retreat from exploring these "new perplexities into the easier realm of our early 'certainties' about international war" but rather try its best to mitigate violence. See FOR National Council and Executive Council, Minutes of Meetings, 1933–1941, March 3, 1933, FOR, reel 102.02.

38. Referendum sent to FOR members from the FOR National Council, FOR National Council and Executive Council, Minutes of Meetings, 1933–1941, November 22, 1933, and December 16, 1933, FOR, reel 102.02. See also Kirby Page, "The Future of the Fellowship," *World Tomorrow* 17, no. 1 (January 4, 1934): 9–11.

39. See FOR National Council and Executive Council, Minutes of Meetings, 1933–1941, January 10, 1934, FOR, reel 102.02; and Howard Kester to John Nevin Sayre, January 16, 1934, JNSP, box 9, folder 6. Kester's resignation was a huge loss for the FOR; as John Egerton has remarked, it "would be difficult to name any white Southerner of the time who had more contacts across racial lines than [Kester] did, or more of a clear-eyed vision of the crippling effects of segregation on blacks and whites alike." John Egerton, *Speak Now Against the Day: The Generation Before the Civil Rights Movement in the South* (Chapel Hill: University of North Carolina Press, 1994), 126.

40. Fox, *Reinhold Niebuhr*, 167–68.

41. Ibid., 168. On liberalism during this period, see Alan Brinkley, *The End of Reform: New Deal Liberalism in Recession and War* (New York: Vintage, 1996); and Rossinow, *Visions of Progress*. For a discussion of Niebuhrian realism and U.S. foreign policy, see Craig, *Glimmer of a New Leviathan*; and Rosenthal, *Righteous Realists*.

42. Harold Fey, "Do Pacifists Uphold Violence?" (ca. 1936), FOR, box 2, folder 4; Harold Fey, "Some Notes on the History and Activities of the Fellowship of Reconciliation Between the Years 1935 and 1940," August 1989, FOR, box 1, folder 1.

43. FOR National Council and Executive Council, Minutes of Meetings, 1933–1941, December 16, 1933, FOR, reel 102.02. See also "Message and Program," *Fellowship* 1, no. 8 (December 1935); Harold Fey, "Realistic Reconciliation," *Fellowship* 1, no. 8 (December 1935); Claude Williams, "Prison Memoir," *Fellowship* 2, no. 1 (January 1936); Delores Ruppersberg, "Labor Tries Non-violence," *Fellowship* 2, no. 3 (March 1936); and Richard Gregg, *The Power of Non-violence* (Philadelphia: J. B. Lippincott, 1934).

44. Gregg, *The Power of Non-violence*, 46–49.

45. Ibid., 46–49, 147–50, 40, and 222–23. See also Kosek, *Acts of Conscience*, esp. 98.

46. See Kosek, *Acts of Conscience*, 110–11. See also Applebaum, *Kingdom to Commune*, 182–83.

47. See Gregg, *The Power of Non-violence*, 75–76, 158, 40, and 222–23. See also Danielson, "'In My Extremity I Turned to Gandhi.'"

48. For example, at the 1935 meeting in which the FOR endorsed nonviolence, pacifists continued to argue that reconciliation "is best exercised by one who remains above or beyond the conflict. . . . Non-violent coercion, on the other hand, is a method whereby ardent believers in the justice of some cause seek to bring to it the victory. Fundamentally, this is not reconciliation at all. It is an instrument of power." See "Message and Program," *Fellowship* 1, no. 8 (December 1935): 3–5.

49. Despite the secular tone of *The Power of Nonviolence*, Gregg was a devout Christian. Indeed, although he promoted nonviolent direct action, his main focus was on nonviolence as a way of life. His wife's mental illness added to his responsibilities and kept him relatively homebound. See Gregg to Muste, March 26, 1942, FOR, box 12, folder 6; Gregg to Muste, March 6, 1943, FOR, box 7, folder 2; Gregg to CNVA Executive Committee (ca. 1962), BDP, box 9, folder 150.

50. Muste, "Sit Downs and Lie Downs," *Fellowship*, no. 3 (March 1937): 5–6; Herbert Bohn, "We Tried Non-Violence," *Fellowship* 3, no. 1 (January 1937): 7–8. Muste's message was enthusiastically embraced by many members of the FOR. See, for example, Jerome Davis, "Non-violent

Techniques for Industrial Justice," *Fellowship* 2, no. 9 (November 1936); Gerald Heard, "The New Pacifism," *Fellowship* 3, no. 6 (June 1937).

51. Robinson, *Abraham Went Out*, 70. See also John Muste to Jo Ann Robinson, February 6, 1979, AJMP-LA, box 2.

52. Muste, "The Church's Responsibility for Peace," address to the General Synod of the Reformed Church in America, June 7, 1937, AJMP, reel 6. The Reformed Church published the speech in pamphlet form. See also Muste, address to Pre-Evangelism Conference of the General Synod, September 2, 1938, AJMP, reel 4. For his reinstatement in the RCA, see Arthur Johnson to Jo Ann Robinson, July 27, 1970, AJMP-LA, box 2.

53. Muste, "The Church's Responsibility for Peace."

54. Muste, quoted in Robinson, "The Pharos of the East Side," 18–37.

55. Robinson, "The Pharos of the East Side," 21; Harold Fey, "Muste to Direct Labor Temple," *Fellowship* 3, no. 6 (June 1937).

56. See, for example, Muste, "Address for CBS's *Church of the Air*," September 3, 1939; Muste, "The Church Cares," *Pageant Magazine*, October 1938, clipping in AJMP, reel 4; Muste, address to the Jersey City YMCA on "Violence in the Labor Movement," October 28, 1937, AJMP, reel 3; Muste, "The Future of Labor Temple," *Presbyterian Tribune*, September 2, 1937, clipping in AJMP, reel 4; Muste, speech entitled "The Problem of the Unorganized Worker," delivered to a student conference held at Paine College, Augusta, Georgia, November 26–28, 1937, AJMP, reel 4; Muste, "Labor Temple's Mission," *Brick Church Record*, May 1938, clipping in AJMP, reel 3.

57. Correspondence between Evan Thomas and Henry Sloan Coffin indicates that Muste's fears were justified. Upon learning that Muste had refused to register for the draft, Coffin published an open letter in the *New York Times* condemning his stance. See letter from Evan Thomas to Henry S. Coffin, November 22, 1940, FOR, box 5, folder 6. For Muste's work with the UPC, see Robinson, *Abraham Went Out*, 76.

58. "Common Discipline of the Mt. Morris Cell," 1950, PMR. See also Muste, *Non-violence in an Aggressive World*, 181–82; Muste to James Farmer and George Houser, June 4, 1943, FOR, box 2, folder 1; "Suggested Draft of 'Message' of FOR Conference," September 1942, FOR, box 5, folder 3; and Muste, "Comments," in Minutes of FOR National Council Meeting, April 11, 1942, FOR, box 3, folder 3.

59. D'Emilio, *Lost Prophet*, 43–44.

60. Marion Bromley, quoted in ibid, 63. Muste clearly cultivated their view of him as mentor. For example, to welcome three young staffers in 1940, he praised them as "heavenly messengers" who feared not for themselves in the spirit of Christian martyrs. See Muste, "The Spirit of the Martyrs," *Fellowship* 6, no. 8 (October 1940): 121–22.

61. Bromley, quoted in D'Emilio, *Lost Prophet*, 63. See also Glenn Smiley, quoted in Robinson, *Abraham Went Out*, 186. The two young pacifists who most resisted Muste's leadership were James Farmer and Dave Dellinger, the reasons for which are discussed below.

62. James Farmer, "Creed and Prejudice," box 2R635, JLFP. See also Farmer, *Lay Bare the Heart*.

63. For details on CORE's organizational history, see Meier and Rudwick, *CORE*.

64. Daniel Levine, *Bayard Rustin and the Civil Rights Movement* (New Brunswick, N.J.: Rutgers University Press, 2000), 20.

65. For Rustin as prophet, see especially D'Emilio, *Lost Prophet*, 47–50. All of Rustin's biographers (and, indeed, Rustin himself) attest to Muste's importance in his personal life and his

political development. See Levine, *Bayard Rustin*; D'Emilio, *Lost Prophet*; and Jervis Anderson, *Bayard Rustin: Troubles I've Seen; A Biography* (New York: HarperCollins, 1997).

66. Glenn Smiley, quoted in D'Emilio, *Lost Prophet*, 63. For Farmer's problems as an organizer, see Rustin to Muste, October 7, 1943, FOR, box 4, folder 7; Muste to Swomley, February 1, 1945, and Muste to Swomley, Sayre, and Irene Ford, May 7, 1945, both in FOR, box 2, folder 1. See also Jo Ann Robinson notes on meeting with James Farmer, AJMP-LA, box 2.

67. Glenn Smiley biography, FOR, box 2, folder 6. See also William T. Martin Riches, *The Civil Rights Movement: Struggle and Resistance*, 2nd ed. (New York: Palgrave Macmillan, 2004), 48–49; Aldon Morris, *The Origins of the Civil Rights Movement: Black Communities Organizing for Change* (New York: Free Press, 1984): 160–62; and Margaret Cavin, "Glenn Smiley Was a Fool: The Use of the Comic as a Strategy of Nonviolence," *Peace and Change: A Journal of Peace Research* 26, no. 2 (April 2001): 223–42.

68. George Houser, interview by author, May 7, 2000, Nyack, New York. See also Houser, "Reflections of a Religious War Objector," in Larry Gara and Lenna Mae Gara, eds., *A Few Small Candles: War Resisters of World War II Tell Their Stories* (Kent, Ohio: Kent State University Press, 1999), 130–51. Similarly, Caleb Foote, Pacific Coast secretary of the FOR, stated, "I could do anything and AJ would support me." Foote, quoted in D'Emilio, *Lost Prophet*, 55.

69. For a discussion of the Student Christian Movement, which has received scant attention from historians, see Warren, *Theologians of a New World Order*. Muste noted that the younger generation of pacifists had roots in the SCM in a letter to Percy Bartlett, secretary of the IFOR [1947], FOR, box 1, folder 5.

70. George Houser and James Farmer, for example, met at one of the annual conferences of the National Council of Methodist Youth, which was affiliated with the SCM. Similarly, Bill Sutherland, an African American student at Bates College, met Dave Dellinger, a white student at Yale University, through the New England SCM. Lula Peterson (who would later marry Farmer) and Marjorie Swann met at Northwestern University, where the latter was active in a Methodist youth group. Both women would become involved in the Evanston chapter of CORE, which Houser would organize soon after moving to Chicago as an organizer for the FOR. See Bill Sutherland, interview by author, April 1, 2000, Austin, Texas; Dave Dellinger, interview by author, February 8, 2001, Austin, Texas; Houser, interview by author; and Marjorie Swann, interview by author, November 25, 2000, Berkeley, California; and Dave Dellinger, *From Yale to Jail: The Life Story of a Moral Dissenter* (Marion, S.D.: Rose Hill, 1993; reprint, 1996), 50.

71. See Sittser, *A Cautious Patriotism*; and Warren, *Theologians of a New World Order*.

72. The Oxford Pledge is quoted in DeBenedetti, *Peace Reform in American History*, 127. For an account of the student movement between the wars, see Robert Cohen, *When the Old Left Was Young: Student Radicals and America's First Mass Student Movement, 1929–1941* (New York: Oxford University Press, 1993). By the end of the decade, divisions had emerged between students who advocated collective security on the one hand and pacifists who called for neutrality on the other.

73. Swann, interview by author.

74. Dorothy Hassler, interview by author, July 4, 2000, by phone.

75. Houser, interview by author

76. Sutherland, interview by author.

77. Dellinger, *From Yale to Jail*, 48. See also William P. Roberts Jr., "Prison and Butterfly Wings," in Gara and Gara, *A Few Small Candles*, 157; Sutherland, interview by author; and

"Newark Colony Gets a Farm," *Catholic Worker* 10, no. 2 (January 1943). For information on the Harlem Ashram, see Farmer, *Lay Bare the Heart*, 149–51; and Wittner, *Rebels Against War*, 63–64. Meanwhile, a group of pacifist students at Antioch College founded Ahisma Farm, an experimental pacifist community that put their ideals into action in a variety of ways, including an effort to desegregate a Cleveland swimming pool. Their activism "caught the interest of leaders" of the FOR and the WRL, and Muste hired Bronson Clark, one of the founders of Ahisma Farm, as the FOR's New England youth secretary. See Gara and Gara, *A Few Small Candles*, 59–60 (Arthur Dole, "My War and My Peace") and 1–19 (Bronson Clark, "Prison Memoir").

78. Appelbaum, *Kingdom to Commune*, 34–38. See also Sittser, *A Cautious Patriotism*, 30–98.

79. Houser, interview by author. Similarly, Rustin recalled that he and other pacifists participated in CORE not only because they wanted to eliminate racial segregation, but also "to justify our own pacifism. . . . We may not be soldiers going to fight in the war but we're not cowards. We're willing to get out and fight for equality, we're willing to get our heads busted in. We're willing to get arrested. . . . Therefore, in a sense, we are doing the job of the true soldier, and there was a lot of that permeating the leadership of the CORE movement." See Oral Memoir, Reminiscences of Bayard Rustin (April 1989), Oral History Research Office, Columbia University. On pacifists as "yellowbellies," see, for example, Gara and Gara, *A Few Small Candles*, 102–3 (John H. Griffith, "War Resistance in World War II") and 34 (Dave Dellinger, "Why I Refused to Register in the October 1940 Draft and a Little of What It Led To."

80. James Robinson was the only non-Protestant in the group, but his commitment to pacifism grew out of his involvement in the Catholic Worker movement while an undergraduate at Columbia University. See Meier and Rudwick, *CORE*, 4–8. See also Farmer, *Lay Bare the Heart*, 75; and George Houser, "Plan for a Nonviolent Campaign Against Jim Crow," June 19, 1944, BRP, reel 5.

81. Farmer, "Memorandum to A. J. Muste on Provisional Plans for Brotherhood Mobilization," January 8, 1942, FOR, box 2, folder 1.

82. Muste to Farmer, January 19, 1942, FOR, box 2, folder 1. In his autobiography, Farmer recalled incorrectly that the meeting was held in Columbus, Ohio.

83. See details in Farmer, *Lay Bare the Heart*, 100–104; Minutes of FOR National Council Meeting, April 11, 1942, FOR, box 3, folder 3; Minutes of FOR National Council Meeting, September 29, 1942, FOR, box 3, folder 4.

84. See Muste statement, in Minutes of FOR Executive Committee Meeting, January 12, 1943; and Minutes of FOR Executive Committee Meeting, February 23, 1943. Both in FOR, box 3, folder 4.

85. Muste, "What the Bible Teaches About Freedom," 261–78

86. Muste et al., "Civil Disobedience, Is It the Answer to Jim Crow? A Symposium with Reinhold Niebuhr and Others," *Non-violent Action Newsbulletin*, nos. 2–3 (1943).

87. See Minutes of FOR Executive Committee Meeting, September 14, 1943, FOR, box 3, folder 4. Historian James Tracy has suggested that one reason Randolph backed away from the plan was that it lacked support from white and black liberals. See Tracy, *Direct Action: Radical Pacifism from the Union Eight to the Chicago Seven* (Chicago: University of Chicago Press, 1997), 34–35.

88. Tracy, *Direct Action*, 64–65. See also D'Emilio, *Lost Prophet*, 150–59.

89. See Meier and Rudwick, *CORE*, 8–9.

90. Ibid., 8, 19–25.

91. Houser quoted in ibid., 20. See also James Farmer, *Freedom—When?* (New York: Random House, 1966), 62.

92. Erna Harris, "It's Time We Outgrew 'Race' Relations," *Fellowship* 11, no. 10 (October 1945). For more on CORE's commitment to interracialism, see Meier and Rudwick, *CORE*, 81; and Farmer, *Lay Bare the Heart*, 168–84.

93. Muste to E. A. Shaal, May 21, 1943, FOR, box 4, folder 7. See also FOR National Council Meeting, May 12, 1942, FOR, box 3, folder 3. For the pacifist critique of the MOWM's all-black character, see James Farmer, "We Cannot Destroy Segregation with a Weapon of Segregation," in August Meier, Elliott Rudwick, and Francis Broderick, eds., *Black Protest Thought in the Twentieth Century* (Indianapolis: Bobbs-Merrill, 1971), 249.

94. Meier and Rudwick, *CORE*, 34–39. The team included pacifists Wally Nelson, Bayard Rustin, George Houser, Homer Jack, James Peck, Igal Roodenko, and Ernest Bromley. See also Marian Mollin, "The Limits of Egalitarianism: Radical Pacifism, Civil Rights, and the Journey of Reconciliation," *Radical History Review* no. 88 (Winter 2004): 113–38.

95. Rustin and Houser, quoted in Meier and Rudwick, *CORE*, 37–38.

96. Meier and Rudwick, *CORE*, 29.

97. For example, Wally Nelson and Caleb Foote, both of whom were active in CORE, called themselves "secular" pacifists, yet both had roots in the SCM and had ministers as fathers. Others, like Bill Sutherland and Dave Dellinger, began to identify as "spiritual" but not Christian pacifists, yet continued to believe in the redemptive power of nonviolence. Nelson, interview in Deena Hurwitz and Craig Simpson, eds., *Against the Tide: Pacifist Resistance in the Second World War; An Oral History* (New York: War Resisters League, 1983): no page numbers; Sutherland, interview by author; Dellinger, interview by author; Dellinger, *From Yale to Jail*; and Meier and Rudwick, *CORE*, 44.

98. Appelbaum, *Kingdom to Commune*, 2–3.

99. Minutes of FOR National Council Meeting, May 29–31, FOR, box 4, folder 3.

100. John Nevin Sayre to Muste, June 23, 1943, JNSP, box 11, folder 5. See also Muste to Sayre, August 13, 1946, FOR, box 11, folder 5, in which he challenged Sayre's argument that the FOR retreat from its experiments with nonviolent direct action and abandon the "racial-industrial" field altogether.

101. Muste, "Comments," April 10, 1942, National Council Meeting, April 10–11, 1942, FOR, box 3, folder 3.

Chapter 9. Conscience Against the Wartime State and the Bomb

Epigraph: Muste, *Not by Might*, ix.

1. Muste, "USA—Arsenal," *Fellowship* 7, no. 4 (April 1941): 59–60.

2. Lichtenstein, *American Capitalism*, 9.

3. Muste, address to the Annual Meeting of the FOR, October 11, 1940, AJMP, reel 3; Muste, "Analysis of Hitler's Reply to Roosevelt," typescript (ca. 1938), AJMP, reel 4; Muste, "Where Are We Going?" (1941), reprinted in Hentoff, *Essays of A. J. Muste*, 234–60; and Muste, *Non-violence in an Aggressive World*, 135–54. See also, for example, "Eight Ways to Build Peace," September 5–7, 1941, FOR, box 5, folder 2; FOR Council, "The Present Crisis," *Fellowship* 6, no. 5 (May 1940): 73–75.

4. Muste, "Where Are We Going?"; and Muste, "Land of Liberty," *Fellowship* 9, no. 4 (April 1943): 70–72.

5. Minutes of FOR National Council Meeting, April 10, 1942, FOR, box 3, folder 3; and Muste, "Land of Liberty." Pacifists not only protested internment, they were quite active in efforts to assist Japanese Americans during the war. See, for example, Joseph B. Hunter, "Problems of Relocation," *Fellowship* 10, no. 9 (September 1944): 156; and Caleb Foote, "A Third Evacuation," *Fellowship* 11, no. 6 (June 1945): 105.

6. Muste, "What Lies Ahead?" *Fellowship* 11, no. 2 (February 1945): 22. See also Muste, "A Modern Tower of Babel," *American Friend*, November 4, 1943, copy in AJMP, reel 4; Muste, "Sowing the Dragon's Teeth," *Fellowship* 9, no. 3 (March 1943): 50–51; and Muste, "Basic World Trends," typescript, January 3, 1944, AJMP, reel 4.

7. For the causes and consequences of the war, see R. J. Overy, *The Origins of the Second World War*, 3rd ed. (Harlow: Longman, 2008); R. A. C. Parker, *The Second World War: A Short History*, rev. ed. (Oxford: Oxford University Press, 2002); John Dower, *War Without Mercy: Race and Power in the Pacific War* (New York: Pantheon, 1986); Michael Sherry, *In the Shadow of War: The United States Since the 1930s* (New Haven, Conn.: Yale University Press, 1997); Elizabeth Borgwardt, *A New Deal for the World: America's Vision for Human Rights* (Cambridge, Mass.: Harvard University Press, 2005); Michael H. Hunt, *The American Ascendancy: How the United States Gained and Wielded Global Dominance* (Chapel Hill: University of North Carolina Press, 2008); and Odd Arne Westad, *The Global Cold War: Third World Interventions and the Making of Our Time* (Cambridge: Cambridge University Press, 2007).

8. See Niebuhr's "Why the Christian Church Is Not Pacifist," in *Christianity and Power Politics*.

9. See *The Collected Works of Mahatma Gandhi*, vol. 18, *July–November 1920* (New Delhi: Government of India, Publications Division, 1965), 132.

10. See, for example, Borgwardt, *A New Deal for the World*; Brinkley, *The End of Reform*; Von Eschen, *Race Against Empire*; and Nelson Lichtenstein, *Labor's War at Home: The CIO in World War II* (Cambridge: Cambridge University Press, 1982).

11. For example, the eight Union Seminary students who refused to register for the draft maintained that war violated "the Way of Love as seen in God through Christ" and that "as followers of Jesus Christ we must overcome evil with good." See Meredith Dallas et al., October 10, 1940, FOR, box 12, folder 2. See Cynthia Eller, *Conscientious Objectors and the Second World War: Moral and Religious Arguments in Support for Pacifism* (Westport, Conn.: Praeger, 1991), esp. 133–34.

12. Meyer, *The Protestant Search for Political Realism*, 362.

13. Muste, typescript for radio address for WEVD, New York (ca. 1938), AJMP, reel 4. See also Muste, "A Plea to Enlist," *Fellowship* 6, no. 7 (September 1940): 103–5; and Meyer, *Protestant Search*, 366.

14. Muste, quoted in Kosek, *Acts of Conscience*, 150. Muste apparently said this at a Quaker meeting in the summer of 1940.

15. Muste, "The Church as a Force in the World," *Christian-Evangelist*, November 10, 1938. copy in AJMP, reel 4; Muste, "The Reign of Terror," *Fellowship* 4, no. 10 (December 1938): 8–9; and "The Course Before Us," statement of the FOR Executive Committee, December 10, 1941, reprinted in *Fellowship* 8, no. 1 (January 1942): 2. For the distinctiveness of the pacifist worldview, see Appelbaum, *Kingdom to Commune*, 182–83; and Kosek, *Acts of Conscience*, 110–11,

159–61. To his credit, Muste always conceded that, in the last analysis, pacifism was based upon "an essentially religious conception of the universe and the nature of man which must inevitably express itself in all relations of life." See Muste, *Not by Might*, 201–2; and Muste, *Non-violence in an Aggressive World*, 174–75.

16. For the paucity of Jewish pacifists during World War II, see Wittner, *Rebels Against War*, 44.

17. Niebuhr, "Why the Christian Church Is Not Pacifist," 29.

18. See Meyer, *The Protestant Search for Political Realism*, 360.

19. Muste, *Non-violence in an Aggressive World*, 33–43.

20. Niebuhr, quoted in Boyer, *By the Bomb's Early Light*, 43. Niebuhr also condoned obliteration bombing. See, for example, Niebuhr, lead editorial, *Christianity and Crisis*, March 9, 1942, 2.

21. Craig, *Glimmer of a New Leviathan*, 79.

22. Muste, "The Foundations of Democracy."

23. See Muste's letters to John and family, August 12, 1960, October 7, 1962, and September 13, 1964, JAH, Muste Collection, box 1; Muste to *New York Herald Tribune*, October 21, 1965, quoted in Hentoff, *Essays of A. J. Muste*, v–vi; and Robinson, *Abraham Went Out*, 85. See also John Muste to Jo Ann Robinson, August 10, 1977, and March 12 [1979], AJMP-LA, box 2. In the latter letter, he suggests that his father was "in many ways very attentive to the family . . . he came frequently to visit me and my family, and Connie and hers, and my own sons have very warm memories of him."

24. For a history of conscientious objectors and Selective Service, see Albert N. Keim and Grant M. Stoltzfus, *The Politics of Conscience: The Historic Peace Churches and America at War, 1917–1955* (Scottdale, Pa.: Herald Press, 1988); and Mulford Q. Sibley and Philip E. Jacob, *Conscription and Conscience: The American State and the Conscientious Objector, 1940–1947* (Ithaca, N.Y.: Cornell University Press, 1952).

25. In early 1943, for example, the Selective Service ordered conscientious objectors working in soil conservation camps to work for private employers, with wages beyond basic maintenance going to the U.S. Treasury. Although the order was made voluntary after pacifists protested, another directive soon followed ordering COs to work for private employers without pay whenever the government declared a crop emergency to exist within a fifteen mile radius of any CPS camp. Another example was when General Lewis B. Hershey, director of the Selective Service System, forbade men in CPS from having meetings on their own time without his permission, an order that many pacifists viewed as authoritarian. See Minutes of FOR Executive Committee Meeting, March 9, 1943, FOR, box 3, folder 4; and Muste, "Memorandum for May 1943 Council Meeting on FOR Relationship to CPS, etc.," FOR, box 7, folder 1.

26. Herbert Wehrly, "Conscription Slows Down," *Fellowship* 12, no. 6 (June 1946): 101; Evan Thomas, "CPS and the Second Mile," *Fellowship* 10, no. 2 (February 1944): 28; "Statement of Aims of Assignees Striking at Civilian Public Service Camp #76," April 30, 1946, FOR, box 7, folder 5; Gara and Gara, *A Few Small Candles*; and Wittner, *Rebels Against War*, 78–80. For Muste's role as advocate for imprisoned COs, and his relationship to the young men, see, for example, correspondence in FOR, box 7, folder 12; and Minutes of FOR Executive Committee Meetings, especially October 27, 1942, April 27, October 11, and November 9, 1943, February 8, March 13, and October 24, 1944, and February 1 and April 24, 1945, all in FOR, box 3, folders 2–5; Muste, partial report on tour of CPS camps, September 11–October 18, 1941, JNSP, box 11,

folder 5; Muste, memorandum on visit to Ashland, Kentucky, Federal Correctional Institution, July 26, 1944, FOR, box 4, folder 7.

27. Paton Price to A. J. Muste, reprinted in the *Conscientious Objector*, March 1943, copy in FOR, box 7, folder 1. See also Caleb Foote to Muste, May 4, 1944, FOR, box 12, folder 10. From the onset of the war in Europe, Muste had maintained that "the clearest and the most consistent position for a Christian and a pacifist to take" was total noncooperation, and he followed this up by refusing to register for the draft when the president ordered all men up to sixty-five years of age to register on April 27, 1942. Yet he also worried that dissent over CPS would disrupt the pacifist "fellowship" and imply "that we regarded some of our members as Grade A and others as Grade B pacifists." Muste's response, as well as the intra-FOR debates on the issue, can be found in Muste to Chris Ahrens, January 13, 1944; and Muste to Paton Price, reprinted in the *Conscientious Objector*, March 1943, both in FOR, box 7, folder 1; Minutes of FOR Executive Committee Meeting, March 24, 1942, FOR, box 3, folder 3; Muste, "Memorandum for May 1943 Council Meeting on FOR Relationship to CPS, etc."; and in the correspondence between him and Evan Thomas, October 29, 1940, March 11 and November 3, 6, 10, and 18, 1941, February 10, March 20, and August 27, 1942, January 6 and 7 and December 28, 1944, and January 2, 1945, all in FOR, box 5, folders 6 and 7. See also list of older nonregistrants, circa April 1942, FOR, box 12, folder 7.

28. Muste, "Memorandum for May 1943 Council Meeting on FOR Relationship to CPS, etc."

29. See Minutes of FOR National Council Meeting, May 14–15, 1943, FOR, box 3, folder 4. For evidence that the council was more conservative than the staff, see, for example, John Nevin Sayre to Harold Fey, June 8, 1944, JNSP, box 5, folder 6; Minutes of FOR Executive Committee Meeting, June 13, 1944, FOR, box 3, folder 3.

30. See "Report on Responses from FOR Membership to Leaflet on 'Shall We Remain in NSBRO?'" November 26, 1943, FOR, box 6, folder 6.

31. Dave Dellinger et al., "Open Letter to the FOR," February 3, 1944, FOR, box 12, folder 10. For more on Dellinger's experiences in prison and his critique of the FOR, see Andrew E. Hunt, *Dave Dellinger: The Life and Times of a Nonviolent Revolutionary* (New York: New York University Press, 2006), 80–86.

32. Muste to Dave Dellinger, July 5, 1944, and Muste to Dellinger, April 4, 1944, both in FOR, box 12, folder 10.

33. See Muste, "Prospectus for Study Conference on Philosophy and Strategy of Revolution-ary Pacifism" (ca. June 1944), FOR, box 5, folder 10.

34. "Report on Study Conference on Revolutionary Pacifism," September 15–17, 1944, FOR, box 5, folder 10. See also David White, "Notes for the Study Conference on the Philosophy and Strategy of Revolutionary Pacifism," August 14, 1944, and Dan West, "Disciplines for Revo-lutionary Pacifism," February 1, 1945, both in FOR, box 5, folders 10 and 11.

35. "Report on Study Conference on Revolutionary Pacifism"; and David White, "Notes for the Study Conference on the Philosophy and Strategy of Revolutionary Pacifism."

36. See White, "Notes for the Study Conference"; "Report on Study Conference on Revolu-tionary Pacifism." For Muste and Kierkegaard, see, for example, Muste, "S. Kierkegaard on the Relation Between Ends and Means," typescript, February 1950, EMBP; and Farmer, *Lay Bare the Heart*, 102.

37. Dellinger et al., "An Open Letter to the FOR," FOR, June 3, 1944.

38. See Caleb Foote to Muste, April 20, 1944, FOR, box 12, folder 10.

39. For example, upon his release from prison, Lowell Naeve wrote in his diary that "I've learned what government means. . . . Government . . . means brute force." See Lowell Naeve, *A Field of Broken Stones* (Glenn Gardner, N.J.: Libertarian Press, 1950), 78–80.

40. Regular column by John Haynes Holmes, *Fellowship* 12, no. 9 (October 1946): 158.

41. Caleb Foote, "Prison Is Revenge," *Fellowship* 12, no. 5 (May 1946): 79. Bill Sutherland (in interview by author) recalled that he and other pacifists developed a similar analysis of society through their experience in prison, and consequently began to reject "the idea that somehow as long as it wasn't an actual physical expression of violence, then you had peace."

42. Roy Finch to Muste, May 20, 1944, FOR, box 1, folder 9.

43. Muste, "The Atomic Bomb and the American Dream," *Fellowship* 10, no. 11 (October 1945): 167. See also Muste, *Not by Might*, 131–32; and Muste, typescript, August 1947, FOR, box 5, folder 3.

44. Muste, "Conscience Against the Bomb," *Fellowship* 11, no. 12 (December 1945): 208. See also Muste, *Not by Might*, 42–43.

45. Dorothy Day, editorial, *Catholic Worker* 12, no. 7 (September 1945): 1.

46. Regular column by John Haynes Holmes, *Fellowship* 11, no. 9 (September 1945): 150.

47. Bent Andersen, "A Message to People of Goodwill," August 1945, FOR, box 6, folder 3. Related documents can be found in the same box.

48. John Nevin Sayre, "The International FOR and the Life of the Age to Come," *Fellowship* 11, no. 11 (November 1945): 190; Elisabeth Dodds and Marion Coddington, "New Methods for New Growth," *Fellowship* 11, no. 10 (October 1945): 178.

49. See, for example, Tracy Mygatt, "Psacifists and World Government," *Fellowship* 13, no. 3 (March 1947): 51, and John Haynes Holmes column, *Fellowship* 12, no. 6 (June 1946): 90. Kant's notion of world government reflected his Enlightenment faith in human progress and reason. Thus it is not surprising that radical pacifists, who were skeptical of world government, also criticized Enlightenment thinking, which they viewed as largely responsible for the creation of the atomic bomb. See Immanuel Kant, *Perpetual Peace* (1795; London: Allen and Unwin, 1917).

50. See, for example, Muste, "World Government: Panacea or Promise?" *Fellowship* 12, no. 10 (November 1946): 177.

51. M. Palmer Bryant, "The Pacifist Bandwagon," *Fellowship* 12, no. 9 (October 1946): 161.

52. Muste, *Not by Might*, 56.

53. Ibid., 106–7; Muste, "The Role of the Pacifist in the Atomic Age," *Fellowship* 12, no. 8 (September 1946): 7. If Muste's argument for unilateral disarmament seems utopian, it is worth noting that starting in the 1960s some countries began to unilaterally place restraints on their nuclear production. See Lawrence Wittner, *One World or None: A History of the World Nuclear Disarmament Movement Through 1953*, vol. 1, *The Struggle Against the Bomb* (Stanford, Calif.: Stanford University Press, 1993).

54. Muste, *Not by Might*, 42.

55. See Wittner, *The Struggle Against the Bomb*; and Boyer, *By the Bomb's Early Light*.

56. Muste to Albert Einstein, May 28, 1946, JNSP, box 11, folder 5. See also Muste to Albert Einstein, September 15, 1947, FOR, box 6, folder 9. In his "Dialogues with Cristina," Don Paolo writes, "He is saved who . . . does not shut himself in a cloister or build himself an ivory tower, or make a cleavage between his way of acting and his way of thinking. He is saved who frees his

own spirit from the idea of resignation to the existing disorder." See Ignazio Silone, *Bread and Wine* (New York: Harper and Brothers, 1937), 290.

57. Albert Einstein to Muste, October 11, 1947, and Muste to Einstein, October 24, 1947, FOR, box 6, folder 9.

58. Much of Muste's extensive correspondence with atomic scientists, as well as his involvement in many of their 1946–47 conferences, can be found in FOR, box 6, folders 3, 4, and 6.

59. Muste, *Not by Might*, 38; Muste to Einstein, October 24, 1947, FOR, box 6, folder 9.

60. Henry Van Dusen to Muste, August 24, 1945, and Niebuhr to Muste, August 21, 1945, both in FOR, box 6, folder 3. John Foster Dulles to Muste, June 17, 1946, FOR, box 1, folder 9. For a recent discussion of nationalism and the religious revival that accompanied the the Cold War, see Stevens, *God-Fearing and Free*.

61. Muste, "Theology of Despair," 303–5. See also Niebuhr to Muste, April 19, 1945; Muste to Niebuhr, April 23, 1945; and Muste to Niebuhr, July 2, 1945, all in FOR, box 3, folder 15.

62. Muste, "Is Our Only Choice Dumbarton Oaks or Chaos?" 69–70; Muste, *Not by Might*, xi; and Muste, "Theology of Despair."

63. Quotes are from Muste to John Foster Dulles, June 11, 1946, FOR, box 1, folder 9; and Muste, *Not by Might*, 4. See also Muste, "On Understanding Russia."

64. Mark G. Toulouse, *The Transformation of John Foster Dulles: From Prophet of Realism to Priest of Nationalism* (Macon, Ga.: Mercer University Press, 1985). For the realist critique of Dulles, see Rosenthal, *Righteous Realists*, 101–7.

65. Muste, "Theology of Despair," 305.

66. Dulles to Muste, June 17, 1946, FOR, box 1, folder 9.

67. Muste to Dulles, July 1, 1946, FOR, box 1, folder 9.

68. Muste, *Not by Might*, 4. Recent scholarship supports Muste's emphasis on the role of race and nationalism in shaping the assumptions that guided American foreign policy during the Cold War. See, for example, Thomas Borstelmann, *The Cold War and the Color Line: American Race Relations in the Global Arena* (Cambridge, Mass.: Harvard University Press, 2001); Gerald Horne, "Who Lost the Cold War? Africans and African Americans," *Diplomatic History* 20, no. 4 (Fall 1996): 613–26; Brenda Gayle Plummer, *Rising Wind: Black Americans and U.S. Foreign Affairs, 1935–1960* (Chapel Hill: University of North Carolina Press, 1996); and Anders Stephanson, *Kennan and the Art of Foreign Policy* (Cambridge, Mass.: Harvard University Press, 1989).

69. Muste, "The World Conference of Christian Youth—Oslo, July 22–31, 1947," AJMP-LA, box 2.

70. See Church Peace Mission, *A Christian Approach to Nuclear War* (Glen Gardner, N.J.: Libertarian Press, 1958). For Muste's role in the CPM, see AJMP, reel 4.

71. Taylor Branch, *Parting the Waters: America in the King Years, 1954–63* (New York: Simon and Schuster, 1989), 73–74, 86–87. Similarly, James Lawson was introduced to "western pacifist thought" when Muste gave a speech at his alma mater in the fall of 1947. From then on, he "incorporated the work and values to which AJM had introduced him into his study-life. When, 13 years later he was expelled from Vanderbilt because of his social activism, that activism was part of a logical progression from the initial contact with and influence of AJM, whom he saw as a major teacher." He also obtained work from the FOR. See Robinson notes from interview with James Lawson, May 11, 1979, AJMP-LA, box 2.

72. Muste, "The H-Bomb as Deterrent," *Christianity and Crisis*, June 14, 1954, 77–79.

73. John C. Bennett, quoted in Hulsether, *Building a Protestant Left*, 33.

74. Petition "To Stop the Pacific Test and Declare a Moratorium on Others," April 1958, AJMP, reel 36.

75. See Hulsether, *Building a Protestant Left*; and Mitchell K. Hall, *Because of Their Faith: CALCAV and Religious Opposition to the Vietnam War* (New York: Columbia University Press, 1990). See also John Bennett to Jo Ann Robinson, AJMP-LA, box 2, in which he recalled that Muste "did much of the best thinking about the theological and ethical bases of pacifism. He was greatly respected by non-pacifists who had disagreed with him about World War II but had many of his concerns."

76. "Record of Proceedings," Retreat Conference on Pacifist Orientation and Strategy, Pendle Hill, Wallingford, Pa., May 20–23, 1947, FOR, box 5, folder 12. See also "Proceedings of Second Pendle Hill Retreat," Wallingford, Pa., November 13–16, 1947, FOR box 5, folder 13.

77. Harold Chance, "Toward Fellowship with God and Man," paper circulated prior to the November 1947 conference, FOR, box 5, folder 13; and "Record of Proceedings."

78. "Record of Proceedings"; "Proceedings of Second Pendle Hill Retreat."

79. "Proceedings of Second Pendle Hill Retreat." Similarly, Milton Mayer, the self-described Jewish-Christian and editor of the *Progressive*, argued that pacifists had to develop a level of "fanaticism" and dramatically demonstrate in their own lives the values they felt other Americans should espouse. As an example, he suggested joining the CP as a protest against the recent suppression of Communist civil liberties by the House Un-American Activities Committee (HUAC). See Milton Mayer to Pendle Hill Conferees, November 5, 1947, FOR, box 5, folder 13.

80. "Proceedings of Second Pendle Hill Retreat."

81. "Crusade for a Changed, Warless World" (ca. November 1947); see also "One World Groups: Draft of Manifesto" (ca. December 1947). Both documents are in FOR, box 5, folder 13. See also Arthur Koestler, *The Yogi and the Commissar, and Other Essays* (New York: Macmillan, 1945).

82. "Call for a Conference on More Disciplined and Revolutionary Pacifist Activity" (ca. spring 1948), PMR; Wittner, *Rebels Against War*, 154–56.

83. Dwight Macdonald, "The Root Is Man," *politics*, April 1946, pp. 98–99, and July 1946, pp. 197–98, and 213.

84. See, for example, Gregory D. Sumner, *Dwight Macdonald and the 'Politics' Circle* (Ithaca, N.Y.: Cornell University Press, 1996); Michael Wreszin, *A Rebel in Defense of Tradition: The Life and Politics of Dwight Macdonald* (New York: Basic Books, 1994); Teres, *Renewing the Left*; Wald, *The New York Intellectuals*; and Pells, *The Liberal Mind in a Conservative Age*.

85. Peacemaker pamphlet, dated 1949, EMBP. See also minutes of the "Continuation Committee of Chicago Conference," Yellow Springs, Ohio, April 20–22, 1948, PMR.

86. Houser, interview by author. See also minutes of the "Continuation Committee of Chicago Conference."

87. Muste, "The Task Ahead," *Fellowship* 9, no. 7 (July 1943): 128–29; Muste to Dellinger et al., July 5, 1944, box 12, folder 10.

88. Houser, interview by author. As Houser put it, "The WRL wasn't as free as a Peacemakers group could be [since the latter] had been put together for the purpose of taking direct action—and in a rather uncompromising way. [Peacemakers] was established for that purpose." See also Bennett, *Radical Pacifism*, 134–72; and Wittner, *Rebels Against War*, 153.

89. See Mel Piehl, "Catholic Worker Pacifism in the Cold War Era," in Anne Klejment and Nancy L. Roberts, eds., *American Catholic Pacifism: The Influence of Dorothy Day and the Catholic Worker Movement* (Westport, Conn.: Greenwood, 1996), 86–88; and Piehl, *Breaking Bread*.

90. "Call for a Conference on Civil Disobedience to the Draft" (ca. July 1948), PMR; see Dave Dellinger and Julius Eichel to the Attorney General, October 27, 1948, PMR; George Houser memo, March 5, 1947, EMBP; and Ernest Bromley's notes for a meeting, circa 1948, EMBP. The withholding system was instituted in 1943.

91. Muste statement, quoted in the *Peacemaker* 2, no. 9 (April 21, 1951): 3. See also *News of Tax Refusal*, January 28, 1950, EMBP; and Ernest Bromley, "The Case for Tax Refusal," *Fellowship* 13, no. 10 (November 1947): 171.

92. Ammon Hennacy statement, quoted in the *Peacemaker* 1, no. 10 (January 30, 1950): 4. Emphasis in original. See also Ammon Hennacy, *Two Agitators: Peter Maurin-Ammon Hennacy* (New York: The Catholic Worker Press,1959).

93. Bayard Rustin to Muste, February 2, 1950, EMBP. Emphasis in original.

94. *Peacemaker* 1, no. 12 (April 25, 1950): 1–2; Muste to Members of the FOR Executive Committee, February 27, 1950, box 4, folder 11, FOR; "Call for Holy Week Fast" issued by Peacemakers Fast Committee, DD-CW, series W-1, box 1, folder 5.

95. *Peacemaker* 1, no. 12 (April 25, 1950): 1–2.

96. "Proceedings of National Committee of Peacemakers," Chicago, Illinois, December 28–30, 1948; and "Proceedings of National Conference of Peacemakers," Chicago, Illinois, April 1–3, 1949, both in PMR. See also *Peacemaker* 1, no. 2 (June 28, 1949): 3; *Peacemaker* 3, no. 1 (June 8, 1951): 2; and *Peacemaker* 2, no. 3 (July 26, 1950): 1. For more on Glen Gardner, see Dellinger, *From Yale to Jail*, 145.

97. Muste, "Sketches," 87–89. The Peacemaker Ernest Bromley recalled, "As time went on, [Muste] had . . . consciously traveled towards the political rather than the spiritually pacifist. The political part of the program, or a pacifist program, that would consider very strongly the number of people you could get to do something and not the qualities so much of the pacifists. Whether you could appeal to numbers of people—in other words, putting that before the central program and efforts of the Peacemaker group. So he really rebuked? [refused?] the Peacemakers around 1954." See Ernest Bromley, interview by Marian Mollin, September 4–7, 1996, Cincinnati, Ohio. David McReynolds (in interview by author) similarly recalled that Muste was "more Marxist than the absolute pacifists within Peacemakers."

98. For example, in 1952, Francis Hall argued that recent events demonstrated that the American people largely agreed with U.S. foreign policy and that radical pacifists should no longer attempt to build "an anti-war revolutionary movement" in the United States or elsewhere. Instead, they should either focus their attention "in areas where there is either racial or colonial subjugation" or concentrate on the "inner revolution" and "the building of community." See *Peacemaker* 3, no. 24 (May 24, 1952): 1–3. Thanks to Doug Rossinow for helping me to develop this critique.

99. Muste, "Problems of Non-Violent Revolution," *Peacemaker* 3, no. 18 (March 1, 1952): 3–4; and *Peacemaker* 3, no. 19 (March 15, 1952): 3.

100. Quoted in D'Emilio, *Lost Prophet*, 183.

101. Muste, "Problems of Non-Violent Revolution," *Peacemaker* 3, no. 18 (March 1, 1952): 3–4; *Peacemaker* 3, no. 19 (March 15, 1952): 3; Muste, working paper "Nehru, the Gandhians and the Communists," and Muste, "Trends," circa 1950, AJMP-LA, box 2. Further evidence of the differences between Muste and his fellow Peacemakers can be found in Lawrence Scott to Albert Bigelow, July 12, 1960, LSP, box 1, folder 1; and Bromley interview by Marian Mollin.

Chapter 10. Speaking Truth to Power

Epigraph: Muste, "Pacifism Enters a New Phase," *Fellowship*, July 1, 1960, 25. Copy in AJMP, reel 1.

1. George Houser, "Thoughts on Organization for Effective Work in Africa," unpublished paper, JLFP, box 2R899; Minutes of FOR National Council Meeting, December 3–4, 1953, FOR, box 4, folder 7; Houser, interview by author; and Bill Sutherland and Matt Meyer, *Guns and Gandhi in Africa: Pan African Insights on Nonviolence, Armed Struggle and Liberation in Africa* (Trenton, N.J.: Africa World Press, 2001): 5; Ernest Dunbar, *The Black Expatriates: A Study of American Negroes in Exile* (New York: E. P. Dutton, 1968), 91; and Sutherland, interview by author. Muste served on the board of both of these organizations. For a discussion of the American Committee on Africa, see Plummer, *Rising Wind*, 233–34, 238.

2. D'Emilio, *Lost Prophet*, 189. See also Muste to the IFOR Council, "World Trends and Pacifist Policy," FOR, box 2, folder 1.

3. Muste, "The Quadruple Revolution: How the Four-fold Revolution Relates to Race," typescript, June 18, 1965, AJMP, reel 5. See also Muste, "Random Thoughts on the Nobel Peace Prize Award," typescript (ca. 1964), AJMP, reel 6.

4. D'Emilio, *Lost Prophet*, 187–89; Rustin interview, Oral History Research Office, Columbia University. The National Committee of the American Committee on Africa also included James Baldwin, Roger Baldwin, Allan Knight Chalmers, Harry Emerson Fosdick, Martin Luther King Jr., Rayford W. Logan, Eugene McCarthy, Reinhold Niebuhr, Sidney Poitier, Jackie Robinson, Howard Thurman, and Mark Van Doren, while the executive board included Muste, Victor Reuther, Bayard Rustin, and Arthur Waskow; JNSP, box 7, folder 16.

5. Sayre, quoted in D'Emilio, *Lost Prophet*, 190. See also Houser, interview by author; report of FOR Policy Committee of May 1950 and Sayre handwritten notes, both in JNSP, box 2, folder 13. According to David McReynolds (in interview with author), the FOR "retired" Muste because he was too radical for the organization, passing a rule that retirement must occur at age sixty-five.

6. Glenn Smiley, quoted in D'Emilio, *Lost Prophet*, 192. For the WRL, see Bennett, *Radical Pacifism*, 172.

7. See D'Emilio, "Homophobia and the Trajectory of Postwar American Radicalism."

8. These views can be found in an undated manuscript (ca. 1946), reviewing Wallace Fowlie's book on contemporary French literature, *Clowns and Angels*, AJMP, reel 5. In it, he observes that modern writers conceive of love naturalistically, as between people rather than as a sacred expression of the love of God. "From this concept of love between man and woman which is an end in itself and not offered as a sacrifice to God and used as a teacher in the love of God it is perhaps a facile step to the homosexuality which is accepted and glorified by [André] Gide, for example, and which plays a not insignificant part in modern decadence—among the Nazis, for example—as in the ancient world." "Hence also the emphasis in much modern literature on the physical aspects of sex." His son, John, recalled that his father "was accepting" of "deviant sexual patterns," while at the same time holding the "belief (common at the time) that homosexuality was a disease that could and should be treated." See John Muste to Jo Ann Robinson, AJMP-LA, box 2.

9. Muste, "Sketches," 90; Muste to CNVA, March 26, 1963, BDP, box 9, folder 151.

10. D'Emilio, *Lost Prophet*, 114–16.

11. This interpretation explains why Muste's contemporaries, gay and straight, described him as nonjudgmental and open-minded, even though they recognized his sexual mores were probably more conventional than their own. Bayard Rustin, for example, stated, "There probably was no one outside of A.J.'s own family who knew him better than I did. We went through many moments of personal and political crisis together. . . . And there was probably no one whom A.J. loved better than he loved me, because there was no one who gave him as much trouble." See Rustin's comments, *WIN Special Supplement on A. J. Muste, 1885–1967*, 16. See also Deming to Jo Ann Robinson, March 25, 1979, AJMP-LA, box 2, in which she writes that she and Muste never discussed sexuality, but that he was "perfectly at ease" with her and her partner, Mary Meigs, "and I never doubted that he was aware that we were lesbians." See also McReynolds, interview with author; Will Inman, interview with author, March 2007; Martin Duberman, *A Saving Remnant: The Radical Lives of David McReynolds and Barbara Deming* (New York: Free Press, 2011); Robinson, *Abraham Went Out*, 221; and Nat Hentoff, *Peace Agitator*, 235–40.

12. D'Emilio, *Lost Prophet*, 116.

13. See previous chapter for a discussion of the role of personal and cell discipline in pacifist political culture. These could involve forms of asceticism, such as periodic fasting and sexual abstinence, and, for some, reflected deeper psychosexual problems. See, for example, Bradford Lyttle, interview by author, Chicago, July 23, 2000.

14. D'Emilio, *Lost Prophet*, 99–104.

15. Ibid., 171–73. For the cultural association between homosexuality and subversion, see Margot Canaday, *The Straight State: Sexuality and Citizenship in Twentieth-Century America* (Princeton, N.J.: Princeton, 2009); David K. Johnson, *The Lavender Scare: The Cold War Persecution of Gays and Lesbians in the Federal Government* (Chicago: University of Chicago Press, 2006); and John D'Emilio and Estelle B. Freedman, *Intimate Matters: A History of Sexuality in America*, 2nd ed. (Chicago: University of Chicago Press, 1997).

16. Evidence of their ideological and political compatibility through the 1950s is ubiquitous in the historical record.

17. Muste to CNVA, March 26, 1963, BDP, box 9, folder 151; Robinson, *Abraham Went Out*, 122. Muste may also have been influenced by the articles on the body, sexuality, and gender published in *Liberation*, such as Esme Wynne-Tyson, "The Masculine-Feminine Balance," *Liberation* 1, no. 5 (July 56): 14–17; Dave Dellinger, "Not Enough Love," *Liberation* 3, nos. 5–6 (August 1958): 28–30; Robert Granat, "Not By Sex Alone," *Liberation* 3, no. 4 (June 1958): 11–13; and "Wilhelm Reich: Two Appraisals," *Liberation* 2, no. 10 (January 1958): 4–9.

18. Muste, "Sketches," 12–13; Robinson, *Abraham Went Out*, 97–99.

19. Hentoff, *Peace Agitator*, 144–45; Robinson, *Abraham Went Out*, 98–99.

20. Robinson, *Abraham Went Out*, 98–99. See also the letters Muste wrote to his son John and his family, dated August 12, 1960; October 7, 1962, and September 13, 1964. All in JAH, Muste Collection, box 1.

21. John Muste to Robinson, March 12 [1979]; John Muste to Robinson, March 27, 1979; Nancy Baker to Robinson, September 12, 1979; Cook to Robinson, August 22, 1978, AJMP-LA, box 2; Cara Cook, unpublished memoir, AJMP, reel 2; Alumnae Biographical Files, Mount Holyoke College Archives and Special Collections, South Hadley, Mass.; Muste to John Muste, February 18, 1958, JAH, Muste Collection, box 1. Perhaps the reason Cook never married Muste was that he was "a revolutionist" who lived "in a way that impeded personal relationship," suggested McReynolds (interview with author).

22. Muste, typescript of position paper, 1956, PMR. See also Muste, "The Camp of Liberation," pamphlet published by *Peace News* (London, 1954); and Muste, "American Radicalism and the Impact of Recent Soviet Developments," pamphlet published by *Liberation* (ca. 1956), both in AJMP, reel 6.

23. Muste, typescript of position paper, 1965, PMR; and Muste, "Neutralism or Third Force," typescript, April 1955, AJMP, reel 4. See also Muste, "Whither Communist Russia?" 3–7; and Homer Jack, "Report on the Bandung Conference," AJMP, reel 4.

24. "Whither Communist Russia?"; Muste, "The Allure of Communism," *Liberation* 1, no. 6 (August 1956): 13–16; and Muste, "The Two War Parties," *Liberation* 1, no. 8 (October 1956): 18–22.

25. Muste, "Proposal for a Bi-Monthly [Bi-Weekly?] Magazine," February 21, 1955, PMR.

26. Ibid.

27. "A Tract for the Times," *Liberation* 1 (March 1956): 3–6.

28. Ibid.

29. "Neither Victims nor Executioners," *Liberation* 4, no. 10 (February 1960): 4–10. See also, for example, Roy Finch, "Religion and the New Generation," *Liberation* 2, no. 3 (May 1957): 11–13.

30. Pells, *The Liberal Mind in a Conservative Age*, 211.

31. For the response of intellectuals to the civil rights movement, see Carol Polsgrove, *Divided Minds: Intellectuals and the Civil Rights Movement* (New York: Norton, 2001). For the magazine's emphasis on the need to break with liberalism, see, for example, Muste, "The Billy Graham Crusade," *Liberation* 2, no. 3 (May 1957): 4–7, 19; and William Appleman Williams, "Go Left or Go Under: American Liberalism at the Crossroads," *Liberation* 2, no. 2 (April 1957): 14–17. For its early support for the freedom movement, see, for example, Martin Luther King Jr., "Our Struggle," *Liberation* 1, no. 2 (April 1956): 3–6; Bayard Rustin, "Montgomery Diary," *Liberation* 1, no. 2 (April 1956): 7–10; editors, "New South, Old Politics," *Liberation* 1, no. 8 (October 1956): 23–26; and Dave Dellinger, "Are Pacifists Willing to Be Negroes?" *Liberation* 4, no. 7 (October 1959): 4–6. The entire December 1956 issue was dedicated to the one-year anniversary of the Montgomery bus boycott.

32. See, for example, Muste, "Nonviolence—A World Movement," *Liberation*, February 1962, 10–16. "The basic fact is that mankind has entered a new era. It is not merely that the age of colonialism, Western expansionism and white domination has come to an end . . . [rather] what we call 'civilization,' which originated some five thousand or more years ago is ending, and that if mankind survives the nuclear age . . . we shall have to speak of 'post-civilization.'"

33. H. Stuart Hughes, quoted in Robinson, *Abraham Went Out*, 159–60. Similarly, Riesman recalled that Muste was never "vindictive" or judgmental toward those who did not share his enthusiasm for radical pacifism and direct action. See Riesman to Jo Ann Robinson, February 9, 1978, AJMP-LA, box 2. For one of Muste's accounts of the drills and his arrest, see Muste, "Riot Squads Surround Court," clipping in AJMP, reel 36. The civil defense protests of the late 1950s have been well described by historians. See, for example, Bennett, *Radical Pacifism*, 207–16; Piehl, "Catholic Worker Pacifism in the Cold War Era," 87; and Dee Garrison, "'Our Skirts Gave Them Courage': The Civil Defense Protest Movement in New York City, 1955–1961," in Joanne Meyerowitz, ed., *Not June Cleaver: Women and Gender in Postwar America, 1945–1960* (Philadelphia: Temple University Press, 1994).

34. *Speak Truth to Power: A Quaker Search for an Alternative to Violence* (Philadelphia: American Friends Service Committee, 1955), see esp. iii–iv, 12, 17, 28.

35. Ibid., 58–70.

36. Robinson, *Abraham Went Out*, 158. See also Arthur Schlesinger Jr., "The Best Hope for Freedom," *Liberation* 1, no. 6 (August 1956): 19.

37. Michael Harrington, letter to editor, *Liberation* 1, no. 5 (July 1956): 9–10.

38. Muste, introduction to Sidney Lens, *Questions for the Left* (New York: American Forum for Socialist Education, 1957), 2. See also Muste, "The Convention and Democratic Socialism," *Liberation* 2, no. 1 (March 1957): 7–10; and Muste, "American Radicalism and the Impact of Recent Soviet Developments."

39. "Communist Heard on Pacifist Forum: Dennis Pleads for a Leftist Alliance—Idea Rejected by Norman Thomas," *New York Times*, May 28, 1956, clipping in FOR, box 1, folder 10; and Muste, "The Convention and Democratic Socialism."

40. Lens, *Questions for the Left*, 3–14.

41. Ibid. See also Sidney Lens, *Radicalism in America*, rev. ed. (New York: Crowell, 1969), 353–54.

42. Muste, "The Convention and Democratic Socialism."

43. "Muste Rejects Senate Inquiry," *New York Times*, May 27, 1957, copy in JNSP, box 11, folder 6. See also Muste to J. Edgar Hoover (ca. April 1957), AJMP-LA, box 2; and Lieberman, *The Strangest Dream*, 140–42.

44. Roy Finch, "A Strange Mistake," *Liberation* 2, no. 4 (June 1957): 13–16. For the opposition of social democrats, see, for example, letters to the editor of *Liberation* 2, no. 4 (June 1957): 18–19; Diana Trilling, letter to the *New Leader* [1957], copy in AJMP, reel 1; and Minutes of American Forum Provisional Working Committee Meeting, April 6, 1957, AJMP-LA, box 2.

45. Roy Kepler to the editors, *Liberation* 2, no. 5 (July–August 1957): 31.

46. Muste, introduction to Lens, *Questions for the Left*, 2.

47. Dave Dellinger, "United Front, No; Public Debate, Yes," *Liberation* 2, no. 4 (June 1957): 13–16.

48. Muste, "Comment on Socialist Rethinking," typescript (ca. 1956), for *Mankind* magazine, AJMP, reel 6.

49. Muste to Paul Krahe et al., February 24, 1953; Muste comments on the Vienna Congress, typescript, March 12, 1955; and "[IFOR] Relations with CP and Peace Front Movements," June 24, 1953. All in FOR, box 2, folder 1.

50. Henri Roser to friends, May 18, 1953, FOR, box 2, folder 1. See also Muste to Roser, October 20, 1952; Muste to Muriel Lester, January 2, 1952, both in JNSP, box 11, folder 6.

51. Muste, quoted in Robinson, *Abraham Went Out*, 154.

52. Muste, "Peace and the Power States," *Liberation* 7, no. 8 (October 1962): 16–19, 23. See also Minutes of CNVA Executive Committee Meeting, July 18, 1961, CNVA, box 1.

53. Muste, "Report on Conversation with Karl Barth at Basel," March 18, 1955, JNSP, box 11, folder 8. See also "AJM—Prospective Trip to Europe," 1955, AJMP, reel 4; and Muste, "The Camp of Liberation," which he published after spending six weeks in Europe over the summer of 1954.

54. Scott to Muste and Cecil Hinshaw, July 4, 1955, LSP, box 1, folder 4; and "Summary of Meeting on H-Bomb Tests," LSP, box 2, folder 1. See also Minutes of Non-Violent Action Against Nuclear Weapons, Executive Committee Meeting, August 25, 1958, and September 17, 1959, CNVA, box 1.

55. Scott, "Words Are Not Enough," *Liberation* 2, no. 3 (May 1957): 14–15. Muste was asked to become national chairman in the fall of 1959. See Minutes of Non-Violent Action

Against Nuclear Weapons, Executive Committee Meeting, September 17, 1959, CNVA, box 1. See also Wittner, *Rebels Against War*, 242–44; and Milton S. Katz, *Ban the Bomb: A History of SANE, 1957–1985* (Westport, Conn.: Greenwood Press, 1986).

56. Jim Peck, quoted in Robinson, *Abraham Went Out*, 163; and Robert Pickus, "The Nevada Project: An Appraisal," *Liberation* 2, no. 6 (September 1957): 2–3. See also Lawrence Scott, "The Nevada Witness," undated typescript, LSP, box 2, folder 1.

57. Albert Bigelow, "Why I Am Sailing into the Pacific Bomb-Test Area," *Liberation* 2, no. 2 (February 1958): 4–6; and Albert Bigelow, *The Voyage of the Golden Rule: An Experiment with Truth* (New York: Doubleday, 1959), 42.

58. Wittner, *Rebels Against War*, 249–50. See also Minutes of Non-Violent Action Against Nuclear Weapons, Executive Committee Meeting, April 25, May 20, 23, 28, June 5–6, and August 25, 1958, CNVA, box 1.

59. Muste to Dwight Eisenhower, June 29, 1959; pamphlet "This Is Omaha Action"; Omaha Action Bulletin, July 1, 1959; CNVA News, June 1959; all in JNSP, box 11, folder 8. See also "Action at Omaha," *Liberation* 4, no. 5 (July–August 1959): 3–4.

60. Bayard Rustin, quoted in Robinson, *Abraham Went Out*, 172. See also Muste, "Africa Against the Bomb" (1960), in Hentoff, *Essays of A. J. Muste*, 394–402; and Minutes of CNVA Executive Committee Meeting, March 19, 1960, CNVA, box 1.

61. Muste, "Africa Against the Bomb," 402. For evidence of Ghanaian enthusiasm for the project, see BRP, reel 1, which has clippings from the *Ghana Times* and leaflets publicizing the protest. See also Kwame Nkrumah, "Against Nuclear Imperialism," *Liberation* 5, no. 3 (May 1960): 16–18.

62. Barbara Deming, "San Francisco to Moscow: Why They Walk," in Deming, *Revolution and Equilibrium* (New York: Grossman, 1971), 51–59, originally published in the *Nation*, July 15, 1961.

63. *CNVA Bulletin*, June 21, August 28, and September 29, 1961, and January 13, 1964. Copies in BDP, box 1, folder 2. For internal debates regarding this question, see Minutes of CNVA Executive Committee Meetings from July and August 1961, CNVA, box 1.

64. Muste, "Berlin, Solomon, Kafka," *Liberation* 6, no. 7 (September 1961): 3–4; and "They Made It to Moscow," *Liberation* 6, no. 9 (November 1961): 7–10. For Muste's role in the Walk for Peace, see *CNVA Bulletin*, June 21, August 28, and September 29, 1961, and January 13, 1964. Copies in BDP, box 1, folder 2; Muste, "They Made It to Moscow"; Joseph Barry, "The Broken Path," *New York Post* (June 27, 1961); and "Peace Marchers Reach Red Square but Soviet Prohibits Speeches," *New York Times*, October 4, 1961, both clippings in AJMP, reel 36.

65. CNVA leaflet, circa 1961, BDP, box 1, folder 2; and "Report of the Committee on General Directions to the Executive Committee of CNVA," September 25, 1962, BDP, box 9, folder 150.

66. See Kosek, *Acts of Conscience*; and Mollin, *Radical Pacifism in Modern America*.

67. Muste, "Saints for This Age," 410–25.

68. The issue first came up in 1958 when some CNVA protesters at the Cheyenne Missile Base in Wyoming tried to prevent trucks from entering the base by lying in the road. It emerged again in the planning of Omaha Action, when the FOR withdrew its support over fears that some of the participants might use "non-violent obstruction." See Minutes of CNVA Executive Committee Meeting, August 25, 1958, and April 14, May 12, June 4, and September 17, 1959, CNVA, box 1; Theodore Olson to Ernest Bromley, May 30, 1959, EMBP; Bradford Lyttle, "On

Nonviolent Obstruction," *Liberation* 3, no. 8 (November 1958): 10–11; Lyttle to Deming, February 2, 1963, BDP, box 20, folder 379.

69. Albert Bigelow to CNVA, June 15, 1960, CNVA, box 5, folder 5. See also Minutes of CNVA Executive Committee Meeting, June 9 and July 23, 1960, CNVA, box 1.

70. Bigelow to CNVA, June 15, 1960. Other examples of these concerns and debates can be found in Minutes of CNVA Executive Committee Meeting, CNVA, box 1; Report of the Committee on General Directions to the Executive Committee of CNVA, September 25, 1962; Minutes of CNVA Informal Executive Committee Meeting, May 31, 1962; George Willoughby to CNVA Committee, October 3, 1962; Marjorie Swann to Members of National Committee for Nonviolent Action, March 7, 1963, BDP, box 9, folders 150 and 151.

71. See, for example, Arthur Harvey to CNVA, March 28, 1962, and Jerry Lehmann to CNVA, May 12, 1962, both in BDP, box 9, folder 150; and the common discipline for the Quebec-Guantanamo Peace Walk; and Bradford Lyttle to CNVA, September 26, 1963, both in BDP, box 9, folder 151. See also Calhoun Geiger to CNVA, June 12, 1963, and CNVA reply to Geiger, June 17, 1963, both in CNVA, box 5.

72. See, for example, "A Rural, Communitarian Base for the Nonviolent Direct Action Peace Movement," BDP, box 20, folder 378; and Bradford Lyttle, position paper, February 24, 1963, CNVA, box 10. For the latter, Lyttle attached the "Principles for Conduct" of the Polaris Project, run by Bob and Marjorie Swann, which included a daily schedule and regulations for personal appearance and behavior, such as: "There is no place in the project for brief, or temporary, or promiscuous sexual relationships."

73. Muste to Bert Bigelow, July 5, 1960, CNVA, box 5, folder 5. See also Muste to CNVA, March 26, 1963, BDP, box 9, folder 151; and Muste, "Reflections on 'Nonviolent Intervention,'" typescript (ca. 1959), AJMP, reel 5. See also Muste, "Saints for This Age," 422–25.

74. Muste to CNVA, March 26, 1963, BDP, box 9, folder 151.

75. Scott to Albert Bigelow, July 12, 1960, LSP, box 1, folder 1.

76. Dellinger, quoted in Robinson, *Abraham Went Out*, 187.

77. Riesman to Robinson, February 9, 1978, AJMP-LA, box 2; "A Psychoanalyst Looks at Peace," *New York Post* magazine, April 22, 1962, 2, clipping in AJMP, reel 36; and Hentoff, *Peace Agitator*, 6. The high regard both Muste and Fromm had for each other is fascinating in light of Lawrence J. Friedman's recent biography of the psychoanalyst, which emphasizes the role of his religious upbringing in shaping his intellectual and political development. Moreover, his preoccupations—with the authoritarian personality, with how to be human in a mass society, and so on—were remarkably similar to those that consumed Muste. See Friedman, *The Lives of Erich Fromm: Love's Prophet* (New York: Columbia University Press, 2013).

78. For example, he resigned as head of the Church Peace Mission and the Council for Correspondence. Still, he continued to be drawn into leadership roles. As he commented in 1960, "I confess that I have occasionally in recent days thought of the utterance of another old man, who said: 'Now lettest thou thy servant depart in peace, Lord, according to thy word.' And if the departing come, I think it would indeed be a departing in peace. But I do not feel like departing and I probably don't know how to quit." See Muste, "Pacifism Enters a New Phase," 25.

79. Muste to George Malloy, August 21, 1964, AJMP, reel 24.

80. Deming to Muste, August 15, 1964, BDP, box 24, folder 459.

81. Edith Snyder to Barbara Deming, circa 1963, BDP, box 24, folder 459.

82. Snyder to Muste, Sunday, October 11 [1964], AJMP-LA, box 2. More letters from her can be found in the same box.

Chapter 11. Muste and the Search for the "Third Way"

Epigraph: Muste to Friends, December 1959, JNSP, box 11, folder 6.

1. Muste, "Nonviolence—A World Movement," *Liberation* 6, no. 2 (February 1962): 10–16; Muste, "Pacifism Enters a New Phase," *Fellowship* (July 1, 1960): 21–25, copy in AJMP, reel 5.

2. See, for example, Muste to J. P. Narayan, January 25, 1963, AJMP, reel 36; Muste, "Report on the Indian Crisis, 1962–63," February 8, 1963, typescript of article for *Peace News*, AJMP, reel 5; and Muste, "Peace and the Power States," 16–19, 23.

3. See Muste to Bill Sutherland and Michael Randle, March 8, 1960; Bill Sutherland to Muste, March 10, 1960; Randall to Muste, dated March 14, 1960, all in AJMP, reel 7.

4. Nkrumah, "Against Nuclear Imperialism." A copy of the conference manifesto followed this reprint of Nkrumah's speech. See also "Some Notes on the Positive Action Conference to Be Held in Accra April 7 to 9" [probably authored by Sutherland], March 20, 1960, and Muste to Harrison Butterworth, April 15, 1960, both in AJMP, reel 7.

5. Sidney Lens, "The Revolution in Africa," published in three parts, *Liberation* 4, no. 10 (January 1960): 8–11, no. 11 (February 1960): 15–19, and *Liberation* 5, no. 1 (March 1960): 7–11.

6. Muste editorial, *Liberation* 5, no. 2 (April 1960): 3.

7. Muste, "Africa Against the Bomb"; Muste editorial, *Liberation* 5, no. 2 (April 1960); and Muste, "Pacifism Enters a New Phase," 21–25.

8. Bill Sutherland to Muste, September 8, 1960, AJMP, reel 7; Muste, "A Strategy for the Peace Movement," *Liberation* 7, no. 4 (June 62): 5–8.

9. Gandhi first proposed forming an international peace army in South Africa in 1906. The idea was revived in late 1949 at the World Pacifist Meeting at Sevagram, India, which Muste attended, but only Belgium and India actually followed through and created "*satyagraha* units." For American plans to form "*satyagraha* units," see *Peacemaker* 2, no. 2 (July 11, 1950): 2; *Peacemaker* 2, no. 4 (August 31, 1950): 2; and *Peacemaker Special Supplement* (September 6, 1950): 1–4. See also Muste to Fellowship Members [1949], JAH, Muste Collection, box 1.

10. Barbara Deming, "International Peace Brigade," in Deming, *Revolution and Equilibrium*, 93–101, originally published in the *Nation*, April 7, 1962. See also Muste, "Some Meanings of the Beirut Conference," typescript (ca. 1960), AJMP, reel 5; and Bradford Lyttle, "Brummana Conference for a World Peace Brigade," unpublished report, BDP, box 20, folder 378.

11. Muste, "Nonviolence—A World Movement," 10–16. See also Muste, "Pacifism Enters a New Phase," 21–25.

12. Sutherland and Meyer, *Guns and Gandhi in Africa*, 96. For the WPB's efforts to raise awareness about apartheid and colonialism in southern Africa, see its leaflet "South Africa—Danger!" (undated); information about its co-sponsorship of a poster walk on October 2, 1962, to protect South African policies; and other documents, all in AJMP, reel 5.

13. See Muste to Al Hassler, May 29, 1962, AJMP, reel 1.

14. Muste, "Prasad's Unique Challenge," *Liberation* 7, nos. 5–6 (July–August 1962): 16–17, 36. For Nehru's dilemmas during this period, see Ramachandra Guha, *India After Gandhi: The History of the World's Largest Democracy* (New York: HarperCollins, 2007), 328–44.

15. Muste, "Report on the Indian Crisis, 1962–63"; Muste, "Tiger at the Gates," *Liberation* 7, no. 12 (February 1963): 4–11. For a detailed account of the Sino-Indian war, see Guha, *India After Gandhi*, 307–41.

16. For problems the WPB encountered, see, for example, James Bristol, "Nonviolence and India Today," Report of the Peace Education Division of the AFSC (which helped to provide

funding and personnel to the march), March 1963; Muste, typescript of editorial, April 23, 1963; Muste "Our Responsibility to the Friendship March," *World Peace Brigade Reports*, July 1963; Shri Siddharaj Dhadda, statement, April 16, 1963; and Devi Prasad, "Friendship Marchers in Difficulties," clipping from *Peace News* (ca. March 1963). All in AJMP, reel 23.

17. On these differences between Indian nationalists, see, for example, Minutes of World Peace Brigade Meeting, December 2, 1962; "In Orbit" (regarding Muste's interview with Vinoba Bhave on "the Indian's pacifist's dilemma"), *Arunodayam*, June 1963; J. P. Narayan, "Delhi-Peking Friendship March: A Bridge of Friendship and Understanding," *Arunodayam*, June 1963; Muste, "India Yet Must Show the Way," *Arunodayam*, June 1963. All in AJMP, reel 23.

18. Narayan to Muste, September 22, 1964; Narayan to Donald Groom, April 4, 1965; Muste, memorandum on the Peace Brigade [1965]; and Devi Prasad to Muste, June 10, 1965. All in AJMP, reel 23. See also Robinson, *Abraham Went Out*, 182–83. The organizations that helped to sponsor the Friendship March were CNVA, AFSC, and FOR.

19. Sutherland and Meyer, *Guns and Gandhi in Africa*, 96; Robinson, *Abraham Went Out*, 182–83.

20. Bill Sutherland, quoted in Robinson, *Abraham Went Out*, 180. See also Sutherland to Muste, May 27, 1966 ("Pacifists have had access to leaders of African Nation-States, but have not been able to provide answers for security of National Interests"); and Minutes of World Peace Brigade Meeting, December 2, 1962," both in AJMP, reel 23.

21. Muste, "Cuba: An Analysis of American and Soviet Foreign Policy" (1962), copy in AJMP, reel 5. For the FOR's support for Cuba, see FOR, box 3, folders 4–9, box 4, folders 1–6, and box 5, folders 5–8.

22. Van Gosse discusses radical pacifists and other Americans who identified with Castro's Cuba in *Where the Boys Are*.

23. For the FOR's efforts at humanitarian aid, see FOR, box 3, folders 4–9, box 4, folders 1–6, and box 5, folders 5–8. The Nonviolent Committee for Cuban Independence included pacifists from the FOR, CNVA, the Catholic Worker movement, and the WRL. See *CNVA Bulletin*, March 10, 1961, copy in BDP, box 1, folder 2.

24. Muste, "Death of the Republic," *Liberation* 6, no. 3 (May 1961): 13–15. See also Muste, "Cuba: An Analysis of American and Soviet Foreign Policy"; and Muste, "Love and Power in Today's Setting," *Christian Century* (ca. 1962), copy in AJMP, reel 5.

25. Finch editorial, "Cycle of Revenge," *Liberation* 3, no. 12 (February 1959): 3. For similar debates within the FOR, see correspondence in FOR, box 4, folders 3–4.

26. Muste, "The Meaning of Albany" (ca. January 1964), AJMP, reel 38.

27. Bradford Lyttle to CNVA, September 17, 1963; and Deming to CNVA, October 9, 1963. Both in BDP, box 9, folder 151.

28. Naomi Eftis to Muste, January 6, 1964, AJMP, reel 37. Emphasis in original.

29. Marian Mollin provides an insightful discussion of the tensions between pacifists and southern African Americans in *Radical Pacifism in Modern America*, 135–38.

30. See Muste to Howard Schomer, March 10, 1964; Muste to Naomi Eftis, January 8, 1964; Muste to Peggy Duff, May 6, 1964, AJMP, reel 37.

31. Evidence of the relationship he built with the African American community of Albany can be found in Muste to Slater King, June 29, 1964; Slater King to Muste, January 18, 1965, AJMP, reel 36. Edith Snyder's letters to Muste in AJMP-LA, box 2, are also suggestive of the relationship.

32. Dave Dellinger to Bradford Lyttle, June 18, 1964; and Dellinger to Dick [?], A. J. [Muste], and Neil Haworth, May 5, 1964. Both in BDP, box 10, folder 173. See also Dellinger to *Liberation* editors, May 13 [1964], BDP, box 20, folder 379; Neil Haworth to Bradford Lyttle, January 23, 1963, CNVA, box 10; and "The Continuing Cuban Crisis: Policy Statement of the Quebec-Guantanamo Walk for Peace," BDP, box 9, folder 151.

33. Dave Dellinger to Bradford Lyttle, June 18, 1964, and Dellinger to Dick [?], A. J. [Muste], and Neil Haworth, May 5, 1964. Both in BDP, box 10, folder 173. See also Dellinger to *Liberation* editors, May 13 [1964], BDP, box 20, folder 379.

34. CNVA, "The Continuing Cuban Crisis: Policy Statement of the Quebec-Guantanamo Walk for Peace," box 9, folder 151. See also Muste and Brad Lyttle to CNVA, July 18, 1964.

35. Muste, "Hurricanes in Miami," typescript, September 1, 1964, AJMP, reel 5.

36. Houser, interview by author.

37. Muste, "Peace and the Power States." See also Muste, "Love and Power in Today's Setting"; and Muste, "Cuba: An Analysis of American and Soviet Policy."

38. See, for example, J. P. Narayan to Muste, May 22, 1964; Muste to J. P. Narayan, June 4, 1964; Muste to Devi Prasad, December 24, 1963; all in AJMP, reel 36.

39. Siddharaj Dhadda, WPB Asian region secretary, to "Friends," May 29, 1963, AJMP, reel 23; telegrams to Muste from Japanese Buddhist Council for World Federations and J. P. Narayan, both circa 1965, AJMP, reel 23; Neil Haworth to Thich Tri Quang, December 30, 1964, CNVA, box 5; Vo Thanh Minh to CNVA, February 21, 1965, and March 18, 1965, BDP, box 10, folder 153. See also Ryokei Onishi of the Kyoto Buddhist Association to Erich Fromm, September 3, 1963; Fromm forwarded the letter to Muste; see AJMP, reel 36.

40. Arthur Mitzman, "Not SANE Enough," *Liberation* 4, no. 7 (October 1959): 16–18.

41. Barbara Deming, "The Ordeal of SANE" (1961), reprinted in *Revolution and Equilibrium*, 46.

42. Muste, "The Crisis in SANE," *Liberation* 5, nos. 5–6 (July–August 1960): 10–14; and Muste, "The Crisis in SANE: Act II," *Liberation* 5, no. 8 (November 1960): 5–8. Muste predicted that SANE's attempts to appease HUAC would not prevent further investigations. Indeed, soon thereafter, HUAC launched an attack on Linus Pauling, one of SANE's sponsors, and subpoenaed thirty-seven more members of the organization.

43. See, for example, Muste, "The Crisis in SANE"; Muste, "The Crisis in SANE: Act II"; Muste, "Getting Rid of War: National Policy and Personal Responsibility," *Liberation* 14, no. 1 (March 1959): 5–7; and Muste, "The Eisenhower-Khrushchev Talks," *Liberation* 4, no. 6 (Sept. 1959): 8–11.

44. Wittner, *Rebels Against War*, 277–78. In an attempt to appear mainstream, SANE explicitly distanced itself from pacifists who advocated unilateralism. See Minutes of FOR Executive Committee Meeting, September 17, 1963, FOR, box 5, folder 8.

45. Scott to CNVA, November 26, 1962, BDP, box 29, folder 581; and "Notes on CNVA Committee Discussions," December 20–21, 1964, BDP, box 9, folder 152.

46. Theodore Olson to CNVA Executive Committee, February 25, 1963, and Marjorie Swann to CNVA Executive Committee, March 7, 1963, BDP, box 150, folder 9; Barbara Deming, "Southern Peace Walk: Two Issues or One," in *Revolution and Equilibrium*, 103, originally published in *Liberation*, July–August 1962; Bradford Lyttle to Marjorie Swann, March 22, 1965, HCP, series B, box 2; and "Notes on CNVA Committee Discussions," December 20–21, 1964.

47. Muste, "The Fall of Man," *Liberation* 9, no. 4 (June–July 1964): 25–30; Muste, "World Perspectives for a Peace Program," *Liberation* 9, no. 1 (March 1964): 17–19; and "Notes on CNVA Committee Discussions," December 20–21, 1964.

48. Muste, "Politics on the Other Side of Despair," *Liberation* 7, no. 2 (April 1962): 6–9.

49. Muste, "Let's Radicalize the Peace Movement," *Liberation* 8, no. 4 (June 1963): 26–30. My emphasis.

50. Muste, "Politics on the Other Side of Despair."

51. Muste, "A Realistic Peace Strategy," *Liberation* 8, nos. 5–6 (Summer 1963): 5–6.

52. "Notes on CNVA Committee Discussions," December 20–21, 1964.

Chapter 12. The "American Gandhi" and Vietnam

Epigraph: Muste, typescript, 1965 speech, AJMP, reel 24.

1. See Muste, *The Camp of Liberation* (London: Peace News, 1954); Muste, "What Really Happened in Korea?" (FOR pamphlet, ca. 1954), copy in AJMP, reel 6; Muste, "The Fall of Man," 25–30; and "Notes on CNVA Committee Discussions," December 20–21, 1964. On the history of the Vietnam War, see Marilyn Young, *The Vietnam Wars, 1945–1990* (New York: HarperPerennial, 1991); George Herring, *America's Longest War: The United States and Vietnam, 1950–1970*, 4th ed. (New York: McGraw-Hill, 2001); and Mark Atwood Lawrence, *Vietnam: A Concise International History* (New York: Oxford University Press, 2010).

2. See Simon Hall, *Peace and Freedom: The Civil Rights and Antiwar Movements of the 1960s* (Philadelphia: University of Pennsylvania Press, 2004), 106–12, 118–19; DeBenedetti, *Peace Reform in American History*, 179–80.

3. Muste and David McReynolds, "Memo on Vietnam," *WRL News*, July 15, 1964. See also Muste and Sid Lens, "Neither Co-existence nor War," typescript (ca. 1962), AJMP, reel 5.

4. Muste, "Problems of the Radical Peace Movement," typescript, September 10, 1964, AJMP, reel 5. See also correspondence between Muste and David Riesman, October 5, 1964, and November 2, 1964, AJMP, reel 36.

5. See Robinson, *Abraham Went Out*, 196–97.

6. Kennan, "A Fresh Look at Our China Policy," *New York Times Magazine*, November 22, 1964. Antiwar sentiment among liberals did, however, grow rapidly over 1965, and especially after the 1968 presidential election. See DeBenedetti, *Peace Reform in American History*, 173–75; and Hall, *Peace and Freedom*, chap. 5.

7. Muste and Kennan, "An Exchange: A Policy for the Far East," 6–8. Muste's argument anticipates Michael Sherry's observation that Americans perceived the threat of war as coming from "outside America to intrude upon their pacific ways." See Sherry, *In the Shadow of War*, ix.

8. Muste and Kennan, "An Exchange," 9–11, 24.

9. See Stephanson, *Kennan and the Art of Foreign Policy*, 173–75.

10. Hans Morgenthau and Reinhold Niebuhr, "The Ethics of War and Peace in the Nuclear Age," *War/Peace Report*, February 1967, 4; Niebuhr, "Vietnam and the Imperial Conflict," *New Leader*, June 6, 1966, 17; and Niebuhr, "Vietnam: An Insoluble Problem," *Christianity and Crisis*, 25, no. 1 (February 8, 1965): 1–2.

11. Muste, "Vietnam: The Political Reality," *Liberation* 9, no. 7 (October 1964): 20–22. Maurice Isserman provides a helpful discussion of the anti-Stalinist left and its views of the Vietnam War. See Maurice Isserman, *The Other American: The Life of Michael Harrington* (New York: PublicAffairs, 2001), 259–64. David McReynolds recalled that the Socialist Party, including himself, was at times "too critical of Muste," viewing him as "too soft on the Soviet Union. On

this basis, McReynolds and other left-wing Socialists initially opposed joining the Fifth Avenue Peace Parade Committee. McReynolds, interview by author.

12. Muste, "Vietnam: The Political Reality."

13. Muste, "Crisis in the World and in the Peace Movement," 465–78. See also Muste memo on CNVA policy, circa 1965, HCP, box 2.

14. Hentoff, *Peace Agitator*, 243; Robinson, *Abraham Went Out*, 197–98.

15. Doug Rossinow, among others, has established the existential roots of New Left activism, an argument that supports my own findings, albeit of radical pacifists. See Rossinow, *The Politics of Authenticity*. See also David Farber, "New Wave Sixties Historiography," *Reviews in American History* 27, no. 2 (June 1999): 298–305; and George Cotkin, *Existential America* (Baltimore: Johns Hopkins University Press, 2005). For the mutual esteem with which Muste and the "sixties" generation held each other, see, for example, Beverly Sterner, interview with author; Will Inman, interview with author; and Tom Cornell, interview with author.

16. See letter from George Willoughby, A. J. Muste, and Neil Haworth, "Tragedy in Vietnam," February 27, 1965, and list of sponsors of "The March on Washington to End the War in Vietnam," April 17, 1965. Both in BDP, box 10, folder 153. See also "Declaration of Conscience," CNVA, box 10.

17. "Declaration of Conscience," CNVA, box 10.

18. See "A Call to Speak Out at the Pentagon," June 16, 1965, AJMP, reel 24; Muste memo, October 8, 1965, BDP, box 24, folder 459.

19. See Robinson, *Abraham Went Out*, 190; and Hall, *Peace and Freedom*, 23–24. Ironically, just prior to this meeting, on March 8, 1965, Muste wrote a memo, "On Problems of Collaboration in Peace Activity," in which he stated that SDS's approach was "on the whole satisfactory" and urging peace groups to adopt an attitude of "experimentation" in a rapidly evolving situation. See AJMP, reel 25.

20. Muste, "Crisis in the World and in the Peace Movement," 477–78. In late spring of 1965, Muste participated in several panel discussions designed to foster closer relations between the peace community and the New Left. For details, see, for example, Homer Jack memo, May 24, 1965, and Jane Billott to Muste, circa May 1965, both in AJMP, reel 38.

21. Bradford Lyttle, Staughton Lynd, and A. J. Muste, "Assembly of Unrepresented People: Three Views." *Liberation* 10, no. 7 (October 1965): 24–29; Muste memo, October 8, 1965, BDP, box 24, folder 459; and Muste, "Assembly of Unrepresented People: A Report," *Liberation* 10, no. 6 (September 1965): 28–29.

22. Their "mandate" was to include "all major approaches to ending the war" and to include representatives of "important social constituencies, i.e., Negroes, Labor, youth, Women, Arts, etc." See Minutes of the Fifth Avenue Peace Parade Committee Meeting, September 17, 1965, AJMP, reel 25.

23. Muste, summary of CNVA experience in united action on the Assembly of Unrepresented People (ca. September 1965), AJMP, reel 6

24. Quotes can be found in Robinson, *Abraham Went Out*, 200. It was by no means an easy task to pull the Parade Committee together, as left sectarianism continued to be a problem. See minutes from September 15, 1965, September 17, 1965, and March 9, 1966, meetings of the Fifth Avenue Peace Parade Committee, all in AJMP, reel 25. Muste preferred working with leftists of the SDS variety. Sectarian groups lacked creativity, a tendency toward anger rather than "outrage," a sentiment that was incompatible with love, Muste wrote to an acquaintance. More

appealing, "more genuinely left," were student radicals of "the C. Wright Mills persuasion." See Muste to Tom Brewer, September 25, 1964, AJMP, reel 24.

25. See Muste to Eric Bentley, March 1, 1965, and March 24, 1964, AJMP, reel 37.

26. The close relationship between Muste and leading radical intellectuals can be found in his correspondence. See, for example, Muste to Fromm, December 3, 1963; Fromm to Muste November 29, 1963; Irving Louis Horowitz to Richard Gilpin, March 11, 1964; Muste to Horowitz, March 12, 1964; Muste to David Riesman, November 2, 1964; Riesman to Muste, October 5, 1964. All in AJMP, reel 36. For the alternative of serving as a "moral" supporter, see, for example, Muste to Martin Luther King Jr., July 11, 1965, AJMP, reel 37.

27. Muste to Artists, Writers, and Professionals Against the War, April 20, 1965, AJMP, reel 23. There are dozens of examples of Muste's participation in university-centered antiwar events in his correspondence, including a speak-out, called by the New Haven-Yale Committee for Peace in Vietnam (other speakers included William Sloane Coffin, Nancy Gitlin, Staughton Lynd, and Norman Thomas); speaking at a Vietnam teach-in at the University of Toronto; leading a rally at San Diego State College to protest South Vietnamese premier Nguyen Cao Ky's visit to the United States; speaking at a 1965 New School symposium on the war; and so on. See letter from Jeffry Larson to Muste, July 29, 1965; John Holland to Muste, October 18, 1966; Murray Thomson to Muste, August 22, 1966; and press release, "New School Committee to Hold Symposium on Vietnam War," December 6, 1965. All in AJMP, reel 37. Joe Stetson to Muste, June 29, 1964, AJMP, reel 36.

28. AFSC Working Party, *Peace in Vietnam: A New Approach in Southeast Asia*, 2nd ed. (New York: Hill and Wang, 1967); the working party gave "special mention to their regard and affection for A. J. Muste" as a leader of the peace movement and as a contributor to the report (p. 126).

29. For a sense of their mutual admiration, see Bennett to Muste, February 22, 1966, and William Sloane Coffin to Muste, June 24, 1966, AJMP, reel 23; Muste to Bennett, March 9, 1964, AJMP, reel 36. Muste continued to actively participate in formal and informal discussions with religious leaders about peace, attending meetings sponsored by such groups as the World Council of Churches, the United Presbyterian Peace Fellowship, the Church Peace Mission, and the Religious Leaders' Conference on Peace, which took place in New York City over the winter of December 1964 and January 1965. See, for example, Rev. Edward G. Murray to Muste, December 3, 1964; "Convention Program," December 4–6, 1964; "Religious Leaders' Conference on Peace" program, January 12–14, 1965; Paul G. Palmer to Muste, March 18, 1966; Muste to Paul Peachey, October 27, 1964; Paul Peachey memo, October 15, 1964; Muste to Paul Peachey, September 22, 1965; Muste to Paul Peachey, December 9, 1963. All in AJMP, reel 37. For the history of CALCAV, see Mitchell Hall, *Because of Their Faith*.

30. See "Vietnam—A Clergyman's Dilemma," a CALCAV position paper for the Spring Mobilization, January 31–February 1, 1967, AJMP, reel 23; Richard Fernandez to CALCAV constituency, first week in May, AJMP, reel 23; and Hall, *Because of Their Faith*.

31. Muste to Jerome Davis, February 1, 1966, AJMP, reel 38.

32. See Robinson, *Abraham Went Out*, 204; and Danielson, "Christianity, Dissent, and the Cold War."

33. Muste called for the "triple revolution" in numerous forums (it later became known as the "quadruple revolution"). See, for example, Muste, "The Primacy of Peace," *Liberation* 9, no.9 (December 1964): 12–15. These efforts to reach out to labor were formalized in a national

committee consisting of Muste, Lens, Michael Harrington, Harvey Swados, Norman Thomas, Paul Jacobs, Erich Fromm, James Farmer, among several others. See "Interim Progress Report on National Committee," May 16, 1963, AJMP, reel 37, and Irving Laucks to Muste, March 24, 1964, AJMP, reel 24.

34. David McReynolds, interview with author.

35. See letter from ACW's secretary-treasurer (name unclear) to Muste, June 2, 1966, AJMP, reel 23. Meetings of antiwar groups were often held at the Textile Workers Hall on University Place.

36. Arnold Johnson to Muste, May 27, 1966; "Support International Days of Protest," leaflet, circa summer 1966. Both in AJMP, reel 23.

37. See Philip S. Foner's classic account, *U.S. Labor and the Vietnam War* (New York: International Publishers, 1989). In the months before his death, Muste closely followed this growing estrangement between Reuther and Meany and hoped that the peace forces could profit from it. While it was unlikely to happen anytime soon, he believed that the mobilization of labor against the war could have "an appreciable impact on the Administration . . . . In such a case, for example, strikes in war industries would become possible, even likely, and that would take the protest out of the 'token' or 'symbolic' category." See Muste, "Cleveland and After," *Mobilizer* 1, no. 1 (December 19, 1966): 6.

38. See Robinson, *Abraham Went Out*, 118–21; and Robinson's notes from interview with James Lawson.

39. Robinson, *Abraham Went Out*, 118–21; and Hall, *Peace and Freedom*, 34–35, 80–104. See also Muste to Harry Boyte (special assistant to MLK), August 26, 1965, and Boyte to Muste, September 10, 1965, AJMP, reel 23. Boyte explained that SCLC was censoring the comments of King and James Bevel that had to do with the war. Still, SCLC proved more willing than other civil rights organizations to condone antiwar sentiment.

40. See, for example, Mary Dudziak, *Cold War Civil Rights: Race and the Image of American Democracy* (Princeton, N.J.: Princeton University Press, 2000); Von Eschen, *Race Against Empire*; and Plummer, *Rising Wind*.

41. See Robinson, *Abraham Went Out*, 119; Dellinger, "Are Pacifists Willing to Be Negroes?"; Muste and Rustin editorial, "Struggle for Integration," *Liberation* 5, no. 3 (May 1960): 5–9. See also Muste, "Our Responsibility to the Friendship March," *World Peace Brigade Reports*, July 1963, copy in AJMP, reel 23. For Muste's support of federal legislation, see Muste, "Nonviolence and Mississippi," reprinted in G. Ramachandran and T. K. Mahadevan, eds., *Gandhi: His Relevance for Our Times* (1964; Canton, Me.: Greenleaf Books, 1983), copy in AJMP, reel 6; and Muste to Howard Schomer, March 10, 1964, AJMP, reel 37.

42. See Muste, "Assembly of Unrepresented People: A Report," 28–29. He also supported two white women who decided, after participating in the Quebec-to-Guantanamo Walk for Peace, to remain in Albany where they focused on antiracist organizing in the white community and building interracial dialogue. See B. Tartt Bell to Muste, September 10, 1964, AJMP, reel 24; Muste to Langston Hughes, July 24, 1964, AJMP, reel 37; Muste to Slater King, June 29, 1964, and Slater King to Muste, January 18, 1965, both in AJMP, reel 36; and Edith May Snyder's letters to Muste in AJMP-LA, box 2.

43. Muste, "Rifle Squads or the Beloved Community" (1964), reprinted in Hentoff, *Essays of A. J. Muste*, 429–30.

44. Ibid, 432–33. See also Muste, "Nonviolence and Mississippi."

45. See Aaron Henry to Muste, April 1, 1964, AJMP, reel 36.

46. See Yvonne [last name?] to Muste, July 3, 1964, AJMP, reel 25.

47. The Mississippi Freedom Democratic Party convention and its impact on grassroots activists have been well documented by scholars. See, for example, accounts by Hall, *Peace and Freedom*, 16–17; Isserman, *The Other American*, 246; and Todd Gitlin, *The Sixties: Years of Hope, Days of Rage*, rev. ed. (New York: Bantam, 1993) 151–62. The divides between nonviolence and self-defense, interracialism and black power may not have been as stark as has often been presented in the historiography, but there was a distinct tendency to associate nonviolent philosophy with weakness and sentimentality. See Peniel Joseph, ed., *The Black Power Movement: Rethinking the Civil Rights–Black Power Era* (New York: Routledge, 2006); Kosek, *Acts of Conscience*, 236; and Leilah Danielson, "The 'Two-ness' of the Movement: James Farmer, Nonviolence, and Black Nationalism," *Peace and Change: A Journal of Peace Research* 29, nos. 3 and 4 (July 2004): 430–53.

48. His friend the poet Kay Boyle was inspired to write "On the Jews," at once a tribute to Muste and a lamentation for Goodman and Schwerner that placed their martyrdom within Jewish history. See Boyle, "A Poem About the Jews" (December 1964), copy in AJMP, reel 23. The poem was not published until the fall of 1966 in the *Harvard Advocate* 6, nos. 3 and 4, pp. 21–23. For Muste and other pacifists' discomfiture with the rising sentiment against nonviolence, see Muste to Peggy Duff, March 16, 1964; and Muste to David Riesman, November 2, 1964, both in AJMP, reel 36; Muste to Harrison Butterworth February 27, 1964, AJMP, reel 24; and Sutherland to Muste, circa June 1964, AJMP, reel 36.

49. For Muste's interest in the A. Philip Randolph Institute, see Beverly Sterner to Randolph, December 30, 1965, AJMP, reel 38; Muste to Lenore Marshall, June 3, 1964, AJMP, 37.

50. Rustin, "From Protest to Politics: The Future of the Civil Rights Movement" (1964), reprinted in Devon W. Carbado and Donald Weise, eds., *Time on Two Crosses: The Collected Writings of Bayard Rustin* (San Francisco: Cleis Press, 2003), 122–23.

51. David McReynolds recalled that Rustin had come to believe that Muste had this "too revolutionary" tendency, lacked caution, and was willing to take "lots of risks." He also recalled that Muste "felt totally betrayed" by Rustin's rejection of radical pacifism, "and he was." David McReynolds, interview by author.

52. Muste, "The Civil Rights Movement and the American Establishment" (1965), reprinted in Hentoff, *Essays of A. J. Muste*, 451–53.

53. Ibid., 458–61.

54. For a more detailed assessment of Farmer's views, see Danielson, "The 'Two-ness' of the Movement." After the publication of his article, Muste continued to push Farmer on the issue, writing to him on April 20, 1965, to request his signature on the Declaration of Conscience. See Muste to Farmer, April 20, 1965, AJMP, reel 25.

55. As it turned out, Muste's analysis proved dead on, as it was later revealed that Farmer's trip had been sponsored by the CIA. See Robinson, *Abraham Went Out*, 131. For Johnson's insistence upon loyalty on the Vietnam War, see Farmer, *Lay Bare the Heart*, 300.

56. Dellinger, "The March on Washington and Its Critics" *Liberation* 10, no. 3 (May 1965): 6–7; Lynd, "Coalition Politics or Nonviolent Revolution?" *Liberation* 10, no. 4 (June 1965): 18–21.

57. Muste, typescript of speech "The Quadruple Revolution: How the Four-fold Revolution Relates to Race," delivered at the Fifth Biennial National Conference of Friends on Race Relations, Earlham College, Richmond, Ind., June 18, 1965. Copy in AJMP, reel 5.

58. See Hall, *Peace and Freedom*, 56–60; Thomas F. Jackson, *From Civil Rights to Human Rights: Martin Luther King Jr., and the Struggle for Economic Justice* (Philadelphia: University of Pennsylvania Press, 2007) , 315.

59. See, for example, Muste to John Lewis, July 8, 1966; Muste to Julian Bond (ca. January 1966); Muste to Robert Browne, December 15, 1965; and Muste to James Bevel, August 26, 1965. All in AJMP, reel 23.

60. Muste to Harry G. Boyte, August 26, 1965, and Boyte to Muste, September 10, 1965; Muste to Ira Sandperl and "Joan" [Baez], January 9, 1966. All in AJMP, reel 23. See also Muste to King, March 30, 1966, and Muste to King, May 17, 1966, AJMP, reel 24; and Muste, "Stop the Lynching" (ca. May 1966), AJMP, reel 6.

61. See notes of conversation between Jo Ann Robinson and James Lawson, May 11, 1979, AJMP-LA, box 2.

62. See also Hall, *Peace and Freedom*, 106–7. Muste also encouraged CNVA, AFSC, and the FOR to sponsor workshops on foreign policy and nonviolence that especially focused on the challenges facing the black freedom movement. See Stewart Meacham, "Report on Exploration of Peace Education and the Freedom Movement," June 1964, AJMP, reel 23. Muste and Rustin spoke at "Nonviolence: Its Relationship to Present Racial Conflict and International Strife," Seabury Conference of the Episcopal Pacifist Fellowship, August 1964, AJMP, reel 38.

63. See Muste, "The Civil Rights Movement and the American Establishment,"456; Floyd McKissick to Muste, February 7, 1967; and Muste et al., "Statement of Support and Congratulations on the Occasion of CORE's Twentieth-Fifth Anniversary," February 3, 1967; and minutes of CORE's National Advisory Committee, January 26, 1967. All in AJMP, reel 23.

64. See Hall, *Peace and Freedom*, 107; Beverly Sterner, interview with author.

65. Hall, *Peace and Freedom*, 107–9.

66. Peter J. Boehmer to Muste, August 8, 1966; Muste to Boehmer, August 14, 1966; and Boehmer to Muste, August 18, 1966. AJMP, reel 23. For anti-Communism and the peace movement, see Lieberman, *The Strangest Dream*.

67. Charles Walker, for example, complained about the thuggish behavior of far left groups in the Philadelphia coalition. See Walker to Muste, August 3, 1966, AJMP, reel 24. Bradford Lyttle's account of the "Times Square Sit Down" on February 2, 1966, describes the various political factions, albeit in a more tolerant tone. See his typescript, February 15, 1966, reel 24, AJMP. For secondary accounts of the factionalism of the white left in the antiwar movement, see Hall, *Peace and Freedom*; and Robinson, *Abraham Went Out*, 203–4.

68. Muste, "Mobilize for Peace," *Liberation* 11, no. 9 (December 1966): 21–25; Muste, "Which Coalition?" typescript, October 1966, AJMP, reel 5.

69. Muste, "Who Has the Spiritual Atom Bomb?" 492–93. For his critique of Rustin, Coser, Harrington, et al., see Muste, "The Movement to Stop the War in Vietnam" (1966), reprinted in Hentoff, *Essays of A. J. Muste*, 503–13.

70. Muste, "The Civil Rights Movement and the American Establishment," 455–56. See also Muste, "Who Has the Spiritual Atom Bomb?"

71. Muste to Guy W. Meyer, January 12, 1966, AJMP, reel 24.

72. Quotes are from Robinson, *Abraham Went Out*, 204. See also Muste, "Stop the Lynching," in which he expressed his "utter bafflement" at liberals and peace activists who suggest that the "president has not been shown a 'practical alternative' and ask Buddhists and other non-Communists in Vietnam, as I have heard them do, to propose a 'sound, practical program' for Vietnam."

73. Muste, "Who Has the Spiritual Atom Bomb?" 494–502.

74. See, for example, Muste to E. J. Lever, January 7, 1965, AJMP, reel 24. See also correspondence between Muste and his son, John, in JAH, Muste collection, box 1; Murray Rosenblith, interview by author, June 2006; and Peter Muste, interview by author.

75. See Robinson, *Abraham Went Out*, 192; Muste to Guy W. Meyer, January 12, 1966, AJMP, reel 24; and Muste to Rabbi Abraham Feinberg, January 17, 1966, AJMP, reel 25.

76. Muste, "Mobilize for Peace."

77. Muste, "Who Has the Spiritual Atom Bomb?" 484. For his participation in the draft-card burnings, see subpoena by United States District Court to Muste, December 17, 1965, and press statement, December 20, 1965, AJMP, reel 25. For the use of draft resistance in the movement against the war in Vietnam, see Michael Foley, *Confronting the War Machine: Draft Resistance During the Vietnam War* (Chapel Hill: University of North Carolina Press, 2003).

78. Marv Davidov to Muste, January 7, 1966, AJMP, reel 24.

79. See Bradford Lyttle, "The Times Square Sit-Down," typescript, February 15, 1966, AJMP, reel 24.

80. Muste to Sid Lens, February 15, 1966, reel 23. See also Muste to Jerome Davis, February 1, 1966, AJMP, reel 38.

81. Muste, "CNVA Asian Project and Related Proposals," circa March 1966; and Minutes of CNVA Subcommittee on the Vietnam Project Meeting, March 10, 1966. Both in AJMP, reel 24.

82. Muste, "CNVA Asian Project and Related Proposals." See also Muste to Claude Bordet, June 13, 1966, AJMP, reel 23.

83. Bradford Lyttle, "Peace Action in Saigon," typescript, ca. May 1966, AJMP, reel 24.

84. Ibid. See also Pete Hamill, "Muste, Unbowed, Back from Saigon," *New York Post*, April 25, 1966, 5.

85. Muste, "A Political Report from Saigon," typescript, April 1966, AJMP, reel 5 (selections subsequently published as "Visit to Saigon," *Liberation* 11, no. 3 [May–June 1966]: 7–10); and Lyttle, "Peace Action in Saigon."

86. Lyttle, "Peace Action in Saigon."

87. Ibid. Lyttle's report contained an appendix with excerpts from these letters. More letters can be found in AJMP, reel 4.

88. The most sympathetic account was by *New York Post* columnist Pete Hamill, who described Muste as modest and courageous in his efforts to make peace, yet also as "the last innocent in America." See Hamill, "Muste, Unbowed, Back from Saigon," 5.

89. Muste, "A Political Report from Saigon."

90. Peter J. Boehmer to Muste, August 8, 1966; Muste to Boehmer, August 14, 1966; and Boehmer to Muste, August 18, 1966. AJMP, reel 23.

91. Sidney Peck to Muste, July 15, 1966, AJMP, reel 23; "New Anti-Vietnam War Group Sets Series of Nationwide Protests," October 11, 1966, and Sidney Peck, memorandum on mobilization event, February 3, 1967, AJMP, reel 6. Related documents can be found in MOBE, box 1.

92. Muste, "Mobilize for Peace," *Liberation* 11, no. 9 (December 1966): 21–25. See also "List of Persons Registered for National Leadership Conference," August 10–11, 1966; "Proceedings, National Leadership Conference," September 10–11, 1966; "Follow Up Meeting to Cleveland Conference, September 14, 1966"; Muste, "Spring Mobilization Committee Meeting," December 18, 1966; Muste to "Friend," November 30, 1966; and Minutes of Spring Mobilization Committee Meeting, November 27, 1966, all in AJMP, reel 6.

93. Beverly Sterner, appeal letter, May 8, 1967, AJMP, reel 6; Nat Hentoff, "A. J.," *Village Voice*, February 23, 1967, copy in AJMP, reel 36; and Muste, "Mobilize for Peace."

94. For example, Muste was part of the Anti-Escalation Committee, which planned for massive civil disobedience in the event of a major escalation of the war. See Muste et al. to "Fellow Peace Worker," November 14, 1966, AJMP, reel 23.

95. Muste to Friend, December 5, 1966, AJMP, reel 38. See also Muste to Adjutant General, July 28, 1966; Muste, telegram to Inspector General, November 1, 1966; Muste to Friend, November 3, 1966; Muste to Robert F. Kennedy, November 10, 1966; Muste to Ivanhoe Donaldson, December 8, 1966. All in AJMP, reel 38. See also statement by Muste on behalf of the Fifth Avenue Peace Parade Committee, October 4, 1966, AJMP, reel 25.

96. Muste to Harrison Butterworth, July 1, 1966, AJMP, reel 23. Hanoi's Vietnam Peace Committee "warmly acclaim[ed]" Muste's efforts to form the Spring Mobilization Committee. See copy of cable they sent to Muste on November 2, 1966, MOBE, box 1.

97. See Robinson, *Abraham Went Out*, 216.

98. Starting in the spring of 1965, Muste began to "feel considerably less energetic" than he was accustomed. He made an appointment for a thorough physical exam. Doctors pronounced him in "exceptionally good health for a person of my age [eighty years old]." See Muste to Ray Kinney, May 25, 1965, AJMP, reel 24.

99. Muste, "An Episode During a Visit of American and British Clergymen to North Vietnam, January 9–19, 1967," handwritten account, AJMP, reel 5. See also Robinson, *Abraham Went Out*, 216.

100. Muste, "Last Speech Back from Hanoi," delivered at a meeting of the National Lawyers Guild on February 9, 1967, in New York City, reprinted in *Liberation* 12, nos. 6 and 7 (September–October 1967): 52–57.

101. Ibid. See also Robinson, *Abraham Went Out*, 217.

102. Muste, "Last Speech Back from Hanoi." See also "Rabbi Warns of Dangers in Bombing North Vietnam," *Denver Post*, date unclear, and "Clergyman Visits Grace Church to Tell About Trip to Hanoi," *East Side News*, April 14, 1967. Both clippings in AJMP, reel 36.

103. "Muste, "Last Speech Back from Hanoi." See also clipping from the *New York Times*, January 24, 1967, AJMP, reel 6.

104. Excerpt from "A. J.," *Peace News*, February 24, 1967, AJMP, reel 36; Robert Gilmore and Joyce Gilmore, "Events Concerning the Death of A. J. Muste" (ca. February 1967), A. J. Muste Memorial Institute; and James Bevel, *WIN Special Supplement on A. J. Muste*, 15.

105. Gilmore and Gilmore, "Events Concerning the Death of A. J. Muste."

106. Cara Cook, quoted in Robinson, *Abraham Went Out*, 220.

107. Gilmore and Gilmore, "Events Concerning the Death of A. J. Muste."

108. Cara Cook to Brookwood Staff and Graduates, February 11, 1967, AJMP-LA, box 2. Excerpts from various telegrams can be found in clippings, AJMP, reel 36, and in *WIN Special Supplement on A. J. Muste*.

109. James Wechsler, "He Never Failed," *New York Post*, February 22, 1967. Those present included figures from all facets of his long life: Norman and Evan Thomas, John Nevin Sayre, Mark and Helen Starr, Bayard Rustin, Bradford Lyttle, Cara Cook, David McReynolds, Joyce and Robert Gilmore, John C. Bennett, Emily Parker Simon, David Dellinger, Frances Witherspoon, Ralph DiGia, Roy Finch, Nat Hentoff, John Oliver Nelson, Milton Mayer, Sidney Lens, and James Wechsler. Flowers for the service had been provided by the British Campaign for Nuclear

Disarmament and the International Confederation for Disarmament and Peace. See clippings, AJMP, reel 36.

110. See clippings, AJMP, reel 36. Also, the night after he died, the radio station WBAI, which often broadcast talks by Muste and other radicals, held a "spur-of-the-moment memorial broadcast" for him. See David McReynolds, in *WIN Special Supplement on A. J. Muste*, 2.

111. Staughton Lynd and Paul Goodman comments on back cover of Hentoff, *Essays of A. J. Muste*; Rustin quote can be found in Wechsler, "He Never Failed"; Reinhold Niebuhr, "Christian Revolutionary," *New York Times*, April 16, 1967; Hugh Black, "He Was a Devoted Pacifist—Was He Also a Dreamer?" undated; for his enjoyment of life's sensual pleasures, see Hentoff, "A. J.," *Village Voice*, February 23, 1967, and John Papworth, "Personal Comment," *Peace News*, February 24, 1967. All can be found in AJMP, reels 36 and 37.

112. Ellen Wertheim to Beverly Sterner, and Sterner to Wertheim, circa March 1967, AJMP, reel 23; Irving Louis Horowitz, "Vietnam Debate Loses Two Intellects," *St. Louis Post Dispatch*, March 12, 1967, clipping in AJMP, reel 36; and Max Lerner, "The Color of War," *New York Post*, April 17, 1967, clipping in AJMP, reel 37.

113. Virtually all of the obituaries of Muste, both in the United States and abroad, referred to him as the "American Gandhi." See clippings in AJMP, reels 1, 36, and 37. For his thoughts on staying in Vietnam, see statement by Rabbi Feinberg in the *New York Times*, February 17, 1967, copy in AJMP, reel 1.

114. See Rossinow, *Visions of Progress*, 253. For the antiwar movement and the decline of the left since the 1960s, see also Hall, *Peace and Freedom*; Kazin, *American Dreamers*; and Gitlin, *The Sixties*.

115. See Kosek, *Acts of Conscience*, 236.

116. For the growth of neoliberalism and American conservatism since the 1970s, see David Harvey, *A Brief History of Neoliberalism* (Oxford: Oxford University Press, 2005); Lichtenstein, *American Capitalism*; Lisa McGirr, *Suburban Warriors: The Origins of the New American Right* (Princeton, N.J.: Princeton University Press, 2001); and Sean Wilentz, *The Age of Reagan: A History, 1974–2008* (New York: Harper, 2009).

117. Deming, "It's a Good Life," *Liberation* 1, nos. 6 and 7 (September–October 1967): 60–61.

118. See Hall, *Peace and Freedom*, 80 (for King's speech) and 106 (for a description of the march. For a description of the march, see Hall, *Peace and Freedom*, 106.

Epilogue

1. "On 5th Ave., a Grandmothers' Protest as Endless as the Wars," *New York Times*, May 7, 2010, A20.

2. Thich Nhat Hanh, *Peace Is Every Step: The Path of Mindfulness in Everyday Life* (New York: Bantam, 1992), 42.

3. See Nelson Lichtenstein, *State of the Union: A Century of American Labor* (Princeton: Princeton University Press, 2002), 141. See also Lichtenstein, "Falling in Love Again?" 18–31; Lichtenstein, "Pluralism, Postwar Intellectuals, and the Demise of the Union Idea"; and Lichtenstein, *American Capitalism*.

4. See Lichtenstein, *State of the Union*; Lichtenstein, "Falling in Love Again"; and Lichtenstein, "Pluralism, Postwar Intellectuals, and the Demise of the Union Idea."

5. Ibid. See also Jefferson Cowie, *Stayin' Alive: The 1970s and the Last Days of the Working Class* (New York: New Press, 2010).

6. Robert Welsh, quoted in Lichtenstein, "Falling in Love Again?" 27.

INDEX

⟿

Abernathy, Ralph, 290
academic freedom, 107, 108, 111, 171
Action Committee of Artists, Writers, and
   Professionals Against the War, 311
Addams, Jane, 48–49
Adler, Felix, 41
adult education movement, 107, 111. *See also*
   workers' education movement
Advance (periodical), 130, 131, 162
Affiliated Schools for Women Workers, 128
African Americans, 104, 157; at Brookwood
   Labor College, 117, 385n12; Cleveland
   postal worker union of, 387n43; CPLA
   and, 128, 129; NAACP and, 224, 386n12;
   pacifism and, 219–20, 237, 296; Vietnam
   War and, 313–15, 319; World War II and,
   233. *See also* civil rights movement; racism
African liberation movements, 261–62,
   290–93, 295, 299
Algeria, 291
All-African Conference on Positive Action
   for Peace and Security of Africa (1960),
   290
Allard, Gerry, 131, 388n54
Allentown, Pa., 148, 191, 194, 195
Amalgamated Clothing Workers (ACW), 3,
   7, 66, 78, 119, 129–30; Brookwood Labor
   College and, 117; housing projects of, 177;
   Lawrence textile workers' strike and,
   73–75; Vietnam War and, 313
Amalgamated Textile Workers of America
   (ATWA), 3, 66, 73–81, 84, 85
American Civil Liberties Union (ACLU), 3,
   56–57, 59, 79, 98
American Committee on Africa, 262, 299,
   421n4
American Fair Play for Cuba Committee, 295
American Federationist (periodical), 87, 97

American Federation of Full-Fashioned
   Hosiery Workers (AFFFHW), 104, 117,
   120, 129, 143, 216
American Federation of Labor (AFL), 61, 68,
   74, 101, 338; anti-intellectualism of, 113,
   141; Brookwood Labor College and, 87,
   91, 105–18, 171; Communist Party and, 5,
   339; CPLA and, 384n4; Marion textile
   workers' strike and, 135, 136, 138; reform
   of, 118–19, 123, 126; Socialist Party and,
   166; worker education programs of, 68,
   81–82, 107–8, 116. *See also individual
   unions*
American Federation of Teachers (AFT), 86,
   97, 112, 117, 167
American Forum for Socialist Education, 14,
   274–76
American Friends Service Committee
   (AFSC), 137, 238, 272–73, 311–12, 327.
   See also Quakers
American Fund for Public Service. *See*
   Garland Fund
American Indians, 249
Americanist approach, 51, 59, 144, 149–50,
   180; Budenz and, 120–21; Debs and, 47;
   Rotzel and, 76
American Labor Associates, 160–61
American Negro Leadership Conference on
   Africa, 317
Americans for South African Resistance, 261
American Woolen Company, 68–74, 78
American Workers Party (AWP), 6, 163–64,
   194–95, 269; Auto-Lite strike and, 185–86;
   CLA's merger with, 180–81, 187–93;
   CPLA and, 159, 162, 165, 179, 190–92;
   founding of, 159, 162, 165, 179
anarchism, 65, 126; Bolshevism and, 70–71;
   individualism and, 13; pacifists and, 241;

ACKNOWLEDGMENTS

OVER THE YEARS, as I have worked on this book, I have benefited from the extraordinary scholarship of other historians of American political culture. I would especially like to thank Michael Kazin and Doug Rossinow for their generous and careful review of my manuscript. The following historians and friends also gave me invaluable support and feedback: Marvin Gettleman, Kip Kosek, Robbie Lieberman, Marian Mollin, Ellen Schrecker, and Geoffrey Smith. Although we have not met, I would like to thank Jo Ann Ooiman Robinson, to whom I am indebted for the meticulous research she conducted for her biography of Muste, *Abraham Went Out*. My editor, Robert Lockhart, has been unflagging in his support and enthusiasm for this project, for which I am grateful.

I also owe a debt to my mentors. My academic interest in the history of American radicalism began many years ago as an undergraduate at the University of Rochester. There I was lucky enough to work with Christopher Lasch and Robert Westbrook, among others, who took ideas and democracy seriously as historians and teachers. I would also like to thank the faculty in the History Department at the University of Texas at Austin, who taught me the beauty and power of social history and black history, and the importance of methodology and theory. I would especially like to acknowledge the support of Robert Abzug, as well as Desley Deacon, Kevin Gaines, Kevin Kenny, Mark Lawrence, Howard Miller, Gunther Peck, Richard Pells, and Penny Von Eschen.

Other historians who aided me in completing this project include Gordon Olson, who drove me around Grand Rapids and directed me to important resources on the city's history and culture; Donald Bruggink of Hope College, who helped me to understand the history of the Reformed Church in America; and Tim Davenport, who helped me to locate circulation numbers for *Labor Age*. Curators and archivists at manuscript collections across the country were also helpful, especially the staff of the Swarthmore College

Peace Collection, the Tamiment Library and Robert F. Wagner Labor Archives, the Kheel Center for Labor-Management Documentation and Archives, the Grand Rapids History and Special Collections Center, and the Manuscripts and Photographs Collection at the Newton History Museum. Chuck Matthei, who has since passed away, generously let me stay at the pacifist farm in Voluntown, Connecticut, and gave me access to the Ernest and Marion Bromley Papers, which are now held at Swarthmore.

I would also like to thank the Schlesinger Library and the Tamiment Library, both of which provided me with funding to help with the costs associated with research, as well as the Faculty Grant Program at Northern Arizona University, which funded several summers of research.

It was my incredible privilege to meet and to interview some extraordinary people in the course of conducting this research. In particular, I would like to thank Christopher Cardinale, Tom Cornell, Dave Dellinger, Dorothy Hassler, George Houser, Will Inman, Bradford Lyttle, David McReynolds, Elizabeth Peterson, Murray Rosenblith, Beverly Sterner, Bill Sutherland, Marjorie Swann Edwin, and George and Lillian Willoughby, all of whom were generous with their time and reminiscences. I am also grateful to A. J. Muste's family members who allowed me to interview them: Doris and Henry Emelander (Muste's niece and her husband), Edwin E. Henry Jr. (Muste's nephew by marriage), Marian Johnson (Muste's niece by marriage), and Peter Muste (Muste's grandson).

My colleagues in the history department at Northern Arizona University have provided a dynamic and intellectually rich community, even as the economic recession and the repressive political climate in Arizona placed a strain on all of us. I would especially like to thank Michael Amundson, George Lubick, and Rick Tillman, who always believed in me, as well as Sanjam Ahluwalia, Susan Deeds, Paul Dutton, Sanjay Joshi, Cynthia Kosso, Marc Matera, and Margaret Morley. My graduate students, especially Jennifer Clark, Carrie Deakin, Jack Reid, and Rich Updegrove, helped to keep me on my toes. Michael Vincent, the dean of the College of Arts and Letters, also provided invaluable support, especially in the last stages of this project.

My friends and community in Flagstaff deserve special mention. We never talked much about history, but I could not have survived the ups and downs of professional life, motherhood, and personal losses without their support, good humor, and commitment to spiritual growth and fun. Monica Brown and Annette McGivney have especially been awe inspiring—I cannot thank you enough—as well as Jeffrey Berglund, Aaron Cohen, Lisa Cohen, Rodrigo de Toledo, Howard Grodman, Patricia Murphey, Raquel Rotnes, Kimberly Sharp, Curtis Smith, Jerry Thull, and Gioia Woods, and all of your wonderful children. I would also like to thank Joe Bader, Lanny Morrison, Lynne Nemeth, and Rabbi Nena Pearlmutter for their mentorship and community.

Most inspiring of all have been my parents, Ross and Susan Danielson. Our family has been reconfigured, but we will always be together. I want you to know that your dream is my dream, though I may have attempted to realize it in a different way. I hope you see that this book is a tribute to both of you. The same goes for my wonderful sisters, Marah and Eliza Danielson. I would also like to thank my parents-in-law, Ron and Maureen Meeks, who have always been supportive, and who generously helped with child care on many occasions. The same goes for my mom, who spent many summers in Flagstaff taking care of Adin and Mira and performing other household responsibilities.

I would also like to thank my children, Adin and Mira Meeks. Not only have they had to put up with an often distracted and busy mother, they have enriched my life and made it more adventurous and fun. It's a cliché, but it's true: Being their mom is the best thing that ever happened to me.

I have dedicated this book to my partner, Eric Meeks. He has been my steady and constant companion and a loving and committed husband throughout this long process, even when I did not deserve it! He is also my colleague and fellow historian; his professional ethics and dedication to the craft of history have served as my example and inspiration. I am forever grateful.

Finally, I would like to thank A. J. Muste, who has also been a constant companion for almost a decade. Although I haven't always agreed with him, he has been endlessly fascinating, challenging, and inspiring. I hope this book does justice to his legacy and vision.